Gender in the 1990s

IMAGES, REALITIES, AND ISSUES

Edited by

E.D. NELSON

B.W. ROBINSON

Nelson Canada

I(T)P An International Thomson Publishing Company

Toronto • Albany • Bonn • Boston • Cincinnati • Detroit • London • Madrid • Melbourne
Mexico City • New York • Pacific Grove • Paris • San Francisco • Singapore • Tokyo • Washington

I(T)P ™

International Thomson Publishing
The ITP logo is a trademark under licence

© Nelson Canada
A division of Thomson Canada Limited, 1995

Published in 1995 by
Nelson Canada
A division of Thomson Canada Limited
1120 Birchmount Road
Scarborough, Ontario M1K 5G4

Canadian Cataloguing in Publication Data

Main entry under title:
Gender in the 1990s : images, realities, and issues

2nd ed.
First ed. published under title: Gender roles :
doing what come naturally?
Includes bibliographical references.
ISBN 0-17-604847-2

1. Sex role. 2. Sexism. I. Nelson, Adie, 1958–
II. Robinson, Barrie W. (Barrie William), 1944–
III. Title: Gender roles : doing what comes naturally?

HQ1075.G46 1995   305.3   C95-930943-8

Gender in the 1990s: Images, Realities, and Issues is the second edition of *Gender Roles: Doing What Comes Naturally?* by E.D. Salamon and B.W. Robinson.

Acquisitions Editor	Charlotte Forbes
Senior Production Editor	Tracy Bordian
Developmental Editor	Heather Martin
Senior Production Coordinator	Sheryl Emery
Art Director	Liz Harasymczuk
Cover Design	Liz Harasymczuk
Cover Photograph	Michael Cooper
Managing Editor, College	Margot Hanis
Senior Composition Analyst	Alicja Jamorski
Input Operators	Elaine Andrews, Michelle Volk

Printed and bound in Canada
1 2 3 4 WC 98 97 96 95

To the memory of Martin Murray Gill.
—E.D.N.

To Darcie and Tracie—with hopes for a better world.
—B.W.R.

Contents

Preface

The first edition of this book, *Gender Roles: Doing What Comes Naturally?*, was published eight years ago. It was born largely of our experiences in teaching classes on the sociology of gender. At the time we felt that no existing reader adequately met our needs for a blend of theoretical and empirical, serious and humorous, as well as descriptive and analytical articles written in Canada and elsewhere. While we crafted the book with what we believed to be the best tools available at the time, we recognized that a new and improved product would be both necessary and possible at some time in the future.

A lot of courses, taught in a variety of academic settings, have disappeared since that time. We, and the entire field of study, have undergone many changes. Role theory, which strongly informed our original volume, increasingly became too constraining to permit the easy integration of new materials drawn from a variety of emerging sources. Feminism in general has become more inclusive in attempting to incorporate many voices, coming from a diversity of perspectives, yet united by certain common themes. The men's movement demonstrates nascent signs of moving in the same direction. We consequently felt that the time was right for a second edition that would, along with a new title, reflect these changes.

Some of the articles from the first edition have endured the test of time and are again included. Our attention has also been drawn to new works, and we have attempted to incorporate a substantial number of them. Yet, a cautionary note must be introduced here. We were cognizant ahead of time, and reminded through examination of the critiques from our many reviewers, that any attempt to be fully inclusive and present the complete variety of gender experiences and perspectives would require a volume weighing slightly more than a brontosaurus. We were also uncomfortably aware that the budget required for the publication—or purchase—of such a reader was likely to both hinder its beginnings and hasten its extinction. We were once again forced to make editorial decisions based on limitations of space and money, decisions that might leave a few readers disappointed on discovering that their preferred image, reality, or issue was not included. Guided by our desire to provide readers with as much stimulating and eclectic material as possible, we believe we have succeeded in being as comprehensive as was feasible. In the process, we have increased the Canadian content of this reader substantially. A number of the articles in this book could easily be placed in any of a number of the chapters, as their contents bear upon topics addressed elsewhere. Our decision regarding their final placement is based on our understanding of the major focal theme presented by the author(s). Instructors and readers are encouraged to alter the presented order in any fashion they desire.

The first edition of this reader was produced through frantic efforts spanning the hallway between our offices at the University of Alberta. This edition was produced through frantic teamwork between offices spanning a distance of over 3000 kilometres and, needless to say, the process acquired a very different dynamic. As is likely the case with any collaborative effort, we will each claim credit for any sections/articles that strike the reader as being particularly provocative; any omissions or inadequacies are, to be sure, the sole responsibility of the other editor.

Acknowledgments

We would like to thank those who took time to review this work at its manuscript stage: Jean Ballard-Kent (University College of the Fraser Valley), Elaine Bazinet-Smith (Algonquin College), Lorraine Davies (University of Western Ontario), Gail Grant (University of Guelph), Fiona Green (University of Manitoba), Alison Hayford (University of Regina), and Bill Moss (Dawson College).

E.D. Nelson and B.W. Robinson

CHAPTER ONE

The Social Construction of Sex, Gender, and Sexuality

Conceptions of sex, gender, and sexuality are simultaneously descriptive, prescriptive, and proscriptive. In other words, they not only attempt to describe the essential characteristics of what the identified biological sexes, genders, and sexualities *are*, but they also implicitly and explicitly constrain and limit what these *should* and *should not be*. Central to the constraints are elemental notions of how many sexes, genders, and sexual orientations actually exist, and how many and which should normatively be allowed to exist. As many commentators have noted, Western societies including Canada are characterized by a belief system decreeing that not only are there (and should there be) only two biological sexes and two genders, but also that everyone must be identified as belonging to *either* one *or* the other. This rigid mind-set precludes the possibilities for multitudinous and multifaceted sexes and genders, and requires the entire social world to be permeated with this "essential" dichotomy.

In this chapter we explore a number of ways in which central assumptions limit and constrain selected images, realities, and issues in our gendered social world. These range from seemingly innocuous choices in clothing to the initial assignment of one's biological sex, from which flows a socially demanded gender socialization, to the "necessity" for surgical realignment of biological appearance to conform to one's sense of a subjectively experienced gender identity, through to certain basic elements of the straight, gay, and lesbian worlds.

Deborah Tannen (Article 1) briefly describes seemingly superficial elements of one's social appearance that demonstrate fundamental conformity to a society's gender expectations and, in the process, serve to refurbish them as well. The works of Kessler and Eichler demonstrate the power of existing beliefs about sex and gender to influence medical decisions that have long-range implications. Suzanne Kessler (Article 2) focuses on instances of children born with ambiguous genitalia in a society where a pronouncement of either "It's a boy!" or "It's a girl!" is deemed an absolute necessity. Within our currently gendered society, permanent ambiguity is unacceptable. Margrit Eichler (Article 3) argues that transsexual surgery functions to reinforce an essential dichotomy by permitting individuals to painfully change their healthy, unambiguous bodies so that they are consistent with their sense of gender identity. Alternative combinations of minds and bodies are thereby denied plausibility and the gender dichotomy is maintained.

M. Rochlin (Article 4) reminds us of the power of language in promoting a heterosexual (or what some deem to be a heterosexist) world. Through inverting traditionally phrased questions, we become aware of our taken-for-granted world wherein gendered heterosexuality is deemed to be "natural and normal" while homosexuality and bisexuality are deemed marginal at best and threatening to our gender foundations at worst. However, even within their disadvantaged status, lesbians and gays are also subject to traditional gender constraints and limitations. Lillian Faderman (Article 5) traces the history of the resurgence within the lesbian community of the models of "butch" and "femme," which draw upon and are negotiated within selected aspects of dominant masculinity and femininity expectations. Gregg Blachford (Article 6) documents various ways in which the gay world complements the traditional male dominance of heterosexual society while also providing limited challenges to our understanding of that society, particularly through the phenomenon of "camp." Readers will note how both lesbian and gay subcultures, as presented by theses authors, evidence variations around the dominant gender themes of our cultures.

1

Wears Jump Suit. Sensible Shoes. Uses Husband's Last Name.

Deborah Tannen

Some years ago I was at a small working conference of four women and eight men. Instead of concentrating on the discussion I found myself looking at the three other women at the table, thinking how each had a different style and how each style was coherent.

One woman had dark brown hair in a classic style, a cross between Cleopatra and Plain Jane. The severity of her straight hair was softened by wavy bangs and ends that turned under. Because she was beautiful, the effect was more Cleopatra than plain.

The second woman was older, full of dignity and composure. Her hair was cut in a fashionable style that left her with only one eye, thanks to a side part that let a curtain of hair fall across half her face. As she looked down to read her prepared paper, the hair robbed her of bifocal vision and created a barrier between her and the listeners.

The third woman's hair was wild, a frosted blond avalanche falling over and beyond her shoulders. When she spoke she frequently tossed her head, calling attention to her hair and away from her lecture.

Then there was makeup. The first woman wore facial cover that made her skin smooth and pale, a black line under each eye and mascara that darkened already dark lashes. The second wore only a light gloss on her lips and a hint of shadow on her eyes. The third had blue bands under her eyes, dark blue shadow, mascara, bright red lipstick and rouge; her fingernails flashed red.

I considered the clothes each woman had wore during the three days of the conference: In the first case, man-tailored suits in primary colors with solid-color blouses. In the second, casual but stylish black T-shirts, a floppy collarless jacket and baggy slacks or a skirt in neutral colors. The third wore a sexy jump suit; tight sleeveless jersey and tight yellow slacks; a dress with gaping armholes and an indulged tendency to fall off one shoulder.

Shoes? No. 1 wore string sandals with medium heels; No. 2, sensible, comfortable walking shoes; No. 3, pumps with spike heels. You can fill in the jewelry, scarves, shawls, sweaters—or lack of them.

As I amused myself finding coherence in these styles, I suddenly wondered why I was scrutinizing only the women. I scanned the eight men at the table. And then I knew why I wasn't studying them. The men's styles were unmarked.

The term "marked" is a staple of linguistic theory. It refers to the way language alters the base meaning of a word by adding a linguistic particle that has no meaning on its own. The unmarked form of a word carries the meaning that goes without saying—what you think of when you're not thinking anything special.

The unmarked tense of verbs in English is the present—for example, *visit*. To indicate past, you mark the verb by adding *ed* to yield *visited*. For future, you add a word: *will visit*. Nouns are presumed to be singular until marked for plural, typically by adding *s* or *es*, so *visit* becomes *visits* and *dish* becomes *dishes*.

The unmarked form of most English words also convey "male." Being male is the unmarked case. Endings like *ess* and *ette* mark words as "female." Unfortunately, they also tend to mark them for frivolousness. Would you feel safe entrusting your life to a doctorette? Alfre Woodward, who was an Oscar nominee for best supporting actress, says she identifies herself as an actor because "actresses worry about eyelashes and cellulite, and women who are actors worry about the characters we are playing." Gender markers pick up extra meanings that reflect common associations with the female gender: not quite serious, often sexual.

Each of the women at the conference had to make decisions about hair, clothing, makeup and accessories, and each decision carried meaning. Every style available to us was marked. The men in our group had made decisions, too, but the range from which they chose was incomparably narrower. Men can choose styles that are marked, but they don't have to, and in this group none did. Unlike the women, they had the option of being unmarked.

Take the men's hair styles. There was no marine crew cut or oily longish hair falling into eyes, no asymmetrical, two-tiered construction to swirl over a bald top. One man was unabashedly bald; the others had hair of standard length, parted on one side, in natural shades of brown or gray or graying. Their hair obstructed no views, left little to toss or push back or run fingers through and, consequently, needed and attracted no attention. A few men had beards. In a business setting, beards might be marked. In this academic gathering, they weren't.

There could have been a cowboy shirt with string tie or a three-piece suit or a necklaced hippie in jeans. But there wasn't. All eight men wore brown or blue slacks and nondescript shirts of light colors. No man wore sandals or boots; their shoes were dark, closed, comfortable and flat. In short, unmarked.

Although no man wore makeup, you couldn't say the men didn't wear makeup in the sense that you could say a woman didn't wear makeup. For men, no makeup is unmarked.

I asked myself what style we women could have adopted that would have been unmarked, like the men's. The answer was none. There is no unmarked woman.

There is no woman's hair style that can be called standard, that says nothing about her. The range of women's hair styles is staggering, but a women whose hair has no particular style is perceived as not caring about how she looks, which can disqualify her for many positions, and will subtly diminish her as a person in the eyes of some.

Women must choose between attractive shoes and comfortable shoes. When our group made an unexpected trek, the woman who wore flat, laced shoes arrived first. Last to arrive was the woman in spike heels, shoes in hand and a handful of men around her.

If a woman's clothing is tight or revealing (in other words, sexy), it sends a message—an intended one of wanting to be attractive, but also a possibly unintended one of availability. If her clothes are not sexy, that too sends a message, lent meaning by the knowledge that they could have been. There are thousands of cosmetic products from which women can choose and myriad ways of applying them. Yet no makeup at all is anything but unmarked. Some men see it as a hostile refusal to please them.

Women can't even fill out a form without telling stories about themselves. Most forms give four titles to choose from. "Mr." carries no meaning other than that the respondent is male. But a woman who checks "Mrs." or "Miss" communicates not only whether she has been married but also whether she has conservative tastes in forms of address—and probably other conservative values as well. Checking "Ms." declines to let on about marriage (checking "Mr." declines nothing since nothing was asked), but it also marks her as either liberated or rebellious, depending on the observer's attitudes and assumptions.

I sometimes try to duck these variously marked choices by giving my title as "Dr."—and in so doing risk marking myself as either uppity (hence sarcastic responses like "Excuse *me!*) or an overachiever (hence reactions of congratulatory surprise like "Good for you!").

All married women's surnames are marked. If a woman takes her husband's name, she announces to the world that she is married and has traditional values. To some it will indicate that she is less herself, more identified by her husband's identity. If she does not take her husband's name, this too is marked, seen as worthy of comment: she has *done* something; she has "kept her own name." A man is never said to have "kept his own name" because it never occurs to anyone that he might have given it up. For him using his own name is unmarked.

A married woman who wants to have her cake and eat it too may use her surname plus his, with or without a hyphen. But this too announces her marital status and often results in a tongue-tying string. In a list (Harvey O'Donovan, Jonathan Feldman, Stephanie Woodbury McGillicutty), the woman's multiple name stands out. It is marked.

I have never been inclined toward biological explanations of gender differences in language, but I was intrigued to see Ralph Fasold bring biological phenomena to bear on the question of linguistic marking in his book "The Sociolinguistics of Language." Fasold stresses that language and culture are particularly unfair in treating women as the marked case because biologically it is the male that is marked. While two X chromosomes make a female, two Y chromosomes make nothing. Like the linguistic markers *s, es* or *ess,* the Y chromosome doesn't "mean" anything unless it is attached to a root form—an X chromosome.

Developing this idea elsewhere, Fasold points out that girls are born with fully female bodies, while boys are born with modified female bodies. He invites men who doubt this to lift up their shirts and contemplate why they have nipples.

In his book, Fasold notes "a wide range of facts which demonstrates that female is the unmarked sex." For example, he observes that there are a few species that produce only females, like the whiptail lizard. Thanks to parthenogenesis, they have no trouble having as many daughters as they like. There are no species, however, that produce only males. This is no surprise, since any such species would become extinct in its first generation.

Fasold is also intrigued by species that produce individuals not involved in reproduction, like honeybees and leaf-cutter ants. Reproduction is handled by the queen and a relatively few males; the workers are sterile females. "Since they do not reproduce," Fasold says, "there is no reason for them to be one sex or the other, so they default, so to speak, to female."

Fasold ends his discussion of these matters by pointing out that if language reflected biology, grammar books would direct us to use "she" to include males and females and "he" only for specifically male referents. But they don't. They tell us that "he" means "he or she," and that "she" is used only if the referent is specifically female. This use of "he" as the sex-indefinite pronoun is an innovation introduced into English by grammarians in the 18th and 19th centuries, according to Peter Mühlhäusler and Rom Harré in "Pronouns and People." From at least about 1500, the correct sex-indefinite pronoun was "they," as it still is in casual spoken English. In other words, the female was declared by grammarians to be the marked case.

Writing this article may mark me not as a writer, not as a linguist, not as an analyst of human behavior, but as a feminist—which will have positive or negative, but in any case powerful, connotations for readers. Yet I doubt that anyone reading Ralph Fasold's book would put that label on him.

I discovered the markedness inherent in the very topic of gender after writing a book on differences in conversational style based on geographical region, ethnicity, class, age and gender. When I was interviewed, the vast majority of journalists wanted to talk about the differences between women and men. While I thought I was simply describing what I observed—something I had learned to do as a researcher—merely mentioning women and men marked me as a feminist for some.

When I wrote a book devoted to gender differences in ways of speaking, I sent the manuscript to five male colleagues, asking them to alert me to any interpretation, phrasing or wording that might seem unfairly negative toward men. Even so, when the book came out, I encountered responses like that of the television talk show host who, after interviewing me, turned to the audience and asked if they thought I was male-bashing.

Leaping upon a poor fellow who affably nodded in agreement, she made him stand and asked, "Did what she said accurately describe you?" "Oh, yes," he answered. "That's me exactly." "And what she said about women—does that sound like your wife?" "Oh, yes," he responded. "That's her exactly." "Then why do you think she's male-bashing?" He answered, with disarming honesty, "Because she's a woman and she's saying things about men."

To say anything about women and men without marking oneself as either feminist or anti-feminist, male-basher or apologist for men seems as impossible for a woman as trying to get dressed in the morning without inviting interpretations of her character.

Sitting at the conference table musing on these matters, I felt sad to think that we women didn't have the freedom to be unmarked that the men sitting next to us had. Some days you just want to get dressed and go about your business. But if you're a woman, you can't, because there is no unmarked woman.

2

The Medical Construction of Gender: Case Management of Intersexed Infants

Suzanne J. Kessler

T he birth of intersexed infants, babies born with genitals that are neither clearly male nor clearly female, has been documented throughout recorded time.[1] In the late twentieth century, medical technology has advanced to allow scientists to determine chromosomal and hormonal gender, which is typically taken to be the real, natural, biological gender, usually referred to as "sex."[2] Nevertheless, physicians who handle the cases of intersexed infants consider several factors beside biological ones in determining, assigning, and announcing the gender of a particular infant. Indeed, biological factors are often preempted in their deliberations by such cultural factors as the "correct" length of the penis and capacity of the vagina.

In the literature of intersexuality, issues such as announcing a baby's gender at the time of delivery, postdelivery discussions with the parents, and consultations with patients in adolescence are considered only peripherally to the central medical issues—etiology, diagnosis, and surgical procedures. Yet members of medical teams have standard practices for managing intersexuality that rely ultimately on cultural understandings of gender. The process and guidelines by which decisions about gender (re)construction are made reveal the model for the social construction of gender generally. Moreover, in the face of apparently incontrovertible evidence—infants born with some combination of "female" and "male" reproductive and sexual features—physicians hold an incorrigible belief in and insistence upon female and male as the only "natural" options. This paradox highlights and calls into question the idea that female and male are biological givens compelling a culture of two genders....

Interviews were conducted with six medical experts (three women and three men) in the field of pediatric intersexuality: one clinical geneticist, three endocrinologists (two of them pediatric specialists), one psychoendocrinologist, and one urologist. All of them have had extensive clinical experience with various intersexed syndromes, and some are internationally known researchers in the field of intersexuality. They were selected on the

From Suzanne J. Kessler "The Medical Construction of Gender: Case Management of Intersexed Infants." *Signs: Journal of Women in Culture and Society,* vol. 16, no. 11 (1990): 3–26. © 1990 by The University of Chicago Press. Reprinted by permission.

basis of their prominence in the field and their representation of four different medical centers in New York City. Although they know one another, they do not collaborate on research and are not part of the same management team. All were interviewed in the spring of 1985, in their offices, and interviews lasted between forty-five minutes and one hour. Unless further referenced, all quotations in this article are from these interviews.

THE THEORY OF INTERSEXUALITY MANAGEMENT

The sophistication of today's medical technology has led to an extensive compilation of various intersex categories based on the various causes of malformed genitals. The "true intersexed" condition, where both ovarian and testicular tissue are present in either the same gonad or in opposite gonads, accounts for fewer than 5 percent of all cases of ambiguous genitals.[3] More commonly, the infant has either ovaries or testes, but the genitals are ambiguous. If the infant has two ovaries, the condition is referred to as female pseudohermaphroditism. If the infant has two testes, the condition is referred to as male pseudohermaphroditism. There are numerous causes of both forms of pseudohermaphroditism, and although there are life-threatening aspects to some of these conditions, having ambiguous genitals per se is not harmful to the infant's health.[4] Although most cases of ambiguous genitals do not represent true intersex, in keeping with the contemporary literature, I will refer to all such cases as intersexed.

Current attitudes toward the intersex condition are primarily influenced by three factors. First are the extraordinary advancements in surgical techniques and endocrinology in the last decade. For example, female genitals can now be constructed to be indistinguishable in appearance from normal natural ones. Some abnormally small penises can be enlarged with the exogenous application of hormones, although surgical skills are not sufficiently advanced to construct a normal-looking and functioning penis out of other tissue.[5] Second, ... the influence of the feminist movement has called into question the valuation of women according to strictly reproductive functions, and the presence or absence of functional gonads is no longer the only or the definitive criterion for gender assignment. Third, contemporary psychological theorists have begun to focus on "gender identity" (one's sense of oneself as belonging to the female or male category) as distinct from "gender role" (cultural expectations of one's behavior as "appropriate" for a female or male).[6] The relevance of this new gender identity theory for rethinking cases of ambiguous genitals is that gender must be assigned as early as possible in order for gender identity to develop successfully. As a result of these three factors, intersexuality is now considered a treatable condition of the genitals, one that needs to be resolved expeditiously.

According to all of the specialists interviewed, management of inter-sexed cases is based upon the theory of gender proposed first by John Money, J. G. Hampson, and J. L. Hampson in 1955 and developed in 1972 by Money and Anke A. Ehrhardt, which argues that gender identity is change-able until approximately eighteen months of age.[7] "To use the Pygmalion allegory, one may begin with the same clay and fashion a god or a goddess."[8] The theory rests on satisfying several conditions: the experts must insure that the parents have no doubt about whether their child is male or female; the genitals must be made to match the assigned gender as soon as possible; gen-der-appropriate hormones must be administered at puberty; and intersexed children must be kept informed about their situation with age-appropriate explanations. If these conditions are met, the theory proposes, the inter-sexed child will develop a gender identity in accordance with the gender assignment (regardless of the chromosomal gender) and will not question her or his assignment and request reassignment at a later age.

Supportive evidence for Money and Ehrhardt's theory is based on only a handful of repeatedly cited cases, but it has been accepted because of the prestige of the theoreticians and its resonance with contemporary ideas about gender, children, psychology, and medicine. Gender and children are malleable; psychology and medicine are the tools used to transform them. This theory is so strongly endorsed that it has taken on the character of gos-pel. "I think we [physicians] have been raised in the Money theory," one endocrinologist said. Another claimed, "We always approach the problem in a similar way and it's been dictated, to a large extent, by the work of John Money and Anke Ehrhardt because they are the only people who have pub-lished, at least in medical literature, any data, any guidelines." It is provocative that this physician immediately followed this assertion with: "And I don't know how effective it really is." Contradictory data are rarely cited in reviews of the literature, were not mentioned by any of the physi-cians interviewed, and have not diminished these physicians' belief in the theory's validity.[9]

The doctors interviewed concur with the argument that gender be assigned immediately, decisively, and irreversibly, and that professional opinions be presented in a clear and unambiguous way. The psychoendocri-nologist said that when doctors make a statement about the infant, they should "stick to it." The urologist said, "If you make a statement that later has to be disclaimed or discredited, you've weakened your credibility." A gender assignment made decisively, unambiguously, and irrevocably contributes, I believe, to the general impression that the infant's true, natural "sex" has been discovered, and that something that was there all along has been found. It also serves to maintain the credibility of the medical profession, reassure the parents, and reflexively substantiate Money and Ehrhardt's theory.

Also according to the theory, if operative correction is necessary, it should take place as soon as possible. If the infant is assigned the male gender, the initial stage of penis repair is usually undertaken in the first year, and further surgery is completed before the child enters school. If the infant is assigned the female gender, vulva repair (including clitoral reduction) is usually begun by three months of age. Money suggests that if reduction of phallic tissue were delayed beyond the neonatal period, the infant would have traumatic memories of having been castrated.[10] Vaginoplasty, in those females having an adequate internal structure (e.g., the vaginal canal is near its expected location), is done between the ages of one and four years. Girls who require more complicated surgical procedures might not be surgically corrected until preadolescence.[11] The complete vaginal canal is typically constructed only when the body is fully grown, following pubertal feminization with estrogen, although more recently some specialists have claimed surgical success with vaginal construction in the early childhood years.[12] Although physicians speculate about the possible trauma of an early childhood "castration" memory, there is no corresponding concern that vaginal reconstructive surgery delayed beyond the neonatal period is traumatic.

Even though gender identity theory places the critical age limit for gender reassignment between eighteen months and two years, the physicians acknowledge that diagnosis, gender assignment, and genital reconstruction cannot be delayed for as long as two years, since a clear gender assignment and correctly formed genitals will determine the kind of interactions parents will have with the child.[13] The geneticist argued that when parents "change a diaper and see genitalia that don't mean much in terms of gender assignment, I think it prolongs the negative response to the baby....If you have clitoral enlargement that is so extraordinary that the parents can't distinguish between male and female, it is sometimes helpful to reduce that somewhat so that the parent views the child as female." Another physician concurred: parents "need to go home and do their job as child rearers with it very clear whether it's a boy or a girl."

DIAGNOSIS

A premature gender announcement by an obstetrician, prior to a close examination of an infant's genitals, can be problematic. Money and his colleagues claim that the primary complications in case management of intersexed infants can be traced to mishandling by medical personnel untrained in sexology.[14] According to one of the pediatric endocrinologists interviewed, obstetricians improperly educated about intersexed conditions "don't examine the babies closely enough at birth and say things just by looking, before separating legs and looking at everything, and jump to conclusions, because 99 percent of the time it's correct....People get upset, physicians I mean. And they say things that are inappropriate." For example, he said that an inexperienced obstetrician might blurt out, "I think you have a boy, or no, maybe you have a girl." Other inappropriate remarks a doctor might make in postdelivery consultation with the parents include, "You have a little boy, but he'll never function as a little boy, so you better raise him as a little girl." As a result, said the pediatric endocrinologist, "the family comes away with the idea that they have a little boy, and that's what they wanted, and that's what they're going to get." In such cases parents sometimes insist that the child be raised male despite the physician's instructions to the contrary. "People have in mind certain things they've heard, that this is a boy, and they're not likely to forget that, or they're not likely to let it go easily." The urologist agreed that the first gender attribution is critical: "Once it's been announced, you've got a big problem on your hands." "One of the worst things is to allow [the parents] to go ahead and give a name and tell everyone, and it turns out the child has to be raised in the opposite sex."[15]

Physicians feel that the mismanagement of such cases requires careful remedying. The psychoendocrinologist asserted, "When I'm involved, I spend hours with the parents to explain to them what has happened and how a mistake like that could be made, *or not really a mistake but a different decision*" (my emphasis). One pediatric endocrinologist said, "[I] try to dissuade them from previous misconceptions, and say, 'Well, I know what they meant, but the way they said it confused you. This is, I think, a better way to think about it.'" These statements reveal physicians' efforts not only to protect parents from concluding that their child is neither male nor female but also to protect other physicians' decision-making processes. Case management involves perpetuating the notion that good medical decisions are based on interpretations of the infant's real "sex" rather than on cultural understandings of gender.

"Mismanagements" are less likely to occur in communities with major medical centers, where specialists are prepared to deal with intersexuality and a medical team (perhaps drawing physicians from more than one teaching hospital) is quickly assembled. The team typically consists of the original referring doctor (obstetrician or pediatrician), a pediatric endocrinologist, a pediatric surgeon (urologist or gynecologist), and a geneticist. In addition, a psychologist, psychiatrist, or psychoendocrinologist might play a role. If an infant is born with ambiguous genitals in a small community hospital, without the relevant specialists on staff, she or he is likely to be transferred to a hospital where diagnosis and treatment are available. Intersexed infants born in poor rural areas where there is less medical intervention might never be referred for genital reconstruction. Many of these children, like those born in earlier historical periods, will grow up and live through adulthood with the condition of genital ambiguity—somehow managing.

The diagnosis of intersexed conditions includes assessing the chromosomal sex and the syndrome that produced the genital ambiguity, and may include medical procedures such as cytologic screening; chromosomal analysis; assessing serum electrolytes; hormone, gonadotropin, and steroids evaluation; digital examination; and radiographic genitography.[16] In any intersexed condition, if the infant is determined to be a genetic female (having an XX chromosome makeup), then the treatment—genital surgery to reduce the phallus size—can proceed relatively quickly, satisfying what the doctors believe are psychological and cultural demands. For example, 21-hydroxylase deficiency, a form of female pseudo-hermaphroditism and one of the most common conditions, can be determined by a blood test within the first few days.

If, on the other hand, the infant is determined to have at least one Y chromosome, then surgery may be considerably delayed. A decision must be made whether to test the ability of the phallic tissue to respond to (HCG) androgen treatment, which is intended to enlarge the microphallus enough to be a penis. The endocrinologist explained, "You do HCG testing and you find out if the male can make testosterone....You can get those results back probably within three weeks....You're sure the male is making testosterone—but can he respond to it? It can take three months of waiting to see whether the phallus responds." If the Y-chromosome infant cannot make testosterone or cannot respond to the testosterone it makes, the phallus will not develop, and the Y-chromosome infant is not considered to be a male after all.

Should the infant's phallus respond to the local application of testosterone or a brief course of intramuscular injections of low-potency androgen, the gender assignment problem is resolved, but possibly at some later cost, since the penis will not grow again at puberty when the rest of the body develops.[17] Money's case management philosophy assumes that while it may be difficult for an adult male to have a much smaller than average penis, it is very detrimental to the morale of the young boy to have a micropenis.[18] In the former case the male's manliness might be at stake, but in the latter case his essential maleness might be. Although the psychological consequences of these experiences have not been empirically documented, Money and his colleagues suggest that it is wise to avoid the problems of both the micropenis in childhood and the still undersized penis postpuberty by reassigning many of these infants to the female gender.[19] This approach suggests that for Money and his colleagues, chromosomes are less relevant in determining gender than penis size, and that, by implication, "male" is defined not by the genetic condition of having one Y and one X chromosome or by the production of sperm but by the aesthetic of having an appropriately sized penis.

The tests and procedures required for diagnosis (and, consequently, for gender assignment) can take several months.[20] Although physicians are anxious not to make a premature gender assignment, their language suggests that it is difficult for them to take a completely neutral position and think and speak only of phallic tissue that belongs to an infant whose gender has not yet been determined or decided. Comments such as "seeing whether the male can respond to testosterone" imply at least a tentative male gender assignment of an XY infant. The psychoendocrinologist's explanation to parents of their infant's treatment program also illustrates this implicit male gender assignment. "Clearly this baby has an underdeveloped phallus. But if the phallus responds to this treatment, we are fairly confident that surgical techniques and hormonal techniques will help this child to look like a boy. But we want to make absolutely sure and use some hormone treatments and see whether the tissue reacts." The mere fact that this doctor refers to the genitals as an "underdeveloped" phallus rather than an overdeveloped clitoris suggests that the infant has been judged to be, at least provisionally, a male. In the case of the undersized phallus, what is ambiguous is not whether this is a penis but whether it is "good enough" to remain one. If at the end of the treatment period the phallic tissue has not responded, what had been a potential penis (referred to in the medical literature as a "clitoropenis") is now considered an enlarged clitoris (or "penoclitoris"), and reconstructive surgery is planned as for the genetic female.

The time-consuming nature of intersex diagnosis and the assumption, based on gender identity theory, that gender should be assigned as soon as possible thus present physicians with difficult dilemmas. Medical personnel are committed to discovering the etiology of the condition in order to determine the best course of treatment, which takes time. Yet they feel an urgent need to provide an immediate assignment and genitals that look and function appropriately. An immediate assignment that will need to be retracted is more problematic than a delayed assignment, since reassignment carries with it an additional set of social complications. The endocrinologist interviewed commented: "We've come very far in that we can diagnose eventually, many of the conditions. But we haven't come far enough....We can't do it early enough....Very frequently a decision is made before all this information is available, simply because it takes so long to make the correct diagnosis. And you cannot let a child go indefinitely, not in this society you can't....There's pressure on parents [for a decision] and the parents transmit that pressure onto physicians." A pediatric endocrinologist agreed: "At times you may need to operate before a diagnosis can be made....In one case parents were told to wait on the announcement while the infant was treated to see if the phallus would grow when treated with androgens. After the first month passed and there was some growth, the parents said they gave it a boy's name. They could only wait a month."

Deliberating out loud on the judiciousness of making parents wait for assignment decisions, the endocrinologist asked rhetorically, "Why do we do all these tests if in the end we're going to make the decision simply on the basis of the appearance of the genitalia?" This question suggests that the principles underlying physicians' decisions are cultural rather than biological, based on parental reaction and the medical team's perception of the infant's societal adjustment prospects given the way her/his genitals look or could be made to look. Moreover, as long as the decision rests largely on the criterion of genital appearance, and male is defined as having a "good-sized" penis, more infants will be assigned to the female gender than to the male.

THE WAITING PERIOD: DEALING WITH AMBIGUITY

During the period of ambiguity between birth and assignment, physicians not only must evaluate the infant's prospects to be a good male but also must manage parents' uncertainty about a genderless child. Physicians advise that parents postpone announcing the gender of the infant until a gender has been explicitly assigned. They believe that parents should not feel compelled to tell other people. The clinical geneticist interviewed said that physicians "basically encourage [parents] to treat [the infant] as neuter." One of the pediatric endocrinologists reported that in France parents confronted with this dilemma sometimes give the infant a neuter name, such as Claude or Jean. The psychoendocrinologist concurred: "If you have a truly borderline situation, and you want to make it dependent on the hormone treatment...then the parents are...told, 'Try not to make a decision. Refer to the baby as "baby." Don't think in terms of boy or girl.'" Yet, when asked whether this is a reasonable request to make of parents in our society, the physician answered: "I don't think so. I think parents can't do it."...

The geneticist explained that when directly asked by parents what to tell others about the gender of the infant, she says, "Why don't you just tell them that the baby is having problems and as soon as the problems are resolved we'll get back to you." A pediatric endocrinologist echoes this suggestion in advising parents to say, "Until the problem is solved [we] would really prefer not to discuss any of the details." According to the urologist, "If [the gender] isn't announced people may mutter about it and may grumble about it, but they haven't got anything to get their teeth into and make trouble over for the child, or the parents, or whatever." In short, parents are asked to sidestep the infant's gender rather than admit the gender is unknown, thereby collaborating in a web of white lies, ellipses, and mystifications.[21]

Even while physicians teach the parents how to deal with others who will not find the infant's condition comprehensible or acceptable, physicians must also make the condition comprehensible and acceptable to the parents, normalizing the intersexed condition for them. In doing so they help the parents consider the infant's condition in the most positive way. There are four key aspects to this "normalizing" process.

First, physicians teach parents normal fetal development and explain that all fetuses have the potential to be male or female. One of the endocrinologists explains, "In the absence of maleness you have femaleness....It's really the basic design. The other [intersex] is really a variation on a theme." This explanation presents the intersex condition as a natural phase of every fetal development. Another endocrinologist "like[s] to show picture[s] to them and explain that at a certain point in development males and females look alike and then diverge for such and such reason." The professional literature suggests that doctors use diagrams that illustrate "nature's principle of using the same anlagen to produce the external genital parts of the male and female."[22]

Second, physicians stress the normalcy of the infant in other aspects. For example, the geneticist tells parents, "The baby is healthy, but there was a problem in the way the baby was developing." The endocrinologist says the infant has "a mild defect, just like anything could be considered a birth defect, a mole or a hemangioma." This language not only eases the blow to the parents but also redirects their attention. Terms like "hermaphrodite" or "abnormal" are not used. The urologist said that he advised parents "about the generalization of sticking to the good things and not confusing people with something that is unnecessary."

Third, physicians (at least initially) imply that it is not the gender of the child that is ambiguous but the genitals. They talk about "undeveloped," "maldeveloped," or "unfinished" organs. From a number of the physicians interviewed came the following explanations: "At a point in time the development proceeded in a different way, and sometimes the development isn't complete and we may have some trouble…in determining what the *actual* sex is. And so we have to do a blood test to help us" (my emphasis); "The baby may be a female, which you would know after the buccal smear, but you can't prove it yet. If so, then it's a normal female with a different appearance. This can be surgically corrected"; "The gender of your child isn't apparent to us at the moment"; "While this looks like a small penis, it's actually a large clitoris. And what we're going to do is put it back in its proper position and reduce the size of the tip of it enough so it doesn't look funny, so it looks right." Money and his colleagues report a case in which parents were advised to tell their friends that the reason their infant's gender was reannounced from male to female is that "the baby was…'closed up down there'…when the closed skin was divided, the female organs were revealed, and the baby discovered to be, *in fact,* a girl" (emphasis mine). It was mistakenly assumed to be a male at first because "there was an excess of skin on the clitoris."[23]

The message in these examples is that the trouble lies in the doctor's ability to determine the gender, not in the baby's gender per se. The real gender will presumably be determined/proven by testing, and the "bad" genitals (which are confusing the situation for everyone) will be "repaired." The emphasis is not on the doctors creating gender but in their completing the genitals. Physicians say that they "reconstruct" the genitals rather than "construct" them. The surgeons reconstitute from remaining parts what should have been there all along. The fact that gender in an infant is "reannounced" rather than "reassigned" suggests that the first announcement was a mistake because the announcer was confused by the genitals. The gender always was what it is now seen to be.[24]

Finally, physicians tell parents that social factors are more important in gender development than biological ones, even though they are searching for biological causes. In essence, the physicians teach the parents Money and Ehrhardt's theory of gender development.[25] In doing so, they shift the emphasis from the discovery of biological factors that are a sign of the "real" gender to providing the appropriate social conditions to produce the "real" gender. What remains unsaid is the apparent contradiction in the notion that a "real" or "natural" gender can be, or needs to be, produced artificially. The physician/parent discussions make it clear to family members that gender is not a biological given (even though, of course, their own procedures for diagnosis assume that it is), and that gender is fluid. The psychoendocrinologist paraphrased an explanation to parents thus: "It will depend, ultimately, on how everybody treats your child and how your child is looking as a person....I can with confidence tell them that generally gender [identity] clearly agrees with the assignment." Similarly, a pediatric endocrinologist explained: "[I] try to impress upon them that there's an enormous amount of clinical data to support the fact that if you sex-reverse an infant...the majority of the time the alternative gender identity is commensurate with the socialization, the way that they're raised, and how people view them, and that seems to be the most critical."

The implication of these comments is that gender identity (of all children, not just those born with ambiguous genitals) is determined primarily by social factors, that the parents and community always construct the child's gender. In the case of intersexed infants, the physicians merely provide the right genitals to go along with the socialization. Of course, at normal births, when the infant's genitals are unambiguous, the parents are not told that the child's gender is ultimately up to socialization. In those cases, doctors do treat gender as a biological given.

SOCIAL FACTORS IN DECISION MAKING

Most of the physicians interviewed claimed that personal convictions of doctors ought to play no role in the decision-making process. The psychoendocrinologist explained: "I think the most critical factors [are] what is the possibility that this child will grow up with genitals which look like that of the assigned gender and which will ultimately function according to gender...That's why it's so important that it's a well-established team, because [personal convictions] can't really enter into it. It has to be what is surgically and endocrinologically possible for that baby to be able to make it...It's really much more within medical criteria. I don't think many social factors enter into it." While this doctor eschews the importance of social factors in gender assignment, she argues forcefully that social factors are extremely important in the development of gender identity. Indeed, she implies that social factors primarily enter the picture once the infant leaves the hospital.

In fact, doctors make decisions about gender on the basis of shared cultural values that are unstated, perhaps even unconscious, and therefore considered objective rather than subjective. Money states the fundamental rule for gender assignment: "Never assign a baby to be reared, and to surgical and hormonal therapy, as a boy, unless the phallic structure, hypospadiac or otherwise, is neonatally of at least the same caliber as that of same-aged males with small-average penises."[26] Elsewhere, he and his colleagues provide specific measurements for what qualifies as a micropenis: "A penis is, by convention, designated as a micropenis when at birth its dimensions are three or more standard deviations below the mean....When it is correspondingly reduced in diameter with corpora that are vestigial...it unquestionably qualifies as a micropenis."[27] A pediatric endocrinologist claimed that although "the [size of the] phallus is not the deciding factor...if the phallus is less than 2 centimeters long at birth and won't respond to androgen treatments, then it's made into a female."

These guidelines are clear, but they focus on only one physical feature, one that is distinctly imbued with cultural meaning. This becomes especially apparent in the case of an XX infant with normal female reproductive gonads and a perfect penis. Would the size and shape of the penis, in this case, be the deciding factor in assigning the infant "male," or would the perfect penis be surgically destroyed and female genitals created? Money notes that this dilemma would be complicated by the anticipated reaction of the parents to seeing "their apparent son lose his penis."[28] Other researchers concur that parents are likely to want to raise a child with a normal-shaped penis (regardless of size) as "male," particularly if the scrotal area looks normal and if the parents have had no experience with intersexuality.[29] Elsewhere Money argues in favor of not neonatally amputating the penis of XX infants, since fetal masculinization of brain structures would predispose them "almost invariably [to] develop behaviorally as tomboys, even when reared as girls."[30] This reasoning implies, first, that tomboyish behavior in girls is bad and should be avoided; and, second, that it is preferable to remove the internal female organs, implant prosthetic testes, and regulate the "boy's" hormones for his entire life than to overlook or disregard the perfection of the penis.[31]

The ultimate proof to these physicians that they intervened appropriately and gave the intersexed infant the correct gender assignment is that the reconstructed genitals look normal and function normally once the patient reaches adulthood. The vulva, labia, and clitoris should appear ordinary to the woman and her partner(s), and the vagina should appear ordinary to the woman and her partner(s), and the vagina should be able to receive a normal-sized penis. Similarly, the man and his partner(s) should feel that his penis (even if somewhat smaller than the norm) looks and functions in an unremarkable way. Although there is no reported data on how much emphasis the intersexed person, him- or herself, places upon genital appearance and functioning, the physicians are absolutely clear about what they believe is important. The clinical geneticist said, "If you have...a seventeen-year-old young lady who has gotten hormone therapy and has breast development and pubic hair and no vaginal opening, I can't even entertain the notion that this young lady wouldn't want to have corrective surgery."

The urologist summarized his criteria: "Happiness is the biggest factor. Anatomy is part of happiness." Money states, "The primary deficit [of not having a sufficient penis]—and destroyer of morale—lies in being unable to satisfy the partner."[32] Another team of clinicians reveals their phallocentrism, arguing that the most serious mistake in gender assignment is to create "an individual unable to engage in genital [heterosexual] sex."[33]

The equation of gender with genitals could only have emerged in an age when medical science can create credible-appearing and functioning genitals, and an emphasis on the good phallus above all else could only have emerged in a culture that has rigid aesthetic and performance criteria for what constitutes maleness. The formulation "good penis equals male; absence of good penis equals female" is treated in the literature and by the physicians interviewed as an objective criterion, operative in all cases. There is a striking lack of attention to the size and shape requirements of the female genitals, other than that the vagina be able to receive a penis.[34]

In the late nineteenth century when women's reproductive function was culturally designated as their essential characteristic, the presence or absence of ovaries (whether or not they were fertile) was held to be the ultimate criterion of gender assignment for hermaphrodites. The urologist interviewed recalled a case as late as the 1950s of a male child reassigned to "female" at the age of four or five because ovaries had been discovered. Nevertheless, doctors today, schooled in the etiology and treatment of the various intersex syndromes, view decisions based primarily on gonads as wrong, although, they complain, the conviction that the gonads are the ultimate criterion "still dictates the decisions of the uneducated and uninformed."[35] Presumably, the educated and informed now know that decisions based primarily on phallic size, shape, and sexual capacity are right.

While the prospect of constructing good genitals is the primary consideration in physicians' gender assignments, another extra-medical factor was repeatedly cited by the six physicians interviewed—the specialty of the attending physician. Although generally intersexed infants are treated by teams of specialists, only the person who coordinates the team is actually responsible for the case. The person, acknowledged by the other physicians as having chief responsibility, acts as spokesperson to the parents. Although all of the physicians claimed that these medical teams work smoothly with few discrepancies of opinion, several of them mentioned decision-making orientations that are grounded in particular medical specializations. One endocrinologist stated, "The easiest route to take, where there is ever any question...is to raise the child as female...In this country that is usual if the infant falls into the hands of a pediatric endocrinologist...If the decision is made by the urologists, who are mostly males,...they're always opting, because they do the surgery, they're always feeling they can correct anything." Another endocrinologist concurred: "[Most urologists] don't think in terms of dynamic processes. They're interested in fixing pipes and lengthening pipes, and not dealing with hormonal, and certainly not psychological issues.... 'What can I do with what I've got.'" Urologists were defended by the clinical geneticist: "Surgeons here, now I can't speak for elsewhere, they don't get into a situation where the child is a year old and they can't make anything." Whether or not urologists "like to make boys," as one endocrinologist claimed, the following example from a urologist who was interviewed explicitly links a cultural interpretation of masculinity to the medical treatment plan. The case involved an adolescent who had been assigned the female gender at birth but was developing some male pubertal signs and wanted to be a boy. "He was ill-equipped," said the urologist, "yet we made a very respectable male out of him. He now owns a huge construction business—those big cranes that put stuff up on the building."

POSTINFANCY CASE MANAGEMENT

After the infant's gender has been assigned, parents generally latch onto the assignment as the solution to the problem—and it is. The physician as detective has collected the evidence, as lawyer has presented the case, and as judge has rendered a verdict. Although most of the interviewees claimed that the parents are equal participants in the whole process, they gave no instances of parental participation prior to the gender assignment.[36] After the physicians assign the infant's gender, the parents are encouraged to establish the credibility of that gender publicly by, for example, giving a detailed medical explanation to a leader in their community, such as a physician or pastor, who will explain the situation to curious casual acquaintances. Money argues that "medical terminology has a special layman's magic in such a context; it is final and authoritative and closes the issue." He also recommends that eventually the mother "settle [the] argument once and for all among her women friends by allowing some of them to see the baby's reconstructed genitalia."[37] Apparently, the powerful influence of normal-looking genitals helps overcome a history of ambiguous gender.

Some of the same issues that arise in assigning gender recur some years later when, at adolescence, the child may be referred to a physician for counseling.[38] The physician then tells the adolescent many of the same things his or her parents had been told years before, with the same language. Terms like "abnormal," "disorder," "disease," and "hermaphroditism" are avoided; the condition is normalized, and the child's gender is treated as unproblematic. One clinician explains to his patients that sex organs are different in appearance for each person, not just those who are intersexed. Furthermore, he tells the girls "that while most women menstruate, not all do... that conception is only one of a number of ways to become a parent; [and] that today some individuals are choosing not to become parents."[39] The clinical geneticist tells a typical female patient: "You are female. Female is not determined by your genes. Lots of other things determine being a woman. And you are a woman but you won't be able to have babies."

A case reported by one of the pediatric endocrinologists involving an adolescent female with androgen insensitivity provides an intriguing insight into the postinfancy gender-management process. She was told at the age of fourteen "that her ovaries weren't normal and had been removed. That's why she needed pills to look normal....I wanted to convince her of her femininity. They I told her she could marry and have normal sexual relations...[her] uterus won't develop but [she] could adopt children." The urologist interviewed was asked to comment on this handling of the counseling. "It sounds like a very good solution to it. He's stating the truth, and if you don't state the truth...then you're in trouble later." This is a strange version of "the truth," however, since the adolescent was chromosomally XY and was born with normal testes that produced normal quantities of androgen. There were no existing ovaries or uterus to be abnormal. Another pediatric endocrinologist, in commenting on the management of this case, hedged the issue by saying that he would have used a generic term like "the gonads." A third endocrinologist said she would say that the uterus had never formed.

Technically these physicians are lying when, for example, they explain to an adolescent XY female with an intersexed history that her "ovaries...had to be removed because they were unhealthy or were producing 'the wrong balance of hormones.'"[40] We can presume that these lies are told in the service of what the physicians consider a greater good—keeping individual/ concrete genders as clear and uncontaminated as the notions of female and male are in the abstract. The clinician suggests that with some female patients it eventually may be possible to talk to them "about their gonads having some structures and features that are testicular-like."[41] This call for honesty might be based at least partly on the possibility of the child's discovering his or her chromosomal sex inadvertently from a buccal smear taken in a high school biology class. Today's litigious climate is possibly another encouragement.

In sum, the adolescent is typically told that certain internal organs did not form because of an endocrinological defect, not because those organs could never have developed in someone with her or his sex chromosomes. The topic of chromosomes is skirted. There are no published studies on how these adolescents experience their condition and their treatment by doctors. An endocrinologist interviewed mentioned that her adolescent patients rarely ask specifically what is wrong with them, suggesting that they are accomplices in this evasion. In spite of the "truth" having being evaded, the clinician's impression is that "their gender identities and general senses of well-being and self-esteem appear not to have suffered."[42]

CONCLUSION

Physicians conduct careful examinations of intersexed infants' genitals and perform intricate laboratory procedures. They are interpreters of the body, trained and committed to uncovering the "actual" gender obscured by ambiguous genitals. Yet they also have considerable leeway in assigning gender, and their decisions are influenced by cultural as well as medical factors. What is the relationship between the physician as discoverer and the physician as determiner of gender? Where is the relative emphasis placed in discussions with parents and adolescents and in the consciousness of physicians? It is misleading to characterize the doctors whose words are provided here as presenting themselves publicly to the parents as discoverers of the infant's real gender but privately acknowledging that the infant has no real gender other than the one being determined or constructed by the medical professionals. They are not hypocritical. It is also misleading to claim that physicians' focus shifts from discovery to determination over the course of treatment: first the doctors regard the infant's gender as an unknown but discoverable reality; then the doctors relinquish their attempts to find the real gender and treat the infant's gender as something they must construct. They are not medically incompetent or deficient. Instead, I am arguing that the peculiar balance of discovery and determination throughout treatment permits physicians to handle very problematic cases of gender in the most problematic of ways.

This balance relies fundamentally on a particular conception of the "natural."[43] Although the deformity of intersexed genitals would be immutable were it not for medical interference, physicians do not consider it natural. Instead they think of, and speak of, the surgical/hormonal alteration of such deformities as natural because such intervention returns the body to what it "ought to have been" if events had taken their typical course. The nonnormative is converted into the normative, and the normative state is considered natural.[44] The genital ambiguity is remedied to conform to a "natural," that is, culturally indisputable, gender dichotomy. Sherry Ortner's claim that the culture/nature distinction is itself a construction—a product of culture—is relevant here. Language and imagery help create and maintain a specific view of what is natural about the two genders and, I would argue, about the very idea of gender—that it consists of two exclusive types: female and male.[45] The belief that gender consists of two exclusive types is maintained and perpetuated by the medical community in the face of incontrovertible physical evidence that this is not mandated by biology.

The lay conception of human anatomy and physiology assumes a concordance among clearly dimorphic gender markers—chromosomes, genitals, gonads, hormones—but physicians understand that concordance and dimorphism do not always exist. Their understanding of biology's complexity, however, does not inform their understanding of gender's complexity. In order for intersexuality to be managed differently than it currently is, physicians would have to take seriously Money's assertion that it is a misrepresentation of epistemology to consider any cell in the body authentically male or female.[46] If authenticity for gender resides not in a discoverable nature but in someone's proclamation, then the power to proclaim something else is available. If physicians recognized that implicit in their management of gender is the notion that finally, and always, people construct gender as well as the social systems that are grounded in gender-based concepts, the possibilities for real societal transformations would be unlimited. Unfortunately, neither in their representations to the families of the intersexed nor among themselves do the physicians interviewed for this study draw such far-reaching implications from their work. Their "understanding" that particular genders are medically (re)constructed in these cases does not lead them to see that gender is always constructed. Accepting genital ambiguity as a natural option would require that physicians also acknowledge that genital ambiguity is "corrected" not because it is threatening to the infant's life but because it is threatening to the infant's culture.

Rather than admit to their role in perpetuating gender, physicians "psychologize" the issue by talking about the parents' anxiety and humiliation in being confronted with an anomalous infant. The physicians talk as though they have no choice but to respond to the parents' pressure for a resolution of psychological discomfort, and as though they have no choice but to use medical technology in the service of a two-gender culture. Neither the psychology nor the technology is doubted, since both shield physicians from responsibility. Indeed, for the most part, neither physicians nor parents emerge from the experience of intersex case management with a greater understanding of the social construction of gender. Society's accountability, like their own, is masked by the assumption that gender is a given. Thus, cases of intersexuality, instead of illustrating nature's failure to ordain gender in these isolated "unfortunate" instances, illustrate physicians' and Western society's failure of imagination—the failure to imagine that each of these management decisions is a moment when a specific instance of biological "sex" is transformed into a culturally constructed gender.

NOTES

1   For historical reviews of the intersexed person in ancient Greek and Roman periods, see Leslie Fiedler, *Freaks: Myths and Images of the Second Self* (New York: Simon & Schuster, 1978); Vern Bullough, *Sexual Variance in Society and History* (New York: Wiley, 1976). For the Middle Ages and Renaissance, see Michel Foucault, *History of Sexuality* (New York: Pantheon, 1980). For the eighteenth and nineteenth centuries, see Michel Foucault, *Herculine Barbin* (New York: Pantheon, 1978); and for the early twentieth century, see Havelock Ellis, *Studies in the Psychology of Sex* (New York: Random House, 1942).

2   Suzanne J. Kessler and Wendy McKenna, *Gender: An Ethnomethodological Approach* (1978; reprint, Chicago: University of Chicago Press, 1985).

3   Mariano Castro-Magana, Moris Angulo, and Platon J. Collipp, "Management of the Child with Ambiguous Genitalia," *Medical Aspects of Human Sexuality* 18 (April 1984): 172–88.

4   For example, infants whose intersexuality is caused by congenital adrenal hyperplasia can develop severe electrolyte disturbances unless the condition is controlled by cortisone treatments. Intersexed infants whose condition is caused by androgen insensitivity are in danger of malignant degeneration of the testes unless they are removed. For a complete catalog of clinical syndromes related to the intersexed condition, see Arye Lev-Ran, "Sex Reversal as Related to Clinical Syndromes in Human Beings," in *Handbook of Sexology II: Genetics, Hormones and Behavior,* ed. John Money and H. Musaph (New York: Elsevier, 1978), 157–73.

5   Much of the surgical experimentation in this area has been accomplished by urologists who are trying to create penises for female-to-male transsexuals. Although there have been some advancements in recent years in the ability to create a "reasonable-looking" penis from tissue taken elsewhere on the body, the complicated requirements of the organ (both urinary and sexual functioning) have posed surgical problems. It may be, however, that the concerns of the urologists are not identical to the concerns of the patients. While data are not yet available from the intersexed, we know that female-to-male transsexuals place greater emphasis on the "public" requirements of the penis (e.g., being able to look normal while standing at the urinal or wearing a bathing suit) than on its functional requirements (e.g., being able to carry urine or achieve an erection) (Kessler and McKenna, 128–32). As surgical techniques improve, female-to-male transsexuals (and intersexed males) might increase their demands for organs that look and function better.

6   Historically, psychology has tended to blur the distinction between the two by equating a person's acceptance of her or his genitals with gender role and ignoring gender identity. For example, Freudian theory posited that if one had a penis and accepted its reality, then masculine gender role behavior would naturally follow (Sigmund Freud, "Some Psychical Consequences of the Anatomical Distinctions between the Sexes" [1925], vol. 18 of *The Complete Psychological Works,* ed. and trans. J. Strachey [New York: Norton, 1976]).

7   Almost all of the published literature on intersexed infant case management has been written or cowritten by one researcher, John Money, professor of medical psychology and professor of pediatrics, emeritus, at the Johns Hopkins University and Hospital, where he is director of the Psychohormonal Research Unit. Even the publications that are produced independently of Money reference him and reiterate his management philosophy. Although only one of the physicians interviewed publishes with Money, all of them essentially concur with his views and give the impression of a consensus that is rarely encountered in science. The one physician who raised some questions about Money's philosophy and the gender theory on which it is based has extensive experience with intersexuality in a nonindustrialized culture where the infant is managed differently with no apparent harm to gender development. Even though psychologists fiercely argue issues of gender identity and gender role development, doctors who treat

intersexed infants seem untouched by these debates. There are no renegade voices either from within the medical establishment or, thus far, from outside. Why Money has been so single-handedly influential in promoting his ideas about gender is a question worthy of a separate substantial analysis. His management philosophy is conveyed in the following sources: John Money, J. G. Hampson, and J. L. Hampson, "Hermaphroditism: Recommendations concerning Assignment of Sex, Change of Sex, and Psychologic Management," *Bulletin of the Johns Hopkins Hospital* 97 (1955): 284–300; John Money, Reynolds Potter, and Clarice S. Stoll, "Sex Reannouncement in Hereditary Sex Deformity: Psychology and Sociology of Habilitation," *Social Science and Medicine* 3 (1969): 207–16; John Money and Anke A. Ehrhardt, *Man and Woman, Boy and Girl* (Baltimore: Johns Hopkins University Press, 1972); John Money, "Psychologic Consideration of Sex Assignment in Intersexuality," *Clinics in Plastic Surgery* 1 (April 1974): 215–22, "Psychological Counseling: Hermaphroditism," in *Endocrine and Genetic Diseases of Childhood and Adolescence*, ed. L. I. Gardner (Philadelphia: Saunders, 1975): 609–18, and "Birth Defect of the Sex Organs: Telling the Parents and the Patient," *British Journal of Sexual Medicine* 10 (March 1983): 14; John Money et al., "Micropenis, Family Mental Health, and Neonatal Management: A Report on Fourteen Patients Reared as Girls," *Journal of Preventive Psychiatry* 1, no. 1 (1981): 17–27.

8   Money and Ehrhardt, 152.

9   Contradictory data are presented in Milton Diamond, "Sexual Identity, Monozygotic Twins Reared in Discordant Sex Roles and a BBC Follow-up," *Archives of Sexual Behaviour* 11, no. 2 (1982): 181–86.

10   Money, "Psychologic Consideration of Sex Assignment in Intersexuality."

11   Castro-Magana, Angulo, and Collipp (n. 3 above).

12   Victor Braren et al., "True Hermaphroditism: A Rational Approach to Diagnosis and Treatment," *Urology* 15 (June 1980): 569–74.

13   Studies of normal newborns have shown that from the moment of birth the parent responds to the infant based on the infant's gender. Jeffrey Rubin, F. J. Provenzano, and Z. Luria, "The Eye of the Beholder: Parents' Views on Sex of Newborns," *American Journal of Orthopsychiatry* 44, no. 4 (1974): 512–19.

14   Money et al. (n. 7 above).

15   There is evidence from other kinds of sources that once a gender attribution is made, all further information buttresses that attribution, and only the most contradictory new information will cause the original gender attribution to be questioned. See, e.g., Kessler and McKenna (n. 2 above).

16   Castro-Magana, Angulo, and Collipp (n. 3 above).

17   Money, "Psychological Consideration of Sex Assignment in Intersexuality" (n. 7 above).

18   Technically, the term "micropenis" should be reserved for an exceptionally small but well-formed structure. A small, malformed "penis" should be referred to as a "microphallus."

19   Money et al., 26. A different view is argued by another leading gender identity theorist: "When a little boy (with an imperfect penis) knows he is a male, he

creates a penis that functions symbolically the same as those of boys with normal penises" (Robert J. Stoller, *Sex and Gender* [New York: Aronson, 1968], 1:49).

20   W. Ch. Hecker, "Operative Correction of Intersexual Genitals in Children," *Pediatric Surgery* 17 (1984): 21–31.

21   These evasions must have many ramifications in everyday social interactions between parents and family and friends. How people "fill in" the uncertainty so that interactions remain relatively normal is an interesting issue that warrants further study. Indeed, the whole issue of parent reaction is worthy of analysis. One of the pediatric endocrinologists interviewed acknowledged that the published literature discusses intersex management only from the physicians' point of view. He asks. "How [do parents] experience what they're told; and what [do] they remember…and carry with them?" One published exception to this neglect of the parents' perspective is a case study comparing two couples' different coping strategies. The first couple, although initially distressed, handled the traumatic event by regarding the abnormality as an act of God. The second couple, more educated and less religious, put their faith in medical science and expressed a need to fully understand the biochemistry of the defect.

22   Tom Mazur, "Ambiguous Genitalia: Detection and Counseling," *Pediatric Nursing* 9 (November/December 1983): 417–31; Money, "Psychologic Consideration of Sex Assignment in Intersexuality" (n. 7, above), 218.

23   Money, Potter, and Stoll (n. 7 above), 211.

24   The term "reassignment" is more commonly used to describe the gender changes of those who are cognizant of their earlier gender, e.g., transsexuals—people whose gender itself was a mistake.

25   Although Money and Ehrhardt's socialization theory is uncontested by the physicians who treat intersexuality and is presented to parents as a matter of fact, there is actually much debate among psychologists about the effect of prenatal hormones on brain structure and ultimately on gender role behavior and even on gender identity. The physicians interviewed agreed that the animal evidence for prenatal brain organization is compelling but that there is no evidence in humans that prenatal hormones have an inviolate or unilateral effect. If there is any effect of prenatal exposure to androgen, they believe it can easily be overcome and modified by psychosocial factors. It is this latter position that is communicated to the parents, not the controversy in the field. For an argument favoring prenatally organized gender differences in the brain, see Milton Diamond, "Human Sexual Development: Biological Foundations for Social Development," in *Human Sexuality in Four Perspectives*, ed. Frank A. Beach (Baltimore: Johns Hopkins University Press, 1976), 22–61; for a critique of that position, see Ruth Bleier, *Science and Gender: A Critique of Biology and Its Theories on Women* (New York: Pergamon, 1984).

26   Money, "Psychological Counseling: Hermaphroditism" (n. 7 above), 610.

27   Money et al. (n. 7 above), 18.

28   John Money, "Hermaphroditism and Pseudohermaphroditism," in *Gynecologic Endocrinology*, ed. Jay J. Gold (New York: Hoeber, 1968), 449–64, esp. 460.

29 Mojtaba Besheshti et al., "Gender Assignment in Male Pseudohermaphrodite Children," *Urology* (December 1983): 604–7. Of course, if the penis looked normal and the empty scrotum were overlooked, it might not be discovered until puberty that the male child was XX, with a female internal structure.

30 John Money, "Psychologic Consideration of Sex Assignment in Intersexuality" (n. 7 above), 216.

31 Weighing the probability of achieving a perfect penis against the probable trauma such procedures might involve is another social factor in decision making. According to an endocrinologist interviewed, if it seemed that an XY infant with an inadequate penis would require as many as ten genital operations over a six-year period in order to have an adequate penis, the infant would be assigned the female gender. In this case, the endocrinologist's practical and compassionate concern would override purely genital criteria.

32 Money, "Psychologic Consideration of Sex Assignment in Intersexuality," 217.

33 Castro-Magana, Angulo, and Collipp (n. 3 above), 180.

34 It is unclear how much of this bias is the result of a general, cultural devaluation of the female and how much the result of physicians' greater facility in constructing aesthetically correct and sexually functional female genitals.

35 Money, "Psychologic Consideration of Sex Assignment in Intersexuality," 215. Remnants of this anachronistic view can still be found, however, when doctors justify the removal of contradictory gonads on the grounds that they are typically sterile or at risk for malignancy (J. Dewhurst and D. B. Grant, "Intersex Problems," *Archives of Disease in Childhood* 59 [July–December 1984]: 1191–94). Presumably, if the gonads were functional and healthy their removal would provide an ethical dilemma for at least some medical professionals.

36 Although one set of authors argued that the views of the parents on the most appropriate gender for their child must be taken into account (Dewhurst and Grant, 1192), the physicians interviewed denied direct knowledge of this kind of participation. They claimed that they personally had encountered few, if any, cases of parents who insisted on their child's being assigned a particular gender. Yet each had heard about cases where a family's ethnicity or religious background biased them toward males. None of the physicians recalled whether this preference for male offspring meant the parents wanted a male regardless of the "inadequacy" of the penis, or whether it meant that the parents would have greater difficulty adjusting to a less-than-perfect male than with a "normal" female.

37 Money, "Psychological Counseling: Hermaphroditism" (n. 7 above), 613.

38 As with the literature on infancy, most of the published material on adolescents is on surgical and hormonal management rather than on social management. See, e.g., Joel J. Roslyn, Eric W. Fonkalsrud, and Barbara Lippe, "Intersex Disorders in Adolescents and Adults," *American Journal of Surgery* 146 (July 1983): 138–44.

39 Mazur (n. 22 above), 421.

40 Dewhurst and Grant, 1193.

41 Mazur, 422.

42 Ibid.

43 For an extended discussion of different ways of conceptualizing "natural," see Richard W. Smith, "What Kind of Sex Is Natural?" in *The Frontiers of Sex Research*, ed. Vern Bullough (Buffalo: Prometheus, 1979), 103–11.

44 This supports sociologist Harold Garfinkel's argument that we treat routine events as our due as social members and that we treat gender, like all normal forms, as a moral imperative. It is no wonder, then, that physicians conceptualize what they are doing as natural and unquestionably "right" (Harold Garfinkel, *Studies in Ethnomethodology* [Englewood Cliffs, N.J.: Prentice Hall, 1967]).

45 Sherry B. Ortner, "Is Female to Male as Nature Is to Culture?" in *Woman, Culture, and Society*, ed. Michelle Zimbalist Rosaldo and Louise Lamphere (Stanford, Calif.: Stanford University Press, 1974), 67–87.

46 Money, "Psychological Counseling: Hermaphroditism" (n. 7 above), 618.

3

Sex Change Operations: The Last Bulwark of the Double Standard

Margrit Eichler

Sex change operations have become increasingly frequent over the past decade. The fact that modern societies are willing to allocate a portion of their scarce resource of highly trained medical personnel and highly sophisticated and expensive medical instruments for such operations suggests a complete acceptance of sex role ideology and therefore an extreme intolerance of sexual ambiguity.

In conventional psychology, people distinguish between people who have a "sex-appropriate gender identity" and those who have a confused gender identity, or exhibit a "gender dysphoria syndrome" (Meyer, 1974). Within the last decade, the treatment of people with gender dysphoria, that is, people who believe that they have the wrong-sexed body for their "real" self, has increasingly been through sex change operations, more commonly referred to in the literature as "sex reassignment surgery."

Sex reassignment surgery has as its goal to make a man as much as is anatomically possible similar to a woman, although it can never make a woman out of a man. The intention of the surgery is to make it possible for the erstwhile male to live as much as possible like a woman, and to be accepted as a woman by his (now her) friends and acquaintances. Vice versa, the surgery aims to make a woman as much as is anatomically possible similar to a man, although, again, it can never make a man out of a woman. Again, the surgery is considered successful if the erstwhile woman is accepted and treated as a man by her (now his) friends and acquaintances. In general, sex reassignment surgery is a costly and long process, and the final surgery which gives it its name is only, if responsibly done, the last step in a several years' process of "changing one's sex"—namely, living in the mode of a member of the opposite sex.

As a rule, transsexualism for a man who wants to become a woman involves, first, hormone treatment, which increases his breast development, effectively sterilises him, and decreases his facial hair growth. A second step

From Margrit Eichler, *The Double Standard* (London: Croom Helm Ltd., 1980), 72–88. Reprinted by permission of the author.

would be electrolysis of his facial hair, of his breast hair and, if necessary, of other parts. After the second hair removal, the hair is usually permanently removed. Sometimes a hair transplant to alter his hair line at the forehead and/or a nose operation are performed. Sometimes breast implants are made to increase his breast size beyond the increase that is due to the hormonal treatment. At this point the patient is often expected to live as a woman for a minimum of six months, and, if possible, for several years. Physicians seem to vary greatly in this requirement, but most seem to be more willing to perform the ultimate sex reassignment surgery the longer the patient has already lived as a member of the sex which he wishes to join. The next step, then, is the removal of the penis and the testes and, lastly, the construction of an artificial vagina (vaginoplasty), with which the person is actually capable of having sexual intercourse, assuming the role of the woman, sometimes to such a degree that her partner is unaware of the fact that the person used to be an anatomical male.

For female-to-male transsexuals, the process is even more complicated. As with male-to-female transsexuals, the first medical step is usually hormone treatments. The androgens tend to lower the voice, and to stimulate facial hair growth. After a prolonged period of time, they also effectively sterilise the erstwhile woman, and periods cease, just as the man with a great influx of estrogens becomes incapable of ejaculation. The next step would be the surgical removal of the breasts, and preceding or succeeding it a hysterectomy (removal of the uterus). This is about as far as many female-to-male transsexuals can go, although there is, by now, a technology which allows the construction of a penis (phalloplasty). The construction of a penis by surgical means is more complicated than the removal of the male sex organs and the construction of an artificial vagina: female-to-male transsexuals can receive a penile construction and an implant of simulated testes which look like male genitals, but the penis cannot get erect, and, of course, cannot ejaculate since there are no functioning testes, and often it cannot even be used for urination. For sexual intercourse it seems to be useless (with the exception of one case that has been reported). The surgical changes are, therefore, of an even more cosmetic nature (since still less functional than the artificial vagina) than those of the male-to-female transsexual.

As can be seen, the whole process is by necessity painful, physically as well as emotionally, and expensive. Persons undergoing sex reassignment surgery need to possess a great deal of determination in order to obtain the desired treatments and operations. Nevertheless, there is no doubt that the incidence of these sex reassignment surgeries has greatly increased over the past few years....Overall, Pauly (1974a:493) estimates the prevalence of male transsexualism as 1:100,000 and of female transsexualism as 1:130,000 of the general population....

The generic term that is utilised to describe a person who wishes to live as a member of the other sex is "transsexual." In the last years, the term has been utilised to designate all those people who seek (but do not necessarily obtain) a sex change operation. The ratio of patients receiving surgery and those requesting it has been estimated as 1:9 (Bentler, 1976:577). The usage of calling all patients requesting surgery transsexual has been criticised by Meyer (1974) as being too vague, and he proposes to call transsexual only those people who have actually managed to live as members of the other sex. It is common to distinguish between post-operative and pre-operative trans-sexuals. This, to me, seems a very questionable custom, since it assumes that all "pre-operative" transsexuals will, some day, become post-operative, which is not the case. More important, it stresses the surgical aspect of transsexualism rather than the cultural aspect by implying that transsexualism culminates in sex reassignment surgery, and that a form of transsexualism which involves living as a member of the opposite sex without surgery is simply a step to having surgery performed. If nothing else, it indicates the mechanical nature of the way in which gender dysphoria is regarded among the clinical experts....

Transsexuals tend to be homosexual in so far as they tend to prefer sexual contacts with a member of the sex to which they belong physically. Since they believe themselves to be people trapped in an anatomically wrong body, this desire is not subjectively experienced as homosexuality, but as heterosexuality, and consequently, a male-to-female transsexual is likely to prefer a man who is not a self-defined homosexual and a female-to-male transsexual is likely to prefer a woman who is not a self-defined lesbian as sexual partners....

...My major thesis here is that transsexual patients have an excessively narrow image of what constitutes "sex-appropriate" behavior, which is reflected in the attitudes of the attending clinicians (psychologists, therapists and medical doctors) and the family of origin of the patient. Were the notions of masculinity and femininity less rigid, sex change operations should be unnecessary. Rather than identify somebody with a "gender identity problem" as sick, we could define a society which insists on raising boys and girls in a clearly differentiated manner as sick. What should be treated as a *social* pathology is treated as if it were normal and when it manifests its effect in individuals it is treated as an *individual* pathology, and is "corrected," rather than any attempts being made to combat the issue at its root: the oppressive (non-human) definition of sex roles, and the lack of recognition of intermediate sexes in Western society and, apparently, Westernised Eastern society, if one can make such a statement on the basis of a few isolated cases.

SEXUAL DIMORPHISM IN TRANSSEXUALITY

Masculinity-Femininity in the Transsexual Patient

Anatomically, contrary to the prevailing notion, the sexes are not "opposites." In many ways we are biologically similar; for example, both males and females have so-called male and female hormones, but the proportions are different for the sexes. Besides the external and internal accessory sexual organs all else is shared between the sexes, although the distributions are, statistically speaking, different.

As far as physical traits are concerned, it is possible to differentiate between different physical characteristics, for example, pitch of voice—at the statistical level—between males and females, but the difference is one of range rather than an absolute difference. As far as character traits are concerned (e.g., gentleness, dependence, emotionality for women; roughness, independence, and non-emotionality for men) we can identify sex stereotypes (as Bem has done for the construction of the Bem Sex-Role Inventory [hereafter BSRI]) and we can observe statistical distributions which point toward differences in the distribution of behavior traits (e.g., greater verbal ability of girls and greater physical aggressiveness of boys). All people encompass in themselves some elements that are stereotypically ascribed to the other sex, and most people seem not to worry about that. However, when we read the accounts of transvestites and transsexuals, we are struck by the very rigid and sharp distinction that is drawn between so-called feminine and masculine attributes, and, more significantly, by the perceived inappropriateness of engaging in behaviors that are seen as being fitting for the other sex.

Jan Morris (1975), for example, in her description of the years of her changeover from male to "female," makes very clear statements as to what she expects a man and a woman to be. She notes that "...my own notion of the female principle was one of gentleness as against force, forgiveness rather than punishment, give more than take, helping more than leading" (p. 12); "...though my body often yearned to give, to yield, to open itself, the machine was wrong" (p. 24)....

Rather, therefore, than permit it to be legitimate for a man to be gentle, give rather than take, help rather than lead or command, Morris perceives of these character traits as only legitimate for a woman (instead of clearly human)—these yearnings that he himself had, were, therefore, for himself illegitimate. He accepts a sexual dimorphism which strictly separates the sexes in terms of character traits, thus trying to live up to an inhuman masculine image, which, after a while, proves to be too much for him. A similar picture emerges from other descriptions (e.g., in Meyer, 1974) and is particularly obvious, also, in transvestites....

Sexual Dimorphism in the Family of Origin of Transsexuals

The etiology of transsexualism has not been determined. The only thing that seems clear is that societal factors play an extremely important role, and that biological factors are, at the very most, contributing towards predisposing a person to become a transsexual, and that possibly they play no role at all....

Clearly, possible explanations of transsexualism are at an early stage. Just as clearly, if people would delineate less sharply between males and females than they do at present, many of the suspected causes would simply cease to exist. The desire to be a member of the opposite sex presupposes very clear and mutually exclusive notions as to what each sex is like....

On the other hand, it seems impossible at this point of time to weigh the familial influences against other social pressures. Since these transsexuals are from a culture which is highly sex-stereotyped and very conscious of "sex-appropriate" behavior, some children who had yearnings to behave in a "sex-inappropriate" manner may have simply found it impossible to overcome the feeling of inappropriateness, and may have thereby been pushed to imagine themselves as members of the other sex who happen to be endowed with the wrong body.

Whatever the role of the family may be, one thing seems certain: clinicians who are attending transsexuals need to believe strongly in "gender differentiation." In order to be willing to offer their services to transsexuals who request them.

Sexual Dimorphism in Attending Clinicians

The prevailing clinical view of transsexuals, transvestites and homosexuals is that they have a gender identity problem, that they have chosen improper sex objects (homosexuality) and that they behave, in a general way, in a gender-inappropriate manner. Indeed, a diagnosis of a gender identity problem is a prerequisite for obtaining sex reassignment surgery. The factor on which surgery seems to hinge is whether or not the patient is judged to have a primary identification as a member of the opposite sex.

It warrants a moment's reflection that the reason for which sex reassignment surgery is performed is gender confusion, and not sex confusion. In other words, the patients are all clearly aware what their anatomical sex is. There is absolutely no "confusion" on this issue. The only "confusion" is their refusal to behave in the manner that is socially prescribed for their sex.

Clinicians need to believe fairly strongly in the appropriateness of "sex-appropriate behavior" and a "proper gender identity" in order to be able to justify, to themselves and others, the removal of physiologically perfectly normal and healthy sex organs in substantial numbers of patients. Clinicians involved with transsexuals—at least those who perform sex reassignment surgery—must not only accept the present sex structure, but must passionately believe in its essential rightness.

There are different ways in which accounts can be read. So far, we have used accounts of transsexuals in order to extract information about the femininity-masculinity attitudes of the patients and their families. However, the same reports (when written by clinicians) can be used to extract not the problems of the patients, but the prejudices of clinicians. One example which is particularly striking is reported by Money, since it reveals at least as much about the clinician's concern with sex role behavior and gender

identity (and the malleability of the human character) as about any problems that the patient may have. It is especially interesting to examine this
example because Money is one of the earliest authors who previously had
advanced the thesis that humans are psychosexually undifferentiated at
birth (Money, 1963:39). According to Money, Hampson and Hampson
(1955:316) "...sexuality is undifferentiated at birth and...becomes differentiated as masculine or feminine in the course of the various experiences of
growing up." These conclusions are based on studies of people with inconsistent sex attributes (hermaphrodites) and, in general, the investigators
found that infants can be successfully raised—irrespective of their biological
sex—in either sex. In this particular example, the raising of a genetic male as
a female is reported.

The case is one of identical male twin brothers, one of whom lost his
penis through an accident at the age of seven months. Consequently, Money
advised the parents to raise this child as a female (1975:67):

> *I gave them advice and counseling on the future prognosis and man-*
> *agement of their new daughter, based on experiences with similar*
> *reassignments in hermaphroditic babies. In particular, they were*
> *given confidence that their child can be expected to differentiate a*
> *female gender identity, in agreement with her sex of rearing.*

By the age of nine years (the age when this case was reported), the two
identical (genetically male) twins showed two clearly differentiated personalities, with different dress preferences, different attitudes towards
cleanliness, very different toy preferences, different duties around the house
which were willingly performed, and generally a sharply differentiated
behavior structure. Money is very laudatory of the successful efforts of the
mother to raise this child as a girl, and reports in positive terms on the mother's
activities in these regards, e.g., "in pointing out the specifics of the female
and male adult reproductive roles," and "their other different roles, such as
wife and husband or financial supporter of the family and caretaker of the
children and house" (p. 69). [Further] (pp. 69–70):

> *Regarding domestic activities, such as work in the kitchen and house*
> *traditionally seen as part of the female's role, the mother reported that*
> *her daughter copies her in trying to help her tidying and cleaning up*
> *the kitchen, while the boy could not care less about it. She encourages*
> *her daughter when she helps her in the housework.*

Through systematically applying a double standard (by differentially
rewarding identical behavior—e.g., the mother encourages the daughter
when she helps her in the housework, but presumably she does not encourage the son) and with the expert guidance of the clinician two different sex
identities of anatomically [sic] identical people are constructed. The result
of the process is likely to be two more adults who will consider it fitting for

the "nature" of a woman to take care of house and children, and fitting for the "nature" of a man to be the breadwinner of a family. The assisting clinician obviously perceives this as the appropriate role division, and actively furthers this outcome. Considering that the girl is anatomically a boy, this case graphically illustrates—perhaps clearer than other cases of transsexualism, because we are here dealing with an involuntary transsexual—the completely arbitrary nature of our sex identity which is thereby shown not to be related to the presence of internal and/or external sex organs, counter to the claims of many psychologists.

In another study, Green (1976) compares 60 boys characterised by "extensive cross-gender behavior" who are seen as potential future transsexuals, and therefore of a pathological inclination. They were so identified if on a "never, occasionally, or frequently trichotomy" they "at least occasionally cross-dressed, role-played as a female, preferred girls' toys and games, related better to girls, avoided rough-and-tumble play, and were called 'sissy' by their peer group." Instead of viewing a situation in which games are rigidly divided by sex, in which boys and girls are supposed not to like to play with each other, etc., as a case of social pathology, children who refuse to participate in this form of social sickness are seen as being individually pathological. It is striking that the discussion of transsexual pathology concerns almost exclusively gender identity rather than sex identity. Patients do not have a confused image about their sexual organs, although they display a strongly negative view of their own sex organs since these symbolise to them at the anatomical level the restrictions that they think they must accept at the personality level. Clinicians further this interpretation by themselves subscribing to a sexual dimorphism at the psychic level.

An alternative route would be not to attempt to convince these people to behave in a "gender-appropriate manner," but to try to get them to accept themselves as men or women, boys or girls who happen to have tastes that are similar to those of many (but not all) members of the other sex rather than to those of many (but not all) members of their own sex. Such an effort may possibly be too late for patients who seek sex reassignment surgery, and in that sense one cannot fault clinicians if they do not succeed in fostering a more positive self-image which includes an acceptance of one's sex organs without any attempt to conform to rigid sex roles. However, this does not alter the fact that individual transsexuals are casualties of an overly rigid sex role differentiation, and that clinicians who perform sex reassignment surgery help to maintain this overly rigid sexual dimorphism which is restrictive to every human being, whether female, male, or transsexual.

There is also evidence of a scientific double standard on the part of clinicians, i.e., a differential interpretation of data according to the sex of the actor. Stoller and Baker (1973:326), for example, when discussing the background of a male-to-female transsexual, note that he took some pride in getting away from his overly protective mother. "When she [previously he] left the house, it was not to express masculine independence but was simply a rebellion against her mother's demands for housekeeping and for just staying in the house." The action reported upon is asexual, but the interpretation offered is sexual.

Sexual dimorphism implies that one does not socially accept the presence of persons who are neither unambiguously male nor female, although in nature such people do exist, and in previous times at least some limited recognition was accorded to them....

The rationale for sex reassignment surgery seems to be based on a circular logic which goes like this. Sex determines character. This is natural. Therefore, cases in which biological sex does not result in the expected sex identities are unnatural. Consequently, we need to change the biological sex (i.e., nature) in order to uphold the principle that biological sex determines one's character.

Transsexuals are people who suffer so deeply from the sex structure that they are willing to endure terrible pain and loneliness in order to reduce their suffering. This group of people would—potentially—be the most potent group of people pressing for changes in the sex structure, because their aversion to their "sex-appropriate" roles is apparently insurmountable. By declaring them, by surgical fiat, as members of the other sex, this change potential is diverted and becomes as conservative as it could have been revolutionary. Each situation is individualized, rather than being recognized as the result of a social pathology, and the social pathology has overcome one more threat to its continued well-being....

REFERENCES

Bem, S. L. 1974. "The Measurement of Psychological Androgyny." *Journal of Clinical Psychology* 42 (2): 155–62.

___. 1977. "On the Utility of Alternative Procedures for Assessing Psychological Androgyny." *Journal of Consulting and Clinical Psychology* 45 (2): 166–205.

Bentler, P.M. 1976. "A Typology of Transsexualism: Gender Identity Theory and Data." *Archives of Sexual Behaviour* 5 (6): 567–83.

Bullough, V. L. 1975. "Transsexualism in History." *Archives of Sexual Behavior* 4 (5): 561–71.

Decision Marketing Research Ltd. 1976. *Women in Canada*. 2d ed. Ottawa: Office of the Coordinator, Status of Women.

Eichler, M. "Power, Dependency, Love and the Sexual Division of Labour: A Critique of the Decision-Making Approach to Family Power and an Alternative Approach." Unpublished paper.

Encyclopedia Britannica. 1973. Vols. 8 and 11.

Evans-Pritchard, E. E. 1945. *Some Aspects of Marriage and the Family among the Nuer*. Rhodes-Livingstone Papers, no. 11. Livingstone, Northern Rhodesia: The Rhodes Livingstone Institute.

Feinbloom, D. H. 1976. *Transvestites and Transsexuals*. New York: Delacorte Press/Seymour Lawrence.

Green, R. 1976. "One-Hundred Ten Feminine and Masculine Boys: Behavioral Contrasts and Demographic Similarities." *Archives of Sexual Behavior* 5 (5): 425–46.

Heiman, E. M., and Le, C. V. 1975. "Transsexualism in Vietnam." *Archives of Sexual Behavior* 4 (1): 89–95.

Holter, H. 1970. *Sex Roles and Social Structure.* Oslo, Bergen, Tromso: Universitetsforlaget.

Hore, B. D., F. V. Nicolle, and J. S. Calnan. [sic] "Male Transsexualism: Two Cases in a Single Family." *Archives of Sexual Behavior:* [sic] 317–31.

Laurie, B. 1977. "An Assessment of Sex-Role Learning in Kindergarten Children: Experimental Application of a Toy Test with Direct Reinforcement of Sex-Typed and of Androgenous Behavior." Master's thesis, Department of Educational Theory, University of Toronto.

Martin, M. K., and B. Voorhies. 1975. *Female of the Species.* Toronto: Methuen.

Meyer, J. K. 1974. "Clinical Variants among Applicants for Sex Reassignment." *Archives of Sexual Behaviour* 3 (6): 527–28.

Money, J. 1963. "Development Differentiation of Femininity and Masculinity Compared." In *Man and Civilization: The Potential of Woman*, 51–65. New York: McGraw-Hill.

___. 1975. "Ablatio Penis: Normal Male Infant Sex—Reassigned as a Girl." *Archives of Sexual Behavior* 4 (1): 65–71.

Money, J., and A. A. Ehrhardt. 1974. *Man and Women, Boy and Girl.* New York: New American Library.

Money, J., J. L. Hampson, and J. G. Hampson. 1955. "An Examination of Some Basic Sexual Concepts: The Evidence of Human Hermaphroditism." *Bulletin of the Johns Hopkins Hospital*, vol. 97, 301–19.

Money, J., and G. Wolff. 1973. "Sex Reassignment: Male to Female to Male." *Archives of Sexual Behavior* 2 (3): 245–50.

Morris, J. 1975. *Conundrum.* New York: Signet.

Pauly, I. B. 1974a. "Female Transsexualism: Part I." *Archives of Sexual Behavior* 3 (5): 487–507.

___. 1974b. "Female Transsexualism: Part II." *Archives of Sexual Behavior* 3 (6): 509–26.

Rosenberg, B. G., and B. Sutton-Smith. 1972. *Sex and Identity.* New York: Holt, Rinehart and Winston.

Sawyer, J. 1976. "On Male Liberation." In *The Forty-Nine Percent Majority*, ed. D. S. David and R. Brannon, 287–90. Reading, Mass.: Addison-Wesley.

Stoller, R. 1972. "Etiological Factors in Female Transsexualism: A First Approximation." *Archives of Sexual Behavior* 2 (1): 47–64.

Stoller, R. J. 1976. "Two Feminized Male American Indians." *Archives of Sexual Behavior* 5 (6): 529–38.

Stoller, R. J., and H. J. Baker. 1973. "Two Male Transsexuals in One Family." *Archives of Sexual Behavior* 2 (4): 323–28.

Swift, J. 1963. *Gulliver's Travels.* New York: Airmont.

4

The Language of Sex:
The Heterosexual Questionnaire

M. Rochlin

1. What do you think caused your heterosexuality?
2. When and how did you decide you were a heterosexual?
3. Is it possible that your heterosexuality is just a phase you may grow out of?
4. Is it possible that your heterosexuality stems from a neurotic fear of others of the same sex?
5. If you have never slept with a person of the same sex, is it possible that all you need is a good gay lover?
6. Do your parents know that you are straight? Do your friends and/ or roommate(s) know? How did they react?
7. Why do you insist on flaunting your heterosexuality? Can't you just be who you are and keep it quiet?
8. Why do heterosexuals place so much emphasis on sex?
9. Why do heterosexuals feel compelled to seduce others into their lifestyles?
10. A disproportionate majority of child molesters are heterosexual. Do you consider it safe to expose children to heterosexual teachers?
11. Just what do men and women *do* in bed together? How can they truly know how to please each other, being so anatomically different?
12. With all the societal support marriage receives, the divorce rate is spiraling. Why are there so few stable relationships among heterosexuals?
13. Statistics show that lesbians have the lowest incidence of sexually transmitted diseases. Is it really safe for a woman to maintain a heterosexual lifestyle and run the risk of disease and pregnancy?

From M. Rochlin, "The Language of Sex: The Heterosexual Questionnaire," *Changing Men* (Spring 1982). Waterloo, ON: University of Waterloo.

14. How can you become a whole person if you limit yourself to compulsive, exclusive heterosexuality?

15. Considering the menace of overpopulation, how could the human race survive if everyone were heterosexual?

16. Could you trust a heterosexual therapist to be objective? Don't you feel s/he might be inclined to influence you in the direction of her/his own leanings?

17. There seem to be very few happy heterosexuals. Techniques have been developed that might enable you to change if you really want to. Have you considered trying aversion therapy?

18. Would you want your child to be heterosexual, knowing the problems that s/he would face?

5

The Return of Butch and Femme:
A Phenomenon in Lesbian Sexuality
of the 1980s and 1990s

Lillian Faderman

> *I got to thinkin'...about how I was s'posed to be so damn butchy—*
> *with my denim, and leather, and studs, and my ducktail; and you*
> *with your heels, your make-up, and skirts...you, so very much the*
> *smoldering woman....Thinkin' 'bout the time when we didn't have no*
> *money and needed gas, and you tore out the station with the nozzle in*
> *the tank....Thinkin' how you **made** me git out on the floor an' dance*
> *with you at the Sweetheart Dance—didn't care **who** saw we was two*
> *women....Got to thinkin', maybe this butch/femme stuff wasn't quite*
> *rule of thumb—maybe leather didn't make you a tough broad, or silk a*
> *sissy; got to realizin' that **maybe** I was always on top 'cause you let me*
> *be, and how soft and warm you made me feel, like sometimes I wanted*
> *to wear long, flowin' skirts, and look pretty just for you...Then I*
> *reached for the keys in my cowboy jacket pocket...and said, "This*
> *time—you drive." [Charlene S. Henderson, "Texas '52," in* Sinister
> Wisdom, *1988]*

The cliché about the 1980s is that it was a far more conservative period than the 1970s for a whole complex of reasons, not the least of which was the fearful connection between sexual pleasure and danger that the AIDS virus brought to public consciousness. It is true that the 1980s ushered into the parent culture a more cautious sexuality, which even rubbed off somewhat on the lesbian culture. For example, the non-monogamy that radical lesbian-feminism encouraged in the 1970s is out and commitment is in in many lesbian circles (although the retreat from open sexuality on the part of both heterosexuals and homosexuals has not yet resulted in an ethos anywhere near as rigid as that of the 1950s). Some lesbian social critics see the contemporary impulse to revive butch and femme relationships as being one more lesbian manifestation of the contemporary right-wing backlash. They have

From Lillian Faderman, "The Return of Butch and Femme: A Phenomenon in Lesbian Sexuality of the 1980s and 1990s," *Journal of the History of Sexuality*, vol. 2, no. 4 (1992): 578–596.

associated it with a 1950s nostalgia à la "Happy Days," a desire for the security of what is naively imagined to have been better times, perhaps a fantasy created out of exhaustion from the battles lesbian-feminists had to fight in the 1970s. But it would be inaccurate to attribute the resurgence of butch/femme roles and relationships in the 1980s to the relative conservatism of the period. Neo-butch/femme may be seen instead as a reaction against the sexual conformity that lesbian-feminism ironically mandated in the course of a radical era. Women who stifled such role identifications in the 1970s dared to examine them and even flaunt them in the next decade. Women who never thought about them in the 1970s began exploring them with curiosity.[1]

Neo-butch/femme may also be related to an attempt to resist cultural assimilation. In the 1970s not only did heterosexual women dress much like the most blatant lesbians of earlier eras, but even the taboos against lesbian sexuality were largely relaxed. What was there to distinguish the radical lesbian—who often wanted to be distinguished—from the run-of-the-mill liberated woman? The resurgence of butch/femme countered such assimilation.

Although a few women who identified as butch or femme in the 1980s (or at present) did so with the same deadly seriousness that characterized the women of the 1950s, many others did it out of a sense of adventure, a historical curiosity, a longing to push at the limits. For them neo-butch/femme roles and relationships often maintain the lessons of feminism that lesbians learned from the 1970s. They are more subtle, complex, flexible. There are few contemporary butches who would entertain the notion that they are men trapped in women's bodies. For these reasons, the meaning of butch and femme over the past decade was very different from what it had been thirty or forty years earlier.

Butch/Femme as "Politically Incorrect" in the 1970s

At the height of radical lesbian-feminism, what was seen as an imitation of heterosexuality was officially frowned upon by the most vocal elements of the subculture. Lesbian-feminists of the 1970s believed that lesbianism was not simply a bedroom issue but also a political issue, and that the personal was political. They regarded butch/femme as roles in which the players were acting out with each other the oppression they had learned from the parent culture. It was a corruption to be eschewed. They had no doubt that butches were trying to mimic men, and their typical response to that was, "I'm not interested in a man *manqué*—in being one or knowing any. I'm not into lesbianism because I like men."[2]

For many women who came to lesbianism through feminism, butch/femme looked like nothing so much as a repetition of that which they left heterosexuality to avoid. Those roles seemed to place a limit on their free growth and expansion, which to them was the most exciting part of feminism. They refused to believe that butch or femme roles came naturally to any women and explained their prevalence in some lesbian communities as resulting from socialization: lesbians had been well brainwashed by the parent culture so that they acquiesced into making their subculture a carbon copy of heterosexuality. Abbott and Love suggested in their popular 1972 book, *Sappho Was a Right-On Woman: A Liberated View of Lesbianism,* that lesbians often came to accept mimicking the roles of heterosexuals through the lesbian bars, which were their entry into "the life." There, a young woman who initially only wanted to find ways to express her love for other women was forced to take on the stereotype of "the Lesbian," whether or not it had anything to do with who she was: "Whereas [before entering the subculture] she has been impersonating a heterosexual woman, now she is impersonating a Lesbian. She gives herself over to a new image, also defined by central casting. The stereotype of the Lesbian becomes self-fulfilling."[3]

Because butch/femme came to be seen as contrary to feminism and "unnatural" to the free woman, lesbian-feminists considered those who assumed the roles "politically incorrect." Such women were accused of shutting themselves off from the benefits women had accrued through feminism, which included not only the recognition that both partners in a relationship could and should be equal but also the freedom to love homogenderally, since feminists challenged the pervasive 1950s belief that only opposites attract.

Lesbian-feminists insisted that while the choice to be butch was understandable in previous years, there was no longer any excuse for it. Some saw that earlier choice as having to do with dress restrictions: women had been drawn to dressing as men because they believed that in men's garb they could do anything that a man could do. But, as one writer for a lesbian journal observed in 1975, dress codes had changed since the 1950s and roles had naturally changed along with them—when women and men are wearing basically the same attire, the roles become less clearly defined. "Men have less power over women; women become less vulnerable." Just as heterosexuals were ostensibly rejecting role divisions, even in their unisex dress, this writer said, so were lesbians, so that butch/femme was bound eventually to be "abolished."[4]

Others blamed the earlier butch/femme divisions on monogamy, which was now a major taboo among lesbian radicals. They argued that the dyad relationship encouraged roles because roles permitted more "efficiency": for example, one person would take care of the house, while the other would go out to work. Radicals saw such efficiency as "part of the whole capitalist trip. A form of social programming." They protested that its purpose was to keep "the old marriage machine going." And their verdict was that it was "boring."[5]

Still others rejected roles because what was most attractive to them about lesbianism were the possibilities they believed it opened for androgyny. They saw themselves as desiring the best elements of what traditionally was defined both as male and as female, and they were attracted to other women who also strove for both elements. Not only was their own favorite attire jeans and a shirt, but they also preferred their partners in the same outfit."[6]

In the 1950s the most readily identifiable lesbians were the butches and the femmes who accompanied them. Consequently, they were the ones who created the dominant lesbian image of the era. In the 1970s the "dyke" was dominant. The dyke image consisted of boots, jeans, "men's" shirts, short hair—and, ideally, aggressive behavior. In effect, it meant that everyone within the radical community looked like what had previously been called butch, but the concept of butch was redefined: a dyke did not look for a femme as a love partner; she looked for another dyke. She did not consider her behavior masculine; rather, it was feminist. According to some critics, sexual expression was often prescribed in dykedom almost as severely as it had been in some areas of butchdom in the 1950s, when the butch had to be the aggressor and could seldom allow herself to be "flipped." Susie Bright, who proclaims herself a femme today, remembers that in the late 1970s dyke relationships had to be heavy on the romance and light on the sex because women were terrified of using each other as sexual objects: "Inserting your fingers into your lover's vagina was considered heterosexual," she says. "Touching her breasts meant that you were just objectifying her. The only thing that was all right was oral sex, and you had to be sure that you both got it for an equal time."[7]

THE 1970S BUTCH/FEMME UNDERGROUND

Although the most vocal lesbians had no interest in butch/femme roles and relationships during the 1970s, some women clearly did. Apolitical women who felt that feminism had little to do with them and who had never even heard of lesbian-feminism, with its precept that roles were politically incorrect, continued to live as they always had. In some ethnic-minority lesbian communities the pressure to adhere to roles were exerted as strongly as it was in earlier decades. H. O., a Chicana woman, says that in Merced, California, where she came out in 1970, all the Chicana lesbians in her small community were into roles. Since she was having a relationship with a woman who "wore lots of make-up, false eyelashes, and had her boobs showing," she felt an obligation during the seven years they were together to project a "macho image," to wear pants and tee shirts, and to be a stone butch (one who does not let herself be touched sexually by her partner), despite what she says was her deep preference for mutuality in a sexual relationship. She explains that both she and her lover "fell into those roles because that's all we knew."[8]

In some black communities as well, butch/femme roles often remained rigid, even throughout the "liberated" 1970s. A study of "lower-lower-class" black lesbians in central Harlem during the mid-1970s observed that only 17 percent of the women in the sample would not identify themselves as either butch or femme, and that while the butch character was considered an anathema outside the area of the study (that is, in middle-class or non-ghetto lesbian life), she was "a fixture on the ghetto scene."[9]

Some black women complained that when they moved outside the ghetto into integrated lesbian communities in certain areas, even in the 1970s, white women sometimes automatically assumed that black women would be butch in a sexual relationship or even manipulated them into being butch. As Iris, a black lesbian from Omaha, Nebraska, remembers, "They didn't like you to wear make-up. They wanted you in masculine dress, but they wanted to be real 'fou-fou' themselves." She attributes the predilection to a covert racism that is blind to femininity in black females.[10]

Among lesbians in prison, the butch/femme division was also strictly maintained throughout the 1970s. Any attempt to diverge from the "mom" and "pop" roles, as they were often called, was met with the same disdain and discomfort that such unorthodoxy elicited among certain groups in the 1950s. As one black lesbian convict described the situation: "I like both parts. They say I'm a faggot because I don't treat any woman the way a butch should. I share with her and do her clothes when she's busy. Sometimes I'm passive and let her be the aggressive one. Both the butches and the femmes get mad."[11]

Some women outside ghettos and prisons also insisted, even in the face of powerful lesbian-feminist opposition, that one or the other of the roles was simply natural to them. In a 1979 interview in *Lesbian Tide* one woman declared that, from her own observations, 80 percent of all lesbians had behavior patterns that could be seen as butch or femme. She admitted that for some years she pretended not to be a butch because it was politically incorrect, but she discovered that she "could just not get it together emotionally" with women who were not femmes. She concluded that although she had had affairs with lesbians who covered the entire spectrum of masculinity and femininity, deep down she always remained a butch: "If I was celibate for the rest of my life, I would still be butch."[12]

Her firm role identification was sometimes echoed in print by other women during the 1970s, despite the fact that that position was generally unpopular with the most vocal of the lesbian community. In another interview for a 1970s lesbian-feminist magazine, a twenty-four-year-old woman named Mickey discussed her own views of butch and femme, which at the height of the lesbian-feminist movement were no different from many of her counterparts twenty years earlier. Relationships, for Mickey, had to be not only heterogenderal but extreme in their divisions. She associated her own butch role with independence, control, "shutting off my emotions when I have to and knocking someone out in the street if I have to." And, she believed, "being a butch you have to be the boss. Most femmes want that. They want you to make the decisions."[13] Not all women who continued to adhere to roles during radical feminism's apogee were so stereotypical in their thinking. Some explained, under the partial influence of feminism, that it was necessary to share powers and privileges in a relationship, regardless of who wore the make-up or the short hair, but that it was unfair of the community to impose a uniform style of behavior on individuals. They protested that pressures to conform had gone from one extreme to the other. In the 1950s one had to be butch or femme in order to be accepted into certain communities. In the 1970s one dared not be butch or femme if she wanted to be accepted in certain communities.

Because the prescriptions, ironically, were so heavy against butch/ femme behavior—which had had its own very heavy prescriptions in the past—many of those who would have preferred the roles believed they had to mask their inclinations. Honey Lee, a San Francisco woman who identifies herself as a working-class butch, remembers that in the early 1970s she realized that the rules were changing and that, although she had never needed to defend her behavior before, suddenly she was open to criticism for being butch: "In the parlance of the '70s I was male-identified, but I socialized with people who assumed I was just a feminist. I had to hide my stuff," she says. "I really felt bad when I learned that what I liked was looked down upon." She explains that she was able to retain her butch self-image, even in the midst of a women's movement that denigrated it, because she always saw herself "as a maverick—never really part of women's lib or gay lib."[14] Such a perception, thinking of oneself as essentially separate from a group, permitted some women to hold out against prescriptions during an era of lesbian-feminist tyranny.

Working-class women in particular, who had identified as butches or femmes and then became genuinely involved in feminism, were often alienated by feminism's attitude toward roles. They perceived that feminists wanted them to repress a large part of themselves for the sake of a political image. Joan Nestle, who, like Honey Lee, identifies herself as being from a working-class background, complained in 1982 that feminism put her in an unconscionable position: if she dressed as a femme to please herself and her lover she would be called a traitor "by many of my own people" because she would be seen as wearing the clothes of the enemy. But if she wore "movement" clothes because she was afraid of the judgment of those same people, she would still be a traitor—to her femme sense of personal style. Her anger was reiterated by many other working-class lesbians who had identified as butch or femme before feminism.[15]

Some women saw the conflict as a class war, fought on the battleground of feminism. It was a war butches and femmes were destined to lose throughout the 1970s, but their convictions often persisted. Sarah, a Boston woman, talks about the battles at the Cambridge Women's Center that took place among the feminists, lesbians, and lesbian-feminists. Wearing make-up, she remembers, was considered "horrible," but being butch was also out of the question: "It made me angry. Who were these people to come out of their middle class and tell us what being lesbian was supposed to mean? They even took over the term 'dyke." Here they were from their rich, sheltered backgrounds wearing their dyke buttons. They didn't have to go through the name-calling we suffered through. Their version of being a lesbian was 'fashionable.' How could they understand what butch meant to those of us who had lived it?"[16]

Those committed butches who did not want to fight a class war and were tired of going against the grain not only in the heterosexual world but in their own lesbian world sometimes chose to opt out of lesbianism altogether, not by developing an interest in men but by becoming men themselves. In San Francisco during the mid-1970s, older masculine women were flocking to the Langley Porter Clinic, asking for sex change operations because, as Phyllis Lyon, codirector of the National Sex Forum, observed, "Lesbians were saying butch was out."[17] If a lesbian was no longer supposed to want to be butch, they reasoned, and yet they themselves still felt butch, it must be because they were really men trapped in women's bodies.

The division between women who saw their lesbianism in images that were popularized in the 1950s and the "new gay" lesbian-feminists led occasionally to heated jockeying for control of the public manifestations of lesbian culture. In one Southern California bar, for example, there was a running battle between old gays and new gays over the issue of playing the song "Under My Thumb" on the jukebox, which to lesbian-feminists was a particularly offensive specimen of male chauvinist piggery and to old gays only a lively expression of dominance and submission in a love relationship. One researcher observed in her study of Albuquerque lesbians and their bars in the 1960s and 1970s that the split was even spatial: "Old dykes would stand on one side, feminists on the other."[18]

BATTLEGROUND IN THE 1980s

The 1980s gave birth to new attitudes toward butch/femme relationships among many lesbian radicals. The midwife to this new view was Joan Nestle, whose poignant articles during the early 1980s pinpointed what came to be seen as the arrogance of lesbian-feminism in trivializing butch/femme in lesbian history. Nestle romanticized 1950s butches and femmes, depicting their open expression of nonconventional sexuality in an antisexual era as a rebellion of a colonized people. The appeal of that heroic image has been tremendous among many lesbians who not only want to honor that aspect of history, as Nestle did, but to live it, though filtered through their own time.

Their enthusiastic romanticizing has sometimes promoted an ahistoricity. Judy Grahn, for example, associates butches with the core members of a minority community who keep the "old ways." She sees them as "its true historians and 'true' practitioners, its fundamentalists, traditionalists, and old timers [who] retain the culture in a continuous line from one century to another." Unfortunately, in this reading of lesbian history romantic friendship, Boston marriage, the lesbian aristocracy of expatriate Paris, and much of middle-class lesbian life as it was lived in twentieth-century America are inadvertently eradicated.[19]

Those who claimed butch or femme identities in the 1980s (or presently, in the 1990s) often see themselves as taboo-smashers and iconoclasts. They are no longer primarily working-class women, as they were in the 1950s and 1960s—they are just as likely in the 1980s and 1990s to be intellectuals whose roots were in the middle class. They see their open role choices as being a defiant proclamation of their lesbianism. To them it is much more honorable than being a lesbian who can "pass for straight" among heterosexuals through her own appearance and that of her lover. As writer Pat Suncircle declares in a lesbian short story: "To love a bulldagger is to be unable to lie."[20]

Some lesbians say they were fed up with the doctrines of lesbian-feminism that wanted to mold all women into a single image. In their view, the lesbian-feminist creation of political propriety that swept into women's bedrooms was far more damaging to lesbian liberty and pursuit of happiness than the rigidity of butch/femme roles in the 1950s and 1960s. In reaction to that propriety they proudly proclaimed, "I like being a butch. I like being with other butches with our nicknames and ballgames—women with muscles and pretty faces," and "When I wear flowing dresses on a hot summer day I believe it is a femme choice coming from my authentic lesbian self.... That real self was denied by a lesbian-feminist analysis fearful...that possibly we were imitating heterosexual roles." The newly proclaimed femmes were now resentful that they had had to "trade in our pretty clothes for the nondescript uniform of that decade." "Let's face it," they said disdainfully of the 1970s style, "feminism is not sexy."[21] Many were furious that the 1970s had forced them into androgyny, which alone became the accepted norm for dress and behavior in the radical feminist community. They see themselves now as virtually doing battle with the lesbian-feminist dragons of conformity.

But confusion has abounded because the usual definition of butchdom in the past decade has been not very different from that of 1970s dykedom or even feminism. Not unlike the early sexologists who explained "aggressive" female behavior not as a challenge to the restrictive concept of woman (as it was believed to be in the 1970s) but as a sign of the invert, in the 1980s and 1990s such behavior has been explained as a sign of the butch. A butch is "the woman who doesn't automatically smile and shuffle for every man she encounters. The woman who walks for her own purpose and not for other people's entertainment. The woman who looks both capable of defending herself and ready to do so. The woman who does not obey. The woman who is in revolt against enforced femininity, who claims for herself the right not to dress and act and talk 'like a woman' (meaning like a toy)." Another lesbian declares that "competence and dignity...are, for me, at the heart of butchdom." But Julia Penelope, who adamantly rejects butch roles, defines the dyke in terms very similar to those in the above definitions of the butch: for example, the dyke is "a woman who resists feminization."[22] And not many feminists, dyke or otherwise, would disagree that women should be subjects instead of objects, or that they should be serious and competent individuals.

The current confusion regarding the butch label may stem from an impatience and disillusionment that some self-identified butches feel with the failure to spread feminist goals quickly and widely enough: if there are still women who shuffle for men and obey them and let themselves be made into toys, then those who resist must be something other than mere women—born-and-bred butches. The historical figure of the butch has thus been metamorphosed into the prime warrior against male chauvinism, replacing for some radicals the feminist and the dyke of the 1970s.

The confusion is compounded by the fact that since the butch image has been presented in such politically attractive terms, not many women are prepared to call themselves femmes. One woman reports having taken an informal head count in a lesbian bar in San Francisco, finding that "butch" was sometimes being used in the 1980s as a substitute for the term "dyke": "One table of eight responded with eight enthusiastic butches, though some were in couple relationships with each other," she reported. As much as many radical femmes have insisted the contrary, it seems that in many lesbians' minds "femme" is associated with feminine, connoting "weak" and "vulnerable"—qualities that women often became lesbians in order to reject. They are too familiar with the stereotype of femininity to be able to believe in the image of femme strength suggested by Charlene Henderson in the passage quoted at the beginning of this essay.[23]

While the 1980s and 1990s consensus among many lesbians seems to be that one should have the freedom of self-definition, the very diversity of homosexual women guarantees that there would be some dissidents from such liberalism. At the one extreme is a group that echoed the 1950s, insisting that all women fall naturally into either butch or femme roles and that the refusal to choose is due to ignorance of self or cowardice or sheer perversity. At the other extreme is a group that maintains the stance of the 1970s, arguing that butches and femmes are backsliders who are demolishing all the sacred tenets of lesbian-feminism. They insist that there is no such thing as an innate butch or femme identity, and they ridicule role divisions by calling themselves "futches" and "bems."[24]

Although butch/femme reemerged in the 1980s essentially as a protest against the doctrinaire conformity and sexual monotony of radical lesbian-feminism, it appears to be gradually bringing with it its own pressures. Perhaps such constant shifts are inevitable in any minority group that is tied together by one factor in the members' identity but fragmented by all the other variables in their personalities. Those who are the most enthusiastic in their newfound butch/femme freedom seem determined to fix one or the other label on all lesbians, insisting that one cannot escape the butch/femme model if one is being honest. They claim, with some homage to Freud, that butch and femme personalities are formed at an early age (generally in response to or reaction against heterosexual indoctrination into feminization) and that they are unchangeable. Judy Grahn suggests that all women fall naturally into one or the other category, even if they try to deny it:

> *Among middle-class American Lesbians, extreme butch-femme polarities are tempered. The dykes simply disguise both members of their relationship in a modified drag known as "Lesbian," with perhaps one haircut a little shorter, one voice thrown a little lower, or some other distinguishing butch mark. The couple probably makes a few jokes about it now and then, meanwhile following feminist movement rhetoric in maintaining the "roles" are "patriarchal" and beneath our advanced consciousness.*[25]

Some women say that butch or femme has less to do with the behavior and appearances that were so intrinsic to those roles in the earlier era than with what they feel in themselves and in other women, what they mystically describe as "the essence of butch" or "the essence of femme." They tell of party conversations in which it was possible to get a consensus among a half-dozen women about who was butch and who was femme in their town, not through dress but rather through what was sensed about the person. In the course of a presentation on lesbian art before 1930, which I attended at the 1987 Berkshire Women's History Conference, the presenters as well as some women in the audience speculated with varying degrees of seriousness on whether the subjects in the paintings had a butch aura or a femme aura. Such mystical knowledge seems to deny refutation. One writer has not so facetiously compared the significance of butch/femme for lesbians today with that of astrology for flower children in the 1960s.[26]

However, the issue of butch/femme has created the most heat among radical lesbian-feminists, who have charged butches and their femmes with being "morally regressive" in their refusal to "think seriously about the meaning of life, the value of developing real human potentials, and the responsibility we each share to enhance the growth of the human community." Some women tell horror stories of their butch/femme encounters, seeing them as insidiously dangerous. Pauline Bart, in a 1986 article entitled "My Brief Career as a Femme," complained that the norms governing femme behavior in the subculture as she experienced it made her life as a Culver City housewife in the 1950s seem like Lesbian Nation. She claims that she soon realized that if she followed those norms, "within a few weeks [many of] the skills I had developed as a woman functioning in the world without a man would be lost." She finds butch/femme relationships irresponsible because dependence on another individual to take care of her leads the lesbian into the same learned helplessness, lack of autonomy, and low self-esteem that is endemic among heterosexual women.[27]

Radical feminists insisted that even the labels butch and femme are dangerous because they form perceptions, limit actions, and perpetuate certain behaviors that are women-oppressing and macho-glorifying. The issue of butch/femme became so heated in the 1980s that it even led to public confrontations and protests, such as the one at Barnard College in 1982. At a conference on "The Scholar and the Feminist," women who identified themselves as "a coalition of radical feminists and lesbian-feminists" handed out leaflets protesting that butch/femme women and those who rally around them constitute a backlash against radical feminism. The feminists accused butches and femmes of internalizing patriarchal messages and advocating those very sex roles that are the psychological foundation of patriarchy.[28] The radical feminists continue to promote the 1970s notion that the personal is political and that even bedroom behavior needs to conform to what is politically correct.

NEO-BUTCH/FEMME

For many of the women who identify as butch or femme today, the concept has little actual connection with the lived experience of those labels in the 1950s. Butch/femme relationships are perhaps more complex now than they were in the earlier era, reflecting the complexity of sexual relationships in the parent culture as well. Heterosexual roles, through the influence of feminism, are no longer universally simple but may legitimately take on all manner of androgynous nuances; so too lesbians who want to identify as butch or femme today have the choice of expressing themselves in an unprecedented variety of images: aggressive butch, passive butch, baby butch, stone butch, clone butch, old-fashioned femme, aggressive femme, and so on. While distinctions in dress between modern butch/femme couples are not unusual, it is also common for both women in the couple to dress in a unisex style.

The more egalitarian day-to-day living arrangements that feminism has brought to the parent culture also seem to be reflected in butch/femme relationships, so that butch/femme may be reduced to who makes the first move sexually (and sometimes not even that). One 1985 study of lesbian couples showed that while almost 70 percent maintained role divisions in sexual relations, in that one or the other woman in the relationship would almost always initiate sex, in other aspects of their lives, such as household responsibility or decisionmaking, there were no clear divisions along traditional lines. Even if sexual initiation or receptivity does indicate butch/femme roles in sexual relations, there seems not to be much left of gender stereotyping in any other area among most lesbian couples.[29]

A few women continue to use stereotypical gender descriptions in talking about their butch/femme relationships, such as Kendall, who identifies as a femme: "I could do all the things my lover does and still not be a butch. It has to do with receptivity and vulnerability; femmes also tend to be more manipulative, willing to express emotions, more concerned with relationships. The butch is the push; the femme is the pull."[30] But too much has happened for history simply to repeat itself. The male hippies of the 1960s challenged the old concept of the masculine: a man could wear his hair to his shoulders and be opposed to violence and wear jewelry. The feminists of the 1970s challenged the old concept of the feminine: a women could be efficient and forceful and demand a place in the world. Except to the most recalcitrant, there is little that remains of the simplistic ideas of gender-appropriate appearance and behavior. And lesbians, who historically have been at the forefront of feminism (in their choice to lead independent lives, if nothing else), cannot easily return to the old fashions in images and behaviors. Most would have a hard time taking such a return seriously. For that reason, butch and femme exists best today in the sexual arena, which invites fantasy and the tension of polarities.

Not even the old fashions in dress could have the same function today: butches who wore pants in the 1950s because it was their symbolic statement of rebellion against the limitations placed on them as women, who were claiming the prerogatives men had reserved for themselves and refusing to be objects and victims, were the mid-century forerunners in the struggle that other women took up in the 1970s. However, the gesture has lost its greatest significance as a political protest, since not only have many of those battles been won, but also heterosexual women who do not consider themselves rebels at all wear pants as much as lesbians do. Yet while there is frequently little distinction in attire between women who identify as butch and women who identify as femme, in the 1980s and 1990s femmes have felt much freer to wear dresses and even extreme feminine garb than they would have in the radical 1970s. It represents play and style, as does the extreme masculine garb that some latter-day butches wear.

Butch/femme roles, styles, and relationships today often appear to be conducted with a sense of lightness and flexibility. As Phyllis Lyon characterizes contemporary butch/femme, "Women 'play at it' rather than 'being it.'" Other lesbians testify to that sense of play. One woman says that she (a butch) and her femme lover complement each other in the roles they play, but they recognize it as play, as a pleasurable game: "She really can find a spark plug, she just prefers not to. Feeling that I have to protect her is an illusion that I enjoy. She allows me my illusion for she enjoys being taken care of like this."[31] Such an awareness of the "game" of roles would have been unlikely in the serious 1950s.

Therefore, for most lesbians the roles are not the life-or-death identity they often were in the 1950s, but rather an enjoyable erotic statement and an escape from the boring "vanilla sex" that they associated with lesbian-feminism. Their purpose is to create erotic tension in a relationship instead of the merging that is being held responsible for what lesbian sexologist Joann Lulan has called lesbian "bed death" (the statistically frequent fading of erotic interest in lesbian relationships after a couple of years).

The resurgence of butch/femme in the 1980s may also reflect reaction to the "drab stylelessness" of lesbian-feminists, as one woman describes the radical group she belonged to in the 1970s. Her friends, she recalls, were philosophically appealing, but they created "the unsexiest environment": "Everyone was doctrinaire about how you should look and act: short hair, no make-up, denim overalls, flannel shirts, hiking boots. It was 'hippy masculine.' I compared it to Mao's China. Plain and sexless. I'd love to see what they're wearing now."[32] As expressed today, butch/femme roles open to lesbians the possibility of wearing fashions that are signals for the erotic in the heterosexual western world in which they grew up, and which would have been ridiculed by lesbian-feminists in the 1970s: high heels, leather, lace, delicate lingerie.

In an only somewhat tongue-in-cheek article, "The Anguished Cry of an '80s Fem: I Want to Be a Drag Queen," Lisa Duggan talks about her last summer at Cherry Grove, where gay male and lesbian positions had been reversed. While gay males came to see drag as a dinosaur—an apolitical holdover, boring and dying—the lesbians at the Grove "were going to Drag Search every Sunday night. We planned our schedules around the drag teas at Cherry's,…and the fems had taken to borrowing boas from the boys to go dancing on Saturday night." Duggan suggests the sense of play in the new femme style when she concludes, with an insouciant verbal pout, "We didn't see why the guys had to be so goddamned serious."[33]

This sense of play and flexibility is also reflected in sexual object choice, even among many butches and femmes. The old sexual dynamic is far from clear in a modern butch/femme relationship. The stone butch, who was common in the 1950s and 1960s, is a rare figure, perhaps because a women who does not want to be reminded of her femaleness by having another woman make love to her has the option today (more easily than she would have had earlier) of eradicating her femaleness through a sex change operation. One lesbian who characterizes herself as a "possible femme" admits that she picks "butchy" women (those who flaunt their unfemininity) as sexual partners, but, she adds, "I cannot stereotype my lovemaking. There, more perhaps than anywhere else, I feel unrestricted enough to do what seems natural to me—and I will not limit myself to *anyone's* code of behavior." She asks that lesbians make no assumptions about what "butchness" and "femmeness" mean to other lesbians, but rather that each woman allow herself to explore and act out unforced role behavior that feels comfortable to her. A Lincoln, Nebraska, woman who says she identifies as a butch admits that she also likes to wear long dresses occasionally, and she does most of the cooking and cleaning chores in the home she shares with a woman who calls herself a femme but is very career-oriented. This "butch's" flexibility is suggested by her attire at a recent function in the lesbian community: "a tuxedo with a matching shade of eye shadow, and a necklace along with a bow tie." Butch and femme today can mean whatever one wants those terms to mean. A woman is a butch or a femme simply because she says she is. The 1966 *Random House Dictionary of the English Language* definition of "butch" as "the one who takes the part of a man" in a lesbian relationship has lost whatever inevitable truth it may have once had.[34]

Lesbian sexual roles have loosened in other ways as well. Just as in recent years it has become easier for a heterosexual to admit homosexual interests, so has it become permissible for a butch to admit interest in another butch, or a femme in another femme. Since the kiki taboo (in which 1950s butches and femmes characterized lesbians who were neither butch nor femme as "confused") no longer exists, women have no external pressure to conform in their selection of partners, although some may be confused over the apparent contradiction in their self-definition. If they can adjust to that ambiguity, there is little to prevent them from identifying however they wish, changing that identity when they wish, and choosing a partner who is either heterogenderal or homogenderal.

But some lesbians even today do not feel such flexibility in their sexual self-image. They are sometimes defensive about their role choice, and in areas as diverse as New York City and Lawrence, Kansas, they have considered it necessary to establish "butch support groups" and "femme support groups" to help them counter what they perceive as hostility from those lesbians who continue to reject roles. They define their preference for butch sexuality or femme sexuality as "a drive that comes from the very deepest core of sexual necessity," having little to do with learned behavior. Amber Hollibaugh, who calls herself a femme, says that her own sexual fantasy life is entirely involved in a butch/femme exchange: "I never come together with a woman sexually outside of those roles. I'm saying to my partner, 'Love me enough to let me go where I need to go and take me there....You map it out. You are in control.'" She hints that perhaps her interest in that kind of dynamic comes from much richer territory than simply that of roles, but like many other women today, she uses the vocabulary that has been revived from the 1950s to explain it.[35]

One woman, who also identifies as a femme although she says she has been butch with inexperienced women, finds that being a femme sexually means playing off feminine stereotypes—the little girl, the bitch, the queen, the sex pot—and making those images into your sexual language. For her it is primarily camp and fantasy, and it does not necessarily have to do with other aspects of personality. Nor are those roles limited in themselves, she explains. One can, for example, be a femme "top" (that is, the sexual dominator) or a butch "bottom."[36]

The roles are often sexually charged in a way that would have been unthinkable in the sexually tame 1970s, when erotic seduction was considered a corrupt imitation of heterosexuality; but the actors who indulge in these roles, femme as well as butch, are now frequently cognizant of the feminist image of the strong woman. The femme fantasy ideal may now be a lesbian Carmen rather than a Camille. One woman, for example, dares to write in a radical lesbian journal of her favorite sexual fantasy, in which she would appear at a lesbian dance in a "sleazy" black silk, low-cut dress with hot pink flowers on it:

> *I would come in, not, I repeat, **not** like a helpless femme-bot [= robot],*
> *but like a bad-ass-no-games-knows-her-own-mind-and-will-tell-you-too*
> *femme. First I would stand there and let my lover wonder. Maybe I*
> *would just stand there altogether and let her come to me. Or maybe,*
> *while all the heads were turning...I would stride across the dance floor*
> *in a bee-line for that green-eyed womon [sic] I love, so that everyone*
> *could see who the one in the black dress was going to fuck tonight.*[37]

As expressed in the 1980s and 1990s, the roles have become both a reflection and a feminist expansion of the early inculcation by the parent culture, and women are using them largely for their own pleasurable aims.

The erotic play that is at the center of neo-butch/femme mirrors Michael Bronski's definition of "gay lib" as it related to gay men: "At its most basic, [it] offers the possibility of freedom of pleasure for its own sake."[38] During the early years of the movement, when lesbians were busy defining the very serious tenets of lesbian-feminism and living by them, the concept of pleasure for its own sake was alien, and the AIDS crisis in the gay male community has now made that definition problematic for men as well as for many lesbians who sympathize with them. Yet in neo-butch/femme as an area of sexual play, a good number of lesbians in the 1980s felt entitled to claim pleasure for its own sake.

It is also a reflection of the current era that even among those lesbians who are mindful of themselves within a lesbian community there is less concern about the strictures of the movement and the group than there was in the 1970s and more interest in self-fulfillment. They claim the liberty to define themselves with fewer references to the expectations of either the parent culture or their immediate society. If butch or femme is part of that self-definition, for whatever reason, they are now likely to claim it. Political correctness is mostly out and individual expression is mostly in.

NOTES

1   I wrote an initial version of this essay intending it to be a chapter in *Odd Girls and Twilight Lovers: A History of Lesbian Life in Twentieth-Century America* (New York, 1991). However, in the course of numerous revisions I cut much of the material, finally using only a fraction of it in the chapter entitled "Lesbian Sex Wars in the

1980s." This essay incorporates most of the material of my original draft for a separate chapter on contemporary butch and femme relationships. My research for *Odd Girls and Twilight Lovers* included 186 unstructured interviews with women from seven states, ranging in age from seventeen to eighty-six, of various socio-economic and racial backgrounds. I also made use of several excellent archives, especially the Lesbian Herstory Archive in New York and the June Mazer Lesbian Collection in Los Angeles.

2   Questionnaire respondent in Dolores Klaich, *Woman + Woman: Attitudes towards Lesbianism* (New York, 1974), p. 117.

3   Sidney Abbott and Barbara Love, *Sappho Was a Right-On Woman: A Liberated View of Lesbianism* (New York, 1972), p. 95.

4   Victoria Brownworth, "Butch/Femme: Myth/Reality, or More of the Same," *Wicce* 4 (Summer 1975): 7–9.

5   Interview with Marty, in Brownworth, p. 9.

6   Personal interview with Paula, age fifty-one, Boston, December 29, 1987; personal interview with Dot, age thirty-seven, Fresno, CA, October 8, 1987.

7   Personal interview with Susie Bright, age twenty-nine, San Francisco, August 11, 1987.

8   Personal interview with H. O., age thirty-six, Merced, CA, October 28, 1987.

9   William A. Fitzgerald, "Pseudo-Heterosexuality in Prison and Out: A Study of Lower-Class Black Lesbians" (Ph.D. diss., City University of New York, 1977), pp. 117, 151.

10   Personal interview with Iris, age thirty-three, Lincoln, NE, October 13, 1988.

11   Fitzgerald, p. 98.

12   Interview with Susan in "Are Roles Really Dead?" *Lesbian Tide* (September/October 1979), p. 10.

13   Interview with Mickey in Brownworth, p. 7. Antoinette Azolakov's character Lester (Celeste) in *Cass and the Stone Butch* (Austin, TX, 1987) is a good fictional portrait of lesbians like Mickey who continue to exist in the 1980s and 1990s.

14   Personal interview with Honey Lee, age forty-one, San Francisco, August 6, 1987.

15   Joan Nestle, "The Fem Question; or, We Will Not Go Away" (paper presented at "The Scholar and the Feminist: Toward a Politics of Sexuality" conference, Barnard College, April 24, 1982).

16   Personal interview with Sarah, age thirty-nine, Boston, July 14, 1987.

17   Personal interview with Phyllis Lyon and Del Martin, San Francisco, August 14, 1987.

18   Bright (n. 7 above); Patricia Franzen, "The Transition Years: Researching the Albuquerque Lesbian Community" (paper presented at the Berkshire Women's History Conference, Wellesley College, June 20, 1987).

19   Judy Grahn, *Another Mother Tongue: Gay Words, Gay Worlds* (Boston, 1984), p. 85. I discuss romantic friendship and Boston marriage in *Surpassing the Love of Men: Romantic Friendship and Love between Women from the Renaissance to the Present* (New York, 1981).

20   Pat Suncircle, "Miriam," in *Lesbian Fiction,* ed. Elly Bulkin (Watertown, MA, 1981).

21   Donna Allegra, "Butch on the Streets," in *Fight Back: Feminist Resistance to Male Violence,* ed. Frederique Delacoste and Felice Newman (Pittsburgh, PA, 1981), pp. 44–45; Paula Mariedaughter, "Too Butch for Straights, Too Femme for Dykes," *Lesbian Ethics* 2 (Spring 1986): 96–100; Norma, "Butch/Fem Relationships Revisited," *Hartford Women's Center Newsletter* 5 (December 1982): 1–2.

22   Julia Penelope, "Whose Past Are We Reclaiming?" *Common Lives/Lesbian Lives* 13 (Autumn 1984): 16–36.

23   Grahn, p. 158; Charlene S. Henderson, "Texas '52," *Sinister Wisdom* 35 (Summer/Fall 1988): 43–45.

24   Isabel Andrews, in "Femme and Butch: A Readers' Forum," *Lesbian Ethics* 2 (Fall 1986): 96–99; personal interview with Paula, age thirty-four, Omaha, NE, October 13, 1988.

25   Grahn, p. 160.

26   Noretta Koertge, "Gender Stereotypes and Lesbian Lifestyles" (paper presented at the International Scientific Conference on Gay and Lesbian Studies, Free University, Amsterdam, December 15–18, 1987), p. 11; De Clarke, in "Femme and Butch: A Readers' Forum"; Lois Anne A., "Butch/Femme; or, I'm Glad I Went to TALF," *Triangle Newsletter,* May 1985, pp. 4–6; Pat Califia, *Sapphistry: The Book of Lesbian Sexuality,* 2d rev. ed. (Tallahassee, FL, 1983), p. 58; Nancy A. F. Langer, "The New Butch/Femme: The '80s Answer to Astrology," *New York Native,* July 29–August 11, 1985. See also Karen Lutzen, "The Return of Butch and Femme," *Hvad Hjertet Begaerer: Kvinders Kaerlighed til Kvinder 1825–1985* (Copenhagen, 1986), pp. 306–9. I am grateful to Karen Lutzen for a translation of this material.

27   Julia Penelope, "Heteropatriarchal Semantics: Just Two Kinds of People in the World," *Lesbian Ethics* 2 (Fall 1986): 58–80; Mary Crane, letter to the editor, *Lesbian Ethics* 2 (Spring 1986): 102–3; Pauline Bart, "My Brief Career as a Femme," *Lesbian Ethics* 2 (Fall 1986): 92–95.

28   Penelope, "Whose Past Are We Reclaiming?"; "We Protest," leaflet distributed by the Coalition for a Feminist Sexuality, New York, April 1982.

29   Jean Lynch and Mary Ellen Reilly, "Role Relationships: Lesbian Perspectives," *Journal of Homosexuality* 12 (Winter 1985/86): 53–69.

30   Personal interview with Kendall, age twenty-five, Berkeley, CA, August 15, 1987.

31   Personal interview with Phyllis Lyon, San Francisco, August 14, 1987; Karen Cameron, in "Femme and Butch: A Readers' Forum"; Norma, "Butch/Fem Relationships Revisited."

32   Bright (n. 7 above).

33   Lisa Duggan, "The Anguished Cry of an '80s Fem: I Want to Be a Drag Queen," *Out/Look* 1 (Spring 1988): 63–65.

34   Laura Rose DancingFire, "Meditations of a Possible Femme," *Common Lives/Lesbian Lives* 14 (Winter 1984): 10–19; personal interview with Neva, age forty-six, Lincoln, NE, October 12, 1988.

35 Amber Hollibaugh and Cherrie Moraga, "What We're Rollin' around in Bed With," in *Powers of Desire: The Politics of Sexuality*, ed. Ann Snitow et al. (New York, 1983), p. 398.

36 Personal interview with S. B., age twenty-nine, San Francisco, September 12, 1987.

37 Jess Wells, "The Dress," *Common Lives/Lesbian Lives* 8 (Summer 1983).

38 Michael Bronski, *Culture Clash: The Making of Gay Sensibility* (Boston, 1984), p. 214.

6

Male Dominance and the Gay World

Gregg Blachford

Homosexual sub-cultures—like other sub-cultures[1]—have typically been seen as massive collective problem-solving devices. Plummer (1975), among others,[2] has suggested that gay sub-cultures may resolve all those problems which flow from the homosexual taboo: secrecy, guilt, identity and access. This is fine as far as it goes, but it generally does not go far enough because it fails to connect the sub-culture back to the dominant culture. The task of this article then will be to begin the empirical and theoretical task of examination of the links between some parts of the male gay sub-culture and the wider social order....[This] framework suggests that all sub-cultures are located at the intersection of the dominant order (which generates problems) and other located cultural forms (which mediate the problems)....

...My discussion of the male gay sub-culture[3] will begin by briefly sketching some themes of the dominant culture in which the gay world must be located. It will then proceed to examine two processes at work in the gay world: those of *reproduction* and *resistance*. The first section examines some characteristics of the male gay sub-culture and how they can be seen to reproduce directly parts of the dominant culture, thereby reinforcing the dominant order through its arch conformity. The second section examines the resistances, alterations and modifications that the homosexual sub-culture makes to the dominant culture that it confronts. It does this as an expression of a partly negotiated opposition to those values....

A final section will then consider the limitations of these resistances, for despite opposition and challenge the gay world remains firmly tied to the dominant order....

THE DOMINANT CULTURE

Justice cannot be done to the complexity of the social order of industrialized societies in this short section.[4] I will only attempt to identify certain core val-

From Gregg Blachford, "Male Dominance and the Gay World," in Ken Plummer (ed.), *The Making of the Modern Homosexual* (London: Century Hutchinson Ltd., 1981), 184–86, 188–204. Reprinted by permission of the publisher.

ues of the social order that can be said to make up its dominant culture, that is, the behaviour that counts as normal, natural, "common sense," against which all other behaviour is measured. It is necessary to identify these values to note how the gay sub-culture is linked to them.

In capitalist societies there is an emphasis on values such as individual achievement, a never ending desire for more consumer goods and a market mentality that extends beyond the commodity market-place to include areas of sexual behaviour and emotional relationships. The majority religion, Christianity, stresses monogamy, sexual fidelity and potentially procreative sexual behaviour within marriage. The homosexual taboo, itself a core value, has its roots in religious doctrine.[5] Finally, age stratification is also prevalent with its stigma against being old in this society and a worship of the idea of youth itself.

Each of these core values (class relationships, consumerism, Christian morality and devaluation of the old) could be examined to see how the gay sub-culture, at the same time, both reproduces and resists them. But in this article I will mainly be dealing with another core value, male dominance, and how it is dealt with by the gay world. In subsequent research, links to the other core values could be examined.

Male Dominance as Part of the Dominant Culture

As with other core values, sex role stereotyping and the resulting domination of men over women is a complex area that cannot adequately be summarized in a few lines.[6]

Men dominate the crucial decision making centres of power in industrialized societies. The economic contributions that women make to society, both at the work-place and at home, are undervalued, if recognized at all.... Berger (1972: 45–47) [states:]

> *According to usage and conventions which are at last being questioned but have by no means been overcome, the social presence of a women is different in kind from that of a man. A man's presence is dependent upon the promise of power which he embodies [which] may be moral, physical, temperamental, economic, social, sexual—but its object is always exterior to the man.... To be born a woman has been to be born, within an allotted and confined space, into the keeping of men. The social presence of women has developed as a result of their ingenuity in living under such tutelage within such a limited space.... One might simplify this by saying: men act and women appear.*

Because of the submissive position that women are given in all aspects of society, their associated gender characteristics of femininity (which are culturally and historically specific) are seen as inferior ways of behaving—for example women's gestures, interests, concerns, dress, mannerisms, language—regardless of whether they are actually taken on by women or men....

REPRODUCTION OF MALE DOMINANCE IN THE GAY SUB-CULTURE

The task now is to see how this particular aspect of the dominant culture, male dominance, is reproduced and resisted in the homosexual sub-culture. I will begin, as I stated earlier, by pointing out how the gay sub-culture *reproduces* male dominance. To do this, I will examine three aspects of the style of the homosexual sub-culture: the practices of language, "pick-ups, cruising and objectification" and, third, the "expressive artefacts and concrete objects" (Willis, 1977:172) found in the gay sub-culture.[7]

The Style of Language

A group's specialized language or slang reflects much about its culture. The homosexual sub-culture, like all others, has its own slang which reflects that manner in which homosexuals perceive and structure the world in which they live. Much of the slang of the male homosexual directly reproduces traditional male attitudes to women. For example, women are often referred to by their sexual organs; "fish" is a common term for a woman and "cunty" is used as an adjective referring to something that possesses the qualities of a woman. The derogatory term "fag hag" is used to describe a woman who enjoys the company of gay men. Besides these peculiarly gay male expressions, most references to women are similar to the way in which heterosexual men can be seen to respond to women: "cow," "old woman," "slag," "tart," "cheap," "scrubber."

Sonenschein (1969) in his study of homosexual language characterized it by four main processes: utilization, effeminization, redirection, invention. The one that is at work here is "utilization," whereby terms used by other groups, in this case heterosexual men, are borrowed and used in a similar way. It reflects a negative attitude to women, who are seen as insignificant, passive objects, not fit for anything except sexual intercourse and/or looking after children. Since gay men neither want sex with women nor have any procreative use for them, they serve no purpose at all; in fact, they may be accused of taking men away from possible homosexual encounters.

There is also slang that refers pejoratively to effeminate homosexuals because they are "like women" and therefore are not worthy of considerate treatment. The slang used is the same as that used by heterosexuals against *all* homosexuals, that is, "queer," "bent," "poof" and "fairy." Bruce Rodgers in *The Queen's Vernacular: A Gay Lexicon* gives examples: "I'm gay, but you're queer"; "We're not the queer ones, they are!" (1972:166). This is said by "normal" homosexuals to those whom they believe are "truly perverted." These would include not only those effeminate homosexuals, but also transvestites, transsexuals and paedophiles.

Perhaps the "normal" homosexual feels threatened by the overtness of the effeminate homosexual. Because of the expectations involved in "being a man," with its attendant homosexual taboo, gay men may want to distance themselves as far as possible from the stereotyped role of the homosexual which they have internalized as negative and undesirable. So effeminate homosexuals are going to be stigmatized by the more "normal" homosexuals, and in rejecting effeminacy they imitate so closely the world of the dominant male culture. Mike Brake relates how one member of a respectable homophile organization (notoriously anti-drag) puffed furiously at his pipe while complaining of being barred from a pub which had banned gays: "They said I was effeminately dressed. I was furious. I may be queer but at least I'm a man" (1076:100).

Aspects of homosexual slang then show the internalization and reproduction of male culture with its particular attitudes towards women and its rejection of deviants who do not fit the prescribed masculine pattern of behaviour (Sagarin, 1970:41).

> *By laughing at homosexuals one ceases to be one, or at least establishes... "role distance" between oneself and other homosexuals. By reserving ridicule for some homosexuals such as the...exhibitionistically effeminate "screaming queen," a distance is placed between oneself who is presumably adjusted and manly, and certain other homosexuals deserving of contempt.*

So the everyday language of homosexual males is in many ways continuous with the everyday language of the heterosexual male culture. Their slang ties them to the dominant order and offers no challenge to a society which labels *all* homosexuals as deviants and oppresses them as such, although effeminate homosexuals are more likely to be singled out for the brunt of any attack because of their visibility.

The Style of Pick-Ups, Cruising and Objectification

Male dominance affects the nature of sexual relationships between men and women. One form of sexual relationship, that of the casual sexual encounter, departs from the strongly sanctioned norms that declare deviant "anything other than monogamous, legally sanctioned, obligated relations" (Hooker, 1967:177). But a man is less likely to suffer sanctions if he engages in promiscuous behaviour, as his powerful position allows him to be the pursuer and the chooser. This stronger position enables him to see his potential female partner as a sexual object with its emphasis on physical appearance to the almost total neglect of other aspects of her character. I want to look for evidence of this form of "sexual objectification" in the gay sub-culture.[8]

The prevalence of homosexual promiscuity has not gone unnoticed. Recent research has found that the average, white, male heterosexual has five to nine sexual partners over his lifetime. The average, white, male homosexual, on the other hand, encounters 1000 partners over his life, most of them strangers (Bell and Weinberg, 1978:12).[9] So sexual activity is important. The sub-culture and common understandings among homosexuals facilitate these encounters (Delph, 1978:9).

> *Two men passing on the street may momentarily glance at each other, drop cues that each is homosexual and interested in each other, hesitate for confirmatory signals and, within a half hour, consummate their "spontaneous" love in the many available niches that are legion in congested N.Y.C.*

Delph's work—an ethnography of public homosexual encounters—describes in detail the social and sexual interactions which occur in a wide variety of settings including streets, public toilets, public parks, subways, cinemas, beaches, empty lorries, public buildings, as well as the more expected gay bars and baths. One characteristic common to almost all of these settings is that verbal utterances are virtually absent. The study illuminates (J. M. Johnson in Delph, 1978:16)[10]

> *how individuals learn to use the special self-presentations, bodily posturing, gestural cues, the manners and informal (but sanctionable) rules unique to the settings; how the distinctive meanings of space, time, and manner (or "self") separate these erotic worlds from the conventional ones; how public sexuality produces a metamorphosis of the individuals who partake in it, thus transforming normal selves into erotic selves.*

Does sexual objectification occur in these casual encounters? People in these situations will not be attracted to someone unless they are attracted by some external feature that fulfils some sexual fantasy. It follows that there must be an emphasis on surface or cosmetic characteristics. And because the criteria of selection can be highly specific, one is, in turn, concerned to present an image of oneself that will attract others. Therefore appearance, dress, manner and body build are very important. The partner is only a means to an impersonal, purely sexual end. "In this meeting of strangers, the disengaged character of activities from any ascriptive characteristics is promoted" (Hooker, 1967: 177).

The ultimate sexual objectification in gay male casual sexual encounters is the glory hole in public toilets.[11] As a wall separates the two participants, they have no contact except for a mouth, a penis and perhaps a hand. Almost total anonymity is maintained as no other attributes are taken into consideration.

Some gay men note the emphasis on outward appearances and resent it (Houston, 1978:14).

> *The gay scene is a market and both sellers and buyers have become used to the coinage of appeal and neither can change it without losing out. The way the compulsive cruisers present themselves is geared to the way the buyers choose: looking no further than skindeep, ignoring what might or what might not be underneath.... The majority of gays are placing their cosmetic selves, not their real selves, on the line.*

In this reproduction of the sexual objectification that even goes beyond that characteristic of heterosexual casual encounters, one is not challenging the ideology of male dominance in our society and its resulting homosexual oppression (Delph, 1978:28).

> *Engaging in public sex, [the public eroticist] does so with no intention of contesting discrimination against homosexuality. There is no drive to change existing moral conditions. The homosexual adapts to the contingencies of the existing order of things. He maintains socially prescribed and expected demeanor in the round of settings through which he travels.*

Gay men have an invested [*sic*] interest in the system as it exists. And so the arch-conformity of the gay sub-culture is further reinforced.

The Style of "Expressive Artefacts and Concrete Objects"

The overall style that is most recognizable and far reaching in the public gay sub-culture in the 1970s is the copying of traditional masculine clothing and its associated artefacts. There are a variety of forms, from "hard" to "soft" masculinity, but the studied virility is to be found almost everywhere. Its extreme is represented by the "leather men" of the gay sub-culture who adopt images of sexual violence and dominance including neo-Nazi adorn- ments, metal-toed boots, studded belts, handcuffs and chains. Then there are those who wear clothes associated with masculine working class labour- ing occupations such as construction workers (overalls, hard boots, construction helmet, tools hanging from belts), mechanics (coveralls) or cowboys (denim jeans, vest and jacket, plaid shirt, cowboy boots, short neck scarves and, in some cases, a cowboy hat and breeches). Different kinds of athletes are represented, and one sees people dressed as joggers (shorts, sleeveless top, white running shoes) or boxers complete with authentic box- ing shorts, a vest or nothing over the chest, long socks and boxing shoes.

Other styles would be a military look including complete uniforms of one of the services. *Him Exclusive,* a British gay magazine, outlines the details of this style for its readers (September 1975:27).[12]

> *If uniforms are your thing the best place you could go seems to be Hampstead Heath....Talking about uniforms I must admit I do have a liking for sailors; there's something about nice short hair and bell bottoms....Somehow a sailor's uniform seems to fit right round the arse and the crotch.*

A popular American disco group in the late 1970s, "Village People," wore clothing and carried artefacts that were clearly intended to represent these gay male styles. The members of this group include a cowboy, Indian chief, policeman, biker/leather freak, GI soldier and construction worker.

But these extremes are not common except in the large "trendy" discos of metropolitan cities. More usual is for an individual to wear only a certain item rather than the complete outfit. Denim for the "Western style" is an example. Peter York describes the general look (1979:59).

> *The costume was Basic Street Gay (for "lumberjack"): straight jeans, cheap plaid shirt, construction worker's yellow lace-up boots, short cropped hair—and the moustache, always the moustache....One of the tightest dress-codes in the world was evolving, and with the costume...the mythology of the hard man, macho.*

These objects and styles have clear meanings in the wider culture: toughness, virility, aggression, strength, potency—essentially, masculinity and its associated machismo. It seems as if there is an attempt, as with language, to achieve through these objects a differentiation between oneself, who becomes a "real man" in these outfits, and the absurd, condemned and ridiculed role of other homosexuals. There is a celebration of masculinity that allows them to distance themselves from the stigmatized label of homosexual. Again the dominant culture with respect to male dominance becomes reproduced in the gay sub-culture (York, 1979:59–60).

> *Reactionary macho had made a cultural reappearance....Mass macho...[was] set solid by the late Seventies into the most archaic possible stereotype: the gay as Ultraman. [Although] there was nothing new, in principle, about gays taking up worker chic, they had been doing it for years...a funny reference to an icon, the straight working man, gays [were now] internalising him, his clothes, his hardman values, his contempt for sissies.*

CHALLENGES THROUGH CAMP

The previous section dealt with some of the ways in which the male gay subculture, through its styles, reproduces characteristics of the dominant culture which are associated closely with male assertiveness and (tacitly at least) female subordination. In this way the gay world reinforces the dominant order through its conformity. But the processes at work in the sub-culture are more complicated than might appear at first glance, for there is some evidence that the gay sub-culture negotiates an oppositional challenge to some aspects of the dominant order. The best way to understand this innovatory style is to examine one phenomenon of the gay sub-culture—camp— and to show how it transforms conformity into a challenge.

What Is Camp?

Very little has been written specifically about camp. It conjures up images of limp wrists and swivelling hips, but camp, Christopher Isherwood (1954:125) says, is much more than

> *a swishy little boy with peroxided hair, dressed in a picture hat and a feather boa, pretending to be Marlene Dietrich....*

Jack Babuscio claims that camp does two things for homosexuals; it gives them a general understanding about what the world is like and their place in it, and it helps them to deal with that world.

What the World Is Like

By being polarized by society into the negative category of homosexuality, which is opposite to the category of heterosexuality and its associated characteristics of normality, natural and healthy behaviour, gay people become aware that to be homosexual is to bear a stigma (Plummer, 1975:160).

> *Homosexuals come to see how the world is socially constructed, and become aware of some of the rules by which it is so constructed, being placed as they are in positions of constantly having to consciously perform roles. Being stigmatised results in the uncommonsense knowledge of commonsense social structures.*

Dealing with That World

Camp can also help homosexuals deal with a hostile environment that forces one to live a "closeted" or two-sided life. It does this by criticizing through mockery the hypocrisy, pretension, self-deceit and prudery that gay people have come to know exist in the wider world. It is a gesture of self-legitimization which has not just a touch of propaganda value. The "normal" world, which makes homosexuality illegitimate and forces homosexuals to pass for straight, is made into the common enemy. "Camp is a solvent of mortality. It neutralizes moral indignation, sponsors playfulness" (Sontag, 1967:290), at least when one is in the sub-culture.

Camp also deals with the world because it is an assertion of identity. It will always be done in the company of others "in the know" where one can "drop the mask" and feel superior to those outside. It is "something of a private code, a badge of identity even, among small urban cliques" (Sontag, 1967:275)....An important aspect of camp is the awareness of another side of what, to "normal" people, has only one meaning.

It should now be possible to look again at the styles of the sub-culture to see if there is an additional way of interpreting the behaviour that we have already examined—especially to see if there is any evidence of these styles challenging, through mockery or otherwise, the dominant male culture, rather than simply copying it.

The Style of Language

While it seems likely that the male gay slang reproduces the dominant male order, it may be at least as plausible to view it simultaneously as containing elements which could be seen as critical: mocking and ridiculing the idea of masculinity, femininity and heterosexual institutions.

There is a massive amount of feminization of nouns, adjectives, pronouns and names among gay men. For example, gay men will constantly "camp it up" by referring to themselves and others as "she," "girl," "woman," "Miss," etc., as well as by changing men's names to women's. Henry becomes Henrice; Stephen becomes Stephanie. "Miss" will be used as a title preceding the first or last name of a gay man. It is also used with nouns or adjectives to describe the characteristics or peculiarities of another homosexual....

Closely connected in usage and meaning is the term "queen," which is a designation among male homosexuals for one another and does not necessarily imply that the individual is effeminate. A "muscle queen" is a gay body builder. It is most frequently, but not always, used affectionately amongst sub-culturalized homosexuals. It can also be put before someone's name. "Queen Cecil didn't give up cigarettes—he gave up quitting" (Rodgers, 1972:164). Or it can be a suffix naming one's locality. "That Hampstead queen is visiting us tonight." It can also indicate one's sexual preference and/or idiosyncrasy. A "size queen" is someone who prefers sex with men who have large penises. A "drama queen" is a fussy person who makes a "scene" at the slightest provocation.

This effeminization can be read as critical of heterosexual norms because it is a recognition that masculinity is a learned behaviour pattern and not necessarily the "normal" or only possible way for men to behave. There are two points to emerge from this. First, it reflects a sharp awareness of conventional expectations that could only come about if one felt divorced from them as a result of being a homosexual. This is illustrated by noting that these same terms (with different meanings) are used to describe heterosexual men. In this case, the slang is used to satirize and point out the ridiculousness of straight men who play at "being a man." It can also be used in this sense to satirize homosexuals who are attempting to hide their homosexuality by engaging in virile activities and responsibilities. "Who does that butch queen think she is—playing football of all things. She'll ruin her manicure." Secondly, this slang indicates that the individual does not think it is an insult to be referred to or thought of as a woman. Masculinity and femininity are just roles to be donned or shunned at different times. Many sub-culturalized homosexuals can "camp it up" or "butch it up," be "butch" or a "screamer" at will.

So the effeminization of language which occurs within the homosexual sub-culture can be seen both to reflect and transform the attitudes about gender and gender expectations of the wider cultures, both to accept and question the position in which homosexuals find themselves.

The Style of Pick-Ups, Cruising and Objectification

Earlier I argued that the promiscuous behaviour of the male homosexual is similar to the heterosexual casual sexual behaviour with its emphasis on seeing others only as physical objects and seeing oneself as a marketable commodity. But the meaning of these rituals is again more complex. There is a sense in which this behaviour is in opposition to the dominant culture's view of sexual behaviour.

First of all, the assumption that a casual sexual encounter involves the "use" of people which is seen as a "bad thing" is giving it a meaning which is not necessarily there. That view reflects the dominant culture's definition of legitimate sex as only that which occurs in the context of love and possible reproduction inside a long-term monogamous relationship, with the resulting stigmatization of sexual behaviour outside of these bounds. Gay casual sex can be seen as a rejection of this narrow definition of legitimate sex, as it expands its range of possible meanings. It includes seeing sex as a form of recreation, simply a game or hobby, as fun. It is divested of all its moral and guilt overtones and is enjoyed as an end in itself. Perhaps the possibility has arisen for this wider and creative range of public meanings because the reproductive aspect of sex is impossible for gay men....Foucault (1979) argues that public sex, anonymous sauna orgies, etc., decentre sex, desubjectivize us as sexed beings, and therefore they are radical or challenging of the society.

Lee's *Getting Sex—A New Approach: More Fun, Less Guilt* offers a legitimation for the sex delivery system of the gay sub-culture in the terms outlined above (1978:viii).

> *It is time to argue that in at least one way, the gay world is better. Gay people are generally less inhibited about the enjoyment of playful and uncommitted sex. Sex with more joy and less guilt is something gay people can teach the rest of the world.*

Instead of being defensive about accusations of promiscuity by insisting that many gay people have long-term relationships (which is true but beside the point, he argues), he feels that it is time to ask what is so wrong with promiscuity. He claims that one cannot talk about objectification and "using and discarding" people when there is a voluntary and reciprocal enjoyment of each other's bodies. Although there are disadvantages and shortcomings, the gay "ecosystem" provides the social arrangements to facilitate mutual sexual pleasure without fear of rape, high costs or unfulfilled expectations. Lee emphasizes the point (ibid:12) that

> *treating sex as a commodity does not mean it is only a commodity. Nothing said of sex in this book prevents anyone from enjoying sex as part of a long-term relationship or faithful marriage.*

Lee claims that there is a great deal of affection in casual sexual relationships that goes unnoticed by outside observers who may only see a continuous flow of bodies. Tripp has also noted that there can be an intensity and a closeness unmatched in even some longer-term relationships (1977:146).

> *Sometimes promiscuity includes surprising elements of affection. Even in fleeting contacts…affection often develops as a by-product of sexual activity.*

But promiscuity is criticized because this affection will only last the length of the encounter and the person may soon be forgotten. Lee asks why sex is centred out for such attention. If we forget the plot of a good book we have read or meet acquaintances through work and forget them a week later, no one is surprised or shocked.

A second challenge to the dominant order through casual gay encounters is that there is no necessary connection between sexual activities and social roles. Male/male sex is more able to ignore the so-called "natural" connection between sexual position (inserter, insertee, for example) and gender role. In other words, if one partner gets fucked, he is not necessarily expected to make the breakfast the next morning or act effeminately (Haist and Hewitt, 1974). In male/female sex there is more likely to be an automatic link between sexual position and gender role. And since there is a power differential between heterosexual women and men, the "use" of the woman by the man is more likely to occur than in male/male sex where, if "use" does occur, it is more likely to be mutual. Sex is invested with different meanings for heterosexual men and women, and although this is changing, women are still meant to see sex as part of an intense emotional relationship, which can lead to unfulfilled expectations in a casual sexual relationship.

There is then the possibility of re-reading the practice of casual sex as an example of a creative transformation of and an opposition to the dominant culture's view of what constitutes legitimate sexual behaviour.

The Style of "Expressive Artefacts and Concrete Objects"

The account of the reactionary nature of the "macho-mania" of the male gay sub-culture assumes that the objects used in the style of the sub-culture have the same meaning there as they do in the wider cultures. An alternative account is that the objects used by gay men have meanings quite different from their original meanings....Clark et al. (1975:178) [state:]

> *The generation of subcultural styles involves differential selection from within the matrix of the existent. What happens is not the creation of objects and meanings from nothing, but rather the **transformation and rearrangement** of what is given (and "borrowed") into a pattern which carries a new meaning, its **translation** to a new context, and its **adaptation**.*

What adaptations then take place? First of all, the clothes are worn differently in the gay sub-culture from the way they are worn by "real men." They are much tighter fitting, especially tailored to be as erotic and sensual as possible. Parts of the body will be purposely left exposed in an attempt to attract others. Some type of jewellery is likely to be worn, including chains on the neck, ear-rings and finger-rings or combinations of these, all of which are unlikely to be found on heterosexual workers or athletes.[13]

These subtle changes and transformations of objects infuse the style with a new meaning of eroticism and overt sexuality—that is, they are used explicitly to make one appear sexy and attractive to other men. This can be seen as distinct from any celebration of masculinity as such. Instead it may be an attempt to show that masculine or "ordinary" men can be homosexual too—a breaking down of the stereotyped image of the homosexual. It forces the wider culture to question its stereotypes and question the legitimacy of linking femininity and homosexuality....

It is true that many gay men find the big, butch, straight image of the macho man very attractive and appealing. But it is possible to separate this fantasy image from the reality of that fantasy, which many of these same gay men would reject. In other words, many of those who don these "costumes" may have no real desire actually to take on the associated characteristics of virile masculinity. It is accepted and seen only as a fantasy and remains at that level....

...In conclusion, objects taken from the male culture can be transformed and given a new oppositional force by their users in an attempt to overcome feelings of stigma and, at the same time, find an alternative life style....

NOTES

1   Most sub-cultural studies have been American and in the field of delinquency, for example, the work of A. K. Cohen (1955), Cloward and Ohlin (1961) and Downes (1966).

2   Some important homosexual sub-cultural studies have been done by Achilles (1967), Hooker (1967), Leznoff and Westley (1967), Hoffman (1968), Warren (1974), Dank (1971), Plummer (1975).

3   I will be concerning myself with the male homosexual sub-culture only, as the female gay sub-culture has different characteristics and origins, and also there is no possibility of me gaining access to this sub-culture. Gagnon and Simon (1967) point to the wider cultural influences of "femininity" (and all that entails in America) on lesbian behaviour which puts lesbians nearer to heterosexual women rather than to homosexual men. I will use the term gay sub-culture rather loosely, but here I stress that it cannot be said to exist in any limited number of settings or times. "The gay world" is multi-faceted, multi-tiered and pluralistic mainly because of its location at the intersection of a large number of other cultural forms. I draw examples more frequently from the public and visible gay world to be found in gay bars, discos and public sex areas. Most homosexuals though (and indeed most people) spend their leisure time with lovers, cliques and friends in a private and less visible world where their behaviour may differ from the more public world.

4   A more detailed discussion can be found in Rock (1974).

5   See Pearce and Roberts (1973).

6   Some of the literature in the sexual divisions field is discussed in Barker and Allen (1976) and Kuhn and Wolpe (1978).

7   The research technique used for this study would have ideally been a full-scale ethnography. What I have relied on as a substitute in this situation is my own retrospectively interpreted personal experiences and observations as a participant homosexual in different aspects of the homosexual sub-culture. This methodological approach and its advantages and disadvantages are outlined and discussed by Riemer (1977).

8   See Schofield (1976) on heterosexual promiscuity.

9   This is an average figure. Many homosexuals, of course, would match the heterosexual average. And many of the "1000 partners" could easily be totted up over a twenty-year period by a fleeting contact with, say, five men on a monthly visit to a gay sauna. Each of the 1000 would not therefore represent an entire night's encounter.

10 Humphreys (1975) discusses casual sexual encounters in public toilets.

11 A "glory hole" is a hole bored through a dividing wall or door of a toilet cubicle that is large enough and placed at the right height to permit passage of the penis through it.

12 Other British gay magazines are *Zipper, Sam, Men In Uniform* and *Mister.* In the USA some magazines are *Blueboy, Macho* and *Numbers.*

13 Interestingly enough, heterosexual workers are taking on some of these "adaptations" themselves. This is not new. In the 1960s aftershave lotion was only for "fairies," but now its use by heterosexual men is close to universal.

REFERENCES

Achilles, N. 1967. "The Development of the Homosexual Bar as an Institution." In *Sexual Deviance*, ed. J. H. Gagnon and W. S. Simon, 228–44. New York: Harper and Row.

Barker, D. L., and S. Allen. 1976. *Sexual Divisions and Society: Process and Change*. London: Tavistock.

Bell, A. P., and M. S. Weinberg. 1978. *Homosexualities: A Study of Diversity among Men and Women*. London: Mitchell Beazley.

Berger, J. 1972. *Ways of Seeing*. London: Penguin.

Brake, M. 1976. "I May Be Queer but At Least I'm a Man: Male Hegemony and Ascribed 'V' Achieved Gender." In *Sexual Divisions and Society: Process and Change*, ed. D. L. Barker and S. Allen, 174–98. London: Tavistock.

Clarke, J., et al. 1975. "Style." In *Resistance through Rituals*, ed. S. Hall and T. Jefferson, 175–91. London: Hutchinson.

Cloward, R., and L. E. Ohlin. 1961. *Delinquency and Opportunity*. London: Routledge and Kegan Paul.

Cohen, A. K. 1955. *Delinquent Boys: The Culture of the Gang*. London: Macmillan.

Dank, B. 1971. "Coming Out in the Gay World." *Psychiatry* 34 (May): 180–97.

Delph, E. W. 1978. *The Silent Community*. London: Sage.

Downes, D. 1966. *The Delinquent Solution: A Study in Subcultural Theory*. London: Routledge and Kegan Paul.

Foucault, M. 1979. *The History of Sexuality*. Vol. 1. London: Allen Lane.

Gagnon, J. H., and W. S. Simon. 1967. "Femininity in the Lesbian Community." *Social Problems* 15.

Haist, M., and J. Hewitt. 1974. "The Butch-Fem Dichotomy in Male Homosexual Behavior." *Journal of Sex Research* 10: 68–75.

Hoffman, M. 1968. *The Gay World: Male Homosexuality and the Social Creation of Evil*. New York: Basic.

Hooker, E. 1967. "The Homosexual Community." In *Sexual Deviance*, ed. J. H. Gagnon and W. S. Simon. New York: Harper and Row.

Houston, R. 1978. "The Way We Wear." *Gay News* 131: 14–15.

Humphreys, L. 1975. *Tea-Room Trade*. 2d. ed. Chicago: Aldine.

Isherwood, C. 1954. *The World in the Evening*. London: Methuen.

Kuhn, D., and A. M. Wolpe. 1978. *Feminism and Materialism: Feminism and Modes of Production*. London: Routledge and Kegan Paul.

Lee, J. A. 1978. *Getting Sex—A New Approach: More Fun, Less Guilt*. Don Mills, Ont.: Musson.

Leznoff, M., and W. A. Westley. 1967. "The Homosexual Community." In *Sexual Deviance*, ed. J. H. Gagnon and W. S. Simon. New York: Harper and Row.

Pearce, F., and A. Roberts. 1973. "The Social Regulation of Sexual Behavior and the Development of Industrial Capitalism." In *Contemporary Social Problems in Britain,* ed. R. Bailey and J. Young. London: Saxon House.

Plummer, K. 1975. *Sexual Stigma: An Interactionist Account.* London: Routledge and Kegan Paul.

Riemer, J. W. 1977. "Varieties of Opportunistic Research." *Urban Life* 5: 467–77.

Rock, P. 1974. "Sociology of Deviancy and Conceptions of Moral Order." *British Journal of Criminology* 14: 139–49.

Rodgers, B. 1972. *The Queen's Vernacular: A Gay Lexicon.* London: Blond and Briggs.

Sagarin, E. 1970. "Languages of Homosexual Sub-Culture." *Medical Aspects of Human Sexuality,* April.

Schofield, M. 1976. *Promiscuity.* London: Gollancz.

Sonenschein, D. 1969. "The Homosexual's Language." *Journal of Sex Research* 5 (4): 281–91.

Sontag, S. 1967. "Notes on Camp." In *Against Interpretation and Other Essays,* 275–92. London: Eyre and Spottiswoode.

Tripp, C. A. 1977. *The Homosexual Matrix.* London: Quartet.

Warren, C. A. 1974. *Identity and Community in the Gay World.* London: Wiley.

Willis, P. 1977. *Learning to Labour.* London: Saxon House.

York, P. 1969. "Machomania." *Harpers and Queen,* February.

CHAPTER TWO

Socialization Influences

Becoming gendered is partly the consequence of lengthy exposure to various influences. While students of socialization acknowledge that our current state of knowledge permits neither an exhaustive listing of the number of such influences, nor a definitive prioritizing of their impact, in this chapter we examine various ways in which messages about gender are transmitted and reinforced.

We begin with Lois Gould's classic fictional account of a family environment seemingly devoid of gender-linked socialization and the problems such a family encounters from a social world based on traditional expectations. After reading Gould's account (Article 7), many students who are either current or prospective parents ask, "How can I attempt to raise an X?" Sandra Bem (Article 8) outlines several major theories of gender acquisition, presents her own gender schema theory, and then outlines some aschematic possibilities for childhood socialization in a gender-schematic world. We offer her latter suggestions not as a definitive set of prescriptive guidelines but rather as a means of provoking and stimulating thought and discussion on the part of the reader.

Of course, socialization is not confined to the home. The work of Jane Gaskell and her associates (Article 9), focuses on the educational system. Asking the question, "What is worth knowing?" they note various answers that have been given to this complex and controversial question. Writing from a socialist feminist perspective, they offer numerous suggestions for changing the structure, content, and process of education in Canada to promote a more egalitarian outcome.

Schools provide the meeting grounds for the development of age-related peer groups, which, because acceptance within them is crucial, are one of the most powerful sources of gender socialization from mid-childhood to at least mid-adolescence. Within gendered peer groups, different criteria for popularity have endured over time and across the international boundary between Canada and the United States. Adler, Kless, and Adler (Article 10) explore different criteria for popularity among male and female elementary school students that have long-range implications for adult gendered behaviour. The authors find that female peer groups evidence change more than male groups do, a common finding among studies of at least the white, middle to upper-middle classes.

Finally, we present the empirical work of Joan Spade and Carol Reese (Article 11), in which findings from a recent study of the work and family plans of college and university students indicate that, despite current calls for greater gender equity in the occupational and family worlds, the pace of social change is indeed slow, attesting in part to the power of existing traditional socialization messages.

7

X: A Fabulous Child's Story

Lois Gould

Once upon a time, a Baby named X was born. It was named X so that nobody could tell whether it was a boy or a girl.

Its parents could tell, of course, but they couldn't tell anybody else. They couldn't even tell Baby X—at least not until much, much later.

You see, it was all part of a very important Secret Scientific Xperiment, known officially as Project Baby X.

This Xperiment was going to cost Xactly 23 billion dollars and 72 cents. Which might seem like a lot for one Baby, even if it was an important Secret Scientific Xperimental Baby.

But when you remember the cost of strained carrots, stuffed bunnies, booster shots, 28 shiny quarters from the tooth fairy...you begin to see how it adds up.

Long before Baby X was born, the smartest scientists had to work out the secret details of the Xperiment, and to write the *Official Instruction Manual*, in secret code, for Baby X's parents, whoever they were.

These parents had to be selected very carefully. Thousands of people volunteered to take thousands of tests, with thousands of tricky questions.

Almost everybody failed because, it turned out, almost everybody wanted a boy or a girl, and not a Baby X at all.

Also, almost everybody thought a Baby X would be more trouble than a boy or a girl. (They were right, too.)

There were families with grandparents named Milton and Agatha, who wanted the baby named Milton or Agatha instead of X, even if it *was* an X.

There were aunts who wanted to knit tiny dresses and uncles who wanted to send tiny baseball mitts.

Worst of all, there were families with other children who couldn't be trusted to keep a Secret. Not if they knew the Secret was worth 23 billion dollars and 72 cents—and all you had to do was take one little peek at Baby X in the bathtub to know what it was.

Finally, the scientists found the Joneses, who really wanted to raise an X more than any other kind of baby—no matter how much trouble it was.

The Joneses promised to take turns holding X, feeding X, and singing X to sleep.

And they promised never to hire any baby-sitters. The scientists knew that a baby-sitter would probably peek at X in the bathtub, too.

The day the Joneses brought their baby home, lots of friends and relatives came to see it. And the first thing they asked was what kind of a baby X was.

When the Joneses said, "It's an X!" nobody knew what to say.

They couldn't say, "Look at her cute little dimples!"

On the other hand, they couldn't say, "Look at his husky little biceps!"

And they didn't feel right about saying just plain "kitchy-coo."

The relatives all felt embarrassed about having an X in the family.

"People will think there's something wrong with it!" they whispered.

"Nonsense!" the Joneses said cheerfully. "What could possibly be wrong with this perfectly adorable X?"

Clearly, nothing at all was wrong. Nevertheless, the cousins who had sent a tiny football helmet would not come and visit any more. And the neighbors who sent a pink-flowered romper suit pulled their shades down when the Joneses passed their house.

The *Official Instruction Manual* had warned the new parents that this would happen, so they didn't fret about it. Besides, they were too busy learning how to bring up Baby X.

Ms. and Mr. Jones had to be Xtra careful. If they kept bouncing it up in the air and saying how *strong* and *active* it was, they'd be treating it more like a boy than an X. But if all they did was cuddle it and kiss it and tell it how *sweet* and *dainty* it was, they'd be treating it more like a girl than an X.

On page 1654 of the *Official Instruction Manual,* the scientists prescribed: "plenty of bouncing and plenty of cuddling, *both.* X ought to be strong and sweet and active. Forget about *dainty* altogether."

There were other problems, too. Toys, for instance, And clothes. On his first shopping trip, Mr. Jones told the store clerk, "I need some things for a new baby." The clerk smiled and said, "Well, now, is it a boy or a girl?" "It's an X," Mr. Jones said, smiling back. But the clerk got all red in the face and said huffily, "In *that* case, I'm afraid I can't help you, sir."

Mr. Jones wandered the aisles trying to find what X needed. But everything was in sections marked BOYS or GIRLS: "Boys' pajamas" and "Girls' Underwear" and "Boys' Fire Engines" and "Girls' Housekeeping Sets." Mr. Jones went home without buying anything for X.

That night he and Ms. Jones consulted page 2326 of the *Official Instruction Manual.* It said firmly: "Buy plenty of everything!"

So they bought all kinds of toys. A boy doll that made pee-pee and cried "Pa-Pa." And a girl doll that talked in three languages and said, "I am the Pres-i-dent of Gen-er-al Mo-tors."

They bought a storybook about a brave princess who rescued a handsome prince from his tower, and another one about a sister and brother who grew up to be a baseball star and a ballet star, and you had to guess which.

The head scientists of Project Baby X checked all their purchases and told them to keep up the good work. They also reminded the Joneses to see page 4629 of the *Manual,* where it said, "Never make Baby X feel *embarrassed* or *ashamed* about what it wants to play with. And if X gets dirty climbing rocks, never say, 'Nice little Xes don't get dirty climbing rocks.'"

Likewise, it said, "If X falls down and cries, never say, 'Brave little Xes don't cry.' Because, of course, nice little Xes *do* get dirty, and brave little Xes *do* cry. No matter how dirty X gets, or how hard it cries, don't worry. It's all part of the Xperiment."

Whenever the Joneses pushed Baby X's stroller in the park, smiling strangers would come over and coo: "Is that a boy or a girl?" The Joneses would smile back and say, "It's an X." The strangers would stop smiling then and often snarl something nasty—as if the Joneses had said something nasty to *them.*

Once a little girl grabbed X's shovel in the sandbox, and zonked X on the head with it. "Now, now, Tracy," the mother began to scold, "little girls mustn't hit little—" and she turned to ask X, "Are you a little boy or a little girl, dear?"

Mr. Joness, who was sitting near the sandbox, held his breath and crossed his fingers.

X smiled politely, even though X's head had never been zonked so hard in its life. "I'm a little X," said X.

"You're a *what?*" the lady exclaimed angrily. "You're a little b-r-a-t, you mean!"

"But little girls mustn't hit little Xes, either!" said X, retrieving the shovel with another polite smile, "What good's hitting, anyway?"

X's father finally X-haled, uncrossed his fingers, and grinned.

And at their next secret Project Baby X meeting, the scientists grinned too. Baby X was doing fine.

But then it was time for X to start school. The Joneses were really worried about this, because school was even more full of rules for boys and girls, and there were no rules for Xes.

Teachers would tell boys to form a line and girls to form another line. There would be boys' games and girls' games, and boys' secrets and girls' secrets.

The school library would have a list of recommended books for girls, and a different list for boys.

There would even be a bathroom marked BOYS and another one marked GIRLS.

Pretty soon boys and girls would hardly talk to each other. What would happen to poor little X?

The Joneses spent weeks consulting their *Instruction Manual.*

There were 249 and one-half pages of advice under "First Day of School."

Then they were all summoned to an Urgent Xtra Special Conference with the smart scientists of Project Baby X.

The scientists had to make sure that X's mother had taught X how to throw and catch a ball properly, and that X's father had been sure to teach X what to serve at a doll's tea party.

X had to know how to shoot marbles and jump rope and, most of all, what to say when the Other Children asked whether X was a Boy or a Girl.

Finally, X was ready.

X's teacher had promised that the class could line up alphabetically, instead of forming separate lines for boys and girls. And X had permission to use the principal's bathroom, because it wasn't marked anything except BATHROOM. But nobody could help X with the biggest problem of all—Other Children.

Nobody in X's class had ever known an X. Nobody had even heard grown-ups say, "Some of my best friends are Xes."

What would other children think? Would they make Xist jokes? Or would they make friends?

You couldn't tell what X was by its clothes. Overalls don't even button right to left, like girls' clothes, or left to right, like boys' clothes.

And did X have a girl's short haircut or a boy's long haircut?

As for the games X liked, either X played ball very well for a girl, or else played house very well for a boy.

The children tried to find out by asking X tricky questions, like, "Who's your favourite sports star?" X had two favorite sports stars: a girl jockey named Robyn Smith and a boy archery champion named Robin Hood.

Then they asked, "What's your favorite TV show?" And X said: "Lassie," which stars a girl dog played by a boy dog.

When X said its favorite toy was a doll, everyone decided that X must be a girl. But then X said the doll was really a robot, and that X had computerized it, and that it was programmed to bake fudge and then clean up the kitchen.

After X told them that, they gave up guessing what X was. All they knew was they'd sure like to see X's doll.

After school, X wanted to play with the other children. "How about shooting baskets in the gym?" X asked the girls. But all they did was make faces and giggle behind X's back.

"Boy, is *he* weird," whispered Jim to Joe.

"How about weaving some baskets in the arts and crafts room?" X asked the boys. But they all made faces and giggled behind X's back, too.

"Boy, is *she* weird," whispered Susie to Peggy.

That night, Ms. and Mr. Jones asked X how things had gone at school. X tried to smile, but there were two big tears in its eyes. "The lessons are okay," X began, "but..."

"But?" said Ms. Jones.

"The Other Children hate me," X whispered.

"Hate you?" said Mr. Jones.

X nodded, which made the two big tears roll down and splash on its overalls.

Once more, the Joneses reached for their *Instructional Manual.* Under "Other Children," it said:

"What did you Xpect? Other Children have to obey silly boy-girl rules, because their parents taught them to. Lucky X—you don't have rules at all! All you have to do is be yourself.

"P.S. We're not saying it'll be easy."

X liked being itself. But X cried a lot that night. So X's father held X tight and cried a little, too. X's mother cheered them up with an Xciting story about an enchanted prince called Sleeping Handsome, who woke up when Princess Charming kissed him.

The next morning, they all felt much better, and little X went back to school with a brave smile and a clean pair of red and white checked overalls.

There was a seven-letter-word spelling bee in class that day. And a seven-lap boys' relay race in the gym. And a seven-layer-cake baking contest in the girls' kitchen corner.

X won the spelling bee. X also won the relay race.

And X almost won the baking contest, Xcept it forgot to light the oven. (Remember, nobody's perfect.)

One of the Other Children noticed something else, too. He said: "X doesn't care about winning. X just thinks it's fun playing boys' stuff *and* girls' stuff."

"Come to think of it," said another one of the Other Children, "X is having twice as much fun as we are!"

After school that day, the girl who beat X in the baking contest gave X a big slice of her winning cake.

And the boy X beat in the relay race asked X to race him home.

From then on, some really funny things began to happen.

Susie, who sat next to X, refused to wear pink dresses to school any more. She wanted red and white checked overalls—just like X's.

Overalls, she told her parents, were better for climbing monkey bars.

Then Jim, the class football nut, started wheeling his little sister's doll carriage around the football field.

He'd put on his entire football uniform, except for the helmet.

Then he'd put the helmet *in* the carriage, lovingly tucked under an old set of shoulder pads.

Then he'd jog around the field, pushing the carriage and singing "Rock-abye Baby" to his helmet.

He said X did the same thing, so it must be okay. After all, X was now the team's star quarterback.

Susie's parents were horrified by her behavior, and Jim's parents were worried sick about his.

But the worst came when the twins, Joe and Peggy, decided to share everything with each other.

Peggy used Joe's hockey skates, and his microscope, and took half his newspaper route.

Joe used Peggy's needlepoint kit, and her cookbooks, and took two of her three baby-sitting jobs.

Peggy ran the lawn mower, and Joe ran the vacuum cleaner.

Their parents weren't one bit pleased with Peggy's science experiments, or with Joe's terrific needlepoint pillows.

They didn't care that Peggy mowed the lawn better, and that Joe vacuumed the carpet better.

In fact, they were furious. It's all that little X's fault, they agreed. X doesn't know what it is, or what it's supposed to be! So X wants to mix everybody *else* up too!

Peggy and Joe were forbidden to play with X any more. So was Susie, and then Jim, and then *all* the Other Children.

But it was too late: the Other Children stayed mixed-up and happy and free, and refused to go back to the way they'd been before X.

Finally, the parents held an emergency meeting to discuss "The X Problem."

They sent a report to the principal stating that X was a "bad influence," and demanding immediate action.

The Joneses, they said, should be *forced* to tell whether X was a boy or a girl. And X should be *forced* to behave like whichever it was.

If the Joneses refused to tell, the parents said, then X must take an Xamination. An Impartial Team of Xperts would Xtract the secret. Then X would start obeying all the old rules. Or else.

And if X turned out to be some kind of mixed-up misfit, then X must be Xpelled from school. Immediately! So that no little Xes would ever come to school again.

The principal was very upset. X, a bad influence? A mixed-up misfit? But X was an Xcellent student! X set a fine Xample! X was Xtraordinary!

X was president of the student council. X had won first prize in the art show, honorable mention in the science fair, and six events on field day, including the potato race.

Nevertheless, insisted the parents, X is a Problem Child. X is the Biggest Problem Child we have ever seen!

So the principal reluctantly notified X's parents and the Joneses reported this to the Project X scientists, who referred them to page 85769 of the *Instructional Manual.* "Sooner or later," it said, "X will have to be Xamined by an Impartial Team of Xperts.

"This may be the only way any of us will know for sure whether X is mixed-up—or everyone else is."

At Xactly 9 o'clock the next day, X reported to the school health office. The principal, along with a committee from the Parents' Association, X's teacher, X's classmates, and Ms. and Mr. Jones, waited in the hall outside.

Inside, the Xperts had set up their famous testing machine: the Super-psychiamedicosocioculturometer.

Nobody knew Xactly how the machine worked, but everybody knew that this examination would reveal Xactly what everyone wanted to know about X, but were afraid to ask.

It was terribly quiet in the hall. Almost spooky. They could hear very strange noises from the room.

There were buzzes.

And a beep or two.

And several bells.

An occasional light flashed under the door. Was it an X ray?

Through it all, you could hear the Xperts' voices, asking questions, and X's voice, answering answers.

I wouldn't like to be in X's overalls right now, the children thought.

At last, the door opened. Everyone crowded around to hear the results. X didn't look any different. In fact, X was smiling. But the Impartial Team of Xperts looked terrible. They looked as if they were crying!

"What happened?" everyone began shouting.

"*Sssh*," ssshed the principal. "The Xperts are trying to speak."

Wiping his eyes and clearing his throat, one Xpert began: "In our opinion," he whispered—you could tell he must be very upset—"in our opinion, young X here—"

"Yes? Yes?" shouted a parent.

"Young X," said the other Xpert, frowning, "is just about the *least* mixed-up child we've ever Xamined!" Xclaimed the two Xperts, together. Behind the closed door, the Superpsychiamedicosocioculturometer made a noise like a contented hum.

"Yay for X!" yelled one of the children. And then the others began yelling, too. Clapping and cheering and jumping up and down.

"*Sssh*!" ssshed the principal, but nobody did.

The Parents' Committee was angry and bewildered. How *could* X have passed the whole Xamination?

Didn't X have an *identity* problem? Wasn't X mixed up at *all*? Wasn't X *any* kind of a misfit?

How could it *not* be, when it didn't even *know* what it was?

"Don't you see!" asked the Xperts. "X isn't one bit mixed up! As for being a misfit—ridiculous! X knows perfectly well what it is. Don't you, X?" The Xperts winked. X winked back.

"But what *is* X?" shrieked Peggy and Joe's parents. "*We* still want to know what it is!"

"Ah, yes," said the Xperts, winking again. "Well, don't worry. You'll all know one of these days. And you won't need us to tell you."

"What? What do they mean?" Jim's parents grumbled suspiciously.

Susie and Peggy and Joe all answered at once. "They mean that by the time it matters which sex X is, it won't be a secret any more!"

With that, the Xperts reached out to hug Ms. and Mr. Jones. "If we ever have an X of our own," they whispered, "we sure hope you'll lend us your instructional manual."

Needless to say, the Joneses were very happy. The Project Baby X scientists were rather pleased, too. So were Susie, Jim, Peggy, Joe, and all the Other Children. Even the parents promised not to make any trouble.

Later that day, all X's friends put on their red and white checked overalls and went over to see X.

They found X in the backyard, playing with a very tiny baby that none of them had ever seen before.

The baby was wearing very tiny red and white checked overalls.

"How do you like our new baby?" X asked the Other Children proudly.

"It's got cute dimples," said Jim. "It's got husky biceps, too," said Susie.

"What kind of baby is it?" asked Joe and Peggy.

X frowned at them. "Can't you tell?" Then X broke into a big, mischievous grin. *"It's a Y!"*

8

Gender Schema Theory and Its Implications for Child Development: Raising Gender-Aschematic Children in a Gender-Schematic Society

Sandra Lipsitz Bem

As every parent, teacher, and development psychologist knows, male and female children become "masculine" and "feminine," respectively, at a very early age. By the time they are four or five, for example, girls and boys have typically come to prefer activities defined by the culture as appropriate for their sex and also to prefer same-sex peers. The acquisition of sex-appropriate preferences, skills, personality attributes, behaviors, and self-concepts is typically referred to within psychology as the process of sex typing.

The universality and importance of this process is reflected in the prominence it has received in psychological theories of development, which seek to elucidate how the developing child comes to match the template defined as sex appropriate by his or her culture. Three theories of sex typing have been especially influential: psychoanalytic theory, social learning theory, and cognitive-developmental theory. More recently, a fourth theory of sex typing has been introduced into the psychological literature—gender schema theory.

This article is designed to introduce gender schema theory to feminist scholars outside the discipline of psychology. In order to provide a background for the conceptual issues that have given rise to gender schema theory, I will begin with a discussion of the three theories of sex typing that have been dominant within psychology to date.

PSYCHOANALYTIC THEORY

The first psychologist to ask how male and female are transmuted into masculine and feminine was Freud. Accordingly, in the past virtually every major

From Sandra Lipsitz Bem, "Gender Schema Theory and Its Implications for Child Development: Raising Gender-Aschematic Children in a Gender-Schematic Society," *Signs: Journal of Women in Culture and Society*, vol. 8, no. 41 (1983): 598–616. Reprinted by permission of The University of Chicago Press.

source book in developmental psychology began its discussion of sex typing with a review of psychoanalytic theory.[1]

Psychoanalytic theory emphasizes the child's identification with the same-sex parent as the primary mechanism whereby children become sex typed, an identification that results from the child's discovery of genital sex differences, from the penis envy and castration anxiety that this discovery produces in females and males, respectively, and from the successful resolution of the Oedipus conflict.[2] Although a number of feminist scholars have found it fruitful in recent years to work within a psychoanalytic framework,[3] the theory's "anatomy is destiny" view has been associated historically with quite conservative conclusions regarding the inevitability of sex typing.

One of the three dominant theories of sex typing, psychoanalytic theory is almost certainly the best known outside the discipline of psychology, although it is no longer especially popular among research psychologists. In part, this is because the theory is difficult to test empirically. An even more important reason, however, is that the empirical evidence simply does not justify emphasizing either the child's discovery of genital sex differences in particular[4] or the child's identification with his or her same-sex parent[5] as a crucial determinant of sex typing.

SOCIAL LEARNING THEORY

In contrast to psychoanalytic theory, social learning theory emphasizes the rewards and punishments that children receive for sex-appropriate and sex-inappropriate behaviors, as well as the vicarious learning that observation and modelling can provide.[6] Social learning theory thus locates the source of sex typing in the sex-differentiated practices of the socializing community.

Perhaps the major virtue of social learning theory for psychologists is that it applies to the development of psychological femaleness and maleness the very same general principles of learning that are already known to account for the development of a multitude of other behaviors. Thus, as far as the formal theory is concerned, gender does not demand special consideration; that is, no special psychological mechanisms or processes must be postulated in order to explain how children become sex typed beyond those already used to explain how children learn other socialized behaviors.

Interestingly, the theory's generality also constitutes the basis of its appeal to feminist psychologists in particular. If there is nothing special about gender, then the phenomenon of sex typing itself is neither inevitable nor unmodifiable. Children become sex typed because sex happens to be the basis of differential socialization in their culture. In principle, however, any category could be made the basis for differential socialization.

Although social learning can account for the young child's acquiring a number of particular behaviors that are stereotyped by the culture as sex appropriate, it treats the child as the relatively passive recipient of environmental forces rather than as an active agent striving to organize and thereby to comprehend the social world. This view of the passive child is inconsistent with the common observation that children themselves frequently construct and enforce their own version of society's gender rules. It is also inconsistent with the fact that the flexibility with which children interpret society's gender rules varies predictably with age. In one study, for example, 73 percent of the four-year-olds and 80 percent of the nine-year-olds believed—quite flexibly—that there should be no sexual restrictions on one's choice of occupation. Between those ages, however, children held more rigid opinions, with the middle children being the least flexible of all. Thus, only 33 percent of the five-year-olds, 10 percent of the six-year-olds, 11 percent of the seven-year-olds, and 44 percent of the eight-year-olds believed there should be no sexual restrictions on one's choice of occupation.[7]

This particular development pattern is not unique to the child's interpretation of gender rules. Even in a domain as far removed from gender as syntax, children first learn certain correct grammatical forms through reinforcement and modelling. As they get a bit older, however, they begin to construct their own grammatical rules on the basis of what they hear spoken around them, and they are able only later to allow for exceptions to those rules. Thus, only the youngest and the oldest children say "ran"; children in between say "runned."[8] What all of this implies, of course, is that the child is passive in neither domain. Rather, she or he is actively constructing rules to organize—and thereby to comprehend—the vast array of information in his or her world.

COGNITIVE-DEVELOPMENTAL THEORY

Unlike social learning theory, cognitive-developmental theory focuses almost exclusively on the child as the primary agent of his or her own sex-role socialization, a focus reflecting the theory's basic assumption that sex typing follows naturally and inevitably from universal principles of cognitive development.... Cognitive-developmental theory postulates that, because of the child's need for cognitive consistency, self-categorization as female or male motivates her or him to value that which is seen as similar to the self in terms of gender. This gender-based value system, in turn, motivates the child to engage in gender-congruent activities, to strive for gender-congruent attributes, and to prefer gender-congruent peers. "Basic self-categorizations determine basic valuings. Once the boy has stably identified himself as male, he then values positively those objects and acts consistent with his gender identity."[9]

The cognitive-developmental account of sex typing has been so influential since its introduction into the literature in 1966 that many psychologists now seem to accept almost as a given that the young child will spontaneously develop both a gender-based self-concept and a gender-based value system even in the absence of external pressure to behave in a sex-stereotyped manner. Despite its popularity, however, the theory fails to explicate why sex will have primacy over other potential categories of the self such as race, religion, or even eye color. Interestingly, the formal theory itself does not dictate that any particular category should have such primacy. Moreover, most cognitive-developmental theorists do not explicitly ponder the "why sex" question nor do they even raise the possibility that other categories could fit the general theory just as well. To the extent that cognitive-developmental psychologists address this question at all, they seem to emphasize the perceptual salience to the child of the observable differences between the sexes, particularly biologically produced differences such as size and strength.[10]

The implicit assumption here that sex differences are naturally and inevitably more perceptually salient to children than other differences may not have cross-cultural validity. Although it may be true that our culture does not construct any distinctions between people that we perceive to be as compelling as sex, other cultures do construct such distinctions, for example, distinctions between those who are high caste and those who are low caste.... What appears to have happened is that the universality and inevitability that the theory claims for the child's cognitive processes have been implicitly and gratuitously transferred to one of the many substantive domains upon which those processes operate: the domain of gender.

This is not to say, of course, that cognitive-developmental theory is necessarily wrong in its implicit assumption that all children have a built-in readiness to organize their perceptions of the social world on the basis of sex. Perhaps evolution has given sex a biologically based priority over many other categories. The important point, however, is that the question of whether and why sex has cognitive primacy is not included within the bounds of cognitive-developmental theory. To understand why children become *sex* typed rather than, say, race or caste typed, we still need a theory that explicitly addresses the question of how and why children come to utilize sex in particular as a cognitive organizing principle.

GENDER SCHEMA THEORY

Gender schema theory[11] contains features of both the cognitive-developmental and the social learning accounts of sex typing. In particular, gender schema theory proposes that sex typing derives in large measure from gender-schematic processing, from a generalized readiness on the part of the child to encode and to organize information—including information about the self—according to the culture's definitions of maleness and femaleness. Like cognitive-developmental theory, then, gender schema theory proposes that sex typing is mediated by the child's own cognitive processing. However, gender schema theory further proposes that gender-schematic processing is itself derived from the sex-differentiated practices of the social community. Thus, like social learning theory, gender schema theory assumes that sex typing is a learned phenomenon and, hence, that it is neither inevitable nor unmodifiable....

Gender-Schematic Processing

Gender schema theory begins with the observation that the developing child invariably learns his or her society's cultural definitions of femaleness and maleness. In most societies, these definitions comprise a diverse and sprawling network of sex-linked associations encompassing not only those features directly related to female and male persons—such as anatomy, reproductive function, division of labor, and personality attributes—but also features more remotely or metaphorically related to sex, such as the angularity or roundedness of an abstract shape and the periodicity of the moon. Indeed, no other dichotomy in human experience appears to have as many entities linked to it as does the distinction between female and male.

But there is more. Gender schema theory proposes that, in addition to learning such content-specific information about gender, the child also learns to invoke this heterogeneous network of sex-related associations in order to evaluate and assimilate new information. The child, in short, learns to encode and to organize information in terms of an evolving gender schema.

A schema is a cognitive structure, a network of associations that organizes and guides an individual's perception. A schema functions as an anticipatory structure, a readiness to search for and to assimilate incoming information in schema-relevant terms. Schematic information processing is thus highly selective and enables the individual to impose structure and meaning onto a vast array of incoming stimuli. More specifically, schematic information processing entails a readiness to sort information into categories on the basis of some particular dimension, despite the existence of other dimensions that could serve equally well in this regard. Gender-schematic processing in particular thus involves spontaneously sorting attributes and behaviors into masculine and feminine categories or "equivalence classes," regardless of their differences on a variety of dimensions unrelated to gender, for example, spontaneously placing items like "tender" and "nightingale" into a feminine category and items like "assertive" and "eagle" into a masculine category. Like schema theories generally,[12] gender schema theory thus construes perception as a constructive process in which the interaction between incoming information and an individual's preexisting schema determines what is perceived.

What gender schema theory proposes, then, is that the phenomenon of sex typing derives, in part, from gender-schematic processing, from an individual's generalized readiness to process information on the basis of the sex-linked associations that constitute the gender schema. Specifically, the theory proposes that sex typing results, in part, from the assimilation of the self-concept itself to the gender schema. As children learn the contents of their society's gender schema, they learn which attributes are to be linked with their own sex and, hence, with themselves. This does not simply entail learning the defined relationship between each sex and each dimension or attribute—that boys are to be strong and girls weak, for example—but involves the deeper lesson that the dimensions themselves are differentially applicable to the two sexes. Thus the strong-weak dimension itself is absent from the schema to be applied to girls just as the dimension of nurturance is implicitly omitted from the schema to be applied to boys. Adults in the child's world rarely notice or remark upon how strong a little girl is becoming or how nurturant a little boy is becoming, despite their readiness to note precisely these attributes in the "appropriate" sex. The child learns to apply this same schematic selectivity to the self, to choose from among the many possible dimensions of human personality only that subset defined as applicable to his or her own sex and thereby eligible for organizing the diverse contents of the self-concept. Thus do children's self-concepts become sex typed, and thus do the two sexes become, in their own eyes, not only different in degree, but different in kind.

Simultaneously, the child also learns to evaluate his or her adequacy as a person according to the gender schema, to match his or her preferences, attitudes, behaviors, and personal attributes against the prototypes stored within it. The gender schema becomes a prescriptive standard or guide,[13] and self-esteem becomes its hostage. Here, then, enters an internalized motivational factor that prompts an individual to regulate his or her behavior so that it conforms to cultural definitions of femaleness and maleness. Thus do cultural myths become self-fulfilling prophecies, and thus, according to gender schema theory, do we arrive at the phenomenon known as sex typing.

It is important to note that gender schema theory is a theory of process, not content. Because sex-typed individuals are seen as processing information and regulating their behavior according to whatever definitions of femininity and masculinity their culture happens to provide, the process of dividing the world into feminine and masculine categories—and not the contents of categories—is central to the theory. Accordingly, sex-typed individuals are seen to differ from other individuals not primarily in the degree of femininity or masculinity they possess, but in the extent to which their self-concepts and behaviors are organized on the basis of gender rather than on the basis of some other dimension. Many non-sex-typed individuals may describe themselves as, say, nurturant or dominant without implicating the concepts of femininity or masculinity. When sex-typed individuals so describe themselves, however, it is precisely the gender connotations of the attributes or behaviors that are presumed to be salient for them.

Empirical Research on Gender-Schematic Processing

Recent empirical research supports gender schema theory's basic contention that sex typing is derived from gender-schematic processing. In a variety of studies using different subject populations and different paradigms, female and male sex-typed individuals have been found to be significantly more likely than non-sex-typed individuals to process information—including information about the self—in terms of gender.[14]

One study, for example, used a memory task to determine whether gender connotations are, in fact, more "cognitively available" to sex-typed individuals than to non-sex-typed individuals, as gender schema theory claims.[15] The subjects in this study were forty-eight male and forty-eight female undergraduates who had described themselves as either sex typed or non-sex typed on the Bem Sex Role Inventory (BSRI).[16]

During the experimental session, subjects were presented with a randomly ordered sequence of sixty-one words that included proper names, animal names, verbs, and articles of clothing. Half of the proper names were female, half were male; one-third of the items within each of the other semantic categories had been consistently rated by undergraduate judges as feminine (e.g., butterfly, blushing, bikini), one-third as masculine (e.g., gorilla, hurling, trousers), and one-third as neutral (e.g., ant, stepping, sweater). The words were presented on slides at three-second intervals, and subjects were told that their recall would be tested. Three seconds after the presentation of the last word, they were given a period of eight minutes to write down as many words as they could, in whatever order they happened to come to mind.

As expected, the results indicated that although sex-typed and non-sex-typed individuals recalled equal numbers of items overall, the order in which they recalled the items was different. Once having recalled a feminine item, sex-typed individuals were more likely than non-sex-typed individuals to recall another feminine item next rather than a masculine or a neutral item. The same was true for masculine items. In other words, the sequence of recall for sex-typed individuals revealed significantly more runs or clusters of feminine items and of masculine items than the sequence of recall for non-sex-typed individuals. Thinking of one feminine (or masculine) item could enhance the probability of thinking of another feminine (or masculine) item in this way only if the individual spontaneously encodes both items as feminine (or masculine), and the gender schema thereby links the two items in memory. These results thus confirm gender schema theory's claim that sex-typed individuals have a greater readiness than do non-sex-typed individuals to encode information in terms of the sex-linked associations that constitute the gender schema.

A second study tested the hypothesis that sex-typed individuals have a readiness to decide on the basis of gender which personal attributes are to be associated with their self-concepts and which are to be dissociated from their self-concepts.[17] The subjects in this second study were another set of forty-eight male and forty-eight female undergraduates who had also described themselves as sex typed or non-sex typed on the Bem Sex Role Inventory. During each of the individual experimental sessions, the sixty attributes from the BSRI were projected on a screen one at a time, and the subject was requested to push one of two buttons, "Me" or "Not Me," to indicate whether the attribute was or was not self-descriptive. Of interest in this study was the subject's response latency, that is, how long it took the subject to make a decision about each attribute.

Gender schema theory predicts and the results of this study confirm that sex-typed subjects are significantly faster than non-sex-typed subjects when endorsing sex-appropriate attributes and when rejecting sex-inappropriate attributes. These results suggest that when deciding whether a particular attribute is or is not self-descriptive, sex-typed individuals do not bother to go through a time-consuming process of recruiting behavioral evidence from memory and judging whether the evidence warrants an affirmative answer—which is presumably what non-sex-typed individuals do. Rather, sex-typed individuals "look up" the attribute in the gender schema. If the attribute is sex appropriate, they quickly say yes; if the attribute is sex inappropriate, they quickly say no. Occasionally, of course, even sex-typed individuals must admit to possessing an attribute that is sex inappropriate or to lacking an attribute that is sex appropriate. On these occasions, they are significantly slower than non-sex-typed individuals. This pattern of rapid delivery of gender-consistent self-descriptions and slow delivery of gender-inconsistent self-descriptions confirms gender schema theory's contention that sex-typed individuals spontaneously sort information into categories on the basis of gender, despite the existence of other dimensions that could serve equally well as a basis for categorization.

Antecedents of Gender-Schematic Processing

But how and why do sex-typed individuals develop a readiness to organize information in general, and their self-concepts in particular, in terms of gender? Because gender-schematic processing is considered a special case of schematic processing, this specific question is superseded by the more general question of how and why individuals come to organize information in terms of any social category, that is, how and why a social category becomes transformed into a cognitive schema.

Gender schema theory proposes that the transformation of a given social category into the nucleus of a highly available cognitive schema depends on the nature of the social context within which the category is embedded, not on the intrinsic nature of the category itself. Given the proper social context, then, even a category like eye color could become a cognitive schema. More specifically, gender schema theory proposes that a category will become a schema if: (a) the social context makes it the nucleus of a large associative network, that is, if the ideology and/or the practices of the culture construct an association between that category and a wide range of other attributes, behaviors, concepts, and categories; and (b) the social context assigns the category broad functional significance, that is, if a broad array of social institutions, norms, and taboos distinguishes between persons, behaviors, and attributes on the basis of this category.

This latter condition is most critical, for gender schema theory presumes that the culture's insistence on the functional importance of the social category is what transforms a passive network of associations into an active and readily available schema for interpreting reality....

From the perspective of gender schema theory, then, gender has come to have cognitive primacy over many other social categories because the culture has made it so. Nearly all societies teach the developing child two crucial things about gender: first, as noted earlier, they teach the substantive network of sex-related associations that can come to serve as a cognitive schema; second, they teach that the dichotomy between male and female has intensive and extensive relevance to virtually every domain of human experience. The typical American child cannot help observing, for example, that what parents, teachers, and peers consider to be appropriate behavior varies as a function of sex; that toys, clothing, occupations, hobbies, the domestic division of labor—even pronouns—all vary as a function of sex.

Gender schema theory thus implies that children would be far less likely to become gender schematic and hence sex typed if the society were to limit functional importance of the gender dichotomy. Ironically, even though our society has become sensitive to negative sex stereotypes and has begun to expunge them from the media and from children's literature, it remains blind to its gratuitous emphasis on the gender dichotomy itself. In elementary schools, for example, boys and girls line up separately or alternately; they learn songs in which the fingers are "ladies" and the thumbs are "men.".....

Because of the role that sex plays in reproduction, perhaps no society could ever be as indifferent to sex in its cultural arrangements as it could be to, say, eye color, thereby giving the gender schema a sociologically based priority over many other categories. For the same reason, it may even be, as noted earlier, that sex has evolved to be a basis category of perception for our species, thereby giving the gender schema a biologically based priority as well. Be that as it may, however, gender schema theory claims that society's ubiquitous insistence on the functional importance of the gender dichotomy must necessarily render it even more cognitively available—and available in more remotely relevant contexts—than it would be otherwise.

It should be noted that gender schema theory's claims about the antecedents of gender-schematic processing have not yet been tested empirically. Hence it is not possible at this point to state whether individual differences in gender-schematic processing do, in fact, derive from differences in the emphasis placed on gender dichotomy in individuals' socialization histories, or to describe concretely the particular kinds of socialization histories that enhance or diminish gender-schematic processing. Nevertheless, I should like to set forth a number of plausible strategies that are consistent with gender schema theory for raising a gender-aschematic child in the midst of a gender-schematic society.

This discussion will, by necessity, be highly speculative. Even so, it will serve to clarify gender schema theory's view of exactly how gender-schematic processing is learned and how something else might be learned in its place....

RAISING GENDER-ASCHEMATIC CHILDREN

Feminist parents who wish to raise gender-aschematic children in a gender-schematic world are like any parents who wish to inculcate their children with beliefs and values that deviate from those of the dominant culture. Their major option is to try to undermine the dominant ideology before it can undermine theirs. Feminist parents are thus in a difficult situation. They cannot simply ignore gender in their child rearing as they might prefer to do, because the society will then have free rein to teach their children the lessons about gender that it teaches all other children. Rather, they must manage somehow to inoculate their children against gender-schematic processing.

Two strategies are suggested here. First, parents can enable their children to learn about sex differences initially without their also learning the culture's sex-linked associative network by simultaneously retarding their children's knowledge of sex's cultural correlates and advancing their children's knowledge of sex's biological correlates. Second, parents can provide alternative or "subversive" schemata that their children can use to interpret the culture's sex-linked associative network when they do learn it. This step is essential if children are not simply to learn gender-schematic processing somewhat later than their counterparts from more traditional homes. Whether one is a child or an adult, such alternative schemata "build up one's resistance" to the lessons of the dominant culture and thereby enable one to remain gender-aschematic even while living in a gender-schematic society.

Teaching Children about Sex Differences
Cultural Correlates of Sex

Children typically learn that gender is a sprawling associative network with ubiquitous functional importance through their observation of the many cultural correlates of sex existing in their society. Accordingly, the first step parents can take to retard the development of gender-schematic processing is to retard the child's knowledge of these cultural messages about gender. Less crudely put, parents can attempt to attenuate sex-linked correlations within the child's social environment, thereby altering the basic data upon which the child will construct his or her own concepts of maleness and femaleness.

In part, parents can do this by eliminating sex stereotyping from their own behaviour and from the alternatives that they provide for their children....

When children are quite young, parents can further inhibit cultural messages about gender by actually censoring books and television programs whose explicit or implicit message is that the sexes differ on non-biological dimensions. At present, this tactic will eliminate many children's books and most television programming....

To compensate for this censorship, parents will need to seek out—and to create—materials that do not teach sex stereotypes. With our own children, my husband and I got into the habit of doctoring books whenever possible so as to remove all sex-linked correlations. We did this, among other ways, by changing the sex of the main character; by drawing longer hair and the outline of breasts onto illustrations of previously male truck drivers, physicians, pilots, and the like; and by deleting or altering sections of the text that described females or males in a sex-stereotyped manner. When reading children's picture books aloud, we also chose pronouns that avoided the ubiquitous implication that all characters without dresses or pink bows must necessarily be male: "And what is this little piggy doing? Why, he or she seems to be building a bridge."

All of these practices are designed to permit very young children to dwell temporarily in a social environment where, if the parents are lucky, the cultural correlations with sex will be attenuated from, say, .96 to .43. According to gender schema theory, this attenuation should retard the formation of the sex-linked associative network that will itself form the basis of the gender schema. By themselves, however, these practices teach children only what sex is not. But children must also be taught what sex is.

Biological Correlates of Sex

What remains when all of the cultural correlates of sex are attenuated or eliminated, of course, are two of the undisputed biological correlates of sex: anatomy and reproduction. Accordingly, parents can make these the definitional attributes of femaleness and maleness.... By teaching their children that whether one is female or male makes a difference only in the context of reproduction, parents limit sex's functional significance and thereby retard gender-schematic processing.... To the extent that young children tend to interpret rules and categories rigidly rather than flexibly, this tendency will serve to enhance their belief that sex is to be narrowly defined in terms of anatomy and reproduction rather than to enhance a traditional belief that every arbitrary gender rule must be strictly obeyed and enforced....

In the American context, children do not typically learn to define sex in terms of anatomy and reproduction until quite late, and, as a result, they... mistakenly treat many of the cultural correlates of sex as definitional. This confusion is facilitated, of course, by the fact that the genitalia themselves are not usually visible and hence cannot be relied on as a way of identifying someone's sex....

We found Stephanie Waxman's picture book *What Is a Girl? What Is a Boy?* to be a superb teaching aid in this context.[18] Each page displays a vivid and attractive photograph of a boy or a girl engaged in some behavior stereotyped as more typical of or more appropriate for the other sex. The accompanying text says such things as, "Some people say a girl is someone with jewelry, but Barry is wearing a necklace and he's a boy." The book ends with nude photographs of both children and adults, and it explicitly defines sex in terms of anatomy.

...Eventually, of course,...[gender-aschematic children] too will begin to learn the culture's sprawling network of sex-linked associations. At that point, parents must take steps to prevent that associative network from itself becoming a cognitive schema.

Providing Alternative Schemata

...How is...a child to understand the many sex-linked correlations that will inevitably begin to intrude upon his or her awareness? What alternative schemata can substitute for the gender schema in helping the child to organize and to assimilate gender-related information?

Individual Differences Schema

The first alternative schema is simply a child's version of the time-honored liberal truism used to counter stereotypic thinking in general, namely, that there is remarkable variability of individuals within groups as compared with the small mean differences between groups. To the child who says that girls do not like to play baseball, the feminist parent can thus point out that although it is true that some girls do not like to play baseball, it is also true that some girls do (e.g., your Aunt Beverly and Alissa who lives across the street) and that some boys do not (e.g., your dad and Alissa's brother Jimmy). It is, of course, useful for parents to supply themselves with a long list of counterexamples well in advance of such occasions.

This individual differences schema is designed to prevent children from interpreting individual differences as sex differences, from assimilating perceived differences among people to a gender schema. Simultaneously, it should also encourage children to treat as a given that the sexes are basically similar to one another and, hence, to view all glib assertions about sex differences as inherently suspect. And it is with this skepticism that feminist consciousness begins.

Cultural Relativism Schema

As the child's knowledge and awareness grow, he or she will gradually begin to realize that his or her family's beliefs and attitudes about gender are at variance with those of the dominant culture. Accordingly, the child needs some rationale for not simply accepting the majority view as the more valid. One possible rationale is cultural relativism, the notion that "different people believe different things" and that the coexistence of even contradictory beliefs is the rule in society rather than the exception.

Children can (and should) be introduced to the schema of cultural relativism long before it is pertinent to the domain of gender. For example, our children needed the rationale that "different people believe different things" in order to understand why they, but not the children next door, had to wear seat belts; why our family, but not the family next door, was casual about nudity in the home. The general principle that contradictory beliefs frequently coexist seems now to have become a readily available schema for our children, a schema that permits them to accept with relative equanimity that they have different beliefs from many of their peers with respect to gender.

Finally, the cultural relativism schema can solve one of the primary dilemmas of the liberal feminist parent: how to give one's children access to the riches of classical literature—as well as to the lesser riches of the mass media—without abandoning them to the forces that promote gender-schematic processing. Happily, the censorship of sex-stereotyped materials that is necessary to retard the initial growth of the sex-linked associative network when children are young can end once children have learned the critical lesson that cultural messages reflect the beliefs and attitudes of the person or persons who created those messages....

Sexism Schema

Cultural relativism is fine in its place, but feminist parents will not and should not be satisfied to pretend that they think all ideas—particularly those about gender—are equally valid. At some point, they will feel compelled to declare that the view of women and men conveyed by fairy tales, by the mass media—and by the next-door neighbors—is not only different, but wrong. It is time to teach one's children about sexism.

Moreover, it is only by giving children a sexism schema, a coherent and organized understanding of the historical roots and the contemporaneous consequences of sex discrimination, that they will truly be able to comprehend why the sexes appear to be so different in our society.... The child who has developed a readiness to encode and to organize information in terms of an evolving sexism schema is a child who is prepared to oppose actively the gender-related constraints that those with a gender schema will inevitably seek to impose....

As feminist parents, we wish it could have been possible to raise our children with neither a gender schema nor a sexism schema. At this historical moment, however, that is not an option. Rather we must choose either to have our children become gender schematic and hence sex typed, or to have our children become sexism schematic and hence feminists. We have chosen the latter.

A COMMENT ON PSYCHOLOGICAL ANDROGYNY

The central figure in gender schema theory is the sex-typed individual, a shift in focus from my earlier work in which the non-sex-typed individual— the androgynous individual in particular—commanded center stage.[19] In the early 1970s, androgyny seemed to me and to many others a liberated and more humane alternative to the traditional, sex-biased standards of mental health. And it is true that this concept can be applied equally to both women and men, and that it encourages individuals to embrace both the feminine and the masculine within themselves. But advocating the concept of androgyny can also be seen as replacing a prescription to be masculine or feminine with the doubly incarcerating prescription to be masculine and feminine. The individual now has not one but two potential sources of inadequacy with which to contend. Even more important, however, the concept of androgyny is problematic from the perspective of gender schema theory because it is based on the presupposition that there is a feminine and a masculine within us all, that is, that "femininity" and "masculinity" have an independent and palpable reality and are not cognitive constructs derived from gender-schematic processing. Focusing on androgyny thus fails to prompt serious examination of the extent to which gender organizes both our perceptions and our social world.

In contrast, the concept of gender-schematic processing directs our attention to the promiscuous availability of the gender schema in contexts where other schemata ought to have priority. Thus, if gender schema theory has a political message, it is not that the individual should be androgynous. Rather, it is that the network of associations constituting the gender schema ought to become more limited in scope and that society ought to temper its insistence on the ubiquitous functional importance of the gender dichotomy. In short, human behaviors and personality attributes should no longer be linked with gender, and society should stop projecting gender into situations irrelevant to genitalia.

NOTES

1   See, e.g., Paul H. Mussen, "Early Sex-Role Development," in *Handbook of Socialization Theory and Research,* ed. David A. Goslin (Chicago: Rand McNally, 1969), 707–31. For a more recent review that does not even mention psychoanalytic the-

ory, see Aletha C. Huston, "Sex-Typing," to appear in *Carmichael's Manual of Child Psychology*, ed. Paul H. Mussen, 4th ed. (New York: John Wiley & Sons, in press).

2   Urie Bronfenbrenner, "Freudian Theories of Identification with Their Derivatives," *Child Development* 31, no. 1 (March 1960): 15–40; Sigmund Freud, "Some Psychological Consequences of the Anatomical Distinction between the Sexes (1925)," in *Collected Papers of Sigmund Freud*, ed. Ernest Jones, 5 vols. (New York: Basic Books, 1959), 5: 186–97; Sigmund Freud, "The Passing of the Oedipus Complex (1924)," ibid., 2: 269–76.

3   E.g., Nancy Chodorow, *The Reproduction of Mothering: Psychoanalysis and the Sociology of Gender* (Berkeley: University of California Press, 1978); Gayle Rubin, "The Traffic in Women: Notes on the 'Political Economy' of Sex," in *Toward an Anthropology of Women*, ed. Rayna Reiter (New York: Monthly Review Press, 1975), 157–210.

4   Lawrence Kohlberg, "A Cognitive-Developmental Analysis of Children's Sex-Role Concepts and Attitudes," in *The Development of Sex Differences*, ed. Eleanor E. Maccoby (Stanford, Calif.: Stanford University Press, 1966), 82–173.; Maureen J. McConaghy, "Gender Permanence and the Genital Basis of Gender: Stages in the Development of Constancy of Gender Identity," *Child Development* 50 (4): 1223–26.

5   Eleanor E. Maccoby and Carol N. Jacklin, *The Psychology of Sex Differences* (Stanford, Calif.: Stanford University Press, 1974).

6   Walter Mischel, "Sex-Typing and Socialization," in *Carmichael's Manual of Child Psychology*, ed. Paul H. Mussen, 2 vols. (New York: John Wiley & Sons, 1970), 2:3–72.

7   William Damon, *The Social World of the Child* (San Francisco: Jossey-Bass, 1977).

8   Courtney B. Cazden, "The Acquisition of Noun and Verb Inflections," *Child Development* 39, no. 2 (June 1968): 433–48; Herbert H. Clark and Eve V. Clark, *Psychology and Language: An Introduction to Psycholinguistics* (New York: Harcourt Brace Jovanovich, 1977).

9   Kohlberg, "A Cognitive-Developmental Analysis," 89.

10 Kohlberg, "A Cognitive-Developmental Analysis," 89; Michael Lewis and Jeanne Brooks-Gunn, *Social Cognition and the Acquisition of Self* (New York: Plenum Publishing Corp., 1979), 270; Dorothy Z. Ullian, "The Child's Construction of Gender: Anatomy as Destiny," in *Cognitive and Affective Growth: Developmental Interaction*, ed. Edna K. Shapiro and Evelyn Weber (Hillsdale, N.J.: Lawrence Erlbaum Associates, 1981), 171–85.

11 Sandra L. Bem, "Gender Schema Theory: A Cognitive Account of Sex Typing," *Psychological Review* 88, no. 4 (July 1981): 354–64; and "Gender Schema Theory and Self-Schema Theory Compared: A Comment on Markus, Crane, Bernstein, and Siladi's 'Self-Schemas and Gender'," *Journal of Personality and Social Psychology* 43, no. 6 (December 1982): 1192–94.

12 Ulric Neisser, *Cognition and Reality* (San Francisco: W. H. Freeman & Co., 1976); Shelley E. Taylor and Jennifer Crocker, "Schematic Bases of Social Information Processing," in *Social Cognition, the Ontario Symposium*, ed. E. Tory Higgins, C. Peter Herman, and Mark P. Zanna (Hillsdale, N.J.: Lawrence Erlbaum Associates, 1981), 1: 89–135.

13   Jerome Kagan, "Acquisition and Significance of Sex Typing and Sex Role Identity," in *Review of Child Development Research,* ed. Martin L. Hoffman and Lois W. Hoffman (New York: Russell Sage Foundation, 1965), 1: 137–67.

14   Susan M. Anderson and Sandra L. Bem, "Sex Typing and Androgyny in Dyadic Interaction: Individual Differences in Responsiveness to Physical Attractiveness," *Journal of Personality and Social Psychology* 41, no. 1 (July 1981): 74–86; Bem, "Gender Schema Theory"; Kay Deaux and Brenda Major, "Sex-Related Patterns in the Unit of Perception," *Personality and Social Psychology Bulletin* 3, no. 2 (Spring 1977): 297–300; Brenda Girvin, "The Nature of Being Schematic: Sex-Role Self-Schemas and Differential Processing of Masculine and Feminine Information" (Ph.D. diss., Stanford University, 1978); Robert V. Kail and Laura E. Levine, "Encoding Processes and Sex-Role Preferences," *Journal of Experimental Child Psychology* 21, no. 2 (April 1976): 256–63; Lynn S. Liben and Margaret L. Signorella, "Gender-Related Schemata and Constructive Memory in Children," *Child Development* 51, no. 1 (March 1980): 11–18; Richard Lippa, "Androgyny, Sex Typing, and the Perception of Masculinity-Femininity in Handwriting," *Journal of Research in Personality* 11, no. 1 (March 1977): 21–37; Hazel Markus et al., "Self-Schemas and Gender," *Journal of Personality and Social Psychology* 42, no. 1 (January 1982): 38–50; Shelley E. Taylor and Hsiao-Ti Falcone, "Cognitive Bases of Stereotyping: The Relationship between Categorization and Prejudice," *Personality and Social Psychology Bulletin* 8, no. 3 (September 1982): 426–32.

15   Bem, "Gender Schema Theory," 356–58.

16   The Bem Sex Role Inventory, or BSRI, is an instrument that identifies sex-typed individuals on the basis of their self-concepts or self-ratings of their personal attributes. The BSRI asks the respondent to indicate on a seven-point scale how well each of sixty attributes describes himself or herself. Although it is not apparent to the respondent, twenty of the attributes reflect the culture's definition of masculinity (e.g. assertive), and twenty reflect its definition of femininity (e.g., tender) with the remaining attributes serving as filler. Each respondent receives both a masculinity and a femininity score, and those who score above the median on the sex-congruent scale and below the median on the sex-incongruent scale are defined as sex typed. That is, men who score high in masculinity and low in femininity are defined as sex typed, as are women who score high in femininity and low in masculinity. The BSRI is described in detail in the following articles: Sandra L. Bem, "The Measurement of Psychological Androgyny," *Journal of Consulting and Clinical Psychology* 42, no. 2 (April 1974): 155–62; "On the Utility of Alternative Procedures for Assessing Psychological Androgyny," *Journal of Clinical and Consulting Psychology* 45, no. 2 (April 1977): 196–205; "The Theory and Measurement of Androgyny: A Reply to the Pedhazur-Tetenbaum and Locksley-Colten Critiques," *Journal of Personality and Social Psychology* 37, no. 6 (June 1979): 1047–54; and *A Manual for the Bem Sex Role Inventory* (Palo Alto, Calif.: Consulting Psychologists Press, 1981).

17   Bem, "Gender Schema Theory," 358–61.

18   Stephanie Waxman, *What is a Girl? What Is a Boy?* (Culver City, Calif.: Peace Press, 1976).

19   Sandra L. Bem, "Sex-Role Adaptability: One Consequence of Psychological Androgyny," *Journal of Personality and Social Psychology* 31, no. 4 (April 1975): 634–

43; Sandra L. Bem, Wendy Martyna, and Carol Watson, "Sex-Typing and Androgyny: Further Explorations of the Expressive Domain," *Journal of Personality and Social Psychology* 34, no. 5 (November 1976): 1016–23; Sandra L. Bem, "Beyond Androgyny: Some Presumptuous Prescriptions for a Liberated Sexual Identity," in *The Future of Women: Issues in Psychology,* ed. Julia Sherman and Florence Denmark (New York: Psychological Dimensions, Inc., 1978), 1–23; Sandra L. Bem and Ellen Lenney, "Sex-Typing and the Avoidance of Cross-Sex Behavior," *Journal of Personality and Social Psychology* 33, no. 1 (January 1976): 48–54.

9

What Is Worth Knowing?
Defining the Feminist Curriculum

Jane Gaskell, Arlene McLaren, and Myra Novogrodsky

... Whe hat kind of education is of most worth, what kind of education is of little worth, and what kind of education is positively destructive? What should the curriculum look like? Who should define it? Who needs what kind of knowledge and why? Feminists have had much to say in answer to these questions, and they are questions which are central to any theory and politics of education.

From an historical perspective, we see that the feminist critique and the feminist vision of the curriculum changed in response to changing social contexts. Already at the turn of the century, the Canadian women's movement was arguing for the inclusion of subjects of particular concern to women in the school curriculum. The Women's Christian Temperance Union argued for including temperance, the Imperial Order of the Daughters of the Empire argued for including citizenship, and the Women's Institutes argued for including all of the above, as well as home economics, or as it was then labelled, "domestic science".[1]

The case of domestic science is interesting, as it highlights some thorny issues that persist today in debates about women's knowledge and the curriculum. In the United States in 1842, Catherine Beecher published *A Treatise on Domestic Economy*, a text which applied moral philosophy, psychology physiology, hygiene, botany, physics, chemistry and architecture to the problems of managing a home and raising children. Her goal was to have women's domestic work raised in status and value by recognizing the complexity of its tasks and the scientific base that should inform them. The importance of this knowledge would be established by its presence in the school curriculum. But the existence of gender differences was not challenged. Women's sphere was domestic, and women were the nurturers, the preservers of family harmony and social welfare. The question of equality was tackled by giving equal importance to the knowledge necessary for these complex tasks.

From Jane Gaskell, Arelene McLaren, and Myra Novogrodsky, "What Is Worth Knowing? Defining the Feminist Curriculum," *Claiming An Education: Feminism and Canadian Schools.* Toronto: Our Schools/Our Selves Education Foundation, 1989. Reprinted by permission.

Adelaide Hoodless was the best known Canadian proponent of domestic science in the schools. She believed that women belonged in the domestic sphere, and that the domestic sphere should have equal status with the public one. Women's work was separate from, but equal to, men's. The school curriculum should reflect both the equality and the separateness.

But when domestic science was widely introduced into the schools, the change was seen only partly as a victory for women. It was also quickly seen to provide a "ghetto" for women, a low status alternative to the academic mainstream, a way to keep women separate and unequal.

The feminist argument later moved to favour an integrated curriculum, where girls and boys learned the same things, thereby bringing an end to the segregation of industrial education (male) and home economics (female). It was convincingly argued that the entrenchment of "women's knowledge" in the curriculum reproduced traditional gender divisions.

Today, the question of women's knowledge and women's ways of knowing are back again on the agenda. Again feminists are arguing that the gendered division of labour has meant that women have distinctive knowledge and tasks, and that these have not been represented adequately in the curriculum. Again women are asking whether sex and gender differences make a substantial difference in the ways women learn, and whether these differences have been respected in the organization of the school.

The issues that arise historically in home economics are issues that need to be addressed systematically for the entire curriculum. How can we combine the rejection of traditional stereotypes, with a positive acknowledgement of the experiences of women? How can we both recognize the importance of gender in the production and incorporation of knowledge, and transcend the way gender has organized our lives and knowledge in a patriarchal society? The feminist critique has no single voice. By exploring some of the debates we can clarify what it means to argue for a curriculum that is equitable for both girls and boys, men and women.

STEREOTYPING IN THE CURRICULUM

In 1970 the Royal Commission on the Status of Women concluded, after examining textbooks used to teach reading, social studies, mathematics and guidance courses, that the problem with the school curriculum was that "a woman's creative and intellectual potential is either underplayed or ignored in the education of children from their earliest years. The sex roles described in these textbooks provide few challenging models for young girls, and they fail to create a sense of community between men and women as fellow human beings."[2]

Numerous studies in the 1970's further documented the findings of the Royal Commission and criticized the omission of women from curricular materials. Studies done by teacher's federations, community groups and academics emphasized the destructive impact of sex stereotyping in the curriculum.[3] These studies revealed that women and girls were underrepresented in school books, and that when they were represented, they were stereotyped. Boys were also stereotyped, but in more powerful and active roles. Little girls in elementary texts played with dolls while their brothers played baseball; mothers wore aprons and baked cookies, while fathers drove off to work; adult women were princesses and witches, while men were doctors and farmers.

The research, in combination with political lobbying, had an effect on the schools. Under pressure from women's groups, publishers and ministries of education across the country appointed advisory groups to screen educational texts and media, issued non-sexist guidelines and developed and published alternative materials. What we see being used in the classrooms has become more diverse and less stereotyped.

This is not to suggest that the problem has disappeared. The old books continue to be used in schools because of the costs of replacing materials. The implementation of non-sexist guidelines is more difficult than their promulgation.[4] In 1988, the Federation of Women Teachers of Ontario published *The More Things Change...the More They Stay the Same*, a study of elementary readers in use in Ontario. They showed that the stereotyping that had been documented 20 years ago was still prevalent in Ontario texts.[5]

The methodology and the assumptions underlying this study reveal the authors' implicit politics of the curriculum. The authors use worksheets to record the numbers of male and female, adult and child characters, and the type of stories involved (fiction, non-fiction, myths/legends). They then indicate the number of pages given to each character, and rate each character on themes like self actualization, moral development, occupation, activities and emotions or descriptive words.

The conclusions support the title—little has changed since 1970. Occupations in these texts continue to reflect a sex-segregated labour market—women are witches and men are truck drivers; women more often care for others while men are less emotional; the man "plays golf" while the woman "is a true and loyal friend"; the man is "charged and sentenced for robbery"; while the woman "joins husband flying to Montreal"; and so on. The authors argue that this is a problem. Stereotyping continues even after two decades of an active women's movement.

We agree there should have been more change, but the lack of change is not evident just in texts: it is in the organization of Canadian society. Labour market statistics tell us that occupations continue to be stereotyped, and studies of the division of labour in the home tell us that women do more nurturing. These texts continue to reflect a fundamental reality—the sexual division of labour. The question is what relationship texts and the school curriculum should have to the world outside the schools. Should texts portray a world that is better than the real world?

The authors of the FWTAO study suggests they should. They argue that texts should portray an ideal and non-sexist world so that youngsters learn what is possible for them, and for the world at large. "Children must meet females and males in equal numbers who are intelligent, independent and competent"; males "should be shown receiving help, friendship and advice from females and as often as females receive these from males", "human failures should be portrayed as learning or growth experiences and not as events which stigmatize individuals for life" and so on.

One problem with these recommendations is that any portrayal of a traditional woman, or of a woman participating in traditional activities becomes a stereotype, and therefore is problematic. Secondly, the notion that all experiences are "positive growth experiences" would make it difficult to discuss the holocaust or slavery or racism. The world in children's books would be a good world. But it would not help children recognize and learn to deal with their own experiences.

We want children to see their experience reflected in their texts, not to create a new world of androgynous superpeople, and not to exclude material that shows women in traditional roles. Women do bake cookies and care for others. These activities must not be identified exclusively with women, of course, but the fact remains that women do them more often than men. A non-sexist curriculum should show mothers as secretaries as well as carpenters and girls playing with dolls as well as playing baseball.

Moreover, the world can be a nasty and unsafe place, with war and pain and racism and suffering. Materials showing racism in that connection are not out of place. We believe that children should be helped to see the world as it is, while being encouraged to develop a critical consciousness, a sense of active and cooperative participation that equips them to engage in the struggle for social change.

What is important is the ideology that underlies the images and the facts that are brought together in the curriculum. The underlying assumptions and story lines in the curriculum—what is being said about those images and characters—these should be the object of our critique. The number of male and female characters, the number of male and female doctors, the number of men and women baking cookies, can tell us something important. But only in context, only in light of the narrative, and its underlying message. The number of positive and negative evaluations of characters that are male and female can also be important, but how they are being judged, by whom and for what purposes, is the important question.

The fundamental issue is our conception of a non-sexist (or gender equitable, or feminist) curriculum and its relationship to a democratic and socialist curriculum. It involves more than avoiding stereotypes. It means incorporating knowledge that reflects the diverse experiences of women into what is deemed to be important school-based knowledge. It involves working from the experience of all children to introduce them to the varieties of experience that are possible, and how that variety can be understood. It involves changing our conceptions of many traditional disciplines and subject areas to make room for this knowledge. It means providing "really important knowledge" for women as well as for men, and it means bringing up gender issues in the classroom, for discussion and examination.

REFORMULATING THE PROBLEM: GIVING A VOICE TO WOMEN

Feminism has meant trying to give a voice to women, and allowing women to examine their own experiences, instead of always examining men's experiences. It has meant an effort to see the world from "the standpoint of women", in Dorothy Smith's phrase, and to make that part of the public discourse. While doing this we must keep in mind the diversity of women's experiences, and not allow white middle-class women's experience to stand for the experience of all women. There is no one place where women stand, and feminism means understanding the ways women have been silenced and women's experience has been misrepresented to themselves and to others....

Feminists must then ask what kind of curriculum can be important and relevant for women; what kind of a curriculum can integrate theory with the practices of women's lives, allowing students to assess critically the grounds of their exploitation and to work for change.

These concerns are not limited to women, of course. At a recent discussion of First Nations education, when students were complaining about the content of courses they were taking at the University of British Columbia, they used similar words, and focussed on the ways in which curriculum did not reflect or illuminate their experience as native people. "The concepts have been developed from the Western world....we need to start by describing our world....we haven't had a chance to reflect on our own experience and develop it...others are talking a different language", and so on. The problems, and the language used to express them, were uncannily similar to the arguments women have been making about the difficulty of using theories and language based in male experience, and the necessity of rethinking everything in order to accommodate their concerns.

And the argument has been made many times in relation to social class. [A]s Ken Osborne [has pointed out,] "There can be no doubt that existing curricula are biased, both in what they include and in what they omit; nor that for many working-class students they have little interest or appeal...It is clear also that schools have been intended to serve as instruments of the dominant ideology, playing their part in reproducing the social order and maintaining cultural hegemony."[6]

The implications of these arguments are that the experiences of women (and of First Nations people, working-class people, visible minorities and other disadvantaged groups) must be incorporated into the curriculum.

Children from all these groups must come to feel that the schools are for and about them, not just for and about privileged white males. The purpose of schooling must be to "empower" (to use an overworked word these days), them, to give them the ability to participate fully in struggles, large and small, to gain respect, dignity and power.

Making the curriculum more "girl-friendly" is one way of thinking about incorporating women's experiences into the school. This is articulated most often in connection with non-traditional courses, and it involves changes in curriculum content as well as in pedagogy. Science classrooms where teachers intervene to ensure equal participation, and where women scientists are discussed, make girls feel that science is for them. Science classes where the social issues associated with scientific discoveries are discussed are more popular with girls, who like to see the social significance and meaning of what they learn.[7] Girl-friendly schooling can also mean adding special classes in mathematics and science to give girls the extra experience with tools and mathematical problems which they need, and may allay their "math anxiety".

Adding women's experience to the curriculum can be done in a wide variety of ways across curriculum areas. In history texts incorporating women means adding discussions of women's suffrage, women's participation in the fur trade, and the changing organization of family life, as well as discussing why women were traditionally excluded from positions of power. In English classes it means examining novels and poems written by women, and seeking to understand why nineteenth century women writers used male names. In art classes it means rediscovering the work of women artists and asking why males produced "art" while women produced "crafts". In short, it means adding the study of women's experience to what has been a curriculum based on male experience. And it means understanding ways in which gender has shaped every discipline by excluding women's experience from that which schools have traditionally deemed worthy of study and analysis.

We must also bear in mind the diversity of the female experience, and not fall into the trap of reifying "the" female experience, which will turn out to be the experience of more privileged women. Curriculum change must involve a dynamic process which enables women to speak from all the places they occupy in the world.

To include women's experience means diversifying the curriculum so that native women, children from single parent homes, businesswomen and Chinese-Canadian women see what they are taught as having some relevance for their lives, so that the enormous variety of women's experience in Canada is represented in instructional settings.[8] It means adding the study of Audre Lorde's poems to the curriculum, alongside Virginia Woolf's novels. It means adding the study of women's work in First Nations families in Labrador as well as adding the study of pioneer women in Nova Scotia.

The so-called "integration" debate around women's studies raises the the question of whether adding women's concerns and women's experiences to the curriculum is a process of addition or a process of transformation.[9] Those who want to keep women's studies as a separate course, department or field argue that cooperative, contextual and interdisciplinary feminist scholarship can only arise and be carried forward among a group of similarly committed educators and students. They argue that the development of women's scholarship depends on a like-minded community of women who are not preoccupied with fighting against male structures. They argue that knowledge is of most value to women, and that women are the ones who must struggle for change, since they are the ones who are the most open to exploring its meaning.

The advocates of integration, on the other hand, argue that feminist scholarship must develop alongside, be incorporated into and ultimately transform the mainstream disciplines, and the curriculum which all students learn. They argue that women's studies becomes a ghetto that allows most students to continue in "men's studies".

We are clearly on the side of those who argue that the ultimate goal is not to continue with two versions of knowledge, the male version and the female version, but to develop a new synthesis that is richer for paying attention to both male and female perspectives. Transforming the entire curriculum, and the entire body of what we count as knowledge must be our ultimate objective. Women's studies programmes are essential in this struggle, but they are not all that is needed.

To add women's experience to the curriculum means fundamental change. It means re-examining the rules that are used for inclusion in the first place and changing the way the entire subject is conceptualized. If the people mentioned in history texts are those who have played an important role in governing the country, clearly women cannot be equally represented. The process of adding women involves changing ideas about what students should learn in history classes and why they should study history in the first place. It means learning about the ways ordinary people lived their lives so children can understand the history of people like themselves. It means including more social history, more studies of how families were organized and work was distributed in other historical periods. It means understanding the ways sex and gender have shaped the organization of Canadian society.

The omission of women is not just a question of oversight. Our very conception of education, of what is worth knowing, and of the disciplines which are studied is challenged by the process of including women. Adding the experiences of women means a reworking of knowledge from its very roots. "Malestream" thought, as Mary O'Brien has dubbed traditional scholarship,[10] is revealed as partial, based in male experience, and therefore inadequate. Seemingly objective and value-free inquiry is revealed to be based on male assumptions.

One of the most influential Canadian documents to address the way feminism must transform all knowledge was published in 1985 by the Social Sciences and Humanities Research Council. Margrit Eichler and Jeanne

Lapointe point out that scholarship that does not take adequate account of women is simply bad scholarship.

As long as women were de facto excluded from intellectual work and higher education, sex-related bias in research was not widely recognized as a problem for the social sciences and humanities. Culture and our way of thinking were shaped by a male perspective which applied even when the life, identity and thought of women were considered. There was little or no awareness that such an androcentric perspective generates serious intellectual problems. Central concepts were seldom examined with respect to their applicability to both sexes, and sexist language was usually uncritically accepted, in spite of its inexactness.[11]

The pamphlet goes on to give specific examples of how male bias operates and what can be done about it. Eichler and Lapointe discuss how research has mistakenly transformed statistical differences into innate differences (as in psychological scales of masculinity and femininity), overgeneralized concepts that apply to males ("universal" suffrage was granted before women got the vote) and failed to consider the way assumptions about sex and gender affect data gathering ("Do you think women doctors are as good as men doctors?" does not allow the response that women are better doctors).

Awareness of these biases in traditional scholarship has informed the development of a feminist scholarship that has been having an impact on academic work in every discipline and field of study. Although the progress remains slow and far from even, the incorporation of this work into the school curriculum will transform it into a non-sexist body of knowledge.

This wide-ranging critique makes the process of putting women back into the curriculum a difficult, indeed revolutionary task. It is relatively straightforward (though we would not want to underplay the difficulty of some of these struggles) to put the suffragists and the First Nations women who organized the fur trade back into the history books, to add a few novels written by women into the literature curriculum, and to add some women artists to the arts syllabus. It is quite another thing to change the way we approach historical, literary and artistic study, and the criteria we use to assess its significance and value. It is nothing less than this that a socialist feminist politics demands.

THE EDUCATED PERSON

The values and politics inherent in any curriculum permeate the organization of classrooms and schools and the interactions between students and teachers, as well as the content of texts. Questions of curriculum content and pedagogy cannot be neatly separated. The question of how well the existing curriculum serves women includes questions about what is taught and how it is taught.

Adrienne Rich states the concerns and issues of the feminist classroom in her essay, *Taking Women Students Seriously*. She says,

> *Listen to the voices of the women and voices of the men; observe the space men allow themselves, physically and verbally, the male assumption that people will listen, even when the majority of the group is female. Look at the faces of the silent and of those who speak. Listen to a woman groping for language in which to express what is on her mind, sensing that the terms of academic discourse are not her language, trying to cut down her thought to the dimensions of a discourse not intended for her...*"[12]

Social science has approached the problems with less nuance, but with some clear findings. There were some early and striking studies on classroom interaction that showed teachers paying much more attention to boys in class, and being quite unaware of this fact. Boys tended to be evaluated by teachers as more intelligent and inquiring, but less well-behaved. Girls were evaluated as more docile, more hardworking, more likely to get the right answer, but less intelligent. Girls were being penalized for doing what the teacher asked, both by getting less attention, and by being thought of as less capable in the long run.

Studies also documented a wide variety of ways in which girls and boys were treated, and how they acted, in clearly stereotyped ways in the classroom. Boys fetched the projectors, and girls cleaned the brushes. Girls did projects on seeds, and boys did projects on electric motors. Girls played in the doll corner while boys played in the big block corner. In science classes, boys "hogged" the equipment, while girls hung back, feeling incompetent. In computer classes, boys excluded girls from the informal groups which gathered around the terminals. Clearly issues of sex equity needed to be attacked in classroom behavior, not just in texts.

Much of this analysis tended to blame the teacher for the problem. Teachers held traditional stereotypes. Teachers needed workshops on gender equity in the classroom. And many teachers did need to re-examine their position on sex and gender issues, in their own lives as well as in relation to their students. But teachers were only part of the problem. Teachers respond to the already gendered behaviors of their students, and teachers work in schools which in a variety of ways are imbued with sexist assumptions.

The question of institutional, "systemic" sexism must be tackled by teachers and parents collectively. In focussing on the teacher, it is important not to forget the context in which s/he works. Policies calling for gender-inclusive language in school communication, affirmative action guidelines for hiring and promotion, commitment to school-based day care and respect for the work of mothering all express the school's interest in gender equity in ways that go beyond an individual teacher's action.

The interactions between student and teacher raise critical questions in relation to the teacher's responsibility in social matters. Some would argue that in democratic classrooms, teachers must respect the values of their students and the surrounding community, even if these values include restrictions on women. This is not a position we find politically responsible. Educators must value the development and growth of all students equally.

But the question of how to intervene effectively to open up possibilities to female students who want, for example, to continue to play only in the doll corner, or who do not want to speak up in class and argue with the boys, can be more complicated. And the question of how to end intimidation by the boys, how to get them to see sexual harassment for the problem it is, and how to encourage them to express their nurturant and expressive selves, can be even more difficult. A skilled teacher must work with patience, empathy and a firm commitment to equity, to create a classroom that works for both boys and girls.

A feminist approach to pedagogy is as complex as a feminist approach to content. We have argued that ridding the schools of stereotyping is a partial approach, based in liberal assumptions, not questioning adequately the organization of schooling. In thinking about feminist pedagogy, we need to examine the underlying assumptions about education and its purposes, to see how these have been based in male experience, and to reframe them in ways that take the experiences of women seriously.

Jane Roland Martin has argued that both the content and the structure of schooling have been designed to prepare young people for a male world. The school has been justified as preparation for the public, productive sphere, for work and for citizenship. In the public sphere, men have played dominant roles, and women have been excluded, by custom, tradition, or law. "The idea of the humanities was tied to civic life and leadership in the public arena...The humanities have been tied to an ideal of human commonality, a unity based on the ideal of the cultivated, educated gentleman."[13]

Schooling has ignored the private sphere. Learning for family life, for the reproductive process of the society have been relegated to the family. As a result, Martin argues, the ideal of the educated person has been based in the male stereotype—objective, analytic, rational, interested in ideas and things, but not nurturing, empathic, intuitive or supportive. Education has emphasized the development and application of reason and objective judgment; it has separated the mind from the body, thought from action and reason from emotion....[14]

[A] burgeoning feminist literature is now exploring the fact that sex and gender do make a difference in the ways we learn and reason. This is not primarily because of biological differences, although there are some provocative arguments about the effect of conceiving and giving birth, and about the effects of hormones and reproductive cycles. It is rather because gender makes a difference to how people live, what toys they play with as children, who their friends are, how much power they are able to exercise in the world, and how others talk to them. It is then not surprising that researchers are able to document differences between men and women in the ways they learn best. And the question of which ways are best, and which ones should be rewarded and taught in schools must be openly examined and explored.

What is good for males is not necessarily good for females in schooling. If female students are learning in institutions which are based on male models of development, which value male skills and ways of reasoning, and which pay more attention to male learning, they are not getting an equal education.

Notions of good moral behaviour are central to any school organization.... Women have been described as holding more often to an ethic of care, basing morality in a sense of connectedness and responsibility, rather than in a version of universal rules and individual rights. Most schools are organized around an ethic of rights, rather than an ethic of caring. An ethics of rights emphasizes individual autonomy, but as Gilligan says, "it may appear frightening to women in its potential justification of indifference and unconcern. At the same time...from a male perspective, a morality of responsibility appears inconclusive and diffuse given its insistent contextual relativism."[15]

A recent book, *Women's Ways of Knowing,*[16] explores differences between the ways men and women learn to understand their relationship to knowledge. The authors argue that women come to understand knowledge as constructed, not given, as connected to, not separated from experience. The authors call for "connected teaching", arguing that women are more likely to learn in ways that explore and relate their experience to the curriculum. They call for problem posing, instead of lecturing, for the teacher as "midwife", instead of imparter of knowledge, for a "yoghurt" class, which provides a culture for growth, as opposed to a "movie" class, where the students are spectators.....

It is radical to insist that schooling recognize the importance of nurturing as well as independence, community as well as individualism, caring as well as responsibility. While it may be possible to formulate plans to stop discrimination against female students and encourage interaction between teachers and female students, it is much more difficult to incorporate a feminist pedagogy that challenges bureaucracy, hierarchy and competition in educational institutions, and a curriculum that joins emotion to reason, and personal experience to knowledge.

These calls for a pedagogical shift have a long and distinguished history. Educators from John Dewey to Paolo Friere to Sylvia Ashton-Warner have argued for a similar shift, and called for an education that will work from the experience of all learners to a pedagogy that is more effective and a society that is more democratic. The feminist critique, in raising questions about who schooling should be for, and how to change it, shares and adds to a long democratic and socialist tradition of educators calling for change.

THE POSSIBILITIES OF CHANGE

Studies of the problems of education frequently make the problems so clear and so overwhelming that they leave little room for hope. A more complete political analysis does not end in despair: it inspires work for change, provides some general vision of alternatives, and leaves people with the energy and enthusiasm to try to bring about changes in their own way.

The feminist movement has brought about change in education, and these changes are ones we should celebrate as well as learn from. In this section we will report some of the changes that have taken place in the Toronto Board of Education. Toronto is not representative of Canadian school districts by any means. It has had a staff person specifically responsible for Women's Studies since 1975. Only seven Boards of Education in Ontario and a few in other Canadian jurisdictions have created similar staff positions. The changes that have taken place in Toronto are changes worth reflecting upon and learning from.

An informal group of Toronto teachers met in 1988 to assess the effects of women's studies and affirmative action efforts in their schools. Members of the group were unanimous in their belief that sex role stereotyping had diminished, that consciousness about the role and contributions of women had been raised, and that numerous sexist practices had been substantially dismantled. Elementary school teachers reported that girls' lines and boys' lines were a thing of the past, that the classroom housekeeping area was now sex-integrated, that *The Paper Bag Princess* has become a modern classic, and that while school libraries had not ditched most sexist children's books, at least they had added numerous titles which portrayed girls and women in a positive light.

Although men still outnumber women in positions of responsibility in elementary as well as secondary schools, the Toronto Board of Education has incorporated affirmative action goals and timetables into its employment policies for teachers to increase the number of women in areas in which they were under-represented. Females in positions of responsibility are clearly more visible and more numerous in this jurisdiction. Few, if any, students now go through public school without seeing and being influenced by women administrators.

As computers are introduced across the curriculum they are accompanied by computer equity guidelines with strategies for encouraging all students to use computers and with specific suggestions for teachers to discourage male dominance around the new technology. Similarly, male dominance in the area of athletics has been recognized and a recent report on equal opportunity in school athletics attempts to move toward equality in what has traditionally been a most unequal arena. What are some of the other areas of change?

Language

Language reflects consciousness. Language describes the way in which we see the world. The conscious use of non-sexist language in both speech and print describes the world in gender-inclusive terms and helps to build a less sexist future.

Heated discussions about changing sexist language habits have raged in many staff rooms. Gradually the shrill voices of opponents to the use of non-sexist language as well as the lethargy of those for whom changing language appeared too large an ordeal, are being challenged by those who see language as an issue of power and who see inclusive language as a positive step toward equity. Many boards, including the Toronto Board of Education, have drafted and are implementing inclusive language policies.

School Action Plans

Reducing sexism in institutions as large and varied as school systems is a formidable task. The Toronto Board of Education requires each elementary and secondary school to appoint a women's studies representative (in large schools this may be a committee) whose task is to design, implement and evaluate a single manageable goal to reduce sexism in each school year. The plan must be discussed and approved by staff members and sometimes includes student and parent voices. A coordinator of women's studies helps schools consider appropriate goals, offers information on ideas which have proven successful in other jurisdictions, and provides some funding to implement plans.

The process of having each school reconsider its women's studies goal(s) on an annual basis gives the message that sexism is deep-rooted and will not be eliminated overnight. At the same time it allows schools to see that their work on the issue can make a difference. At the Toronto gathering in 1988, teachers whose schools had designed and implemented plans for ten years unanimously indicated that they felt their school plans had helped raise consciousness and reverse overt sexist practices. These teachers are now prepared to work on identifying and dealing with covert sexist practices and habits.

When each school is allowed to identify its own goal(s) rather than having to respond to centrally-dictated, system-wide priorities, the uniqueness of each school community is recognized and local initiatives can be developed. In 1988, one school took advantage of the Olympics and focussed its plan on equal opportunity in sports. Students researched and produced a school-wide visual display on women's contributions and achievements in sports through the 20th century. The same school is also in the process of analyzing budgets for athletic programs and making recommendations to assure that funding of men's and women's physical and health education programmes is equalized.

Another school identified math anxiety among girls as its key area of concern. The school implemented a family math programme in which English and non-English speaking parents spent five evenings in the school library playing math-based games and doing activities with their children. More games were distributed to parents for the summer so that male and female children would continue to experience parental involvement in mathematics-based activities.

A third school decided its key goal was to encourage girls in the sciences. This school organized a school-based Mini-Science Fair and all staff encouraged female students to participate in preparing projects for the fair.

A fourth school designed a 3-week block in which the role and contribution of women in every discipline was emphasized. The art course studied women's contribution to ceramics and sculpture. The science programme focused on ecology and emphasized women's contribution to the environmental protection movement. English students read women authors and history students looked at the role of women in the anti-apartheid struggle in South Africa. The block ended with a full-day school celebration of "Women in Action" which featured participatory discussions, a panel discussion on Prostitution and Sex Trade Workers, and entertainment.

While school-based plans do allow each school to consider its own needs, some larger jurisdictions are simultaneously designing system-wide projects which are not financially feasible for a single school.

A popular initiative has been launched in Toronto and other Ontario boards of education with the *Expanding Your Horizons* conferences for young women students. The goal of these conferences is to encourage young women to consider mathematics, science and computer education for their future career choices. With hands-on activities and female role models who use those disciplines in their work, these special days encourage young women to pause and explore options beyond stereotyped career choices for women and to consider the kind of preparation students will need to enter these fields. Borrowing a model developed in California, boards of education have run these special days for students from Grades 7–12/13. The Toronto Board of Education has also designed a workshop for parents which not only gives parents information about math/science education and their daughters' career choices, but also allows parents to come to terms with their own anxieties and uncertainties about the world of work awaiting their daughters.

Another system-wide initiative which can be adopted by single schools involves the *Job Site Visits* project sponsored by the Toronto Board of Education. In this programme teachers and students visit work sites in which career people (usually women) are working in mathematics or science-related careers. Rather than have the community visit the school (as in *Expanding Your Horizons*) in *Job Sites* the school visits the community and students get to see various work processes first hand, and to meet positive female role models in non-traditional career settings.

Learning Materials

The Toronto Board of Education now screens every curriculum document for sexist (as well as racist and class-biased) language and images. An Advisory Council on Bias in the Curriculum which includes teachers, principals, vice-principals, as well as parent representatives from ethnic liaison groups, performs an important monitoring function. Many suggestions from this committee have been incorporated in completed documents. At the recommendation of the committee, all curriculum writers will soon be given in-service training on race, sex and class bias before writing projects begin.

The Ontario Ministry of Education has developed criteria for defining bias in curriculum; all documents submitted for inclusion on Circular 14, an annual publication of approved texts for use in Ontario schools, are now sent to outside evaluators who specifically analyze texts for sex role stereotyping as well as ethnocultural and racial bias. In 1984, 29 of 179 submissions for inclusion on the list were rejected because of perceived bias and/or stereotyping.

Because of budget constraints, the shelf life of many text books is 15 to 20 years. Even some of the new materials are disappointing in their portrayal of women. Nevertheless, conscious and energetic educators have much better materials to use than were available in 1970. The Toronto Board of Education has opened a Women's and Labour Studies Resource Room which includes thousands of books, vertical files, photographs, audiotapes, posters, slides and other learning materials for teacher and student use. While Canadian materials are not as abundant as American sources (the U.S. based National Women's History Project publishes a 36-page catalogue of outstanding classroom materials), the long drought of materials portraying women's experience in all facets of life is mercifully coming to an end.

In the meantime, it is the responsibility of boards of education to train teachers to deal critically with stereotyped materials. One lesson plan designed by the California-based National Women's History Project and adapted from Stereotypes, Distortions and Omissions in U.S. Texts by the Council on Interracial Books for Children, could be used by Canadian teachers. The activity involves identifying sexist, racist, or class-biased passages from their own textbooks. Based on traditional material and their own research, students are asked to rewrite these offensive and distorted passages.

What About the Boys?

Education programmes are being developed to increase awareness of a broad range of work options based on skill and interest rather than on stereotyped notions of what is appropriate for each sex. While many of these programmes place their emphasis on getting girls and young women to consider non-traditional occupations, few are directed to young men who need encouragement to explore the possibility of entering arts-based careers or nurturing occupations. While the economic motivation for women to move into non-traditional careers far exceeds the personal reasons for males to consider what have been "female careers", our eventual goal must be to eliminate gender as a factor in all people's career selection.

A unique programme run in the Toronto area is *Boys for Babies*. This brief hands-on course is designed for pre-adolescent males (grades 5–6), and attempts to break down male stereotypes about sex-appropriate behaviour and activities. Boys are withdrawn from their regular school programme and are given an opportunity to care for, learn about, and bond with infants who are brought in from the community. At the beginning most boys express the stereotyped belief that infant care is "women's work". Over the course of a month, however, the boys begin to change their own notions about whether care-giving should be restricted to one sex. In this environment the nurturing, caring, and sensitive behaviour of the boys is encouraged. At the end of four two-hour sessions most young men have had a positive experience and have reflected on the ways in which care-giving can be satisfying and positive.

In a draft manual entitled *Snakes and Snails*, the Toronto Board of Education suggests dozens of activities for students in grades 4–8 which focus on male sex role stereotyping. The Introduction of *Snakes and Snails* makes the point that "young boys need permission and encouragement to learn about nurturing. Girls also need to see models of male nurturers." The manual includes interviews with males doing non-traditional work, suggests community service experiences that will give students practice in being care-givers, and includes improvisations, tableaux, and role plays which encourage discussion about male and female sex role stereotyping. Practical work in classrooms with *Snakes and Snails* not only encourages males to consider non-traditional work and to redefine maleness, but also encourages boys to accept a broader range of options for their female peers. This is important because research has shown that male peer expectations are an important influence on girls' academic course choices and career selections.

Gender Communications

Researchers Myra and David Sadker have found that in the United States, "Male students receive more attention from teachers and are given more time to talk in the classroom."[17] Male students are generally involved in more interactions than female students. The Sadkers found that males receive more positive comments, more criticism, and more remediation.

Males tend to clog the air waves. A Toronto teacher, disturbed by the domination of male students in his secondary school classroom, asked students to use a stop watch to measure how much males and females were speaking in the class. Students themselves were shocked by the results. Males were speaking 75–80% of the time.

Most educators are generally unaware of gender communication bias. They believe that they treat males and females equally but are unaware of gender difference in the way they question male and female students, in the waiting time allowed for male or female students to answer questions, in the patterns of interruption, and in the kind of feedback given to male or female students. According to the Sadkers, brief but focussed training is effective in changing teacher behaviour.

Representing the Diversity of Women's Experiences

In our efforts to create more choices for women, we must not invalidate women who make traditional choices. In preparing a curriculum guide for Grade 4 students in Toronto called *Working in the City: Kids Talk to Workers About What They Do,* educators debated whether to include a portrayal of women whose work was secretarial along with a portrayal of a female electrician. Some educators argued that children see enough women in traditional roles in real life and that progressive curriculum should only portray women in non-stereotyped roles. Others argued that in our frenzy to create new images we must not invalidate the role and contribution of those who have done, now do, and will in the future do traditional female work. We must not insult these women, and we should not be in the business of judging which occupational categories are "superior" for our daughters and female students. In the end, both portrayals were included in the text.

Empowering Young Women

Mary Kay Thompson Tetreault has stated "There is little in the schools which educates female students to think about their rights and responsibilities in shaping their own lives."[18] She implores teachers "to help girls of various classes and races think about their futures."

A systematic effort is needed to develop curriculum that includes necessary information about the work force, the changing family, the legal system, services available in the community, and ways to make responsible changes in one's personal life and in the work place. Schools can also help empower female students through cooperative learning in classrooms, and through full participation in student government, in school athletics, in science fairs and in cultural events. Schools can recognize, acknowledge and use the cooperative, nurturing and organizational skills young women bring to schools, and they can teach young women leadership skills such as how to chair meetings and how to facilitate discussions. In Toronto, the *Expanding Your Horizons* Conference uses trained female senior high school students to facilitate discussions among grade 7 and 8 students.

Toronto has also run a special conference called *Life After High School* to give graduating students information about women's issues they are likely to encounter at home, in the work place and in the community.

Staffing and Funding

The creation of equal opportunity for female students in schools has a price tag. More and better materials have to be developed and purchased; staff training and retaining are necessary; research needs to be done on girl-friendly curricula; positive workshop models must be developed for parents and teachers so that both school and home can give students a consistent message about the goal of equality for women in society; leadership pro-grammes for female students and staff as well as curriculum that supports nurturing behaviour in males and male acceptance of a wide range of oppor-tunities for girls need to be developed, tested and implemented.

Even "progressive" boards of education hire only one person in a large school system to create women's studies programmes and affirmative action programmes; they allocate a pitiful budget, and consider the job done. Yet even inexpensive and simple things can make a big difference in the life of an individual learner....

When Alice Baumgartner and colleagues at the Institute for Equality of Education and the University of Colorado surveyed 2000 children asking the question: "If you woke up tomorrow and discovered that you were a (boy/girl) how would your life be different?" she found that male and female students were almost unanimous in feeling that boys are better off than girls.[19] If schools are successful in reducing the level of sexism, and if Alice Baum-gartner's research were repeated in the year 2000, perhaps we will find different results. In the next millennium we can strive for a population of females who do not feel that they will lose opportunities because of their sex and a population of males who will have learned to appreciate and acknowl-edge the contribution of females.

Addressing the content of the curriculum—what we teach our children about the world in which they live—is central to the agenda of feminism. We must ensure that what is taught and learned in schools does not degrade women, does not misrepresent our experience, or interpret it through the categories of malestream scholarship.

We must keep in mind that the demand is a radical one that involves restructuring our conceptions of worthwhile knowledge for all students.

FOOTNOTES

1   N. Sheehan, "National Issues and Curricula Issues: Women and Educational Reform: 1900–1930" in Gaskell and McLaren, *Women and Education: A Canadian Perspective*. Calgary: Detselig, 1987.

2   Royal Commission on the Status of Women, Ottawa, 1970.

3   S. Pyke, "Children's Literature: Conceptions of Sex Roles" in E. Zureik and R. Pike, (eds.) *Socialization and Values in Canadian Society.* Toronto: McClelland and Stewart, 1975; J. Gaskell, "Stereotyping and Discrimination in the Curriculum"

in J. D. Wilson and H. Stevenson, *Precepts, Policy and Process: Perspectives on Contemporary Education.* Calgary: Detselig, 1977; L. Fisher and J. A. Cheyne, "Sex Roles: Biological and Cultural Interactions as Found in Social Science Research and Ontario Educational Media," Toronto: Ontario Ministry of Education, 1977; Batcher et al., "And Then There Were None..." A Report commissioned by the Status of Women Committee, Federation of Women Teachers of Ontario, Toronto, 1975; "Women in Teaching Text Book Study," British Columbia Teachers Federation, Vancouver, 1975; C. Pascoe, *Sex Stereotyping Study,* Halifax: mimeo, 1975; L. Cullin, *A Study into Sex Stereotyping in Alberta Elementary Textbooks.* Edmonton: mimeo 1972.

4   P. Galloway, *What's Wrong With High School English? It's Sexist...unCanadian...outdated.* Toronto: OISE Press, 1980. National Film Board, Report of the National Film Board/Education Forum on Women's Studies in Secondary School. Ottawa, 1986.

5   FWTAO. "The More Things Change...The More they Stay the Same." Toronto: 1988.

6   Ken Osborne, *Educating Citizens: A Democratic Socialist Agenda for Canadian Education.* Toronto: Our Schools/Our Selves, 1988.

7   "See Who Turns the Wheel," J. Whyte, *Girls into Science and Technology,* London: Routledge and Kegan Paul, 1986; and B. Collis, "Adolescent Females and Computers: Real and Perceived Barriers" in Gaskell and McLaren, *Women and Education.*

8   See, for example, *All in a Day's Work,* and *ESL Kit on the Value of Housework* by the Committee to Advance the Status of Housework, Toronto, 1981; *A Shared Experience: Bridging Cultures: Resources for Cross-cultural Training,* Cross Cultural Learning Centre, London, Ontario, 1983; Barb Thomas, *Multiculturalism at Work: A Guide to Organized Change,* Toronto, YWCA, 1987.

9   V. Strong-Boag, "Mapping Women's Studies in Canada: Some Signposts." *Journal of Educational Thought* 17:2, pp. 94–111, 1983; M. Boxer, "For and About Women: The Theory and Practice of Women's Studies in the United States" in N. Keohan (ed.) *Feminist Theory: A Critique of Ideology,* Chicago: University of Chicago Press, 1982.

10   M. O'Brien, *The Politics of Reproduction.* London: Routledge and Kegan Paul, 1981.

11   M. Eichler and J. Lapointe, *On the Treatment of the Sexes in Research,* Ottawa: Social Sciences and Humanities Research Council, 1985, p. 5.

12   Adrienne Rich, "Taking Women Seriously" in *On Lies Secrets and Silence,* New York: Norton 1979, pp. 237–246.

13   J. R. Martin, "The Ideal of the Educated Person in Philosophy of Education 1981," Daniel R. DENicola (ed.). Illinois: Philosophy of Education Society, 1982.

14   J. R. Martin, *Reclaiming a Conversation: The Ideal of the Educated Woman.* New Haven: Yale University Press, 1985, pp. 197–98.

15   C. Gilligan, *In a Different Voice.* Cambridge: Harvard University Press.

16   M. Belenky et al., *Women's Way of Knowing.* New York: Basic Books, 1986.

17   Myra Sadker and David Sadker, "Sexism in the Classroom: From Grade School to Graduate School." *Phil Delta Kappa,* March 1986.

18   Mary Kay Thompson Tetreault, "It's So Opinioney," *Journal of Education.* Vol. 168, no. 2, 1986.

19   Carol Tauris and Alice Baumgartner, *How Would Your Life Be Different.*

10

Socialization to Gender Roles: Popularity among Elementary School Boys and Girls

Patricia A. Adler, Steven J. Kless, and Peter Adler

Considerable effort has been invested in the past two decades toward understanding the nature of gender differences in society. Critical to this effort is knowledge about where gender differences begin, where they are particularly supported, and how they become entrenched.

Elementary schools are powerful sites for the construction of culturally patterned gender relations. In what has been called the "second curriculum" (Best 1983) or the "unofficial school" (Kessler et al. 1985), children create their own norms, values, and styles within the school setting that constitute their peer culture, what Glassner (1976) called "kid society." It is within this peer culture that they do their "identity work" (Wexler 1988), learning and evaluating roles and values for their future adult behavior, of which their "gender regimes" (Kessler et al. 1985) are an important component.

Children's peer cultures may be further stratified by gender, with boys and girls producing differential "symbolic identity systems" (Wexler 1988). Segregated sexual cultures have been observed as early as preschool (Berentzen 1984; Gunnarsson 1978), as boys and girls separate and begin to evolve their own interests and activities. By elementary school, boys' and girls' distinct and autonomous peer cultures are clearly established (Best 1983; Lever 1976, 1978; Thorne and Luria 1986; Whiting and Edwards 1973), although in situations and patterns of social organization, boys and girls cross gender lines to interact in both organized and casual manners (Goodwin 1990; Thorne 1986). These peer cultures contribute significantly to the creation of gender differences because they constitute enclaves in which boys and girls can escape the well-intentioned efforts of their schools and parents to shape or individualize them, freeing them to cleave instead to their own normative molds.

Studies of preadolescent and adolescent gendered peer cultures have examined the influence of several factors on the social construction of gender roles. For example, in analyzing the differences between boys' and girls' play, Lever (1976, 1978) and Best (1983) noted that boys' games were highly

From Patricia Adler, Steven J. Kless, and Peter Adler, "Socialization to Gender Roles: Popularity among Elementary School Boys and Girls," *Sociology of Education*, vol. 65 (July 1992): 169–187. Reprinted by permission.

complex, competitive, rule infused, large in size, and goal directed, whereas girls played in small, intimate groups; engaged in similar, independent activities; and focused on enjoying themselves more than on winning. Borman and Frankel (1984) argued that boys' play more closely approximates the structure, dynamics, and complexity inherent in the managerial world of work and thus prepares boys for success in this organizational realm.

Eder and Hallinan (1978) compared the structure of boys' and girls' friendship patterns and found that girls have more exclusive and dyadic relationships than do boys, which leads to their greater social skills, emotional intimacy, and ease of self-disclosure. Boys' and girls' extracurricular involvements also differ (Eder 1985; Eder and Parker 1987), with boys' activities (e.g., sports) emphasizing such masculine values as achievement, toughness, endurance, competitiveness, and aggression and girls' activities (e.g., cheerleading) fostering emotional management, glamour, and a concern with appearance. Studies of differences in cross-gender orientations (Eisenhart and Holland 1983; Goodwin 1980a, 1980b; Thorne 1986) have shown that girls become interested in bridging the separate gender worlds earlier than do boys for both platonic and romantic relationships, but that their attention is perceived by boys as sexually infused and, hence, threatening. Finally, studies of conversational patterns and rules (Gilligan 1982; Maltz and Borker 1983) have suggested that girls speak "in a different voice" from boys—one that emphasizes equality and solidarity while avoiding disagreement and contains "supportive" forms of collaboration that diminish girls' power relative to boys.

Yet these studies have not examined one of the most important dimensions of elementary school children's lives: the role of popularity in gender socialization. Boys and girls arrange themselves into cliques and into strata within cliques according to their perceptions of each other as relatively popular or unpopular. The determinants of popularity vary greatly between boys and girls, with gender-appropriate models relevant to each. Embedded within these idealized models of masculinity and femininity are the gender images that children actively synthesize from the larger culture and apply to themselves and to each other. As they learn and direct themselves to fit within these perceived parameters of popularity, they socialize themselves to gender roles. In this article, we examine the factors that constitute the determinants of popularity for elementary school boys and girls and in so doing, assemble the cultural norms of appropriate gender identity constructed by these children.

Studies of children's gender roles have suggested that boys have traditionally displayed an *active* posture and girls, a *passive* one (Coleman 1961; Eder and Parker 1987; Lever 1976). The role of boys has encompassed rough play, the command of space, competition with peers, and a certain toughness designed to show independence and masculinity (Eder and Parker 1987; Lever 1976; Willis 1977). Girls' behavior has historically included a focus on relational and intimacy work, nurturance and emotional supportiveness, and a concern with developing feminine allure (Eder and Parker 1987; Eisenhart and Holland 1983; Gilligan 1982; Lever 1976; Thorne 1986; Valli 1988).

Yet changes in society, influenced by the women's movement and the vast entry of women into the work force, have profoundly affected adult women's gender roles, expanding and androgenizing them. Much concern has focused on whether these changes have filtered down to children, narrowing the differences in boys' and girls' child-rearing experiences within the home. Noting these societal trends, Hoffman (1977) and Best (1983) investigated whether children are being raised in ways that differ significantly from past generations; both found that shifts in the traditional gender roles were slight, at best, with children displaying fairly conservative gender orientations....

METHODS

This article draws on data gathered by all three authors from 1987 to 1991 through participant observation with elementary-school students, who we observed and interacted with inside and outside their schools. The children attended two public schools drawing predominantly on middle- and upper-middle class neighborhoods (with a smattering of children from lower socioeconomic areas) in a large, mostly White university community....

In interacting with children, we varied our behavior. At times, we acted naturally, expressing ourselves fully as responsible adults, and at other times, we cast these attitudes and demeanors aside and tried to hang out with the children, getting into their gossip and adventures (or misadventures) ....thereby taking on what Mandell (1988) called the "least-adult" role....

STRATIFICATION AND SOCIALIZATION

In educational institutions, children develop a stratified social order that is determined by their interactions with peers, parents, and others (Passuth 1987). According to Corsaro (1979), children's knowledge of social position is influenced by their conception of status, which may be defined as popularity, prestige, or "social honor" (Weber 1946). This article focuses primarily on the concept of popularity, which can be defined operationally as the children who are liked by the greatest number of their peers, who are the most influential in setting group opinions, and who have the greatest impact on determining the boundaries of membership in the most exclusive social group. In the school environment, boys and girls have divergent attitudes and behavioral patterns in their gender-role expectations and the methods they use to attain status, or popularity, among peers.

BOYS' POPULARITY FACTORS

Boys' popularity, or rank in the status hierarchy, was influenced by several factors. Although the boys' popularity ordering was not as clearly defined as was the girls', there was a rationale underlying the stratification in their daily interactions and group relations.

Athletic Ability

The major factor that affected the boys' popularity was athletic ability (cf. Coleman 1961, Eder and Parker 1987, Eitzen 1975, Fine 1987, Schofield 1981). Athletic ability was so critical that those who were proficient in sports attained both peer recognition and upward social mobility. In both schools we observed the best athlete was also the most popular boy in the grade. Two third- and fourth-grade boys considered the question of what makes kids popular:

> **NICK:** *Craig is sort of mean, but he's really good at sports, so he's popular.*

> **BEN:** *Everybody wants to be friends with Gabe, even though he makes fun of most of them all the time. But they still all want to pick him on their team and have him be friends with them because he's a good athlete, even though he brags a lot about it. He's popular.*

In the upper grades, the most popular boys all had a keen interest in sports even if they were not adept in athletics. Those with moderate ability and interest in athletic endeavors fell primarily into lower status groups. Those who were least proficient athletically were potential pariahs.

Because of the boy's physicality, contact sports occasionally degenerated into conflicts between participants. Fighting, whether formal fights or informal pushing, shoving, or roughhousing, was a means of establishing a social order. The more popular boys often dispensed these physical actions of superiority, while the less popular boys were often the recipients. The victors, although negatively sanctioned by the adults in the school, attained more status than did the defeated, who lost considerable status. The less popular boys were the ones who were most frequently hurt and least frequently assisted during games in the playground. For example, Mikey, an unpopular boy with asthma who was fairly uncoordinated and weak, was often the victim of rough playground tackles in football or checks in soccer. Boys knew they could take the ball away from him at will. When he was hurt and fell down crying, he was blamed for the incident and mocked.

Coolness

Athletics was a major determinant of the boys' social hierarchy, but being good in sports was not the sole variable that affected their popularity. For boys, being "cool" generated a great deal of peer status. As Lyman and Scott (1989, p. 93) noted, "a display of coolness is often a prerequisite to entrance into or maintenance of membership in certain social circles." Cool was a social construction whose definition was in constant flux. Being cool involved individuals' self-presentational skills, their accessibility to expressive equipment, and their impression-management techniques (Fine 1981). Various social forces were involved in the continual negotiation of cool and how the students came to agree on its meaning. As a sixth-grade teacher commented:

The popular group is what society might term "cool." You know they're skaters, they skateboard, they wear more cool clothes, you know the "in" things you'd see in ads right now in magazines. If you look at our media and advertising right now on TV, like the Levi commercials, they're kinda loose, they skate and they're doing those things. The identity they created for themselves, I think, has a lot to do with the messages the kids are getting from the media and advertising as to what's cool and what's not cool.

There was a shared agreement among the boys as to what type of expressive equipment, such as clothing, was socially defined as cool. Although this type of apparel was worn mostly by the popular boys, boys in the other groups also tried to emulate this style. Aspects of this style included (1) high-top tennis shoes, such as Nike Air Jordans or Reeboks, which were often unlaced at the top eyelets or left untied; (2) baggy designer jeans that were rolled up at the cuff; (3) loose-fitting button-down shirts, which were not tucked into their pants (or were tucked in only in front) so that the shirttails hung out, or T-shirts with surfing and skateboarding logos, such as Maui Town and Country, Bugle Boy, Vision, and Quicksilver; (4) hairstyles, in which the back and sides were cut short so that the ears were exposed, with the top left longer and moussed to give the hair a "wet look" or to make it stand up straight; (5) denim jackets; (6) Sony Walkm[ans] or other brands of portable stereo receivers–cassette players; and (7) in the sixth grade especially, roller-blades.

Toughness

In the schools we studied, the popular boys, especially in the upper grades, were defiant of adult authority, challenged existing rules, and received more disciplinary actions than did boys in the other groups. They attained a great deal of peer status from this type of acting out. This defiance is related to what Miller (1958) referred to as the "focal concerns" of lower-class culture, specifically "trouble" and "toughness." Trouble involves rule-breaking behavior, and, as Miller (1958), p. 176) noted, "in certain situations, 'getting into trouble' is overtly recognized as prestige conferring." Boys who exhibited an air of nonchalance in the face of teacher authority or disciplinary measures enhanced their status among their peers. Two fourth-grade boys described how members of the popular group in their grade acted:

> **MARK:** *They're always getting into trouble by talking back to the teacher.*
>
> **TOM:** *Yeah, they always have to show off to each other that they aren't afraid to say anything they want to the teacher, that they aren't teachers' pets. Whatever they're doing, they make it look like it's better than what the teacher is doing, 'cause they think what she's doing is stupid.*
>
> **MARK:** *And one day Josh and Allen got in trouble in music 'cause they told the teacher the Disney movie she wanted to show sucked. They got pink [disciplinary] slips.*
>
> **TOM:** *Yeah, and that's the third pink slip Josh's got already this year, and it's only Thanksgiving.*

Toughness involved displays of physical prowess, athletic skill, and belligerency, especially in repartee with peers and adults. In the status hierarchy, boys who exhibited "macho" behavioral patterns gained recognition from their peers for being tough. Often, boys in the high-status crowd were the "class clowns" or "troublemakers" in the school, thereby becoming the center of attention.

In contrast, boys who demonstrated "effeminate" behavior were referred to by pejorative terms, such as "fag," "sissy," and "homo," and consequently lost status (cf. Thorne and Luria 1986). One boy was constantly derided behind his back because he got flustered easily, had a "spaz" (lost his temper, slammed things down on his desk, stomped around the classroom), and then would start to cry. Two fifth-grade boys described a classmate they considered the prototypical "fag:"

> **TRAVIS:** *Wren is such a nerd. He's short and his ears stick out.*
>
> **NIKKO:** *And when he sits in his chair, he crosses one leg over the other and curls the toe around under his calf, so it's double-crossed, like this [shows]. It looks so faggy with his "girly" shoes. And he always sits up erect with perfect posture, like this [shows].*
>
> **TRAVIS:** *And he's always raising his hand to get the teacher to call on him.*
>
> **NIKKO:** *Yeah, Wren is the kind of kid, when the teacher has to go out for a minute, she says, "I'm leaving Wren in charge while I'm gone."*

Savoir-faire

Savoir-faire refers to children's sophistication in social and interpersonal skills. These behaviors included such interpersonal communication skills as being able to initiate sequences of play and other joint lines of action, affirmation of friendships, role-taking and role-playing abilities, social knowledge and cognition, providing constructive criticism and support to one's peers, and expressing feelings in a positive manner. Boys used their social skills to establish friendships with peers and adults both within and outside the school, thereby enhancing their popularity.

Many of the behaviors composing savoir-faire depended on children's maturity, adroitness, and awareness of what was going on in the social world around them. Boys who had a higher degree of social awareness knew how to use their social skills more effectively. This use of social skills manifested itself in a greater degree of sophistication in communicating with peers and adults. One teacher commented on some of the characteristics she noted in the group leaders:

> *Interpersonal skills, there's a big difference there. It seems like I get a more steady gaze, more eye contact, and more of an adult response with some of the kids in the popular group, one on one with them. The ones who aren't [in the popular group] kind of avert their gaze or are kind of more fidgety; they fidget a little more and are a little more uneasy one on one....*

Many boys further used their savoir-faire to their social advantage. In their desire to be popular, they were often manipulative, domineering, and controlling. They set potential friends against each other, vying for their favors. They goaded others into acting out in class and getting into trouble. They set the attitudes for all to follow and then changed the rules by not following them themselves....

Group leaders with savoir-faire often defined and enforced the boundaries of an exclusive social group. Although nearly everyone liked them and wanted to be in their group, they included only the children they wanted. They communicated to other peers, especially unpopular boys, that they were not really their friends or that play sessions were temporary. This exclusion maintained social boundaries by keeping others on the periphery and at a marginal status.

These kinds of social skills did not seem to emerge along a developmental continuum, with some children further along than the rest. Rather, certain individuals seemed to possess a more proficient social and interactional acumen and to sustain it from year to year, grade to grade.

In contrast, those with extremely poor savoir-faire had difficult social lives and low popularity (cf. Asher and Renshaw 1981). Their interpersonal skills were awkward or poor, and they rarely engaged in highly valued interaction with their peers. Some of them were either withdrawn or aggressively antisocial. Others exhibited dysfunctional behavior and were referred to as being "bossy" or mean. These boys did not receive a great deal of peer recognition, yet often wanted to be accepted into the more prestigious groups....

Many of the boys who lacked savoir-faire to an extreme were thus disagreeable in conversations with their peers. Not only did they lack the social skills necessary to make it in the popular group, they could not maintain relationships with other less popular individuals.

Cross-Gender Relations

Although cross-gender friendships were common in the preschool years, play and games became mostly sex segregated in elementary school, and there was a general lack of cross-sex interaction in the classroom (cf. Hallinan 1979). After kindergarten and first grade, boys and girls were reluctant to engage in intergender activities. Social-control mechanisms, such as "rituals of pollution" and "borderwork" (Thorne 1986),[1] reinforced intragender activities as the socially acceptable norm. Also, intergender activities were often viewed as romances by the children's peers, which made them highly stigmatized and therefore difficult to maintain. The elementary school boys often picked out one girl that they secretly "liked," but they were reluctant to spend much time talking with her or to reveal their feelings to anyone for fear of being teased. When these secrets did get out, children were made the butt of friends' jokes. Most boys, whatever their popularity, were interested only in the select girls from the popular group.

Sometime during the fourth or fifth grade, both boys and girls began to renegotiate the social definition of intergender interactions because of pubertal changes and the emulation of older children's behavior[2] (cf. Thorne 1986). Eder and Parker (1987, p. 201) commented that preadolescence is the stage during which "cross sex interactions become more salient." During the later elementary years, it generally became more socially acceptable for the members of male and female groups to engage in intergender interactions, which took the form of boys talking with girls in the protected enclave of their social group. The boys would tease girls or ask them silly or awkward questions. They sometimes wrote anonymous prank letters with their friends to girls they secretly liked, asking or challenging these girls about "mysterious" features of puberty.

By the sixth grade, the boys began to display a stronger interest in girls, and several of the more popular boys initiated cross-gender relations....

As Fine (1987) pointed out, sexual interest is a sign of maturity in preadolescent boys, yet it is difficult for inexperienced boys who are not fully cognizant of the norms involved. For safety, boys often went through intermediaries (cf. Eder and Sanford 1986) in approaching girls to find out if their interests were reciprocated. They rarely made such dangerous forays face to face. Rather, they gathered with a friend after school to telephone girls for each other or passed notes or messages from friends to the girls in question. When the friends confirmed that the interest was mutual, the interested boy would then ask the girl to "go" with him. One sixth-grade boy described the Saturday he spent with a friend:

We were over at Bob's house and we started calling girls we liked on the phone, one at a time. We'd each call the girl the other one liked and ask if she wanted to go with the other one. Then we'd hang up. If she didn't say yes, we'd call her back and ask why. Usually they wouldn't say too much. So sometimes we'd call her best friend to see if she could tell us anything. Then they would call each other and call us back. If we got the feeling after a few calls that she really was serious about no, then we might go on to our next choice, if we had one.

Getting a confirmation from a girl that she accepted the commitment affected the interaction between them in school only to a certain degree. Boy-girl relations posed considerable risks by representing "innovative situations" (Lyman and Scott 1989) that called for displays of coolness. Yet the boy was now free to call the girl on the phone at home and invite her to a boy-girl party, to a movie or to the mall with another couple or two.

Once the connection was established, boys pressured each other to "score" with girls. Boys who were successful in "making out" with girls (or who claimed that they were) received higher status from their friends. Boys' need for status in the male subculture put considerable pressure on their relationships with girls....

A boy who was successful in getting a girl to go with him developed the reputation of being a "ladies' man" and gained status among his peers.

Academic Performance

The impact of academic performance on boys' popularity was negative for cases of extreme deviation from the norm, but changed over the course of their elementary years for the majority of boys from a positive influence to a potentially degrading stigma.

At all ages, boys who were skewed toward either end of the academic continuum suffered socially. Thus, those who struggled scholastically, who had low self-confidence in accomplishing educational tasks, or who had to be placed in remedial classrooms lost peer recognition. For example, one third-grade boy who went to an afterschool tutoring institute shielded this information from his peers, for fear of ridicule. Boys with serious academic problems were liable to the pejorative label "dummies." At the other end of the continuum, boys who were exceedingly smart but lacked other status-enhancing traits, such as coolness, toughness, or athletic ability, were often stigmatized as "brainy" or "nerdy."...

In the early elementary years, academic performance in between these extremes was positively correlated with social status. Younger boys took pride in their work, loved school, and loved their teachers. Many teachers routinely hugged their students at day's end as they sent them out the door. Yet sometime during the middle elementary years, by around third grade, boys began to change their collective attitudes about academics. This change in attitude coincided with a change in their orientation, away from surrounding adults and toward the peer group.

The boys' shift in attitude involved the introduction of a potential stigma associated with doing too well in school. The macho attitudes embodied in the coolness and toughness orientations led them to lean more toward group identities as renegades or rowdies and affected their exertion in academics, creating a ceiling level of effort beyond which it was potentially dangerous to reach. Boys who persisted in their pursuit of academics while lacking other social skills were subject to ridicule as "cultural dopes" (Garfinkel 1967). Those who had high scholastic aptitude, even with other culturally redeeming traits, became reluctant to work up to their full potential for fear of exhibiting low-value behavior. By diminishing their effort in academics, they avoided the disdain of other boys....

Some boys who were scholastically adept thus tried to hide their academic efforts or to manage good performance in school with other status-enhancing factors to avoid becoming stigmatized. They gave their friends answers when the friends were called on by the teacher and were disruptive and off-task during instructional periods, socializing with their friends and occasionally playing the "class clowns." These behaviors nullified the label of being a "goody-goody" or a "teacher's pet" by demonstrating a rebellious attitude to adult authority. Thus, by the second half of elementary school, the environment provided more of a social than an educational function for them, and this function had a negative effect on their desire for academic success (cf. Coleman 1961).

GIRLS' POPULARITY FACTORS

The major distinction between the boys' and girls' status hierarchies lay in the factors that conferred popularity. Although some factors were similar, the girls used them in a different manner to organize their social environment. Consequently, the factors had different effects on the girls' and boys' status hierarchies.

Family Background
Similar to the middle-school girls studied by Eder (1985), the elementary school girls' family background was a powerful force that affected their attainment of popularity in multiple ways. Their parents' socioeconomic sta-

tus (SES) and degree of permissiveness were two of the most influential factors.

SES. Maccoby (1980) suggested that among the most powerful and least understood influences on a child are the parents' income, education, and occupation (SES). In general, many popular girls came from upper-class and upper-middle-class families and were able to afford expensive clothing that was socially defined as "stylish" and "fashionable." These "rich" girls had a broader range of material possessions, such as expensive computers or games, a television in their room, and a designer phone with a separate line (some girls even had a custom acronym for the number). They also participated in select extracurricular activities, such as horseback riding and skiing and vacationed with their families at elite locations. Some girls' families owned second houses in resort areas to which they could invite their friends for the weekend. Their SES gave these girls greater access to highly regarded symbols of prestige. Although less privileged girls often referred to them as "spoiled," they secretly envied these girls' life-styles and possessions. As two fourth-grade girls in the unpopular group stated:

ALISSA: *If your Mom has a good job, you're popular, but if your Mom has a bad job, then you're unpopular.*

BETTY: *And, if, like, you're on welfare, then you're unpopular because it shows that you don't have a lot of money.*

ALISSA: *They think money means that you're great—you can go to Sophia's [a neighborhood "little store" where popular people hang out] and get whatever you want and stuff like that. You can buy things for people.*

BETTY: *I have a TV, but if you don't have cable [TV] then you're unpopular because everybody that's popular has cable.*

Family background also influenced the girls' popularity indirectly, through the factor of residential location. Neighborhoods varied within school districts and girls from similar economic strata usually lived near each other. Not only did this geographic proximity increase the likelihood of their playing together, and not with girls from other class backgrounds, but the social activities in which they engaged after school were more likely to be similar, and their parents were more apt to be friends. In addition, the differences in their houses could be considerable, intimidating some and embarrassing others. One girl, who lived in one of the poorer areas in the district, often referred to the houses of her classmates as "mansions." When she invited these girls to her house, she felt uncomfortable bringing them into her room because her clothes were kept in cardboard Pampers boxes, out of which her mother had fashioned a dresser....

Thus, although some popular girls were not affluent, most of the popular girls came from families with high SES. The girls believed that having money influenced their location in the social hierarchy.

Laissez-faire. Laissez-faire refers to the degree to which parents closely supervised their children or were permissive, allowing them to engage in a wide range of activities. Girls whose parents let them stay up late on sleepover dates, go out with their friends to all kinds of social activities, and gave them a lot of freedom while playing in the house were more likely to be popular. Girls who had to stay home (especially on weekend nights) and "get their sleep," were not allowed to go to boy-girl parties, had strict curfews, or whose parents called ahead to parties to ensure that they would be adult "supervised" were more likely to be left out of the wildest capers and the most exclusive social crowd.

Whether for business, social, or simply personal reasons, permissive or absentee parents oversaw the daily nuances of their children's lives less closely. They had a less tightly integrated family life and were less aware of their children's responsibilities, activities, and place in the social order. Their daughters thus had a valuable resource, freedom, that they could both use and offer others. These girls were also the most likely to socialize away from their houses or to organize activities with their friends that others perceived as fun and appealing. Their freedom and parental permissiveness often tempted them to try out taboo activities, which was a source of popularity among their peers. Their activities sometimes led their group to become a wild or fast crowd, which further enhanced their status.

In some instances, girls who received less support or supervision in their home lives developed an "external locus of control" (Good and Brophy 1987) and became major figureheads in the popular crowd. Using the peer group as a support mechanism, they manipulated others in the group to establish their central position and to dominate the definition of the group's boundaries. These ringleaders could make life difficult for members of their own clique, as one member of the popular group lamented:

> *I've really been trying to break away from Laura this year because she can be so mean, and I don't know when I go in to school every day if she's been calling up other girls talking about me behind my back and getting everybody against me or not. Like, if I don't call everyone in my clique every night, I might find myself dropped from it the next day. Or she might decide at school that I've done something she doesn't like and turn everyone against me. That's why I'd like to break away from her, but I'm afraid, because she controls everybody, and I wouldn't have any friends.*

Physical Appearance

Another powerful determinant of girls' location in the stratification system was their physical attractiveness. Others (Coleman 1961; Eder and Parker

1987; Eder and Sanford, 1986; Schofield 1981) have noted that appearance and grooming behavior are not only a major topic of girls' conversation, but a source of popularity. The norms of popular appearance included designer clothing, such as Calvin Klein, Gitano, Forenza, and Esprit. In the upper grades, makeup was used as a status symbol, but as Eder and Sanford (186) observed, too much makeup was highly criticized by other members of the group, thereby inhibiting social mobility. Finally, girls who were deemed pretty by society's socially constructed standards were attractive to boys and had a much greater probability of being popular.

Girls were socialized into these norms of appearance at an early age. A group of five kindergarten girls voiced their feelings of upset about another girl in their class because they felt that she was popular and they were not....

The perception that popularity was determined by physical traits was fully evidenced by these kindergartners. These aspects of appearance, such as clothing, hairstyles, and attractiveness to boys, were even more salient, with the girls in the upper grades. As an excerpt from one of our field notes indicated:

> *I walked into the fifth-grade coat closet and saw Diane applying hair-spray and mousse to Paula's and Mary's hair. Someone passed by and said, "Oh, Mary I like your hair," and she responded, "I didn't do it; Diane did it." It seemed that Diane, who was the most popular girl in the class, was socializing them to use the proper beauty supplies that were socially accepted by the popular clique. I asked what made girls unpopular, and Diane said, "They're not rich and not pretty enough. Some people don't use the same kind of mousse or wear the same style of clothing."*

As girls learn these norms of appearance and associate them with social status, they form the values that will guide their future attitudes and behavior, especially in cross-gender relationships (cf. Eder and Sanford 1986). This finding correlates with other research (Hatfield and Sprecher 1986) that suggested that physical appearance is closely related to attaining a mate, that people who perceive themselves as being unattractive have difficulty establishing relationships with others, and that there is a correlation between opportunities for occupational success and physical attractiveness.

Social Development

Social factors were also salient to girls' popularity. Like the boys, the most precocious girls achieved dominant positions, but they were also more sensitive to issues of inclusion and exclusion. Precocity and exclusivity were thus crucial influences on girls' formation of friendships and their location on the popularity hierarchy.

Precocity. Precocity refers to girls early attainment of adult social characteristics, such as the ability to express themselves verbally, to understand the dynamics of intra- and intergroup relationships, to convince others of their point, and to manipulate others into doing what they wanted, as well as interest in more mature social concerns (such as makeup and boys). As with the boys, these social skills were only partly developmental; some girls just seemed more precocious from their arrival in kindergarten....

The most precocious girls showed an interest in boys from the earliest elementary years.[3] They talked about boys and tried to get boys to pay attention to them. This group of girls was usually the popular crowd, with the clothes and appearance that boys (if they were interested in girls) would like. These girls told secrets and giggled about boys and passed boys [sic] notes in class and in the halls that embarrassed but excited the boys. They also called boys on the phone, giggling at them, asking them mundane or silly questions, pretending they were the teacher, singing radio jingles to them, or blurting out "sexy" remarks. One second-grade boy described the kinds of things a group of popular girls said to him when they called him on the phone:

> *Well, usually they just call up and say, like "This is radio station KNUB and we're here to call you," but sometimes they say things like, "Babe will you go out with me tonight," or one time Jim (his brother) answered the phone and they said, "Get your sexy brother on the phone right now." And one time last year when we were out to dinner, they called and filled up our whole phone machine with messages, around 20 of them, and my mom had to call their moms and tell them to stop it.*

Other girls who did not participate in these kinds of interactions often looked down on these girls as boy crazy, but these girls' behavior sharpened the boys' interest. Although boys could not let their peers know they liked it, they appreciated the attention. The notice they repaid to the girls then enhanced these girls' popularity (cf. Schofield 1981).

By around the fourth to sixth grade, it became more socially acceptable for girls to engage in cross-gender interactions without being rebuked by their peers. The more precocious girls began to experiment further by flirting with boys; calling them on the telephone; "going" with them; going to parties; and ultimately, dating. Although some girls were adventurous enough to ask a boy out, most followed traditional patterns and waited for boys to commit themselves first. One fourth-grade girl described what it meant to "go" with a boy: "You talk. You hold hands at school. You pass notes in class. You go out with them, and go to movies, and go swimming....We usually double date."

In the upper grades, if a girl went with a popular boy, she was able to achieve a share of his prestige and social status. Several girls dreamed of this possibility and even spoke with longing or anticipation to their friends about it.[4] When popular girls went with popular boys, it reinforced and strengthened the status of both. This was the most common practice, as a fifth-grade girl noted: "It seems that most of the popular girls go out with the popular boys; I don't know why." One fourth-grade girl referred to such a union as a "Wowee" (a highly prestigious couple), because people would be saying "Wow!" at the magnitude of their stardom. Yet, to go out with a lower-status boy would diminish a girl's prestige....

A high-status girl would thus be performing a form of social suicide if she interacted with a low-status boy in any type of relationship. Although the girls acknowledged that they were sensitive to this issue, they were doubtful whether a popular boy's rank in the social hierarchy would be affected by going with a girl from a lower stratum. They thought that boys would not place as much weight on such issues.

Exclusivity. Exclusivity refers to individuals' desire, need, and ability to form elite social groups using such negative tactics as gossiping, the proliferation of rumors, bossiness, and meanness. One or two elite groups of girls at each grade level jointly participated in exclusionary playground games and extracurricular activities, which created clearly defined social boundaries because these girls granted limited access to their friendship circles. In one fourth-grade class, a clique of girls had such a strong group identity that they gave themselves a name and a secret language....

This group of girls restricted entrée to their play and friendship activities, although they did not want to be perceived as pretentious and condescending. Many girls in the less popular groups did not like the girls in the highest-status crowd, even though they acknowledged that these girls were popular (cf. Eder 1985)....

[O]ne of the most common forms of boundary maintenance among friendship groups, both intra- and interclique, involved the use of rumors and gossip (Parker and Gottman 1989). Shared secrets were passed among friends, cementing their relational bonds (Simmel 1950), while derisive rumours were told about outsiders. These were tactics girls used to create and maintain exclusivity. During classroom instructional periods, many of the girls were preoccupied with passing notes to one another. These behaviors primarily involved the girls in the popular cliques, who often derided the girls in the unpopular groups. This type of behavior not only separated the groups, but maintained the popular crowd's position at the top of the social hierarchy. As Simmel (1950, p. 314) stated: "The lie which maintains itself, which is not seen through, is undoubtedly a means of asserting intellectual superiority and of using it to control and suppress the less intelligent (if intelligence is measured as knowledge of the social situation)."

Academic Performance

In contrast to the boys, the girls never seemed to develop the machismo culture that forced them to disdain and disengage from academics. Although not all popular girls were smart or academic achievers, they did not suffer any stigma from performing well scholastically. Throughout elementary school, most girls continued to try to attain the favor of their teachers and to do well on their assignments. They gained status from their classmates for getting good grades and performing difficult assignments. The extent to which a school's policies favored clumping students of like abilities in homogeneous learning groups or classes affected the influence of academic stratification on girls' cliques. Homogeneous academic groupings were less common during the early elementary years, but increased in frequency as students approached sixth grade and their performance curve spread out wider. By fifth or sixth grade, then, girls were more likely to become friends with others of similar scholastic levels. Depending on the size of the school, within each grade there might be both a clique of academically inclined popular girls and a clique composed of popular girls who did not perform as well and who bestowed lower salience on schoolwork.

DISCUSSION

One of the major contributions of this work lies in its illustration of the role of popularity in gender socialization. Gaining and maintaining popularity has enormous significance on children's lives (cf. Eder 1985), influencing their ability to make friends, to be included in fun activities, and to develop a positive sense of self-esteem. In discerning, adapting to, and creatively forging these features of popularity, children actively socialize themselves to the gender roles embodied in their peer culture.

Our research suggests that many of the features of popularity described here arise and become differentiated at an earlier age than previous studies have shown. Factors that were considered primarily salient only to adolescent gendered cultures can now be seen as having their roots in elementary school. Thus, the girls we observed were already deriving status from their success in grooming, clothes, and other appearance-related variables; social sophistication and friendship ties; romantic success, measured through popularity and going with boys; affluence and its correlates of material possessions and leisure pursuits; and academic performance. Boys, even in the predominantly White middle-class schools that we studied, were accorded popularity and respect for distancing themselves from deference to authority and investment in academic effort and for displaying traits, such as toughness, trouble, domination, coolness, and interpersonal bragging and sparring skills. These peer focal concerns, the determinants of popularity, embody the models of children's idealized gender roles.

A second contribution of this research lies in the gender images of elementary school children it portrays. As we noted earlier, previous characterizations of boys' and girls' gender roles have emphasized differences in their *active* and *passive* natures. Our research suggests that these depictions are of mixed validity: the images still exist, but boys' and girls' behavior incorporates some elements of both features. In addition to these dimensions, however, girls' and boys' popularity factors and gender roles incorporate elements of an *achieved* versus *ascribed* dichotomy that has not been addressed in the literature. Both these dimensions can be seen, to some extent, in overlapping and independent fashions in the gender models. Our research suggests that the following images embody the focal concerns of boys' and girls' gender roles.

Boys prosper in the youthful popularity system and carve out their gender identities through a successful internalization and expression of the male ethos. Their focal concerns evince an awareness of and aspiration to the *cult of masculinity,* through which they can demonstrate their growth, maturity, and distance from the femininity characterizing their early family-oriented lives. They try to adopt elements of the machismo posture through their toughness and defiance of adult authority, challenging prescribed rules and roles in class, and distancing themselves from academics. They also strive for admiration and reputation among peers by bragging and boasting about their exploits (despite norms of modesty) in sports, experiments with deviant behavior, success with girls, and dominance over other boys.

Boys' culture also embodies their *expression of physicality* in its central focus on active participation and prowess in sports. Boys spend most of their free time outdoors, carving out and conquering space, filling it up with their play and games, and overrunning the play of girls and younger boys (cf. Thorne 1986). Their physicality is competitive and dominating, structured to involve contests in which one individual or team bests the other and revels in the victory. Physical displays, both within and outside the game structure, can also culminate in physical aggression and fights between boys, through which masculinity is tested and dominance is established.

The active nature of boys' lives is tied to their *orientation of autonomy.* Boys know that part of growing up involves measuring up, or proving themselves as men. Thus, they prepare themselves for this eventuality by regularly measuring themselves against each other. They strive for independence from adult authority figures, for self-reliance, and for toughness. They cut themselves and each other off from the cult of coddling with sharp remarks and derogations against "babylike" behavior, toughening themselves in preparation for their adult role.

Finally, boys enter the *culture of coolness,* assuming suitably detached postures and attitudes, both within and outside their groups. They act cool in distancing themselves from things they used to like, but now define as feminine or nerdy. They act cool by repressing emotionality and dealing with others on a physical level. Most especially, they try to act cool to protect themselves in cross-gender relations, to avoid excessively weakening themselves because of their structural position of having to expose their interest in girls and to face possible rejection. They are not always successful in this regard, however, for they sometimes become emotional and show it in dealing with girls, hanging on, despite rejection, to the hope that a girl will like them and go with them.

The focal concerns of the girls' peer culture and gender role revolve around a different set of skills and values. In contrast to the boys' defiance, girls become absorbed into a *culture of compliance and conformity*. Especially at school, they occupy themselves with games and social interactions in which they practice and perfect established social roles, rules, and relationships. They not only follow explicitly stated rules, but extrapolate upon them, enforcing them on others as well. Their superior performance in school reflects, not necessarily their greater innate intelligence, but their more passive adherence to the normative order. Yet they do have instances of assertiveness, rebellion, or misbehavior, which are likely to be directed into social channels, toward other girls, or at home, toward their families.

From an earlier age than boys, girls are attracted to the *culture of romance* (cf. Eisenhart and Holland 1983; Simon, Eder, and Evans 1992; Valli 1988). They fantasize about romantic involvements with boys and become interested, sooner, in crossing gender lines for relationships, both platonic and otherwise. They absorb idealized images of gendered ways of relating to boys that are based partly on traditional roles. This romantic ideal fosters flirtatious behavior that is more active in its teasing and chasing than were previous models and more egalitarian in relationship power (girls go "dutch," arrange transportation, initiate more activities, and are not content merely to acquiesce to boys' wishes). Its ultimate aim, however, is to lure boys into the feminine realm of intimacy, emotions, and relationship work. Girls who accomplish romance successfully by attracting a boy, gain status among other girls.

Passivity is also inherent in the *ideology of domesticity* (Valli 1988) that characterizes girls' play and interaction. Unlike the boys, who search for the physical limits of their bodies and the social limits of their school, group, and society through their efforts to challenge these limits, the girls carve out inner space. They live indoor lives; draw indoor scenes; and concern themselves with gathering others around them. They focus on the emotional dimension of expression and become more adept at intimacy and cooperation than at openly competing against others (cf. Deaux 1977; Gilligan 1982; Karweit and Hansell 1983). In this way, they prepare themselves for the domestic and maternal roles.

Hovering over all this is an *orientation of ascription* that is found, although in an eroded form compared to years past. From their families and the mass-media culture, they learn that the woman's role has been to attract a man who will bestow his status on her. Although many more of their mothers have careers than in previous generations, they see that these jobs are often accorded secondary stature within the family and may be located within the sphere of "women's occupations." Many elementary school girls plan to have careers in addition to being mothers, yet they also perceive that women still get status partly by its being attached to them. Therefore, they look to see what is attached to other girls. This orientation comes out in their preoccupation with ascribed features of potential playmates, such as their material possessions, life-styles, houses, and appearance (cf. Eder 1985). As part of this reflected role, girls also learn that women have often gotten what they want through indirection and manipulation, rather than through direct action (a component of their flirting), and that indirection and manipulation remain part of their behavioral repertoire.

These ascribed-achieved and active-passive divergences are found in the popularity factors and the idealized gender images, yet oppositional elements are also clearly present. Boys are passive in leveling themselves academically to conform to peer-group norms and manipulative and indirect, like girls, in their jockeying to maintain both boundaries around their friendship groups and their own positions within these groups. They may not be as concerned about ascribed characteristics and social class as are girls, but they are cognizant of appearance and material possessions. At the same time, girls are active in their everyday behavior. They work to get good grades, to participate in sports (a greatly expanded realm, although not as yet a strongly popularity-inducing one), to be involved in extra-curricular activities, and to stay embedded within their cliques.

Hence, boys and girls are both active and passive within their own realms. They employ agency within the structural framework provided by their gender roles, socially constructing their behavior so it accords with the impressions they seek to achieve popularity among their peers. Under the guise of passivity and being attached, girls actively produce their peer status (although they may do so indirectly), while boys engineer images of themselves as forthright, active, and democratic, all the while working the back channels and scanning others for ascribed traits. Thus both boys and girls actively create their roles of relative passivity and activity, achievement and ascription, in accord with their perceptions of the larger culture. These are patterns and roles that they learn in childhood and that they will continue to evince as adults.

As a third contribution of this research, we compare these children's gender roles with models from earlier times. Looking at the composition of these images, we see that in their complexity, their integration of oppositional elements that expand and androgenize them, they represent a slight historical shift from previous generations. This has been a focus of concern for those studying changes in the gender roles of men and women in society. In our middle-class sample, we found more achievement-oriented female role models for girls and more structural avenues open for them to be active and accomplished. The girls knew and espoused the rhetoric of feminism, that they had rights and expectations within society. To a greater extent than did the boys, then, they attained some gender-role expansion: They could more acceptably pursue the traditionally male avenues of sports, achievement, autonomy, and initiative toward the opposite sex. Such a cross-over among boys into "feminine" areas was less acceptable, however, and still negatively sanctioned.

These changes have created some modification in the traditional gender roles, especially for girls. Thus, compared to previous studies that found only minimal changes in children's gender socialization (Best 1983; Hoffman 1977), the notions of appropriate roles and behaviors of the girls in our study accord somewhat greater with societal transformations. At the same time, the boys still predominantly sought and attained popularity and acceptance through traditional gendered behavior. This "progressive" population is precisely where one would expect the greatest changes in gender roles to begin appearing, for many of these children came from highly educated, professional, and dual-career families. While these modifications are becoming more visible among this group, researchers should note that they may well be weaker among a broader spectrum of other racial and class groups. Future research could profit from examining divergences and affinities in the gender roles of elementary school children across such racial and class lines.

NOTES

1   Rituals of pollution refer to intergender activities in which each gender accuses the other of having "germs" or "cooties." Thorne (1986, pp. 174–75) noted that girls are perceived as being more polluting than boys, and this perception anticipates and influences cross-cultural patterns of feminine subordination. Borderwork refers to boundary maintenances.

2   Children with older siblings were often more precocious than were others, overcoming their reluctance to approach girls and initiating rites of flirtation and dating.

3   In the second grade, a group of popular girls, centered on an extremely precocious ringleader, regularly called boys. They asked the boys silly questions, giggled, and left long messages on their telephone answering machines. At one school outing, the dominant girl bribed a boy she liked with money and candy to kiss her, but when he balked at the task (after having eaten the candy and spent the money), she had to pretend to her friends that he had done so, to avoid losing face.

4   One girl even lied to her friends about it, pretending to them that she was going with a popular boy. When they found out that she had fabricated the story, they dropped her, and she lost both her status and her friends.

REFERENCES

Asher, Steven R. and Peter D. Renshaw. 1981. "Children without Friends: Social Knowledge and Social Skill Training." Pp. 273–96 in *The Development of Children's*

Friendships, edited by S. R. Asher and J. M. Gottman. New York: Cambridge University Press.

Berentzen, S. 1984. *Children's Constructing their Social Worlds.* Bergen, Norway: University of Bergen.

Best, Raphaela. 1983. *We All Have Scars.* Bloomington: Indiana University Press.

Borman, Kathryn M. and J. Frankel. 1984. "Gender Inequalities in Childhood Social Life and the Adult Work Life." Pp. 55–83 in *Women in the Workplace: Effects on Families,* edited by S. Gideonse. Norwood, NJ: Ablex.

Coleman, James. 1961. *The Adolescent Society.* Glencoe, IL: Free Press.

Corsaro, William. 1979. "Young Children's Conceptions of Status and Role." *Sociology of Education* 52: 46–59.

Deaux, K. 1977. "Sex Differences." Pp. 357–77 in *Personality Variables in Social Behavior,* edited by T. Blass. New York: John Wiley.

Douglas, Jack D. 1976. *Investigative Social Research.* Beverly Hills, CA: Sage.

Eder, Donna. 1985. "The Cycle of Popularity: Interpersonal Relations among Female Adolescents." *Sociology of Education* 58:154–65.

Eder, Donna and Maureen T. Hallinan. 1978. "Sex Differences in Children's Friendships." *American Sociological Review* 43: 237–50.

Eder, Donna and Stephen Parker. 1987. "The Central Production and Reproduction of Gender: The Effect of Extracurricular Activities on Peer-Group Culture." *Sociology of Education* 60: 200–13.

Eder, Donna and Stephanie Sanford. 1986. "The Development and Maintenance of Interactional Norms Among Early Adolescents." Pp. 283–300 in *Sociological Studies of Child Development* (Vol. 1) edited by P. A. Adler and P. Adler, Greenwich, CT: JAI Press.

Eisenhart, Margaret A. and Dorothy C. Holland. 1983. "Learning Gender from Peers: The Role of Peer Groups in the Cultural Transmission of Gender." *Human Organization* 42: 321–32.

Eitzen, D. Stanley. 1975. "Athletics in the Status System of Male Adolescents: A Replication of Coleman's *The Adolescent Society.*" *Adolescence* 10: 267–76.

Fine, Gary Alan. 1981. "Friends, Impression Management, and Preadolescent Behavior." Pp. 29–52 in *The Development of Children's Friendships,* edited by S. Asher and J. Gottman. New York: Cambridge University Press.

———. 1987. *With the Boys.* Chicago: University of Chicago Press.

Fine, Gary Alan and Kent Sandstrom. 1988. *Knowing Children.* Newbury Park, CA: Sage.

Garfinkel, Harold. 1967. *Studies in Ethnomethodology.* Englewood Cliffs, NJ: Prentice-Hall.

Gilligan, Carol. 1982. *In a Different Voice.* Cambridge, MA: Harvard University Press.

Glassner, Barry. 1976. "Kid Society." *Urban Education* 11: 5–22.

Good, Thomas L. and Jere E. Brophy. 1987. *Looking in Classrooms* (4th ed.). New York: Harper & Row.

Goodwin, Marjorie H. 1980a. "'He-Said-She-Said:' Formal Cultural Procedures for the Construction of a Gossip Dispute Activity." *American Ethnologist* 7: 674–95.

————. 1980b. "Directive/Response Speech Sequences in Girls' and Boys' Task Activities." Pp. 157–73 in *Women and Language in Literature and Society*, edited by S. McConnell-Ginet, R. Borker, and N. Furman. New York: Praeger.

————. 1990. *He-Said-She-Said*. Bloomington: Indiana University Press.

Gunnarsson, L. 1978. *Children in Day Care and Family Care in Sweden*. Stockholm, Sweden: Department of Educational Research.

Hallinan, Maureen T. 1979. "Structured Effects on Children's Friendships and Cliques." *Social Psychology Quarterly* 42: 43–54.

Hatfield, Elaine and Susan Sprecher. 1986. *Mirror, Mirror...The Importance of Looks in Everyday Life*. Albany: State University of New York Press.

Hoffman, Lois Wladis. 1977. "Changes in Family Roles, Socialization, and Sex Differences." *American Psychologist* 42: 644–57.

Karweit, Nancy and Stephen Hansell. 1983. "Sex Differences in Adolescent Relationships: Friendship and Status." Pp. 115–30 in *Friends in School*, edited by J. L. Epstein and N. Karweit. New York: Academic Press.

Kessler, S., D. J. Ashenden, R. W. Connell and G. W. Dowsett. 1985. "Gender Relations in Secondary Schooling." *Sociology of Education* 58: 34–48.

Lever, Janet. 1976. "Sex Differences in the Games Children Play." *Social Problems* 23: 478–87.

————. 1978. "Sex Differences in the Complexity of Children's Play and Games." *American Sociological Review* 43: 471–83.

Lyman, Stanford and Marvin Scott. 1989. *Sociology of the Absurd* (2nd ed.). Dix Hills, NY: General Hall.

Maccoby, Eleanor. 1980. *Social Development*. New York: Harcourt, Brace Jovanovich.

Maltz, Daniel N. and Ruth A. Borker. 1983. "A Cultural Approach to Male-Female Miscommunication." Pp. 195–216 in *Language and Social Identity*, edited by J. J. Gumperz. New York: Cambridge University Press.

Mandell, Nancy. 1988. "The Least-Adult Role in Studying Children." *Journal of Contemporary Ethnography* 16: 433–67.

Miller, Walter. 1958. "Lower Class Culture and Gang Delinquency." *Journal of Social Issues* 14: 5–19.

Parker, Jeffrey G. and John M. Gottman. 1989. "Social and Emotional Development in a Relational Context." Pp. 95–131 in *Peer Relationships in Child Development*. edited by T. J. Berndt and G. W. Ladd. New York: John Wiley.

Passuth, Patricia. 1987. "Age Hierarchies within Children's Groups." Pp. 185–203 in *Sociological Studies of Child Development* (Vol. 2), edited by P. A. Adler and P. Adler. Greenwich, CT: JAI Press.

Schofield, Janet Ward. 1981. "Complementary and Conflicting Identities: Images and Interaction in an Interracial School." Pp. 53–90 in *The Development of Children's Friendships*. edited by S. Asher and J. Gottman. New York: Cambridge University Press.

Simmel, Georg. 1950. *The Sociology of Georg Simmel*. Translated and edited by K. Wolff. New York: Free Press.

Simon, Robin, Donna Eder, and Cathy Evans. 1992. "The Development of Feeling Norms Underlying Romantic Love Among Adolescent Females." *Social Psychology Quarterly* 55: 29–46.

Thorne, Barrie. 1986. "Girls and Boys Together, But Mostly Apart: Gender Arrangements in Elementary Schools." Pp. 167–84 in *Relationships and Development*, edited by W. Hartup and Z. Rubin. Hillsdale, NJ: Lawrence Erlbaum.

Thorne, Barrie and Zella Luria. 1986. "Sexuality and Gender in Children's Daily Worlds." *Social Problems* 33: 176–90.

Valli, Linda. 1988. "Gender Identity and the Technology of Office Education." Pp. 87–105 in *Class, Race and Gender in American Education*, edited by L. Weis. Albany: State University of New York Press.

Weber, Max. 1946. "Class, Status, and Party." Pp. 180–95 in *From Max Weber*, edited by H. Gerth and C. W. Mills. New York: Oxford University Press.

Wexler, Philip. 1988. "Symbolic Economy of Identity and Denial of Labor: Studies in High School Number 1." Pp. 302–15 in *Class, Race and Gender in American Education*, edited by L. Weis. Albany: State University of New York Press.

Whiting, Beatrice and Carolyn Pope Edwards. 1973. "A Cross-Cultural Analysis of Sex Differences in the Behavior of Children Aged 3 Through 11." *Journal of Social Psychology* 91: 171–88.

Willis, Paul. 1977. *Learning to Labour.* New York: Columbia University Press.

11

We've Come a Long Way, Maybe: College Students' Plans for Work and Family[1]

Joan Z. Spade and Carole A. Reese

As men and women in college today think about their future and plan for work and family, they are exposed to a variety of mixed messages relating to gender. Gender socialization continues to influence young people's identities and stereotypes from the past frame choices (e.g., Angrist & Almquist, 1975; Komarovsky, 1985; Machung, 1989) for students as they move into a society which, at least theoretically, permits equality of opportunities regardless of gender. Yet, participation of women in the work force has increased significantly and attitude surveys indicate that we are much more accepting of women taking active roles in our society (e.g., Mason & Lu, 1988). Nevertheless, women still face considerable occupational segregation (Blau & Ferber, 1985). It is these contradictions between how gender roles are defined for work and family and how individuals respond to a supposedly changing society which we explore in this paper.

Gender is more than simple expectations for us to behave "as a woman or a man." In many ways gender dichotomizes human existence and dominates our lives. Recent assessments of gender socialization focus on the process by which gender differences are constructed either in response to social constraints (Risman, 1981) or embedded in the daily interactions of males and females (West & Zimmerman, 1987). Consequently, gender does not stand alone as an identity issue, but rather becomes part of a complex social process whereby men and women take on masculine and feminine roles and responsibilities.

However, things are changing and the gender socialization of today's college students differs from that of previous generations. Young girls see women working in proportions that make a traditional family in which Mommy stays home with the children while Daddy goes off to work a rarity—only 21% of all families in 1988 (U.S. Department of Commerce, 1989). Furthermore, in terms of their own activities, males and females in college today

From Joan Z. Spade and Carole A. Reese, "We've Come a Long Way, Maybe: College Students' Plans for Work and Family," *Sex Roles*, vol. 24, nos. 5/6 (1991): 309–321. Reprinted by permission of Plenum Publishing Corporation.

have been socialized more equally than previous cohorts. Females had the opportunity to play Little League baseball along with the boys, and their parents are just as likely to have encouraged them to pursue higher education as their brothers.

Yet, there remain embedded in society strongholds of traditional male and female roles, particularly in the family and work. Research suggests that women continue to oversee management of home, children and social activities of the family, while men "help" with household tasks (Hochschild, 1989; Bernardo, Shehan, & Leslie, 1987; Coverman & Sheley, 1986, Berk, 1985). Since discrimination results in women earning less money for equal time at work, men can justify their non-involvement in household chores because they must "provide" for the family. Thus, despite many changes, today's college students have grown up in traditional families where women have had to assume the majority of household tasks, whether they worked outside of the home or not. Consequently, many traditional gender expectations are maintained by the structural inequality in our society.

This paper explores students' plans, attitudes, and orientations in response to these mixed signals. We ask whether college students will incorporate the increased opportunities for women and their more androgenous socialization into their plans for their futures. Are today's college students expecting to have symmetrical roles, with both men and women sharing work and family responsibilities? Or, will students continue to hold traditional gender orientations for family and work, expecting that women will care for hearth and home and men will provide? Although college students today have been exposed to a more liberal socialization, we expect that they will maintain traditional expectations because many structural barriers remain to symmetrical relationships.

Gender and Career Expectations

Various models have been developed to explain the multitude of influence on career decisions, including gender. Although research suggests that social factors (e.g., input from significant others) as well as the ability and personality characteristics of the individual can mediate the influence of gender (Farmer, 1987), there remain significant gender differences in career aspirations and behaviour. Eccles (1987) builds upon these paradigms but emphasizes the subjective value individuals place on different choices. According to Eccles, women's career choices will differ from men's because they place more value on family relationships.

Research findings highlight the influence of gender on future plans. Fiorentine (1988) expected to find a masculinization model in which men and women place increasing emphasis on career goals while downplaying the importance of domestic and nurturing activities. Instead, he found that females are acquiring career goals similar to males but not relinquishing the value they place on domestic and nurturing activities, a model he calls amalgamation. Machung's (1989) interviews with 30 graduating Berkeley seniors, illustrates the contradictions which occur between the changing role of women in society and the traditional roles we still hold for women and men in the family. The women whom Machung interviewed wanted careers, but recognized that their career paths would be interrupted by family and children. The men she spoke to, on the other hand, planned their career with the expectation of having a support system (wives) to care for their homes and families. The women in other studies (e.g., Komarovsky, 1985; Maines & Hardesty, 1987; Angrist & Almquist, 1975) also express a tentativeness about plans for their work life, in which career planning becomes contingency planning or planning around husbands and children. Women in these studies expect to be working most of their adult life, but also expect that their family will take priority over work as needed. Given the responses of the men in Machung's (1989) and Fiorentine's (1988) studies as well as what we know about men's participation in household tasks (e.g., Bernardo *et al.*, 1987; Coverman & Sheley, 1986; Berk, 1985), the expectations of these women may be realistic.

Our research explores how gender influences work and family plans for men and women. We asked undergraduates about their college experience and plans for the future, and use their responses to examine how gender influences their attitudes and orientations toward work and family. As in the research of Machung (1989) and Fiorentine (1988), we include both males and females, but are able to extend their findings using a larger sample and expanded measures. The following questions are explored.

1. How do males and females prepare for their futures in terms of their college experiences? That is, how do males and females perceive their place in the educational structure, achieve, and pursue educational goals?

2. What attitudes and value orientations do males and females hold toward the roles of men and women in work and family as well as their own role in the household?

3. What expectations do males and females have for their future, relative to both work and family?

RESEARCH DESIGN AND METHODOLOGY

Sample

The data used in this study were collected in a 1989 random telephone survey of undergraduates at an independent, nondenominational, coeducational school with an undergraduate population of approximately 4,500 students from primarily upper-middle class families. The college, which was all-male until 1972, is highly competitive and well-known for its engineering program, although the majority of students are in other programs.

A random sample of 320 students (46% female [148] and 54% male [172]) was obtained by using a directory of all currently-registered under-graduates. The telephone interviews were conducted by graduate and undergraduate students in a social science research course. The sample is fairly representative of the college population in terms of distribution by sex and class rank. However, we find the sample overrepresents students in the College of Engineering, while underrepresenting students in the College of Arts and Science, particularly for males. The differences here may be due to the higher proportion of students in the sample who reported having declared a major (84% versus the only 54% who were listed by major in the college data).[2]

RESULTS

Educational Experience

Relative to students' current educational experiences, we examined charac-teristics assessing seriousness toward the educational experience as well as factors related to future work patterns. Measures used are number of math-ematics and science courses taken, perceived ability relative to other students, and grade point average. These items are indicative of the steps stu-dents have taken toward future work roles as well as their status in the college community.

Number of Math and Science Courses. The number of mathematics and sci-ences courses taken is included as a measure of preparation for particular fields of study which have been male dominated. Females are less likely to take as many mathematics and science courses as males (see Table 1). Although the absolute differences are slight, they lend some support to the argument that females are not preparing for jobs which require mathemat-ics and science backgrounds, jobs which are generally male-dominated and characterized by higher salaries.

Grade Point Average. There are also statistically significant differences in grade point average with females outperforming males by .15 points (2.84 vs. 2.69—see Table 1). Yet when students are asked to compare their ability to other students at the college, females rank themselves lower than males. Males are more likely to say they are about average compared to other stu-dents at the college (62.1% vs. 47% for females) and, within this category, males are more likely than females to say they are among the brightest stu-dents at the college (11.6% vs. 4.1% for females). However, a comparison of only those students who considered themselves above average revealed that the grade point average for females is still significantly higher ($M = 3.05$ and 2.86, for females and males respectively, $t(162) = -2.90$, $p < .01$). The rela-tionship between grade point average and gender would not be clarified by

TABLE I

Means and Standard Deviations for Dependent Variables by Gender

	Males		Females		
	M	SD	M	SD	t-test, p
Educational experience					
Number of mathematics courses taken	3.22	1.86	2.61	1.69	t(316) = 3.09, p < .01
Number of science courses taken	2.64	2.43	2.16	1.92	t(313) = 1.99, p < .05
Grade point average	2.69	.50	2.84	.42	t(306) = −2.83, p < .01
Attitudes toward men's and women's roles in work and family					
Combining work and family roles	−.42	1.02	.48	.72	t(304) = −9.09, p < .001
Orientation toward house hold roles	−.22	1.02	.25	.92	t(317) = −4.35, p < .001
Expectations for the future					
Expected age to marry	26.97	2.30	26.09	1.86	t(268) = 3.50, p < .001
Expected age to begin having children	29.13	2.67	28.42	2.23	t(259) = 2.37, p < .05
Hours expect to work at age 30	42.77	11.64	38.19	12.42	t(367) = 3.23, p < .001
Income expected at age 30 (in thousands)	68.15	90.00	57.07	82.41	t(204) = .97, p = .33

controlling for ability of the student since males have slightly higher SAT scores than incoming female students.

Attitudes Toward Men's and Women's Roles in Work and Family

Students in this sample expect to have both work and family in their futures. Respondents overwhelmingly agree that having a good marriage and family was important to them (99%) with no differences by gender. Furthermore, there is almost equal commitment to work, with 94% of the males and 93% of the females expecting that work will be a central part of their lives. However, their orientations toward men's and women's roles in work and family differ.

Combining Work and Family Roles. Attitudes toward work and family is a factor score based upon factor analysis (using a confirmatory model and principal component analysis) for several questions relating to men's and women's future roles in work and family... All factor loadings are at .50 or higher, with an eigenvalue of 2.86 (41% of variance explained). Items loaded on two poles—one representing traditional views in which women's sphere is seen as being in the home and men's in the work place (negative loadings) and the other representing an orientation toward symmetrical relationships in which males and females see their roles as similar and overlapping (positive loadings)....

Using these factor scores, we find that men are significantly more likely to express traditional orientations toward combining work and family roles whereas women are more likely to hold orientations which envision symmetrical role relationships in work and family (see Table 1).

In examining other variables which might contribute to differential orientations toward work and family roles, we again computed multiple regressions including gender along with controls for educational experiences (grade point average, how capable they are compared to others at the college, and year in school), social class (mothers' and fathers' educational backgrounds), and measures of future plans (plans to attend graduate school, whether they expect to work and the earnings they expect to age 30, as well as the age they intend to marry and have their first children). Although the multiple regression is of moderate strength in predicting orientations toward work and family (R Square = .24, $p < .01$), only gender and grade point average are statistically significant predictors. Males and individuals with lower grade point averages are much more likely to hold traditional orientations toward work and family (see Table 2).

Orientation Toward Household Roles. Orientation toward future household roles is a computed factor score based upon questions assessing the importance respondents placed on taking care of the home, visiting and writing relatives, organizing family recreational activities, and caring for preschool children. These items are taken from Nye and Gecas's Family Role Inventory (1976) and ask respondents how important it is for them to do these activities even if someone else was available to do them.[3] Again, computation of the factor scores uses a confirmatory model and principal component analysis. All factor loadings are at .42 or higher, with an eigenvalue of 1.46 (37% of variance explained). A high value on this factor indicates that the individual places high importance on these four family roles, a low value indicates that the individual does not place importance on performing these family roles....

Using the factor scores measuring orientation toward household activities, again we find that men are expressing traditional orientations in view of the fact that they place less importance on assuming household responsibilities. Men are significantly less likely to say that performing these four household roles was of great importance to them (see Table 1).

As we did with attitudes toward combining work and family roles, we ran a multiple regression including gender and controlling for education experiences, social class background, and future plans (see Table 2). The regression predicting importance of household roles is weak (R Square = .13, $p < .05$), however, once again gender is a significant predictor of future roles, along with age at which they want to begin having children.

TABLE 2

Regressions Predicting Orientations Toward Work and Family and Importance of Household Roles

	Orientations toward work and family		Importance of household roles	
	Beta	B	Beta	B
Gender (0 = Male, 1 = Female)	.35[a]	.74	.26[a]	.53
Grade point average	.18[b]	.00	−.02	−.00
Ability compared to others	.16	.24	−.10	−.14
Year in school	.03	.03	.05	.04
Mother's education	.11	.09	−.03	−.02
Father's education	.05	.03	.00	.00
Plans to attend grad school	.14	.13	−.09	−.08
Job plans for age 30 (0 = no occupational plans, 1 = occupation specified)	−.09	−.25	−.00	−.01
Earning expected at age 30	.02	.00	.02	.00
Age intend to marry	.00	.00	.18	.08
Age intend to have 1st child	.08	.03	−.31[b]	−.12
R Square	.24[a]		.13[b]	

[a]Significant at < .01
[b]Significant at < .05

Expectations for the Future

Expectations for the future include items measuring plans for family and work activities. Relative to family plans, respondents were asked when they expect to marry and have children, and if they prefer to have their spouse employed. Expectations for future work roles included measures of the hours, earnings, and job they expect to have at age 30.

Plans for Family and Children. Although females expect to marry and have children at an earlier age than males, the differences are less than a year (see Table 1).

Preference of Spouse to Be Employed. The majority of the sample expect that their spouse will work (66%), as indicated in Table 3, however, males are much more likely than females to respond that they did not want their spouse to work or that they are uncertain about their feelings in this regard (Gamma = .76, p < .001). Equally interesting is that 89% of the women expect their spouse to be employed even if the women make enough to support their families.

Expectations for Employment. Responses to what type of job they expect to have at age 30 are recorded into two categories—undecided versus a stated occupational category. Our findings indicate that males (78%) are only slightly more likely than females (73%) to have a specific career in mind and this difference is not statistically significant (Gamma = .12, p = .36).

In addition, respondents were asked how many hours they expect to be working at age 30. There is a statistically significant difference, with males expecting to be working more hours than females (43 hours per week vs. 38 hours). The difference in number of hours students expect to be working at age 30 indicates that most males expect to be working full-time, while at least some females are considering part-time work.

When asked what they expect to be earning at age 30, males expect to be earning over $10,000 more than females (see Table 1), although the difference is not...significant. These salary figures are somewhat high, considering the fact that at least some of the females expect to be working part time. Although 39% of the students in the sample are training for a career in engineering and 25% for a career in business, both male and female students have unusually high expectations for future salaries.

CONCLUSION

In examining these findings we ask "how far have we come?" The results indicate some signs of change, however, contradictions in expectations for work and family roles, which can lead to potential conflict, also are indicated.

In terms of areas where males and females are becoming more similar, we find that females are performing as well, if not better, than males in college, with a higher mean grade point average. We also find that males and females have equally strong commitments to family and work, with women

TABLE 3
Prefer that Spouse Is Employed by Gender of Respondent

| | | Gender | | |
		Male	Female	
Do you prefer that your spouse be employed if you make enough to support your family?	Yes	47% (80)	89% (130)	66% (210)
	Uncertain	27% (46)	6% (8)	17% (54)
	No	27% (46)	6% (8)	17% (54)
	Total	54% (172)	46% (146)	100% (318)
Gamma .76		Chi square 63.69		$p < .001$

just as decisive as men when specifying a job at age 30 and males equally committed to having a good family life. Furthermore, although women expect to earn less than men, they have similarly high (and perhaps unrealistic) expectations for income as their male peers. Lastly, although males and females differ slightly in the age at which they expect to marry and have children, both are expecting to postpone families until their late 20's, suggesting that both males and females wish to establish themselves in careers prior to beginning a family.

However, we also find many differences between males and females which imply that traditional gender roles may be influencing plans for their futures. Of particular interest is the gender difference in self-perception. Although females have higher grade point averages than their male counterparts in this sample, they are likely to see themselves as less able than their male peers. The difference in self-perception is particularly perplexing, since these female students are enrolled in a very competitive university. These findings support a traditional gender socialization model in which males and all things masculine are valued and females and all things feminine are devalued. Women may be socialized to devalue their own achievements whereas males, despite lower GPA's, would be pressured to overestimate their abilities. Therefore, responses such as these may be appropriate for both young men and women of marriageable age *if* they live in a world where men are expected to be superior (Eccles, 1987).

We also find that men and women have very different expectations for roles in the home and work place. Although both sexes feel that a good marriage and family are important, men do not feel it is important for them to maintain household activities. Furthermore, males hold more traditional values about women combining work and family, and are more likely to want their wives to remain at home. Likewise, women place more importance on household roles, expect to be employed for fewer hours, and are more likely than males to expect their spouse to work.

Inherent in these plans for work and family are some contradictions and potential conflicts, only vaguely acknowledged by the respondents. These students want to have it all—a good family life and a job which is central in their lives, but their plans are somewhat unrealistic because they have not considered the amount of labor it takes to maintain both activities. Although the ability to purchase services may lessen potential pressures in the home (cf., Hertz, 1988), these students are certain to face conflict as the needs of family life force them to reconsider their work plans.

These responses also suggest that the primary burden of combining work and family will fall upon the females. These value orientations and plans do not support plans for symmetrical relationships in which both men and women share household and work responsibilities. The males we sampled see their role in the workplace as most central to their future plans and do not picture themselves in as strong a family role as they see for their wives. As they approach these roles in their lives, the males find it easier to reconcile the demands between work and family by reverting to the traditional definition of father as provider.

The females, however, face conflict in their futures if they continue to maintain and combine strong commitments to work and family because females as well as males view family activities as mainly women's responsibilities. Although the orientation of these women toward work and family may change considerably over the coming years (c.f., Gerson, 1985), at this point they have adopted the amalgamation model proposed by Fiorentine (1988). That is, these women are similar to their male peers in the value they place on work, but they also place high importance on family activities. If, as Eccles (1987) has argued, women hold different value orientations and place more importance on family, then perhaps these women have considered the possible contradictions between adult roles in work and family as they plan for their careers. Perhaps these women recognize that they will either have to be 'superwomen' or give up their careers during the most intensive child-rearing years and have chosen the latter because they value family more than work. There is some evidence which suggest that women have chosen the latter (e.g., the number of hours they plan to work).

Clearly, the value orientation of the men and women we interviewed do not support plans for symmetrical relationships in which both men and women share household and work responsibilities. However, their orientations may be realistic since they face a world in which women are discriminated against in the labor market and where employment policies do not accommodate family needs. Even in Sweden where policies respond to demands of the family, few men take paid leaves to care for children and those who do are likely to be ridiculed by their co-workers (Moen, 1989). Thus, for the future to be significantly different for young men and women today, we will not only have to change the structure of work to allow both men and women to better meet the needs of their families, but we will also have to challenge the definitions of gender ascribed to men and women in their roles as parents and workers. Until then, it appears that, as DiBenedetto and Tittle (1990) have suggested, women's plans for work and family will be interdependent, with preferences for work and children seen as trade-offs, whereas men will view work and family decisions as independent issues.

NOTES

1   We are grateful to Brenda K. Hawks, Sue Curry Jansen, and Judith Lasker for their careful readings of earlier drafts of this paper. Special thanks go to the students in SR377/477 for their major contribution in collecting the data which are analyzed herein.

2   Detailed descriptions of the sample and college population are available from the authors.

3   Although the wording of the questions frees females from the responsibility of having to do the work " if someone else was available to do them" it contains bias in that males will be more likely to assume that someone else will be available to do the task—their wives.

REFERENCES

Angrist, S. S., & Almquist, E. M. (1975). *Careers and contingencies: How college women juggle with gender.* Port Washington, NY: Kennikat Press Corp.

Berk, S. F. (1985). *The gender factory: The apportionment of work in American households.* New York: Plenum Press.

Bernardo, D. H., Shehan, C. L., & Leslie, G. R. (1987). A residue of tradition: Jobs, careers, and spouses' time in housework. *Journal of Marriage and the Family, 49,* 381–390.

Blau, F. D., & Ferber, M. A. (1985). Women in the labor market: The last twenty years, L. Larwood, A. H. Stomberg, & B. A. Gutek (Eds.), *Women and work: An annual review* (Vol. 1). Beverly Hills CA: Sage Publications.

Coverman, S., & Sheley, J. F. (1986). Change in men' s housework and child care time, 1965-1975. *Journal of Marriage and the Family, 48,* 413–422.

DiBenedetto, B., & Tittle, C. K. (1990). Gender and adult roles: Role commitment of women and men in a job-family trade-off context. *Journal of Counseling Psychology, 37,* 41–48.

Eccles, J. S. (1987). Gender roles and women's achievement-related decisions. *Psychology of Women Quarterly, 11,* 35–72.

Farmer, H. S. (1987). A multivariate model for explaining gender differences in career and achievement motivation. *Educational Researcher, 16,* 5–9.

Fiorentine, R. (1988). Increasing similarity in the values and life plans of male and female college students? Evidence and implications. *Sex Roles, 18,* 143–158.

Gerson, K. (1985). *Hard choices: How women decide about work, career, and motherhood.* Berkeley, CA: University of California Press.

Hertz, R. (1988). *More equal than others: Women and men in dual-career marriages.* Berkeley, CA: University of California Press.

Hochschild, A., with Machung, A. (1989). *The second shift: Working parents and the revolution at home.* New York: Viking.

Komarovsky, M. (1985). *Women in college: Shaping new feminine identities.* New York: Basic Books.

Machung, A. (1989). Talking career, thinking jobs: Gender differences in career and family expectations of Berkeley seniors. *Feminist Studies, 15,* 35–58.

Maines, D. R., & Hardesty, M. J. (1987). Temporality and gender: Young adults' career and family plans. *Social Forces, 66,* 102–120.

Mason, K. O. (1975). *Sex-role attitude items and scales from U.S. sample surveys.* National Institute of Mental Health.

Mason, K. O., & Lu, Y. (1988). Attitudes toward women's familial roles: Changes in the United States, 1977-1985. *Gender & Society, 2,* 39–57.

Moen, P. (1989). *Working parents: Transformations in gender roles and public policies in Sweden.* Madison, WI: The University of Wisconsin Press.

Nye, F. I., & Gecas, V. (1976). *Family role analysis: The Washington family role inventory.* Technical Bulletin 82, Washington State University.

Risman, B. J. (1987). Intimate relationships from a microstructural perspective: Men who mother. *Gender & Society, 1,* 6–32.

U.S. Department of Commerce, Bureau of the Census. (1989). *Household and family characteristics.* Current Population Report, Series P20, Report No. 437.

West, C., & Zimmerman, D. H. (1987). Doing gender. *Gender & Society, 1,* 125–151.

CHAPTER THREE

Gender and the Workplace

The focus of this chapter is paid employment. Much of our lives are currently played out within the workplace, but this has not always been the case. In her classic article, Jessie Bernard (Article 12) traces historical changes in the role of the provider in North America. Even though gender expectations since the time of the Industrial Revolution have generally been that men be the primary providers for themselves and their families, Bernard notes that changes have led to the decline of this "good provider" role. The article draws our attention to many of the connecting points between family, work, and gender—themes we return to in subsequent articles and chapters.

D.W. Livingstone and Meg Luxton (Article 13) examine both one's general sense of "gender consciousness" and the specific connection between being a provider and attendant norms of gender. The authors then examine these issues in an empirical study of a blue-collar occupational setting in Hamilton, Ontario. Shifting our focus to the national scene, Nancy Zukewich Ghalam (Article 14), presents data on the proportion and distribution of women in the Canadian labour force.

Numerous authors, such as Spade and Reese in Chapter 2, have noted the reluctance of the business world to accommodate the needs of the family, particularly the needs of the employed mother. The realization that women's family responsibilities frequently have a negative impact upon their career-advancement possibilities lead to the creation of the "mommy track" proposal. According to this proposal, businesses should establish two different career ladders for women. The traditional ladder would evaluate and reward women according to the same criteria as those used for male employees. The "mommy track" ladder would use different evaluative criteria and a temporarily different reward structure for women who wished to lessen their work responsibilities while meeting their family and child care responsibilities. Barbara Ehrenreich and Dierdre English (Article 15) critically examine the "mommy track" and note several direct and indirect problems with this proposal.

Susan Ehrlich Martin (Article 16) focuses on one of the significant problems women face within the workplace, namely, sexual harassment. Martin argues that understanding sexual harassment requires scrutiny of the sociostructural environment in which such "coercive sexuality" is enacted. More specifically, she directs our attention toward the nature of the workplace environment, existing norms for male and female sociosexual behaviour, and sexual harassment as a means of limiting women's mobility both in and out of the workplace.

12

The Good-Provider Role: Its Rise and Fall

Jessie Bernard

I have not searched the literature to determine when the concept of the good provider entered our thinking. The term *provider* entered the English language in 1532, but was not yet male sex typed, as the older term *purveyor* already was in 1442. Webster's second edition defines the good provider as "one who provides, especially, colloq., one who provides food, clothing, etc. for his family; as, he is a good or an adequate provider." More simply, he could be defined as a man whose wife did not have to enter the labor force. The counterpart to the good provider was the housewife. However the term is defined, the role itself delineated relationships within a marriage and family in a way that added to the legal, religious, and other advantages men had over women.

Thus, under the common law, although the husband was legally head of the household and as such had the responsibility of providing for his wife and children, this provision was often made with help from the wife's personal property and earnings, to which he was entitled (Babcock, Freedman, Norton, and Ross, 1975:561):

> He owned his wife's and children's services, and had the sole right to collect wages for their work outside the home. He owned his wife's personal property outright, and had the right to manage and control all of his wife's real property during marriage, which included the right to use or lease property, and to keep any rents and profits from it.

So even when she was the actual provider, the legal recognition was granted the husband. Therefore, whatever the husband's legal responsibilities for support may have been, he was not necessarily a good provider in the way the term came to be understood. The wife may have been performing that role....

The good provider as a specialized male role seems to have arisen in the transition from subsistence to market—especially money—economies that accelerated with the industrial revolution. The good-provider role for males

From Jessie Bernard, "The Good-Provider Role: Its Rise and Fall," *American Psychologist*, vol. 36, no. 1 (January 1981): 1–12. Copyright © 1981 by the American Psychological Association. Reprinted by permission.

emerged in this country roughly, say, from the 1830s, when de Tocqueville was observing it, to the late 1970s, when the 1980 census declared that a male was not automatically to be assumed to be head of the household....

As a psychological and sociological phenomenon, the good-provider role had wide ramifications for all of our thinking about families. It marked a new kind of marriage. It did not have good effects on women. The role deprived them of many chips by placing them in a peculiarly vulnerable position. Because she was not reimbursed for her contribution to the family in either products or services, a wife was stripped to a considerable extent of her access to cash-mediated markets. By discouraging labor force participation, it deprived many women, especially affluent ones, of opportunities to achieve strength and competence. It deterred young women from acquiring productive skills. They dedicated themselves instead to winning a good provider who would "take care of" them....

EXPRESSIVITY AND THE GOOD-PROVIDER ROLE

The new industrial order that produced the good provider changed not so much the division of labor between the sexes as it did the site of the work they engaged in. Only two of the concomitants of this change in work site are selected for comment here, namely, (a) the identification of gender with work site as well as with work itself and (b) the reduction of time for personal interaction and intimacy within the family.

It is not so much the specific kinds of work men and women do—they have always varied from time to time and place to place—but the simple fact that the sexes do different kinds of work, whatever it is, which is in and of itself important. The division of labor by sex means that the work group becomes also a sex group. The very nature of maleness and femaleness becomes embedded in the sexual division of labor. One's sex and one's work are part of one another. One's work defines one's gender.

Any division of labor implies that people doing different kinds of work will occupy different work sites. When the division is based on sex, men and women will necessarily have different work sites.... When the factory took over much of the work formerly done in the house, the separation of work space became especially marked. Not only did the separation of the sexes become spatially extended, but it came to relate work and gender in a special way. The work site as well as the work itself became associated with gender; each sex had its own turf. This sexual "territoriality" has had complicating effects on efforts to change any sexual division of labor. The good provider worked primarily in the outside male world of business and industry. The homemaker worked primarily in the home.

Spatial separation of the sexes not only identifies gender with work site and work but also reduces the amount of time available for spontaneous emotional give-and-take between husbands and wives. When men and women work in an economy based in the home, there are frequent occasions for interaction. (Consider, for example, the suggestive allusions made today to the rise in the birth rate nine months after a blackout.) When men and women are in close proximity, there is always the possibility of reassuring glances, the comfort of simple physical presence. But when the division of labor removes the man from the family dwelling for most of the day, intimate relationships become less feasible. De Tocqueville was one of the first to call our attention to this. In 1840 he noted (p. 212) that

> *almost all men in democracies are engaged in public or professional life, and...the limited extent of common incomes obliges a wife to confine herself to the house, in order to watch in person and very closely over the details of domestic economy. All these distinct and compulsory occupations are so many natural barriers, which, by keeping the two sexes asunder, render the solicitations of the one less frequent and less ardent—the resistance of the other more easy.*

Not directly related to the spatial constraints on emotional expression by men, but nevertheless a concomitant of the new industrial order with the same effect, was the enormous drive for achievement, for success, for "making it" that escalated the provider role into the good-provider role....As a result of this male concentration on jobs and careers, much abnegation and "a constant sacrifice of her pleasures to her duties" (de Tocqueville, 1840:212) were demanded of the American woman. The good-provider role, as it came to be shaped by his ambience, was thus restricted in what it was called upon to provide. Emotional expressivity was not included in the role. One of the things a parent might say about a man to persuade a daughter to marry him, or a daughter might say to explain to her parents why she wanted to, was not that he was a gentle, loving, or tender man but that he was a good provider. He might have many other qualities, good or bad, but if a man was a good provider, everything else was either gravy or the price one had to pay for a good provider.

Lack of expressivity did not imply neglect of the family. The good provider was a "family man." He set a good table, provided a decent home, paid the mortgage, bought the shoes, and kept his children warmly clothed. He might, with the help of the children's part-time jobs, have been able to finance their educations through high school and sometimes, even college....The good provider made a decent contribution to the church.... Loving attention and emotional involvement in the family were not part of a woman's implicit bargain with the good provider.

By the time de Tocqueville published his observations in 1840, the general outlines of the good-provider role had taken shape. It called for a hardworking man who spent most of his time at his work. In the traditional conception of the role, a man's chief responsibility is his job, so that "by definition any family behaviors must be subordinate to it in terms of significance and [the job] has priority in the event of a clash" (Scanzoni, 1975:38). This was the classic form of the good-provider role, which remained a powerful component of our societal structure until well into the present century.

COSTS AND REWARDS OF THE GOOD-PROVIDER ROLE FOR MEN

There were both costs and rewards for those men attached to the good-provider role. The most serious cost was perhaps the identification of maleness not only with the work site but especially with success in the role. "The American male looks to his breadwinning role to confirm his manliness" (Brenton, 1966:194) [1] To be a man one had to be not only a provider but a *good* provider. Success in the good-provider role came in time to define masculinity itself. The good provider had to achieve, to win, to succeed, to dominate. He was a bread*winner*. He had to show "strength, cunning, inventiveness, endurance—a whole range of traits henceforth defined as exclusively 'masculine' " (Demos, 1974:436). Men were judged as men by the level of living they provided. They were judged by the myth "that endows a money-making man with sexiness and virility, and is based on man's dominance, strength, and ability to provide for and care for 'his' woman" (Gould, 1974:97). The good provider became a player in the male competitive macho game. What one man provided for his family in the way of luxury and display had to be equaled or topped by what another could provide. Families became display cases for the success of a good provider.

The psychic costs could be high (Brenton, 1966:194):

> *By depending so heavily on his breadwinning role to validate his sense of himself as a man, instead of also letting his roles as husband, father, and citizen of the community count as validating sources, the American male treads on psychically dangerous ground. It's always dangerous to put all of one's psychic eggs into one basket.*

The good-provider role not only put all of a man's gender-identifying eggs into one psychic basket, but it also put all the family-providing eggs into one basket. One individual became responsible for the support of the whole family. Countless stories portrayed the humiliation families underwent to keep wives and especially mothers out of the labor force, a circumstance that would admit to the world the male head's failure in the good-provider role. If a married woman had to enter the labor force at all, that was bad enough. If she made a good salary, however, she was "co-opting the man's passport to masculinity" (Gould, 1974:98) and he was effectively castrated. A wife's earning capacity diminished a man's position as head of the household (Gould, 1974:99).

Failure in the role of good provider, which employment of wives evidenced, could produce deep frustration. As Komarovsky (1940:20) explains, this is "because in his own estimation he is failing to fulfill what is the central duty of his life, the very touchstone of his manhood—the role of family provider."

But just as there was punishment for failure in the good-provider role, so also were there rewards for successful performance. A man "derived strength from his role as provider" (Komarovsky, 1940:205). He achieved a good deal of satisfaction from his ability to support his family. It won kudos. Being a good provider led to status in both the family and the community. Within the family it gave him the power of the purse and the right to decide about expenditures, standards of living, and what constituted good providing. "Every purchase of the family—the radio, his wife's new hat, the children's skates, the meals set before him—were all symbols of their dependence upon him" (Komarovsky, 1940:74–75). Such dependence gave him a "profound sense of stability" (p. 74). It was a strong counterpoise vis-à-vis a wife with a stronger personality. "Whether he had considerable authority within the family and was recognized as its head, or whether the wife's stronger personality...dominated the family, he nevertheless derived strength from his role as a provider" (Komarovsky, 1940:75). As recently as 1975, in a sample of 3,100 husbands and wives in 10 cities, Scanzoni found that despite increasing egalitarian norms, the good-provider still had "considerable power in ultimate decision-making" and as "unique provider" had the right "to organize his life and the lives of other family members around his occupation" (p. 39).

A man who was successful in the good-provider role might be freed from other obligations to the family. But the flip side of this dispensation was that he could not make up for poor performance by excellence in other family roles. Since everything depended on his success as a provider, everything was at stake. The good provider played an all-or-nothing game.

DIFFERENT WAYS OF PERFORMING THE GOOD-PROVIDER ROLE

Although the legal specifications for the role were laid out in the common law, in legislation, in legal precedents, in court decisions, and, most importantly, in custom and convention, in real-life situations the social and social-psychological specifications were set by the husband or, perhaps more accurately, by the community, alias the Joneses, and there were many ways to perform it.

Some men resented the burdens the role forced them to bear. A man could easily vent such resentment toward his family by keeping complete control over all expenditures, dispensing the money for household maintenance, and complaining about bills as though it were his wife's fault that shoes cost so much. He could, in effect, punish his family for his having to perform the role. Since the money he earned belonged to him—was "his"—he could do with it what he pleased. Through extreme parsimony he could dole out his money in a mean, humiliating way, forcing his wife to come begging for pennies. By his reluctance and resentment he could make his family pay emotionally for the provisioning he supplied.

At the other extreme were the highly competitive men who were so involved in outdoing the Joneses that the fur coat became more important than the affectionate hug. They "bought off" their families. They sometimes succeeded so well in their extravagance that they sacrificed the family they were presumably providing for to the achievements that made it possible (Keniston, 1965).[2]

The Depression of the 1930s revealed in harsh detail what the loss of the role could mean both to the good provider and to his family, not only in the loss of income itself—which could be supplied by welfare agencies or even by other family members, including wives—but also and especially in the loss of face.

The Great Depression did not mark the demise of the good-provider role. But it did teach us what a slender thread the family hung on. It stimulated a whole array of programs designed to strengthen that thread, to ensure that it would never again be similarly threatened. Unemployment insurance was incorporated into the Social Security Act of 1935, for example, and a Full Employment Act was passed in 1946. But there proved to be many other ways in which the good-provider role could be subverted.

ROLE REJECTORS AND ROLE OVERPERFORMERS

Recent research in psychology, anthropology, and sociology has familiarized us with the tremendous power of roles. But we also know that one of the fundamental principles of role behavior is that conformity to role norms is not universal. Not everyone lives up to the specifications of roles, either in the psychological or in the sociological definition of the concept. Two extremes have attracted research attention: (a) the men who could not live up to the norms of the good-provider role or did not want to, at one extreme, and (b) the men who overperformed the role, at the other. For the wide range in between, from blue-collar workers to professionals, there was fairly consistent acceptance of the role, however well or poorly, however grumblingly or willingly, performed....

Poorly or well performed, the good-provider role lingered on. World War II initiated a challenge, this time in the form of attracting more and more married women into the labor force, but the challenge was papered over in the 1950s with an "age of togetherness" that all but apotheosized the good provider, his house in the suburbs, his homebody wife, and his third, fourth, even fifth, child. As late as the 1960s most housewives (87%) still saw bread-winning as their husband's primary role (Lopata, 1971:91).[3]...

INTRINSIC CONFLICT IN THE GOOD-PROVIDER ROLE

Since the good-provider role involved both family and work roles, most people believed that there was no incompatibility between them or at least that there should not be. But in the 1960s and 1970s evidence began to mount that maybe something was amiss.

De Tocqueville had documented the implicit conflict in the American businessman's devotion to his work at the expense of his family in the early years of the 19th century; the Industrial Workers of the World had proclaimed that the good-provider role which tied a man to his family was an impediment to the great revolution at the beginning of the 20th century; Fiedler (1962) had noted that throughout our history, in the male fantasy world, there was freedom from the responsibilities of this role; about 50 years ago Freud (1930/1958: 50–51) had analyzed the intrinsic conflict between the demands of women and the family on one side and the demands of men's work on the other:

> *Women represent the interests of the family and sexual life; the work of civilization has become more and more men's business; it confronts them with ever harder tasks, compels them to sublimations of instinct which women are not easily able to achieve. Since man has not an unlimited amount of mental energy at his disposal, he must accomplish his tasks by distributing his libido to the best advantage. What he employs for cultural [occupational] purposes he withdraws to a great extent from women, and his sexual life; his constant association with men and his dependence on his relations with them even estrange him from his duties as husband and father. Woman finds herself thus forced into the background by the claims of culture [work] and she adapts an inimical attitude towards it.*

In the last two decades, researchers have been raising questions relevant to Freud's statement of the problem. They have been asking people about the relative satisfactions they derive from these conflicting values—family and work. Among the earliest studies comparing family-work values was a Gallup poll in 1940 in which both men and women chose a happy home over an interesting job or wealth as a major life value. Since then there have been a number of such polls, and a considerable body of results has now accumulated. Pleck and Lang (1979) and Hesselbart (Note 1) have summarized the findings of these surveys. All agree that there is a clear bias in the direction of the family. Pleck and Lang conclude that "men's family role is far more psychologically significant to them than is their work role" (p. 29), and Hesselbart—however critical she is of the studies she summarizes—believes they should not be dismissed lightly and concludes that they certainly "challenge the idea that family is a 'secondary' valued role" (p. 14).[4] Douvan

(Note 2) also found in a 1976 replication of a 1957 survey that family values retained priority over work: "Family roles almost uniformly rate higher in value production than the job role does" (p. 16).[5]

The very fact that researchers have asked such questions is itself interesting. Somehow or other both the researchers and the informants seem to be saying that all this complaining about the male neglect of the family, about the lack of family involvement by men, just is not warranted. Neither de Tocqueville nor Freud was right. Men do value family life more than they value their work. They do derive their major life satisfactions from their families rather than from their work.

It may well be true that men derive the greatest satisfaction from their family roles, but this does not necessarily mean they are willing to pay for this benefit. In any event, great attitudinal changes took place in the 1960s and 1970s.

Douvan (Note 2), on the basis of surveys in 1957 and 1976, found, for example, a considerable increase in the proportion of both men and women who found marriage and parenthood burdensome and restrictive. Almost three fifths (57%) of both married men and married women in 1976 saw marriage as "all burdens and restrictions," as compared with only 42% and 47%, respectively, in 1957. And almost half (45%) also viewed children as "all burdens and restrictions" in 1976, as compared with only 28% and 33% for married men and married women, respectively, in 1957. The proportion of working men with a positive attitude toward marriage dropped drastically over this period, from 68% to 39%. Working women, who made up a fairly small number of all married women in 1957, hardly changed attitudes at all, dropping only from 43% to 42%. The proportion of working men who found marriage and children burdensome and restrictive more than doubled, from 25% to 56% and from 25% to 58%, respectively. Although some of these changes reflected greater willingness in 1976 than in 1957 to admit negative attitudes toward marriage and parenthood—itself significant—profound changes were clearly in process. More and more men and women were experiencing disaffection with family life.[6]

"ALL BURDENS AND RESTRICTIONS"

Apparently, the benefits of the good-provider role were greater than the costs for most men. Despite the legend of the flight of the America male (Fiedler, 1962), despite the defectors and dropouts, despite the tavern habitué's "ball and chain" cliché, men seemed to know that the good-provider role, if they could succeed in it, was good for them. But Douvan's (Note 2) findings suggest that recently their complaints have become serious, bone-deep. The family they have been providing for is not the same family it was in the past.

Smith (1979) calls the great trek of married women into the labor force a subtle revolution—revolutionary not in the sense of one class overthrowing a status quo and substituting its own regime, but revolutionary in its impact on both the family and the work roles of men and women. It diluted the prerogatives of the good-provider role. It increased the demands made on the good provider, especially in the form of more emotional investment in the family, more sharing of household responsibilities. The role became even more burdensome.

However men may now feel about the burdens and restrictions imposed on them by the good-provider role, most have, at least ostensibly, accepted them. The tramp and the bum had "voted with their feet" against the role; the hobo or Wobbly had rejected it on the basis of a revolutionary ideology that saw it as enslaving men to the corporation; tavern humor had glossed the resentment habitués felt against its demands. Now the "burdens-and-restrictions" motif has surfaced both in research reports and, more blatantly, in the male liberation movement. From time to time it has also appeared in the clinicians' notes.

Sometimes the resentment of the good provider takes the form of simply wanting more appreciation for the life-style he provides. All he does for his family seems to be taken for granted. Thus, for example, Goldberg (1976:124), a psychiatrist, recounts the case of a successful businessman:

> *He's feeling a deepening sense of bitterness and frustration about his wife and family. He doesn't feel appreciated. It angers him the way they seem to take the things his earnings purchase for granted. They've come to expect it as their due. It particularly enrages him when his children put him down for his "materialistic middle-class trip." He'd like to tell them to get someone else to support them but he holds himself back....*

Sometimes there is even more than expressed resentment; there is an actual repudiation of the role. In the past, only a few men like the hobo or Wobbly were likely to give up. Today, Goldberg (1976:184) believes, more are ready to renounce the role, not on theoretical revolutionary grounds, however, but on purely selfish ones:

> *Male growth will stem from openly avowed, unashamed, self-oriented motivations....Guilt-oriented "should" behavior will be rejected because it is always at the price of a hidden buildup of resentment and frustration and alienation from others and is, therefore, counterproductive.*

The disaffection of the good provider is directed to both sides of his role. With respect to work, Lefkowitz (1979) has described men among whom the good-provider role is neither being completely rejected nor repudiated, but diluted. These men began their working lives in the conventional style, hopeful and ambitious. They found a job, married, raised a family, and "achieved a measure of economic security and earned the respect of...colleagues and neighbors" (Lefkowitz, 1979:31). In brief, they successfully performed the good-provider role. But unlike their historical predecessors, they in time became disillusioned with their jobs—not jobs on assembly lines, not jobs usually characterized as alienating, but fairly prestigious jobs such as aeronautics engineer and government economist. They daydreamed about other interests. "The common theme which surfaced again and again in their histories, was the need to find a new social connection—to reassert control over their lives, to gain some sense of freedom" (Lefkowitz, 1979:31). These men felt "entitled to freedom and independence." Middle-class, educated, self-assured, articulate, and for the most part white, they knew they could talk themselves into a job if they had to. Most of them did not want to desert their families. Indeed, most of them "wanted to rejoin the intimate circle they felt they had neglected in their years of work" (p. 31).

Though some of the men Lefkowitz studied sought closer ties with their families, in the case of those studied by Sarason (1977), a psychologist, career changes involved lower income and had a negative impact on families. Sarason's subjects were also men in high-level professions, the very men least likely to find marriage and parenthood burdensome and restrictive. Still, since career change often involved a reduction in pay, some wives were unwilling to accept it, with the result that the marriage deteriorated (p. 178). Sometimes it looked like a no-win game. The husband's earlier career brought him feelings of emptiness and alienation, but it also brought financial rewards for the family. Greater work satisfaction for him in lower paying work meant reduced satisfaction with life-style. These findings lead Sarason to raise a number of points with respect to the good-provider role. "How much," he asks, "does an individual or a family need in order to maintain a satisfactory existence? Is an individual being responsible to himself or his family if he provides them with little more than the bare essentials of living?" (p. 178). These are questions about the good-provider role that few men raised in the past.

Lefkowitz (1979) wonders how his downwardly mobile men lived when they left their jobs. "They put together a basic economic package which consisted of government assistance, contributions from family members who had not worked before and some bartering of goods and services" (p. 31). Especially interesting in this list of income sources are the "contributions from family members who had not worked before" (p. 31). Surely not mothers and sisters. Who, of course, but wives?...

WOMEN AND THE PROVIDER ROLE

The assault on the good-provider role in the Depression was traumatic. But a modified version began to appear in the 1970s as a single income became inadequate for more and more families. Husbands have remained the major providers, but in an increasing number of cases the wife has begun to share this role. Thus, the proportion of married women aged 15 to 54 (living with their husbands) in the labor force more than doubled between 1950 and 1978, from 25.2% to 55.4%. The proportion for 1990 is estimated to reach 66.7% (Smith, 1979:14). Fewer women are now full-time housewives.

For some men the relief from the strain of sole responsibility for the provider role has been welcome. But for others the feeling of degradation resembles the feelings reported 40 years earlier in the Great Depression. It is not that they are no longer providing for the family but that the role-sharing wife now feels justified in making demands on them. The good-provider role with all its prerogatives and perquisites has undergone profound changes. It will never be the same again.[7] Its death knell was sounded when, as noted above, the 1980 census no longer automatically assumed that the male member of the household was its head.

THE CURRENT SCENE

Among the new demands being made on the good-provider role, two deserve special consideration, namely, (a) more intimacy, expressivity, and nurturance—specifications never included in it as it originally took shape—and (b) more sharing of household responsibility and child care.

As the pampered wife in an affluent household came often to be an economic parasite, so also the good provider was often, in a way, a kind of emotional parasite. Implicit in the definition of the role was that he provided goods and material things. Tender loving care was not one of the requirements. Emotional ministrations from the family were his right; providing them was not a corresponding obligation. Therefore, as de Tocqueville had already noted by 1840, women suffered a kind of emotional deprivation labeled by Robert Weiss "relational deficit" (cited in Bernard, 1976). Only recently has this male rejection of emotional expression come to be challenged. Today, even blue-collar women are imposing "a host of new role expectations upon their husbands or lovers....A new role set asks the blue collar male to strive for...deep-coursing intimacy" (Shostak, Note 4, 75). It was not only vis-à-vis his family that the good provider was lacking in expressivity. This lack was built into the whole male role script. Today not only women but also men are beginning to protest the repudiation of expressivity prescribed in male roles (David and Brannon, 1976; Farrell, 1974; Fasteau, 1974; Pleck and Sawyer, 1974).

Is there any relationship between the "imposing" on men of "deep-coursing intimacy" by women on one side and the increasing proportion of men who find marriage burdensome and restrictive on the other? Are men seeing the new emotional involvements being asked of them as "all burdens and restrictions?" Are they responding to the new involvements under duress? Are they feeling oppressed by them? Fearful of them?

From the standpoint of high-level pure-science research there may be something bizarre, if not even slightly absurd, in the growing corpus of serious research on how much or how little husbands of employed wives contribute to household chores and child care. Yet it is serious enough that all over the industrialized world such research is going on. Time studies in a dozen countries—communist as well as capitalist—trace the slow and bungling process by which marriage accommodates to changing conditions and by which women struggle to mold the changing conditions on their behalf. For everywhere the same picture shows up in the research: an image of women sharing the provider role and at the same time retaining responsibility for the household. Until recently such a topic would have been judged unworthy of serious attention. It was a subject that might be worth a good laugh, for instance, as when an all-thumbs man in a cartoon burns the potatoes or finds himself bumbling awkwardly over a diaper, demonstrating his—proud—male ineptness at such female work. But it is no longer funny.

The "politics of housework" (Mainardi, 1970) proves to be more profound than originally believed. It has to do not only with tasks but also with gender—and perhaps more with the site of the tasks than with their intrinsic nature. A man can cook magnificently if he does it on a hunting or fishing trip; he can wield a skillful needle if he does it mending a tent or a fishing net; he can even feed and clean a toddler on a camping trip. Few of the skills of the homemaker are beyond his reach so long as they are practiced in a suitably male environment. It is not only women's work in and of itself that is degrading but any work on female turf. It may be true, as Brenton (1966:211) says, that "the secure man can wash a dish, diaper a baby, and throw the dirty clothes into the washing machine—or do anything else women used to do exclusively—without thinking twice about it," but not all men are that secure. To a great many men such chores are demasculinizing. The apron is shameful on a man in the kitchen; it is all right at the carpenter's bench.

The male world may look upon the man who shares household responsibilities as, in effect, a scab....We are fairly familiar with the trauma associated with the invasion by women of the male work turf, the hazing women can be subjected to, and the male resentment of admitting them except into their own segregated areas. The corresponding entrance of men into the traditional turf of women—the kitchen or the nursery—has analogous but not identical concomitants.

Pleck and Lang (1979:1) tell us that men are now beginning to change in the direction of greater involvement in family life. "Men's family behavior is beginning to change, becoming increasingly congruent with the long-standing psychological significance of the family in their lives." They measure this greater involvement by way of the help they offer with homemaking chores. Scanzoni (1975:38), on the basis of a survey of over 3,000 husbands and wives, concludes that at least in households in which wives are in the labor force, there is the "possibility of a different pattern in which responsibility for households would unequivocally fall equally on husbands as well as wives." A brave new world indeed. Still, when we look at the reality around us, the pace seems intolerably slow. The responsibilities of the old good-provider role have attenuated far faster than have its prerogatives and privileges.

A considerable amount of thought has been devoted to studying the effects of the large influx of women into the work force. An equally interesting question is what the effect will be if a large number of men actually do increase their participation in the family and the household. Will men find the apron shameful? What if we were to ask fathers to alternate with mothers in being in the home when youngsters come home from school? Would fighting adolescent drug abuse be more successful if fathers and mothers were equally engaged in it? If the school could confer with fathers as often as with mothers? If the father accompanied children when they went shopping for clothes? If fathers spent as much time with children as do mothers?

Even as husbands, let alone as fathers, the new pattern is not without trauma. Hall and Hall (1979), in their study of two-career couples, report that the most serious fights among such couples occur not in the bedroom, but in the kitchen, between couples who profess a commitment to equality but who find actually implementing it difficult....The stresses involved in reworking roles may have an impact on health. A study of engineers and accountants finds poorer health among those with employed wives than among those with nonemployed wives (Burke and Wier, 1976). The processes involved in role change have been compared with those involved in deprogramming a cult member. Are they part of the increasing sense of marriage and parenthood as "all burdens and restrictions?"

The demise of the good-provider role also calls for consideration of other questions: What does the demotion of the good provider to the status of senior provider or even mere coprovider do to him? To marriage? To gender identity? What does expanding the role of housewife to that of junior provider or even coprovider do to her? To marriage? To gender identity? Much will of course depend on the social and psychological ambience in which changes take place....

NOTES

1   Rainwater and Yancey (1967), critiquing current welfare policies, note that they "have robbed men of their manhood, women of their husbands, and children of their fathers. To create a stable monogamous family we need to provide men with the opportunity to be men, and that involves enabling them to perform occupationally" (p. 235).

2   Several years ago I presented a critique of what I called "extreme sex role specialization," including "work-intoxicated fathers." I noted that making success in the

provider role the only test for real manliness was putting a lot of eggs into one basket. At both the blue-collar and the managerial levels, it was dysfunctional for families. I referred to the several attempts being made even then to correct the excesses of extreme sex role specialization: rural and urban communes, leaving jobs to take up small-scale enterprises that allowed more contact with families, and a rebellion against overtime in industry (Bernard, 1975:217–39).

3   Although all the women in Lopata's (1971) sample saw breadwinning as important, fewer employed women (54%) than either nonemployed urban (63%) or suburban (64%) women assigned it first place (p. 91).

4   Pleck and Lang (1979) found only one serious study contracting their own conclusions: "Using data from the 1973 NORC [National Opinion Research Centre] General Social Survey, Harry analyzed the bivariate relationship of job and family satisfaction to life happiness in men classified by family life cycle stage. In three of the five groups of husbands...job satisfaction had a stronger association than family satisfaction to life happiness" (pp: 5–6).

5   In 1978, a Yankelovich survey on "The New Work Psychology" suggested that leisure is now becoming a strict competitor for both family and work as a source of life satisfactions: "Family and work have grown less important than leisure; a majority of 60 percent say that although they enjoy their work, it is not their major source of satisfaction" (p. 46). A 1977 survey of Swedish men aged 18 to 35 found that the proportion saying the family was the main source of meaning in their lives declined from 45% in 1955 to 41% in 1977; the proportion indicating work as the main source of satisfaction dropped from 33% to 17%. The earlier tendency for men to identify themselves through their work is less marked these days. In the new value system, the individual says, in effect, "I am more than my role. I am myself" (Yankelovich, 1978). Is the increasing concern with leisure a way to escape the dissatisfaction with both the alienating relations found on the work site and the demands for increased involvement with the family?

6   Men seem to be having problems with both work and family roles: Veroff..., for example, reports an increased "sense of dissatisfaction with the social relations in the work setting" and a "dissatisfaction with the affiliative nature of work" (p. 47). This dissatisfaction may be one of the factors that leads men to seek affiliative-need satisfaction in marriage, just as in the 19th century they looked to the home as shelter from the jungle of the outside world.

7   Among the indices of the waning of the good-provider role are the increasing number of married women in the labor force; the growth in the number of female-headed families; the growing trend toward egalitarian norms in marriage; the need for two earners in so many middle-class families; and the recognition of these trends in the abandonment of the identification of head of household as a male.

REFERENCES

Babcock, B., A. E. Freedman, E. H. Norton, and S. C. Ross. 1975. *Sex Discrimination and the Law: Causes and Remedies.* Boston: Little, Brown.

Bernard, J. 1975. *Women, Wives, Mothers.* Chicago: Aldine.

————. 1976. "Homosociality and Female Depression." *Journal of Social Issues* 32: 207–24.

Boulding, E. 1976. "Familial Constraints on Women's Work Roles." *Signs* 1: 95–118.

Brenton, M. 1966. *The American Male.* New York: Coward-McCann.

Burke, R., and T. Weir. 1976. "Relationship of Wives' Employment Status to Husband, Wife and Pair Satisfaction and Performance." *Journal of Marriage and the Family,* 38: 279–87.

David, D. S., and R. Brannon, eds. 1976. *The Forty-Nine Percent Majority: The Male Sex Role.* Reading, Mass.: Addison-Wesley.

Demos, J. 1974. "The American Family in Past Time." *American Scholar* 43: 422–46.

Farrell, W. 1974. *The Liberated Man.* New York: Random House.

Fasteau, M. F. 1974. *The Male Machine.* New York: McGraw-Hill.

Fiedler, L. 1962. *Love and Death in the American Novel.* New York: Meredith.

Foner, P. S. 1979. *Women and the American Labor Movement.* New York: Free Press.

Freud, S. [1939] 1958. *Civilization and Its Discontents.* New York: Doubleday, Anchor Books.

Goldberg, H. 1976. *The Hazards of Being Male.* New York: New American Library.

Gould, R. E. 1974. "Measuring Masculinity by the Size of a Paycheck." In *Men and Masculinity,* ed. J. E. Pleck and J. Sawyer. Englewood Cliffs, N.J.: Prentice-Hall.

Hall, D., and F. Hall. 1979. *The Two-Career Couple.* Reading, Mass.: Addison-Wesley.

Jones, C. A. 1976. *A Review of Child Support Payment Performance.* Washington, D.C.: Urban Institute.

Keniston, K. 1965. *The Uncommitted: Alienated Youth in American Society.* New York: Harcourt, Brace & World.

Komarovsky, M. 1940. *The Unemployed Man and His Family.* New York: Dryden Press.

Lefkowitz, B. 1979. "Life without Work." *Newsweek,* 14 May, 31.

Lein, L. 1979. "Responsibility in the Allocation of Tasks." *Family Coordinator* 28: 489–96.

Liebow, E. 1966. *Tally's Corner.* Boston: Little, Brown.

Lopata, H. 1971. *Occupation Housewife.* New York: Oxford University Press.

Mainardi, P. 1970. "The Politics of Housework." In *Sisterhood is Powerful,* ed. R. Morgan. New York: Random House, Vintage Books.

Pleck, J. H., and L. Lang. 1979. "Men's Family Work: Three Perspectives and Some New Data." *Family Coordinator* 28: 481–88.

Pleck, J. H., and J. Sawyer, eds.: 1974. *Men and Masculinity.* Englewood Cliffs, N.J.: Prentice-Hall.

Rainwater, L., and W. L. Yancey. 1967. *The Moynihan Report and the Politics of Controversy.* Cambridge, Mass.: MIT Press.

Sarason, S. B. 1977. *Work, Aging, and Social Change.* New York: Free Press.

Scanzoni, J. H. 1975. *Sex Roles, Life Styles, and Childbearing: Changing Patterns in Marriage and the Family.* New York: Free Press.

————. 1979. "An Historical Perspective on Husband-Wife Bargaining Power and Marital Dissolution." In *Divorce and Separation in America*, ed. G. Levinger and O. Moles. New York: Basic Books.

Smith, R. E., ed. 1979. *The Subtle Revolution*. Washington, D.C.: Urban Institute.

Smuts, R. W. 1959. *Women and Work in America*. New York: Columbia University Press.

Snyder, L. 1979. "The Deserting, Non-Supporting Father: Scapegoat of Family Non-Policy." *Family Coordinator* 38: 594–98.

Tocqueville, A. de. 1840. *Democracy in America*. New York: J. & H. G. Langley.

Warner, W. L., and J. O. Ableggglen. 1955. *Big Business Leaders in America*. New York: Harper.

Yankelovich, D. 1978. "The New Psychological Contracts at Work." *Psychology Today*, May, 46–47, 49–50.

Zborowski, M., and E. Herzog. 1952. *Life Is with People*. New York: Schocken Books.

13

Gender Consciousness at Work: Modification of the Male Breadwinner Norm Among Steelworkers and Their Spouses

D.W. Livingstone and Meg Luxton

INTRODUCTION

The contemporary women's movement has seriously challenged both the naturalization of gender differences and the assumed necessity of the subordination of women to men. The women's movement and the lesbian and gay liberation movements have also directly challenged traditional distinctions between the categories of 'man'/'woman' and 'masculine'/'feminine'. As a result, the social construction of gender has become an increasingly visible and problematic process....

But one issue which scholars have only begun to investigate is the nature and content of 'gender consciousness'. Since the re-emergence of the women's movement, gender consciousness is increasingly revealed in common-sense, everyday expressions such as 'she's a real women's libber...'; 'that man is in the stone age as far as his attitudes to women are concerned'; 'she doesn't laugh at the guys' jokes anymore—she says they're sexist'. Such comments demonstrate that people rank gradations of attitudes, negotiate or confront differences in gender consciousness, and notice changes over time in the gender consciousness of individuals or groups. At present, in the social sciences, this concept is poorly articulated, and is used differently in various scholarly traditions. For the most part, studies of gender consciousness have been limited to discussions of women and much work tends, incorrectly, to equate gender and women (Porter, 1983; Gurin, 1985; Maroney and Luxton, 1987a). Very few studies have been done of men's gender consciousness (Tolson, 1977; Willis, 1979; Cockburn, 1983; Buchbinder, 1987; Kaufman, 1987) and even fewer on the interactions of the gender consciousness of women and men. For the most part, what exists at present is a working

From D.W. Livingstone and Meg Luxton, "Gender Consciousness at Work: Modification of the Male Breadwinner Norm Among Steelworkers and Their Spouses," *Canadian Review of Sociology and Anthropology*, vol. 26 (1989): 240–275. Reprinted by permission.

assumption that there is such a thing as gender consciousness and that it describes significant attitudes and behavioral dispositions on the part of (usually) women (Gurin, 1985)....

CONCEPTUALIZING GENDER CONSCIOUSNESS

Many analysts have identified three main tendencies within the contemporary women's movement as liberal, radical, and socialist feminism (e.g., Jaggar, 1983). While these perspectives often overlap, influence each other and are constantly evolving, they represent distinct theoretical orientations with particular political implications. These theoretical perspectives have placed different emphases on issues of gender consciousness.

Liberal feminism has emphasized socialization, particularly the way 'sex stereotyping' produces and transmits 'sex roles'. This perspective has been primarily concerned with sex role or more recently, 'gender identity' based on shared perceptions of normal female/male attributes.[1] Radical feminism has generally tended to take the biological sex dichotomy of women and men as a set of established categories, focussing on the power relations between them in terms of 'sexual politics' and 'patriarchy'. This approach has stressed the importance of consciousness raising and women's feminist consciousness, based on recognition of and opposition to the subordination of women. Socialist feminism, also recognizing the political power of consciousness raising and the importance of feminist consciousness for political action, has traced the continuing construction of both gender identity and feminist consciousness through the power relations of women and men in specific spheres of social practice and has paid particular attention to working class women. Thus, at present in the literature related to gender consciousness there are three main concepts—sex role identity and attitudes, feminist consciousness, and gender consciousness per se.

Sex Role Identity and Attitudes Research

Sex role socialization theories have focussed on the processes through which female and male personalities are created. This approach may be traced back to the psychoanalytic revolution, but received its major impetus in social science through the functionalist paradigm that prevailed in academic social science in the immediate post-World War II period (Komarovsky, 1946; Mead, 1950; Parsons and Bales, 1953). Its resurgence over the past 15 years has been preoccupied with documenting dominant perceptions of the social meaning of the categories of 'women' and 'men'. Some of the principal cumulative findings with regard to personal sex identities are: 1/ that popular notions of 'women' and 'men' are not simply bi-polar but multi-dimensional, with some overlapping personal attributes (Spence and Helmreich, 1978; Bem, 1981); 2/ that images of men remain centred around a

quite sharply defined concept of heterosexual masculinity in terms of instrumental competence and power-dominance, while images of women have
become somewhat more diffuse and flexible—including loosely-related
dimensions of nurturing and expressiveness, and submissiveness and emotional vulnerability, but also with more specific female subtypes (e.g.,
'housewife,' 'woman athlete,' 'sexy woman,' 'businesswoman') commonly
perceived to have diverse combinations of personal attributes (Ruch, 1984;
Thompson et al., 1985; Deux et al., 1985); but 3/ that, in descriptive terms of
the fundamental dimensions of instrumentality/expressivity and power/
submissiveness, sex role stereotypes have changed very little over the past
generation (Werner and La Russa, 1985; Gibbs, 1985).

Sex role researchers have also surveyed general social attitudes and their
demographic correlates, and have increasingly assessed popular attitudes
about appropriate social roles for women and men. Notable among the
empirical findings are: 1/ a growing recognition of the multi-dimensionality
of sex roles and of the inconsistency of sex role attitudes across public or
societal, family and general interpersonal spheres (Mason and Bumpass,
1975; Giordano and Cernkovich 1979; Figueira-McDonough, 1985); 2/ a
definite trend toward more egalitarian conceptions of women's social roles
(Thornton et al., 1984; Boyd, 1984; Anderson and Cook, 1985; Gurin, 1985;
Mansbridge, 1986); and 3/ consistent verification that women's engagement in paid employment, as well as youthfulness and higher educational
attainment are associated with more egalitarian views of women's roles
(Smith and Fisher, 1982; Thornton et al., 1983; Boyd, 1984; Smith, 1985)....

Informative as this research may be in descriptive terms (and certainly
our findings confirm its conclusions), it remains limited by the inherent
weaknesses of functionalist role theory. As Gerson (1985: 32–37) has
observed, sex role socialization theories tend to oversimplify the relations
between internalized norms and behavior, to underestimate ambivalent
socializing influences, and to overemphasize individual conformity, while
ignoring the dynamics of individual and social change. Most fundamentally,
as Connell (1985: 263) puts it:

> *The problem is that role theory cannot grasp social change as history,
> that is, as transformation generated in the interplay of social practice
> and social structure. Change is always something that happens to
> sex roles, that impinges on them. It comes from outside, as in discus-
> sions of how technological and economic changes demand a shift to a
> 'modern' male role for men. Or it comes from inside the person, from
> the 'real self' that protests against the artificial restrictions of con-
> straining roles. Sex role theory has no way of grasping change as a
> dialectic arising within gender relations themselves.*

More specifically, changes in attitudes of and about women continue to be
regarded, in sex role research, either as necessary responses to externally

imposed structural changes or as a clearer expression of women's internalized interests. Such assumptions fail to recognize either the connections with specific changes in the economic, domestic and political power that men exercise over women, or the impact of the political mobilization of feminism (see Bashevkin, 1984 for graphic examples).

Studies of Feminist Consciousness

Approaches that emphasize the power dynamics of sex and gender relations found one of their earliest sustained expressions in the writing of Simone de Beauvoir (1949), and have been given more systematic forms since by radical feminists, who have focussed on men's sexual domination and violence toward women and society as a whole (especially through militarism and the violation of the environment), and on the institutional dynamics of women's general subordination to men especially in the family sphere and sexuality (Firestone, 1970; Mitchell, 1971; Delphy, 1979; Daly, 1978; O'Brien, 1981). Although more recent radical feminist scholarship appears to have placed greater emphasis on differences among women, (recognizing in particular the importance of race), there has been a strong tendency to treat 'women' and 'men' as undifferentiated universal categories (Stimpson, 1984).[2] This is clearly the case in most attempts to date to define feminist consciousness (Mitchell and Oakley, 1986). The growth of the women's movement in the 1960s produced widespread usage of the concept of feminist consciousness. Many women joined small 'consciousness raising' groups in which they discussed their own personal lives, and through that sharing came to understand the ways in which 'the personal is political'; that is, the ways in which their individual experiences were shaped by social patterns common to most women. Those who recognized that women are oppressed were said to have a feminist consciousness. For example, Gerda Lerner (1986: 242) defines feminist consciousness as the recognition of a collective wrong suffered and efforts to remedy those wrongs in political, economic and social life. Appeals to the solidarity of sisterhood, often in terms comparable to earlier Marxist appeals to the solidarity of the working class, were commonly made during the 'consciousness raising phase' of the women's movement (Shulman, 1980) and continue to be made (Morgan, 1984). Even among those who reject such conceptions as the imposition of arbitrary stages (i.e., movement from false consciousness through consciousness raising to true revolutionary consciousness), and argue instead for a multiplicity of contextually grounded feminist consciousnesses, the oppression of women has tended to be treated as a primitive universal term (Stanley and Wise, 1983).

Some feminists have argued that there is a consciousness shared by women of all societies. Merle Thornton (1980) and Mary O'Brien (1981: 50, 189–90) argue that 'reproductive consciousness' generated by the labor of birth is universal among women. Temma Caplan (1982: 546) similarly claims that within all cultures, women share an essential consciousness: 'the bedrock of women's consciousness is the need to preserve life'. She argues that, as a result, women's domestic responsibilities in class societies reinforce a revolutionary potential of their consciousness, for when women's responsibilities are threatened, especially their responsibility to preserve life, women mobilize as a group through traditional female networks to protest and resist. While the shared material bases of women's condition should be recognized, other feminists have argued that women's experiences of biological reproduction vary greatly and are shaped by diverse historical and cultural conditions....

The basic limitations of radical feminist studies of women's consciousness to date have been: an overemphasis on, and often an ahistorical treatment of, the force of patriarchal structures to the exclusion of the active practices of actual women and men as motivated social agents; an undemonstrated assumption that all women and all men, respectively, share not only common experience but unified, internally consistent sets of interests; and a tacit denial that material and emotional needs for mutual support both diminish most men's motivation to dominate women and generate contradictions in most women's relations with most men (cf. Gerson, 1985: 24–29).

Studies of Women's Gender Consciousness

While whole societies may be gender divided in such a way that some aspects of gender consciousness hold for all women or men of that society, in most large-scale societies there are significant differences within genders based on class, race, region, ethnicity or generation.[3] Most pertinently, socialist feminist historical studies have recognized that, while a pervasive ethos of heterosexual masculinity and femininity has been intimately connected with the institutionalization of men's dominance over women in industrial capitalist societies, this ethos has had distinctive bases in ruling class, middle class and working class settings (Barrett and McIntosh, 1982; Davidoff and Hall, 1987). Much socialist feminist research pertaining to gender consciousness has focussed on the construction of women's gendered subjectivity as domestic laborers, family members, and sexual beings, especially in the context of family households as a central institutional site of women's oppression (Mitchell, 1966; Rowbotham, 1974; Rapp, 1978). Over the past decade, the topic of female wage labor in capitalist society has gained greater attention, as have employment-based influences on women's gender identities and political orientations (Vogel, 1986: 13–15).

The most detailed insights into the historical development of women's gender consciousness have come from studies of working class women in Britain and America....Some historical studies demonstrate the existence among working class women of a collective sense of themselves which certainly provided them with resources for struggle. For example, Susan Benson (1983) shows how women's work culture has provided department store saleswomen with a framework for understanding and resources for coping with their jobs....However, there is no evidence in the existing studies that such women were critical of the dual categories, 'feminine' and 'masculine,' or that their gender consciousness ever took on a sustained oppositional form. Furthermore, the idea of gender consciousness has been utilized by historians to describe phenomena rather than as a concept to be theorized.

Comparative studies of societies in which women and men are sharply differentiated and confined to same-sex groups have noted that common economic responsibilities, often shared residence and social expectations of shared characteristics do result in gender-specific cultures (Pettigrew, 1981; Chafetz, 1984). So, within one society there may be a men's culture and a women's culture, each of which has its own understanding of itself, the other culture and of the social totality (Turnbull, 1981). When, as is often the case, the society as a whole is male-dominated, women's material condition may be dictated by men and of benefit to men; nevertheless, the internal workings and meanings of women's culture may be only partially understood by the men. While these situations are often very oppressive for women, the existence of a distinct women's culture offers the potential for certain efforts on the part of women to at least provide themselves with support and solidarity—in a sense, a culture of consolation (Abu-Lughad, 1985; Smith-Rosenberg, 1980). Discussing middle-class women in nineteenth century American society, Nancy Cott (1977: 100) argues that:

> *The cannon of domesticity intensified women's gender group identification by assimilating diverse personalities to one work-role that was also a sex role signifying a shared and special destiny.*

In certain circumstances, where the women are able to wield relative power, their shared women's culture offers the potential for them to challenge their domination by the men's culture and to offer alternative definitions to the male interpretation of the social totality (Murphy and Murphy, 1974). In so far as women share some collective sense of their common experience, they may be said to share a gender consciousness.

Other, often socialist feminist, researchers have begun to document carefully women's gender consciousness in contemporary capitalist societies. The main focus of this work has been on the ways in which awareness of gender and class interests are related. Ethnographies of working class couples have illustrated how women's greater concern with home affairs than men influences both their attitudes toward social relations in employment and their connection with broader social issues (Hunt, 1980; Porter, 1983). More detailed case studies of women's recent paid work experience show that gender consciousness is often negotiated between the work culture and the world of home and family. For example, Heidi Gottfried and David Fasenfest (1984), Sallie Westwood (1984) and Louise Lamphere (1985) all argue that working class women use women's family related interests and concerns (for example, the celebration of weddings, pregnancies and births) to create a social space which male workers and bosses find difficult to penetrate. This allows women to provide themselves with some measure of control over the workplace. Women's collective experience of wage labor itself has shown to lead to their growing, if often ambivalent, awareness that the male family wage is a myth and the ideal of a male breadwinner is inappropriate, that they themselves are essential earners, and that their own shared work cultures provide a key resource in struggles for both job rights and fairer domestic division of labor (Pollert, 1981; Costello, 1985).

An Emergent Approach to Understanding Gender Consciousness

These cumulative findings, particularly from socialist feminist research, have provoked a rethinking of the theoretical underpinnings of both gender consciousness and class consciousness (Bartky, 1975; Tiano and Bracken, 1984; Wilson and Sennott, 1984). Conventional Marxist notions of class consciousness which ignore gender relations and which focus narrowly on the relations between workers and bosses at the point of production, often explicitly denying the significance of other experiences, are seen as inadequate for proper understanding of class consciousness (Livingstone and Mangan, forthcoming), as are global assertions of feminist consciousness on the basis of class-blind gender relations. Roberta Goldberg (1984: 84) concludes her study of the consciousness of women clerical workers:

> *How consciousness develops to enable people to challenge their roles is a question that cannot be answered using classical theories of class consciousness. A new theory of consciousness encompassing the two major areas of production, work and the family, must take into account the profound expectations of gender roles and the accompanying consciousness that arises when people are confronted by the contradictory expectations of the workplace and the family.*

This understanding of social consciousness from a Marxist feminist perspective is explicitly based on an expanded conception of the capitalist mode of production which recognizes the family household as well as the paid workplace as two equally important points of production (Seccombe, 1980; Goldberg, 1984: 76). Our own general view is that class and gender relations in capitalist societies, as well as race and ethnic relations, are constituted through practices in three primary spheres of activity, paid workplaces, households and communities; we conceive of a hierarchy of determination such that paid workplace production relations tend to constrain the autonomy of household activities more than vice versa, while communities extending from both household and paid workplace spheres take up residual and more discretionary parts of people's time and energies (Luxton, Livingstone and Seccombe, 1982; Corman, forthcoming; Livingstone and Mangan, forthcoming). Certainly, research findings to date appear to support a general assumption that, in addition to family household-based relations, class-specific, gender-based changes in contemporary paid workplace relations are critical to understanding both women's resistance and the gender consciousness of women and men in contemporary capitalist societies (Pollert, 1983: 113–14; Game and Pringle, 1983).

The existence of well-developed Marxist conceptualizations of class consciousness offers a suggestive framework for thinking about gender consciousness. Marxists have commonly distinguished at least three aspects of class consciousness: 1/class identity, which is awareness of classes and identification with one's own class; 2/oppositional class consciousness, which is recognition of antagonistic interests with another class or classes; and 3/hegemonic class consciousness, which is readiness to act to achieve or maintain a form of society based on the assumption of specific class interests as universal ones.[4]

Simple comparable distinctions are not directly applicable to gender consciousness. Where class differences are entirely social, gender differences and gender identity have a basis in sex differences. Furthermore, at least in contemporary capitalist societies, an individual's sex (female or male) is explicitly stressed from the moment the birth is announced and reiterated daily in almost all activities including the most intimate ones; class membership is more rarely acknowledged and many people are able to live unaware of their class location. In addition, the elimination of ruling classes is possible in a way that the elimination of men is not (except in the daydreams of frustrated feminists). Thus gender identity and some form of gender consciousness are fundamental to social relations in a way that class membership and consciousness are not.

Nevertheless, using the analogy of class consciousness as a starting point, we might think of gender consciousness in contemporary society in terms of: 1/gender identities, as our understanding of the normal meanings of femininity and masculinity, and our personal sentiments of affinity with those distinctions; 2/oppositional gender consciousness, as a sense that gender identities of feminine and masculine have been arbitrary and constraining for both women and men and a recognition that gender relations have involved domination and oppression of women by men; and 3/hegemonic gender consciousness, as the willingness to either maintain or create a form of society based on the assumption that one's own gender interests can be generalized for all.

At one extreme, we could distinguish those with hegemonic masculinist consciousness, that is, a strong heterosexual masculine personal identity and affinity, a consistent sense of resistance to men's sharing power with women in any sphere, and the continual assertion in practice of male dominance as the natural state of life. Conversely, a counter-hegemonic feminist consciousness might involve a strong sense of one's own personal identity as a woman and a clear sense of commonality with other women, a coherent belief in women's right to contest male dominance in any sphere, and a disposition to create a future society organized on principles consistent with women's complete liberation. Just as people of dominant class origins have sometimes developed profound sympathies with and taken the standpoint of subordinate classes, men can develop a pro-feminist consciousness—that is, sympathies with women's interests and a rejection of male power and masculinist discourse—without denying their own male identities. Similarly, just as some working class people can ally themselves with the ruling class in an apparent opposition to their own long-term class interest, so many women support systems of male domination.

We could further expect that most people would exhibit more mixed forms of gender consciousness in most circumstances. Partly as a consequence of inconsistencies between ruling class ideology/discourse and the lived experiences of subordinate class cultures, working class people have commonly exhibited forms of 'contradictory class consciousness' (Gramsci, 1971; Emmison, 1985). Similarly, the dominant masculine ideology/discourse that many women have had imposed on them often contrasts sharply with their lived personal experiences and results in bifurcated forms of gender consciousness (Smith, 1978; Kasper, 1986).

While construing forms of gender consciousness in these terms may be useful, we need to be wary of a gender reductionism that, in effect, repeats common Marxist errors of class reductionism....

The current practice, by which studies of gender consciousness are conflated with studies of women's consciousness, must be avoided. Hence, studies of men's gender consciousness, alone and in interaction with women's are much needed (Brod, 1987; Kaufman, 1987). Such studies must recognize that experiences of gender relations are not only class-specific, but also grounded in race/ethnic and age relations as equally irreducible features of social reality (Davis, 1981; Enthuse and Yuval-Davis, 1983; Dixon, 1983; Britan and Maynard, 1985)....But everyone's social consciousness presumably remains constrained and mediated by their own class, gender, age and racial identities in complex ways (Simpson and Mutran, 1981; Hraba and Yarborough, 1983). At this stage of knowledge, the extension of more modest inquiries into the interplay of specific aspects of gender identities and oppositional gender consciousness among men and women in specific class and racial settings may be most fruitful....

GENDER CONSCIOUSNESS AT WORK: A STUDY OF STEELWORKERS AND THEIR SPOUSES

Probably the most predominant ideological notion connected with gendered social practices in advanced capitalist societies maintains that heterosexual marriage is the ideal for all women and men and that within such marriages the preferred division of labor is one where the man is the breadwinner and the woman is the homemaker (Hunt, 1980: 180). Whatever the actual extent of this practice (and where it actually has been practiced most extensively is among white, urban populations), the ideology is profoundly pervasive, affecting most aspects of contemporary life from building codes, tax laws and health care plans to access to the labor market and wage levels (Luxton, 1987).[5] As Archer and Lloyd (1984: 242) summarize:

> *Perhaps the most pervasive [gender] stereotype is the belief that a man's main responsibility is to go out to work and a women's is to look after her family. One consequence of this belief is that a working man is seen as the breadwinner and a woman as merely working for 'pin money'. This view may also be used as a reason for undervaluing the contribution of women workers, for justifying lower pay for women, and for regarding men's careers as being of greater importance than women's. Despite this belief, a large proportion of women workers ...were the chief economic supporters of households in the 1970s...*

The class, race and gender composition of the employed workforce in most advanced capitalist societies, including Canada, has changed dramatically in the post World War II period, with changing patterns of immigration and the increasing participation of married women especially in working class jobs (Armstrong, 1984). The infusion of women into paid employment has forced both men and women to rethink the mother-wife-homemaker role as the taken-for-granted female gender identity in society. Where women have found employment in so-called 'women's jobs,' the dominant ideology has been modified; when women take on so-called 'men's jobs' that ideology is seriously challenged.[6]

The remainder of this paper focusses on particular aspects of gender consciousness by investigating the reproduction and modification of the male breadwinner norm in a factory in the steel industry—which is widely regarded to be one of the strongest preserves of traditional white working class masculine identity and opposition to women trying to do a 'man's job.' By examining the shop floor cultural practices and expressed attitudes of married white working class men employed in the steel industry, the perceptions of their spouses and the experiences of a small number of women who were hired in the steel plant, the paper documents the articulation of the male breadwinner norm and assesses the various experiences which either lead to a modification of or actually challenge that norm.

Views on the gendered division of labor, as expressed most explicitly through acceptance or rejection of the male breadwinner norm, are among the most basic ingredients of oppositional gender consciousness. Whether one is inclined to a feminist, male chauvinist or more ambivalent sense of oppositional gender consciousness is likely to be intimately related to both dispositions on fundamental dimensions of gender identity, and predispositions to act to maintain or create alternative forms of gender relations.

The Hilton Works of the Steel Company of Canada (Stelco), in Hamilton, Ontario, is one of the largest manufacturing plants in Canada. With a labor force of between 8,000 and 14,000, it has been the major employer in the city of Hamilton since the early 20th century. Unionized in the late 1940s by the United Steelworkers of America (Local 1005), its relatively high wages and benefits have made it one of the most desirable industrial workplaces in the city. The production labor force has been almost entirely white and male.[7]

Until recently, because of the relatively high wages and the relative job security, the vast majority of men at Stelco were economically able to support dependent wives and children, thus realizing the male breadwinner ideal. Indeed, from 1945 to 1981 when there was a world decline in steel manufacturing, Hamilton consistently had among the lowest rates of women's employment in Canada, a fact made possible by the wages from the heavy industry which dominates the city and of course supported by the discriminatory hiring practices by those same industries (Webber, 1986). During World War II, women were employed to replace male workers who had joined the army and after the war almost all those women were let go. Between 1946 and 1961, a few women were hired occasionally, but by 1961 they were all employed in one particular work site—the tin mill. Between 1961 and 1978, no women were hired although approximately 30,000 women applied for jobs during those 19 years (Luxton, forthcoming). By 1978, there were 28 women working in the tin mill; the rest of the production workers were men. In 1979–80, a union-supported committee, The Women Back Into Stelco Committee, launched a highly public campaign, which included a discrimination complaint with the Ontario Human Rights Commission, to force Stelco to hire women for production jobs in the Hilton Works. As a result, Stelco hired approximately 200 women. The highly publicized campaign and the subsequent hiring of a number of women focussed attention on the question of gender and paid employment and for the women and men involved posed sharply the issue of gender identity (Eason, Field and Santucci, 1983).

We examined patterns of gender consciousness among white married male steelworkers and their spouses, and among white female steelworkers who entered Stelco as a result of their political campaign. Our study was conducted in 1983–84 in the wake of massive lay-offs by Stelco, including most of the women hired in this campaign. We interviewed a random sample of 184 married steelworkers (182 were men), drawn from the Local 1005 membership list, who were living with their spouses and employed at Stelco. We also interviewed their spouses (76 of the women spouses were full-time housewives and 106 were in paid employment; the 2 male spouses were employed). In-depth follow-up interviews were also conducted selectively. For comparative purposes, a representative sample of individuals living with partners in the Greater Hamilton Area was given a similar interview ($N = 795$). We also interviewed the leaders of the Women Back Into Stelco Campaign and 25 women who, though not part of the original campaign, were hired as a result of it. This paper investigates patterns of gender conscious-ness among men and women who, for the most part, are living in nuclear families where the man's income forms the greater part of the household income. It also looks at the impact on that consciousness of the women who got jobs at Stelco. We consider what factors foster support for a sharply dif-ferentiated sex/gender division of paid labor and, particularly, the ideal of the male breadwinner, and conversely what leads to a recognition that women and men can and ought to do the same paid work for the same remu-neration. Most specifically, we attempt to investigate the links of masculine shop floor culture with ideologies of work and the male breadwinner norm in this core of the Hamilton working class.

Masculine Shop Floor Culture

In occupational settings where the large majority of workers are male, there is often an equation of paid work with masculinity. It is assumed that workers in that field are, and should be, male. Such ideas are part of a larger ideology which accepts the existence of a decisive sex/gender division of labor, fun-damental to which is the belief that women should be first and foremost wives and mothers and that men are primarily breadwinners. In describing professional occupations, this assumption is articulated in phrases which call attention to the exception such as 'a lady doctor,' 'a woman pilot' or 'a female professor'.[8] As Paul Willis (1970) and Cynthia Cockburn (1983) have demonstrated, the equation of paid work with masculinity is frequently char-acteristic of large scale industrial settings where much of the work involves manual labor or where the work environment is particularly noisy, dirty and noxious. Existing studies of masculine shop floor culture also describe the meaning and pleasure that men extract in the midst of boring and alienating work situations. The assertion of masculinity is partially a defence, a way of insisting on the exclusion of women to protect specific jobs and more gen-eral job skills from increased competition (Cockburn, 1985). It is also an integral part of the ideology of the male breadwinner. Such studies show why male camaraderie, based on masculinity, is important and why the men are often threatened if their culture is challenged (for example by the presence of women).

In workplaces such as Stelco where many parts of the plant have involved dangerous or heavy work, and where—with the exception of the cafeteria, the cleaning and office staff and the tin mill—all workers were men from 1945 until the challenge in 1979, manual labor, dangerous work or even work with large machinery is often identified as men's work. This may mili-tate against individuals recognizing the class nature of this work and therefore retard their sense of class identity. A male steelworker described the qualities needed to work at Stelco: 'You got to be tough and you got to be willing to take risks. You got to be strong. It takes a real man to work here.'

The shared experience of work, the camaraderie of co-workers, is shaped by their shared masculinity (Stewart, 1981). As John Lippert (1977: 208) observed of his experience as an auto worker:

> *Each member of the group seems concerned mainly with exhibiting sexual experience and competency through the competition...None of what happens between men in the plant is considered 'sexuality'. That remains as what we do with (or to) our women when we get home... But even through this competition, it is easy to see that many, many men enjoy their physical interaction and that they receive a kind of physical satisfaction from it that they just don't get [from the work itself or] when they go home.*

The unpleasantness and the brutality of the working situation is sometimes reinterpreted into a heroic exercise by manly confrontation with the task. In this way, a potential for developing oppositional class consciousness may be modified or even deflected by a gender consciousness that validates certain stereotypic notions of masculinity. Difficult, uncomfortable or dangerous working conditions are not seen directly as employer-imposed hazards for the workers, but as challenges to masculine prowess: A male steelworker noted: 'The coke oven, where I am, is really rough. The men who work there, they got to be really tough you know, just to keep at it, day after day.'

Discontent with work in male-dominated factory environments is often not articulated as political discontent directed against the bosses but rather is mediated through forms of language and interplay among workers that express sexual competition and antagonism (Gray, 1984; Meissner, 1986). Sexually antagonistic language pervades the steel mill. Work itself—especially difficult work—is characterized as feminine and to be conquered: 'it's a real bitch,' 'give her hell'. Similarly, malfunctioning machinery is called by derogatory terms for women—bitch, slut—which often have explicit sexual connotations. Disliked bosses are similarly described by terms which cast aspersion either on their masculinity and sexual ability—wimp, cream puff, dick—or identify them with negative female terms—bitch. Specific anger is expressed using terms for sexual intercourse and workers' descriptions of their exploitation by management are usually articulated using rape terms— 'we're getting fucked' or 'we're getting screwed around'.

Gender codes are central to the ways in which male workers approach other aspects of their work. One of the few ways workers can influence the design of the work sites is in their choice of pictures on the walls. Frequently lunch rooms are wallpapered with pinups of apparently sexually available women—imagery which both continues the theme of sexual symbolism and suggests a potential alternative activity which sharply contrasts with the workplace. This alternative for men involves both fantasized sexual activity which is deemed to be physically and emotionally pleasurable in ways that the reality of work is not, and sexual domination where the male (at least as viewer) is in a position of power over (at least the image of) the women in ways that the worker never has power at work.

Even when discontent at work is expressed as direct political opposition to management, it is filtered through a language of masculinity. Male workers describe standing up to management in masculine terms. One male Stelco worker described another approvingly: 'He never takes any shit from the foreman and when they give him a hard time, he fights back hard—he's a real man.' In plant floor confrontations, and in contract negotiations, masculine characteristics and behaviors are commonly mobilized. As Paul Willis has noted (1979: 198), the spectacle, especially of the potential fist fight, and the bluff, or strong and combative language, register real expressions of anger and opposition. These may be very effective in the short run and certainly represent a strong force. But this 'masculine style of confrontation demands an appropriate and honourable resolution: visible and immediate concessions' (Willis, 1979: 198). As a consequence, contract negotiations often result in cash settlements, gains which are immediately visible but which may 'actually conceal longer-term defeats over the less visible issues of control and ownership' (Willis, 1979: 198; Winter and Robert, 1980). Most significantly, such masculinist worker consciousness is usually taken for granted as a normal part of how work is understood. Even men who don't like it tend rather to distance themselves from particular manifestations of it, objecting to swearing or to food throwing for example, than to develop a critique or opposition to the total culture. It is only when challenged explicitly that the dynamics of this gender consciousness can be seen at work. The Women Back Into Stelco campaign posed such a challenge.

The Challenge from Women and the Modification of the Male Breadwinner Norm

When women attacked the policies which had excluded them from employment at the Hilton works, they were also, intentionally or not, attacking the legitimacy and attending beliefs both of the equation of steelmaking and masculinity and of the male breadwinner ideal. In so doing they were challenging existing ideologies of gender. The mere presence of female steelworkers, whatever their personal gender consciousness or motivation for seeking Stelco employment, acted as a 'consciousness raising' for those involved.

There were about 14,000 men employed at Stelco when the first women walked through the doors after the success of the campaign. Their responses to women's employment at Stelco varied. One of the women noted:

Some of them feel if you can do your job you got a right to be here. And others feel you got a right to be there if you are the only breadwinner. And then others...you shouldn't be there. And then there are others, that you should be there.

Male steelworkers, their spouses, and women steelworkers almost unanimously supported, in the abstract, the general principle of equal opportunities for women in the labor market. This is not surprising given that over the past 30 years, Canadian opinion surveys have found growing majority support among both women and men for the general principle of sex equality in paid workplaces; by 1970, over four-fifths of Canadian women and men supported equal pay for the same kind of work, and by the early 1980s support for the view that women could run most businesses as well as men had grown to about four-fifths of both women and men (Boyd, 1984). Similarly, in our interview survey, male steelworkers and their spouses both expressed strong consensus (>70%) on the general statement: 'If given the chance, women would and should do the same work as men now do, and men could and should do the same work as women now do (except for pregnancy)'. They also demonstrated support for the principle of equal pay for equal work when they strongly disagreed (>85%) with the proposition that 'women should not be paid the same as men'....

However, despite this general support in principle for women's right to paid employment and equal pay for equal work, attitudes toward more specific aspects of full sex/gender equality are much more mixed. Canada-wide opinion survey responses suggest that support for the male breadwinner norm also generally appears to be diminishing; by the early 1980s, the majority of Canadian women and men expressed support for equal job opportunities for married women. However, in spite of growing support in recent years, small majorities are still opposed to married women with young children taking a job outside the home (Boyd, 1984; Reid, 1987). This pattern appears to be confirmed by our Hamilton surveys.

The most pertinent questions asked in both our Hamilton-wide and steelworker household surveys dealt with priority for jobs in hard times, and affirmative action in traditionally male jobs....Overall, the pattern of responses indicated that Hamilton couples also remained quite divided on these more specific issues of gender equality, that male Stelco workers were somewhat less supportive than Hamilton men in general, and that employed women were more supportive than homemakers.[9]

...[S]mall majorities of women and men in Hamilton couples rejected men's priority for jobs in hard times. A bare majority of Stelco wives did as well. Only among male Stelco workers was there a small majority in favor of giving men priority for jobs. As one male steelworker insisted: 'Between a single mother with kids and a guy supporting a family, I would take the guy first'.

Women's employment typically had a significant effect on the views of both spouses. Among Hamilton couples generally, over 60 per cent of employed women and of men with employed spouses supported women's equal right to paid employment in times of high unemployment. Both Hamilton women presently working exclusively as homemakers and men with homemaker spouses were about equally divided on the issue. Male Stelco workers and their spouses exhibited fairly similar differences by employment status of the woman. The employed wives of Stelco workers showed a virtually identical pattern of majority support to Hamilton working women in general. Conversely, definite majorities of both male steelworkers with homemaker wives and their wives themselves expressed agreement with men's priority for jobs. Perhaps most notably, male Stelco workers with employed wives remained about equally divided, and therefore less moved by their wives' employment than Hamilton men in general to support women's equal right to jobs. However, the general pattern...supports the not surprising conclusion of several prior studies that people in both middle class and working class households with wives in paid employment are more likely to reject the male breadwinner norm (cf. Huber and Spitze, 1983; Ferree, 1983; Anderson and Cook, 1985; Smith, 1985; Black and Creese, 1986). Also, as in prior studies, significant correlations of youthfulness and higher educational attainment with more egalitarian views on women's employment rights have been found both for men and women, whether the wife is employed or not.

On the issue of affirmative action in traditionally male jobs, the overall pattern of responses was again similar... Most notably, the majority of women in all categories—including Stelco homemaker wives—were likely to support such affirmative action practices, while men in general remained more divided and a small majority of male Stelco workers expressed opposition.

While these Hamilton survey results are consistent with a general trend of declining support for male breadwinner power, they therefore also confirm that at least some aspects of the male breadwinner norm remain accepted in some form by the majority of Stelco workers as well as by many of their wives. The results further confirm that many male Stelco workers with employed wives also continue to defend male breadwinner power even if their wives disagree.

Our in-depth interviews with Stelco workers and their spouses offer further insight into the complexities and dynamics of the current renegotiation of these features of breadwinner power and, by implication, of gender identities in general. The other side of the argument that certain occupations, such as steelmaking, are only for men is the insistence that men must be breadwinners. So, while there is rarely any overt denial of women's right to paid work, an underlying identification of breadwinner status with men's work remains strong among many male steelworkers. While some men actively supported the efforts of the women to get hired at Stelco and welcomed them when they succeeded (and the union formally and practically gave full support to the campaign), many men insisted that steelmaking, especially given the dirty, dangerous and heavy work at Stelco, must be men's work....

The notion of steelmaking as essentially men's work is not merely a simplistic assertion of male chauvinism, but is typically bound to a deeper sense of responsibility to provide for their families. Both the wages earned and the very sacrifice and strength required to do the work offer a basic self-esteem and self-worth. The wage packet is seen as conferring breadwinner power and status and confirming that the man has fulfilled his obligation as family provider....But in virtually every case, the steelworker's male identity appeared to be integrally tied to his perceived capacity to bring home a 'decent' or 'living' wage.

Homemaker wives of steelworkers most frequently expressed the concomitant belief that women's place is in the home: 'I think a mother should be home with her children. It's better for them, isn't it.' But some homemaker wives' comments reflected both an awareness of the centrality of their own domestic work to the reproduction of their husband's labor power, and also asserted their own continuing right to seek paid work:

> *I make sure he goes to work happy and in a good mood every day. So he is going into his workplace not thinking about things. He can go and put his mind into his job, not worry about what is worrying at home...I gave up my job when we got married, but that was a mutual agreement. I didn't do it for him. He didn't make me quit my job, you know. I could probably go back to work somehow.*

Homemaker wives of steelworkers frequently reiterated versions of the male breadwinner norm, but those who supported women working in steel typically did so on the same basis as they supported their husbands working there, the wage packet....

Employed wives frequently showed both a deeper appreciation of the negative side of male breadwinners' responsibility and a determination to maintain their own employment, albeit generally in low paid or part-time jobs:

> *The man might think it's terrible because he has to go to work every day. He can't afford to take a day off. The way society has put it, the man is the breadwinner in the family. And that must be a lot of stress on you, like thinking—'I have to go to work, I have no choice, I have to work full-time. If I don't work full-time, then we don't get our money and we don't survive'...I never thought of staying home for long. I really enjoy getting out....*

Steelworkers' wives, whether employed or full-time homemakers, tended to be quite pragmatic about the possibility of women's employment at Stelco, not articulating any notion that the work is too much for women....

The employed wives of steelworkers in general expressed support for women steelworkers, and some also saw benefits to male entry into female job ghettos:

> *I think the Women into Stelco Campaign was a good idea. I feel work should be shared, no matter, anywhere. We've just hired our first male nurse. Some said there was just no way that there'd ever be men in our*

workplace. It's good, because they're stronger and a lot of those patients are just dead weight, you know...Surely if they go through nursing school, they're just as smart as we are. It's just so silly. So, really, I can't see that it would be any problem down at the steel mill. If there's girls that can do the work, why not?

Women steelworkers noted the extensive resistance to their presence and explained it in terms of masculine ideologies:

I think a lot of the men were threatened...here was a woman coming along who said she could do it just as well as they could.

Despite the common tendency for male steelworkers to construe their gender identities through their perceptions of their jobs as tough and dangerous, the presence of committed, full-time women steelworkers through the divisions of the Hilton Works began to seriously erode the basis of the masculinist ideology of steelwork.

The women recognized the masculine shop floor culture and argued that men felt very threatened when women entered those previously all-male terrains. In particular, they suggested that men were embarrassed to have their shop floor cultural practices made public to women:

It is like a sub-culture at Stelco...The men at Stelco whose every second word is fuck...you meet them on the street with their families and a bad word would never cross their lips...Some of us women who lived in Hamilton and maybe had their wives for neighbours saw the other side and I think that was a threat to some of them....

They also noted that the presence of women challenged and undermined the basic premises of the male breadwinner ideology and the sex/gender division of labor itself:

The man goes out and does the job, it doesn't matter how he does it, he's got to make a lot of money and the women stay home and take care of the children...It's a very nice, well-ordered life and we were changing that order. Not only were we working with them, many of us were also going home and doing what their wives were doing as well and it was very difficult for some of them.

In fact, the challenge to the masculine ideology of work potentially reveals the actual oppressive character of that work. Occasionally the words of the men themselves offered a glimmer of insight into the way in which concepts of masculinity at the workplace hinder a clear critique of the work itself. In defending the principle that steelmaking is men's work and unsuitable for women, one man implied that there are problems with anyone doing the work:

> *It's dirty, heavy, it's no climate for a woman. The men's world is a lit-*
> *tle rougher than the women's. Physically a man is in better shape.*
> *Men are more mechanically minded...There is nothing wrong with*
> *women, it's just that sometimes with heavy work...Everywhere you*
> *find place for some women, could be as strong as men, you know. But*
> *if you take the overall picture, masculinity has always been the man's.*
> *It doesn't mean that he has more brains because that is not true, but*
> *muscularity. I think that women should be outside. It is no place for*
> *women. I hate it.*

Women steelworkers have most clearly perceived the limits of the mas-culinist ideology of steel work: 'I've never seen a job that I couldn't do or any other women couldn't do. Men will say this is no place for a woman, but it's not really good for men either.'

Some men who defended women's general employment rights dis-played ambivalence about them as steelworkers either because their capabilities may be more limited or on the basis that they are taking jobs away from men:

> *Philosophically, I have to agree that [women] have the same right in*
> *the marketplace as I do...In an environment like Stelco, I agree she has*
> *the right to be there, but in a life threatening situation, I wouldn't*
> *want my life being dependent on how she is going to react to that sit-*
> *uation at that time, and we do get into some precarious positions...If*
> *you were to carry it a step farther, if you are going to allow them into*
> *the marketplace, you are going to have to at some time or other*
> *approach the subject of them in positions of supervision, and how well*
> *a female supervisor on a bull gang would go I really wouldn't even*
> *like to speculate. But we can't promote them all to the main office and*
> *we can't keep them all at the lower end.*

Other men expressed more direct antagonism to women steelworkers, arguing that they posed a direct threat to men's breadwinner power:

> *There were a lot of men who could do those jobs. We've had quite a few*
> *cases of women who have gone to Stelco to work whose husbands work*
> *there. There were a lot of men who have families who got laid off.*
> *That's what most guys object to—I was laid off, she's taking over my*
> *job. They were making $500 to $600 a week. You lose your house, you*
> *lose your car, you lose your wife...*

Some of the women steelworkers noted that men were opposed to hir-ing women because so many men were unemployed: 'They figured it was a man's job, a man's world, and there a lot of unemployed men still out there.'

Steelworkers and their spouses were very aware of actual or threatened unemployment. At the same time of the study, about 5,000 Stelco production workers had been let go and many more had received layoff notices. As many other workplaces in Hamilton were also laying off, most Hamilton residents had close contact with someone unemployed (Webber, 1986). This fear and the realistic assessment of the basic injustice of wealth engendered in many a strong sense that it is unfair that some households have two 'good incomes' while others have none. A male steelworker explained:

> *What really bothers me is where there are two breadwinners. That's not fair. I don't care who the breadwinner is, the man or the woman, but there shouldn't be two breadwinners in some families when some people have no jobs. I know everyone wants to get ahead, but it's not fair when some have no jobs.*

While the vast majority were unable to think about this in class terms, not able to make the leap to criticizing the existence of the real inequalities of wealth (Livingstone and Mangan, forthcoming), they found it hard to break with the notion of one primary breadwinner. Most acknowledged circumstances in which the woman might well be the breadwinner but still felt that ideally the man should be. They could also accept circumstances in which both men and women were employed but the woman had a conventional (lower paid) 'woman's job'. However, they were strongly hostile to households in which both partners in a couple were employed in 'good' paying jobs....

For many women and men who accepted the idea of the male breadwinner norm, the employment of women at Stelco could only be tolerated if those women were required by necessity to take on that breadwinner role themselves. Unmarried women or women with husbands who were unemployed were acceptable; women married to employed men, especially those employed at Stelco or at equally well-paying jobs, were not....

Other men were more ambivalent about the issue:

> *Well, of course there are so many different things to look at today because with single parenthood, some of these women doing jobs, you know. But sometimes I see women going in, taking jobs away from a family man or something like that. But I don't feel no animosity towards them...I guess everybody wants a job. The way it is today, it's hard to survive unless you have got a job. So I don't know, I wouldn't say it's good and I wouldn't say it's bad. I just have a middle of the road feeling about it.*

Because so many male steelworkers were outright antagonistic to or at best ambivalent about the employment of women in the plant, the women who started at Stelco were at least initially greeted with considerable resistance. As a result of the campaign and because there were so few women, each was highly noticeable in her work site. Most of them described being tested by male co-workers. Several, especially those who had led the campaign, were harassed both by fellow workers and by foremen (Gray, 1984; 1986). They felt management was not seriously committed to gender equality in hiring. Despite this, most expressed satisfaction with their jobs and said that after a few months they ceased to be perceived merely as women intruders and became Stelco workers like everyone else (Luxton, forthcoming)....

The actual experience of working closely with women was the most effective antidote to male skepticism about women's capacity to do the work:...

> *One woman that worked in our department was good and better than some of the young fellows. She had the right personality and the right character to fit into our department...She knew her job. It took her a while but she knew her job. I have no qualms about working with a woman like that.*

The recognition that women can actually do most of the work (cf. Deaux and Ullman, 1983) has encouraged some male steelworkers, particularly those with employed wives and more secure jobs, to express explicit support for the principle of gender equality even in Stelco:...

> *Me, I don't care if it is a man or woman. Black, white or purple, it don't matter to me, you know...I am not prejudiced about anything. If the woman wants to come with me driving the truck, and if she can do it. There is only one thing. If she cannot do the job, then I think there should be something done about it, because then it is not fair.*

CONCLUDING REMARKS

Our findings show that male steelworkers, who are widely regarded as occupying one of the strongest bastions of working class masculinist ideology, strongly supported a general rhetoric of gender equality, as well as giving formal support through their union to the campaign to hire women. Some of these men were fully committed to women's equality. However, many men continued to believe that steelmaking should be men's work and that men should be primary breadwinners. Those male steelworkers who were more ambivalent about asserting the validity of the male breadwinner norm, and those who, despite massive layoffs in Stelco, expressed support for women's equal right to scarce jobs, tended to be men who had had direct experiences of women's employment. Either their wives had significant employment experience or they themselves had worked with women. Among the wives of steelworkers, their own employment experiences obviously sharply affected their adherence to male breadwinner ideologies, but even a majority of full-time housewives expressed general support for women working in traditional male jobs like steel. Clearly, the male bread-winner norm as a basis of gender identity is undergoing modifications in steelworker families, as well as in Canadian society generally. Such changes in gender consciousness are occurring primarily in response to the growing importance of married women as essential wage earners, but are also stimulated by the women's movement (in this case the explicitly feminist Women Back into Stelco campaign).

These findings are suggestive in several ways. They indicate that a strong adherence to a hegemonic masculinist ideology—to the male breadwinner norm and the assumption that steelmaking is men's work—can inhibit the development of oppositional working class consciousness in settings that are usually presumed to be most conducive to such development. Many other factors, besides production relations per se, particularly household relations and gender, race, ethnicity and age, shape people's consciousness. Further analyses of class and gender consciousness need to account for the complex interplay of various formative experiences rather than assume the determining force of one.

Our study further suggests that claims for a widespread 'women's consciousness' do not appear to be very useful at the level of particular household and workplace analyses. At this level, there appears to be very little shared consciousness; instead, the range and variation of gender consciousness, for both women and men, requires explanation. This case study confirms the usefulness of recent Marxist feminist perspectives which recognize that class and gender relations are constituted through practices in at least two primary spheres of activity, paid workplaces and households.

Finally, the study also shows that, despite the discernible impact of feminism on Canadian trade union practices, (Maroney, 1983) including steelworkers Local 1005 at Stelco, the language forms and prevalent social practices of the steel mill shop floor culture clearly remain assertively masculine. Gender-based power asymmetries, and the male gender consciousness that accompanies them, are still strongly entrenched.

Women may have demonstrated that steelmaking is not exclusively 'men's work,' but the majority of male steelworkers remain skeptical. With the massive layoffs in steel, almost all of the women have been laid off from Stelco; thus the challenge to traditions of masculine shop floor culture has been, for the moment, aborted. However, while the majority of men in steel still defend their right to employment before women, asserting the primacy of the male breadwinner norm over women's full equality, there is clearly a growing tension between that ideology and women's increasing demonstration of their employment capabilities even in the most exclusive male preserves.

NOTES

1   As Weigert et al. (1986: 68–69) point out, gender identity (internalized sociocultural meanings and expectations accompanying the normal sense of maleness or femaleness), sex identity (based on biological criteria of genetic and physiological classifications) and sexual identity (in terms of preference for sexual activity with a particular gender) are often conflated in the general literature; all three interactively influence the individual's personal identification with self and others.

2   For a fuller critical review of this tendency see Connell (1985).

3   For an excellent critical review of the literature on women's consciousness, see Lynne Marks (1987). We are also grateful for her important work theorizing the concept of 'women's culture' (personal communication).

4   For more detailed discussion of these aspects, see for example, Mann (1973), and Livingstone (1976, 1985).

5   This set of beliefs corresponds to dominant liberal ideology. Liberalism, and particularly liberal feminism, has a major contradiction at its heart. On the one hand, liberalism calls for equality of opportunity for all, treating both men and women as potentially equal individuals. However, classical liberal theory supports a sex-based division of labor in which men should be breadwinners for women who should be dependent wives and mothers. This contradiction has proved very difficult for liberalism. An early proponent of liberal feminism, John Stuart Mill, resolved it by insisting that women could do anything they wanted, but the vast majority would (should) desire to be dependent wives and mothers.

6   However, recent ethnographic studies of the experiences and perceptions of ruling class and working class boys and girls in school and family settings (Connell et al., 1982; Anyon, 1984; Russell, 1987; Valli, 1987) show how this stereotype at the root of gender consciousness continues to be reproduced and modified in the 'next generation,' despite dramatic changes in women's work.

7   In our 1983 random sample of steelworkers, less than 2% were women. Less than 2% of male steelworkers and no stewards were born outside European or North American locations. One steward was a Canadian Indian; other respondents may of course have been 'black' or some other 'visible non-white'. All of the men steelworkers and their wives who were interviewed in the follow-up study were 'white'. All of the women steelworkers interviewed were 'white'.

8   It is interesting that most studies of masculine ideology at work are of working class jobs; there are few, if any, of professional occupations. The closest are Kanter (1977), Lafontaine (1983) and Patterson and Engelberg (1978). More comparable work is necessary on proprietary class and professional and managerial class occupations in which the incumbents typically exercise more discretionary control over subsequent conditions of entry and exit and thereby the continuing creation of workplace culture.

9   All statistical differences reported in the text are significant at least at the .05 level of confidence.

REFERENCES

Abu-Lughad, Lila 1985 'Community of secrets: the separate world of Bedouin women.' *Signs,* Summer

Anderson, Kristi, and Elizabeth A. Cook 1985 'Women, work and political attitudes.' *American Journal of Political Science* (August) 29(3): 606–25

Anthias, F., and N. Yuval-Davis 1983 'Contextualizing feminism—gender, ethnic and class divisions.' *Feminist Review* (November) 15: 62–75

Archer, John, and Barbara Lloyd 1984 *Sex and Gender.* New York: Cambridge University Press

Armstrong, Pat 1984 *Labour Pains: Women's Work in Crisis.* Toronto: Women's Press

Barrett, Michele, and Mary McIntosh 1982 *The Anti-social Family.* London: Verso

Bartky, S. 1975 'Toward a phenomenology of feminist consciousness.' *Social Theory and Practice* (Fall) 3(4): 425–39

Bashevkin Sylvia B. 1984 'Social feminism and the study of American public opinion.' *International Journal of Women's Studies* (January–February) 7(1): 47–56

Bem, S. L. 1981 'Gender schema theory: a cognitive account of sex typing.' *Psychological Review* 88: 354–64

Benson, Susan 1983 'The customer ain't God: the work culture of department store saleswomen 1890–1940.' In Michael Frisch and Daniel Walkowitz, *Working Class America.* Urbana: University of Illinois Press

Black, D., and G. Creese 1986 'Class, gender and politics in Canada.' Unpublished paper, Department of Sociology, Carletan University, Ottawa

Blumberg, R. L. 1978 *Stratification: Social, Economic and Sexual Inequality.* Dubuque, Iowa: W. C. Brown

Boyd, Marilyn S. 1981 *Women's Liberation Ideology and Union Participation: A Study.* Saratoga, California: Century 21 Publishing

Boyd, Monica 1984 *Canadian Attitudes Toward Women: Thirty Years of Change.* Ottawa: Minister of Supply and Services

Brittan, A., and M. Maynard 1985 *Sexism, Racism and Oppression.* Oxford: Basil Blackwell

Brod, H. (ed.) 1987 *The Making of Masculinities: The New Men's Studies.* Beverley Hills: Sage

Buchbinder, Howard 1987 'Male Heterosexuality: The Socialized Penis Revisited.' In H. Buchbinder, V. Burstyn, D. Forbes and M. Steadman, *Who's on Top: The Politics of Heterosexuality.* Toronto: Garamond

Campbell, Beatrix 1984 *Wigan Pier Revisited: Poverty and Politics in the Eighties.* London: Virago

Caplan, Temma 1982 'Female consciousness and collective action: the case of Barcelona 1910–1918.' *Signs* (Spring) 7(3): 545–66

Carrigan, T., R. W. Connell, and J. Lee 1985 'Toward a new sociology of masculinity.' *Theory and Society* 14: 551–604

Chafetz, Janet Saltzman 1984 *Sex and Advantage: A Comparative Macro-Structural Theory of Sex Stratification*. Totowa, N.J.: Rowman and Allanheld

Cockburn, Cynthia 1983 *Brothers, Male Dominance and Technological Change*. London: Pluto Press

———. 1985 *Machinery of Dominance: Women, Men and Technical Know-How*. London: Pluto Press

Connell, R. W. 1985 'Theorizing Gender.' *Sociology* (May) 19(2): 260–22.

Connell, R. W., et al. 1982 *Making the Difference: Schools, Families and Social Division*. Sydney: Allen and Unwin

Corman, J. 1988 'Employment and Household Constraints on the Number of Social Ties.' Paper presented at Canadian Sociology and Anthropology Meetings, University of Windsor June 1988

Costello, Cynthia B. 1985 'WEA're worth it! Work culture and conflict at the Wisconsin Education Association Insurance Trust.' *Feminist Studies* 11(3): 496–518

Cott, Nancy 1977 *The Bonds of Womanhood: 'Women's Sphere' in New England 1780–1835*. New Haven [sic]

Daly, Mary 1978 *Gynaecology, the metaethics of radical feminism*. Boston: Beacon

Davidoff, L., and C. Hall 1987 *Family Fortunes: Men and Women of the English Middle Class 1780–1850*. London: Hutchinson

Davis, Angela 1981 *Women, Race and Class*. London: Women's Press

Deaux, K., and J. Ullman 1983 *Women of Steel: Female Blue-Collar Workers in the Basic Steel Industry*. New York: Praeger

Deaux, Kay, et al. 1983 'Level of categorization and content of gender stereotypes.' *Social Cognition* 3(2): 145–167

de Beauvoir, S. 1949 (1972) *The Second Sex*. Harmondsworth: Penguin

Delphy, C. 1979 *The Main Enemy*. London: Women's Research and Resource Centre

Dixon, Marlene 1983 *The Future of Women*. San Francisco: Synthesis Publication

Eason, J., D. Field, and J. Santucci 1983 'Working Steel.' Pp. 191–218 in Jennifer Penney (ed.), *Hard Earned Wages: Women Fighting for Better Work*. Toronto: Women's Educational Press

Emmison, M, 1985 'Class images of "the economy": Opposition and ideological incorporation within working class consciousness.' *Sociology* (February) 19(1): 19–38

Ferree, Myra Marx 1983 'The women's movement in the working class.' *Sex Roles* 9(4): 493–505

Figueira-McDonough, Josefina 1985 'Gender, race and class: differences in levels of feminist orientation.' *The Journal of Applied Behavioral Science* (May) 21(2): 121–42

Firestone, S. 1980 *The Dialectic of Sex*. New York: Bantam

Game, A., and R. Pringle 1983 *Gender at Work*. Sydney: Allen and Unwin

Gerson, Kathleen 1985 *Hard Choices: How Women Decide about Work, Career and Motherhood*. Berkeley: University of California Press

Gibbs, Margaret S. 1985 'The instrumental-expressive dimension revisited.' *Academic Psychology Bulletin* (Summer) 7(2): 145–55

Giordano, P.C., and S.A. Cernkovich 1979 'On complicating the relationships between liberation and delinquency.' *Social Problems* 26: 467–81

Goldberg, Roberta 1984 'The determination of consciousness through gender, family, and work experience.' *The Social Science Journal* (October) 21(4): 75–85

Gottfried, Heidi, and D. Fasenfest 1984 'Gender and class formation: female clerical workers.' *Review of Radical Political Economy* 16(1): 89–103

Gramsci, A. 1971 *Selections from the Prison Notebooks*. New York: International Publishers

Gray Stan 1984 'Sharing the shop floor.' *Canadian Dimension* (June) 18(2): 17–32; 1986 'Fight to survive—the case of Bonita Clark.' *Canadian Dimension* (May) 20(3): 15–20

Gurin, Patricia 1985 'Women's gender consciousness.' *The Public Opinion Quarterly* (Summer) 49(2): 143–63

Huber, Joan, and Glenna Spitze 1983 *Sex Stratification: Children, Housework and Jobs.* New York: Academic Press

Hunt, Pauline 1980 *Gender and Class Consciousness*. London: Macmillan

Hraba, Joseph, and Paul Yarborough 1983 'Gender consciousness and class action for women: a comparison of black and white female adolescents.' Youth and Society (December) 15(2): 115–31

Jaggar, Alison 1983 *Feminist Politics and Human Nature*. New York: Rowman and Allanheld

Kanter, Rosabeth 1977 *Men and Women of the Corporation*. New York: Basic Books

Kasper, A. S. 1986 'Consciousness Re-evaluated: Interpretive Theory and Feminist Scholarship.' *Sociological Inquiry* 65(1): 30–49

Kaufman, M. (ed.) 1987 *Beyond Patriarchy: Essays by Men on Pleasure, Power, and Change.* Toronto: Oxford University Press

Komarovsky, M. 1946 'Cultural contradictions and sex roles.' *American Journal of Sociology* 52: 184–89

LaFontaine, Edward 1983 'Forms of False Consciousness among Professional Women.' *Humboldt Journal of Social Relations* (Spring/Summer) 10(2): 26–46

Lamphere, Louise 1985 'Bringing the family to work: women's culture on the shop floor.' *Feminist Studies* (Fall) 11(3): 519–40

Lerner, Gerda 1986 *The Creation of Patriarchy*. London: Oxford

Lippert, J. 1977 'Sexuality as consumption.' Pp. 207–13 in J. Snodgrass (ed.), *For Men Against Sexism*. Albion, CA: Times Change Press

Livingstone, D. W. 1985 *Social Crisis and Schooling*. Toronto: Garamond Press

Livingstone, D. W., and J. M. Mangan forthcoming 'Class, gender and expanded class consciousness in Steeltown.' In M. Dobkowski and I. Wallimann (eds.), *Research in Inequality and Social Conflict*. Greenwich: JAI Press

Luxton, Meg 1980 *More than a Labour of Love: Three Generations of Women's Work in the Home*. Toronto: Women's Press

—— 1983 'Two hands for the clock: changing patterns in the gendered division of labour in the home.' *Studies in Political Economy* (Fall) 12: 27–44

—— 1987 'Thinking about the Future.' In K. Anderson et al. (eds.), *Family Matters: Sociology and Contemporary Canadian Families.* Toronto: Methuen

—— forthcoming 'Getting to work: The challenge of the women back into Stelco campaign.'

Luxton, M., D. W. Livingstone, and W. Seccombe 1982 'Steelworker families: Workplace, household and community in Hamilton.' A research proposal to the SSHRC

Mansbridge, Jane 1986 *Why We Lost the ERA.* Chicago: University of Chicago Press

Maroney, H. J. 1983 'Feminism at Work.' *New Left Review* (September–October) 141: 51–71

Maroney, H. J., and Meg Luxton 1987a 'From feminism and political economy to feminist political economy.' In Maroney and Luxton (eds.), *Feminism and Political Economy.* Toronto: Methuen

Mason, K., and L. Bumpass 1975 'U.S. women's sex role ideology, 1970.' *American Journal of Sociology* 80: 1212–19

Mead, M. 1950 *Male and Female.* London: Gollancz

Meissner, Martin 1986 'The Reproduction of Women's Domination in Organizational Communication.' In L. Thayer (ed.), *Organization–Communication: Emerging Perspectives I.* Norwood: Ablex

Mitchell, J. 1966 'Women: The Longest Revolution.' *New Left Review* (November–December) 40

—— 1971 *Women's Estate.* Harmondsworth: Penguin

Mitchell, Juliet, and Ann Oakley (eds.) 1986 *What is Feminism: A Re-examination.* New York: Pantheon

Morgan, Robin 1984 *Sisterhood is Global: the International Women's Movement Anthology.* Garden City, New York: Anchor Press

Murphy, Yolanda, and Robert Murphy 1974 *Women of the Forest.* New York: Columbia University Press

O'Brien, M. 1971 *The Politics of Reproduction.* London: Routledge and Kegan Paul

Parsons, T., and R. F. Bales 1953 *Family, Socialization and Interaction Process.* London: Routledge and Kegan Paul

Patterson, Michele, and Laurie Engelberg 1978 "Women in male dominated professions." In A. Stomberg and S. Harkess (eds.), *Women Working: Theories and Facts in Perspective.* Palo Alto, CA: Mayfield Publishing Co.

Pettigrew, Joyce 19[8]1 'Reminiscences of fieldwork among the Sikhs.' In Helen Roberts (ed.), *Doing Feminist Research.* London: Routledge and Kegan Paul

Pollert, Anna 1981 *Girls, Wives, Factory Lives.* London: Macmillan

—— 1983 'Women, gender relations and wage labour.' Pp. 96–114 in Eva Gamarnikow et al. (eds.), *Gender, Class and Work.* London: Heinemann

Porter, Marilyn 1983 *Home, Work and Class Consciousness.* Manchester: Manchester University Press

Rapp, Rayna 1978 'Family and Class in Contemporary America: Notes Toward and Understanding of Ideology.' *Science and Society* (Fall) 42(3): 278–300

Reid, Angus 1987 *Canadians' Views of the Role of Women in Society.* Winnipeg: Angus Reid Associates, January 24

Rowbotham, S. 1973 *Women, Resistance and Revolution.* Harmondsworth: Penguin

—— 1974 *Woman's Consciousness, Man's World.* Harmondsworth: Penguin

Ruch, Libby O. 1984 'Dimensionality of the Bem sex role inventory: a multidimensional analysis.' *Sex Roles* (January) 10(1–2): 99–117

Seccombe, Wally 1980 'Domestic labour and the Working Class Household.' Pp. 25–99 in B. Fox (ed.), *Hidden in the Household.* Toronto: Women's Educational Press

—— forthcoming 'Explaining Men's Participation in Domestic Labour: Evidence from Hamilton Steelworker Households'

Shulman, A. K. 1980 'Gender and Power: Gender Bases of Radical Feminism.' *Signs* (Summer) 5: 590–604

Simpson, J., and E. Mutran 1981 'Women's Social Consciousness: Sex or Worker Identity.' Pp 335–50 in R. L. Simpson and I. H. Simpson (eds.), *Research in the Sociology of Work I.* Greenwich, Conn.: JAI Press

Smith, D. E. 1978 'A Peculiar Eclipsing: Women's Exclusion from Man's Culture.' *Women's Studies International Quarterly* 1: 281–95

Smith, M. D., and L. J. Fisher 1982 'Sex role attitudes and social class: a reanalysis and clarification.' *Journal of Comparative Family Studies* (Spring) 77–88

Smith, Tom 1985 'Working wives and women's rights: the connection between the employment status of wives and the feminist attitudes of husbands.' *Sex Roles* (March) 12(5–6): 501–8)

Smith-Rosenberg, Carol 1980 'Politics and history in women's culture.' *Feminist Studies* (Spring) 6(1): 55–64

Spence, J. T., and R. L. Helmreich 1978 *Masculinity and Femininity: Their Psychological Dimensions, Correlates and Antecedents.* Austin, Texas: University of Texas Press

Stanley, Liz, and Sue Wise 1983 *Breaking Out: Feminist Consciousness and Feminist Research.* London: RKP

Stewart, Katie 1981 'The Marriage of Capitalist and Patriarchal Ideologies: Meanings of Male Bonding and Male Ranking in U.S. Culture,' In L. Sargent (ed.), *Women and Revolution.* Montreal: Black Rose

Stimpson, Catharine R. 1984 'Women as Knowers.' Pp. 15–24 in D. Fowlkes and C. McClure (eds.), *Feminist Visions: Toward a Transformation of the Liberal Arts Curriculum.* University, Alabama: University of Alabama Press

Thompson, Edward H., et al. 1985 'Attitudes toward the male role and their correlates.' *Sex Roles* (October) 13(7–8): 413–27

Thornton, G., D. Alwin, and D. Camburn 1983 'Causes and consequences of sex-role attitudes and attitude change.' *American Sociological Review* 48: 211–17

Thornton, M. 1980 'Work and Consciousness.' Pp. 198–229 in P. Boreham and G. Dow (eds.), *Work and Inequality II*. London: Macmillan

Tiano, S., and Bracken, K. 1984 'Ideology on the Line: A Typology for the Analysis of Assembly Line Workers' Images of Class and Gender Relations.' *Quarterly Journal of Ideology* (October) 8(4): 60–71

Tolson, A. 1988 *The Limits of Masculinity*. London: Tavistock

Turnbull, C. 1981 'MBUTI womanhood.' Pp. 205–19 in F. Dahlberg (ed.), *Woman, the Gatherer*, New Haven: York [sic] University Press

Valli, Linda 1987 *Becoming Clerical Workers*. London: Routledge and Kegan Paul

Vogel, L. 1986 'Feminist Scholarship: The Impact of Marxism.' Pp. 1–34 in B. Ollman and E. Vernoff (eds.), *The Left Academy 3*. New York: Praeger

Webber, M. J. 1986 'Regional Production and the Production of Regions: The Case of Steeltown.' Pp. 197–224 in A. J. Scott and M. Storper (eds.), *Production Work, Territory: The Geographical Anatomy of Industrial Capitalism*. Boston: Allen and Unwin.

Werner, Paul D., and Georgina W. La Russa 1985 'Persistence and change in sex-role stereotypes.' *Sex Roles* (May) 12(9–10): 1098–100

Westwood, Sallie 1984 *All Day Every Day: Factory and Family in the Making of Women's Lives*. London: Pluto Press

Willis, P. 1979 'Shop-floor culture, masculinity and the wage form.' Pp. 185–98 in J. Clarke et al. (eds.), *Working Class Culture: Studies in History and Theory*. London: Hutchinson

Wilson, M., and R. Sennott 1984 'Means of Knowing in the Neutralization of Women's Consciousness.' *Quarterly Journal of Ideology* (October) 8(4): 12–18

Winter, M. F., and E. F. Robert 1980 'Male dominance, late capitalism, and the growth of instrumental reason.' *Berkeley Journal of Sociology* 24–25: 249–80

Wolf, Margery 1972 *Women and the Family in Rural Taiwan*. Stanford, California: Stanford University Press

14

Women in the Workplace

Nancy Zukewich Ghalam

One of the most dramatic social changes in Canada over the past several decades has been the increase in the number of women in the workplace.[1] In fact, women currently make up almost one-half of all employed Canadians. However, women are still over-represented in part-time jobs, and, despite increased participation in most professional occupations, they remain concentrated in traditionally female jobs. Also, women's earnings are still well below those of men. Even when employed, women remain primarily responsible for family care and housework.

RISE IN EMPLOYMENT

Over the past two decades, most of the growth in Canada's employment levels has been attributable to the influx of women into the workforce. In fact, women aged 15 and over accounted for almost three-quarters (72%) of the rise in employment between 1975 and 1991. During this period, the total number of working women increased 65%, from 3.4 million to 5.6 million, whereas the number of men with jobs rose only 14%, from 5.9 million to 6.8 million. As a result, by 1991, women made up 45% of the workforce, compared with 36% in 1975.

Indeed, by 1991, 53% of women were employed, up from 41% in 1975. In contrast, male employment declined over the same period, falling to 67% from 74%.

Female employment levels vary widely across Canada. The proportion of women in the workforce in 1991 ranged from a high of 59% in Alberta to a low of 39% in Newfoundland. The percentages were around the national average in Ontario (55%), Saskatchewan (55%), Manitoba (54%) and British Columbia (53%). In contrast, less than one-half of women were employed in Prince Edward Island (49%), Quebec (48%), Nova Scotia (47%) and New Brunswick (45%). Employment levels of women, however, rose in every province between 1975 and 1991.

From Nancy Zukewich Ghalam, "Women in the Workplace," *Canadian Social Trends*, Cat. No. 11-008E (Winter 1992): 2–6. Reprinted by permission.

MORE WOMEN WORKING PART-TIME

Much of women's employment is part-time. In 1991, 26% of employed women worked part-time, compared with only 9% of employed men. In fact, women have consistently accounted for at least 70% of all part-time employment in Canada over the past fifteen years.

Many women, though, work part-time by "choice". In 1991, 36% of women employed part-time reported they did not want a full-time job, while another 22% were going to school.

However, many women work part-time either because they can't find a full-time position or because of personal or family commitments. In 1991, almost 400,000 women, 27% of all female part-time workers, indicated that they wanted full-time employment, but could only find part-time positions. Another 187,000 women, 13% of the total, worked part-time because of personal or family responsibilities.

Among both women and men, young adults are the most likely to work part-time. However, many older women also work part-time, in contrast to very few older men. In 1991, 20% of employed women aged 25–44 and 25% of those aged 45 and over worked part-time, compared with only 3% of employed men aged 25–44 and 6% of those aged 45 and over.

Not surprisingly, the reasons women work part-time vary by age, the stage of life, and the values associated with the different age groups. For example, most women aged 15–24 employed part-time in 1991 cited going to school as their reason (66%). On the other hand, 40% of women aged 25–

Percentage of Women and Men Employed, 1975–1991

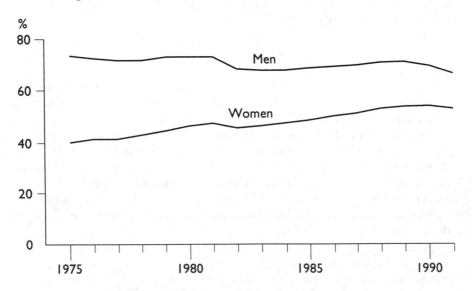

Sources: Statistics Canada, Catalogues 71-001, 71-220, and 71-529.

Percentage of Women Employed, by Province, 1981–1991

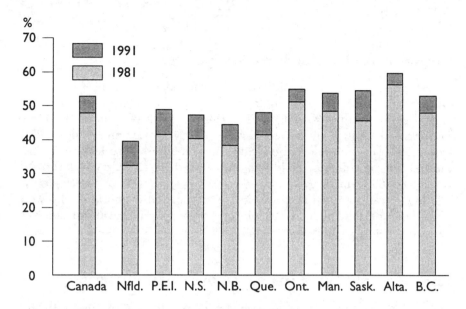

Sources: Statistics Canada, Catalogues 71-220 and 71-529.

44 and fully 65% of those aged 45 and over working part-time did not want full-time jobs. Personal or family responsibilities were cited by 24% of female part-time workers aged 24–44 (the prime child-rearing age-group) as their reason for working part-time.

MORE MARRIED WOMEN WORKING

Married women are now much more likely to be in the workforce than they were in previous years. In 1991, 56% of married women were employed, up from 47% in 1981. Nonetheless, they are still considerably less likely than their male counterparts to be employed, although the percentage of married men with jobs dropped to 71% from 80% over the same period.

In contrast to trends among married women, the proportion of both separated/divorced and widowed women who were employed declined over the last decade. By 1991, 56% of separated/divorced women were employed, down from 59% in 1981. Over the same period, the proportion for widowed women dropped to 12% from 18%. Declines also occurred in the percentage of comparable men with jobs, although the proportion of these men employed remained higher than for women. In 1991, 65% of separated/divorced men and 20% of widowed men were employed.

Over the last decade, employment levels of single (never-married) women and men remained about the same. In 1991, 59% of such women and 60% of single men were in the workforce.

GROWTH IN THE EMPLOYMENT OF MOTHERS

There has also been very rapid growth in the employment of women with children. In 1991, 63% of mothers with children under age 16 were employed, up from 50% in 1981. The rise in the proportion of employed mothers with children under age 6 was even more dramatic, rising to 57% from 42% over the same period. Still, these mothers were less likely than mothers whose youngest child was school-aged (6–15 years) to be in the workforce (69%) in 1991.

In contrast to sharp increases in the proportion of mothers who were employed, the percentage of employed married women without children rose only to 45% in 1991 from 41% in 1981.

LONE MOTHERS LESS LIKELY EMPLOYED THAN OTHERS

Female lone parents are considerably less likely than other women with children to be in the workforce. In 1991, just 52% of lone mothers with children less than age 16 were employed, compared with 65% of mothers in two-parent families.

In addition, employment among female lone parents was slightly lower in 1991 than in 1981 (54%). This decline can be traced largely to substantial drops in employment levels among lone mothers during the recessions of the early 1980s and 1990s, a trend contrary to that for women in general.

The labour force activity of female lone parents is particularly influenced by the presence of young children. For example, in 1991, 31% of lone mothers with children under age 3 and 47% of those whose youngest child was aged 3–5 were employed. These proportions were much lower than the 62% of lone mothers whose youngest child was aged 6–15.

OCCUPATION

Most women continue to work in traditionally female-dominated fields. In 1991, 71% of women were employed in just five occupational groups— teaching, nursing or related health occupations, clerical, sales, and service. In contrast, only about 30% of employed men worked in one of these occupational groupings. The percentage of women currently employed in these areas, however, is down from around 76% during the early 1980s.

The largest single concentration of female workers is in clerical occupations. This category accounted for 29% of female employment in 1991,

Percentage of Employed Women and Men Working Part-time, by Age, 1991

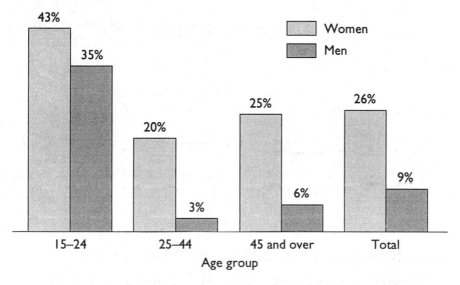

Source: Statistics Canada, Catalogue 71-220.

compared with 6% of that of men. At the same time, 17% of employed women had service jobs, 10% worked in sales, 9% were nurses or related medical professionals such as technicians, and 6% were teachers.

Women have made gains in several professional occupations. For example, in 1991, women accounted for 27% of all doctors, dentists, and other health diagnosing and treating professionals, up from 18% in 1982. At the same time, however, women made up 87% of nurses, therapists, and other medical assistants and technologists in 1991.

Women also represent a growing proportion of those working in management and administrative positions. In 1991, 40% of those working in one of these categories were women, up from 27% in 1981. Much of this increase is attributable to changes in occupational definitions, such as some clerical jobs being reclassified into the management/administrative category. Even without this artificial boost, though, there was considerable growth in women's employment in these areas.

On the other hand, women remain very much under-represented in the natural sciences, engineering, and mathematics. For example, in 1991, women made up only 18% of professionals in these fields, up just slightly from 16% in 1981.

Women also remain under-represented in most traditionally male-dominated goods-producing occupations. Women accounted for 15% of employment in primary, manufacturing, construction, transportation, and materials handling jobs in 1991, ranging from 22% in the primary industries to only 2% in construction.

Earnings of Women as a Percentage of Those of Men,[1] 1967–1991

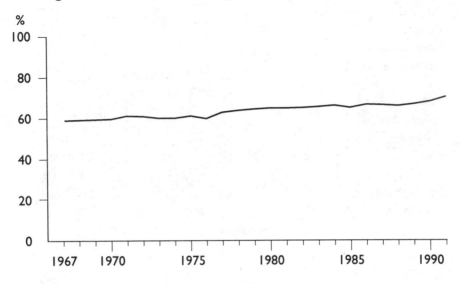

[1] Includes earnings of full-time, full-year workers.
Source: Statistics Canada, Catalogue 13-217.

SELF-EMPLOYMENT LOWER FOR WOMEN

Women are less likely than men to be self-employed. In 1991, approximately 525,000 women worked for themselves, representing just 9% of all female employment. This compared with almost 1.3 million self-employed men, accounting for 19% of total male employment. As a result, women represented only 29% of all self-employed workers in 1991, a figure well below their share of total employment (45%).

AVERAGE EARNINGS[2]

Employed women in Canada earn substantially less than their male counterparts. In 1991, women working on a full-time, full-year basis earned an average of $26,800, just 70% as much as comparable men. Furthermore, this pattern changed little over the last decade: in 1981, women's earnings had been 64% of those of men.

Earnings of Women as a Percentage of Those of Men,[1] by Occupation, 1991

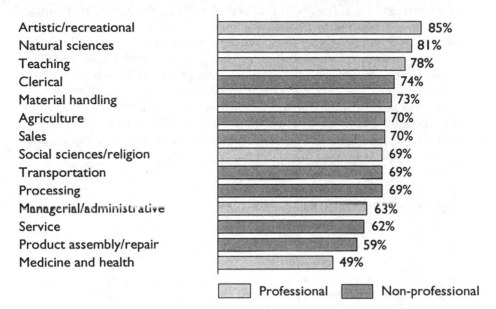

Artistic/recreational	85%
Natural sciences	81%
Teaching	78%
Clerical	74%
Material handling	73%
Agriculture	70%
Sales	70%
Social sciences/religion	69%
Transportation	69%
Processing	69%
Managerial/administrative	63%
Service	62%
Product assembly/repair	59%
Medicine and health	49%

Professional   Non-professional

[1] Includes earnings of full-time, full-year workers.
Source: Statistics Canada, Catalogue 13-217

Within several professional fields, the gap between women's and men's earnings is smaller than that for all occupations. In 1991, for instance, women employed in teaching earned 78% as much as their male colleagues.

Nonetheless, there were several professional occupations in which the female-to-male earnings ratio was quite low. In 1991, for example, the earnings of female managers/administrators were, on average, 63% of those of their male counterparts, and among health technicians and other related workers, just 58%. The earnings ratio was also very low, just 49% in 1991, for medical and health professionals. This reflects in part, though, the fact that women employed in these fields tend to be concentrated in lower-paying occupations such as nursing, whereas, men are more likely to be treatment and diagnosis professionals, such as doctors and dentists.

For women employed in some non-professional occupations, the earnings ratio was above the national rate: female clerical workers' earnings were 74% of those of their male counterparts. However, both women's and men's earnings in these occupational groups were quite low. In contrast, in the remaining non-professional occupations, women's earnings were less than 70% of those of men.

CONTRIBUTION TO FAMILY INCOME

With the influx of married women into the workplace, both spouses are employed in the majority of Canadian families. By 1990, dual-earner families made up 62% of all husband-wife families, compared with 55% in 1981 and 32% in 1967.

Although the average earnings of women remain considerably less than those of men, women are making an increasingly important contribution to family income. The earnings of wives made up 29% of family income in 1990, compared with 26% in 1967. At the same time, husbands' contribution to family income fell from 63% in 1967 to 56% in 1990. The relative shares of income received from investments and transfer payments also increased over the same period.

ABSENCES FROM WORK

Women in Canada remain primarily responsible for family-related matters, regardless of their employment status. This is reflected in the fact that women are more than twice as likely as men to be absent from work because of personal or family responsibilities. During an average week in 1991, 3.0% of all employed women, versus 1.2% of employed men, lost some time from work for these reasons.

The presence of young children has a particularly strong influence on work absences of women. In 1991, 11% of women in two-parent families with at least one child under age 6, and 6% of comparable lone mothers, missed time from work each week because of personal or family responsibilities. Absentee rates dropped to around 2% for both lone mothers and mothers in dual-parent families whose youngest child was aged 6–15. In contrast, the presence of young children had little effect on the work absences of fathers. Only 2% of fathers in two-parent families with preschool-age children and 1% of those whose youngest child was aged 6–15 lost time from work.[3]

Time Use

Women who are active in the workplace still take on most household duties. In 1986, employed women spent almost an hour and a half more per day (averaged over a seven-day week) than men performing unpaid household work, including domestic work, primary child care, and shopping. That year, employed women spent 3.2 hours per day on these activities, compared with only 1.8 hours for men.

However, when all time devoted to paid work, education and unpaid work is combined, employed women and men spend nearly the same amounts of time on "productive activities". In 1986, women spent an average of 9.2 hours per day (averaged over a seven-day week) on these activities, compared with 9.0 hours for men. Given that women do more unpaid work, it follows that the productive activity of employed men is more heavily oriented towards paid work. Indeed, in 1986, women devoted an average of 6.0 hours per day to paid work and education, compared with 7.2 hours for men.

Employed women generally have less free time than their male counterparts. In 1986, working women averaged about 4.2 hours of free time per day, compared with 4.8 hours for men. On the other hand, employed women devoted nearly half an hour more per day than men to personal care activities such as sleeping and eating.

Child Care

The need for child care services has grown as a result of the increasing number of mothers entering the workforce. According to the National Child Care Study[1], 1.1 million preschool-age children and 1.6 million school-age children required some form of child care in the fall of 1988 to accommodate the work or study schedules of their parents.

Informal arrangements were the major source of child care support for families in 1988. In fact, regulated or organized care, including daycare centres, licensed family day care, before and after school care, and kindergarten and nursery schools was the main method of care for only 11% of children under age 13. Not surprisingly, preschool-age children were the most likely to be cared for through one of these arrangements. In 1988, this was the case for 19% of children under age 6, compared with only 5% of those aged 6–12.

In 1988, parents themselves were the main source of care for 28% of all children under age 13. The employed parent most responsible for child care (usually the mother) looked after 9% of children while working, while 20% of children were cared for by that parent's partner to cover work or school hours. It is likely that many parents arrange their work schedules so as to be able to care for their children themselves. In 1988, 45% of employed parents primarily responsible for child care arrangements worked weekends, evening or irregular hours. For these people, the availability of child care outside of daytime, weekday hours may be critical to their availability for jobs.

Babysitters and relatives are an important source of child care services, particularly for children under age 6. For example, in 1988, babysitters were the main source of care for 37% of children under age 3 and 31% of those aged 3–5. Reliance on a relative was the main child

---

[1] For additional information, see *Parental Work Patterns and Child Care Needs*, Statistics Canada, Catalogue 89-529, by D.S. Lero, H. Goelman, A.R. Pence, L.M. Brockman and S. Nuttall.

care arrangement for 24% of children under age 3 and 16% of those aged 3–5. Among children aged 6–12, babysitters were the main care giver for 16%, and relatives, for 11%.

School-aged children tended to rely more on themselves or on a sibling, or had no specific arrangements. In 1988, 23% of children this age either looked after themselves or were looked after by a sibling. No formal child care arrangement outside of school was necessary for another 16%.

NOTES

1 Throughout this article, involvement in the workplace or workforce refers to employment. Statistics Canada's Labour Force Survey defines employed persons as those who have a job performing work for pay or profit. This includes paid work in the context of both an employer-employee relationship and self-employment. It also includes unpaid family work where the work contributes directly to the operation of a farm, business, or professional practice owned or operated by a related member of the household.

2 Unless stated otherwise, the figures in this section are for women and men employed on a full-time, full-year basis.

3 See *Absenteeism at Work*, by Ernest B. Akyeampong, in Canadian Social Trends, Summer 1992, Statistics Canada, Catalogue 11-008.

15

Blowing the Whistle on the "Mommy Track"

Barbara Ehrenreich and Deirdre English

W hen a feminist has something bad to say about women, the media listen. Three years ago it was Sylvia Hewlett, announcing in her book *A Lesser Life* that feminism had sold women out by neglecting to win child-care and maternity leaves. This year it's Felice Schwartz, the New York-based consultant who argues that women—or at least the mothers among us—have become a corporate liability. They cost too much to employ, she argues, and the solution is to put them on a special lower-paid, low-pressure career track—the now-notorious "mommy track."

The "mommy track" story rated prominent coverage in the New York *Times* and *USA Today,* a cover story in *Business Week,* and airtime on dozens of talk shows. Schwartz, after all, seemed perfectly legitimate. She is the president of Catalyst, an organization that has been advising corporations on women's careers since 1962. She had published her controversial claims in no less a spot than the *Harvard Business Review* ("Management Women and the New Facts of Life," January–February 1989). And her intentions, as she put it in a later op-ed piece, seemed thoroughly benign: "to urge employers to create policies that help mothers balance career and family responsibilities."

Moreover, Schwartz's argument seemed to confirm what everybody already knew. Women haven't been climbing up the corporate ladder as fast as might once have been expected, and women with children are still, on average, groping around the bottom rungs. Only about 40 percent of top female executives have children, compared to 95 percent of their male peers. There have been dozens of articles about female dropouts: women who slink off the fast track, at age 30-something, to bear a strategically timed baby or two. In fact, the "mommy track"—meaning a lower-pressure, flexible, or part-time approach to work—was neither a term Schwartz used nor her invention. It was already, in an anecdotal sort of way, a well-worn issue.

Most of the controversy focused on Schwartz's wildly anachronistic "solution." Corporate employers, she advised, should distinguish between two categories of women: "career-primary" women, who won't interrupt their careers for children and hence belong on the fast track with the men, and "career-and-family" women, who should be shunted directly to the mommy track. Schwartz had no answers for the obvious questions: how is the employer supposed to sort the potential "breeders" from the strivers? Would such distinction even be legal? What about *fathers*? But in a sense, the damage had already been done. A respected feminist, writing in a respected journal, had made a case that most women can't pull their weight in the corporate world, and should be paid accordingly.

Few people, though, actually read Schwartz's article. The first surprise is that it contains *no* evidence to support her principal claim, that "the cost of employing women in management is greater than the cost of employing men." Schwartz offers no data, no documentation at all—except for two unpublished studies by two *anonymous* corporations. Do these studies really support her claim? Were they methodologically sound? Do they even exist? There is no way to know.

Few media reports of the "mommy track" article bothered to mention the peculiar nature of Schwartz's "evidence." We, however were moved to call the *Harvard Business Review* and inquire whether the article was representative of its normal editorial standard. Timothy Blodgett, the executive director, defended the article as "an expression of opinion and judgment." When we suggested that such potentially damaging "opinions" might need a bit of bolstering, he responded by defending Schwartz: "She speaks with a tone of authority. That comes through."

(The conversation went downhill from there, with Blodgett stating sarcastically, "I'm sure your article in *Ms.* will be *very* objective." Couldn't fall much lower than the *Harvard Business Review,* we assured him.)

Are managerial women more costly to employ than men? As far as we could determine—with the help of the Business and Professional Women's Foundation and Women's Equity Action League—there is no *published* data on this point. A 1987 government study did show female managerial employees spending less time with each employer than males (5 years compared to 6.8 years), but there is no way of knowing what causes this turnover or what costs it incurs. And despite pregnancy, and despite women's generally greater responsibility for child-raising, they use up on the average only 5.1 sick days per year, compared to 4.9 for men.

The second surprise, given Schwartz's feminist credentials, is that the article is riddled with ancient sexist assumptions—for example, about the possibility of a more androgynous approach to child-raising *and* work. She starts with the unobjectionable statement that "maternity is biological rather than cultural." The same thing, after all, could be said of paternity. But a moment later, we find her defining maternity as "...a continuum that begins with an awareness of the ticking of the biological clock, proceeds to the anticipation of motherhood, includes pregnancy, childbirth, physical recuperation, psychological adjustment, and continues on to nursing, bonding, and child-rearing."

Now, pregnancy, childbirth, and nursing do qualify as biological processes. But slipping child-rearing into the list, as if changing diapers and picking up socks were hormonally programmed activities, is an old masculinist trick. Child-raising is a *social* undertaking, which may involve nannies, aunts, grandparents, day-care workers, or, of course, *fathers*.

Equally strange for a "feminist" article is Schwartz's implicit assumption that employment, in the case of married women, is strictly optional, or at least that *mothers* don't need to be top-flight earners. The "career-and-family woman," she tells us, is "willing" and "satisfied" to forgo promotions and "stay at the middle level." What about the single mother, or the wife of a low-paid male? But Schwartz's out-of-date—and classbound—assumption that every woman is supported by a male breadwinner fits in with her apparent nostalgia for the era of the feminine mystique. "Ironically," she writes, "although the feminist movement was an expression of women's quest for freedom from their home-based lives, *most women are remarkably free already* [emphasis added]."

But perhaps the oddest thing about the "mommy track" article—even as an "expression of opinion and judgment"—is that it is full of what we might charitably call ambivalence or, more bluntly, self-contradictions. Take the matter of the "glass ceiling," which symbolized all the barriers, both subtle and overt, that corporate women keep banging their heads against. At the outset, Schwartz dismisses the glass ceiling as a "misleading metaphor." Sexism, in short, is not the problem.

Nevertheless, within a few pages, she is describing the glass ceiling (not by that phrase, of course) like a veteran. "Male corporate culture," she tells us, sees both the career-primary and the career-and-family women as "unacceptable." The woman with family responsibilities is likely to be seen as lacking commitment to the organization, while the woman who *is* fully committed to the organization is likely to be seen as "abrasive and unfeminine." She goes on to cite the corporate male's "confusion, competitiveness," and his "stereotypical language and sexist...behavior," concluding that "with notable exceptions, men are still more comfortable with other men."

And we're supposed to blame *women* for their lack of progress in the corporate world?

Even on her premier point, that women are more costly to employ, Schwartz loops around and rebuts herself. Near the end of her article, she urges corporations to conduct their own studies of the costs of employing women—the two anonymous studies were apparently not definitive after all—and asserts confidently ("of course I believe") that the benefits will end up outweighing the costs. In a more recent New York *Times* article, she puts it even more baldly: "The costs of employing women pale beside the payoffs."

Could it be that Felice Schwartz and the editors of the *Harvard Business Review* are ignorant of that most basic financial management concept, the cost-benefit analysis? If the "payoffs" outweigh the costs of employing women—runny noses and maternity leaves included—then the net cost may indeed be *lower* than the cost of employing men.

In sum, the notorious "mommy track" article is a tortured muddle of feminist perceptions and sexist assumptions, good intentions and dangerous suggestions—unsupported by any acceptable evidence at all. It should never have been taken seriously, not by the media and not by the nation's most prestigious academic business publication. The fact that it was suggests that something serious *is* afoot: a backlash against America's high-status, better paid women, and potentially against all women workers.

We should have seen it coming. For the past 15 years upwardly mobile, managerial women have done everything possible to fit into an often hostile corporate world. They dressed up as non-threatening corporate clones. They put in 70-hour workweeks; and of course, they postponed childbearing. Thanks in part to their commitment to the work world, the birthrate dropped by 16 percent since 1970. But now many of these women are ready to start families. This should hardly be surprising; after all, 90 percent of American women do become mothers.

But while corporate women were busily making adjustments and concessions, the larger corporate world was not. The "fast track," with its macho camaraderie and toxic work load, remains the only track to success. As a result, success is indeed usually incompatible with motherhood—as well as with any engaged and active form of fatherhood. The corporate culture strongly discourages *men* from taking paternal leave even if offered. And how many families can afford to have both earners on the mommy track?

Today there's an additional factor on the scene—the corporate women who *have* made it. Many of them are reliable advocates for the supports that working parents need. But you don't have to hang out with the skirted-suit crowd for long to discover that others of them are impatient with, and sometimes even actively resentful of, younger women who are trying to combine career and family. Recall that 60 percent of top female executives are themselves childless. Others are of the "if I did it, so can you" school of thought. Felice Schwartz may herself belong in this unsisterly category. In a telling anecdote in her original article, she describes her own problems with an executive employee seeking maternity leave, and the "somewhat awkward conversations" that ensued.

Sooner or later, corporations will have to yield to the pressure for paid parental leave, flextime, and child care, if only because they've become dependent on female talent. The danger is that employers—no doubt quoting Felice Schwartz for legitimization—will insist that the price for such options be reduced pay and withheld promotions, i.e., consignment to the mommy track. Such a policy would place a penalty on parenthood, and the ultimate victims—especially if the policy trickles down to the already low-paid female majority—will of course be children.

Bumping women—or just fertile women, or married women, or whomever—off the fast track may sound smart to cost-conscious CEOs, but eventually it is the corporate culture itself that needs to slow down to a human pace. No one, male or female, works at peak productivity for 70 hours a week, year after year, without sabbaticals or leaves. Think of it this way. If the price of success were exposure to a toxic chemical, would we argue that only women should be protected? Work loads that are incompatible with family life are themselves a kind of toxin—to men as well as women, and ultimately to businesses as well as families.

16

Sexual Harassment: The Link Between Gender Stratification, Sexuality, and Women's Economic Status

Susan Ehrlich Martin

... Until recently, if sexual harassment received any attention, it tended to be regarded as an individual problem, either a not-too-serious matter brought on by the woman of dubious virtue whose demeanor or attire "asked for it" or a complaint initiated by a woman as an illegitimate way to get ahead on the job. Until 1976, when the term *sexual harassment* apparently first came into use, the phenomenon was literally unspeakable (MacKinnon, 1979). Since that time there has been a growing recognition of its pervasiveness and its negative consequences, as well as an emerging view that it is a serious social problem. ...

Understanding sexual harassment requires recognizing that it is central to maintaining women's subordinate social, economic, and sexual statuses and thus is closely related to other feminist issues. Along with rape, wife beating, prostitution, and pornography, it is one of the ways in which male control of women's sexuality shapes women's experience. ...

DEFINITIONS OF SEXUAL HARASSMENT

Various definitions of sexual harassment have been proposed. For example, Safran (1976: 49) defined it as "sex that is one-sided, unwelcome, or comes with strings attached"; Farley (1978: 14–15) called it "unsolicited, nonreciprocal male behavior that asserts a woman's sex role over her functioning as a worker"; a survey by New Responses, Inc. (1979: 2) defined it as behavior that makes an individual feel that her employment situation will in some way suffer unless sexual demands are met. The definition of sexual harassment applicable throughout the federal civil service is "deliberate or repeated unsolicited verbal comments, gestures, or physical contact of a sexual nature which are unwelcome" (U.S. House of Representatives, 1980: 8). What is common to these definitions is that sexual harassment (1) is physical or verbal behavior that is sexual in nature (i.e., it makes the victim's sex salient over her occupational or other statuses); (2) is unwanted; and (3) implicitly or explicitly is experienced as a threat to the woman's job or ability to perform her work or educational activities.[1]

Problems arise in defining and identifying incidents of sexual harassment because harassing behavior is not always clearly different from other acts. The same action, such as a man's putting an arm around a woman's shoulder, may be regarded by its recipient either as intentionally offensive or as a friendly gesture and may be welcome or repugnant depending on the woman's interpretation of the man's intentions, her view of him, and the situation.[2]

Several types of sexual harassment have been identified. MacKinnon (1979) distinguishes between *quid pro quo harassment* and *harassment as a continuing condition of work*. Quid pro quo harassment involves a more or less explicit exchange: a woman must comply sexually or forfeit an employment or educational benefit. In such instances the harasser tends to be an employer, supervisor, or teacher because his power to punish or reward rests on his occupational status. Male coworkers, classmates, and clients, however, may use informal authority in the work or academic setting or the power to give or withhold business or sales in order to harass. Quid pro quo harassment situations involve three elements: an advance, a response, and a consequence. Four different outcomes are possible: (1) an employer or instructor makes an advance, the woman declines it, and she is punished; (2) the employer or instructor makes an advance, the woman complies, but she does not receive the promised benefit; (3) the employer or instructor makes an advance, the woman complies, and she gains the benefit; (4) the employer or instructor makes an advance, the woman declines, and she receives no subsequent harassment or reprisal. Although each situation involves harassment, all successful legal cases against quid pro quo harassment have dealt with the first type.

Sexual harassment may also occur as a condition of work. Such harassment rarely involves outright sexual demands but includes a variety of behaviors, such as touching, teasing, and comments about a woman's appearance or sexuality; these require no response but make the woman's work environment unpleasant. Often such harassing behavior is less blatant or threatening than quid pro quo harassment, is condoned by management, and is regarded as "normal" male behavior or as an extension of the male prerogative of initiation in male-female interaction. For these reasons women often do not define such behavior as sexual harassment and, when they do, tend to be more reluctant to make formal complaints about it than about quid pro quo harassment.

Loy and Stewart (n.d.) identify four types of harassment along two dimensions: its form (whether it is verbal or physical) and the level of coerciveness involved and the response required (whether it requires only tolerance by the woman or evokes reciprocation or resistance). The four types are verbal commentary, which includes sexual messages delivered through teasing, off-color jokes, and animal sounds; verbal negotiation, which includes explicit sexual propositions and negotiation; manhandling, which includes unwanted touching, such as patting, brushing against, or pinching; and sexual assault, which involves the use of physical force.

SURVEY FINDINGS REGARDING SEXUAL HARASSMENT

Knowledge is still limited about the frequency of various types of sexual harassment, the characteristics of victims and harassers, the conditions under which it occurs, its psychological and physical effects on the victims, and their responses to it. Most of the early studies involved nonrandom surveys with self-selected respondents, lacked a standard definition of sexual harassment, failed to specify the time period within which the respondent was to answer, and provided evidence that was stark but impressionistic rather than scientific (Safran, 1976; Carey, 1977; Kelber, 1977; Silverman, 1976–77). Several recent studies have used random samples that permit more conclusive statistical analyses of the distribution of harassing behavior (Loy and Stewart, n.d.; Gutek et al., 1980; Gutek, 1981; MSPB, 1981; Benson and Thomson, 1982). ... The study by the U.S. Merit Systems Protection Board (MSPB) involved a stratified random sample of more than twenty-three thousand civilian employees of the executive branch of the federal government and thus provides the fullest and most reliable picture of sexual harassment to date.[3]

Extent of Sexual Harassment

In the early studies estimates of the proportion of women experiencing sexual harassment on the job were so high that *Redbook* observed: "The problem is not epidemic; it is pandemic—an everyday, everywhere occurrence" (Safran, 1976: 217). Recent studies support this conclusion. The MSPB study found that 42 percent of the female federal employees had experienced some form of sexual harassment in the workplace during the previous two years. One percent of the women in the sample were victims of actual or attempted rape or sexual assault (hereafter referred to as *rape/assault*); 29 percent experienced "severe sexual harassment" (including unwanted letters, phone calls, or materials of a sexual nature; unwanted pressure for sexual favors; or unwanted touching, pinching, or being leaned over or cornered); and 12 percent were victims of "less severe sexual harassment" (including unwanted pressure for dates; unwanted suggestive looks or gestures; or unwanted sexual teasing, jokes, remarks, or questions) (MSPB, 1981: 34–8). ...

Benson and Thomson (1982:241) found that about 30 percent of the Berkeley seniors who responded had personally experienced at least one incident of sexual harassment during their college career, although a larger proportion knew of incidents involving someone else and agreed that such occurrences are not rare. These incidents tended to take the form of gradual inducements not overtly linked to grades or immediate sexual obligations. Instead, instructors displayed friendliness and offered extra help and flexible deadlines, which laid the groundwork for subsequent overtures.

Victim Characteristics

Women of all backgrounds and in all positions have been victims of harassment, although a woman's age, marital status, and education affect the likelihood of harassment. The MSPB found that the rate of harassment was directly proportional to the youth of the victim. Twice as many women between sixteen and nineteen years of age (67 percent) reported being harassed as did women between forty-five and fifty-four (33 percent) (MSPB, 1981: 43). More single (53 percent) and divorced (49 percent) women reported harassment than married (37 percent) and widowed women (31 percent). Surprisingly, harassment was found to increase with the woman's education. The higher victimization rate of the more educated female employees appears to be related both to the difference in their attitudes (i.e., they defined more behaviors as harassment) and to their presence in nontraditional jobs (MSPB, 1981:44). The race and ethnic background of the victim, however, made virtually no difference (MSPB, 1981: 44–5).

Organizational Characteristics

A number of organizational characteristics were also found by the MSPB study to be related to sexual harassment, including agency, job classification, traditionalism of the job, sex of the victim's supervisor, and sexual composition of the victim's work group. Incidence of harassment varied by federal agency, ranging from 56 percent in the Department of Labor to 31 percent in the Department of Agriculture (MSPB, 1981: 47). The job classification of the victim showed modest relationship to victimization. The highest frequency of harassment occurred among trainees (51 percent reported harassment), which may be related both to their age and to their relative powerlessness on the job. Of the women in professional and technical positions, 41 percent reported harassment; in clerical positions, 40 percent; and in blue-collar jobs, 38 percent (MSPB, 1981: 50). It is noteworthy that 53 percent of the women in nontraditional jobs but only 41 percent in traditional jobs reported unwanted sexual attention on the job (MSPB, 1981: 51). Women with a male supervisor were somewhat more likely to be sexually harassed (45 percent) than those with a female supervisor (38 percent). In addition, the male-female ratio of the work group was strongly related to harassment: the greater the proportion of men in the work group the more likely the women were to be harassed: 55 percent of those who work in virtually all-male groups and 49 percent of those in predominantly male groups were subjected to harassment: 37 percent in predominantly female and only 22 percent in all-female work groups were victims of harassment (MSPB, 1981: 52). This may be related both to the statistically greater number of men in jobs that are nontraditional for women and to deliberate harassment by men as an expression of resentment of the presence of women in these jobs. Differences among salaries and grade levels and by region were minor, as were several other organizational characteristics, including privacy on the job, length of federal service, work schedule, typical working hours, and the size of the immediate work group (MSPB, 1981:52–4).

The Harassers

The typical harasser of federal female employees was a male coworker who was married, older than the victim, of the same race or ethnic background, and likely to have harassed others at work, according to the descriptions of the victims. Of the women who reported being harassed (and described the incident in some detail), 79 percent indicated that the harasser was a lone man; 16 percent reported that the incident involved two or more men; 2 percent said the incident involved both male and female harassers; and 3 percent said they were harassed by one or more women. In 37 percent of the cases women reported harassment by an immediate or higher level supervisor; 65 percent were bothered by a coworker or other federal employee with no supervisory authority over the victim; and only 4 percent were bothered by a subordinate (MSPB, 1981: 59–60). (Since some respondents reported that more than one person had harassed them, these figures total more than 100 percent.) For the victim of rape/sexual assault, however, the supervisor was the perpetrator in 51 percent of the cases.

Loy and Stewart report somewhat different proportions of harassment by coworkers and supervisor. They found that 48 percent of the women reporting harassment had been victimized by an immediate or higher level supervisor, and 50 percent reported harassment by a coworker (Loy and Stewart, n.d.: Table 8).

Effects of Sexual Harassment on Victims

Sexual harassment has psychological, social, and physical effects on its victims. Like rape victims, sexually harassed women feel humiliated, ashamed, and angry. In one survey in which women could report more than one reaction, 78 percent reported feeling angry, 48 percent were upset, 23 percent were frightened, and an additional 27 percent mentioned feeling alienation, aloneness, helplessness, guilt, or some other emotion. Only 7 percent reported feeling indifference (Silverman 1976–77). The harassed women tended to feel the incident was their fault and that they were individually responsible as well as demeaned. Some have reported strained relations with men, including their husbands, as a result of the harassment (Safran, 1976; Lindsey, 1977). Others reported developing physical symptoms and attitude changes, including loss of ambition and self-confidence and a negative view of their work (Safran, 1976; Silverman, 1976–77; New Responses, Inc., 1979). A third of all the victims—and 82 percent of the victims of rape/assault—reported suffering emotional or physical consequences (MSPB, 1981: 81).

Sexual harassment also had harmful effects on female students. It disrupted the process of intellectual development and caused confusion, uncertainty, self-doubt, and distrust of male faculty in general (Benson and Thomson, 1982: 246–7). It also led to feelings of helplessness—that nothing was likely to be done about a complaint, that the student was not likely to be believed when a tenured professor denied a complaint, and that she would be labeled a "troublemaker" or suffer reprisal in the form of lowered grades and poor recommendations.

While there is no way to estimate costs to individual victims, the MSPB estimated that the sexual harassment of women cost the federal government $101 million. This figure encompasses the costs of job turnover, including the costs of offering a job, doing background checks, and training new employees; dollar losses due to emotional and physical stress, measured in terms of increased use of governmental health benefit plans; and dollar losses due to absenteeism and lost individual and work-group productivity over a two-year period (MSPB, 1981: 77).

ANALYSIS OF SEXUAL HARASSMENT

Sexual harassment is traditionally explained as either biologically based, "natural" behavior or the idiosyncratic personal proclivity of a minority of men. One variation of this traditional perspective assumes that the human sex drive is stronger in men, leading them to act in sexually aggressive ways toward women. Another variation maintains that men and women are naturally attracted to each other and therefore inevitably engage in sexually oriented behavior in the workplace. A third variation suggests that sexually harassing behavior stems from the personal peculiarities of isolated, highly sexed individuals. What these variations have in common is their denial that sexual harassment at work has the intent or effect of discriminating against women or that it reduces their chances to achieve social equality.

This traditional approach has several notable shortcomings. Most important is the failure to see that men and women are gender groups that are socialized into learned sex roles and work behaviors. Sexual behavior, like other kinds of social behavior, is learned, shaped by social rules and norms, and best understood in a social rather than an isolated individual context. Most individuals can and do control their impulses, in conformity with existing social rules. In addition, the traditional view trivializes the problem of sexual harassment by asserting that such behavior is "normal" or that it is futile to try to change human nature, thereby making any systematic effort to remedy the problem hopeless.

A feminist approach to sexual harassment views it as the use of power derived from the economic or occupational sphere to gain benefits or impose punishments in the sexual sphere. Thus, economic inequality (i.e., the employer's control of workers) and sexual inequality (i.e., men's dominance over and control of women) reinforce each other to undercut women's potential for social equality in two interlocking ways. Women's confinement to dead-end, low-paying, sex-typed jobs and their subordination to male supervisors, employers, and instructors make them systematically vulnerable to sexual coercion. At the same time the sex-role expectations of women as wives, mothers, and sex objects get carried into the workplace and are used to coerce women economically.

Women in the Occupational System

Women's place in the occupational world is characterized by (1) lower pay than men on the average and lower pay for doing the same job; (2) subordination to male supervisors and dependence on their goodwill and approval for getting, keeping, and advancing on a job; and (3) concentration in sex-typed occupations considered appropriate for women with limited opportunities for mobility into other types of work or up a career ladder. Limited alternatives and subordination to male supervisors make it difficult for female workers to reject sexual advances by males in positions of authority. Occupational segregation contributes to the sexual harassment of women employed in both traditionally "female" and traditionally "male" jobs through a phenomenon termed *sex-role spillover* (Gutek and Morash, 1982). Sex-role spillover occurs when gender-based expectations for behavior get carried into the workplace, so that workers in their work roles are expected to behave as males or females.

"Women's jobs" not only offer low pay, little prestige, and routine tasks, but they also require women to serve, emotionally support, and be sexually attractive to men. Thus their jobs are extensions of the female sex role into the workplace. The secretary, for example, is the "office wife," who, in addition to performing her official duties, is expected to make coffee, run her boss's personal errands, and maintain his sense of masculinity through flattery and deference (Kanter, 1977). Similarly, the scanty attire required of some waitresses and the former requirement that airline stewardesses be unmarried and younger than thirty years old indicate that female sexuality is an integral part of what is being sold by their employers. Indeed (MacKinnon, 1979: 23),

> the very qualities which men find sexually attractive in the women they harass are the real qualifications for the jobs for which they hire them. It is this good-girl sexiness ... that qualifies a woman for her job

*that leaves her open to sexual harassment at any time and to the accu-
sation that she invited it.*

Women who enter male-dominated occupations or high-status positions, as conspicious "token" exceptions to women's position in the
occupational world, also suffer from sexual harassment. For them, too, sex-
role expectations spill over into work-role expectations. But their jobs
require behaviors regarded as masculine—behaviors seen as incongruent
with their sex role. The tendency of male coworkers in this situation is to
behave toward these women in accordance with the men's primary conception of them, i.e., as women rather than as workers. The women's sex
becomes salient, and the men cast them into stereotyped female roles,
including "the mother," "the sister," and "the seductress," whose sexuality
blots out all other characteristics (Kanter, 1977: 234–5). While similar stereotyping of women in traditionally female jobs occurs, it is less visible
because the expected behavior is perceived to be a part of the woman's job.

In addition, women in "men's jobs" are sexually harassed as a condition
of work. Men view the presence of these women as an invasion of male economic turf (i.e., as a challenge to the men's better pay and supervisory
authority), an invasion of their social turf (e.g., army barracks, board rooms,
and police stations), and a threat to their definition of their work and selves
as "masculine." They often harass women to keep them from working effectively, thereby "proving" women's unfitness for a "man's job" and, in some
instances, driving out the female "invaders."

Sex-Role Socialization and Cultural Norms

Sexual harassment, as well as the position of women in the occupational
world, rests on the social arrangements between the sexes and the perpetuation of these arrangements through sex-role socialization. Sex-role
socialization is the process by which people learn the cultural norms for attitudes and behaviors appropriate to their sex; that is, they learn how to think
and act as men or as women. These sex-role norms also express the relative
positions of the sexes. Male and female sex roles are not simply different;
they reflect sexual inequality and, in their enactment, perpetuate it. Women
are not born weak, passive, dependent, and receptive to male initiation; they
are socially conditioned to develop these qualities. Similarly, men learn that
they are expected to be strong, dominant, independent, aggressive, and the
initiators of sexual interaction. These expectations and norms permit men
as a group to dominate women as a group through the privilege of initiating—and thereby controlling—intimate relationships. The social and sexual
power that sex-role norms give men over women is carried into the workplace and reinforced through male economic control of women's
livelihood.

Acquiescence to Sexual Harassment

Despite folklore about "women who sleep their way to the top," there is little evidence that women advance on the job by using their sexuality to gain employment benefits. On the contrary, there is strong indication that acquiescence to sexual harassment has harmful effects on women's efforts to gain social and economic equality. Allegations of women's sexual complicity to gain employment benefits trivializes the magnitude of the problem of sexual harassment and obscures the nature of the situation faced by most women by putting it in false moral terms. For example, Phyllis Schlafly asserted that "sexual harassment on the job is not a problem for the virtuous woman except in the rarest of cases" (Rich, 1981: A2). Such a statement implies that sexual harassment is the woman's fault. Rather than perceiving the woman as a victim of unwanted attention from someone with power over her livelihood, Schlafly blames the woman who "allows" herself to be harassed—or worse, elicits the harassment—because she is of dubious virtue. However, sexual harassment is not a question of "virtue"; it is a question of power. Women who acquiesce often are not in position to refuse; their surrender is the price of survival. And while some women may gain benefits by providing "sexual favors," statistics on women's employment clearly indicate that these must be few in number, since as a group women fail to attain jobs for which they are qualified, much less obtain undeserved advancement.

Both women and men feel injured by the benefits given to acquiescent women. But they direct their anger at the victims rather than looking at the system that permits the victimization. The acquiescence of a few women divides women as a group, thereby diminishing their ability to unite in fighting economic and sexual discrimination. Compliant women become the scapegoats for women's anger, which should properly focus on the men who offer economic rewards at a price, the work organization that permits harassment (often informally regarding it as a perquisite of male employees), or the sexual stratification system that gives men power over women's livelihood and sexuality and perpetuates women's subordination and dependence.

Women's acquiescence to sexual harassment also reinforces the hostility of men to female coworkers. Many men who tolerate or accept a variety of other forms of favoritism in the distribution of job-related rewards, including relationships cultivated on the ball field, in the locker room, or at all-male clubs, are infuriated by the thought that women have and use "advantages" men do not have, making them feel "disadvantaged as a class" (Martin, 1980). Men's anger at this form of injustice, however, is directed at both the compliant women and all women on the job, rather than at their male bosses (since it would be dangerous to express such jealousy and anger) or at the system that evades the merit principles it espouses. Such anger also serves as a convenient ego-protecting device, particularly for men of average competence. Stories or rumors about compliant women protect such men's sense of masculinity, which is threatened by the possibility that female coworkers are being advanced ahead of them because the women are more competent. By implying that the only way a woman can succeed is by using her sexuality rather than by performing better than male colleagues, the men can rationalize their failures, redirect their anger at a less threatening target, and thereby reassert their superiority as males.

Responses to Sexual Harassment

Individual Response Strategies and Their Outcomes

Victims of sexual harassment have limited options for dealing with unwanted sexual attention. They can adopt informal approaches, which include ignoring the harassment and asking the harasser to stop. They can quit the job or seek a transfer; students can change majors or courses. They can use formal grievance and complaint procedures or take legal action. Or they can acquiesce. Each strategy has risks and costs. Informal approaches may be ineffectual and may trigger escalation of the situation or retaliation. Escapist approaches can have substantial economic consequences: the loss of seniority, accumulated job knowledge, personal work-based ties, and income during the transition; the possibility of finding a new job only at a lower salary; and the acquisition of a reputation as an unstable worker. Formal complaints risk reprisals (including failure to be promoted, reduction in duties, dismissal, or, for students, lowered grades and poor recommendations); acquisition of a reputation for being a "troublemaker" among coworkers, who often "blame the victim"; and considerable expense if legal action is taken.

Given these options most women workers seek to handle the situation informally—by either ignoring the behavior, avoiding the harasser, or asking him to stop. In the MSPB study (1981: 67), 61 percent of the victims reported ignoring the harassment and 48 percent asking the harasser to stop. Loy and Stewart (n.d.) found 32 percent ignoring the harasser and 39 percent asking him to stop. Respondents in both studies indicated that ignoring the harassment failed to end it and often made it worse. Asking the harasser to stop was effective for 54 percent of the women (MSPB, 1981: 67)—but ineffective in almost half the cases.

Findings from several studies suggest that the high job-turnover and absenteeism rates for female workers are related to sexual harassment. In the MSPB study, 6 percent of all sexually harassed women (but 14 percent of the rape victims and 10 percent of the severely harassed women) reported subsequently quitting or transferring from their jobs (MSPB, 1981: 80). Loy and Stewart (n.d.: Table 4) found that 17 percent of victims reported quitting or transferring.

Only a small proportion of victimized women adopt the option of seeking a formal remedy: 18 percent according to Silverman (1976–77), 4 percent according to New Responses, Inc. (1979), 12.5 percent according to

Loy and Stewart (n.d.: Table 4), and almost 3 percent according to the MSPB (1981: 70). The vast majority of female victims do not complain through official channels, due to ignorance of available remedies, the belief that formal action is less effective than informal treatment, and fear of making the situation worse. Fear of reprisals and negative outcomes appears to be well founded. Among MSPB respondents who had taken formal action, 41 percent found that their actions had no effect or made things worse (MSPB, 1981: 88–92).

Acquiescence is also an option. In the case of the less severely harassed, this generally means tolerating suggestive looks, jokes, teasing, or pressure to go on dates. According to the MSPB study, 18 percent of the less severely harassed, 3 percent of the severely harassed, and 14 percent of the rape/ assault victims reported that they "went along with the behavior," but only 8 percent of these women found that things had improved as a result (MSPB, 1981: 67).

Female students manage unwanted sexual attention in ways similar to those adopted by working women. Some, fearful of making a direct complaint, try to ignore the harassing behavior or use indirect strategies for stopping it. These include directing discussion with the instructor back to the academic issue, bringing a friend to the instructor's office to avoid being alone with the instructor, and talking about a husband or boyfriend to indicate sexual unavailability. About 30 percent of the student victims did not directly communicate their displeasure to the harassing instructor; for almost all of these women (thirteen out of fifteen) his unwanted behavior continued (Benson and Thomson, 1982: 244). The 70 percent who directly communicated their displeasure were more successful in stopping the harassment, although the professor's power tended to affect this outcome. Power was measured by three factors: whether the professor had tenure, whether he was in the student's chosen major field, and whether the student aspired to attend graduate school. The sexual harassment stopped in twenty-one of the twenty-four cases in which one or two of the three conditions were present. However, the harassment stopped in only five of the eleven instances in which all three were present (Benson and Thomson, 1982: 244). Even when the harassment stopped, however, students who did not reciprocate sexual attention were often punished by the instructor's withdrawal of intellectual support and encouragement, critical comments about work that formerly had been praised and lower grades. ...

CONCLUSION

Sexual harassment in the university and the workplace must be recognized and treated as an oppressive form of sex discrimination that undercuts women's potential for independence and equality. It disrupts women's drive for autonomy outside of the home and family by sexualizing women's work role and by making sexuality a condition of economic survival. Women as a group suffer from two inequalites: inequality based on socially defined patterns of sexual initiative and acquiescence, and economic inequality maintained by women's separate and subordinate place at work. Sexual harassment links these inequalities by expressing the unequal social power of women, sexualizing their subordination, and deepening their powerlessness as women.

NOTES

1   Although men have been victims of sexual harassment as well as women, the vast difference between the sexes in victimization rates and the meaning attached to sexual initiatives make it primarily a problem of women. Only research findings on the sexual harassment of women are presented here, and the analysis of harassment is from the perspective of female victims.

2   One study found that more than 70 percent of the women surveyed would not call a behavior sexual harassment if the person doing it did not mean to be offensive (U.S. Merit Systems Protection Board [MSPB], 1981: 29).

3   In 1978 the Civil Service Reform Act reorganized the Civil Service Commission by dividing it into two agencies: MSPB and the Office of Personnel Management. The MSPB hears and adjudicates appeals by federal employees complaining of adverse personnel actions, resolves cases charging prohibited personnel practices, and conducts special studies on the civil service and other executive branch merit systems. The Office of Personnel Management administers a merit system for federal employees, which includes recruitment, examination, training, and promotion of people on the basis of their knowledge and skill.

REFERENCES

Benson, D.J., and G.E. Thomson. 1982. "Sexual Harassment on a University Campus: The Confluence of Authority Relations, Sexual Interest and Gender Stratification." *Social Problems* 29: 236:–51.

Carey, S. H. 1977. "Sexual Politics in Business." Unpublished paper. University of Texas, San Antonio.

Farley, L. 1978. *Sexual Shakedown: The Sexual Harassment of Women on the Job.* New York: McGraw-Hill.

Carey, S. H. 1977. "Sexual Politics in Business." Unpublished paper. University of Texas, San Antonio.

Gutek, B. A. 1981. "The Experience of Sexual Harassment: Results from a Representative Survey." Paper presented at the American Psychological Association annual meeting, Los Angeles.

Gutek, B., and B. Morash. 1982. "Sex Ratios, Sex Role Spillover, and Sexual Harassment of Women at Work." *Journal of Social Issues* 38: 55–74.

Gutek, B. A., C. Y. Nakamura, M. Gahart, I. Handschumacher, and D. Russell. 1980. "Sexuality in the Workplace." *Basic and Applied Social Psychology* 1: 255–65.

Jensen, I.W., and B. Gutek. 1982. "Attributions and Assignment of Responsibility in Sexual Harassment." *Journal of Social Issues* 38: 121–36.

Kanter, R.M. 1977. *Men and Women of the Corporation.* New York: Basic.

Kelber, M. 1977. "Sexual Harassment … The UN'S Dirty Little Secret." *Ms.*, November.

Lindsey, K. 1977. "Sexual Harassment on the Job." *Ms.*, November.

Livingston, J. 1982. "Responses to Sexual Harassment on the Job: Legal, Organizational, and Individual Actions." *Journal of Social Issues* 38: 5–22.

Loy, P., and Stewart, I. n.d. "Sexual Harassment: Strategies and Outcomes." Unpublished paper.

MacKinnon, C.A. 1979. *Sexual Harassment of Working Women: A Case of Sex Discrimination.* New Haven, Conn.: Yale University Press.

—— 1982. "Feminism, Marxism, Method and the State: An Agenda for Action." *Signs* 7: 515–44.

Martin, S.E. 1980. *"Breaking and Entering": Policewomen on Patrol.* Berkeley: University of California Press.

MSPB. See U.S. Merit System Protection Board.

Munich, A. 1978. "Seduction in Academe." *Psychology Today*, February.

New Responses, Inc. 1979. *Report on Sexual Harassment in Federal Employment.* Prepared by M.A. Largen.

Pogrebin, L.C. 1977. "Sex Harassment: The Working Woman." *Ladies Home Journal*, June.

Project on the Status of Women in Education. 1978. *Sexual Harassment: A Hidden Issue.* Washington, D.C.: American Association of Colleges.

Rich, S. 1981. "Schlafly: Sex Harassment on Job No Problem For Virtuous Woman." *Washington Post*, 22 April, A-2.

Ripskis, A. 1979. "Sexual Harassment Rampant at HUD." *Impact* 7 (July/Aug.): 1, 5, 7.

Safran, C. 1976. "What Men Do to Women on the Job: A Shocking Look at Sexual Harassment." *Redbook*, November.

Seymour, W.C. 1979. "Sexual Harassment: Finding a Cause of Action under Title VII. *Labor Law Journal* (March).

Silverman, D. 1976–77. "Sexual Harassment: Working Women's Dilemma." *Quest: A Feminist Quarterly* 3 (Winter).

U.S. House of Representatives. 1980. *Hearings on Sexual Harassment in the Federal Government.* Committee on the Post Office and Civil Service, Subcommittee on Investigations.

U.S. Merit Systems Protection Board (MSPB). 1981. *Sexual Harassment in the Federal Workplace: Is It a Problem?* Washington, D.C.: U.S. Government Printing Office.

CHAPTER FOUR

Gender and Intimate Relationships

This chapter examines elements of the intimate relationships between men and women both within and outside the context of marriage. E.D. Nelson and Barrie Robinson (Article 17) set the stage by providing a partial overview of structural and personal factors that limit the freedom women and men possess in their quest for an intimate partner. Sex ratios, mating gradients, trade-offs and comparison levels, and changing gender expectations and behaviours all place different, yet interrelated, constraints on the options today's questers confront. A preliminary difficulty facing both men and women is how to meet eligible potential partners. We have witnessed a proliferation in recent years of innovative, technological ways for individuals to make first contact without the risk of face-to-face rejection. Of the various techniques that are currently part of the intimacy marketplace, including telephone and cable television advertising, personal ads in newspapers appear to be the most utilized form. Simon Davis (Article 18) examines the underlying themes found in advertisements created by women and men for a Vancouver newspaper. While the means of advertising are new, the qualities stressed by each gender in their self-descriptions are not.

An intense amount of personal and professional interest in gender differences has long been evident, but with very little attention devoted to similarities pertaining to two key dimensions of intimate relationships, namely, love and sexuality. Elaine Hatfield (Article 19) provides a classic summary of research knowledge pertaining to these differences as found primarily among studies of university-age men and women. Since the publication of her article, little has changed in both the subject matter itself and in our knowledge of gender and love. Some change has occurred, however, with respect to gender and sexuality. Bernie Zilbergeld (Article 20), in his witty and thought-provoking analysis of images of male sexuality forwarded by the mass media, has updated his fantasy model to acknowledge a major new requirement being placed upon men in the form of increased expectations of sexual performance and technique.

To state the obvious, doing intimacy in the context of marriage (and cohabitation) involves two people performing roles that are significantly influenced by gender expectations. Meg Luxton's (Article 21) two-part study of attitudes and behaviours regarding domestic work as exemplified by inhabitants of Flin Flon, Manitoba, puts a human face on this issue. Her identification of three distinct strategies taken towards balancing the demands of housework, paid work, and family life offers insight into certain of the dynamics of intimate relationships rarely considered in romance novels. On the national level, Katherine Marshall (Article 22) presents the most recent comprehensive Canadian data on the distribution of household tasks among dual-earner couples who now constitute the majority of married couples. Both the Luxton and Marshall articles demonstrate an essentially unchanging lack of egalitarianism with the "division" of domestic labour among Canadian couples.

17
The Quest for Intimacy

E.D. Nelson and Barrie W. Robinson

We begin this article by drawing the reader's attention to the fact that much of the material presented here focuses upon women and their quest for intimacy. We are not trying to suggest or imply that the quest is solely or even primarily a female issue or "problem" to be resolved. While it is true that females have been, and to a lesser extent today still are, defined by their relationship to males much more so than the reverse, both men and women actively seek an intimate partner.

Much of the research and theorizing about intimate relationships today is still located within the context of the once seemingly inevitable connection between sexual intimacy and reproduction. Demographers and sociologists interested in predicting future reproductive patterns have been concerned with projecting what proportion of the female population will most likely be involved in those types of relationships apt to produce children. Given that, from a record-keeping point of view, maternity is virtually always known while paternity is not always as certain, and that the vast majority of reproduction occurs within the context of legal marriage, social scientists as well as government policy planners and others focus their attentions more upon females than upon males and particularly upon such phenomena as female marriage, divorce, and mortality patterns.

For a variety of reasons including the greater availability and use of contraceptives, an increasing rejection of legal marriage as the necessary context for reproduction, decreases in marriages and increases in cohabitation, the traditional focus now appears to be too narrow. However, we are still forced to draw upon research generated from those traditional sources. The strait jacket of necessity thus forces us for the moment to emphasize the female more than the male perspective on the intimacy quest.

Despite the existence of popular myths proclaiming that everyone in contemporary society is totally free to seek out the marriage or relationship partner of their unique choice, empirical research clearly indicates that the intimacy quest operates within a context of structurally and personally imposed constraints. Success in finding an intimate partner is significantly influenced by the existing proportional balance between the number of eli-

Adapted from Adie Nelson and Barrie W. Robinson, *Gigolos and Madames Bountiful: Illusions of Gender, Power, and Intimacy*. Toronto: University of Toronto Press, 1994, Chapter 2. Reprinted by permission.

gible males and females in the population. This ratio is influenced by a combination of factors such as birth and mortality rates for the sexes; norms regarding appropriate matching of the personal characteristics of potential partners; marriage, singlehood, cohabitation, and divorce rates; and changing gender expectations and behaviours.

SEX RATIOS AND MATING GRADIENTS

Perhaps first and foremost among these factors is the proportional balance between the number of females and males in the population. In order for everyone to have an intimate partner, an equal number of potential partners of the other sex must exist, assuming that everyone is interested in a heterosexual relationship (a questionable assumption at best but one that must be made nonetheless given the general unreliability of estimates of the gay/lesbian population distributed across different age-sex categories). The proportional balance of males to females in the population is referred to by demographers as the *sex ratio* and is usually calculated with the following formula:

$$\frac{\text{total number of males in the population of interest} \times 100}{\text{total number of females in the population of interest}} = \text{sex ratio}$$

A resulting figure larger than 100 indicates an "excess of males" (e.g., a sex ratio of 105 means there are 105 males to every 100 females), while a figure below 100 indicates an "excess of females" (e.g., a sex ratio of 90 means that there are 90 males to every 100 females). As noted earlier, the sex ratio itself within any given society is determined by the combined historical influences of births and deaths, as well as migration patterns. The ratio can be calculated for the total or only specific segments of the population. Calculating the sex ratio for the population as a whole (known as a "crude sex ratio") can be misleading since it includes men and women who are not eligible for participation in a quest for intimacy, such as very young children. It is possible to calculate more "refined" ratios for certain age-specific segments of the population to reflect those who would truly be eligible for participation in a socially acceptable intimate relationship.

Who is truly and at least minimally eligible deserves careful consideration here. This issue has recently been resurrected by Faludi (1991:9–14) in her consideration of the largely media-created "Man Shortage" or "Marriage Crunch" controversy. The original controversy revolved around unpublished research on American female marriage patterns by Neil Bennett, David Bloom and Patricia Craig (the so-called "Harvard-Yale" study) that was reported and sensationalized in a mass circulation weekly newsmagazine, and a subsequent unpublished report by Jeanne Moorman of the United States Census Bureau. While both unpublished studies had the same goal of predicting female age-specific marriage patterns (that is, the proportion of the female population who would be married by specific ages), they differed primarily in the assumptions the researchers made about whether college-educated females would follow the same marriage patterns as females with only a high school education.

Specifically, Bennett *et al.* assumed that the college educated would adopt the same patterns and Moorman assumed that they would establish new patterns. Based upon their assumptions, the two groups of researchers used different methods of analysis (with the Bennett *et al.* choice of method being rather questionable) which yielded different outcomes. The Bennett *et al.* findings were what could be termed "pessimistic" and the Moorman findings were more "optimistic." The former study concluded that single females aged 35 or older had only a miniscule chance of ever marrying (media sensationalism translated this into less of a likelihood than being shot by a terrorist), while the latter study suggested that the chances would be significantly higher. The Harvard-Yale study, the Moorman response, and even Faludi's own contribution to this portion of the controversy were alike in one thing. All of them focused almost exclusively upon the marriage patterns of "single" (never married) females (a point that Faludi fails to stress) although Faludi includes aged widows in one small portion of her presentation.

The actual eligible population is much larger, especially for certain age groups. Farber (1964) argues that North America is moving toward a condition of "permanent availability" in which every adult, outside of the incest taboo, can or will be considered to be potentially eligible as a mate, regardless of their marital status. Being currently married does not necessarily remove one from circulation, as evidenced at the very least by the existence of extramarital affairs some of which lead to divorce and the subsequent marrying of former lovers. Most researchers, however, do not include the currently married in their calculations of those eligible for the intimacy quest.

Obviously, more is involved in the quest for intimacy than just the number of potentially eligible partners. Even if the numbers of eligibles were perfectly equal, there is no guarantee that all of them would eventually select each other for a relationship of some kind. Further constraints are imposed upon the selection process by contemporary aspects of our dating and courtship norms. These norms or rules exert social pressures on questers to select partners from what are deemed appropriate social categories. One set of rules comprise what may be called the "dating differential" or, depending upon the desired outcome, the "marriage gradient." For the sake of simplicity we shall refer to this as the *mating gradient*.

Regardless of what our most cherished values may tell us—all people are not equal. They vary at the very least in age, physical size and attractiveness, educational attainment, intelligence, and current and/or potential income and therefore we can and—even if we do not wish to admit it—do rank order men and women from high to low along sex-linked continuums in terms of their possession of these characteristics. When it comes to selecting a potential intimate partner, the norms are quite simple—men are supposed to select "down" the other-sex continuum whereas women are supposed to select "up" (Saxton, 1990:190–191).

In other words, women are socialized from an early age to select a partner who is, for example, somewhat older, bigger, more educated, and possessing greater current or potential income. Conversely, men are taught to prefer a partner who is somewhat younger, physically smaller, possessing comparable but lesser education, and less income (real or potential). Conventional wisdom or "common sense" claims that significant departures from these norms will result in subsequent problems for the relationship. It must be stressed that the differences in desirable characteristics being sought after do not emphasize large differences. The "Cinderella-Prince Charming" myth is just that—a myth. Reality demands relatively smaller, but still noticeable, differences between potential partners. In this regard, and as an indicator of our changing times, South (1991), in a random sample of respondents aged 19 to 35, finds that men now report being generally unwilling to marry a woman who does not now have, or is unlikely in the near future to have, steady unemployment. The difference being sought here is not between some versus no income, but rather a difference in relative income.

One of the immediate consequences of these rules is that, assuming everyone performs according to societal expectations, we will have two very different groups of unselected men and women. The unselected males will be those who possess the lowest desired qualities (except for age at certain periods in the life span) because they will not be able to find females of lower quality. In contrast, the unselected females will be those who possess the highest qualities (again, excepting age for certain portions of the life span) (Saxton, 1990:190–191). This phenomenon of the mating gradient helps to explain, at least in part, why unmarried women in our society are often from relatively higher-status populations than are unmarried men of the same or a similar age.

Spreitzer and Riley (1983) note that higher levels of intelligence, education and occupation are associated with singlehood among women. Marshall's (1987:7) examination of Canadian women in male-dominated professions finds that these women are "more likely than women in other occupations to have never married." Nagnur and Adams (1987:4) observe that "highly educated women typically marry later, if they marry at all." Eshleman (1994:546) concludes that "professional women were more likely never to have married, were more likely to divorce if they had married, and were less likely to remarry if they divorced." Elizabeth Haven (1978) suggests that high-achieving women tend to consider marriage too confining and thus elect to remain single. Those women who do seek the intimacy of a long-term relationship frequently cannot find anyone of the other sex who possesses higher sought-after characteristics and their equals on the other-sex continuum appear to find such females too intimidating.

Obviously the imbalance of desired characteristics has, as one of its consequences, a reinforcing of power differentials in relationships between men and women within our society. Balancing those characteristics, or even an imbalance wherein the female possesses more of the higher qualities than her partner, would upset the traditional power structure. Despite general appeals over the past 25 years for a redressing of power imbalances in private relationships, such a condition currently still appears to be too threatening to one or both participants, according to the available empirical evidence on patterns of mate selection. For the moment, the different compositions of the undated and unmated pools of males and females, and the typical power imbalance within relationships, appear to be the products of societies which have yet to fully embrace the principles and practices of true equality between women and men.

If we focus solely upon the issue of age, the dating/mating norms of Canadian society suggest that the most desirable relationship would be one between a younger woman and a slightly older man. In terms of marriage, data this century from Canada indicate that the average age difference between males and females at first marriage has consistently been around 1–3 years, although variations do exist at different points in the life span (Oderkirk, 1994:2–5). Unfortunately, it is impossible to obtain reliable information on the average age differential between intimate, but not married, partners; however, it seems safe to assume that such relationships generally follow the same pattern, particularly among younger age groups. Based upon an assumption of an average two-year age difference, it is possible to calculate more refined sex ratios for eligible males and females in a population. Table 1 presents sex ratios for selected age groups of eligibles (never married + widowed + divorced) derived from estimates of the Canadian population for 1991 and compared to actual figures for 1981.

As we can see from the table, at the younger ages, basically under age 35, we currently have an excess of men in Canada. These conditions stand in stark contrast to the situation 25–30 years ago when females who were born on the leading edge of the baby boom immediately following the Second World War and into the early 1950s were, in their late teens and early twenties and in accordance with the dictates of the mating gradient, looking for potential partners from among the male birth cohort born prior to the baby boom. These males comprised a very small birth cohort and the females in question were confronted by what was termed the "marriage squeeze" (Glick, Heer, and Beresford, 1963). They faced the demographic reality of an excess of younger women of marriageable age compared to a deficit of "older" men of appropriate age and were consequently squeezed out of the marriage market. Their younger sisters (literally or figuratively), however, do not face the same conditions when they reach the age of seeking suitable partners as the baby boom and subsequent fertility patterns have resulted in an excess of males among the younger age groups. However, returning to Table 1, we also note that from about age 29 in 1981 and age 34 onwards in

TABLE I
Sex Ratios for Marital Eligibles, Selected Age Groups, Canada: 1981 and 1991

Female's Age	Male's Age	1981	1991
15 years	17 years	117.4	102.4
16 years	18 years	107.7	104.6
17 years	19 years	100.0	110.1
18 years	20 years	100.0	113.8
19 years	21 years	98.1	111.4
20 years	22 years	94.6	102.2
21 years	23 years	95.2	101.8
22 years	24 years	97.4	107.4
23 years	25 years	97.4	116.0
24 years	26 years	101.3	127.3
25 years	27 years	103.4	127.5
26 years	28 years	98.9	119.6
27 years	29 years	101.8	114.7
28 years	30 years	100.6	117.7
29 years	31 years	98.3	116.8
30 years	32 years	97.9	109.8
31 years	33 years	99.0	108.3
32 years	34 years	99.1	108.1
33 years	35 years	80.6	103.1
34 years	36 years	70.0	99.6
35 years	37 years	84.4	97.9
36 years	38 years	86.6	92.3
37 years	39 years	81.6	89.0
38 years	40 years	80.6	89.0
39 years	41 years	81.7	88.0
40 years	42 years	80.5	85.6
41 years	43 years	80.8	85.3
42 years	44 years	80.2	84.1

Note: Eligibles = Never Married + Divorced + Widowed

Source: Adapted from Wayne W. McVey and Warren E. Kalbach, *Canadian Population.* Toronto: Nelson, 1995.

1991, women find themselves confronting a deficit of eligible men which becomes greater with increasing age.

The reader may well question whether individuals in a society are actually cognizant of the excess or deficit numbers of one sex or the other. Although most individuals are unaware of the precise sex ratio statistics for any given year, they are likely to have a general impression of the ratio of available males and females in their particular community and the implications this has for competition, or lack thereof, for establishing relationships with members of the other sex. Such statistics might subtly be recognized in statements from younger males today such as: "Where have all the good women gone?" The answer obviously is: "They exist, but not in sufficient numbers for everyone."

Of course, such a question assumes that the males are interested in looking for female intimacy partners. This assumption, that *all* males as well as *all* females are actively involved in the quest for intimacy, is a difficult assumption to prove. A certain portion of the population may be, and probably are, completely uninterested in forming intimate partnerships. Since their actual numbers are unknown, they cannot accurately be taken into consideration when developing eligibles estimates for various portions of the population. An additional number of those who are potentially eligible, according to official statistics, have essentially removed themselves from contention through cohabitation or long-term noncohabitation relationships and their numbers cannot adequately be estimated. Such considerations must be taken into account when interpreting the tables presented here.

Among thirtysomething or older questers seeking intimacy, divorced men and women (who were not a significant factor for younger age groups) contribute to an expansion of the pool of eligibles. Since the mid-1960s, divorce rates have more than doubled in Canada (Larson, Goltz, and Hobart, 1994:428), which releases substantial numbers of people for "recycling" as potential intimate partners. As well, with increasing age, another factor begins to affect the number and social characteristics of the eligibles, namely mortality and survivorship. Available data indicate that females born in Canada in 1976, for example, could expect to live 77.5 years and males could expect to live 70.2 years. This "life expectancy gap" creates problems for whose who wish to share their life with a relational/romantic partner. Given the typical age difference at first marriage, and assuming their marriage lasts until the death of one of the partners, we would expect that these females will be widows for approximately nine years (a difference in age at marriage of two years plus the difference in life expectancy of seven years). Does this mean that currently young university- and college-age women must begin cruising junior high school gymnasiums in search of a potentially suitable and healthy partner for comfort in one's old age? We will explore the issue of departing from the mating gradient's expectations with regard to age in a later section of this article.

Regardless of whether one examines the 1960s, 1980s or early 1990s, a group of females exists for whom the problem has always been one of an imbalance between the eligible sexes, namely, divorced, widowed, and never-married females over age 55 who are at a distinct demographic disadvantage. Table 2 provides sex ratios of marital eligibles calculated for selected age categories based upon Canadian 1991 census data. The two-year age differential assumption used to construct Table 1 is no longer applicable since the age differential between partners who form relationships at older ages tends to be greater in comparison to those who form relationships during their teenage or twentysomething years (Oderkirk, 1994:4). As we can see from Table 2, the sex ratio continues to decline dramatically with increasing age and demonstrates both a combination of differential mortality (particularly at the oldest ages) and the greater propensity of divorced and widowed men to remarry, thereby taking themselves out of eligible circulation. Here, females seeking intimate partners who ask "Where have all the good men gone?" must confront the answer: "They are either confirmed bachelors, gay, currently in relationships of some form, or dead."

Such sentiments will be expressed with greater or lesser frequency depending also upon one's geographical location. Table 3 focuses upon the largest major urban centres whose combined numbers of inhabitants accounted for a little over 61 percent of the total Canadian population in 1991. Since research indicates that the fundamental factor influencing the possibility of establishing an intimate relationship is propinquity, or simply having physical access to eligibles (see Adams, 1979; Wells, 1984), geographic location must also be acknowledged.

T A B L E   2
Sex Ratios for Marital Eligibles, Selected Age Groups, Canada, 1991

Age	Sex Ratio	Age	Sex Ratio
45–49 years	78	60–64 years	49
50–54 years	70	65–69 years	37
55–59 years	60	70–74 years	29

Note: Eligibles = Never Married + Divorced + Widowed

Source: Calculations based on Table 3, "Population by Marital Status and Sex showing Five-year Age Groups for Canada, Provinces, Territories, and Census Metropolitan Areas, 1986 and 1991 – 100% Data" in *Age, Sex and Marital Status: The Nation.* (Catalogue 93–310) Ottawa: Minister of Industry, Science and Technology, 1992.

TABLE 3

Sex Ratios of Marital Eligibles for Selected Ages, Census Metropolitan Areas, Canada, 1991

CMA	Ages 20–69	Ages 20–44	Ages 45–69
Thunder Bay	108	128	65
Calgary	107	126	54
Edmonton	107	124	60
Oshawa	105	127	52
Vancouver	104	122	61
Kitchener	104	126	48
Hamilton	98	120	51
Windsor	97	119	52
Winnipeg	96	117	51
Toronto	96	115	48
Sudbury	96	113	58
Chicoutimi–Jonquière	95	127	48
Ottawa-Hull	95	114	49
St Catharines–Niagara	95	121	48
Regina	95	110	54
Victoria	94	118	48
Montréal	92	116	51
Halifax	91	106	51
Saskatoon	90	106	48
Saint John	89	107	53
St. John's	89	102	50
Québec City	88	112	49
London	88	107	44
Trois-Rivières	88	115	50
Sherbrooke	85	107	48

Note: Marital Eligibles = Single, Never Married + Widowed + Divorced

Source: Calculations based on Table 3, "Population by Marital Status and Sex, Showing Five-year Age Groups, for Canada, Provinces, Territories and Census Metropolitan Areas, 1986 and 1991—100% Data" in *Age, Sex and Marital Status: The Nation.* (Catalogue 93–310) Ottawa: Minister of Industry, Science and Technology, 1992.

TRADES-OFFS AND COMPARISON LEVELS

Thus far we have focused upon some of the most basic structural constraints influencing whether one will likely achieve initial success in the quest for intimacy. However, focusing upon sex ratios, mating gradients, and geographical location by no means paints the complete picture. Operating within this broad framework are a number of other factors. While all of us sometime during our lives create a picture of our "ideal mate," we typically do not expect to find that perfect intimate partner. Most of us discover ourselves to be in the situation described by Walster and Walster (1978:141) wherein "our selection of a mate appears to be a delicate compromise between our desire to capture an ideal partner and our realization that we must eventually settle for what we deserve."

Typically, we find ourselves attracted to a person who (in a simplified case) possesses sufficient or even more-than-sufficient quantities of one desired characteristic but insufficient quantities of another desired characteristic. We then frequently decide (sometimes consciously, sometimes not) that we can live with this combination. In other words, we "trade off" the lower quality for the higher quality. Such trade-offs are more common than we often would wish to admit. One person will trade off a less-than-desirable age of a potential partner for a high income. Another will trade off a less-than-desirable intelligence level for a striking physical attractiveness. Usually, we have some point below which we will be unwilling to make a trade-off regardless of the other person's higher qualities, but rarely can we easily put that "cut-off" point into precise words. Since not everyone shares the same cut-off point, we often hear parents, friends, and acquaintances remark: "I just can't understand what he/she sees in that loser anyway!" In the absence of available research, readers are encouraged to speculate about the qualities that males and females are most likely to consider in their trade-off "decisions" about potential intimate partners.

The trade-off factor applies to those qualities and characteristics which exist within a partner. However, we additionally make relationship decisions based upon factors which exist outside of the other person. When we expand our focus beyond the partner we take into consideration one's "comparative level of alternatives" (see Adams 1979). In other words, "what other choices do I have?" Not only do questers have to examine a potential intimacy partner's "résumé" to see if he or she can meet or beat a cut-off point, but we also have to evaluate the present possibility in comparison to whatever else appears to be available both now and in the foreseeable future. Questers find themselves selecting a partner from among what they perceive to be a limited number of available choices. Outsiders may not understand the selection of an apparent "runt of the litter," but they don't always appreciate that one may see that partner as being not all that bad—considering the alternatives.

GENDER IN TRANSITION

Another important element that cannot be ignored is the performance and display of one's gender. All of us are familiar with the intense examination and transformation processes the female gender role has undergone since the mid-1960s. The male gender role has undergone significantly less intense examination and transformation but, since the mid-1970s, that intensity level has been elevated. The most accurate term to describe the current gender situation appears to be—confusion!

This confusion takes two basic forms. On the one hand, we currently have many men and women who are personally confused about what they want and expect from a member of the other sex, as well as what they themselves should be thinking, feeling and doing in any and all relationships with that other sex. On the other hand, many people have very definite opinions regarding what they consider to be the one and only proper way for each gender's behavior. The problem is that these people are seldom in agreement. Consequently, both men and women from the 1970s to the present day have been, and still are, sending out contradictory and confusing messages to each other about the gender requirements of a desirable potential mate.

While some males still adhere to the notion of wanting their desirable female to possess only homemaking and people-nurturing skills, most males now appear to want a female who is not only economically capable and psycho-emotionally strong in public life, but one who will defer to them in private life and largely take responsibility for managing her home, children and husband—a sort of super-cuddly Superwoman who can not only take care of business but also channel considerable energies into making and sustaining intimate relationships. On the other side of the coin, Dennis (1992:61) suggests that men are now being directed to transform themselves "from dull but dutiful breadwinner, in the Ozzie Nelson mold, to androgynous danger-boy, in the Mick Jagger mold, to caring-sharing-and-relating soul-mate, in the Phil Donahue mold, to risk-taker with a vulnerable heart, in the Bruce Willis mold, to sensitive but sexy man-boy, in the Kevin Costner mold"—in other words, a super-cuddly Superman who still takes care of business but also meaningfully sustains an intimate relationship with his partner in all of the desired dimensions. Consider also, for example, Starhawk's (1992:27–28) answer to the question of "what women really want":

> *We dream of a world full of men who could be passionate lovers, grounded in their own bodies, capable of profound loves and deep sorrows, strong allies of women, sensitive nurturers, fearless defenders of all people's liberation, unbound by stifling conventions yet respectful of their own and others' boundaries, serious without being humorless, stable without being dull, disciplined without being rigid, sweet with-*

out being spineless, proud without being insufferably egotistical, fierce
without being violent, wild without being, well, assholes.

Once again, we must bear in mind that not everyone shares these prescriptions.

The directions being provided in the last examples are those primarily, but not exclusively, from women to men. But, at this point in time, we are also witnessing the generation and development of what is arguably a new ground swell men's "movement" that is in large part predicated upon a rejection of what may be termed "women-defined men," and in favor of creating a new image of "men-defined men." Whether it be a search for "Wild Men" (see Bly, 1990), or "warriors," all with "fire in their bellies" (see Keen 1991), increasing numbers of men are investing in books, seminars and weekend retreats designed to promote the creation of a new alternative to the modern male; an alternative that is supposed to be generated from within themselves in the context of other men's support. At the very least, the current process and ultimate goal appears to reinforce the theme of "independence" that has long been a part of the major underpinnings of the male gender role (Cicone and Ruble, 1978). Such independence promises to clash eventually with the demands, from both male and female sources, for more "relational-oriented" men. Considerable personal and societal work remains to be done before the independent and autonomous Wild Man can also be a loving and nurturing relationship partner.

It must be stressed that we are not witnessing battle lines being drawn between the sexes with all males on one side and all females on the other. Rather, males and females array themselves along both sides of these designs for ideal gender roles and ideal intimate partners. That alignment, in large part, contributes to the existing turmoil of the day. Confusing and competing messages are being directed towards an individual male or female, of whatever age, to be this or that, either to adopt wholeheartedly the total package being proffered from one source or another, or to create, on one's own, some blend from the vast cafeteria of choices on display. While a smorgasbord of choice initially appeals to one's sense of freedom, it can in many cases become daunting, even immobilizing, to the chooser. It can also lead to a nostalgia for the supposedly "good old days," when "men were men and women were women" and everybody knew the difference and was supposedly content to perform a prescribed and limited role. Nostalgia, however, tends to be very selective, and yet seductive and comforting, in its reduction of complexity into apparent simplicity.

At the moment, both sexes appear to be succumbing to rising expectations and projecting intimate partner "job descriptions" that few realistically qualify for. One result, partly evidenced by the reduction in the marriage rate since the mid-1970s (Oderkirk, 1994), is a more deliberate and active choice of many men and women to not commit themselves to a relationship they feel will not meet their intimacy and other needs. Such freedom of choice is more possible than in the past particularly because of the increasing economic independence, but not necessarily affluence, of women with a consequent lessening of financial dependence upon men.

Existing concurrently with this increased freedom of choice is the still dominant ideology of a couples society. This Noah's Ark mentality, which expects all people to line up in "two by two" formation, depicts the unattached person in a social situation as an oddity, a sorrowful being whose presence should be discomforting to all persons concerned. Our cardinal etiquette still demands that one should have an escort/companion for most social functions, partly for appearances' sake and partly for protection against unwanted advances from members of the other sex (particularly men). The couples society ideology contains socialization messages which insist that, since everyone is basically incomplete of and in themselves (a message traced back to a mythology developed by Plato [Saxton 1990:9–10]), an intimate partner is necessary for a sense of personal and socially approved completion or wholeness

CONTRADICTORY ALTERNATIVES

We thus have two seemingly contradictory societal expectations. On one hand, we have slowly been developing a social environment for the accepted existence of single-by-choice individuals. On the other hand, having an appendage who seemingly walks and talks independently is still *de rigueur* for most social situations. While this latter pressure is experienced by both males and females, it would appear that both blatant and subtle societal messages stressing the importance of an intimate relationship for one's public and private identity have been and still are directed more towards women than towards men. Responses to these contradictory conditions have been forecast by Guttentag and Secord (1983) who suggest that, when men are in demographic "short supply," combined with the fact that men typically control the basic legal, political, and economic social institutions, contradictory pressures yielding two different outcomes for females and their gender roles will result.

Guttentag and Second suggest that a real or perceived shortage of men, and a reduced likelihood of commitment from them given their greater alternatives for potential partners, produces pressures towards increasing female independence since male economic and emotional support can no longer be counted upon. While some commentators continue to blame women for making dumb choices of men under these conditions, many suggest that women should channel their energies towards changing those conditions. Efforts should be directed towards increasing female power over the structure of a society particularly in the arenas of government, business and the law to increase independence from rather than dependence upon men; develop women-centered values as opposed to values based upon what men want women to be; and develop independent identities. In other words, according to proponents of this point of view, the range of options for women beyond marriage and motherhood must be increased and acted upon.

Simultaneously, according to Guttentag and Secord, that very same combination of a deficit of men who nonetheless possess disproportionate power also leads to alternative pressures being placed upon women to increase their positive appeal to men in order to obtain male commitment and support. Females will receive "traditional" female value messages in a variety of forms stressing the priority of acquiring housekeeping and home-making skills; maintaining a positive orientation towards motherhood; being physically attractive to men; and developing their ability to provide a strong supportive role for men, as opposed to doing anything that might be perceived as "threatening." Even the most casual observer of Canadian society over the past twenty years will have noticed both of these alternatives being promoted by self-proclaimed experts via all forms of the media.

THE OPTIONS

For women of certain ages both now and in the recent past, the available options appear to be both somewhat limited and potentially in conflict at one and the same time. One could seek out a mate to cohabit with or marry. One could choose to opt for a status of permanent singlehood with or without the required walking appendage for social functions. One could choose to create a lifestyle revolving solely around other females, which may or may not include a sexual dimension. At younger ages one could choose to maintain high expectations for a desirable mate and, if one cannot be found initially, wait until later years for the next cohort of males being recycled (through divorce in particular) and perhaps find one "the second time around" when love is supposedly lovelier. During the interim, and as part of an important element of one's continuing identify and lifestyle, one could establish and maintain independent economic and career foundations for one's life.

Another option one could take is to ignore the traditional constraints of the mating gradient and select a much older—or younger—intimate partner. This latter option has appealed to a sizable minority of women during the 1980s and early 1990s. Valerie Gibson (in Creighton, 1992), a 53-year-old writer, veteran of five marriages, and currently married to a man in his thirties claims that "many older women in the 1990s will be choosing youth and virility over maturity." Gibson notes the lack of acceptance accorded such relationships—from society in general ("Many people believe the older woman is either a raging nymphomaniac or the younger man is after her money") or from the man's mother in particular ("That problem is obvious. You are often her age or close to it…not who they would choose for their son."). However, she claims that "Young men say that younger women… want to get married immediately or they want to know what kind of car the young man is driving or if he has a good job" while older women are more worldly, independent and stimulating. According to Banner (1992:5):

Many of my own middle-aged women friends have formed such relationships. They are joined in this behavior by well-known entertainment figures like Mary Tyler Moore and Olivia Newton-John, whose relationships with younger husbands and lovers have been emblazoned in gossip sheets and family magazines alike…Popular writers cite statistics showing that cross-age relationships between older women and younger men are on the increase. Thus, for example, of the marriages that took place in 1983 [in the United States], more than 30 percent of the women aged twenty-five to thirty-four married younger men. In that year, among women aged thirty-five to forty-four, nearly 40 percent married younger men.

Faludi (1991:467) claims that in 1986 "nearly one-fourth of [all American] brides were older than their grooms, up from 16 percent in 1970." Unfortunately, general statistics such as those provided by Banner and Faludi give us no indication of how much "younger" than their brides these grooms actually were.

Our more precise examination and analysis of marriage data published by Statistics Canada (1993) for the year 1991 indicates that for each five-year age group between 25–29 and 70–74 (all women and men over the age of 75 are lumped into one category and are not amenable to analysis and less than one percent of brides in the 20–24 age category chose younger grooms) the percentage of women marrying men from younger age groups ranges from 11 to 33 percent. The percentages increase from ages 25–29 to the peak at ages 35–39 and then slowly decline to ages 60–64 when they once again increase among the last two age groups. The second highest percentage (31) is found among women in the 40–44 age group. (The same patterns were found for the years 1989 and 1985.) While these figures are intriguingly high of and in themselves, it must be stressed that, within these age categories for 1991, 67 to almost 90 percent of women marrying in these years still married men from either the same or older age groups. This basic fact is typically ignored by the media (and some writers) since it is simply part of the taken-for-granted normalcy of everyday life and does not lend itself to sensationalistic claims.

Further analysis of the data indicates that at least 50 percent of women in all five-year age groups who married younger men chose men from the adjacent age group, that is, men who were from one to five years younger. However, with increasing age up to the category of 50–54 years, the percentage choosing from this adjacent age group decreases. For example, in 1991, among females aged 25–29 who married a younger man, 99 percent selected a man 1–5 years younger. Among women aged 50–54 who married a younger man, 50 percent chose a man 1–5 years younger, 31 percent selected a man 6–10 years younger, 11 percent a man 11–15 years younger and five percent a man 16–20 years younger. In other words, among women up to age 54 who marry a younger man, the older the woman, the greater the likelihood she will select a much younger mate. In the absence of any information to the contrary, we can only assume that such age differences are also characteristic of intimate liaisons occurring outside marriage.

The reader must bear in mind several important facts in attempting to interpret the meaning of these findings. First, these marriage data do not distinguish between first versus second or subsequent marriages. In general, age differences between brides and grooms tend to be greater with each subsequent marriage. Second, and closely related, the age differences reported here are in large part attributable to a wider range of alternatives available to older women. Obviously a woman of age 25 cannot marry a man 15 years her junior, but a woman of 50 can marry a 35-year-old man. Opportunity is obviously an important consideration to be taken into account here. Up to a point, older women simply have a wider range of possibilities to select from.

Third, older people tend to feel less constrained by age expectations than do younger people. Of the analyzed data, the lowest percentages of women marrying younger men in 1991 are found to occur in the 20–24 (one percent) and the 25–29 year age categories (11 percent). We find greater conformity among younger women in meeting social expectations to marry someone of an appropriate age as defined by the mating gradient. It appears that, with increasing age, there is less concern among these women with social approval. Fourth and finally, the available statistical information indicates only the ages of the marital partners and nothing else. We know nothing about social factors such as the participants' education, income, social class background and physical attractiveness or personal factors such as comparison levels of alternatives and trade-offs that may or may not have existed as these partnerships were negotiated and formalized.

All we do know from such information is that men are not the only ones who select a younger marital partner. The mass media and especially popular gossip magazines, sensationalistic "newspapers," and television talk shows are quick to provide details about the marriages of older celebrity women and their younger men. But these details probably cannot be generalized to fit the circumstances surrounding the marriages of most anonymous women to their younger men. For our purposes here, it must be sufficient to note that, while still in a relatively small statistical minority, marriages between older women and younger men are not exceptional nor completely outside of the range of available options.

We conclude our presentation by reminding the reader that, despite what appears to be an expanding range of available alternatives, the quest for intimacy is not solely a unique, highly personalized, journey. Rather, it is still undertaken within the context of a number of constraints operating upon a socially imposed gendered reality.

REFERENCES

Adams, Bert N. 1979. "Mate Selection in the United States: A Theoretical Summarization," in Wesley R. Burr *et al. Contemporary Theories About the Family.* Volume I. New York: The Free Press.

Banner, Lois W. 1992. *In Full Flower: Aging Women, Power and Sexuality,* New York: Alfred A. Knopf.

Bly, Robert. 1990. *Iron John: A Book about Men.* Reading, Mass.: Addison-Wesley.

Cicone, Michael V. and Diane N. Ruble. 1978. "Beliefs about Males." *Journal of Social Issues* 34:5–16.

Creighton, Judy. 1992. "Older Woman, Younger Man." *The Edmonton Journal.* November 12.

Dennis, Wendy. 1992. *Hot and Bothered: Men and Women, Sex and Love in the 90s.* Toronto: Key Porter.

Eshleman, J. Ross. 1994. *The Family.* Seventh edition. Boston: Allyn and Bacon.

Faludi, Susan. 1991. *Backlash: The Undeclared War Against American Women.* New York: Simon and Schuster.

Farber, Bernard. 1964. *Family Organization and Interaction.* San Francisco: Chandler.

Glick, Paul C., D. Heer and J. C. Beresford. 1963. "Family Formation and Family Composition: Trends and Prospects." In M. B. Sussman (ed.) *Sourcebook of Marriage and the Family.* New York: Houghton Mifflin, 30–40.

Guttentag, Marcia and Paul F. Secord. 1983. *Too Many Women? The Sex Ratio Question.* Beverley Hills, Calif.: Sage.

Havens, Elizabeth. 1978. "Women, Work and Wedlock: A note on female marital patterns in the United States." *American Journal of Sociology* 78:975–981.

Keen, Sam. 1991. *Fire in the Belly: On Being a Man.* New York: Bantam.

Larson, Lyle E., J. Walter Goltz, and Charles Hobart. *Families in Canada: Social Context, Continuities and Changes.* Scarborough, Ontario: Prentice Hall Canada.

Marshall, Katherine. 1987. "Women in Male Dominated Professions." *Canadian Social Trends.* Winter: 7–11.

Nagnur D. and O. Adams. 1987. "Tying the Knot: An Overview of Marriage Rates in Canada." *Canadian Social Trends.* Autumn: 1–6.

Oderkirk, Jillian. 1994. "Marriage in Canada: Changing Beliefs and Behaviours 1600–1990." *Canadian Social Trends.* Summer: 2–7.

Saxton, Lloyd, 1990. *The Individual, Marriage, and the Family.* Seventh edition. Belmont, Calif.: Wadsworth.

South, Scott. 1991. "Sociodemographic Differentials in Mate Selection Preferences." *Journal of Marriage and the Family*. 53:928–940.

Spreitzer, E. and L. Riley. 1983. "Factors Associated with Singlehood." *Journal of Marriage and the Family*. 36:533–542.

Starhawk, 1992. "A Men's Movement I Can Trust," In Kay Leigh Hagan (ed.) *Women Respond to the Men's Movement*. San Francisco: Pandora, 27–28.

Statistics Canada, 1993. *Marriages, 1991*. Catalogue No. 84–212. Ottawa: Minister of Industry, Science and Technology, Table 4.

Walster, Elaine and G.William Walster. 1978. *A New Look at Love*. Reading, Mass.: Addison-Wesley.

Wells, J. Gipson. 1984. *Choices in Marriage and Family*. Jackson, Miss.: Piedmont.

18

Men as Success Objects and Women as Sex Objects: A Study of Personal Advertisements

Simon Davis

P revious research has indicated that, to a large extent, selection of opposite-sex partners is dictated by traditional sex stereotypes (Urberg, 1979). More specifically, it has been found that men tend to emphasize sexuality and physical attractiveness in a mate to a greater extent than women (e.g., Harrison & Saeed, 1977; Deaux & Hanna, 1984; Nevid, 1984); this distinction has been found across cultures, as in the study by Stiles and colleagues (1987) of American and Icelandic adolescents.

The relatively greater preoccupation with casual sexual encounters demonstrated by men (Hite, 1987, p. 184) may be accounted for by the greater emotional investment that women place in sex; Basow (1986, p. 80) suggests that the "gender differences in this area (different meaning attached to sex) may turn out to be the strongest of all gender differences."

Women, conversely, may tend to emphasize psychological and personality characteristics (Curry & Hock, 1981; Deaux & Hanna, 1984), and to seek longevity and commitment in a relationship to a greater extent (Basow, 1986, p. 213).

Women may also seek financial security more so than men (Harrison & Saeed, 1977). Regarding this last point, Farrell (1986, p. 25) suggests that the tendency to treat men as success objects is reflected in the media, particularly in advertisements in women's magazines. On the other hand, men themselves may reinforce this stereotype in that a number of men still apparently prefer the traditional marriage with working husband and unemployed wife (Basow, 1986, p. 210).

Men have traditionally been more dominant in intellectual matters, and this may be reinforced in the courting process: Braito (1981) found in his study that female coeds feigned intellectual inferiority with their dates on a number of occasions. In the same vein, Hite, in her 1981 survey, found that men were less likely to seek intellectual prowess in their mate (p. 108).

The mate selection process has been characterized in at least two ways. Harrison and Saeed (1977) found evidence for a matching process, where

From Simon Davis "Men as Success Objects and Women as Sex Objects: A Study of Personal Advertisements," *Sex Roles*, vol. 23, nos. 1/2 (1990): 43–50. Reprinted by permission of Plenum Publishing Corporation.

individuals seeking particular characteristics in a partner were more likely to offer those characteristics in themselves. This is consistent with the observation that "like attracts like" and that husbands and wives tend to resemble one another in various ways (Thiessen & Gregg, 1980). Additionally, an exchange process may be in operation, wherein a trade-off is made with women offering "domestic work and sex for financial support" (Basow, 1986, p. 213).

With respect to sex stereotypes and mate selection, the trend has been for "both sexes to believe that the other sex expects them to live up to the gender stereotype" (Basow, 1986, p. 209).

Theoretical explanations of sex stereotypes in mate selection range from the sociobiological (Symons, 1987) to radical political views (Smith, 1973). Of interest in recent years has been demographic influences, that is, the lesser availability of men because of population shifts and marital patterns (Shaevitz, 1987, p. 40). Age may differentially affect women, particularly when children are desired; this, combined with women's generally lower economic status [particularly when unmarried (Halas, 1981, p. 124)], may mean that the need to "settle down" into a secure, committed relationship becomes relatively more crucial for women.

The present study looks at differential mate selection by men and women as reflected in newspaper companion ads. Using such a forum for the exploration of sex stereotypes is not new; for instance, in the study by Harrison and Saeed (1977) cited earlier, the authors found that in such ads women were more likely to seek financial security and men to seek attractiveness; a later study by Deaux and Hanna (1984) had similar results, along with the finding that women were more likely to seek psychological characteristics, specific personality traits, and to emphasize the quality and longevity of the relationship. The present study may be seen as a follow-up of this earlier research, although on this occasion using a Canadian setting. Of particular interest was the following: Were traditional stereotypes still in operation, that is, women being viewed as sex objects and men as success objects (the latter defined as financial and intellectual accomplishments)?

METHOD

Personal advertisements were taken from the *Vancouver Sun,* which is the major daily newspaper serving Vancouver, British Columbia. The *Sun* is generally perceived as a conservative, respectable journal—hence it was assumed that people advertising in it represented the "mainstream." It should be noted that people placing the ads must do so in person. For the sake of this study, gay ads were not included. A typical ad would run about 50 words, and included a brief description of the person placing it and a list of the attributes desired in the other party. Only the parts pertaining to the attributes desired in the partner were included for analysis. Attributes that pertained to hobbies or recreations were not included for the purpose of this study.

The ads were sampled as follows: Only Saturday ads were used, since in the *Sun* the convention was for Saturday to be the main day for personal ads, with 40–60 ads per edition—compared to only 2–4 ads per edition on weekdays. Within any one edition *all* the ads were included for analysis. Six editions were randomly sampled, covering the period of September 30, 1988, to September 30, 1989. The attempt to sample through the calendar year was made in an effort to avoid any unspecified seasonal effect. The size of the sample (six editions) was large enough to meet goodness-of-fit requirements for statistics tests.

The attributes listed in the ads were coded as follows:

1. *Attractive:* specified that a partner should be, for example, "pretty" or "handsome."
2. *Physique:* similar to 1; however, this focused not on the face but rather on whether the partner was "fit and trim," "muscular," or had "a good figure." If it was not clear if body or face was being emphasized, this fell into variable (1) by default.
3. *Sex:* specified that the partner should have, for instance, "high sex drive," or should be "sensuous" or "erotic," or if there was a clear message that this was an arrangement for sexual purposes ("lunchtime liaisons—discretion required").
4. *Picture:* specified that the partner should include a photo in his/her reply.
5. *Profession:* specified that the partner should be a professional.
6. *Employed:* specified that the partner should be employed, e.g., "must hold steady job" or "must have steady income."
7. *Financial:* specified that the partner should be, for instance, "financially secure" or "financially independent."
8. *Education:* specified that the partner should be, for instance, "well educated" or "well read," or should be a "college grad."
9. *Intelligence:* specified that the partner should be "intelligent," "intellectual," or "bright."
10. *Honest:* specified, for instance, that the partner should be "honest" or have "integrity."
11. *Humor:* specified "sense of humor" or "cheerfulness."
12. *Commitment:* specified that the relationship was to be "long term" or "lead to marriage," or some other indication of stability and longevity.
13. *Emotion:* specified that the partner should be "warm," "romantic," "emotionally supportive," "emotionally expressive," "sensitive,"

"loving," "responsive," or similar terms indicating an opposition to being cold and aloof.

In addition to the 13 attribute variables, two other pieces of information were collected: The length of the ad (in lines) and the age of the person placing the ad. Only if age were exactly specified was it included: if age was vague (e.g., "late 40s") this was not counted.

Variables were measured in the following way: Any ad requesting one of the 13 attributes was scored once for that attribute. If not explicitly mentioned, it was not scored. The scoring was thus "all or nothing," e.g., no matter how many times a person in a particular ad stressed that looks were important it was only counted as a single score in the "attractive" column; thus, each single score represented one person. Conceivably, an individual ad could mention all, some, or none of the variables. Comparisons were then made between the sexes on the basis of the variables, using percentages and chi-squares. Chi-square values were derived by cross-tabulating gender (male/female) with attribute (asked for/not asked for). Degrees of freedom in all cases equaled one. Finally, several of the individual variables were collapsed to get an overall sense of the relative importance of (a) physical factors, (b) employment factors, and (c) intellectual factors.

RESULTS

A total of 329 personal ads were contained in the six newspaper editions studied. One ad was discarded in that it specified a gay relationship, leaving a total sample of 328. Of this number, 215 of the ads were placed by men (65.5%) and 113 by women (34.5%).

The mean age of people placing ads was 40.4. One hundred and twenty seven cases (38.7%) counted as missing data in that the age was not specified or was vague. The mean age for the two sexes was similar: 39.4 for women (with 50.4% of cases missing) and 40.7 for men (with 32.6% of cases missing).

Sex differences in desired companion attributes are summarized in Table 1. It will be seen that for 10 of the 13 variables a statistically significant difference was detected. The three largest differences were found for attractiveness, professional and financial status. To summarize the table: in the case of attractiveness, physique, sex, and picture (physical attributes) the men were more likely than the women to seek these. In the case of professional status, employment status, financial status, intelligence, commitment, and emotion (nonphysical attributes) the women were more likely to seek these. The women were also more likely to specify education, honesty and humor, however not at a statistically significant level.

The data were explored further by collapsing several of the categories: the first 4 variables were collapsed into a "physical" category, Variables 5–7 were collapsed into an "employment" category, and Variables 8 and 9 were collapsed into an "intellectual" category. The assumption was that the collapsed categories were sufficiently similar (within the three new categories) to make the new larger categories conceptually meaningful; conversely, it was felt the remaining variables (10–13) could not be meaningfully collapsed any further.

Sex differences for the three collapsed categories are summarized in Table 2. Note that the Table 2 figures were not derived simply by adding the numbers in the Table 1 categories: recall that for Variables 1–4 a subject could specify all, one, or none, hence simply adding the Table 1 figures would be biased by those individuals who were more effusive in specifying various physical traits. Instead, the Table 2 categories are (like Table 1) all or nothing: whether a subject specified one or all four of the physical attributes it would only count once. Thus, each score represented one person.

In brief, Table 2 gives similar, although more exaggerated results to Table 1. (The exaggeration is the result of only one item of several being needed to score within a collapsed category.) The men were more likely than the women to specify some physical attribute. The women were considerably more likely to specify that the companion be employed, or have a profession, or be in good financial shape. And the women were more likely to emphasize the intellectual abilities of their mate.

One can, incidentally, also note from this table an overall indication of attribute importance by collapsing across sexes, i.e., it is apparent that physical characteristics are the most desired regardless of sex.

DISCUSSION

Sex Differences

This study found that the attitudes of the subjects, in terms of desired companion attributes, were consistent with traditional sex role stereotypes. The men were more likely to emphasize stereotypically desirable feminine traits (appearance) and deemphasize the nonfeminine traits (financial, employment, and intellectual status). One inconsistency was that emotional expressiveness is a feminine trait but was emphasized relatively less by the men. Women, on the other hand, were more likely to emphasize masculine traits such as financial, employment, and intellectual status, and valued commitment in a relationship more highly. One inconsistency detected for the women concerned the fact that although emotional expressiveness is not a masculine trait, the women in this sample asked for it, relatively more than the men, anyway. Regarding this last point, it may be relevant to refer to Basow's (1986, p. 210) conclusion that "women prefer relatively androgynous men, but men, especially traditional ones, prefer relatively sex-typed women."

These findings are similar to results from earlier studies, e.g., Deaux and Hanna (1984), and indicate that at this point in time and in this setting sex role stereotyping is still in operation.

TABLE I
Gender Comparison for Attributes Desired in Partner

| | Gender | | |
| | Desired by men | Desired by women | |
Variable	($n = 215$)	($n = 113$)	Chi-square
1. Attractive	76 (35.3%)	20 (17.7%)	11.13[a]
2. Physique	81 (37.7%)	27 (23.9%)	6.37[a]
3. Sex	25 (11.6%)	4 (3.5%)	6.03[a]
4. Picture	74 (34.4%)	24 (21.2%)	6.18[a]
5. Profession	6 (2.8%)	19 (16.8%)	20.74[a]
6. Employed	8 (3.7%)	12 (10.6%)	6.12[a]
7. Financial	7 (3.2%)	22 (19.5%)	24.26[a]
8. Education	8 (3.7%)	8 (7.1%)	1.79 (ns)
9. Intelligence	22 (10.2%)	24 (21.2%)	7.46[a]
10. Honest	20 (9.3%)	17 (15.0%)	2.44 (ns)
11. Humor	36 (16.7%)	26 (23.0%)	1.89 (ns)
12. Commitment	38 (17.6%)	31 (27.4%)	4.25[a]
13. Emotion	44 (20.5%)	35 (31.0%)	4.36[a]

[a] Significant at the .05 level.

One secondary finding that was of some interest to the author was that considerably more men than women placed personal ads—almost a 2:1 ratio. One can only speculate as to why this was so; however, there are probably at least two (related) contributing factors. One is that social convention dictates that women should be less outgoing in the initiation of relationships: Green and Sandos (1983) found that women who initiated dates were viewed less positively than their male counterparts. Another factor is that whoever places the ad is in a "power position" in that they can check out the other person's letter and photo, and then make a choice, all in anonymity; one could speculate that this need to be in control might be more an issue for the men.

Methodological Issues

Content analysis of newspaper ads has its strengths and weaknesses. By virtue of being an unobtrusive study of variables with face validity, it was felt some reliable measure of gender-related attitudes was being achieved. That the mean age of the men and women placing the ads was similar was taken as support for the assumption that the two sexes in this sample were demo-

TABLE 2
Gender Comparison for Physical, Employment, and Intellectual Attributes Desired in Partner

	Gender		
	Desired by men	Desired by women	
Variable	($n = 215$)	($n = 113$)	Chi-square
Physical (collapsing Variables 1–4)	143 (66.5%)	50 (44.2%)	15.13[a]
Employment (collapsing Variables 5–7)	17 (7.9%)	47 (41.6%)	51.36[a]
Intellectual (collapsing Variables 8 and 9)	29 (13.5%)	31 (27.4 %)	9.65[a]

[a]Significant at the .05 level.

graphically similar. Further, sex differences in desired companion attributes could not be attributed to differential verbal ability in that it was found that length of ad was similar for both sexes.

On the other hand, there were some limitations. It could be argued that people placing personal ads are not representative of the public in general. For instance, with respect to this study, it was found that the subjects were a somewhat older group—mean age of 40—than might be found in other courting situations. This raises the possibility of age being a confounding variable. Older singles may emphasize certain aspects of a relationship, regardless of sex. On the other hand, there is the possibility that age differentially affects women in the mate selection process, particularly when children are desired. The strategy of controlling for age in the analysis was felt problematic in that the number for analysis were fairly small, especially given the missing data, and further, that one cannot assume the missing cases were not systematically different (ie., older) from those present.

REFERENCES

Basow, S. (1986). *Gender stereotypes: Traditions and alternatives,* Brooks/Cole Publishing Co.

Braito, R. (1981). The inferiority game: Perceptions and behavior. *Sex Roles, 7,* 65–72.

Curry, T., & Hock, R. (1981). Sex differences in sex role ideals in early adolescence. *Adolescence, 16,* 779–789.

Deaux, K., & Hanna, R. (1984). Courtship in the personals column: The influence of gender and sexual orientation. *Sex Roles 11,* 363–375.

Farrell, W. (1986). *Why men are the way they are.* New York: Berkley Books.

Green, S., & Sandos, P. (1983). Perceptions of male and female initiators of relationship. *Sex Roles, 9,* 849–852.

Halas, C. (1981). *Why can't a woman be more like a man?* New York: Macmillan Publishing Co.

Harrison, A., & Saeed, L. (1977). Let's make a deal: An analysis of revelations and stipulations in lonely hearts advertisements. *Journal of Personality and Social Psychology, 35,* 257–264.

Hite, S. (1981). *The Hite report on male sexuality.* New York: Alfred A. Knopf.

Hite, S. (1987). *Women and love: A cultural revolution in progress.* New York: Alfred A. Knopf.

Nevid, J. (1984). Sex differences in factors of romantic attraction. *Sex Roles, 11,* 401–411.

Shaevitz, M. (1987). *Sexual static.* Boston: Little, Brown & Co.

Smith, D. (1973). Women, the family and corporate capitalism. In M. Stephenson (Ed.), *Women in Canada,* Toronto: New Press.

Stiles, D., Gibbon, J., Hardardottir, S., & Schnellmann, J. (1987). The ideal man or women as described by young adolescents in Iceland and the United States. *Sex Roles, 17,* 313–320.

Symons, D. (1987). An evolutionary approach. In J. Geer & W. O'Donohue (Eds.), *Theories of human sexuality.* New York: Plenum Press.

Thiessen, D., & Gregg, B. (1980). Human assortive mating and genetic equilibrium: An evolutionary perspective. *Ethology and Sociobiology, 1,* 111–140.

Urberg, K. (1979). Sex role conceptualization in adolescents and adults. *Developmental Psychology, 15,* 90–92.

19

What Do Women and Men Want from Love and Sex?

Elaine Hatfield

THE MEANING OF LOVE

What do we mean by "love?" Lee (1977) and Hatkoff and Lasswell (1979) argue that "love" means very different things to different people. Hatkoff and Lasswell (1979) have concluded that men and women differ in the way they conceptualize love. They interviewed 554 blacks, whites, and Asians as well as members of several other ethnic groups. The lovers' ages ranged from under 18 to 60. They concluded that men are more romantic and self-centered lovers. Women are more dependent, companionate, and practical. No one is very altruistic.

Research by other investigators suggests that their conclusions might have some validity. Let us consider the evidence regarding gender differences in the different kinds of love.

ROMANTIC LOVE

Several theorists agree with Hatkoff and Lasswell's (1979) finding that men are more romantic than are women. In 1958, sociologist Charles Hobart asked 923 men and women to respond to a series of statements related to romanticism. Why not try seeing how you feel about Hobart's 12 statements? You might also want to ask your current dating partner how he or she feels (see Table 1).

Hobart (1958) found that men had a somewhat more romantic view of male-female relationships than did women. On the average, women agreed with about four of the romanticism items. Men agreed with about five of them.

Recently, social psychologists tried to replicate Hobart's work in an effort to determine if it is still men who are the real romantics. They found

---

evidence to indicate that men may still be the more romantic sex (see Dion and Dion, 1973, 1979; and Knox and Sporakowski, 1968).

Other researchers support Hatkoff and Lasswell's findings that men—as the romantics—are more likely to fall in love at first sight, become deeply committed to a romantic dream, and suffer bitterly when their romantic fantasies fall apart. For example, Kanin, Davidson, and Scheck (1970) inter-

---

TABLE I
Romanticism Scale

		AGREE	DISAGREE
*1.	Lovers ought to expect a certain amount of disillusionment after marriage.	——	——
*2.	True love should be suppressed in cases where its existence conflicts with the prevailing standards of morality.	——	——
3.	To be truly in love is to be in love forever.	——	——
*4.	The sweetly feminine "clinging vine" girl cannot compare with the capable and sympathetic girl as a sweetheart.	——	——
5.	As long as they at least love each other, two people should have no trouble getting along together in marriage.	——	——
6.	A girl should expect her sweetheart to be chivalrous on all occasions.	——	——
7.	A person should marry whomever he loves regardless of social position.	——	——
8.	Lovers should freely confess everything of personal significance to each other.	——	——
*9.	Economic security should be carefully considered before selecting a marriage partner.	——	——
*10.	Most of us could sincerely love any one of several people equally as well.	——	——
11.	A lover without jealousy is hardly to be desired.	——	——
*12.	One should not marry against the serious advice of one's parents.	——	——

Note: What's your romanticism score? If you agreed with Items 3, 5, 6, 7, 8, or 11 (the items without an asterisk), give yourself one point per item. If you disagreed with Items 1, 2, 4, 9, 10, or 12 (the items with an asterisk), give yourself one point per item. Record your total score here _____.

Source: C. W. Hobart, "The Incidence of Romanticism during Courtship," *Social Forces* 36 (1958): 364. Copyright © 1958 by The University of North Carolina Press. Used by permission.

viewed 700 young lovers. "How early," they asked, "did you become aware that you loved the other?" Of the men, 20 percent fell in love before the fourth date; only 15 percent of the women fell in love that early. At the other extreme, 30 percent of the men, compared to 43 percent of the women, were not sure if they were in love by the twentieth date. Men seemed willing to fall headlong into love; women were far more cautious about getting involved.

There is also some evidence that it is men who cling most tenaciously to an obviously stricken affair and who suffer most when it finally dies. A group of Harvard scientists (Hill, Rubin, and Peplau, 1976) charted the course of 231 Boston couples' affairs for two years. They found that usually it was the women who decided whether and when an affair should end; men seemed to stick it out to the bitter end. When an affair finally did flicker out, the men suffered most. The men felt most depressed, most lonely, least happy, and least free after a breakup. They found it extremely hard to accept the fact that they were no longer loved, that the affair was over and there was nothing they could do about it. They were plagued with the hope that if only they said the right thing or did the right thing everything would be as it was. Women were far more resigned, and thus were better able to pick up the pieces of their lives and move on. And the contention that it is men who suffer most when an affair flickers out, is consistent with the fact that three times as many men as women commit suicide after a disastrous love affair (Bernard, 1979).

Six Definitions of Love

Romantic Love
Romantic lovers believe in love at first sight. They're in love with love. They can remember when they met, how they met, and what their partners were wearing when they first touched. They expect their partners to remember, too. Romantic lovers want to know everything about their beloved; to share their joys and sorrows and their experiences. They identify totally with one another. They are thoroughly committed to their lovers. Theirs is a sexual kind of love. Romantic lovers try hard to please their loved ones. They give generous presents.

Self-Centred Love
Self-centred lovers play at love affairs as they would play at games. They try to demonstrate their skills or superiority; they try to win. Such lovers may keep two or three lovers on the string at one time. For them, sex is self-centred and exploitative. As a rule, such lovers have only one sexual routine. If that doesn't work, they move on to new sexual partners. Self-centred lovers care about having fun. They get frightened off if someone becomes dependent on them or wants commitment. If a partner ends the relationship, they take loss gracefully: "You win a few, you lose a few—there'll be another one along in a minute."

Dependent Love

Dependent lovers are obsessed. They are unable to sleep, eat, or even think. The dependent lover has peaks of excitement, but also depths of depression. They are irrationally jealous, and become extremely anxious when their loved ones threaten to leave, even for a short time.

Companionate Love

Companionate lovers are basically good friends. They take it for granted that their relationships will be permanent. The companionate relationship is *not* an intensely sexual one. Sex is satisfying, but not compelling. Temporary separations are not a great problem. If their relationship breaks up, such lovers remain close and caring friends for the rest of their lives.

Practical Love

Practical lovers are intensely pragmatic. They look realistically at their own assets, assess their market value, and set off to get the best possible deal in their partners. They are faithful in love so long as the loved one is a good bargain. Practical lovers think carefully about education, make sensible decisions about family size, and so on. They carefully check out their future in-laws and relatives.

Altruistic Love

Altruistic lovers are forgiving. They assume the best. If their lovers cause them pain, they assume the lovers didn't mean to do so. Altruistic lovers are always supportive, self-sacrificing. They care enough about their lovers' happiness to give them up, if their lovers have a chance for greater happiness elsewhere.

SELF-CENTERED LOVE

Self-centered lovers see love as a pleasant pastime. Following the Roman poet Ovid's advice, they play the game of love for their own purposes. The rules of the game are to exploit a relationship to its fullest without getting deeply involved.

Few social psychologists have explored self-centered love, probably because most people don't consider it to be love at all. Hatkoff and Lasswell (1979) do, and they found that men are far more likely to be self-centered lovers than women. Replicating their findings, Dion and Dion (1973) also found that men can be more exploitative in love relationships than women.

DEPENDENT LOVE

A number of scientists have studied dependent love, although they have chosen to label this intense state as "passionate love" (the term we prefer), "puppy love," "infatuation," or "falling in love" (as opposed to "being in love").

Hatfield and Walster (1981:9) defined passionate love as "A state of intense absorption in another. Sometimes lovers are those who long for their partners and for complete fulfillment. Sometimes lovers are those who are ecstatic at finally having attained their partners' love, and, momentarily, complete fulfillment. A state of intense psychological arousal." Tennov (1979) argues that passionate love has the following basic components:

1. Lovers find it impossible to work, to study, to do anything but think about the beloved.
2. They long to be loved in return.
3. Their mood fluctuates wildly; they are ecstatic when they hope they might be loved, despairing when they feel they're not.
4. They find it impossible to believe that they could ever love again.
5. They fantasize about how it would go if their partner declared his or her love for them.
6. They're shy in the other's presence.
7. When everything seems lost, their feelings are even more intense than usual.
8. They search for signs (a squeeze of the hand, a knee that doesn't move away, a gaze that lingers) that signify that the other desires them.
9. Their heart aches when they imagine they might lose the other.
10. They feel like walking on air when the other seems to care.
11. They care so desperately about the other that nothing else matters; they are willing to sacrifice anything for love.
12. Love *is* blind; lovers idealize one another.

Contrary to the evidence presented earlier that men tend to be more romantic, researchers have found that, while a relationship is at its highest pitch, women experience the euphoria and agony of romance more intensely than do men. Kanin, Davidson, and Scheck (1970) asked men and women to rate (on the following scale: 1 = none; 2 = slight; 3 = moderate; 4 = strong; 5 = very strong) how they felt when they were in love; that is, to what extent did they experience the following love reactions:

( ) Felt like I was floating on a cloud
( ) Felt like I wanted to run, jump, and scream
( ) Had trouble concentrating
( ) Felt giddy and carefree
( ) Had a general feeling of well-being
( ) Was nervous before dates

( ) Had physical sensations: cold hands, butterflies in the stomach, tingling spine, and so on

( ) Had insomnia

In this study, the women appeared to be the most passionate. They generally experienced the symptoms of passionate love with some intensity. Men did not, with one exception: men and women were both nervous before dates. The recent work of Tennov (1979) provides additional support for the contention that women feel more "symptoms" of love than do men.

Researchers have found only one exception to this conclusion. Traupmann and Hatfield (1981) interviewed men and women at all stages of life about their feelings for their partners. They interviewed 191 dating couples and 53 newlywed couples right after their marriages and then again a year later. They also interviewed 106 older women, but (unfortunately, for our purposes) they did not interview women's husbands. These people were asked how much passionate love they felt for their partners and how much love they thought their partners felt for them. Possible answers were (1) "None at all," (2) "Very little," (3) "Some," (4) "A great deal," and (5) "A tremendous amount." Unlike previous researchers, they found that during courtship and the early years of marriage, men and women felt equally passionate about one another. Both steady daters and newlywed men and women felt "a great deal" of passionate love for their partners. It was only in old age that men *may* begin to love their partners with slightly more passion than they are loved in return. Older women reported that their husbands loved them with "some" passion. They reported feeling slightly less passionate about their husbands. Whether or not their husbands agree with this assessment is unknown....In summary, women appear to love the most passionately, at least until old age.

COMPASSIONATE AND PRACTICAL LOVE

Women appear to *like* their partners more than their partners like them in return. Researchers have talked about this friendly kind of love as companionate love, practical love, or just plain love. For most people, this is the essence of love.

Hatfield and Walster (1981:9) agree that liking and companionate love have much in common. They define companionate love as "The affection we feel for those with whom our lives are deeply entwined." Rubin (1970) explores some of the components of love. He argued that love includes such elements as idealization of the other, tenderness, responsibility, the longing to aid and be aided by the loved one, intimacy, the desire to share emotions and experiences, sexual attraction, the exclusive and absorptive nature of the relationship, and finally, a relative lack of concern with social norms and constraints.

Again, researchers find that, from the first, women are the friendly lovers. Traupmann and Hatfield (1981), also asked dating, newlywed, and older people how *companionately* they loved their partners and how much they thought they were loved in return. They found that from the dating period until very late in life, women admitted they loved their partners more companionately than they were loved in return. Both steady daters and newlyweds expressed a "great deal" to "tremendous amount" of companionate love for their partners. By age 50, most people still expressed "a great deal" of companionate love for their mates—even after many years of marriage....At each point in time women feel more companionate love than do men. It is only in the final years of life that men and women come to love one another companionately with equal intensity. With long experience, equal respect and love evidently comes.

For many women, the fact that they love more passionately and companionately than they are loved in return is deeply unsettling. They continue to long for love throughout their marriages.

ALTRUISTIC LOVE

Altruism is a classical form of love—love that is patient, kind, that never demands reciprocity. All the great religions share this concept of love....

The data on who is most altruistic—men or women—are confusing. Sociologist John Lee asked Americans, Canadians, and Britons about their love experiences. He didn't find anyone, man or woman, who was very altruistic. Lee (1974:50) admits,

> *I found no saints in my sample. I have yet to interview an unqualified example of [altruism], although a few respondents had brief [altruistic] episodes in relationships that were otherwise tinged with selfishness....*

...Psychologists have begun to study couples' implicit "marriage contracts"—men and women's unconscious understandings as to what sort of give-and-take is fair. In his book on marriage contracts, for example, Sager (1976:4–5) observes,

> *The concept of...marriage contracts has proven extremely useful.... But what must be emphasized above all is the reciprocal aspect of the contract: What each partner expects to give and receive in exchange are crucial. Contracts deal with every conceivable aspect of family life: relationships with friends, achievements, power, sex, leisure time, money, children, etc.*

And researchers have attempted to determine how fair men and women perceive their respective "contracts" to be (Hatfield, Walster, and

Traupmann, 1979; Utne et al., in press; Traupmann and Hatfield, in press; Traupmann, Hatfield, and Sprecher, 1982). The researchers contacted dating couples, newlyweds, and elderly couples who had been married for up to 60 years, and asked them how fair they thought their relationships were.

Couples in this series of studies were asked to focus on four possible areas of concern:

1. *Personal concerns:* How attractive were they and their partners? How sociable? Intelligent?

2. *Emotional concerns:* How much love did they express for one another? How much liking, understanding, and acceptance? How much sexual pleasure did they give and get? Were they faithful? How committed to one another? Did they respect their partners' needs for freedom?

3. *Day-to-day concerns:* How much of the day-to-day maintenance of the house did they and their partners do? How about finances? Companionability? Conversation? Decision making? Remembering special occasions? Did they fit in with one another's friends and relatives?

4. *Opportunities gained and lost:* How much did they gain simply from going together or being married? (For example, how much did they appreciate the chance to be married? To be a parent or a grandparent? Having someone to grow old with?) How about opportunities forgone?

After considering all these things, men and women were asked how fair they thought their relationships were. Were they getting more than they felt they deserved? Just what they deserved? Or less than they thought they had coming from their relationships?

Researchers found that regardless of whether couples were dating, newlyweds, or long marrieds, both men and women agreed that the men were getting the best deal. Both men and women agreed that, in general, men contribute less to a marriage than women do and get more out of marriage than do women.

Bernard (1972:27) provides additional support for the notion that women sacrifice more for love than men do. In her review of the voluminous literature contrasting "his marriage" versus "her marriage," she observes a strange paradox. Women are generally thought to be more eager to marry (and marry anyone) than are men. Yet women are the "losers" in marriage. She notes that "being married is about twice as advantageous to men as to women in terms of continued survival." As compared to single men, married men's mental health is far better, their happiness is greater, their earning power is greater, after middle age their health is better, and they live longer. The *opposite* is true for married as compared to single women. For example, all symptoms of psychological distress show up more frequently than expected among married women: nervous breakdowns, nervousness, inertia, insomnia, trembling hands, nightmares, perspiring hands, fainting, headaches, dizziness, and heart palpitations. They show up much less frequently than expected among unmarried women.

These data, then, suggest that, like it or not, women sacrifice the most for love. Perhaps for women, marriage should carry a warning label: "This relationship may be hazardous to your health."...

CONCERN WITH SEX

The second type of gender difference that scientists have investigated is in concern with sex. Traditionally, theorists have assumed that sex is far more important for men than for women. According to cultural stereotypes, men are eager for sexual activity; women set limits on such activity....

Regardless of theorists' debates as to *why* men and women may differ in their enthusiasm for sex, they generally agree that men and women *do* differ. But, as we have seen earlier, cultural stereotypes are not always correct. What does research indicate?

In the earliest sex research, scientists found fairly sizable gender differences. In more recent research, researchers find that although gender differences still exist, they are not always so strong as theorists have assumed. Gender differences have begun to narrow, or disappear.

GENDER DIFFERENCES IN LIKING FOR EROTICA

Early research supported the traditional assumption that men, not women, are interested in erotica (Kinsey, et al., 1948, 1953). Recently, however, researchers have found that there are few, if any, gender differences in response to literary erotica (Veitch and Griffitt, 1980) or to audiotapes of sexual encounters (Heiman, 1977)....

WILLINGNESS TO INITIATE SEXUAL ACTIVITY

In Kinsey's day, a double standard existed. Men were allowed, if not encouraged, to get sex whenever and wherever they could. Women were supposed to save themselves for marriage. In light of the double standard, it was not surprising that both men and women agreed that men were more likely to initiate sex and that women were more likely to resist sexual advances (see Baker, 1974; Ehrmann, 1959; Kaats and Davis, 1970; Reiss, 1967; Schofield, 1965; Sorensen, 1973).

Recent evidence suggests that traditional standards, although changing, are not yet dead. Contemporary college students reject a sexual double standard (Hopkins, 1977; Komarovsky, 1976; Peplau, Rubin, and Hill, 1976). Yet, this new single standard does not seem to have changed the cultural stereotype of male as sexual initiator and female as limit setter. Even today, it is almost always the man who initiates sexual activity....In a recent study of unmarried students, the man was found to have more say than the woman about the type and frequency of sexual activity (Peplau, Rubin, and Hill, 1976) except when a dating couple had decided to abstain from coitus in which case the woman's veto was the major restraining influence (Peplau, Rubin, and Hill, 1977).

GENDER DIFFERENCES IN SEXUAL EXPERIENCE

There is compelling evidence that men and women are becoming very similar with regard to sexual experience, however.

In the classic studies of sexuality, researchers found that society's double standard influenced sexual experience. For example, Kinsey and his colleagues (1948, 1953) tried to assess how sexually active men were throughout their lives, compared to women. They found that (1) indeed, men did seem to engage in more sexual activity than did women, and (2) men and women had strikingly different sexual histories....

Since Kinsey's day, researchers (DeLamater and MacCorquodale, 1979; Ehrmann, 1959; Schofield, 1965; Reiss, 1967, Sorensen, 1973) continued to interview samples of young people about their sexual behavior....

When responses from these studies are compared, we find that indeed, a sexual revolution *is* occurring. In the early studies, in general, men were far more experienced than were women. By the end of the 1970s, these differences had virtually disappeared. As DeLamater and MacCorquodale (1979:58) observe,

> *There are virtually no differences in the incidence of each of the behaviors. Unlike most earlier studies which generally reported lower frequencies of more intimate activities among females, we find that women are as likely as men to have ever engaged in these behaviors. The only exception occurs with coitus, which women...are less likely to have experienced. (**Among students,** 75 percent of men and 60 percent of women had had intercourse. **Among nonstudents,** 79 percent of men and 72 percent of women had had intercourse.)*

DeLamater and MacCorquodale continue (p. 58):

> *Thus, the gender differences in lifetime behavior which were consistently found in studies conducted in the 1950s and 1960s have narrowed considerably. This is also an important finding; it suggests that those models which have emphasized gender as an explanatory variable are no longer valid.*

When men and women are together in a close, loving relationship, they seem equally likely to desire to engage in sexual activity. There is only one type of situation in which scientists find women are still more reserved than men: if men and women are offered a chance to participate in uncertain, unconventional, or downright bizarre sexual activities, men are more willing to take the risk than are women.

For example, in the Clark and Hatfield (1981) study...college men and women were hired to approach Florida State University students of the other gender. If a woman requested a date, suggested that the man visit her apartment, or even go to bed with her, she was generally very successful in getting the stranger to agree. Men were generally at ease with such requests. They said such things as "Why do we have to wait until tonight?" or "I can't tonight, but tomorrow would be fine." When a man made such a request, however, he was much less successful. Although the majority of women would date a man who approached her, few would go to his apartment, and none would agree to go to bed with him. Typical responses to males were "You've got to be kidding" or "What's wrong with you? Leave me alone."...

DESIRE FOR INTIMACY

The third way in which theorists agree men and women differ is in desire for intimacy. What is intimacy? Intimacy is not a static state, but a *process*. Intimacy may be defined as a process by which a couple—in the expression of thought, emotion, and behavior—attempts to move toward more complete communication on all levels....

According to family therapists, men have the easiest time achieving an independent identity; women have the easiest time achieving closeness with others. Napier (1977) describes two types of people who seem, with uncanny accuracy, to attract one another. Type I (usually a woman) is only minimally concerned with maintaining her independence. What she cares about is achieving emotional closeness. She seeks "fusion with the partner," "oneness" or "we-ness" in the marriage. She puts much energy into planning "togetherness" activities. Type I fears rejection and abandonment. She feels rejected when her partner chooses to spend an evening alone, or with other friends. Her feeling of rejection may even extend to times when her partner is engaged in necessarily exclusive activities—such as earning an income, studying for exams, or writing a manuscript.

Type I's partner, Type II (usually a man), is most concerned with maintaining his sense of self and personal freedom and autonomy. He feels a strong need to establish his territory within the common household: to have "my study," "my workshop," "my car." Similarly, he feels compelled to draw sharp lines around psychological space: "my night out," "my career," "my way of handling problems." What he fears is being "suffocated," "stifled," or "engulfed,"...or in some manner intruded on by his spouse....

Psychologist Sidney Jourard (1964) developed one of the most commonly used measures of intimacy, the Jourard Self-Disclosure Questionnaire (JSDQ). The JSDQ consists of 60 questions in all. It asks people to think about how much they typically disclose to others in six different areas of life. A few of these items are shown here [in Table 2]....

In self-disclosure research, four findings have consistently emerged. First, both men and women disclose far more about themselves in intimate than in casual relationships. In casual encounters, most people are willing to reveal only the sketchiest, most stereotyped information about themselves....In intimate relationships, more of the complexities and contradictions are revealed. In deeply intimate relationships, friends and lovers feel free to reveal far more facets of themselves. As a consequence, intimates share profound information about one another's histories, values, strengths and weaknesses, idiosyncracies, hopes, and fears (Altman and Taylor, 1973; Huesmann and Levinger, 1976; Jourard, 1964; Worthy, Gary, and Kahn, 1969).

Second, in their deeply intimate relationships, men and women often differ little, if at all, in how much they are willing to reveal to one another. For example, Rubin and his colleagues (1980) asked dating couples via the Jourard Self-Disclosure Questionnaire how much they had revealed themselves to their partners....The authors found that, overall, men and women did *not* differ in how much they were willing to confide in their partners.

There was a difference, however, in the *kind* of things men and women were willing to share with those they love. Men were more willing to share their views on politics and their pride in their strengths. Women were more likely to disclose their feelings about other people and their fears. Interestingly enough, Rubin and his colleagues found that the stereotyped form of communication is most common in traditional men and women.

Some authors have observed that neither men nor women may be getting exactly the amount of intimacy they would like. Women may want more intimacy than they are getting; men may want far less. There is evidence that couples tend to negotiate a level of self-disclosure that is bearable to both....

Third, in less intimate relationships, women disclose far more to others than do men (Jourard, 1971; Cozby, 1973). Rubin and his colleagues (1980: 306) point out that "The basis for such differences appears to be in socialization practices. Whereas women in our culture have traditionally been encouraged to show their feelings, men have been taught to hide their feelings and to avoid displays of weakness" (Pleck and Sawyer, 1974). As Kate Millett (1975) has put it: "Women express, men repress." The authors argue that it is traditional men and women who differ most on emotional sharing. They discovered that more egalitarian couples were more likely to disclose themselves fully to one another.

Fourth, and last, women receive more disclosures than do men. This is not surprising in view of the fact that the amount of information people reveal to others has an enormous impact on the amount of information they receive in return (see Altman, 1973; Davis and Skinner, 1974; Jourard, 1964; Jourard and Friedman, 1970; Marlatt, 1971; Rubin, 1975; Worthy, Gary, and Kahn, 1969).

TABLE 2

The Jourard Self-Disclosure Questionnaire

0 = Have told my friend nothing about this aspect of me.

1 = Have talked in general terms about this item. My friend has only a general idea about this aspect of me.

2 = Have talked in full and complete detail about this aspect; my friend could describe me accurately.

ATTITUDES AND OPINIONS

1. What I think and feel about religion; my personal religious views. _____

2. My views on the present government—the president, government, policies, etc. _____

3. My personal views on sexual morality—how I feel and how others ought to behave in sexual matters. _____

TASTES AND INTERESTS

1. My favorite food, the ways I like food prepared, and my food dislikes. _____

2. The kind of party, or social gathering I like best, and the kind that would bore me, or that I wouldn't enjoy. _____

WORK (OR STUDIES)

1. What I find to be the worst pressures and the strains in my work. _____

2. What I feel are my special strong points and qualifications for my work. _____

3. What I feel are my shortcomings and handicaps that prevent me from working as I'd like to, or that prevent me from getting further ahead in my work. _____

MONEY

1. How much money I make at my work, or get as an allowance. _____

2. My most pressing need for money right now; e.g., outstanding bills, some major purchase that is desired or needed. _____

3. My total financial worth, including property savings, bonds, insurance, etc. _____

PERSONALITY

1. What feelings, if any, that I have trouble expressing or controlling. _____

2. The aspects of my personality that I dislike, worry about, that I regard as a handicap to me. _____

3. Things in the past or present that I feel ashamed and guilty about. _____

4. The kinds of things that make me just furious. _____

5. The kinds of things that make me especially proud of myself, elated, full of self-esteem or self-respect. _____

BODY

1. How I wish I looked: my ideas for overall appearance. _____
2. Any problems or worries that I had with my appearance in the past. _____
3. My feelings about different parts of my body—legs, hips, waist, weight, chest or bust, etc. _____

Source: S.M. Jourard, *"The Transparent Self,"* rev. ed. Copyright © 1971 by Litton Educational Publishing, Inc. Reprinted by permission of Wadsworth Publishing Company, Belmont, Calif. 94002.

There does seem to be some evidence, then, that women feel slightly more comfortable with intense intimacy in their love relationships than do men, and are far more comfortable revealing themselves in more casual relationships than are men. Tradition dictates that women should be the "intimacy experts." And today, women *are* more comfortable sharing their ideas, feelings, and behavior than are men. But what happens if this situation changes? Rubin and his colleagues (1980:316) suggest that such changes have already begun....

> *Men and women should have the freedom to decide for themselves when they will reveal themselves—and when they will listen to another's revelations. "Full disclosure" need not be so full that it eliminates all areas of privacy, even within the most intimate relationships...[given that] we believe the ethic of openness is a desirable one. Especially when contemplating marriage, it is valuable for women and men to be able to share rather fully—and equally—their thoughts and feelings about themselves, each other, and their relationship....It is encouraging to discover that a large majority of the college students we studied seem to have moved, even if incompletely, and sometimes uneasily, toward the ethic of openness.*

There is one final way in which theorists have speculated that men and women may differ—in their desire to flow with the moment versus to dominate, to achieve.

DESIRE FOR CONTROL

...According to theorists,...there are marked gender differences in three areas: (1) desire to be "in control," (2) desire to dominate their partners or submit to them, and (3) desire to "achieve" in their love and sexual relations.

Unfortunately, although a great deal has been written about these topics, there is almost no research documenting that these differences do in fact exist. Let us review what scientists do know.

Desire to Be in Control

As I said in the previous section, it appears that even in love relationships, men are more concerned than women about possessing and expressing appropriate thoughts, feelings, and behaviors. It is especially difficult for men to acknowledge their weaknesses.

Desire to Dominate or Submit to Others

Sociobiologists have argued that gender differences in dominance-submission are genetically "wired in." Males can ensure the survival of their genes by dominating women; women, by submitting to one man.

There is little evidence, however, to support such a contention. The only study relevant to this issue examined gender differences in the desire for dominance-submission on couples' intimate sexual encounters (Hatfield et al., 1981). The study reviewed a number of reasons why men's and women's desires might differ.

Most men and women accept traditional roles. They believe that men and women ought to be very different: men "should" be dominant; women "should" be submissive (Broverman et al., 1972). In fact, however, men and women are surprisingly similar in dominance-submission (Maccoby and Jacklin, 1974). Thus, perhaps both men and women secretly fear they do not "measure up." Men may worry that they're not sufficiently "masculine"— they may feel compelled to exaggerate their "macho" image, to deny any hint of weakness. They want their partners to be as submissive as possible. Women, worried about their "femininity," may wish to deny any hint of strength; they may want their partners to be "real men," dominant and strong. If such a dynamic is operating, men might be expected to wish secretly that their partners would be more feminine, women, to wish their mates would be more dominant.

That's one possibility, but there is another. Gender roles are limiting. Modern men and women may secretly wish that they could express themselves more honestly, but they may be afraid to do so. Some men may want to express their submissive side, and some women may want to express their dominant side in sexual relations. Some theorists have argued that men, forced to be more dominant than they wish to be in their daily activities, are especially attracted to masochistic sexual experiences (Gibson, 1978; Green and Green, 1973; Kamiat, 1936; Krafft-Ebing, 1903/1939). According to this same logic, we might expect women to find sadism equally appealing. Few theorists, however, have ever suggested that they do (Robertiello, 1970; for an exception to this statement, see Stoller, 1978). According to this reasoning, then, we might expect to find that *both* men and women wish their sexual repertoires could be expanded—men wishing their partners would sometimes take the lead, women wishing their partners would sometimes behave more submissively.

To determine which, if either, of these possibilities is true, I and my colleagues (Hatfield et al., 1981) asked dating and newlywed couples how they *wished* things were in their sexual relationships. We measured men and women's desire for dominance/submission via such questions as

1. "During sex, I wish my partner would…" (Answers range from "Give many more instructions and requests" to "Give many less instructions and request.")
2. "I wish my partner was …" (Answers range from "Much more willing to do what I want sexually" to "Much less willing to do what I want sexually.")
3. "I wish my partner would play …" (Answers range from "The dominant role in sex much more" to "The dominant role in sex much less.")
4. "I wish my partner would play …" (Answers range from "The submissive role in sex much more" to "The submissive role in sex much less.")

When we examined men and women's reactions to these items, a surprising result emerged: there is no evidence that couples wish men could be more dominant and women could be more submissive—nor any evidence that they wish they could be more androgynous in their sexual lives. What *do* the data show? Interviews suggested two surprising conclusions. First, as family therapists have noted, couples seem to have a communication problem. Both men and women wish *their partners* would be a little clearer about what they want sexually, but these same men and women are evidently reluctant to say what *they* want. Second, in general, if anything, *both* men and women wish their partners would be more assertive about what they want sexually. Of the two, men are the more eager for their partners to take an active role. Evidently, in spite of some therapists' concerns… women have not yet become so dominant and demanding that they frighten men away….

CONCLUSIONS

In this [article] I have explored what is known about gender differences in four areas: love, sex, intimacy, and control. Many theories have seen men and women as very different—to the point of almost being incompatible. A consideration of the evidence, however, indicates that nature has arranged things more sensibly. Men and women are surprisingly similar in what they want out of their most intimate relations. Everyone, male *and* female, wants love *and* sex, intimacy *and* control. Yet, if one is determined, one can detect some slight differences between the genders. Women may be slightly more concerned with love; men, with sex. Women may be somewhat more eager for a deeply intimate relationship than are men. Men may be a little more eager to be in control of things, perhaps to dominate their partners, to "achieve" at love than are women. This last contention is badly in need of research; the available research clearly indicates far greater similarities than differences in the feelings of men and women about sex and love.

REFERENCES

Altman, I. "Reciprocity of interpersonal exchange." *Journal for the Theory of Social Behavior,* 1973, 3, 249–261.

Altman, I., & Taylor, D.A. *Social penetration: The development of interpersonal relationships.* New York: Holt, Rinehart & Winston, 1973.

Baker, M.J., *The effects of inequality on heterosexual behavior: A test for compensation in inequitable relationships.* Unpublished manuscript, Department of Sociology, University of Wisconsin, 1974.

Bernard, J. *The future of marriage.* New York: Bantam Books, 1972.

Broverman, I., Vogel, S., Broverman, D., Clarkson, F., & Rosenkrantz, P. "Sex role stereotypes: A current appraisal." *Journal of Social Issues,* 1972, 28, 59–78.

Clark, R.D., III, & Hatfield, E. *Gender differences in receptivity to sexual offers.* Unpublished manuscript, 1981. (Available from Dr. Elaine Hatfield, Psychology Department, 2430 Campus Road, Honolulu, HI 96822).

Cozby, P.C. "Self-disclosure: A literature review." *Psychological Bulletin,* 1973, 79, 73–91.

Davis, J.B., & Skinner, A.E., "Reciprocity of self-disclosure in interviews: Modeling of social exchange." *Journal of Personality and Social Psychology,* 1974, 29, 779–784.

DeLamater, J., & MacCorquodale, P. *Premarital sexuality: Attitudes, relationships, behavior.* Madison: University of Wisconsin Press, 1979.

Dion, K.L., & Dion, K.K. "Correlates of romantic love." *Journal of Consulting and Clinical Psychology,* 1973, 41, 51–56.

Dion, K.L. & Dion, K.K. "Personality and behavioral correlates of romantic love." In M. Cook & G. Wilson (Eds.), *Love and attraction: An international conference.* New York: Pergamon, 1979.

Ehrmann, W. *Premarital dating behavior.* New York: Holt, Rinehart & Winston, 1959.

Gibson, I. *The English vice: beating sex and shame in Victorian England and after.* London: Duckworth, 1978.

Green, C., & Green, G. *S–M: The last taboo.* New York: Grove Press, 1973.

Hagen, R. *The bio-social factor.* New York: Doubleday, 1979.

Hatfield, E., & Walster, G.W. *A new look at love.* Reading, Mass.: Addison-Wesley, 1981.

Hatfield, E., Walster, G.W., Traupman, J. "Equality and premarital sex." In M. Cook & G. Wilson (Eds.) *Love and attraction: An international conference.* New York: Pergamon Press, 1979. (Reprinted from *Journal of Personality and Social Psychology,* 1978, 37, 82–92.)

Hatkoff, T.S. & Laswell, T.E. "Male-Female similarities and differences in conceptualizing love." In M. Cook & G. Wilson (Eds.), *Love and attraction: An international conference.* New York: Pergamon Press, 1979.

Heiman, J.P. "A psychophysiological exploration of sexual arousal patterns in females and males." *Psychophysiology,* 1977, 14, 266–274.

Hill, C.T., Rubin, Z., & Peplau, L.A. "Breakups before marriage: The end of 103 affairs." *Journal of Social Issues,* 1976, 32, 147–168.

Hobart, C.W. "The incidence of romanticism during courtship." *Social Forces,* 1958, 36, 362–367.

Hopkins, J.R. "Sexual behavior in adolescence." *Journal of Social Issues.* 1977, 33, 67–85.

Huesmann, L.R., & Levinger, G. "Incremental exchange theory: A formal model for progression in dyadic social interaction." In L. Berkowitz & E. Walster (Eds.), *Advances in Experimental Social Psychology* (Vol. 9). New York: Academic Press, 1976.

Jourard, S.M. *The transparent self.* Princeton, N.J.: D. Van Nostrand, 1964.

Jourard, S. *Self-disclosure: An experimental analysis of the transparent self.* New York: Wiley, 1971.

Jourard, S., & Friedman, R. "Experimenter-subject distance in self-disclosure." *Journal of Personality and Social Psychology,* 1970, 15, 278–282.

Kaats, G.R., & Davis, K.E., "The dynamics of sexual behavior of college students." *Journal of Marriage and the Family,* 1970, 32, 390–399.

Kamiat, A.H. "Male masochism and culture." *Psychoanalytic Review,* 1936, 23, 84–91.

Kanin, E.J., Davidson, K.D., & Scheck, S.R. "A research note on male/female differentials in the experience of heterosexual love." *The Journal of Sex Research,* 1970, 6, 64–72.

Kinsey, A.C., Pomeroy, W.B. & Martin, C.E. *Sexual behavior in the human male.* Philadelphia: Saunders, 1948.

Kinsey, A.C., Pomeroy, W.B., Martin, C.E., & Gebhard, P.H. *Sexual behavior in the human female.* Philadelphia: Saunders, 1953.

Knox, D.H., & Sporakowski, M.J. "Attitudes of college students toward love." *Journal of Marriage and the Family,* 1968, 30, 638–642.

Komarovsky, M. *Dilemmas of masculinity: A study of college youth.* New York: Norton, 1976.

Krafft-Ebing, R. von. [*Psychopathia sexualis: A medico-forensic study.*] New York: Pioneer, 1939. (Trans. of 12th edition, originally published, 1903.)

Lee, J.A. "The styles of loving." *Psychology Today,* 1974, 8, 43–51.

_____. *The colors of love.* New York: Bantam Books, 1977.

Maccoby, E.E., & Jacklin, C.N. *The psychology of sex differences.* Stanford, Calif.: Stanford University Press, 1974.

Marlatt, G.A. "Exposure to a model and task ambiguity as determinants of verbal behavior in an interview." *Journal of Consulting and Clinical Psychology,* 1971, 36, 268–276.

Millett, K. "The shame is over." *Ms.*, January, 1975, pp. 26–29.

Napier, A.Y. *The rejection-intrusion pattern: A central family dynamic.* Unpublished manuscript, School of Family Resources, University of Wisconsin, Madison, 1977.

Peplau, L., Rubin, A., & Hill, C. "The sexual balance of power." *Psychology Today*, 1976, 10, 142–147; 151.

_____. "Sexual intimacy in dating couples." *Journal of Social Issues*, 1977, 33, 86–109.

Pleck, J.J., & Sawyer, J. (Eds.). *Men and masculinity.* Englewood Cliffs, N.J.: Prentice-Hall, 1974.

Reiss, I.L., *The social context of premarital sexual permissiveness.* New York: Holt, Rinehart & Winston, 1967.

Robertiello, R.C. "Masochism and the female sexual role." *Journal of Sex Research*, 1970, 6, 56–58.

Rubin, Z., "Measurement of romantic love." *Journal of Personality and Social Psychology*, 1970, 16, 265–273.

_____. "Disclosing oneself to a stranger: Reciprocity and its limits." *Journal of Experimental Social Psychology*, 1975, 11, 233–260.

Rubin, Z., Hill, C.T., Peplau, L.A., & Dunkel-Schetter, C. "Self-disclosure in dating couples: Sex roles and the ethic of openness." *Journal of Marriage and the Family*, 1980, 42, 305–317.

Sager, C. *Marriage contracts and couple therapy.* New York: Brunner/Mazel, 1976.

Schofield, M. *The sexual behavior of young people.* Boston: Little, Brown, 1965.

Sorenson, R.C. *Adolescent sexuality in contemporary America.* New York: World, 1973.

Stroller, R.J. *Sexual excitement.* New York: Pantheon Books, 1978.

Tennov, D. *Love and limerance.* New York: Stein & Day, 1979.

Traupmann, J. & Hatfield, E. "Love: Its effects on mental and physical health." In J. March, S. Kiesler, R. Fogel, E. Hatfield, & E. Shanas (Eds.), *Aging: stability and change in the family.* New York: Academic Press, 1981.

Traupmann, J. & Hatfield, E. "How important is fairness over the lifespan?" *International Journal of Aging and Human Development*, in press.

Traupmann, J., Hatfield, E., & Sprecher, S. *The importance of "fairness" for the material satisfaction of older women.* Unpublished manuscript, 1982. (Available from Dr. Elaine Hatfield, Department of Psychology, University of Hawaii, 2430 Campus Rd., Honolulu, HI 96822.)

Utne, M.K. Hatfield, E., Traupmann, J. & Greenberger, D. "Equity, marital satisfaction and stability." *Basic and Applied Social Psychology*, in press.

Vietch, R. & Griffit, W. "The perception of erotic arousal in men and women by same- and opposite-sex peers." *Sex Roles*, 1980, 723–733.

Worthy, M.A., Gary, L., & Kahn, G.M. "Self-disclosure as an exchange process." *Journal of Personality and Social Psychology*, 1969, 13, 63–69.

20

It's Two Feet Long, Hard As Steel, Always Ready, and Will Knock Your Socks Off: The Fantasy Model of Sex

Bernie Zilbergeld

When I started working with men with sex problems over twenty years ago, I was immediately struck by the absolutely fantastic beliefs they held. They seemed to believe, for example, that they needed a penis as big and hard as a telephone pole to satisfy a woman, that male and female orgasm were absolutely necessary, that intercourse was the only real sexual act, that good sex had to be spontaneous, without planning or talking, and that it was a crime against humanity if a man had any questions, doubts, or problems about sex. As I reflected on these beliefs, I was shocked to realize that my clients weren't the only ones who held them. I shared many of them myself, and so did most men who weren't clients, and many women as well....

Whether we know it or not, whether it's intended or not, sex education goes on all the time, from the day we're born until the day we die, with an especially heavy dose coming during puberty....Because all the media portray essentially the same sexual messages, it's virtually assured that all men and women will learn the same model of sex, although, to be sure, the messages are filtered through the different gender training males and females have undergone....

The sexual messages conveyed in our culture are the stuff of fantasy, of overheated imaginations run wild, and that's why I call them collectively the fantasy model of sex. It is a model of total unreality about how bodies look and function, how people relate, and how they have sex. The main actors in this model are not actually people, but sexual organs, especially the penis. These penises are not like anything real but instead are, according to historian Steven Marcus, "magical instruments of infinite powers." The men these penises are attached to are not exactly average either. They are always well-built and muscular, even if they're over sixty and even if they do nothing but shuffle papers all day. They are usually tall, with "strong, intelligent" faces,

From *The New Male Sexuality: The Truth about Men, Sex, and Pleasure*, by Bernie Zilbergeld, Ph.D. Copyright © 1992 by Bernie Zilbergeld, Ph.D. Used by permission of Bantam Books, a division of Bantam Doubleday Dell Publishing Group, Inc.

they "radiate power," most are extremely successful at work, and sexual energy oozes from every pore.

The women in fantasyland are incredible. With beautiful faces, sensuous lips and hips, lustrous hair, slim bodies, full breasts always pointing outward and upward, and long, shapely legs you wouldn't believe. It might be thought that the combination of slimness and big breasts would create a problem of balance but fear not, none of the women ever keel over. And these women are mainly young, meaning in their twenties or early thirties. The few older women we encounter, except for those who are someone's mother, don't look half their age and could pass for college sophomores. For instance: "She was a month away from her fortieth birthday and looked thirty, even on a bad morning."

Regardless of age, these women have some interesting features. Barbara, in John Gardner's *Secret Houses,* is, well, kind of perfect: "As she leaned over him he noticed that her hair, like her breasts, stayed in perfect order." Wouldn't do to have any hair or breasts flopping about. Her breasts are worth another few words. They "remained the same whichever way she turned. They did not even seem to flatten when she was on her back, as some girls' did." Ain't life wonderful?

Another interesting feature of women in fantasyland is that they are seriously into sex. They go around with dripping panties, are ready for action at a moment's notice, and can express their desires as some men have always done: "That's right, honey, eat me, hurt me, talk dirty to me, and fuck me. That's all I want." Unless they're virgins, foreplay is not something they need much of. Orgasms, dozens of them, come quickly and easily to them.

Some women complain that this emphasis on perfect female forms is a male conspiracy, but the women created by female writers—for example, most of those who write romance novels—also tend to be young and physically perfect. The fantasy model is equally hard on men and women. The male bodies, organs, and performances are just as far out of reach for the ordinary man as the female bodies and performances are out of reach for the average woman.

Here's a little passage from a Harold Robbins novel that sums a lot of the action of the fantasy model. Try to keep in mind that this book is not only not pornographic by any of the usual definitions, but for decades has been available at many drugstores and supermarkets; Robbins is one of the best-selling authors of fiction in the world. He, along with other popular writers like Henry Miller, Norman Mailer, Mario Puzo, Sidney Sheldon, Erica Jong, Judith Krantz, and Jackie Collins—all of whose books have sold millions of copies and all of whom share some rather interesting ideas about sex—may be far more influential sex educators than Masters and Johnson and Dr. Ruth.

The man in the story is a wealthy businessman and the woman is his wife's dressmaker, whom he has just met. He got aroused and asked her how much. She indicated she wanted to open a small shop, and he said, "You've got it." With that for introduction and foreplay, we begin:

Gently her fingers opened his union suit and he sprang out at her like an angry lion from its cage. Carefully she...took him in both hands, one behind the other as if she were grasping a baseball bat. She stared at it in wonder....

[After placing his hands under her armpits and lifting her in the air] he began to lower her on him. Her legs came up, circling his waist, as he began to enter her. Her breath caught in her throat. It was as if a giant of white hot steel were penetrating her. She began to moan as it opened her and climbed higher into her body, past her womb, past her stomach, under her heart, up into her throat. She was panting now, like a bitch in heat....[He then lifts her off him and throws her onto the bed.] Then he was posed over her....His hands reached and grasped each of her heavy breasts as if he wanted to tear them from her body. She moaned in pain and writhed, her pelvis suddenly arching and thrusting toward him. Then he entered her again.

"My God," she cried, "my God!" She began to climax almost before he was fully inside her. Then she couldn't stop them, one coming rapidly after the other as he slammed into her with the force of the giant body press she had seen working in his factory. She become confused, the man and the machine they were one and the same and the strength was something she had never known before. And finally, when orgasm after orgasm had racked her body into a searing sheet of flame and she could bear no more, she cried out at him: "Take your pleasure...Quick, before I die!"

A roar came from deep inside his throat...she felt the hot onrushing gusher of his semen turning her insides into hot, flowing lava. She discovered herself climaxing again.

You may be wondering what's wrong with this kind of material. Isn't it more exciting and more fun to view, read about, and fantasize about perfectly built people and flawless performances than about real people? I admit it can be great fun to get away from the shortcomings and hassles of real life and imagine only perfection. That's one of the main purposes of fantasy. But there is a problem. Because we don't have any realistic models or standards in sex, of what is customary or even possible in the real world, we tend to measure ourselves against these fantasies. We often don't remember that what we're comparing ourselves to is for the most part unattainable by human beings. We usually aren't even aware that we're comparing ourselves to anything. We just know that we feel bad because our equipment and performances aren't what we wish they were.

In a society that doesn't give realistic models of sexuality, where else would people go for standards? It's rare, for example, to read of or see an average-looking couple having sex, so we end up feeling inadequate about our bodies and our partners'. It's rare, for example, to read of or see a couple having the kind of sex that is possible in the real world, so we feel bad about our less than cataclysmic experiences. It's rare to read of or see a couple discussing a sexual problem, so we learn that sex problems don't or shouldn't exist, and we fail to learn how to deal with them when they do occur....Good sex is always somewhere else with someone else.

[What follows are] some of the main destructive myths men hold about connecting and sex.

MYTH 1: WE'RE LIBERATED FOLKS WHO ARE VERY COMFORTABLE WITH SEX

Beginning with the sexual revolution of the 1960s and '70s, the idea has spread that we have overthrown and overcome the prudishness and inhibitions of our Victorian ancestors. Sexual pleasure is our birthright, and we don't much care what our religions or churches or parents say about it. We're going to do what we want with whom we want, and we're going to enjoy it. In other words, we are fairly calm about and accepting about sex. This view is now held by many people, especially men.

This belief is reinforced by media portrayals of erotica. Everyone in movies and books seems so comfortable with sex. No woman is concerned with her weight or the state of her breasts, thighs, or hips, or about her ability to lubricate and be orgasmic. No man is concerned about the size and hardness of his penis or his sexual endurance. No one questions his ability to provide a mind-blowing experience for himself and his partner. Everyone is comfortable with everything: vaginal, oral and anal sex, sex with and without drugs, sex in public places, sex with several partners at the same time, and sex without protection against pregnancy and disease. In fact, people in fantasyland are usually so comfortable that it doesn't make any difference whether the partners know each other. In the Harold Robbins story I quoted earlier, the man and woman had barely exchanged a dozen words; he didn't even know her name until ten seconds before sex. But, hey, no problem! Once they decide to have sex, everything is just fine. And this is far from the only example in popular literature where people who don't know each other, haven't exchanged a word, and maybe don't even like each other just do it and have a wonderful time.

...[I]t certainly would be nice if we were more comfortable with our bodies, our sexual organs, and sexuality in general than we are now....I have yet to meet a man or woman who I think is totally comfortable with sex, and that of course includes myself. We all seem to have hang-ups of one kind or another....

MYTH 2: A REAL MAN ISN'T INTO SISSY STUFF LIKE FEELINGS AND COMMUNICATING

...Women want to talk, men want to do. She can't understand why he doesn't say more about how he feels and isn't more interested in her personal expressions. He can't understand why she wants to talk so much and why she doesn't want to just get down to sex or whatever else he wants to do.

Because men have trouble directly expressing feelings except for sexual ones, they tend to get sneaky. In one scene in the movie *Three Men and a Baby,* Tom Selleck asks his woman friend to spend the night and the subject of feelings comes up. She says: "I thought sentiment made you uncomfortable." His reply: "I can handle it, as long as it's disguised as sex."...

MYTH 3: ALL TOUCHING IS SEXUAL OR SHOULD LEAD TO SEX

Boys and girls learn different things about touching, and men and women use touch in different ways. Women tend to see touching as a goal in itself; that is they hug in order to hug, not in order to get someplace else. For men, touching is more often a means to an end; hugging is a part of the foreplay to sex. As a result, misunderstanding and conflicts over touch are common....

The idea that touching is sexual is so deeply ingrained that many men don't consider having physical contact unless it is part of or going to lead to sex. Women complain about not getting as much touching as they want, but they aren't the only ones being deprived. Men need touching, if only they knew it, and cheat themselves as well. If sex isn't possible—because of illness, a sexual problem or something else—touching becomes even more important as a source of support and bonding. But many men don't see this and distance themselves physically from their partners in times of trouble....

This myth robs us of the joys of "just" touching, it confuses us as to what we want, and it puts pressure on us to be sexual whenever we touch or are touched.

MYTH 4: A MAN IS ALWAYS INTERESTED IN AND ALWAYS READY FOR SEX

...A real man is someone who's always interested in sex and ready for it. Here's an example from a novel about a man's needs: "Ike Vesper had had his fill of girlie magazines. Ten weeks without a women was nine weeks and six days too long." Poor baby!...

Having to be over-eager for sex makes it difficult for a man to refuse a sexual invitation. If someone within five miles is interested in sex, far be it from him to say no. Not being able to say no leads to trouble, because there's nothing more likely to result in a sex problem than having sex when you're not interested....

This myth also puts tremendous pressure on young men to be sexual as early as possible....If you aren't ready to talk to someone about sex and if you aren't ready to ask them for a back-rub or a hug, you're definitely not ready to have good sex with them.

MYTH 5: A REAL MAN PERFORMS IN SEX

You've got to have good equipment and you've got to use it right. Sex isn't mainly for enjoyment or to express love or caring or lust, it's mainly to prove that you're a man. This performance orientation explains why men are so much into measurement. If sex is to enjoy and express personal feelings, then you just do and enjoy. But if you're into proving something, then you have to know how to measure up. How big is it, how long did it last, how many orgasms were there? The performance orientation also explains why some men brag about sex to their friends. What's the point of a great performance if no one knows about it?

The quote from Harold Robbins earlier in the chapter is one kind of great performance. Here's another one, from Erica Jong's best-seller *Parachutes and Kisses:*

> He heaped the pillows in front of her for her to lean on, and cupping her breasts, he took her from behind, ramming her harder than before. Her cunt throbbed, ached, tingled. She screamed for him to ram her even harder, to smack her, to pound her....
>
> Never had she so surely met her sexual mate—a man who never tired of fucking, who liked to fuck until the point of soreness and exhaustion, a man who had as few hang-ups about sweat and smell and blood as she had....
>
> She had never come before in this position—but when she did it was as if thirty-nine years of comes were released and she howled and growled like an animal—whereupon he was aroused beyond containment and he began to come with a pelvis and cock gone wild, pounding her fiercely, filling her with come....

Whew! I get tired just reading this stuff.

One fascinating fact is that fictional accounts of sex almost invariably depict male *performance* and female *pleasure*. He *acts* (rams, pounds, thrusts, bangs) and she *feels* ("unbearable pleasure," "overwhelming joy," "delirious ecstasy," "a sublime moment of climax in which all the stars in the heavens seemed to explode in her mind"), the usual male-female dichotomy. Although she sometimes performs (she too can thrust and bang), it's rarely clear what he feels and experiences. It's as if his feelings and pleasure are beside the point. Now let's look at the main performance specifications.

Myth 6: Sex is Centered on a Hard Penis and What's Done with It

The adolescent male's fixation on his penis remains constant throughout life. When men think of sex, they think of what they can do with, or what can be done to, their erections. That's what it's all about. And not any old penis or erection will do. Men have a set of specifications for what's required.

Size: Penises in fantasyland come in only three sizes: large, extra large, and so big you can't get them through the door. "Massive," "huge," and "enormous" are commonly mentioned in fiction. "She reached inside his pants and freed his huge erection. "He was so big that she could not reach her fingers all around him." Sometimes we get numbers: "She swears that her Italian singer's cock is over ten inches long." In Mario Puzo's *Godfather,* Sonny Corleone's main claim to fame is the possession of the biggest cock in the known universe. Here's the experience of one of his many lovers with it: "Her hand closed around an enormous, blood-gorged pole of muscle. It pulsated in her hand like an animal and almost weeping with grateful ecstasy she pointed it into her own wet, turgid flesh." And this is what happens in Harold Robbin's *Dreams Die First* to women who witness the unveiling of a male model appropriately called King Dong: "I've seen them go absolutely glassy-eyed and come right in their pants the minute he takes out his tool."

Not only are penises huge to begin with, they can get still bigger during intercourse. "She wailed in hot flooding ecstasy. It went on and on, one climax after another, and as Craig's penis lengthened unbelievably, his semen erupting within her, she wailed again this time in unison with him." With that penis expanding the way it was, it's no wonder everyone was wailing.

Hardness: These organs that might be mistaken for phone poles are not mere flesh and blood but "hard as steel," "hard as a rock," or a "diamond cutter." Something that could cut a diamond, the toughest substance in the world, must really be hard. One wonders whether we're talking about making war or making love with these tools. There is, of course, no joy in a penis that's sort of hard, semihard, or "only 70 percent" erect.

Activity: The rocklike monstrosities manifest an excess of exuberance, for they are forever leaping, surging, springing, and, in general, behaving in a manner that might be considered dangerous for objects so large and hard. Two examples from novels: "He sprang swollen into her hand" and "She captured his surging phallus." Sounds like that one almost got away. Nowhere does one read of a penis that quietly moseyed out for a look at what was going on before springing and crashing into action.

The desired penis functions automatically and predictably just like a well-oiled machine. It should immediately spring into full readiness and whenever its owner decides he will use it. If you're dancing close with someone, your penis should be fully erect, pressing mightily against your pants and making its presence clearly felt. If a woman unzips your fly, your erection ought to spring out at her. If you kiss, well, here's how one novel puts it: "The lingering kiss [the first one that day, it should be said] induced an immediate erection." The way some men talk about it, I have the impression they think their penises should stand fully erect if a woman even says hello to them.

Automatic functioning means that the penis should function regardless of any other considerations. Neither rain, nor snow, nor sleet shall keep the almighty penis from its appointed rounds. No matter if you're sick or well, tired or fresh, preoccupied or fully present, if you like your partner or not, if you're angry or not, if you're anxious or relaxed, or if you've gotten any stimulation or not—your penis should immediately come to full attention and do its manly thing.

Penises in fantasyland are also distinguished by their ability to last. They can literally go all night. The admiring wife in one novel: "With Dax it's like having a machine gun inside you. It never stops shooting and neither does he." In one scene, she and Dax have intercourse and both have orgasms (naturally). Immediately after; "She looked at him in surprise. 'You're still hard,' she exclaimed, a note of wonder coming into her voice. She threw her head back...as he thrust himself into her again."

The clear message to men and to women is that a man showing up at a sexual event without a rock-hard penis is as inappropriate as a carpenter showing up for work without his hammer and tape measure. You simply can't leave home without your stiff dick. Almost needless to say, these requirements make a man feel inadequate about the size and power of their penises and under a bit of pressure to achieve and keep erections.

MYTH 7: SEX EQUALS INTERCOURSE

Both men and women learn that the main thing in sex is intercourse, and for most of us the two terms are synonymous. Almost all resources that deal with sex—medical books, textbooks, popular books, and articles, as well as erotic materials—treat sex and intercourse as if they were the same. Kissing, caressing, and manual and oral stimulation of genitals are all fine, but mainly as preliminaries to the ultimate: having the penis in the vagina. The very term we use to describe these other activities—*foreplay*—indicates their lowly status relative to intercourse. They're presumably important only as means to that main event.

This is silly. Since the goal of the vast majority of sexual encounters is *not* conception, there is no good reason why they have to include or end in intercourse, unless that is what the participants desire. There is no "normal" or "natural" way for sex to proceed. There are lots of possibilities, most of which do not include intercourse....

Insisting on intercourse as a necessary part of sex—as the only real way to go—creates a number of problems. One is that it reinforces our performance orientation and makes it difficult to enjoy other aspects of what's going on because we're so focused about getting to intercourse. In this way we rob ourselves of pleasure and of fully experiencing the stimulation necessary for an enjoyable sexual response.

Because intercourse requires some kind of erection (not as much as most men think, but still some hardness), making it a mandatory part of sex reinforces our anxiety about erections. And this, not surprisingly, is likely to result in erection problems....

MYTH 8: A MAN SHOULD BE ABLE TO MAKE THE EARTH MOVE FOR HIS PARTNER, OR AT THE VERY LEAST KNOCK HER SOCKS OFF

There has been an important change in men's view of their role in sex in the last twenty-five years or so. It used to be that scoring was all that mattered. Any man who got a lot of sex could consider himself successful in the sex department. But now we are much more focused on the pleasure of our partners. You can't consider yourself a good lover unless you give your partner an earthshaking experience.

Here is an example of what a man should be able to bring about:

> *Then Jeff rolled on top of her and was inside of her and it began again, more exciting than before, a fountain spilling over with unbearable pleasure, and Tracy thought,* **Now I know. For the first time, I know.**

...[A]nother popular author found the words: "Alix felt as if she had been thrown into a fire, felt as if her bones were melting. She could not catch her breath. She had never felt such overwhelming pleasure." Once her bones start melting, you know you're doing it right.

If you're in doubt, she'll probably tell you. In a novel by Irving Wallace, a man receives the ultimate accolade from his lover: "You're good, Erza, very good. You're the best I know. You're spoiling me for all other men." And a woman in one of Harold Robbin's books: "You're the most man I ever had."

In fantasyland, sex is always the best, the greatest, the most wonderful. The earth always moves.

One result of this myth is added pressure on a man to perform. Not only does he have to get it up and keep it up, he also has to use his tool, and everything else he has, to give his partner a mind-blowing experience. And, of course, no one ever tells him exactly how he's supposed to accomplish that. This belief has another unfortunate consequence. It can make it difficult for a man to feel good about a sexual encounter that consists primarily of being pleasured by his partner....

But because of the idea that sex isn't complete unless the woman has convulsions, many men disparage such activities as "servicing" and say they aren't interested. So the man may deprive himself of the sex he could have had and feel frustrated, annoyed, or angry. The woman may also be in a bad place. What she was able and willing to provide isn't good enough, and now she's got an upset partner. Should she just accept that, or should she try to force feelings that aren't there or even fake them? This kind of stuff does not make for happy relationships.

MYTH 9: GOOD SEX REQUIRES ORGASM

It has always been accepted that the goal of sex for men is their own ejaculation/orgasm. I've never seen or read of a sexual experience that didn't include clear indication that the man had "come," "finished," "shot his load," "exploded inside of her," and so on.

And now women have to have orgasms as well. It is rare these days to view a sexual scene in a movie or read of one in a book that doesn't include at least one per experience. Ever since Masters and Johnson's research showed that some women are capable of multiple orgasms, these have become the rage, and expectations have soared. "One climax after another" is a common way of putting it in novels. Here's one happy woman: "Deeper, harder, faster, until she cried out again, barely recovered from her first overwhelming orgasm before she was thrust into her second." Any man who can't generate at least a dozen or so orgasms in his partner is hardly worth considering.

There's also concern about the type of orgasm that women have. In fantasyland they are quick and furious. Women have orgasms "instantaneously" or "almost before he was fully inside her," always accompanied by screams and thrashing limbs. "With three violent thrusts he brought her to orgasm" is one example, as is, "Within seconds they reached orgasm simultaneously."...

Many men try to force their own orgasms by thrusting wildly and calling up every fantasy they can think of. Although it surprises many people when I say this, more than a few men I've talked to have faked orgasm. They felt bad about doing this, but they didn't want their partners to know they hadn't come. Besides, they had no idea of how to stop the activity without an orgasm.

Men also put pressure on their partners to have quick, loud orgasms so they, the men, will be able to feel good about themselves. No wonder that faking orgasms on the part of the women hasn't gone out of style. Even if she has a real one, she may feel pressured to fake several more, or to make it more dramatic than it really is....

MYTH 10: MEN DON'T HAVE TO LISTEN TO WOMEN IN SEX

Despite the increasing emphasis on giving women a good time in bed, there is also a contradictory myth that men can do whatever they want regardless of what the woman says.

One form of this myth is that females don't necessarily mean it when they say no to sex and that it pays to push on regardless of their protests. In popular novels and movies, it's common for a man to be rewarded for not taking a woman's rebuff seriously. He forces himself on her, and somewhere along the way, she gets into it and they both have a wonderful time.

A quote from a piece of pornography from Victorian England sums up the idea:

> *He pressed me in his arms. "Robert, let me go—where are you drawing me—you will make me fall. Oh! what do you mean—don't push your knees there—don't attempt to raise my dress. Robert, what are you about—I won't let you—take it away—you must not do it—Oh! Oh!—you are hurting me—Oh, my! what are you pushing in—yes, I do feel it—hold me in your arms—yes, I like that—you may fuck me, Robert, as hard as you like. ".*...

MYTH 11: GOOD SEX IS SPONTANEOUS, WITH NO PLANNING AND NO TALKING

Fantasyland sex is spontaneous. People get turned on to each other and one thing leads to another, as we like to say. Of course, one or both partners may have been thinking about sex beforehand, hoping for it, anticipating it. And the partners may hint, flirt, tease, and seduce. But apparently it's not okay to talk openly and plan together for sex.

A quote from the best-selling author Jackie Collins illustrates part of this myth. A man and woman who don't know each other and who have barely exchanged a dozen words start having sex. "There was nothing awkward about their lovemaking. He entered her smoothly and she moved with him as if they had been together many times before. Instinctively she knew his rhythm and he knew hers." Isn't that nice? Nothing was awkward and each "instinctively" knew the other's rhythm and presumably desires as well. Just like in real life, right? Later, as the man recalls the experience, he thinks this; "No corny lines or bullshit. Just wonderfully uninhibited sex." The message is clear: Discussing sex, or even getting to know one another—all this is "corny lines or bullshit." Only silent sex is real and meaningful.

This shows why fantasy sex is so popular. It feeds into the childish fantasies we all carry around, where people instinctively know what the other wants and willingly provide it, where there are no serious problems, where we can have whatever we want and all we want of it.

We have no trouble planning dates, dinners, vacations, and social events. Few people show up at airports, laden with suitcases, asking, "Do you have planes going to any interesting places today?"...But because we still view sex, even in marriage, as not quite all right, we'd rather sneak our way into it—and call it spontaneity....

MYTH 12: REAL MEN DON'T HAVE SEX PROBLEMS

In fantasyland there are no sexual problems or difficulties. It's all perfect and wonderful, just like in a fairy tale, which is exactly what it is.

It's as if sex problems don't exist. Despite the fact that millions of American men and women have sexually transmitted diseases—herpes, chlamydia, and genital warts, to name only the most common—no one in popular fiction has them, so there's no discussion of how to tell a partner about them and how to manage a sex life to avoid infecting others....

It's bad enough for a man to have a problem of any kind, but for "his manhood" not to be in perfect order—that's an incredible blow....These and similar myths have made men and women anxious, created problems and dissatisfactions and made resolution of existing problems more difficult. But we are not stuck with these destructive notions. We can reject them and put in their place more realistic and more constructive ideas....

21

Two Hands for the Clock: Changing Patterns in the Gendered Division of Labour in the Home

Meg Luxton

When I first got a job, I just never had any time, what with looking after the children and the housework. But now my husband has started to help me. He cooks and picks up the kids and is even starting to do other stuff! What a difference! Before, I used to feel like the second hand on the clock—you know, always racing around. Now, with his help, it feels like there are two hands for the clock—his and mine—so I get to stop occasionally.

More and more married women with young dependent children are employed outside the home. Studies conducted in the early and mid-1970s suggested that when married women took on paid employment, their husbands did not respond by increasing the amount of time they spent on domestic labour. These studies reached the general conclusion that married women were bearing the burden of the double day of labour almost entirely by themselves.[1]

Underlying women's double day of labour is the larger question of the gendered division of labour itself. The gendered division of labour, and particularly women's responsibility for domestic labour, have been identified as central to women's oppression in the capitalist societies as a whole, and specifically to women's subordination to men within families.[2]...

A recent Gallup poll on the sharing of general housework is suggestive. The poll, conducted across Canada in August 1981, reports that during the years 1976 to 1981, Canadians changed their opinions substantially about whether husbands should share in general housework. When asked the question, "In your opinion, should husbands be expected to share in the general housework or not?" 72 per cent responded "yes" in 1981 as compared with 57 per cent in 1976. Only 9 per cent (11 per cent of all men and 7 per cent of all women) replied that men should not share the work.

From Meg Luxton, "Two Hands for the Clock: Changing Patterns in the Gendered Division of Labour in the Home," *Studies in Political Economy* 12 (Fall 1983): 27–44.

However, changes in attitudes do not necessarily indicate changes in behaviour. The Gallup poll goes on to suggest that there has apparently been little change in what husbands do. It also implies that women and men disagree on the extent to which men are helping regularly. In 1976, 44 per cent of men polled said they helped regularly with housework, while in 1981, 47 per cent said they did. By contrast, in 1976, 33 per cent of women polled said men regularly helped while in 1981, 37 per cent of women polled said men regularly helped.[3]

FLIN FLON REVISITED

In 1976–77 I investigated women's work in the home through a case study of one hundred working class households in Flin Flon, a mining town in northern Manitoba.[4] Five years later, in 1981, I carried out a follow-up study to discover whether or not changes had occurred over the preceding five years. As Flin Flon is a small, fairly remote, single-industry town, it is not a Canadian pace setter. Changes occurring in Flin Flon probably indicate more widespread developments. While this case study does not dispute the finding of earlier studies (that when married women get paying jobs they continue to do most of the domestic labour), it does suggest that the situation is considerably more complex than had previously been perceived. It illustrates some of the factors underlying the emergence of the different patterns of attitudes and behaviours reflected in the Gallup poll. It also shows that in some working-class households, important changes in the division of labour are beginning to occur, as women exert pressure on their husbands to take on more domestic labour.

In the first study, I interviewed women of three generations. The first generation set up households in the 1920s and 1930s, the second in the 1940s and 1950s, and the third in the 1960s and 1970s. With just a few exceptions, women of the third generation were the ones with young children under the age of twelve. Just over half the women interviewed had held paid work outside the home for some period after their marriage. None of them, however, had worked outside the home while their children were young. Most had worked for pay before their children were born, but then had not worked for pay again until the children were of school-age. Regardless of whether or not they held paid jobs outside the home, these women identified themselves primarily as housewives and considered domestic labour their responsibility. They generally maintained that they did not expect their husbands to help with domestic labour. Those few men who did some work were praised as wonderful exceptions.

In the follow-up study I sought out only women of the third generation and was able to locate forty-nine of the original fifty-two. In striking contrast to the previous study, I found that these women, all of whom had children twelve years of age or less, were for the most part working outside the home for pay. Over half of these women had pre-school children, and nineteen had had another baby between 1976 and 1981. Despite their continued child care responsibilities, forty-four women had full-time employment. Of these, fourteen said they would prefer to be in the home full-time; nine said they would prefer part-time paid work; and almost half (21) said they were satisfied with the situation they were in. Four women had part-time paid work. Of these, two were satisfied while one wanted, but had not yet been able to find, a full-time paid job. One wanted to return to full-time domestic labour, but could not afford to quit her job. Only one woman was still working full-time in the home and she said she was there by choice.

What emerged from the interviews was that regardless of whether or not they wanted to be employed, these women were changing their identification of themselves as being primarily housewives. As one of the women who was working for pay full-time, but who wished she could stay at home, put it:

> *I am a housewife. That's what I always wanted to be. But I have also been a clerk for four years so I guess I'm one of those working mothers—a housewife, a mother and a sales clerk.*

Given the demands of their paid work, these women were forced to reorganize their domestic labour in some way. Both interviews and time budgets showed that the attitudes women have towards their work responsibilities (both paid and domestic) affect the way they reorganize domestic labour. A key factor was the extent to which they were willing to envisage a change in the gendered division of labour inside the family household.

Labour-force participation did not necessarily reflect their approval of "working mothers." In 1981 all of the women were asked what they thought about married women who had dependent children and who worked outside the home. Seven flatly opposed it under any circumstances, although all of them were in that situation. Nine did not think it was right for them personally, although they felt such a decision should be made on an individual basis. Eight women said it was fine if the woman needed the money, although they opposed mothers working outside the home for any other reasons.[5]

In contrast, over half of the women interviewed (25) maintained that mothers with dependent children had every right to work outside the home if they wanted to. Many of them (14) went further and argued that it was better for mothers to be working outside the home. For these women, economic need was only one of several valid reasons that women would take paid employment.

There was a direct correspondence between the attitudes these women expressed toward paid employment for mothers and their views on the gendered division of labour in the home. All of the women were asked who they thought should be responsible for domestic labour. Their responses show three distinct strategies in balancing the demands of domestic labour, paid employment and family. I have identified these distinct positions, based on their conceptualization of appropriate gender relations, as follows:

1. separate spheres and hierarchical relations;
2. separate spheres and co-operative relations;
3. shared spheres and changed relations.[6]

I. Separate Spheres and Hierarchical Relations

Seven respondents (14 per cent) advocated a strict gender-based division of labour. They flatly opposed women working outside the home because doing so would both violate women's proper role and detract from their ability to do domestic labour. These women argued that men, as males, were breadwinners and were "naturally" also household or family heads. Women were to be subordinate to their husbands—this was described by several women as "taking second place to my husband." They argued that women's wifely duties included acquiescence in relation to their husbands' demands and putting their families' needs before their own. These women maintained that they themselves held paid jobs outside the home only because their earnings were crucial. They intended to stop work as soon as the "emergency" was over.

They insisted that their paid work must never interfere with their ability to care for their husbands and children or to run their households. Because they assumed that domestic labour was entirely women's responsibility, they did not expect their husbands to help. They maintained that boy children should not be expected to do anything at all around the house and argued that they were teaching their girl children domestic labour skills, not because the mothers needed help, but as training for the girls' future roles as wives and mothers. Accordingly, these women sustained the full double day of labour entirely by themselves.

To deal with the contradiction between their beliefs and their actions, these women worked even harder at their domestic labour. In what appears to be a rigorous overcompensation, they actually raised their standards for domestic labour. They were determined to behave as though paid work made no difference to their domestic performance. Many of them insisted, for example, that every evening meal include several courses made from scratch as well as home-made desserts.

As a result, these women set themselves up in a never-ending vicious circle and ran themselves ragged. Their fatigue and resulting irritability and occasional illnesses only served to convince them that their original prognosis was correct: paid employment is bad for women and harmful to their families.

2. Separate Spheres and Co-Operative Relations

Seventeen women (35 per cent) said that women and men are different. Each gender moves in a separate sphere and marriage, in uniting a woman and man requires cooperation between the two spheres, with each person pulling his or her own weight. These women considered it acceptable for women to "help out" by earning money when necessary but, they argued, women's real work was in the home.

There were two identifiable currents within this general position. Nine women advocated full-time domestic labour for themselves though they agreed that might not be the best option for all women. These women maintained that they should not be working outside the home because they thought it interfered with their family responsibilities. While they were more flexible in their attitudes than those in the first group of women, they argued generally for the maintenance of the gendered division of labour. Particularly in their childrearing attitudes and behaviour, they adhered to a strict notion that boys should not be expected to engage in domestic labour while girls should be encouraged to do so.

Like the first group of women, these women also did most of the domestic labour on their own. Their way of trying to cope with the enormous strain this created, however, was to ease up their standards for domestic labour. They were much more willing to purchase "convenience foods" or to eat in restaurants. They talked about doing less around the house and about feeling vaguely disappointed that they could not keep their place nicer. They were, however, prepared to accept that they could not work outside the home and continue to do full-time domestic labour as well.

Taking a slightly different approach, eight women stated that paid work was acceptable for women with children, if the woman's income was necessary for her household economy. While these women also indicated that they were in favour of maintaining a traditional gendered division of labour, they often engaged in contradictory practices. They would argue that domestic labour was women's work, but in day-to-day activities they frequently asked their husbands to lend a hand, and they all expected their boy children as well as the girls to learn and take on certain domestic tasks.

To a large extent, it appears that the discrepancy between their beliefs and their behaviour lies in an experienced necessity. Unlike those who argued for hierarchical relations, these women were unwilling to become "super-women." They acknowledged the pressures on them and were willing to ask for help. The extent to which they asked for, and received, assistance varied from household to household. In most cases, children had assigned chores such as washing the dishes or setting the dinner table which they were expected to do on a regular basis. Husbands were not assigned regular jobs but were usually expected to "lend a hand" when they were specifically asked.

3. Towards Shares Spheres and Changing Relations

Twenty-five women—just over half the sample (51 per cent)—stated that regardless of necessity, women with young children had the right to paid employment if they wanted it. For them, wives and husbands were partners who should share the responsibilities for financial support and domestic labour. They supported the idea of changing the division of labour and in practice they were instituting such changes by exerting increasing pressure on their husbands and children to redistribute both the responsibility for, and the carrying out of, domestic labour. As it is these women who are challenging the existing ideology and practice of the gendered division of labour, and especially the place of women and men in the family home, I want to look more closely at the changes they have enacted in the last five years.

A REDISTRIBUTION OF LABOUR TIME

While the women who argued for separate spheres were defending a gendered division of labour within the household, statements made by the third group reflected the trends indicated in the Gallup poll. When these twenty-five women were asked in the 1976 study if they thought husbands should help with domestic labour, most agreed that they did not expect their husbands to do anything, although six said their husbands actually did help. By 1981, however, they unanimously insisted that husbands should help out and all said their husbands did some domestic labour on a regular basis.

An examination of time budgets for these households shows that men have in fact increased the amount of time they spend on domestic labour. By themselves, the figures seem to be quite impressive; men increased their domestic labour time from an average of 10.8 hours per week in 1976 to 19.1 hours in 1981—an increase of 8.3 hours.

By contrast, in 1976 full-time housewives spent an average of 63 hours per week on domestic labour while women working a double day spent an average of 87.2 hours per week working, of with 35.7 hours were spent on domestic labour. In 1981, women doing both jobs averaged 73.9 hours per week of which 31.4 hours were spent on domestic labour. This is a decrease of only 4.3 hours per week. While one would not expect a direct hour for hour substitution of one person's labour for another, there is a discrepancy between the increase in men's work and the relatively insignificant reduction in women's work. Women on an average were spending 12.3 hours a week more than men on domestic labour. Furthermore, there is a discrepancy between the women's insistence that domestic labour should be shared equally and the actual behaviour of household members. These discrepancies generate considerable tension between wives and husbands—tension which reflects the power struggle inherent in the redistribution of domestic labour.

WOMEN AND MEN'S DOMESTIC LABOUR

The women who want their husbands to be more involved have developed a variety of strategies and tactics with which to get the men to take on more work. These range from gentle appeals to fairness or requests for assistance to militant demands for greater (or equal) participation. In a few cases, women discussed the situation with their husbands and they mutually agreed on a sharing of tasks that both partners considered fair and reasonable. In the majority of cases, however, negotiations appeared to be out of the question. Instead the couples seemed locked into tension-generating, manipulative power struggles.

For the women, the impetus to change comes from the pressures of their two jobs. It is fuelled further when they compare their experiences with those of their husbands. Some contrasted their own working time at home with their husband's leisure time.

> *I come home from work dead tired and I still have to cook and be with the kids and clean up. And he just lies around, drinking beer, watching TV and I get so mad, I could kill him.*

Others compared the standards their husbands expected from their wives with those the men held for themselves. They noted that when living alone, some men kept their households immaculately clean; others lived in a total mess. Whatever their standards for themselves, when the women were around, men changed their behaviour, altered their expectations and pressured the women to meet male standards.

> *When my husband is on his own, he's quite happy to live in a pig sty. Mess doesn't bother him. But the minute I get back he insists that he can't live in the house unless it is spotless.*
>
> *Before we were married he lived on his own and his place was so clean and tidy. But as soon as we got married, he somehow never felt he could clean up. It was all up to me.*

Despite the obvious interest these women have in redistributing domestic labour, and despite their motivating anger, there are numerous forces operating which make it difficult for women to insist that their spouses actually share the work.

Because inequalities in the division of labour are based on male power, when women demand equalization of the work, they are challenging that power. Some women were afraid that if they pushed for more male participation, they would provoke their husbands' anger and rage. At least one woman said her husband had beaten her for suggesting he help with domestic labour.

While there is evidence to suggest that when women have paid employment they increase their own power in marriage, all of these women earned considerably less than their husbands. As a result, the men retained economic power (bread-winner power). Men can also use their greater earnings as a justification for not doing domestic labour. They often argued that with their earnings they discharged the responsibility to the household. Under present circumstances it is up to the individual women to initiate changes in the patterns of domestic labour. For many, economic dependency makes it difficult to challenge their husbands.

Furthermore, the actual task of getting men to do domestic labour is often difficult. If women want their husbands to begin doing domestic labour, they must be prepared to take responsibility not only for overcoming male resistance but also for helping the men overcome both the accumulated years of inexperience and the weight of traditional assumptions about masculinity. Generally, the women assumed that their husbands were unfamiliar with domestic labour and therefore neither knew what needed doing nor had the necessary skills to carry out the work. Taking on this training of resisting and unskilled workers is often in itself an additional job.

When men do start doing domestic labour, women begin to lose control. Domestic labour has traditionally been the one sphere of female control and power. For most women, the kitchen is the closest they ever come to having a "room of one's own." It is difficult for many women to relinquish this, particularly if they are not compensated for that loss by gains made elsewhere—for example in their paid work. While the women were uniformly pleased that their husbands had increased their contribution, they were troubled by the way domestic labour was being redistributed.

MEN AND DOMESTIC LABOUR

That men increase the amount of time they spend on domestic labour does not in itself convey much about changing work patterns. Most significantly, it was still assumed that women were primarily responsible for domestic labour and that men were "helping out." When women do domestic labour they often juggle several tasks at once. One of the ways that men have increased the amount of time they spend on domestic labour is by taking over some of that simultaneous work. Many women reported that their husbands were willing to watch the children while the women prepared dinner or did other household chores. While such actions obviously relieved some of the pressures and tensions on women, they did not reduce the amount of time required of women for domestic labour.

Often when men (and children) took on certain tasks, they ended up generating even more domestic work. A number of women indicated that their husbands cooked, but when they did so they seriously disrupted the orderliness of the kitchen, emptying cupboards to find something and not putting things back or using an excessive number of dishes in preparation. Another commonly cited example was that when men agreed to look after the children, they actually paid more attention to their visiting friends or the TV. Unattended, the children ran "wild" through the house so that when the woman returned she had to spend a great deal of time tidying the house and calming the children. Further, many women pointed out that getting their husbands to do domestic labour required a considerable amount of their time and energy. Sometimes, women argued, it took more work to get the man to do the work than it did to do the work themselves.

Furthermore, men tended to take over certain specific tasks which had clearly defined boundaries. They did not take on the more nebulous, on-going management tasks and they rarely took responsibility for pre-task planning. For example, a number of men did the grocery shopping on a regular basis but they insisted that the woman draw up the basic list of things needed. Some men would do the laundry, if all the dirty clothes were previously collected and sorted and if the necessary soap and bleach were already at hand.

A recurring theme throughout the interviews was that men preferred jobs that involved working with machinery. A number of men were willing to do the vacuuming because they enjoyed playing with the vacuum cleaner. One woman described how her husband had refused to cook until they purchased a food processor. After that he was forever reading the recipe book and planning new techniques for meal preparation. Several women noted that their husbands had increased their participation in meal preparation after they bought microwave ovens.

The redistribution that is occurring is selective. The husbands tend to take the path of least resistance. The trend has been for men to take on those tasks that are the most clearly defined, or sociable and pleasant ones, while leaving the more ill-defined or unpleasant ones to the women. Repeatedly women noted that their husbands had taken on reading the children a bed-time story and staying with them until they feel asleep, thus "freeing" the women to wash the dishes and tidy the kitchen. Men were often willing to feed their infant children or take older ones to the park, but on the whole they would not change soiled diapers or wash their children's hair. They would wash the dishes but not the kitchen floor or the toilet. One man would vacuum the living room rug but refused to do the stairs because they were too awkward.

A number of women expressed concern about this pattern. They noted that when men took on the more pleasant aspects of domestic labour, they were left with the most onerous and boring tasks. They were particularly concerned when the man took on more of the playtime with children. As one woman expressed it:

> *I'm really glad he's spending more time with the children. They really enjoy it. But it's beginning to make me look like the meany. Daddy plays with them and tells them stories and other nice things while I do the disciplining, make them wash up, tidy their toys and never have time to play because I'm cooking supper.*

One of the most significant transformations of men's involvement in domestic labour has been in the area of child care. While most fathers have always spent some time with their children, particularly with older children, increasingly they are doing more of the day-to-day caregiving, especially with younger children. Perhaps the most significant change of all has been with the birth process itself.[7] In 1976 only 4 out of 25 men had been present at the birth of at least one of their children. However, of the babies born between 1976–1981, 10 of the 19 new fathers had been present at the birth (and only 2 of these were of the original 4).The wives indicated that they felt very strongly that having their husbands involved in the birth also drew the men into the whole process of pregnancy, child birth and infant care. Men who were willing to attend the birth were subsequently more inclined to get up at night with the baby, to take over certain feedings and to be generally more involved with their small babies.

Despite this very promising shift, women were still responsible for overall child care. All twenty-five women said it was up to them to arrange day care for their children when they worked outside the home. If the child care arrangements fell through on any particular day, it was the woman who had to get time off work to stay home, although this can in part be explained by her lower pay and in part by his unavailability when underground.

Furthermore, men "babysat" their own children—something that women never did. The implication of this typical reference was that the children were the responsibility of the mother, and the father "helped out." This attitudinal difference was often carried out in behaviour as well. Women repeatedly described situations where men would agree to watch the children, but would then get involved in some other activity and would ignore the children. As children grew up, they learned from experience that their mothers were more likely to be helpful, and so they would turn to the woman rather than the man for assistance, thus actively perpetuating the traditional division of labour.

The ambivalent and often reluctant way in which these men have moved into domestic labour reflects a combination of valid reasons and invalid excuses. In "The Politics of Housework," Pat Mainardi describes with biting sarcasm the various forms of male resistance developed in response to a wife's attempt to share housework:

> **Husband:** *"I don't mind sharing the work, but you'll have to show me how to do it."*

> **Meaning:** *I'll ask a lot of questions and you'll have to show me everything every time I do it because I don't remember so good. And don't try to sit down and read while I'm doing my jobs because I'm going to annoy the hell out of you until it's easier to do them yourself.*[8]

Flin Flon women described various forms of male behaviour that were obviously intended to resist attempts to draw them into domestic labour.... Some women talked suspiciously of the way household machinery "broke down" when their husbands tried to use it. Several women told of incidents where their husbands agreed to do the work but then repeatedly "forgot" to do it, complained when the women "nagged" them about it, and finally told the women to do it themselves if they did not like the way the men did it. One man explained his position quite clearly:

> *Look, I'm not interested in doing stuff around the house. I think that's her job, but since she's working she's been on my back to get me to help out so I say "sure I'll do it." It shuts her up for a while and sometimes I do a few things just to keep her quiet. But really, I don't intend to do it, but it prevents a row if I don't say that....*

Because the majority of men have, until recently, not been expected to do domestic labour, they have not been taught either implicitly, the way girls learn via their dolls and play kitchens, or explicitly, through "helping" mother or in home economics classes. As a result, they often lack knowledge and are unskilled and awkward. Working at a job for which one is ill-prepared often generates feelings of anxiety, inadequacy and incompetence which are easily translated into a generalized rēluctance to continue the job....

This fear of public ridicule was illustrated by two neighbours. Both families visited together frequently, and the men were friends. They also did a considerable amount of cooking and cleaning. Both, however, insisted that their wives not let the other couple know of the extent to which the men did domestic labour. The fear of public ridicule may reflect a deeper fear. When wives insist that men move into an area that has traditionally been defined as "women's work," men face a challenge to their conventional notions of femininity and masculinity. This may arouse deep psychological and emotional resistances, and stimulate anxiety and fear....

CONCLUSION

Because people tend to evaluate their experiences in light of existing social explanations and ideologies, the response of Flin Flon women can be set in a broader context. The three perspectives expressed reflect ideologies which are currently prominent.

Those women who put forward a "separate spheres and hierarchical relations" position were defending the traditional conservative view which locates women inside the family, subordinates women's interests to men's, and places priority above all on the preservation of the breadwinner husband/dependent wife nuclear family.

Because the beliefs these Flin Flon women held conflicted directly with the activities they engaged in, they were compelled to mediate the contradiction. Their attempts to defend a strict gendered division of labour forced them deeper into the hardship of the double day. Their actual experiences highlight the conditions under which support for right-wing "pro-family" reform movements is generated, for in their opinion, it is their paid work that creates the problem.

Those women who argued for "separate spheres and co-operative relations" were expressing a classic liberal view of appropriate female/male relations in the family. This "different but equal" perspective echoes the maternal feminism of some early twentieth-century theorists. It is also found in many sociologists of the family such as Young and Willmott, who argue that marriages are now symmetrical or companionate.[9]

Those women who argued for "shared spheres and changing relations" were expressing contemporary feminist views which hold that the existing gendered division of labour is a major factor in women's oppression. In challenging the way work is divided in the home, they are questioning the existing relationships between women and men, and between children and adults. Discussing existing family relationships, Hartmann has argued that "Because of the division of labour among family members, disunity is thus inherent in the 'unity' of the family."[10]

This study suggests that a large-scale social transformation is occurring as traditional patterns are eroding and new ones are emerging, but to date the change has been acted out on the level of the individual household, and may, in the short run, be intensifying family disunity. What emerged from these interviews was the total isolation both women and men felt. Women involved in active, collective organizing to change the division of labour in the paid workforce have the women's liberation movement, the trade union movement, Status of Women committees, and sometimes the law and other organizations or institutions such as the Human Rights Commissions, to back them up. In contrast, women challenging the gendered division of labour in the home do so on an individual basis. Similarly, there is a complete lack of social and material support for men with regard to domestic labour. Very few unions have won paternity leave, for example, so it is very difficult for new fathers to get time off work to be with their new children. This makes it very difficult for men actually to take equal responsibility for their infants.[11] Accordingly, any man who takes on domestic labour places himself at odds with current social practices. It takes a certain amount of self-confidence and courage to do so.

As a result, the majority of respondents implied that they considered that the changes in their domestic division of labour were specific to their individual households. They perceived these changes not as part of a large scale transformation in the patterns of work and family life, but as a personal struggle between them and their spouse. Such a perception only exacerbated the tensions between women and men.

As material conditions change and new ideologies emerge, many individuals and families are floundering, trying to decide what they want, how to get it, and most problematically, how to resolve conflicts between various possibilities and needs. There are currently no social policies or clear-cut, developing social norms to provide a context in which individuals can evaluate their own actions. Instead, there are several contending ideologies and related social movements, such as the "pro-family" movement and the women's liberation movement.[12] While these movements articulate positions on what female/male relations should entail, they rarely organize to provide support for women to achieve the desired end. The current situation is thereby generating a great deal of confusion and often pain and interpersonal conflict, especially between women and men.

Finally, this study demonstrates that until the exclusive identification of women with domestic labour is broken, there is no possibility of achieving any kind of equality between women and men. If the necessary labour is not redistributed, women end up with a dramatically increased work load. Unlike earlier studies, the findings of this research suggest, that despite all the problems, some working-class women are contesting male power and challenging male privilege and some men are responding by assuming more responsibility for domestic labour.

NOTES

This paper reports the results of research carried out in Flin Flon, Manitoba, in 1981. All the quotes cited in the paper without references are from interviews conducted as part of that research.

The article is a revised version of a paper presented at the Canadian Sociology and Anthropology Association meeting in Ottawa in 1982. For critical comments I am grateful to Margaret Benston, Pat Connelly, Heather Jon Maroney, Pat Marchak, Ester Reiter, Harriet Rosenberg and Wally Seccombe.

1   Heidi Hartmann, "The Family as the Locus of Gender, Class and Political Struggle; The Example of Housework," *Signs* 6: 3 (Spring 1981), 377–86.

2   Rayna Rapp, "Family and Class in Contemporary America: Notes Towards an Understanding of Ideology," *Science and Society* 42 (Fall 1978), 278–301; Michelle Barrett, *Women's Oppression Today* (London: Verso, 1980); Michelle Barrett and Mary MacIntosh, *The Anti-Social Family* (London: 1983).

3   Canadian Institute of Public Opinion, *The Gallup Report* (Toronto, 7 October 1981), 1–2.

4   Meg Luxton, *More Than a Labour of Love, Three Generations of Women's Work in the Home* (Toronto: The Women's Press, 1980).

5   The problem here, however, lies in trying to determine what constitutes economic need. All of these women (24) maintained that they were working outside the home for economic reasons, because their families needed the money. In all likelihood, this is true. However, it may be that these women, like most employed housewives who have been studied, also have non-economic reasons for accepting paid employment. Economic necessity is a more socially legitimated reason and some of these women may be dealing with the contradictory feeling they have toward their family obligations and their

pleasure in employment by convincing themselves and others that they are only working because they "have to."

6   There were no obvious sociological factors that might explain the differences in opinion and behaviour. While a large-scale survey might reveal correlations between these different strategies and such factors as political or religious affiliation, ethnicity, and husbands' attitudes, at least among this group of women, and given the available data, no such patterns emerged.

It is also important to point out that while these three approaches are typical, they are not the only available options. Some women have fully egalitarian relations with the men they live with; others live alone or with other women.

A creative strategy was developed by one couple (not included in the study). The man worked a forty-hour week in the mines; the woman was a housewife. They determined mutually what work she was responsible for during a forty-hour week. She did child care while he was at work, as well as heavy cleaning and certain other chores. The rest of the domestic labour—child care, cooking, cleaning, laundry, shopping—they divided equally between them. As a result, each worked a forty-hour week at their own work and shared all remaining labour.

7   It seems to me that the involvement of men in the actual birth of their children is of enormous significance—something which has not yet been appreciated, or studied.

8   Pat Mainardi, "The Politics of Housework," in *Sisterhood Is Powerful*, ed. Robin Morgan (New York: Random House, 1970), 449–51.

9   Nellie McClung, *In Times like These* (1915; Toronto: University of Toronto Press, 1972); Michael Young and Peter Willmott [sic], *The Symmetrical Family* (London: Routledge and Kegan Paul, 1973).

10   Hartmann, "Family as the Locus," 379.

11   In Québec the unions of CEGEP teachers have won paternity leave. This has made it possible for some men to take equal responsibility for infant care.

12   Susan Harding, "Family Reform Movements: Recent Feminism and Its Opposition," *Feminist Studies* 7: 1 (Spring 1981), 57–75.

22

Dual Earners: Who's Responsible for Housework?

Katherine Marshall

Women employed full-time and in dual-earner families, particularly those with young children, are the most pressured for time. This is not surprising, given that these women carry the double burden of paid work and unpaid housework. More than one-half of full-time working wives in dual-earner families with children at home[1] are solely responsible for all daily household chores, according to the 1990 General Social Survey (GSS). However, husbands of these women generally take a greater role in domestic chores than do other husbands. Sharing of household work tends to be most common among younger, well-educated couples with few children. Nonetheless, the division of housework is still far from equal.

MOST COUPLES ARE DUAL EARNERS

Balancing family and job obligations has become a challenge for more Canadian couples than ever before. According to the 1990 GSS, 71% of couples, with children under age 19 in the household, were dual earners (both partners had at least some employment outside the home) that year. In contrast, just over 20 years ago, only 30% of such families were dual earners.

In 1990, both the wife and the husband were employed full-time in 51% of two-parent families. In 19% of two-parent families, the husband worked full-time, while the wife was employed part-time. Single-earner families, in which the husband was employed full-time and the wife was at home full-time, accounted for 27%.

WIVES' RESPONSIBILITY FOR HOUSEWORK VARIES WITH EMPLOYMENT STATUS

As wives' involvement in the workforce increases, their responsibility for housework declines, but their husbands' contribution does not increase enough to approach parity. For example, 72% of wives aged 15–64 working

From Katherine Marshall "Dual Earners: Who's Responsible for Housework?" *Canadian Social Trends*, Cat. No. 11–008E (Spring and Winter 1993): 11–14. Reprinted by permission.

full-time who had children living at home were solely responsible for meal preparation, compared with 86% of wives employed part-time and 89% of those not in the labour force.

Husbands in dual-earner families, with both partners employed full-time and with children at home, were the most likely of all husbands to assume responsibility for domestic chores. The proportions who did so, however, were relatively low. Meal clean-up was the task that these men most often shared (15%) or did on their own (16%). Slightly fewer shared (12%) or had sole responsibility (13%) for meal preparation. And although 13% of husbands shared the cleaning and laundry, these were the chores that they were least likely to do alone (7%).

Men maintained responsibility for chores such as repairs, maintenance and yard work, regardless of whether their wife was employed or stayed at home. In 1990, for example, the husband had sole responsibility for these tasks in 79% of full-time dual-earner families with children at home. In families where the wife stayed at home, the proportion was 77%.

WOMEN WORKING FULL-TIME OFTEN RESPONSIBLE FOR ALL HOUSEWORK

In one-half of couples with children under age 19, both spouses are employed full-time, and consequently, have less time for domestic chores than do those with other employment patterns. With both partners sharing responsibility for paid work, it would appear that these couples deviate from traditional gender roles. However, this is not the case in the home, where wives still are usually responsible for the routine household chores of meal preparation and clean-up, as well as cleaning and laundry.[2] Over half of wives employed full-time (52%) had all of the responsibility for daily housework, while another 28% had most of this responsibility. Only 10% of dual-earning couples working full-time shared responsibility for housework equally. In the remaining 10% of couples, the husband had all or most of the responsibility.

WHO SHARES...WHO DOESN'T?

Only a small minority of dual-earner couples, with both partners working full-time and with children at home, had an egalitarian division of housework. Generally, the younger the partners, the less likely was the wife to be the only one responsible for housework. For example, 47% of wives under age 35, in dual-earner families and employed full-time, were solely responsible for daily housework, compared with 69% of those wives aged 45–64. Some of this variation is due to attitudinal differences across age groups.

Although husbands and children may help with household tasks, women assume more responsibility for housework as the number of children

CANADIAN SOCIAL TRENDS BACKGROUNDER

Primary responsibility for work around the house among couples aged 15–64 with children under age 19, 1990

Household chore and type of couple	Total[1]	Primary responsibility			
		Wife only	Husband only	Wife and husband equal	Others[2]
Meal preparation					
Dual-earner, both full-time	100	72	13	12	2
Dual-earner, wife part-time[3]	100	86	7	6	—
Single-earner, husband full-time	100	89	5	5	—
Meal clean-up					
Dual-earner, both full-time	100	59	16	15	6
Dual-earner, wife part-time[3]	100	72	9	10	3
Single-earner, husband full-time	100	78	7	8	3
Cleaning and laundry					
Dual-earner, both full-time	100	74	7	13	3
Dual-earner, wife part-time[3]	100	86	4	6	—
Single-earner, husband full-time	100	86	4	7	—
House maintenance and outside work					
Dual-earner, both full-time	100	7	79	4	9
Dual-earner, wife part-time[3]	100	9	80	3	6
Single-earner, husband full-time	100	8	77	5	9

[1] May not add to 100 due to rounding and the exclusion of Not Stated.
[2] Someone other than the wife or husband has primary responsibility for the chore.
[3] In this type of couple, the husband works full-time.

Source: Statistics Canada, 1990 General Social Survey.

in the household increases. The percentage of full-time employed wives in dual-earner families who had all responsibility for housework increased from 44% of those with one child at home to 83% of those with four or more children. It appears that women are more likely than men to do the extra

Wives largely responsible for housework in dual-earner families with both spouses employed full-time, 1990

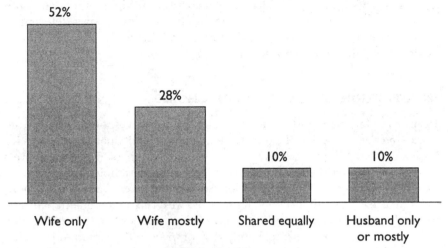

Source: Statistics Canada. 1990 General Social Survey.

work required to maintain a home with several children. It is also possible that parents with several children at home may have retained many traditional values, despite the mother working at a paid job.

Women in common-law unions where both partners work full-time were somewhat less likely than those in marriages to do all the housework. The wife had sole responsibility for housework in 46% of common-law unions, compared with 52% of marriages.

Women with high educational attainment were less likely than others to assume full responsibility for domestic chores in dual-earner families. University-educated women employed full-time with children living at home had sole responsibility for daily housework in 45% of their households. This was the case in 58% of households where women had less than high school graduation. Husbands with higher education were more likely than others to share responsibility for household chores. This may be because there is less of an income differential between wives and husbands as education level rises. More equality in income earned may lead to more equal sharing of responsibilities for housework.

The relationship between domestic responsibility and income differed for women and men. In dual-earner families with both partners working full-time, the wife's likelihood of having sole responsibility for housework declined as her income rose. Whereas 67% of women whose income was under $20,000 had sole responsibility for housework, this was the case for 53% of those whose income was $40,000 or over. As a husband's income increased, his propensity for doing housework declined, leaving an increasing proportion of wives with sole responsibility for domestic chores. Thirty-nine percent of wives whose husband's income was under $20,000 had sole responsibility for housework, compared with 45% of those whose husband's income was $40,000 or over. This pattern corresponds to the theory that the relative social and economic power between husbands and wives determines who does household chores.[3] In other words, having greater economic power "buys" time out of housework.

SATISFACTION WITH DIVISION OF CHORES

Despite the fact that most women are solely or mostly responsible for housework, the vast majority of both women and men in dual-earner families indicated that they were satisfied with the allocation of domestic chores. Almost all husbands (97%) and wives (98%) in households where housework was shared equally, as well as spouses with little responsibility for these tasks (at least 94%), reported being satisfied with this arrangement. Not surprisingly, spouses least satisfied were those with sole responsibility for household chores. For example, only 75% of wives in this situation reported being satisfied with the division of labour.

DUAL EARNERS' TIME FOR ACTIVITIES AND BALANCE BETWEEN FAMILY AND JOB

Spouses with sole responsibility for housework are less satisfied than their partners with the amount of time they have to pursue other interests. In dual-earner families where both partners were working full-time, 58% of women with sole responsibility for housework were satisfied, compared with 70% of their partners. In those families where the husband had sole or most of the responsibility, 54% of men were satisfied, compared with 74% of their spouses. In other dual-earner families, around 60% of both husbands and wives were satisfied with the amount of time they had for other activities.

Regardless of the allocation of responsibility for housework, around 80% of spouses in dual-earner families said that they were satisfied with the balance between job and family. Experience with other surveys has shown, however, that reported levels of satisfaction tend to be somewhat exaggerated because many people consider it more socially acceptable to express satisfaction than dissatisfaction with their personal life.

TRADITIONAL DIVISION OF LABOUR

Although in many families today, both spouses are working, traditional roles still persist in the home. Women, even those employed full-time, continue to be primarily responsible for housework, whereas men maintain responsibility for tasks such as repairs, outside work and maintenance.

Responsibility for a chore goes beyond the actual performance of the task to include anticipating, planning and organizing what needs to be done and managing people, resources and time. The routine tasks of housework—such as meal preparation, meal clean-up, and cleaning and laundry—are time-consuming and often must be performed daily or at least weekly. In contrast, many repair, yard work and maintenance chores are done infrequently and, in some cases, can be delayed indefinitely.

Because of the differences in the nature of the responsibilities, it is usually more difficult to manage the daily household chores in conjunction with full-time employment than to manage the more infrequent repairs, yard work and maintenance. Without a more equal division of responsibility for housework, women will have to continue to juggle employment, household chores and family time. This, in turn, will leave them more limited time for professional or personal development.

The General Social Survey

Statistics Canada established the General Social Survey (GSS) in 1985 to monitor changes in the living conditions and well-being of Canadians, and to provide information on various social issues of current or emerging interest. Data are collected annually from a random sample of households. Approximately 13,500 people were interviewed in 1990. The target population consists of all people aged 15 and over, except full-time residents of institutions and residents of the Yukon and the Northwest Territories. For further information on the survey, contact Josephine Stanic at (613) 951-8644.

Determining level of responsibility for housework

A point system was used to determine responsibility for housework. Individuals scored a point each time they were acknowledged as having primary responsibility for meal preparation, meal clean-up, and cleaning and laundry. If responsibility for a chore was shared equally, each partner scored a point. Since daily housework consisted of three chores, the maximum score was three points. For example, "wife mostly" comprises scores of W=3 H=2; W=3 H=1; and W=2 H=1.

Because one respondent reported for all family members, the data reflect that person's perception of who was responsible for household chores. Husbands collectively perceived themselves as doing more than wives observed them doing, and vice versa. Since results were based on responses from both husbands and wives, differences in perception generally averaged out. In the case of income, however, the analysis of husbands' income and housework was based on male respondents only, which results in a male perspective on the division of household chores. The same is true for female income and housework. This produces some bias in reporting.

Percentage of wives employed full-time and in dual-earner families with sole responsibility for housework, 1990

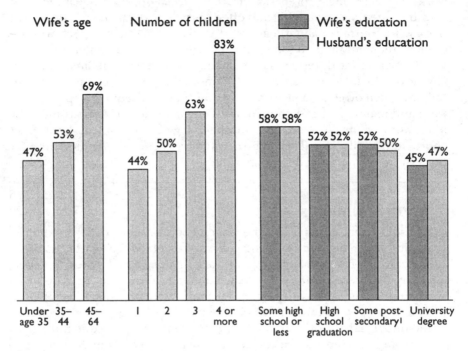

1 Includes certificate or diploma.
Source: Statistics Canada, 1990 General Social Survey.

NOTES

1   The population examined in this article consists of married or common-law couples with both partners aged 15–64 and with dependent children under age 19 at home.

2   Throughout the rest of this article, the terms "housework" or "household chores" refer to the tasks of meal preparation, meal clean-up, and cleaning and laundry.

3   Brayfield, April A., "Employment Resources and Housework in Canada," in *Journal of Marriage and the Family*, Vol. 54, No. 1, February 1992, pp. 19–30.

CHAPTER FIVE

Gender, Families, and Parenting

W e devote a separate chapter to gender, families, and parenting in order to present a sampling of the increasing number of articles being written on these topics. The nature of parenting, within or outside the traditional definition of "family," has become the focus of intense research and theorizing in recent years. Contemporary issues concern whether family structure (one versus two parents) or sexual orientation (heterosexual versus homosexual) or simply process (the provision of a caring and sharing environment) is the key and essential ingredient of families and adequate parenting. An inclusive orientation acknowledges and celebrates differences in structural numbers and sexual orientation while still contributing to what is considered to be the key ingredient, namely, that of care providing. Before exploring these issues, we present a work by Harriet Rosenberg (Article 23) that examines the nature of mothering, or "motherwork," within Canadian society and concludes that its socially structured isolation is associated with significant levels of stress and depression. Although her comments appear to be directed mainly toward full-time mothers, readers are invited to speculate on how or whether the context of parenting has significantly changed in recent times.

Many pathways to motherhood exist and several articles are devoted to examining various dimensions of them. Katherine Arnup (Article 24) examines the arguments in support of the claim of lesbian mothers as equally deserving of the label "family." This is obviously more than a definitional exercise, for it has major political and economic implications that are certain to provoke discussion for decades to come in Canada. Another social issue certain to have far-reaching significance in our country is addressed by Rona Achilles (Article 25) in her examination of the new assisted reproductive technologies currently or potentially available to Canadians. As is often the case when technology outpaces the growth of our beliefs about it and the norms regarding its use, Canadians are now just beginning to contemplate what these technologies can or will mean for families, parenting, and some of our most basic understandings and expectations of gender.

Ralph LaRossa (Article 26) explores social changes pertaining to the "culture" of fatherhood as opposed to the actual behavior of fathers. He argues that while the culture of fatherhood promoted within the media and by various special interest groups has changed, behavioral reality has failed to keep pace. This argument has particular relevance when applied to the issue of who is awarded custody of a child or children upon the formal dissolution of a marriage. Divorce dissolves the legal relationship between husband and wife but not necessarily the relationship between parents and their children. Janice Drakich (Article 27) examines changes over the past hundred years in the guiding principles used to formulate decisions over who should retain custody of the children of divorce. She then evaluates recent demands for "joint custody" decisions within the Canadian courts in light of what is known about fathering behaviour.

Just as there are many pathways to parenthood in general, there are also many paths leading to lone parenthood in particular. Jillian Oderkirk and Clarence Lochhead (Article 28) present recent data on gender differences in the nature and distribution of lone parenthood in Canada. Fuelled largely by the combined effects of rising numbers of divorces and births unaccompanied by marriage, increasingly large numbers of women find themselves being the lone parent to one or more children. Lesley Harman (Article 29) focuses on the attendant economic problems women face, problems related to what has come to be known as the "feminization of poverty." While many treatments of the phenomenon suggest that this is a new problem on the Canadian scene, Harman argues that such is not the case. Her basic point is that women in Canada, both today and in the past, are and have been just one man away from poverty. She further notes that some categories of women have been and still are more vulnerable to the poverty experience.

23

Motherwork, Stress, and Depression: The Costs of Privatized Social Reproduction

Harriet Rosenberg

INTRODUCTION: THE POLITICAL ECONOMY OF PAIN[1]

"Mother who killed two sons says she's paid price," announced a front-page headline. In 1970 a woman smothered her six-week-old; two years later she smothered a second infant. Both deaths were recorded at the time as crib death. In 1984, "frayed by more than a decade of struggling for her sanity," she said that she wanted to warn other women about the postpartum depression that led to the killing. "At the first signs of that, don't hesitate to…For God's sake, ask for help," she said. "I just wouldn't want any women to go through what I went through." (*Toronto Star*, March 3, 1984).

Why did this happen? Such violence is usually explained in individual psychological terms: people go crazy and do violent things. yet other violent crimes such as rape, murder, and suicide have been linked to underlying social causes. The correlation between increases in suicide rates, for example, and rising levels of unemployment (Brenner 1973, 1977, 1979) establishes a link between crisis in individual lives and crisis in an economic system. But, because childbirth and childbearing are widely considered to be a "natural" female condition, the possibility of social structural origins of "postpartum depression" have rarely been investigated (Friedan 196[3]; Oakley 1972). Rather, the dominant contemporary explanatory model, constructed and maintained by a powerful medical establishment, is explicitly asocial. It defines the emotional distress of mothers as an exclusively individual problem called "postpartum depression" and has developed a variety of individual therapies including psychoanalysis, drugs, and vitamins to deal with it. To combat the tendencies which constantly push analysis of motherhood and depression in a personalistic direction we must start with a fresh perspective—one that has both feminist and political economy underpinnings.

From Harriet Rosenberg "Motherwork, Stress, and Depression: The Cost of Privatized Social Reproduction," in Heather J. Maroney and Meg Luxton (eds.), *Feminism and Political Economy*. Toronto: Methuen, 1987, pp. 181–196. Reprinted by permission.

Producing or not producing human beings is part of the political discourse of most societies. Historically, as nation-states developed, debates about population grew with them. From the mercantilists to Malthus, demography, taxation, and militarization all became intertwined problematics (Seccombe, 1983; Davin, 1978). Furthermore, the institutions which turned children into soldiers, taxpayers, and workers have always been part of the public debate on how societies organize to reproduce themselves. Public funds are now being legitimately allocated to these tasks, through school systems and the armed forces, for example. It is the proportions which are debated, not the appropriateness of the undertaking.

And yet the daily work of childbearing within the household/family is almost entirely eclipsed from political discussion and considered to be a private matter. The fact that motherwork is integral to social reproduction and not a personal pastime is obscured. In the public domain debates rage about sexuality, abortion, and birth control, but not about the social condition of motherwork.

This radical separation of motherwork from social reproduction has a variety of consequences, including depression, anxiety, and violence. But if we start with the premise that the personal is political and that political economy is a significant component of even the most seemingly personal experience, we can analyze motherhood as an integral part of social reproduction.

Such an approach enables us to view postpartum depression not just as an issue of private medicine but as one of public health, and to explore the consequences of the denial of parenting as a form of social labour under capitalism. Ultimately, a central aim of the socialist feminist project is to stimulate inquiry into the deep structural links between so-called private and public spheres and to locate apparently private pain in its socio-political context.

EMOTIONAL PAIN AFTER BIRTH OR ADOPTION

When they say to me, "Oh, what a wonderful baby. How lucky you are," I look around in a daze to see who they're talking to. I'm in a fog all the time. I'm so tired I can't think straight. I hate it. I want my life back.

In Western societies, between 60 percent and 80 percent of mothers have emotional problems after childbirth (Davidson 1972; Dalton 1971; Yalom 1968; Hamilton 1962; Balchin 1975; Kruckman 1980). Depression and anxiety are also experienced by women who adopt[2] and by men (Bucove 1964). About 20 percent of women continue to experience depression for many months after birth or adoption, or even occasionally throughout life (Kruckman 1980; Welburn 1980; Rosenberg 1980).

In the medical and popular literature the terms "postpartum depression," "baby blues," and "postpartum psychosis" are often used interchangeably. "Baby blues" is frequently applied to all forms of postnatal psychological problems. Ideologically dismissive, it is akin to the blame-the-victim connotation of "blue-collar blues." However, more precise medical usage distinguishes different forms of the depressed experience. More carefully defined, the term "blues" is restricted to a depressed mood and transitory tearfulness that is experienced by about 80 percent of mothers on the third or fourth day after birth. This mild postpartum depression lasts for a few hours only. Although some explanations have associated it with hormonal changes on the onset of lactation (Dalton 1971), others have pointed out that there is little cross-cultural evidence for such a claim and have argued that there is a historical link in North America between the medicalization of birth and the appearance of mild postpartum depression (Catano and Catano 1981).

At the other extreme, "postpartum psychosis" is also frequently conflated with postpartum depression, especially in medical literature. This confusion results from the fact that medical studies are frequently based on hospitalized populations. Actual psychosis is relatively rare, occurring in one in a thousand cases. It is treated by psychiatric intervention, hospitalization, and electroconvulsive therapy (ECT).

There is also a "mid-range" depression which may be expressed as slow, tired, hopeless, eyes filled with unshed tears or constant crying, or by intense anxiety and frantic behaviour. In this form, feelings of anger and conflict with children or mates is common. About 65 percent of the 1,000 women who sought the services of the Post-Partum Counseling Service (see note 1) expressed fears of harming their children, although very few actually did so. Physiological symptoms like constant colds, and rashes, as well as frequent accidents and alcohol and drug abuse, are all associated with this form of postpartum depression (PPCS files). It is a terrifying and debilitating experience, made all the more frightening by the fact that it is rarely mentioned. "You never hear about this," said one woman. "No one ever talks about it. Are they all lying?"

It is this mid-range form of postpartum depression which will be discussed in this paper. It is this type of depression which can be clearly seen to have social structural causes amenable to a socialist feminist political economy analysis.

TREATMENT: MEDICAL MODELS, FEMINIST MODELS

My doctor is very squelching. He says, "It's just cabin fever, dearie. Don't worry."

Sometimes I think my volunteer [at Post-Partum Counselling Service] is the only person in the world who puts the mother first.

There are two competing general models for the treatment of postpartum depression. The medical model stems from an analysis of depression as an individual problem; the feminist model identifies it as a problem related to the oppressed social position of women.

Although there have been different explanations of the etiology of postpartum depression and consequently different fashions in its treatment, the medical model has consistently tried to "cure" the individual. Treatment has included the use of drugs, sleep cures, and prolonged hospitalization in the nineteenth century and electroconvulsive, insulin shock, and psychoanalytic therapies in the twentieth century (Kruckman 1980). One practitioner in the 1940s was so fond of shock therapy that he claimed a 75 percent recovery rate and was not at all alarmed by the 5 percent death rate resulting from it (Kruckman 1980). By the mid-1950s, a new psycho-pharmacological approach had come to dominate in research and treatment. Psychoactive drugs, also coupled with hormonal injections, were widely used by doctors claiming phenomenal success rates.

The psychoanalytic theories of postpartum depression which developed in the 1930s rested upon the normative conception that biological mothering was the essential mark of femininity. A pioneer of this approach, Zilboorg, stated that depression after childbirth was related to "symbolic castration" and was common "in narcissistic, frigid, latent homosexual women" (cited in Kruckman 1980: 8). The psychiatric literature still characterizes women with postpartum depression as infantile, immature, having unresolved conflicts with their mothers, failing to adjust to the feminine role, and having penis envy. And contemporary medical analyses continue to rely heavily on theories of biological causality (Butts 1969; Karacan and Williams 1970; Seltzer 1980).

> *Therapy is usually directed at the conflictual areas—helping the patient accept the feminine role or express jealous feelings toward the child, occasioned by thwarted dependency needs...(Seltzer, 1980: 2549)*

However, the studies of hormonal and genetic causes of depression tend to be poorly designed and yield insufficient and even contradictory results (Weissman and Klerman, 1977; Parlee, 1980; Livingston, 1976). The poor quality of research on the physiological causes of postpartum depression should not cause us to discount this line of inquiry, but should alert us to the inadequacy of relying on the simplistic, unicausal models which medical research tends to favour.

A path-breaking alternative feminist model has been developed by the Vancouver Post-Partum Counselling Service (PPCS) after over a decade of experience in working with more than a thousand women (Robertson 1980; Robertson with Howard 1980). The PPCS model is explicitly woman-centred, and looks to find the causes of depression in the structure of society rather than solely in individual pathology or hormonal imbalance. This perspective has informed the PPCS definition of depression, the population at risk, and the organization of treatment.

> *Basically we redefined the term. We invented a definition separate from blues and psychosis.*

A social perspective has enabled them to identify situations likely to generate postpartum depression. Since they do not see the causes of postpartum depression to be either exclusively physiological or a manifestation of failed femininity, the counsellors and volunteers at PPCS are able to respond to symptoms of depression in all new parents, including men and adoptive parents. It has also enabled them to draw a profile of the person who is most likely to get postpartum depression. The most striking feature of the profile is that the woman who is expected to make the most trouble-free transition to motherhood is the one who is most at risk.

The average woman seen by PPCS is twenty-seven, married, middle-class (in terms of occupation and income),[3] and has had at least two years of post-secondary education. She has held responsible paying jobs (e.g., nurse, teller, social worker, hairdresser, secretary, teacher). The pregnancy was planned. Both parents attended prenatal classes. The father was present at the delivery. The woman chose to breast-feed. No significant prior incidents of depression were found among these women. PPCS also found that there was no significant correlation between Caesarean sections and depression, although many of the mothers had negative hospital experiences. [4] Nor have they found that the supposed closeness or bonding said to be inherent in non-medicated childbirth and in breastfeeding has been a mitigating factor (Arney 1980; Robertson 1976).

The societal model used by PPCS has identified loss, isolation, and lack of social support as significant factors contributing to depression. Women who have lost their connection with their paid workplace are particularly vulnerable to depression. Some women keenly feel the loss of status as a "girl" in this youth-oriented culture, an ironic situation when we consider that many societies count motherhood to be the resolution of a crisis period and the onset of social adulthood for women (Silverman 1975). Other feelings of loss stem from the very real experience of many women who report feeling deserted by their friends and family members after the first few weeks of their child's life (Saulnier, forthcoming). They have few sources of reassurance, advice, or assistance in their work as mothers. They feel their husbands do not understand the pressures of "full-time mothering." And even men who "help'" can be undermining because they define the problem solely as the woman's. They do not seem to be able to offer emotional support ("I want a hug and he vacuums the living room"). Past miscarriages, the recent or past death of a parent, or loss of emotional contact with a significant person because of illness or alcoholism can also contribute to feelings of depression.

In an overall sense, postpartum depression is an expression of social isolation accompanied by loss over personal identity, loss of confidence in one's ability to cope. To understand why this should be so, we need to look at how motherhood and motherwork are structured in our society.

MOTHERING AS SOCIAL AND PERSONAL WORK

Defining mothering as work is crucial to the PPCS strategy for postpartum depression.

> *It is very important for women to realize that what they are doing is work. When I talk to women, I consciously change the language I use. I talk about the job and the fact that the woman is the manager. That's one of the hardest parts about the job and it usually isn't even recognized as work—even by husbands who are "nice guys" and "help" [with housework and childcare]. They don't seem to realize that helping is not the same thing as carrying the weight of responsibility that mothers carry.*

This redefinition is also a prerequisite for a feminist analysis of the political economic determinants of mothering as an aspect of social reproduction under capitalism. The overlapping organization of gender relations and the division between what are called "the public" and "the private" (or the domestic household and the economy) effectively assigns the major responsibility for the social work of reproduction to women without any social recognition or social support. Geographical mobility and segmented households, combined with the ideology of family privacy, mean that women with babies get very little on-the-job training from experienced workers.

For many women, becoming a parent is often devastating and confusing because they suddenly find themselves in unfamiliar work situations. Although they have prepared for childbirth by taking classes and reading books, they suddenly find that they have not just given birth to a baby but to an endlessly demanding human being. The care of that human being is not defined as work: it is seen as a private, natural, and essentialist enterprise. When women complain or despair they are frequently told, "Well, you were the one who wanted this baby…" But raising a baby is not a personal hobby like raising begonias, it is an undertaking which reproduces society as well as expressing the individual need to love and cherish children.

Examples from kin-ordered societies demonstrate that childbearing is usually viewed as being both social and personal, and most cultures have provided very rich systems of social support to new parents (Lewis 1958; Mead

1962; Oakley 1976; Bettelheim 1954; Metraux 1963; Dawson 1929; Kupferer 1965; Newman 1966). While postpartum customs and rituals may seem obscure or unusual to Western eyes, they serve the very concrete social function of making a public statement that a new birth is significant to the community as a whole and that social attention must be focused on care for the new child. In industrial capitalist societies the spotlight tends to be on the fetus, the doctor, and the technology of hospital births (Arms 1977; Jordan 1978). After a mother leaves the hospital, the thousands and thousands of socially approved dollars and hours and hours of work energy crystallized in the hospital setting evaporate. The woman is on her own: she moves from the public realm of hospital medicine to the private world of her household.

In contrast, in kin-based communities mothers can usually command social support as their right in custom and ritual. Mothers can expect kin to cook, clean, protect, and advise. A new mother may be ritually prohibited from preparing food, thus placing the onus of meal preparation on her kin (Solway 1984). In such settings new mothers are not expected to know or do everything for themselves. They are seen to be at the centre of a social drama and are understood to be entitled to help with caregiving and household tasks. The existence of amulets, special foods, and behavioural taboos constantly reinforce the sensibility that mothering is a public concern and not a private pastime.

In part these social concerns reflect fears for the health of mother and child in societies with high rates of infant and maternal mortality. Postpartum ritual is at one level a communal attempt to deal with a time of real danger for babies and mothers. But such cultural supports can persist and have other effects even when mortality rates are not obviously an issue. By maintaining these rituals communities symbolically testify to their collective responsibility for children and mothers. In one study, Mexican-American women in Chicago who adhered to customary rituals in the postpartum period had no incidence of depression (Kruckman 1980). The confidence these mothers had in the social importance of childrearing was revealed in their attitude toward the evil eye. Mothers felt that if a stranger were to look at a baby he or she must immediately touch the child to ward off the evil eye. One woman recounted how when she spied a man looking at her baby, she crossed a crowded restaurant and insisted that he touch the infant. This belief, which defines uninvolved onlookers as dangerous, presses encorporating claims which prohibit looking without touching. What may look like "superstition" to those outside the culture is actually a cultural safety-net which asserts community responsibility for infant and maternal well-being. The women in this study, unlike those that PPCS found to be vulnerable in their isolation, did not find that they had to solve all problems by themselves.

For most women in North America and western Europe, however, the capacity to override claims of social non-involvement in childcare is quite limited. Unwaged caregiving in the household is rarely recognized as either a contribution to social reproduction or as real work; rather, it is seen in essentialist biological terms for women and as a private and personal reward for waged work for men. Mothers are not supposed to need, nor have the right to need, social services or social funds. Public funding for social services to alleviate the work done by mothers in households is identified as a "frill"—an unnecessary expenditure which is unwarranted, especially in times of economic decline...

Furthermore, for women who do the work of caregiving there are contradictions between the low status of the work they do and the seemingly high status of the role.[5] "Mother," "motherhood," and "mothering" are words that bring forth flamboyant, extravagant, romantic images. In contrast, the work itself includes many tasks which are not socially respected. Motherwork involves dealing with infant bodily functions: people who clean up human wastes have low status (Luxton, 1983). Few jobs have this contradiction so deeply ingrained.

Equally significant to the stress of mothering tasks is the fact that many women do not really know what motherwork involves until they are faced with doing it. They have only a series of platitudes to go on, about it being "the most important job in the world." It is as if one were hired for a new job with the understanding that the job description would be so vast and so vague as to be undoable, that little assistance would be provided, and that any errors would be the employee's sole responsibility. Motherwork, like any other job, must be learned. Books and courses have become the major means of learning: for most it is an inadequate method, because it is not based on experience. There is no apprenticeship period in our society as there is in small-scale kin-ordered societies where young girls learn the ropes as caregivers to younger children. In industrialized societies, a falling birthrate has resulted in small families in which girls (and boys) grow up playing in peer-oriented, age-segregated groups. Many leave home having experienced little or no contact with newborns and infants. Said one North American mother, "When the baby is born, I knew I wasn't ready. I hadn't gone through the reading list."

One should add that the experts, the writers of childrearing guides, are often men who in fact rarely do the daily work of caregiving themselves.[6] ("Provide a stimulating environment for the infant but don't overstimulate him," says one TV advice-giver.) Advice-givers define the job goals, and they judge the outcome. They garner wealth, prestige, and status by explaining the day-to-day working conditions of mothers. This separation between expert and worker can lead to condescending attitudes on the part of the expert. For example, Dr. Frederick W. Rutherford, in *You and Your Baby*, has some inkling that all may not go well for mothers. He had no index entry under depression but does mention "baby blues." His advice:

If you are feeling blue, pour out your troubles to someone who will make no moral judgments, someone who will understand that no matter how little real basis there is for your depression you nevertheless feel it

*strongly, but who also knows that with a little help you will manage
nicely before very long. Try not to wallow in the blues, but don't be
ashamed to express your feelings. You don't have to act like a cheerful
cherub when you feel like a Pitiful Pearl. (Rutherford 1971: 167;
emphasis added)*

To the non-worker, the pain of the worker is not quite real.

Contradictory, guilt-inducing "how-to" books, magazines, and TV talk
shows cater to the isolated model of caregiving and miss the social context—
people with whom to talk, ask questions, share experiences. Some doctors
fill the role, but the medicalization of parenting has been a risky business for
mothers. Visits to the doctor can further reinforce the isolated and individ-
uated nature of childrearing. Medical consultations are usually brief and
centre on the health of the child, not the work of childrearing or the mental
health of the mother. Simple-minded measures like weight gain can become
an index for whether the mother is doing a good job. The fact that the child
may be gaining and the mother falling apart may not be perceived by the
doctor. Furthermore, family doctors may be reluctant to raise the issue of
postpartum depression because they feel that women are suggestible and
will get the symptoms if the issue is discussed.

Yet women are very dependent on advice from the medical establishment. Mothers may be labelled overinvolved or hysterical, but since they so
rarely have alternative methods of assessing health and nutrition matters,
they must rely on their doctors. If they go outside the doctor-patient dyad,
women risk criticism for listening to "old wives' tales" (i.e., other women) or
for negligence (e.g., attacks on home birth). Thus the privatized, asocial
model of childrearing is constantly reinforced.

STRESS, DEPRESSION, BURNOUT

*This is a very scattered job. I can't think any thoughts more than half-
way. At least when my husband goes to work he gets silences.*

*I work 24 hours a day. He [her husband] doesn't. At night when
the baby cries, he never wakes up first. I have to wake him and he goes
to the baby. Then he's so proud because he let me sleep!*

*I wish I could remember what it felt like not to have a knot in my
stomach.*

If we step back from the issue of mothers learning a new job, to the
larger context of workplace stress, we gain some useful insights into the pre-
dicament in which many women find themselves.

The effects of stress (Selye 1980, 1975, 1956; Holmes and Rahe 1967;
Lumsden 1981) on mental health are now being widely studied. Unions representing police, firefighters, public employees, and teachers in Canada and
the U.S.A. have become very concerned with psychosocial stress in the work-

place. Unions, employers, and courts are increasingly reading symptoms like chronic anxiety, depression, fatigue, and substance abuse (alcohol, drugs, overeating) as signals of strain produced on the job (Ellison and Genz 1978).

Some extreme forms of mental strain and emotional exhaustion have been called "burnout" (Freudenberger and Richelson 1980). It has been argued that "...any kind of frontline person—teacher, social worker, therapist, nurse—who is at the beck and call of needy individuals is prone to burnout" (Murdoch 1981:6). The literature on burnout among professionals offers some important insights into what unwaged mothers experience in the home. Burned-out front-line workers complain of unrelenting demands, little time away from intense personal interaction with clients or patients, shift work, and constant responsibility for two or more things at once (Maslach and Pines 1977). Burned-out professional childcare workers are reported to experience feelings of "inarticulated personal distress" and fatigue as do lawyers, psychiatrists, nurses, and clinical psychologists when faced with the tense conditions of their jobs (Mattingly 1977; Maslach and Pines 1977; Maslach 197[9]; Pines and Kafry 1978).

If they are not alerted to burnout as a potential response to these stressors, professionals may respond by blaming themselves and seeking psychiatric help for what they perceive to be personal deficiencies. Those who have studied the process among daycare workers, for example, argue that it is the structure and intensity of the job, and not personal idiosyncrasies, that cause some workers to develop feelings of worthlessness. Psychiatric intervention, according to this research, rarely succeeds unless the work situation is taken into account (Maslach and Pines 1977).

These stressful job conditions are also true of motherwork. Most of the psychological and physical symptoms associated with burnout are the same as those reported by mothers diagnosed as having postpartum depression. Thus I would argue that postpartum depression, like burnout, is actually a syndrome in response to the organization of work.

Not all professionals have emotional problems; nor do all mothers. But there are times in any worker's life when job demands deplete, exhaust, and undermine. Motherwork, especially in relation to an infant, is a job of high demands. For many women it is a job of perpetual shift work—of always being on call (see Stellman and Daum 1973 on health and shift work). In that respect it is like policing or nursing, with the exception that in motherwork there are rarely shifts off. Furthermore, unlike other workers, mothers are not encouraged to separate home and work life. Since mothering is seen as a role, and not as work, mothers are supposed to always remain in character. They rarely get restorative "time outs," let alone extended vacations or sick leave. The disorientation caused by lack of sleep and the disappearance of predictable routines of eating, sleeping, and waking contribute to a "twilight zone" atmosphere. In addition, women who do motherwork also do housework and frequently must combine both jobs in a space like the kitchen that can be unsafe for infants and young children (Rosenberg 1984). Time-budget studies (Meissner et al. 1975; Proulx 1978) and case studies (Luxton 1980, 1983) tell us just how unrelenting these jobs are.

LOW CONTROL AND HIGH DEMANDS

Those who study industrial workers argue that the most stressful job situations are not caused by high demand levels alone. Multiple demands, under the right circumstances, can create positive work experiences. It is situations of high demand combined with low levels of control in decision making that cause the highest levels of worker stress, measured in terms of exhaustion and depression (Karasek 197[9]). Daycare workers who feel that they have high levels of participation in their centres, or social workers who feel they participate in agency decision making, express high levels of job satisfaction (Maslach and Pines 1977; Pines and Kafry 1978).

Mental strain from high demands and low control occurs more commonly among assembly-line workers, whose movements are often rigidly contained, than it does among executives, who can set hours and control working conditions (Karasek 1970). Mothering is usually thought to be more similar to an executive job than to assembly-line work. But for many women

> *It's a myth that we are our bosses or that we can have a cigarette and a coffee when we want. You can't plan a thing, especially when they are young. You are lucky if you can find time to go to the bathroom. And even then, you don't go alone.*

Women as mothers are like women in many other work situations: they have the appearance of wide "decision-making latitude" or control,[7] but in reality they have little power to define their work situations. Typically, women's waged work (nursing, teaching, social work, working as bank tellers, as well as pink-collar jobs) is structured by institutionalized gender hierarchies. Female teachers have responsibilities within classrooms, but major decisions are usually made by predominantly male administrators. Men supervise women in social service agencies, banks, department stores, and beauty shops (Armstrong and Armstrong 1984; Howe 1975; Bank Book Collective 1979; Tepperman 1976). Women who quit underpaid, undervalued jobs for the "freedom" of domestic work and childrearing may find themselves escaping into more of the same. They may make trivial consumer choices between brands of detergent, but ultimately they can be very dependent. Women who give up waged work become financially dependent on mates; they become dependent on "expert" advice-givers; and they are tied to infant-defined schedules, the schedules of other children, and the schedule of the wage-earner.

In motherwork, one of the most devastating aspects of lack of control is the absence of feedback. The isolation of the job severely limits the feedback which is so essential to decision making. Daycare workers who work with under-two-year-olds argued that isolation from adult company is what they felt most distinguished motherwork from daycare work. As one teacher said,

> *Even though the job description is sometimes vague, I know I will get support and feedback from other [teachers] on how I am doing and how a child is doing. That's the big difference between us and mothers.*

Some mothers have compared their isolation to being a prisoner of war. Said the nursing mother of a two-month-old whose mate was frequently absent because of job commitments,

> *It's pure torture. Your street clothes are taken away and you wear a bathrobe, since all you do all day is [breast-] feed the baby. Just as you fall asleep, you are woken again. You're afraid to fall asleep anyway. What's the point? But God, the worst is that there is no one to talk to.*

STRATEGIES FOR JOB REDESIGN

Occupational health and safety research on stress and social science studies of burnout situate the problems of exhaustion and depression in the workplace. They argue that solutions are social and structural, and lie in redesigning the job to lessen demands and increase control.[8] This is also true for motherwork stress and burnout, and is a solution that was first suggested by nineteenth-century feminists.

Over ninety years ago, feminist economist Charlotte Perkins Gilman wrote a short story called "The Yellow Wallpaper" ([1899] 1973). It is a nightmarish account of postpartum depression based on Gilman's own experience. Gilman's pioneering economic and architectural writings go further. They outline plans for job redesign which take up the whole question of how housework and motherwork should be socially structured, albeit from a somewhat elitist perspective (Hayden 1979). Other thinkers and activists struggled to bring housework and motherwork overtly into the public sphere through daycares and producers' and consumers' cooperatives (Hayden 1981). But by the 1930s these movements were defeated. Housework and motherwork became thoroughly identified as women's individual, private projects, and as "natural" expressions of femininity.

The reawakened women's movement of the 1960s once again introduced housework and mothering as social issues. Such a task is not easy and has led to reassessments of stereotyped patterns of the division of labour. With the exception of breastfeeding, motherwork is not sex-typed labour.

Caregiving may be performed by other adults, including men, or by older children, within and outside the nuclear family unit. This work is not "help," which still pins organizational responsibility on a supposedly all-knowing mother, but rather inclines toward the development of strategies for sharing responsibility, which may require women to relinquish some of the pleasures of feeling indispensable. Said one woman,

> *When it was his shift with the baby, I had to leave the house. Otherwise, I just hovered over him the whole time. He got anxious and insecure and then I'd take over. It took me a long time to let go and let him be really in charge.*

Such a restructuring of jobs and responsibilities forces women and men to face very deep currents of internalized socialization about what mothers and fathers should do and how they should act. It may require constant struggle with previously unacknowledged feelings and fears. At times it may seem that the struggle to assign tasks fairly is just too difficult. But discussions within the household and actions which aim to deliberately involve community members (e.g., drop-in centres, paid maternity/paternity leave or paid leave for a designated caregiver, flexible work hours, choice of workplace or community daycare, babysitting exchanges, co-operative non-profit daycare and political pressure groups that lobby for the maintenance and enhancement of locally controlled social services for parents) all ultimately serve to create dense networks of involvement which can lessen the ambivalences, stresses, and burnout of motherwork.

At the level of political practice, the women's movement has provided the context for this kind of debate. Local self-help groups, such as the Vancouver Post-Partum Counselling Service, have provided immediate crisis support and have helped to reduce women's dependency on experts, enhanced self-perceptions of competence, and enabled women to break down the tendency to personalize domestic problems. Since the 1960s, the lesson of conscious-raising groups has always been that groups of women who have shared experiences begin to see that their private pain has social roots. This type of collective experience has often served as a prelude to the formation of a variety of helping organizations, from rape crisis centres to shelters for battered wives to groups like PPCS.

However, attempts to socialize childcare outside the household—a project crucial to the redesign of motherwork and parenting—continues to meet with enormous resistance. In North America there is still much popular and official hostility to "institutionalized" daycare. While it may be tolerated for "working mothers," the ideas that women who do not work for wages should have access to publicly funded childcare arrangements raises even stronger negative reactions.[9] The intensity of the "fight for good daycare," defined as top quality, universally accessible, twenty-four-hour-a-day and community controlled (Ross 1979), illustrates that redesigning the job of parenting is deeply ideological, because it challenges the essentialist ideologies of "the nuclear family" and "motherhood," and the allocation of resources and funds.[10] But such struggles—economic, ideological, and political—are necessary to dismantle the crazy-making structures of privatized mother work and in its place to create the social job of caregiving.

NOTES

1   Data for this paper were collected during visits to the Post-Partum Counselling Service (PPCS), Ministry of Human Resources, Vancouver, British Columbia, in 1980, 1981, 1982. PPCS was founded in 1971 and has served over 1,000 women. Despite the efforts of hundreds of people, PPCS was closed by the Social Credit government of British Columbia in 1983. This paper is dedicated to Joann, Jim, Penny, Allison, and Fran, former counsellors who truly fought the good fight.

I would also like to thank the men, women, and children whom I interviewed in New York, Toronto, and Vancouver for their time and the effort they made to share their understanding of parenting with me.

Thanks, too, to Gloria Gordon, Jeanne Stellman, Lawrence Kruckman, Jan Schneider, Rayna Rapp, Joan Jacobson, Don Hale, Meg Luxton, and Richard Lee for their encouragement and suggestions.

2   Based on interviews with Post-Partum Counselling counsellors and interviews with adoptive parents in Toronto.

3   Most of the women who went to PPCS are middle class in terms of income level, lifestyle, and education. The counsellors have assumed that this self-selection was an artifact of a class-based society in which middle-class people have better access to services. However, some poor women do come to PPCS. They tend to be young (late teens or early twenties) single parents on welfare. PPCS counsellors concluded that their depressions were so concretely rooted in economic and social deprivation ("Dealing with the welfare system is automatically depressing") that their situation was not technically postpartum depression.

Over the years PPCS has received letters from women across Canada in response to various radio and television broadcasts they have done. This admittedly informal and unscientific survey seems to indicate that postnatal depression does cut across geographical, occupational, and ethnic lines.

Since so little research has been done on the question of postpartum depression and class, we cannot make any assumptions about differential rates between working-class, upper-class, and middle-class women. One community study in London on depression and marriage (i.e., not specifically the postnatal period) found that, subject to equivalent levels of stress, working-class women were five times more likely to become depressed than middle-class women. Working-class married women with young children living at home had the highest rate of depression (Brown, Bhrolchain, and Harris 1975; Rice 1937).

This data should caution one against assuming that working-class women are automatically plugged into networks of support that mitigate the effects of stress and depression.

4   J. Croke, *Postpartum Depression* (Master's thesis, School of Social Work, Carleton University, Ottawa, 1982) shows that women who have had home births are less

likely to experience depression after birth. However, her sample is small and further research is needed to obtain more significant data.

5   There exists a body of literature (reviewed by Parlee 1980) which links postpartum depression to a women's difficulty in her *role* as a mother. With the exception of Luxton (1980), however, there has been little discussion of the actual work that women do as mothers on a day-to-day basis.

Since mothering is constantly defined as a role, women who don't like to do some parts of the job may be considered crazy. See Boszormenyi-Nagy and Spark (1973) for family therapists who criticize women who do not fulfill the female domestic role, and Ehrenreich and English (1979) for criticism of the experts.

6   See L. Bloom (1976) for a short summary of the vagaries of childcare advice from the mid-nineteenth century to the late 1960s, as well as Ehrenreich and English (1979).

7   The terms "control," "decision-making latitude," and "discretion" as used in Karasek's study deserve a closer look. Karasek based his data on male labour force statistics in the USA and Sweden. "Control" was defined through the questions in the questionnaire that received a yes answer to whether the job was at a high skill level; one learned new things; the job was non-repetitious; creative; allowed freedom; permitted one to make decisions; and to have a say on the job. These were collapsed into the definition of "control" over tasks and conduct during the day. Two measures—"decision authority" and "intellectual discretion" are highly correlated. He argued that highly skilled work rarely combined with low decision-making authority.

This combination may be rare in male jobs, but it is more common in female jobs, where the contradiction of high skill but low authority is built into a sex-segregated labour force. Thus female nurses, teachers, tellers, and social workers are usually in the position of knowing that male authority can override their decisions. This sexist structure, coupled with the fact that women are more vulnerable to layoffs than men, argues for more sensitive measures in aggregate data studies to pick up the special stressors to which women are subject. Furthermore, in relation to (unwaged) domestic labour like motherwork, we find the contradiction between high skill levels and low authority levels to be important. The popular myth that housewives/mothers are autonomous and have high degrees of decision-making power in their jobs is belied by their economic dependence on a male breadwinner (Smith 1973; Zaretsky 1976; Luxton 1980).

8   Karasek (1979) argues for work teams rather than single-task assembly lines. Maslach and Pines (1977), Pines and Kafry (1978), Freudenberger and Richelson (1980), and Mattingly (1977) all include mention of techniques which can give professionals more control in their workplace, including rotations and times off from the constant face-to-face patient or client contact. Collegial support, awareness sessions, and variations in tasks are considered useful ways of restructuring work situations.

Other stress-reducing techniques operate on an individual level. They include strenuous exercise (Freudenberger 1977) and biofeedback (Greenspan 1978). These individual solutions are frequently difficult for mothers of new infants, who may be overwhelmed by lack of energy, time and money, and by the difficulty of finding babysitters to take over while they go out.

The mother of an infant said in this regard, "I know exactly why I didn't get postpartum depression. I bought my way out. We hired a housekeeper to come in five days a week, make meals, clean, and babysit. I went out and just sat in the library. Eventually, I got a job and felt less guilty about the housekeeper."

9   When I proposed this solution to a group of previously quite sympathetic upper-middle-class women, they balked. Said one woman, "Sure, it sounds like a good idea, but our husbands would never give us the money. It'll never work."

10   In Toronto, it now seems that over $225 million of public funds will be allocated for a domed sports stadium. This money could provide more than 10,000 new daycare spots for five years. A group of anti-dome pro-day-care fathers demonstrated in opposition to the project but met with little success.

REFERENCES

Arms, Suzanne. 1977. *Immaculate Deception*. New York: Bantam.

Armstrong, Pat and Hugh Armstrong. 1984. *The Double Ghetto: Canadian Women and their Segregated Work.* rev. ed. Toronto: McClelland and Stewart.

Armstrong, Pat and Hugh Armstrong. 1987. "Looking Ahead: the Future of Women's Work in Australia and Canada." In *Feminism and Political Economy: Women's Work, Women's Struggles.* Toronto: Methuen.

Arney, W. R. 1980. "Maternal Infant Bonding: the Politics of Falling in Love with Your Child." *Feminist Studies* 6, no. 3.

Balchin, P. 1975. "The Midwife and Puerperal Psychosis." *Midwife Health Visitor* 11, no. 2.

Bank Book Collective. 1979. *An Account to Settle: The Story of the United Bank Workers (SORWUC).* Vancouver: Press Gang.

Bettleheim, Bruno. 1954. *Symbolic Wounds: Puberty Rites and the Envious Male.* New York: Free Press.

Brenner, M. H. 1973. *Mental Illness and the Economy.* Cambridge MA: Harvard University Press.

Brenner, M. H. 1977. "Health Costs and the Benefits of Economic Policy." *International Journal of Health Services* 7, no. 4.

Brenner, M. H. 1979. "Unemployment and Economic Growth and Mortality." *Lancet,* March 24.

Catano J., and V. Catano. 1981. "Mild Post-partum Depression: Learned Helplessness and the Medicalization of Obstetrics." Unpublished ms., St. Mary's University, Halifax.

Dalton, Katharina. 1971. Puerperal and Premenstrual Depression." *Proceedings of the Royal Society of Medicine* 64, no. 12: 1249–52.

Davidson, J. R. 1972. "Postpartum Mood Change in Jamaican Women: A Description and Discussion of its Significance." *British Journal of Psychiatry* 121: 659–63.

Davin, A. 1978. "Imperialism and Motherhood." *History Workshop* 5 (Spring): 9–65.

Dawson, W. R. 1929. *The Custom of Couvade*. Manchester: Manchester University Press.

Ellison, K., and J. L. Genz. 1978. "The Police Officer as a Burned Out Samaritan." *FBI Law Enforcement Bulletin* 47, no. 3 (March).

Freudenberger, H. J., and G. Richelson. 1980. *Burn-Out*. New York: Doubleday.

Friedan, Betty. 1968. *The Feminine Mystique*. New York: Dell.

Gilman, Charlotte Perkins. [1899] 1973. *Women and Economics*. Edited by Carl Degler. New York: Harper Torchbooks.

Hamilton, J. A. 1962. *Postpartum Psychiatric Problems*. St. Louis MO: C. V. Mosby.

Hayden, D. 1979. "Charlotte Perkins Gilman and the Kitchenless House." *Radical History Review* 21: 225–47.

Hayden, D. 1981. *The Grand Domestic Revolution: A History of Feminist Designs for American Homes, Neighbourhoods and Cities*. Cambridge: MIT Press.

Holmes, T., and R. Rahe. 1967. "The Social Adjustment Rating Scale." *Journal of Psychosomatic Research* 1, no. 2.

Howe, Louise Kapp. 1975. *Pink Collar Workers*. New York: Avon Books.

Jordan, Brigitte. 1978. *Birth in Four Cultures: A Cross-cultural Investigation of Childbirth in Holland, Sweden and the United States*. Montreal: Eden Press.

Karacan, I., and R. L. Williams. 1970. *Current Advances in Theory and Practice Relating to Postpartum Syndromes*. Psychiatry in Medicine: 1: 307–208.

Karasek, R. A. 1979. "Job Demands Job Decision Latitude, and Mental Strain: Implication for Job Redesign." *Administrative Science Quarterly* 24: 285–308.

Kruckman, L. 1980. "From Institutionalization to Self-Help: a Review of Postpartum Depression Treatment." Chicago: School of Public Health, University of Illinois Medical Center. Photocopy.

Kupferer, H. J. K. 1965. "Couvade: Ritual or Illness?" *American Anthropologist* 67: 99–102.

Lewis, O. 1958. *Village Life in North India*. Urbana: University of Illinois Press.

Livingston, J. E. 1976. *An Assessment of Vitamin B_6 Status in Women with Postpartum Depression*. M.Sc. Thesis, Department of Medical Genetics, University of British Columbia.

Lumsden, D. P. 1981. "Is the Concept of 'Stress' of Any Use, Anymore?" In *Contributions to Primary Prevention in Mental Health*, ed. D. Randall. Toronto: Canadian Mental Health Association.

Luxton, Meg. 1980. *More Than a Labour of Love: Three Generations of Women's Work in the Home*. Toronto: Women's Press.

—————. 1983. "Two Hands for the Clock: Changing Patterns in the Domestic Division of Labour." *Studies in Political Economy* 12.

Maslach C. and A. Pines. 1977. "The Burn-out Syndrome in the Day Care Setting." *Child Care Quarterly* 6, no. 2 (Summer): 100–113.

Mead, Margaret. 1962. "A Cultural Anthropological Approach to Maternal Deprivation." In *Deprivation of Maternal Health Care: A Re-assessment of its Effects*, ed. World Health Organization. Geneva: WHO.

Meissner, M. et al. 1975. "No Exit for Wives: Sexual Division of Labour and the Cumulation of Household Demands." University of British Columbia. Photocopy. *Canadian Review of Sociology and Anthropology* 125, no. 4, part I (November).

Metraux, A. 1963. "The Couvade." In *Handbook of South American Indians,* Vol. 5, ed. J. H. Stewart. New York: Cooper Square.

Newman, Lucille. 1966. "The Couvade: A Replay to Kupferer." *American Anthropologist* 68.

Oakley, Ann. 1972. *Sex, Gender and Society.* London: Temple-Smith.

Oakley, Ann. 1976. *Housewife.* Harmondsworth: Penguin.

Parlce, M. B. 1980. "Psychological Aspects of Menstruation, Childbirth and Menopause." In *Psychology of Women: Future Directions Research,* eds. J. A. Sherman and F. L. Denmark. New York: Psychological Dimensions.

Pines, A. and B. and Kafry. 1978. "Occupational Tedium in the Social Services," *Social Work* (November) 499–508.

Proulx, M. 1978. *Five Million Women: A Study of the Canadian Housewife.* Ottawa: Advisory Council on the Status of Women.

Robertson, J. 1976. "The Abusive Parent: A Different Perspective." *Canada's Mental Health 24,* no. 4 (December): 18–19.

Robertson, J. 1980. "A Treatment Model for Post-Partum Depression." *Canada's Mental Health* (Summer).

Robertson, J. with A. Howard. 1980. *The Post-Partum Counselling Service Manual.* British Columbia: Ministry of Human Resources.

Rosenberg, Harriet. 1980. "After Birth Blues." *Healthsharing* (Winter): 18–20.

Rosenberg, Harriet. 1984. "The Home is the Workplace." In *Double Exposure: Women's Health Hazards on the Job and at Home,* ed. Wendy Chavkin. New York: Monthly Review Press.

Ross, Kathleen Gallagher. 1979. *Good Day Care: Fighting for It, Getting It, Keeping It.* Toronto: Women's Press.

Rutherford, F. W. 1971. *You and Your Baby: From Conception Through to the First Year.* New York: Signet.

Seccombe, Wally. 1983. "Marxism and Demography." *New Left Review* no. 137.

Seltzer, A. 1980. "Postpartum Mental Syndrome." Canadian Family Physician 26 (November): 1546–50.

Selye, Hans. 1956. *The Stress of Life.* New York: McGraw-Hill.

Selye, Hans. 1975. "Confusion and Controversy in the Stress Field." *Journal of Human Stress* I, no. 2.

Sely, Hans. 1980. Preface to *Selye's Guide to Stress Research,* Vol. 1. New York: Van Nostrand Reinhold.

Silverman, S. 1975. "The Life Crisis as a Social Function." In *Toward an Anthropology of Women,* ed. Rayna Reiter. New York: Monthly Review Press.

Solway, J. 1984. "Women and Work Among the Bakgalagadi of Botswana." Paper presented at the Canadian Ethnology Society, Montreal.

Stellman, Jeanne M. and S. Daum. 1973. *Work is Dangerous to Your Health*. New York: Vintage.

Tepperman, J. 1976. *Not Servants, Not Machines*. Boston: Beacon Press.

Weissman, M. M. and G. Klerman. 1977. "Sex Differences and the Epidemiology of Depression." *Archives of General Psychiatry* 34 (January): 98–111.

Welburn, V. 1980. *Postnatal Depression*. Glasgow: Fontana.

Yalom, D. I. 1968. "'Postpartum Blues' Syndrome." *Archives of General Psychiatry* 18: 16–27.

24

"We Are Family": Lesbian Mothers in Canada[1]

Katherine Arnup

When you see a woman pushing a stroller down the street, it probably never crosses your mind that this woman might be a lesbian mother. Yet, it has been estimated that 10 percent of women are lesbians and that between 20 and 30 percent of lesbians are mothers. In the United States alone, this represents some 3 to 4 million lesbian mothers.[2] Although no figures are available in Canada, we can assume that the proportion of lesbian mothers is equally high. Despite these rather staggering numbers, very little is known about lesbian motherhood. In recent years, however, lesbian mothers have moved increasingly into the public eye through child custody battles, the lesbian "baby boom," and the fight for spousal benefit coverage for same-sex partners and their children. In this article, I will discuss lesbian mothers' struggles and their implications for the women's movement and for Canadian society as a whole.

It is important to recognize that the "typical" lesbian mother exists only in the minds of judges, legislators, and social science researchers. As discussions of difference within feminist theory in recent years have revealed the multiple experiences and identities of the category of women, so we must also conclude that no unified category of lesbian mother exists. Lesbian mothers differ on many dimensions: how they became mothers (before becoming a lesbian, after coming out, by choice, by accident); how they view their lesbianism (as a private matter of sexual orientation or preference; as one facet of an entire challenge to the established social order); and how, of course, they behave as mothers. Lesbian mothers may be women of colour or white; they may be working class or middle class; they may be rich or poor. Lesbian mothers reflect all the differences among women. And finally, the world in which lesbian mothers function may range in attitude from acceptance to rejection, as ex-husbands, children, work mates, parents and siblings respond and react to the revelation of a lesbian mother's sexual orientation. Some lesbian mothers, whether through fear or a desire for privacy, choose to remain "closeted," living a life that resembles that of a het-

From Katherine Arnup, "'We Are Family': Lesbian Mothers in Canada," *Resources for Feminist Research* (RFR/DRF), vol. 20, nos. 3/4 (1991): 101–107. Reprinted by permission.

erosexual single mother. Others "come out" to family and friends, school and day care, sharing their stories and hoping for the best. Regardless of how they choose to live, however, lesbian mothers, like all women, are affected by the political and judicial climate within which they live and raise their children. In many jurisdictions, lesbianism still constitutes a "crime against nature," and a revelation of lesbianism can lead to criminal charges and imprisonment. As Minnie Bruce Pratt reminds us, "how I love is outside the law."[3] We ignore that political reality at our peril.

CHILD CUSTODY

Prior to the 1970s, few lesbian mothers contested custody in court. Fearing the implications of such a battle for their daily lives and jobs and almost assured of defeat at the hands of a decidedly homophobic legal system, they often "voluntarily" relinquished custody, in the hopes of securing liberal access rights to their children. On occasion, lesbian mothers were able to make a private arrangement with their former husbands, often lying about their sexual identity in order to retain custody of the children. During the 1970s and 80s, with the support of the gay and lesbian movements and of feminist lawyers and friends, increasing numbers of lesbians began to contest and, in a limited number of cases, win the custody of children conceived within heterosexual marriages. Only a handful of cases have appeared in Canadian law journals since the first one was reported in 1974.[4] While the outcome for the most part has been far from positive, the cases have forced judges and the public to deal with the existence of lesbian mothers.

The few reported child custody cases in Canada involving lesbian mothers have been well documented.[5] Here it is important to highlight the distinction which judges have increasingly drawn between what they determine to be "good" and "bad" lesbian mothers. Good lesbian mothers, women who live quiet, discreet lives, who promise that they will raise their children to be heterosexual, who appear to the outside world to be heterosexual single parents, have in recent years succeeded in winning custody of their children. At the other end of the spectrum, "bad" lesbian mothers, women who are politically active, who attend gay and lesbian demonstrations, and who view their lesbianism as one aspect of an entire challenge to society, are almost certain to lose custody of their children to their ex-husbands. As Mary Eaton has observed, "essentially, the bad lesbian mother is a woman who is certain that she is a lesbian, is not ashamed of being a lesbian, and who is committed to changing the social status of lesbians. A good lesbian mother will be completely and utterly secretive..."[6]

That such analysis is not merely the result of paranoia on the part of lesbian researchers is revealed by the judicial reasoning provided by judges to explain their determinations of custody. Under current family law provisions in Canada, the paramount standard applied in custody is "the best interests of the child." No precise rule or formula exists, however, for determining *which* household or family arrangement operates in the child's best interests. Under legislations in force until recently in Canada, and still in place in many jurisdictions in the United States and elsewhere, parental fitness represented a key element of the "best interests" criteria. Judges relied on a variety of factors for determining the "fitness" of each parent, including past and present sexual conduct, the grounds for the termination of the marriage, the guilt or innocence of each party, and the "quality" of the home to assist them in determining the best custody arrangements for the children. It was these tests which served to brand virtually every lesbian who attempted to contest custody as an "unfit" mother. With the passage of family law reform legislation in the early 1980s, criteria for determining custody were amended and, as a result, parental behaviour *in and of itself* could no longer be considered a bar to custody. In Ontario, for example, the Children's Law Reform Act specifies that the "best interests of the child" shall be the determining factor. The legislation directs the judge to consider "all the needs and circumstances of the child," including the relationship between the child and those persons claiming custody, the preferences of the child, the current living situation of the child, the plans put forward for the child, the "permanence and stability of the family unit with which it is proposed that the child will live," and the blood or adoptive links between the child and the applicant.[7] The section explicitly states that "the past conduct of a person is not relevant to a determination of an application...unless the conduct is relevant to the ability of the person to act as a parent of a child."[8]

While the revised legislation may appear on the surface to improve the chances for success of a custodial application by a lesbian mother, there are a number of ways in which these provisions may mitigate against her application. First, a judge may refuse to recognize a "homosexual" family as a permanent and stable family unit. Homosexuals, after all, are not permitted to marry and therefore do not meet the standard measure of "stability" in heterosexual relationships. As well, the "closeted" nature of many gay and lesbian relationships renders it virtually impossible for counsel to offer statistical evidence of the degree of the longevity of same-sex relationships. In this respect, then, a lesbian mother might find herself unable to demonstrate the "permanence and stability" of her lesbian household.

Other aspects of a "lesbian life-style" may also be deemed to render a lesbian mother unlikely to provide a suitable home for her child. Attending lesbian rallies and dances, exposing the child to other lesbian and gay people, and discussing lesbian issues openly in the home have all been deemed to be negative factors by judges considering the application of lesbian mothers for custody of their children.[9] Thus, despite the apparently fair-minded language of family law reform, lesbian mothers may still find that their "lesbian lifestyle" remains a crucial barrier to gaining custody of their children.

The continued presence of such criteria in family law provisions provides the lesbian mother seeking custody of her children with a number of difficult choices. If she presents herself in court as an "avowed lesbian," if she admits to coming out at work, at school, and so on, she stands little chance of winning custody of her children, especially in the face of a determined challenge by her ex-husband. Faced with the dilemma, most lesbians choose to act as "straight" as possible in court in order to win their custody battle. Such women have met with harsh criticism from some elements of the lesbian community, however, for sustaining an oppressive familial ideology, rather than standing up for their rights as open and proud lesbian mothers. One author writes:

> *It is wrong for society to deny lesbian mothers their children, and it is right to oppose that effect of homophobia. But when we constantly assert in the public arena that we will raise our children to be heterosexual, and that we will protect them from manifestations of our sexuality and from the larger lesbian and gay community, we lose something that affects all lesbians and gay men. We essentially concede it is preferable to be heterosexual, thereby foreclosing an assertion of pride and of the positive value in homosexuality.* [10]

Lesbian mothers who choose not to contest custody, attempting instead to secure liberal access rights to their children, may also meet with criticism from the lesbian community, as they are accused of "giving up" too easily. Minnie Bruce Pratt, a poet and a lesbian mother who lost custody of her two sons, writes of such judgments in the following excerpt from her poem, "The Child Taken from the Mother":

> *I could do nothing. Nothing. Do you*
> *understand? Women ask:* **Why didn't you...?**
> *like they do of women who've been raped.*
> *And I ask myself: Why didn't I? Why*
> *didn't I run away with them? Or face*
> *him in court?* [11]

She concludes: "I did the best I could. It was not enough. It was about terror and power. I did everything I could. Not enough." As we engage in our political theorizing, we must not forget the incredible toll of pain and grief faced by lesbian mothers who lose custody of their children. We must remember as well that contested custody cases take an enormous financial toll on women, costing as much as one hundred thousand dollars in legal fees, with no assurance of victory at the end of it all. Even if a lesbian mother wins her case, she lives with the ever-present danger of the case being reopened because of allegations of "changed circumstances."[12] Most lesbian mothers still face these battles virtually alone.[13]

"LESBIAN BABY BOOM"

Initially, most lesbian mothers who came to public attention were women who had conceived and given birth to children within heterosexual partnerships or marriages. In the past fifteen years, however, increasing numbers of lesbians have chosen to conceive and bear children, either on their own, or with a lesbian partner. Relying primarily on artificial or alternative[14] insemination as a means of conception, these women have become part of what the mainstream and lesbian media have termed the "lesbian baby boom." While lesbians have probably been practising self-insemination for many years, their activities came to public attention in the early 1980s through articles in the mainstream media, bearing sensational titles like "'Turkey-baster babies' kept secret in lesbian world."[15] Although few lesbians actually employed a turkey baster for the inseminations, finding it a crude and inefficient tool, newspaper columnists took a prurient delight in conjuring up images of lesbian insemination practices for their readers. A decidedly less sensational approach to self-insemination was taken by the lesbian media, as self-help manuals and articles in women's newspapers offered practical advice on the best methods of insemination.[16]

Beginning in the late 1970s, lesbians began to apply for artificial insemination at infertility clinics and sperm banks across North America. Many of these requests for insemination were denied once an applicant's sexual orientation was revealed. In some instances women were informed that the clinic had decided not to inseminate *any* single women, claiming that they feared single mothers would launch child support suits against the medical facility should the insemination be successful. To date, no legal challenge to infertility clinics which discriminate against single women or lesbians has reached the courts. In the only documented case, a woman launched a legal action against Wayne State University when its medical centre rejected her application for artificial insemination. Fearing the repercussions of a protracted legal battle, the clinic abandoned its restrictive policy, granting her application for insemination before the case could be heard by the courts. Thus, clinic policies which discriminate against single women and lesbians have yet to be tested in the courts in either the United States or Canada.[17]

Faced with such discriminatory practices, many lesbians have chosen private insemination arrangements. In some American jurisdictions, most notably California, and in at least one instance in Canada, groups of lesbians and heterosexual and single women established their own woman-controlled sperm banks, to insure safe and easy access to insemination services. Once again, their efforts came to the attention of the mainstream media, and were reported with an attitude that ranged from curiosity to shock. In an article on the Windsor, Ontario, insemination service, Dr. Albert Yuzpe of London's University Hospital, observed: "It's another women's self-help group taking medicine out of the hands of physicians." While he acknowledged that such a development might not be an entirely bad thing, he warned that the women would need some [unspecified] input from "professionals."[18] Finding a sufficient number of suitable donors, and raising the money to purchase the necessary medical equipment to preserve sperm proved to be insurmountable obstacles, at least in the case of the Windsor clinic, and it was forced to close its doors shortly after it had begun operations.[19] The failure of these efforts has meant that most women must make private insemination arrangements. In the early 1980s many lesbians relied upon the help of their gay male friends, but the AIDS epidemic has threatened that practice. Many gay men prefer not to be tested for the HIV virus, and have removed themselves from the pool of available donors. Faced with the risk of AIDS infection, many lesbians are once again forced to turn to medical clinics and hospitals for insemination services or to heterosexual donors willing to undergo testing to ensure their HIV-free status.

The issues raised by lesbians seeking to become mothers through artificial insemination are complex and varied. On the legal front, both the right of access to clinical insemination services and the status of private alternative insemination practices remains untested. Legislative initiatives in a number of jurisdictions in the United States have already restricted access to insemination services to married women.[20] While no such Canadian legislation yet exists, recommendations to this effect have been made by a number of commissions.[21] One of the critical issues which access to insemination services raises is whether a fundamental right to procreate is constitutionally or legislatively protected. If it can be demonstrated that such a right exists, then, arguably, lesbians seeking access to artificial insemination services will have a legal basis for their claims. In this respect, legislation such as the Canadian Charter of Rights and Freedoms and human rights legislation explicitly barring discrimination on the grounds of sexual orientation may be helpful in securing access rights for lesbians and single women.

In recent years, a number of jurisdictions in the United States and elsewhere have passed legislation declaring artificial insemination to be a practice of medicine and thereby restricting its use to licensed practitioners. The Ontario Law Reform Commission recommended the passage of similar legislation in 1985.[22] Should such a measure be implemented, it would force lesbians and single women engaging in private insemination arrangements to remain "clandestine" about their activities in order to avoid legal sanctions.

Lesbians who arrange private insemination already face the risk of paternity claims by sperm donors. To date, no Canadian cases have been reported, but in all five American cases which have appeared before the courts and have been reported, sperm donors seeking paternity rights have had their claims upheld by the courts. They have ranged from placing the sperm donor's name on the child's birth certificate to granting access rights. One case in which a sperm donor is seeking joint custody of the child is still before the courts in California.[23]

In marked contrast to sperm donors, the legal status of non-biological lesbian mothers—the partners of lesbians who are the biological mothers of children—has for the most part been denied by the courts in both the United States and Canada.[24] While many of these women have helped to care for and financially support the children of lesbian families, courts have repeatedly refused to grant their claims for visitation rights upon dissolution of the lesbian relationship or custody rights upon the death of the biological mother. In the only reported Canadian case to date, the judge rejected a lesbian mother's application for support for herself and her children born during the course of her relationship with her former lesbian partner. The court held that the non-biological mother had no legal obligation to support either the biological mother or the children.[25]

Within the lesbian community itself, lesbian motherhood has created a storm of controversy. Authors like Nancy Polikoff, a well-known American lawyer and lesbian mother, have argued that lesbians' "personal" decision to have children can be seen to represent a retreat into private life, and a rejection of lesbian political activism. "What does this mean for the full-time political activist who can no longer get enough help sending out mailings," Polikoff asks. "For the feminist candidate with fewer campaign workers? For lesbians who are not mothers but who have pressing responsibilities and get little sleep...Who nurtures them?[26] "To the extent that motherhood drains the available pool of lesbians engaging in ongoing political work, its long-term significance is overwhelming," Polikoff concludes.[27]

Such a view rests on an extremely narrow definition of "political work." For on the other side of the debate stand lesbian mothers who argue that our alliances with the heterosexual mothers may in fact help to bring about social change. As our children come into contact with children of so-called normal families at day care and schools, they break down the artificial barriers between the heterosexual and lesbian worlds. Lesbian families, often headed by two female parents, are not simply a replica of the heterosexual family; our differences expand and stretch people's notions of the acceptable, challenging long-standing notions about family. These friendships have led to a growing awareness of lesbian families and, hopefully, to an acceptance of our way of life.

Alliances based on shared experiences of discrimination and prejudice can also be made between white women and women of colour—both lesbian and heterosexual—who must raise their children in a profoundly racist society. While encouraging their children to be strong and proud, women of colour must nevertheless teach their children about racism. They might tell their children that they will be subjected to harassment and discrimination because of the colour of their skin. All lesbian mothers face a similar and/or additional task of explaining to their children that the family which has provided their love and security may be regarded by others as deviant or perverted. While a lesbian mother has the option of disguising her sexual orientation, such an option becomes increasingly difficult as children grow older, as their friends' contact with the "other" mother becomes more frequent and the "unusual" nature of the family becomes obvious.

Difficult as this process of telling may be, we cannot afford to avoid it. As Audre Lorde explains: "If we raise our children in the absence of an accurate picture of the world as we know it, then we blunt their most effective weapons for survival and growth, as well as their motivation for social change."[28] While Lorde acknowledges the hurt that the lessons of discrimination may cause, these lessons equip children with the skills they will need to survive and to change the world. Elsewhere Lorde explains: "Black children of lesbian couples have an advantage because they learn, very early, that oppression comes in many different forms, none of which have anything to do with their own worth."[29] Through dealing with experiences of discrimination, links can be made between mothers and between our children.

Once again, however, some lesbian theorists are appalled at the prospect of the intermingling of lesbian and heterosexual families. Nancy Polikoff, for example, expresses a particular horror of the lesbian mother who "believes she has more in common with a heterosexual, usually married, mother than with a lesbian who has no children. I have seen lesbians whose social lives have come to revolve around families, usually straight, with other children close in age to their own. I have seen child care plans made with other heterosexual families of unknown politics because it was the most convenient arrangement." "The perception that one's interest as a mother supercedes one's interest as a lesbian is politically devastating," Polikoff concludes.[30] To examine the basis of her concerns, I will turn now to the subject of the struggle for spousal benefits.

SPOUSAL BENEFITS

The issue of lesbian motherhood has also come to public attention through the fight by lesbians for entitlement to family benefit coverage for their partners and their children.[31] In many respects, this campaign is an offshoot of lesbians having babies and of lesbian mothers, now in relationships, creating lesbian families. Raising children is expensive: they need dental care, prescription drugs for their seemingly interminable ear infections, braces, and glasses. Lesbians faced with these expenses have begun to take a long hard look at benefits packages most of us had virtually ignored in the carefree days of our youth. While the biological mother might have a benefits package under which she could include her children, it is not unusual for one member of a partnership to have a better benefits package, or for the mother to lack any workplace benefits, whether because she is a student, self-employed, or working part time. In such instances, many lesbian and gay couples have found themselves face to face with one of the more blatant examples of heterosexual privilege in our society. Heterosexual couples can opt to include their children under either parent's benefit package; a lesbian couple cannot. While a lesbian who is the non-biological parent of children must participate in her workplace benefits plan, she is not entitled to pay family premiums and thereby provide benefits coverage for her partner and their children.

One of the first people to confront discriminatory benefits policies was Karen Andrews, a library worker with the Toronto Public Library System. Supported by her union, the Canadian Union of Public Employees (CUPE) Local 1996, Andrews challenged the Ontario Health Insurance Plan's refusal to accept her application for family coverage. The case reached the Supreme Court of Ontario, where Andrews' claim was based on Section 15 of the Canadian Charter of Rights and Freedoms, which provides as follows:

> *Every individual is equal before and under the law and has the right to equal protection and equal benefit of the law without discrimination and, in particular, without discrimination based on race, national or ethnic origin, colour, religion, sex, age or mental or physical disability.*[33]

Under the test in force at the time, Mr. Justice McRae reasoned that "homosexual couples" could claim discrimination under Section 15 of the Charter only if they could demonstrate that they were "similarly situated" to heterosexual couples. Mr. Justice McRae found that they were not. He explained:

> *Homosexual couples are not similarly situated to heterosexual couples. Heterosexual couples procreate and raise children. They marry or are potential marriage partners and most importantly they have legal obligations of support for their children whether born in wedlock or out and for their spouses…A same sex partner does not and cannot have these obligations.*[34]

Since that decision, the Supreme Court of Canada has ruled in an unrelated case that the rights provided under the Charter do extend to groups not specifically identified under Section 15.[35] Heartened by that ruling, lesbians and gays have continued to fight for spousal benefits and a number of cases involving such claims continue to work their way through the courts. Despite proclamations by both John Crosbie and Kim Campbell that discrimination against gays and lesbians will be redressed by the current federal government, no concrete actions have yet been taken. A major victory in the struggle for spousal benefits was achieved in December 1990, when the government of Ontario, led by the New Democratic Party, extended same-sex spousal benefits to all its employees, effective January 1, 1991.[36]

The campaign for spousal benefits has become a highly contentious issue within the lesbian and gay movements. Critics of the "rights" strategy charge that the campaign is appropriating and perpetuating oppressive familial ideology. Commenting on the Karen Andrews' case, Mary Eaton and

Cynthia Petersen noted that, "in order to be successful in an equality application, a claimant must make herself look as much as possible like her oppressor. In this case, Ms. Andrews and Ms. Trenholm personified the idealized nuclear family except for the fact that they were lesbians..." In their efforts to demonstrate that they were "similarly situated" to heterosexual couples, Eaton and Petersen charged that lesbians and gays were forced to "engage in a methodology of cooptation, buying into the male white heterosexual culture."[37] Such actions, critics charge, will inevitably depoliticize the lesbian and gay movements, as we move from "a discourse of liberation to one of rights."[38] "By claiming our rights as spouses, rather than our rights/ needs as people, we emulate and legitimize the ideological norm and we also compound the marginization of others," charges Didi Herman, in a searing critique of the rights perspective.[39] "By appropriating familial ideology, lesbians and gay men may be supporting the very institutional structures that create and perpetuate women's oppression"—the nuclear family and heterosexual coupledom.[40] Rights activists rejoin that their campaign *challenges* rather than sustains the heterosexual nuclear family, as they seek to extend and expand the notion of family.

To some extent, the debate over spousal benefits has polarized the lesbian and gay communities between single people and those in partnerships or family relationships.[41] At the Coalition for Gay Rights in Ontario Conference on spousal benefits in August 1989, Chris Bearchell, a longtime gay activist, argued that "privileges" for people in couples would inevitably translate into "penalties" for those who were not in couples.[42] As one critic of the critics has pointed out, however, single heterosexuals and single gays and lesbians have the same access to benefits and pensions provided through their workplace. Lesbians and gay men who choose to live in partnerships with or without children do not have the same access to benefits as their heterosexual counterparts. For many lesbians and gay men, the issue is one of fairness. Few lesbians and gay men who advocate the extension of spousal benefits to same-sex couples believe that such a move will eliminate discrimination from our society. On the contrary, most advocate the extension of medical and dental benefits as well as other fundamental social benefits to all members of society, regardless of sexual orientation, family status, or income level.[43] The debate over spousal benefits is, needless to say, far from resolved.

The issues of child custody, lesbian insemination, and spousal benefits have given lesbian mothers a public presence; in all three instances, lesbian mothers have challenged traditional notions about mother and family. What has this meant for lesbian mothers? For the women's movement and the lesbian and gay movements? For all women? It is to these questions which I will now turn my attention.

The women's movement has moved a considerable distance since the first lesbian mother took to the stage at International Women's Day (1978) with a paper bag over her head to disguise her identity. While her need for anonymity was understandable, the presentation of the issue alarmed many women in the lesbian community. Under increasing pressure from the lesbian and gay movements, the women's movement began to include custody rights for lesbian mothers in its "shopping list" of feminist demands. This support often amounted to little more than a statement of sympathy, however, as the issue was framed primarily in terms of discrimination against an oppressed minority. Seldom was the issue of lesbian custody rights seen to have far reaching implications either for the women's movement itself or for heterosexual mothers.

During the 1980s, however, the terrain of motherhood begins to shift dramatically. In a pronatalist period reminiscent of the 1950s, new reproductive technologies, including in vitro fertilization and surrogate motherhood, placed issues of motherhood front and centre on the feminist agenda. While no unified feminist position has emerged, developments in new reproductive technology have forced feminists to grapple with the meaning of motherhood for all women. On another front, heterosexual mothers have increasingly found themselves facing vicious custody battles with embittered husbands backed by "father's rights" organizations. Coupled with a move away from the maternal presumption in custody cases in this era of "equal rights," these battles have forced many feminists to examine the thorny issue of the rights of mothers, heterosexual or lesbian, to their children.

As feminists begin to explore the history of child custody, links between the situation of heterosexual and lesbian mothers become clearer. Until very recently, for example, a woman who has committed adultery was routinely denied custody of, and often access to, her children. Many cases have been documented of women engaged in inter-racial heterosexual relationships who were denied custody of their children on the grounds of the social stigma attached to such a family. These prejudicial rulings have slowly changed, but only through a long history of struggles against such discriminatory and racist practices.[44]

As increasing numbers of "good enough"[45] mothers lose custody of their children, the issue of the rights of all mothers, heterosexual or lesbian, becomes crucial. In courtroom battles involving lesbian mothers, maternal fitness, disguised as a factor which might adversely affect the best interests of the child, continues to be used as a determining factor in denying custody rights. Increasingly, the "best interests of the children" tests are being negatively applied against heterosexual mothers on the grounds of their political or sexual activity or even their failure to secure a well paid job because of their years devoted to full-time mothering.

Clearly, the issues involved are complex ones, particularly in an era when many fathers are assuming an increasingly visible role in the parenting process. All too often, however, the significance of the primary caregiver function is undermined, in favour of such gender-based criteria as income, social status, or future prospects. In a day when women still earn less than two-thirds of a male wage, such criteria penalize all mothers, heterosexual or lesbian.

I would be presenting a false picture to suggest that lesbian and heterosexual mothers' situations and concerns were identical, or that all lesbian mothers share the same views of themselves or their children. As I have already noted, lesbians are divided as to the best strategy to pursue in order to obtain our rights. Regardless of their strategic objectives, as women-identified women, all lesbian mothers stand outside of the structures of heterosexuality and the so-called traditional nuclear family. In posting a positive alternative to marriage and the family, lesbian mothers can be seen as a "threat" to traditional social values. I frankly doubt that the structures of heterosexuality will crumble as a result of our existence. More likely, we will force some people to question notions about what constitutes a "family." As our children form friendships at their day care centres and schools, as our work mates socialize with our partners and children, as "ordinary" people realize how "ordinary" we are, long held notions of deviance and perversion are discredited. We are lesbians, yes. But we are mothers too. Devoted to our children, worried when they are sick, proud when they do well, concerned about violence and nuclear war, and the quality of education in our schools.

The feminist movement will be strengthened by the degree to which it can incorporate lesbian mothers and our concerns. Lesbian mothers too realize long forgotten bonds with our heterosexual sisters as we face the joys and dilemmas of mothering in a patriarchal society. Sharing these concerns, supporting one another's struggles, perhaps we can raise a generation of children more accepting of difference, more prepared to fight for fairness and dignity, than any of us was reared to be.

NOTES

1   I wish to acknowledge the financial assistance provided by a postdoctoral fellowship from the Social Sciences and Humanities Research Council of Canada. I am grateful to Mary Ellen Cummings and to Susan Genge for their thoughtful readings of an earlier draft of this article and for their insights into the family debate. Finally, I wish to thank Karen Andrews for her courage in taking on the fight for spousal benefits for lesbian and gay families.

2   Ellen Herman, "The Romance of Lesbian Motherhood," *Sojourner: The Women's Forum*, March 1988, p. 12. Other estimates range as high as 6 to 10 million lesbian mothers. See ABA Annual Meeting Provides Forum for Family Law Experts, *Family Law Reporter* (BNA) 1512, 1513 (August 25, 1987), p. 13.

3   Minnie Bruce Pratt, "Poetry in Time of War," in *Rebellion: Essays 1980–1991* (Ithaca, New York: Firebrand Books, 1991), p. 228.

4   Not all cases which appear before the courts are reported in legal journals. It is a common occurrence in cases in which homosexuality or lesbianism is a factor to seal the records, ostensibly to protect the privacy of the individuals involved. This

practice presents a problem for both lawyers and researchers in the field of lesbian custody. Those cases which are reported become accessible to judges and lawyers for their use in future cases, and thereby assume an importance beyond their individual significance.

5   See Wendy Gross, "Judging the Best Interests of the Child: Child Custody and the Homosexual Parent," *Canadian Journal of Women and the Law* vol. 1, no. 2 (1986), pp. 505–31; Katherine Arnup, "Mothers Just Like Others: Lesbians, Divorce and Child Custody in Canada," *Canadian Journal of Women and the Law* vol. 3, no. 1 (1989), pp. 18–32.

6   Mary Eaton, "Lesbians and the Law," in Sharon D. Stone, ed., *Lesbians in Canada* (Toronto: Between the Lines, 1990), p. 118.

7   Children's Law Reform Act, R.S.O. 1980, c. 68, section 24.

8   Ibid., section 24.

9   See, in particular, Case *v.* Case (1974), 18 R.F.L. 138 (Sask. Queen's Bench). Although this case was decided prior to the family law reforms referred to above, the judicial reasoning applied by Mr. Justice MacPherson would still be allowed under current family law. In evaluating the relative fitness of each parent, the judge stated: "I hesitate to put adjectives on the personality of the mother but the evidence shows, I think, that her way of life is irregular." His primary concern was expressed as follows: "I greatly fear that if these children are raised by the mother they will be too much in contact with people of abnormal tastes and proclivities."

10   Nancy D. Polikoff, "Lesbian Mothers, Lesbian Families: Legal Obstacles, Legal Challenges," in Sandra Pollock and Jeanne Vaughn, eds. *The Politics of the Heart: A Lesbian Parenting Anthology*, (Ithaca, NY: Firebrand Books, 1987), p. 326.

11   Minnie Bruce Pratt, "The Child Taken From the Mother," in *Crime Against Nature* (Ithaca, New York: Firebrand Books, 1990), p. 24.

12   Custody cases can be brought back to the courts for reconsideration on the basis of "changed circumstances." These can range from the marriage of one of the parties to the "discovery" of a lesbian mother's sexual orientation.

13   From its formulation in 1978 until its demise in 1987, the Lesbian Mothers' Defence Fund (LMDF) provided lesbian mothers with invaluable legal, financial, and emotional support. The LMDF produced *The Grapevine*, a newsletter reporting on custody cases across North America, assisted in fundraising, and organized monthly potluck suppers for lesbian mothers and their children. For a discussion of LMDF, see Sharon Dale Stone, "Lesbian Mothers Organizing," in *Lesbians in Canada*, pp. 198–208.

14   Many feminists prefer to use the term alternative insemination or alternative fertilization, since there is nothing inherently "artificial" in the process of insemination. Susan Robinson and H.F. Pizer point out: "Alternative fertilization is as natural a means for producing a normal baby as the method employed over millions of years of human evolution—it is different only in that sexual intercourse is not needed," in *Having a Baby Without a Man: The Woman's Guide to Alternative Insemination* (New York: Simon and Schuster, 1985), p. 36. For a discussion of the lesbian feminist perspective on insemination, see Mary Anne Coffey, "Of Fathers Born: A Lesbian Feminist Critique of the Ontario Law

Reform Commission Recommendations on Artificial Insemination," *Canadian Journal of Women and the Law* vol. 1 (1986), pp. 424–33.

15 *The Globe and Mail*, August 29, 1979, A11.

16 See, for example, Martha Heath, "Do It Yourself: Artificial Insemination," *Lesbian Tide* September/October 1978, pp. 26–7; Moira Fran, "Lesbian Self Insemination: Life Without Father?" *Off Our Backs* January 1982, pp. 12–13; Renate Duelli Klein, "Doing it Ourselves: Self Insemination," in *Test-Tube Women: What Future for Motherhood*, Rita Arditti, Renate Duelli Klein, and Shelley Minden, eds. (London: Routledge and Kegan Paul, 1984), pp. 382–90; "Choosing to Have Children: A Lesbian Perspective," *Women—A Journal of Liberation* vol. 6, no. 2 (1979).

17 Smedes *v.* Wayne State University, No. 80–725–83, (E.D. Mich., filed July 15, 1980). The case was widely reported in the American press: e.g., "Woman Sues to be Mother," *Bulletin* (Philadelphia), July 17, 1980; and "A Single Sues for Artificial Insemination," *Seattle Times* July 17, 1980, p. A5.

18 "Artificial insemination service bypasses MDs," *Toronto Star*, June 29, 1982. An article describing the efforts of the Oakland Feminist Health Clinic appeared in *The Globe* that year. "Sperm bank established by feminists," *The Globe and Mail* October 7, 1982.

19 For a discussion of these efforts, see Kathleen A. Lahey, "Reproduction, Male Technology and 'Lifestyle' Conflicts: The Lesbian Challenge." Unpublished paper presented to the National Association of Women and the Law Biennial Conference, Ottawa, Ontario, February 21–24, 1985.

20 On this issue, Robert H. Blank notes: "[T]he question of allowing single or lesbian women access to AID has been approached explicitly in a few jurisdictions and rejected in virtually all," in Blank, *Regulating Reproduction* (New York: Columbia University Press, 1990), p. 151.

21 See, for example, Saskatchewan, Law Reform Commission of Saskatchewan, *Proposals for a Human Artificial Insemination Act* (March 1987).

22 Ontario, Ministry of the Attorney General, Ontario Law Reform Commission, *Report on Artificial Reproduction and Related Matters*, 1985.

23 See "Sperm donor wins fight with lesbians," *Toronto Star* July 26, 1991, p. F1.

24 For an in-depth discussion of the parental rights of non-biological mothers, see Nancy D. Polikoff, "This Child Does Have Two Mothers; Redefining Parenthood to Meet the Needs of Children in Lesbian-Mother and Other Nontraditional Families," *Georgetown Law Journal* vol. 78 (1990–91), pp. 459–575.

25 Anderson *v.* Luomo (1986), 50 R.F.L. (2d) 127 (B.C.S.C.)

26 Nancy D. Polikoff, "Lesbians Choosing Children: The Personal is Political Revisited," in *The Politics of the Heart*, p. 50.

27 Ibid., p. 51.

28 Audre Lorde, "Turning the Beat Around: Lesbian Parenting 1986," in *A Burst of Light: Essays* (Ithaca, New York: Firebrand Books, 1988), p. 41.

29 Audre Lorde, "Man Child: A Black Lesbian Feminist's Response," in *Sister Outsider: Essays and Speeches* (Trumansburg, New York: The Crossing Press, 1984), p. 75.

Gender, Families, and Parenting

30   Ibid., p. 52.

31   For a critique of the spousal benefits strategy, see Didi Herman, "Are We Family?: Lesbian Rights and Women's Liberation," *Osgoode Hall Law Journal* vol. 24, no. 4 (Winter 1990), pp. 789–815.

32   The Ontario Supreme Court ruled against Andrews' application in March, 1988.

33   Canadian Charter of Rights and Freedoms, Section 15(1).

34   Andrews, *v*, Ontario (Minister of Health), 64 O.R. (2d), 258; 49 D.L.R. (4th) 584. For a discussion of the decision, see Mary Eaton and Cynthia Petersen, Case Comment, Andrews *v.* Ontario (Minister of Health), *Canadian Journal of Women and the Law*, vol. 2 (1987–88), pp. 416–21.

35   The Law Society of British Columbia et al. *v.* Andrews and Kinersly et al. [1989] 1 S.C.R. 143.

36   The Ontario government is currently in the process of reviewing all provincial legislation with regard to the issue of same-sex partners. The passage of Bill 7 in 1986 provided a major impetus for these measures. This bill added sexual orientation as a prohibited ground for discrimination in the areas of housing, employment and the provision of services.

37   Mary Eaton and Cynthia Petersen, "Andrews *v.* Ontario (Minister of Health), p. 419.

38   Didi Herman, "Are We Family?", p. 790.

39   Ibid., p. 799.

40   Ibid., p. 797.

41   There are, of course, "single" lesbians on both sides of the debate; as well, there are lesbians in "family" relationships who oppose the spousal benefits strategy.

42   On Our Own Terms, C.L.G.R.O., 5, 6 August 1989.

43   The recent elimination of OHIP premiums in Ontario is one example of the elimination of income barriers to access to medical services and of family-based coverage for OHIP. Many activists continue to lobby for universal access to dental and other medical services. The campaign for spousal benefits does not in and of itself prevent the extension of such benefits to all citizens. Rather, it extends those benefits to additional members of society who are eligible but who do not currently enjoy access to such services solely because of their sexual orientation.

44   For a discussion of changing practices of child custody, see Constance Backhouse, *Petticoats and Prejudice: Women and the Law in Nineteenth Century Canada* (Toronto: Women's Press, 1991), chapter 7; and "Shifting Patterns in Nineteenth-century Canadian Custody Awards," in David Flaherty, ed. *Essays in the History of Canadian Law* vol. 1 (1981), pp. 212–48.

45   For a discussion of mothers' loss of custody, see Phyllis Chesler, *Mothers on Trial: The Battle for Children and Custody* (New York: McGraw Hill, 1986).

REFERENCES

Arnup, Katherine, "Lesbian Mothers and Child Custody." In *Gender and Society: Creating a Canadian Women's Sociology*, Arlene Tigar McLaren, ed. Toronto: Copp Clark Pitman, 1988.

Arnup, Katherine, "Mothers Just Like Others: Lesbians, Divorce and Child Custody in Canada." *Canadian Journal of Women and the Law* vol. 3, no. 1 (1989).

Bell, Laurie. *On Our Own Terms: A Practical Guide for Lesbian and Gay Relationships.* Toronto: Coalition for Lesbian and Gay Rights in Ontario, 1991.

Day, Dian. "Lesbian/Mother." In *Lesbians in Canada*, Sharon Dale Stone, ed. Toronto: Between the Lines, 1990.

Eaton, Mary. "Lesbians and the Law." In *Lesbians in Canada.* Sharon D. Stone, ed. Toronto: Between the Lines, 1990.

Ferris, Kathryn, "Child Custody and the Lesbian Mother: An Annotated Bibliography." *Resources for Feminist Research* vol. 12, no. 1 (March 1983), pp. 106–9.

Gross, Wendy. "Judging the Best Interests of the Child: Child Custody and the Homosexual Parent." *Canadian Journal of Women and the Law* vol. 1, no. 2 (1986), pp. 505–31.

Hanscombe, Gillian E. and Jackie Forster, *Rocking the Cradle—Lesbian Mothers: A Challenge in Family Living.* Boston: Alyson Publications Ltd., 1982.

Herman, Didi. "Are We Family?: Lesbian Rights and Women's Liberation," *Osgoode Hall Law Journal* vo. 24, no. 4 (Winter 1990), pp. 789–815.

Leopold, Margaret and Wendy King. "Compulsory Heterosexuality, Lesbians and the Law: The Case for Constitutional Protection." *Canadian Journal of Women and the Law* vol. 1 (1985).

Pollock, Sandra and Jeanne Vaughn, eds. *Politics of the Heart: A Lesbian Parenting Anthology.* Ithaca, New York: Firebrand Books, 1987.

Ryder, Bruce. "Equality Rights and Sexual Orientation: Confronting Heterosexual Family Privilege." *Canadian Journal of Family Law* (1990).

Stone, Sharon Dale, "Lesbian Mothers Organizing." In *Lesbians in Canada*, Sharon Dale Stone, ed. Toronto: Between the Lines, 1990.

Wyland, Francie. *Motherhood, Lesbianism and Child Custody.* Bristol: Falling Wall Press, 1977.

25

Assisted Reproduction: The Social Issues

Rona Achilles

Women's dominant role in the reproduction of the species is the source of both their power and their powerlessness. Reproductive autonomy—the ability and right to control fertility—is fundamental to women's health and well-being. Reproductive technologies can empower or disempower women, depending on how they are used and on the social context in which they are used.

Reproductive technology is a very broad term. It can refer to something as simple and user-controlled as a diaphragm and to technologies as complex and physician-controlled as *in vitro* fertilization. Most reproductive technologies fall into three basic categories: those that inhibit the development of new life, those that monitor the development of new life, and those that involve the creation of new life. Those involved in the inhibition of new life are the most familiar: birth control, sterilization, and abortion. Medical advances in the monitoring of new life are more recent and involve techniques such as ultrasound, amniocentesis, chorionic villi sampling, foetal monitoring, and foetal surgery.[1]

Developments in both of these spheres—in the inhibition of new life and the monitoring of new life—have a tremendous impact on women's reproductive autonomy. Foetal surgery, for example, creates a situation where, potentially, the foetus still in a woman's uterus can be defined as a patient separate from the carrying mother. The capacity to monitor, 'correct,' and artificially sustain foetal life at increasingly earlier stages of pregnancy may, in practice, work against the individual mother's reproductive autonomy. Ruth Hubbard documents two instances in the United States where women were forced to undergo Caesarean sections through a court order.[2] The checkered health record of the Pill and I.U.D. further illustrates the extent to which the technological 'hope chest' for reproductive autonomy and choice may become a 'Pandora's box' under the prevailing social, economic, political, and medical conditions. The central question is simply

From Rona Achilles, "Assisted Reproduction: The Social Issues," in Sandra Burt, Lorraine Code, and Lindsay Dorney (eds.), *Changing Patterns Women in Canada* (2nd ed.). Used by permission of the Canadian Publishers, McClelland & Stewart, Toronto.

choice, but choice for whom, and under what conditions? And from what range of alternatives?

Feminist efforts in relation to reproduction have largely been devoted to ensuring women's right to avoid unwanted pregnancies and the right to plan and space pregnancies. The availability of safe and effective birth control and equal access to legal abortion have been major concerns for feminists in the past two decades.[3] More recently, the right to control the conditions of birth and the right to have access to midwives have emerged as feminist issues. All of these remain important arenas for feminist analysis and action. However, even before these issues are resolved, we are moving into an era that has and will continue to have an unprecedented impact on women's reproductive choice....

Artificial insemination, sperm banks, preconception contracts, *in vitro* fertilization, and related techniques including freezing of sperm, ova, and embryos are some of the developments in the field of assisted reproduction.... The media tend to sensationalize their coverage and label every new form of conception as 'test-tube.' An authentic 'test-tube' baby would require conception, gestation, and birth to occur completely outside of a woman's body; the technical term for this is 'ectogenesis.' The technology for an authentic 'test-tube' baby has yet to be fully developed, although it may not be too far off in the future. The media's inaccurate description of current procedures, however, has sown the seeds for its public reception.

Reproductive choice, once limited to concerns about avoiding or planning pregnancies, is an issue that takes on a new meaning through the use of assisted reproductive procedures. New dilemmas, choices, and responsibilities accompany their introduction into society.... In concert with the issues surrounding freedom from motherhood, feminists must now analyze and understand the need to mother expressed by women who will utilize these technologies.

There is a striking absence of social and psychological research on the impact of infertility on either women or men, and infertile women argue that their plight has not been of concern to feminists.[4] Infertility is very simply the inability to reproduce oneself biologically. In the past, the discovery that a wife was 'barren' constituted grounds for divorce; and it currently elicits public sympathy as well as social stigma. The quest for fertility through assisted reproduction, which is taxing emotionally, physically, and sometimes financially, testifies to the strength of women's desire for motherhood despite few publicly sanctioned rewards for this role in our culture. Increased participation in the paid labour force and the opening of opportunities for women to enter professions, limited as they may be, have not eradicated motherhood's centrality to women's identity and self-esteem. The social reasons for this are complex: family pressures, full adult status, gender identity, and the importance of biological continuity or lineage are some of the factors that induce women (and men) to seek fertility through these costly measures. 'It hurts to be infertile,' as Barbara Menning states in her defence of *in vitro* fertilization....[5]

These technologies definitely do provide the opportunity for some women to bear children who perhaps otherwise could not do so. But they also close down some choices while introducing new pressures and dilemmas for women. A woman confronted with infertility today will feel the pressure to pursue every possible avenue to overcome or circumvent her or her partner's infertility. As with the prenatal diagnostic techniques of amniocentesis and ultrasound, which have become commonplace for many 'high-risk' women, the mere availability of various reproductive technologies may foreclose the option of *not* using them. Furthermore, the causes of infertility may be ignored because they can be bypassed technologically.

Infertility is estimated to affect up to 15 per cent of couples and is considered to be on the increase. At present, approximately one-third of all cases of infertility are attributed to women, one-third are attributed to men, and one-third are either unexplained or shared by both partners. In Canada, infertility is defined as one year of attempting to achieve pregnancy without success. The definition of fertility varies culturally; in France, for example, the definition is five years of unsuccessful attempts to achieve pregnancy. The definition of infertility itself, therefore, is socially defined and structured. Currently, assisted reproduction technologies are used only to assist couples who have fertility problems, or in some instances, for women without a male procreative partner. However, the potential exists for these technologies to be used for other reasons. For example, a woman or couple might hire another woman to bear her or their child for a number of reasons—for convenience, economic reasons, or simply to avoid the discomforts and health concerns of pregnancy.[6]

As well as the prevalence of infertility, a number of social factors indicate that the demand for these procedures is assured and will likely increase.[7] These include: the decline in availability of children for adoption (particularly healthy white babies, and because of the difficulties and costs of international adoption); the strong emphasis in our culture on having genetically related children (which is possible with some of these technologies but not with others); late childbearing, which sometimes incurs fertility problems; the use of permanent contraceptive methods such as vasectomies or tubal ligations by individuals who later change their mind about childbearing;[8] and the increase in genetic counselling, which may forewarn potential parents about possible genetic defects in their offspring. In addition, the increase in single women who want to be mothers and in lesbian couples who want children without contact with a male promises to increase the demand for some procedures such as donor insemination.

Technically there are two major categories of assisted reproduction technologies: artificial insemination and *in vitro* fertilization. A fundamental difference between these two procedures is that artificial insemination is potentially a very simple procedure not necessarily requiring medical assistance. Artificial insemination simply replaces sexual intercourse, and fertilization occurs within the body. In *in vitro* fertilization, conception occurs outside a woman's body in a petri dish (*in vitro* is Latin for 'in glass'). For each of these two categories there are several different procedures, and in some cases they overlap and are used together. Preconception contracts, for example, might use a simple version of artificial insemination, which usually involves lawyers and physicians. It is useful to explain and analyse each procedure individually.

ARTIFICIAL INSEMINATION

Artificial insemination is the oldest, least visible, and most widespread of what we now call assisted reproduction technologies. It is arguable, given the simplicity of the procedure, whether it is appropriate to call artificial insemination a technology since it is very simply a replacement for sexual intercourse. Semen, obtained through masturbation, is inserted into a woman's vagina at the time of her ovulation. Sometimes a small cap or diaphragm-like device is used to keep the semen in place. Although most artificial insemination takes place in clinical settings, the simplicity of the procedure makes it possible for women to inseminate themselves without the assistance of physicians. Self-insemination groups, who organize the transfer of sperm from donors to women, are springing up in many countries, including Canada.[9] Since conception, gestation, and birth occur through natural processes (or as 'naturally' as pregnancies that occur through sexual intercourse), the term 'artificial' is slightly misleading. Kathleen Lahey argues, for example, that a more appropriate term is 'alternative insemination.'[10]

There are three types of artificial insemination: artificial insemination by husband or male partner (AIH), donor insemination (DI), and artificial insemination combined (AIC).[11] Artificial insemination with a husband's or partner's sperm might be used in a variety of different situations, such as when the male partner's sperm count is low or when he is undergoing treatment that might damage his sperm—such as chemotherapy. The sperm may be concentrated and treated with chemicals to increase its fertility, or frozen and stored for future use. In other instances, the female partner's cervical mucous may be reacting to her husband's sperm; to bypass the cervix, sperm is placed in the uterus. In these cases, in which a medical condition is being overcome, AIH is a treatment for infertility. In other cases, reasons for use may be socially motivated—such as its use after sperm has been treated for sex selection. In donor insemination, because the man who donates the sperm is not the woman's partner, many more complex psychological and social issues are raised. It is for these reasons that DI has had a surprisingly long but quiet history.

Donor insemination is not a new procedure: the first recorded instance of DI occurred in the United States in 1884.... Opponents of the procedure argued that it was against the laws of God and nature; that the use of another man's sperm was adulterous; that the legitimacy of the child was questionable; and that the procedure was dishonest and immoral. Advocates perceived the possibility of improving the quality of the species (an early form of eugenics) and argued that the source of sperm was irrelevant.[12] Over one hundred years later, we have yet to resolve some of these dilemmas. The Roman Catholic church, for example, still considers donor insemination to be adulterous. Furthermore, the issue of secrecy is unresolved and the eugenic potential of DI remains problematic.

Because there is no regulation or monitoring of artificial insemination, its incidence is unknown. Estimates for the early 1980s in Canada range from 1,500 to 6,000 babies born a year through donor insemination alone. Since these estimates were made several years ago and do not include women inseminating themselves outside of clinical settings, the numbers are probably conservative. In the United States a recent survey estimates that in 1986–87, 172,000 women underwent artificial insemination with a resulting 35,000 births for AIH and 30,000 births for DI.[13] Other estimates put the total population of DI offspring at over one million.[14]

Donors are solicited from a variety of sources. A common assumption is that most donors are medical students or medical personnel, but an exploratory study of participants in donor insemination indicates a broader spectrum, varying from postal workers to accountants.[15] Donors are usually paid about $15–$75 for time and expenses, which has led George Annas to argue that sperm donors are more accurately called sperm vendors.[16] In Canada we do not pay blood donors, and there is evidence to indicate that the quality of blood is lower in countries where blood is bought and sold.[17] Payment for reproductive capacities becomes even more problematic when we look at the practice of preconception contracts. The risk of individuals conceived through DI meeting and marrying a half-sibling (unknown to each other as such) increases with the number of DI children produced by each donor. Guidelines generally suggest that donors should father no more than ten children. However, there are frequently poor adherence to professional guidelines and no method of enforcement. As well, poor record-keeping practices and inadequate follow-up procedures make it impossible to monitor the number of pregnancies, births, and the linkages between recipients and donors. One donor in an explanatory study estimated that he had donated approximately 240 times, suggesting that he would have more than ten biological children through DI.

Similarly, with the screening of donors for sexually transmitted diseases including HIV (which may result in AIDS), guidelines are rigorous but not all practicing DI physicians will adhere to the guidelines. A 1987 U.S. survey reports haphazard screening of donors. Less than one-half of the physicians surveyed tested donors for HIV antibodies, one out of four did not screen for infertility, and one out of five did not screen for sexually transmitted diseases.[18] There has been no survey of Canadian DI practitioners; however, at least two women have been infected with HIV through donor sperm. In a precedent-setting case, one woman successfully sued the physician for negligence for not informing her of the risk of acquiring HIV through the insemination.[19]

With donor insemination, the structure of the practice informs us about our attitudes towards it. Although the specifics may vary from physician to physician, the most common practice (which is supported by most legal, medical, and ethical reports) is that donors and recipients remain unknown to each other. Anonymity, it is argued, is essential to avoid emotional complications, to ensure "the stability of the family and the welfare of the child."[20] The fear that conflicting emotional ties might arise if anonymity is not protected is based on the assumption that biologically linked individuals may develop curiosity or other feelings about each other that could threaten the coherence of the family unit created through DI. For example, DI offspring may become interested in the identity of their biological father, the DI mother might become curious about the man who is the biological father of her DI child, or the infertile husband may feel threatened by the sperm donor who was able to impregnate his wife when he was unable to. Consequently, the couple or woman usually have no information about the donor, and the donor is usually not told whether a pregnancy or birth has occurred. Usually there is an attempt to 'match' the physical characteristics of the sperm donor to the DI mother's partner (if present) or to herself. Women using self-insemination (outside of clinical settings) may choose to know or not to know their donors.

This issue of anonymity, in itself, is a momentous shift in reproductive relations. Although neither marriage nor parenthood has always been based on individual choice—our choices are socially structured in any event—neither to know nor to choose the biological father of one's child is an unprecedented social act. In the case of donor insemination, physicians are choosing the reproductive partner, the man who will be the biological 'father' of a DI mother's child....

There are, as yet, no laws to protect the participants in DI except in Quebec, where the child is legally considered to be affiliated with the social father, and in the Yukon, where donors are protected from possible legal suits by offspring or recipients. In 1985 the Ontario Law Reform Commission undertook a major study of the legal problems posed by assisted reproduction and proposed amendments to legislation. However, despite the fact that its study purports to protect the 'best interests of the child,' the report agrees with most other reports in viewing donor anonymity as essential to the success of the procedure. Some individuals conceived through DI may have no interest in knowing the identity of their biological father.

However, given the current increase in genetic counseling, access to medical information on sperm donors may be considered important by some, and increasingly so by recipients....

In medical literature, DI is described as a treatment for male infertility. It does not, however, cure infertility but circumvents it through the use of another man's sperm. Ironically, but not surprisingly, it is the fertile woman who becomes the patient. Despite the simplicity of the procedure, when it is practised in clinical settings it is frequently accompanied by other medical procedures to increase efficiency and the success rate. The presumably fertile woman may undergo a series of tests to ensure that she is fertile and that sperm is not 'wasted' on a woman with her own fertility problems....

PRECONCEPTION CONTRACTS

Preconception contracts are what is popularly referred to as 'surrogate motherhood'—a misnomer since 'surrogate' means substitute and the so–called "surrogate" is the biological mother of the child. A preconception contract is a much more socially visible procedure than is donor insemination. This is partially because paternity is a less visible event than maternity. It is also a more controversial social arrangement because biological motherhood is more complex and involved relationship than biological fatherhood. Physiologically, fatherhood (in DI) involves sperm donation, and motherhood (in preconception contracts) involves nine months gestation in which a relationship develops with the baby-to-be. Preconception contracts have captured the attention of the media more than any other assisted reproduction technology. This arrangement is generally used by couples when the wife is infertile. The husband's sperm is used to artificially inseminate a woman (the contractual mother) who agrees (contractually) to surrender the child at birth and who is generally paid a fee for her 'services.' The method has the potential, however, to be used by anyone willing and able to pay a women to bear a child for them for any reason.

Several questions are raised by the practice of preconception contracts. It is somewhat reminiscent of wet-nursing, when poor working-class women were used to provide breast milk for babies of wealthier women. By logical extension, it sets the groundwork for some women to become breeders for others—with some contractual mothers being more highly valued according to prevailing standards of beauty or intelligence. Margaret Atwood's novel *The Handmaid's Tale* provides a dystopian vision of this possibility....

Preconception contracts began as an organized practice in the mid-1970s.[21] So far, there are no organized preconception services in Canada. However, media reports indicate that these services do exist as an underground practice, and that Canadians are participating in preconception arrangements (both as contractual mothers and commissioning couples) through U.S. organizations. A 1988 U.S. study reports that fifteen organizations provide the services and concludes that about six hundred arrangements have occurred to date. The report estimates that a typical contract involves a $10,000 fee for the 'contractual mother' and an additional $20,000 to $30,000 for living expenses, medical expenses, and attorney's fees. In these situations about one dollar in four is estimated actually to go to the woman carrying the child.[22] However alarmed we may be at the idea of women bearing children for a fee, it is the lawyers who are making a profit from this practice.

In contrast to donor inseminations, the recipients of preconception services generally pick their contractual mother out of a catalogue and may have contact with her during the pregnancy. (This varies according to the particular organization.) There has been a mixed response from the feminist community about preconception contracts, but whatever the response it has been strongly stated. On the one hand it is argued that it is exploitation, similar to prostitution or concubinage, and that the contractual mother is acting as a 'surrogate wife' to the biological father. On the other hand some feminists have said, 'Why not? Isn't it about time that women were paid for their reproductive labour?' Most paid work for women remains low-status, low-paid, and with little opportunity for advancement. The fee of $10,000—although less than minimum wage if calculated on an hourly basis—is still a substantial amount of money, which could alter the short-term economic circumstances of a person's life. Additionally, some contractual mothers say it provides 'all the magic of pregnancy' without the responsibility of rearing a child.

To separate themselves emotionally from the child they will surrender at birth, the contractual mothers describe themselves as 'vehicles' or 'vessels.' Nevertheless, there is frequently a grief reaction (called 'transient grief') after the child is given up to the contracting couple or individual. There are already self-help groups for contractual mothers, organized to provide support after the child is surrendered....

Although it remains unclear as to what extent these arrangements are enforceable in Canada, contracts potentially divest the contractual mother of her rights over her body throughout the terms of the contract. Interventions include extensive controls over diet, lifestyle, and activities. In 1987 in the United States a contractual mother was charged with a misdemeanor for taking drugs during her pregnancy. The contractual mother may also be required to undergo medical procedures such as ultrasound or amniocentesis to ensure a 'quality product.' If the foetus is discovered to be 'defective' she may be asked to undergo an abortion late in the pregnancy and forfeit the majority or all of her fee. There is also the question of what happens if the contractual mother decides that she does not want to give up the child. In current adoption practice, the birth-mother usually has a period of approximately two weeks after birth to make her final decision. There have already been several instances of contractual mothers changing their minds about surrendering the child after birth. In addition, since the ideal contractual mother is married with children of her own, the effect of the arrangement on other family members such as her other children, husband (or partner), and parents is crucial, but remains unknown....

Another version of preconception contracts involves IVF and embryo transfer (ET), with the 'contractual mother' carrying a child genetically unrelated to her. This procedure allows the commissioning couple to preserve their genetic tie to the child and sever the genetic tie of the carrying mother. The 'contractual mother,' who is the gestational/biological mother but not the genetic mother, becomes a vessel to carry the child for the couple. As might be expected, there is already a U.S. case in which the biological mother changed her mind and decided to keep the child she carried for the commissioning couple. The egg and sperm of the commissioning couple were fertilized *in vitro* and the embryo implanted in the 'contractual mother.'....

IN VITRO FERTILIZATION AND RELATED TECHNIQUES

In the IVF method of assisted conception, the process moves firmly into the hands of physicians. IVF involves very sophisticated medical technology and medical expertise. The process for recipients is stressful, invasive, and financially and emotionally draining. What most people do not know when the media report with awe the birth of another IVF child is that the success rate is very low. An additional problem is that success rates may be presented in a way that disguises the low rates, such as giving 'pregnancy rates' rather than how many couples have a child through this method—the 'take-home baby rate.' One Canadian study that presents careful results reports a pregnancy rate of 26.1 per cent and a take-home baby rate of 15 per cent.[23] Other estimates of Canadian clinics range from 3 per cent to 13 per cent.[24] The history of IVF is short, with the first successful IVF child having been born in Britain in 1978. Nevertheless, this is definitely a growth industry within the medical profession. There are already fifteen or so IVF clinics in Canada, all of them with very long waiting lists, indicating the prevalence of infertility and the willingness of couples to undergo invasive and uncertain medical treatments to achieve their own genetically linked children.

IVF was initially used when the problem of infertility was on the part of the woman, usually because her fallopian tubes were blocked. Its use has been expanded to couples where the male partner has a low sperm count. Linda Williams, in a preliminary study of IVF candidates, also found IVF being used as a diagnostic tool to define further the source of infertility.[25]

In contrast to artificial insemination, this procedure is not simple. The first step is the retrieval or 'harvesting' of the eggs (note the language of animal husbandry, where all of these techniques were first developed), which involves taking drugs to stimulate egg production, daily blood tests, pelvic examinations, and ultrasound. Then, usually, because drugs have been used to stimulate the ovaries to produce more than one egg at a time, between two to six eggs are removed surgically through a laparoscopy.[26] In the second step, the eggs and sperm (usually the woman's partners sperm, but not necessarily) are joined in a culture dish, where fertilization may or may not take place. If fertilization does take place, the third step is the transfer of the fertilized egg into the woman's uterus in the hope that implantation and pregnancy will ensue. Usually more than one fertilized egg is transferred to increase the possibilities of implantation. This is why IVF births frequently involve twins, triplets, or quintuplets. Fertilized eggs, technically referred to as *concepti*, may also be frozen and stored for future use by the genetic mother or another woman.

A more recent technique, very similar to IVF and ET, is called GIFT (gamete intrafallopian transfer) and can be used with women with at least one functioning fallopian tube. In this procedure, eggs are removed in the same way as with IVF but are then combined with sperm in a catheter threaded into the fallopian tube. Fertilization then occurs naturally in the woman's body—in the fallopian tube. The success rates for this procedure are reportedly much higher than with IVF—as high as 30 to 35 per cent. However, as with IVF a broad range of success rates is reported.[27]

Another version of GIFT is ZIFT, in which the egg and sperm are fused to form a zygote (hence zygote intrafallopian transfer) before transfer into the body. Other more experimental techniques include the freezing of embryos, freezing of eggs, and the micromanipulation of sperm. That is, when several embryos are available for transfer (more than three or four), rather than implant all of them, some are frozen for future use to reduce the risk of multiple pregnancies. Although this method was still considered experimental in 1988, sixty children had been born in Australia and Europe using frozen embryos.[28] When the technique of freezing eggs is perfected it will likely supplant the freezing of embryos in order to avoid the ethical issues of freezing an already fertilized egg. Like men who are currently able to store their sperm, women who face a loss of fertility due to pelvic disease, surgery, radiation, or chemotherapy will be able to freeze their eggs for future use. The eggs could be used for themselves or for another woman.

The final technique, the micromanipulation of sperm into ova, which is still experimental, is used when a man has a low sperm count, a lot of abnormal sperm, or sperm that do not move very well (non-motile). It could also be used for sex selection. In this procedure a sperm cell is injected into an egg. In one type of micromanipulation, sperm is inserted under the egg's outer membrane with a fine glass needle. In another type the egg's outer member is etched chemically to create an opening for sperm penetration. Because these are fertilizations that could not occur otherwise, the consequences of the procedures are as yet unknown....

.... [W]e still know very little about who actually uses the technologies and what their experiences are. The legal questions alone raised by these technologies are overwhelming.[29] There is currently a wealth of legal literature that identifies the problems and attempts to resolve them. But the resolution of legal issues will not entirely settle the social problems created by the use of the procedures. Since most of these procedures are still in experimental stages, much is unknown about their short-term or long-term social implications. However, at least [three] social issues can be identified: the further medicalization of the reproductive process; the impact on family ...and the potential eugenic uses of assisted reproduction technologies.

MEDICALIZATION

Among the most obvious social processes involved in the use of assisted reproductive technologies is the further medicalization of women's reproductive experience. Although reproduction requires the biological contribution of both sexes, it is notable that all of these technologies involve women becoming patients, even in the case of DI, where the woman is presumably fertile. Medicalization...is the expansion of medical expertise and influence into previously non-medical arenas of society. The medicalization of women's reproductive experience is an ongoing social process. The introduction of assisted reproductive technologies is not a bold leap into Huxley's Brave New World. Rather, it is a significant furthering of already existing social trends. The medical profession is already very involved in making decisions about reproductive matters, including the choice and distribution of most birth control methods, prenatal and postnatal care, and birthing, all of which increasingly involve reproductive technologies. The development of assisted reproduction technologies may be perceived as a logical (but extreme) extension of the 'planned parenthood' mentality pervasive in our culture. The further involvement of the medical profession provided by the development of assisted reproduction raises new questions about control and about responsibility and influence. In short, these new techniques precipitate a host of social consequences, which reflect, in a heightened manner, already existing social forces.

Society has always attempted to regulate who has sexual intercourse with whom, where, and under what conditions. Informal and sometimes formal sanctions govern sexual behaviour according to, for example, age, race, religion, class, and marital status. Before the development of assisted reproduction, conception occurred through the private, intimate interaction of two individuals—sexual intercourse between a man and a woman. All of these technologies separate the act of sexual intercourse from reproduction. The fact in itself is not necessarily problematic. However, with the exception of self-insemination, assisted reproduction technologies as practised in clinical settings move conception out of the private and into the public realm. Members of the medical profession, in other words, are now deciding who will have access to these services and, therefore, who will or will not become parents. This is not a realm of decision-making for which physicians are trained. Furthermore, the movement of conception into the public realm raises the question of whether every individual has a fundamental right to procreate and whether this right includes access to these services. The potential for discrimination exists on the grounds of class (those who can afford to pay for these services), race, marital status, and sexual preference. Most physicians will presumably attempt to uphold the cultural standard that a heterosexual couple provides the best possible parents for a child.

FAMILY STRUCTURE

...Few Canadian families conform to the presumed cultural norm of a married heterosexual couple who rear their biological offspring to adulthood. Nevertheless, the image and norm of the family persist as a normative structure. When we use the term 'parent,' we generally assume that the biological and social components of the role merge in one person. Exceptions to this are families formed through adoption, foster-parenthood, and step-parenting. In these situations, the term 'parent' is modified by an additional descriptor indicating some deviation from the presumed cultural norm. With adoption, for example, biological parents are referred to as birth parents and social parents are referred to as adoptive parents.

Assisted reproduction technologies make possible further diversity in family configurations. The assortment of parental roles is reflected in the current linguistic and conceptual confusion in describing these roles. With DI, fathering is split into two roles: the generally unknown biological father (sperm donor) and the social or rearing father. The family configuration presumes that the recipients are a heterosexual couple. If the DI mother is single there will be no rearing or social father. If she is part of a lesbian couple, then the second parent will be another mother (a co-mother) who is not biologically linked to the child. The biological father is in all cases the possibly unknown sperm donor.

The role of 'mother'—traditionally the genetic, uterine, and social mother of a child—is potentially fragmented into six different roles through the use of one or a combination of assisted reproduction technologies: (1) an egg donor—a woman who provides an egg but does not carry or rear the child; (2) a uterine mother—a woman who provides the gestational environment for a child who is not hers genetically, and who will not rear the child; (3) an egg and uterine mother (popularly referred to as a 'surrogate' mother or contractual mother)—a woman who is the biological mother, but who will not rear the child (a situation somewhat analogous to a birth mother who gives up a child for adoption at birth); (4) a uterine and social mother—a woman who is the recipient of an egg donation; (5) an egg (or genetic) and social mother—a woman whose fertilized (*in vitro*) egg is carried by another woman who returns the child after birth; and (6) a social mother, not genetically related to the child—the recipient of a preconception contract arrangement. This situation is similar to that of an adoptive mother or stepmother or any woman who raises children to whom she is not genetically related. An even more complex picture emerges when we consider that each of the individuals involved may marry, divorce and remarry—possibly even several times. Although not all of these roles are socially unprecedented, the manner in which they are created is new. The full implications of this fragmentation of women's reproductive and mothering experience have yet to be realized.

A child conceived through a combination of these procedures could potentially have five parents: two fathers and three mothers. The two fathers are the sperm donor or biological father and the social father. The three possible mothers are the egg donor, the uterine mother, and the mother who rears the child (the social mother). Again, these family constellations are based on the presumption that the recipients are a heterosexual couple. Even more possibilities emerge when the recipients are single or in lesbian couples.

The practice of freezing eggs, sperm, or embryos, technically referred to as 'cryopreservation,' further complicates our common understanding of the process of reproduction. Conception, for example, could occur in a petri dish in Australia. The embryo could be frozen, stored, and transported to Canada, where it could be implanted in a woman who (if pregnancy is successful) could give birth to a child, conceived many years earlier, to whom she has no genetic ties and whose genetic parents may no longer be alive. These possibilities alter both our temporal and geographical assumptions about the boundaries of the reproductive process, as well as the common cultural assumption that the parents of a child are genetically linked....

A woman who donates an egg for another woman who will carry and rear a child takes on a role somewhat similar to that of a sperm donor. [30] The potential exists, therefore, for women to 'father' children by providing only genetic material, as do men who donate sperm or biological fathers who do not assist in rearing their offspring....

The success of families created through assisted reproduction rests, to some extent, not on the technologies themselves but on our capacity as a society to redefine what constitutes family. In concert with other changes in family forms, assisted reproduction technologies challenge the sanctity and increasingly mythological image of the biologically linked nuclear family as normative. If the emphasis on the blood-tied nuclear family persists, it is likely that a preference will develop for technologies that preserve the genetic links of parents and offspring wherever possible. This emphasis could result in the use of more expensive and invasive methods over simpler, less costly procedures. For example, in the case of a male with a low sperm count, IVF or the micromanipulation of sperm may be used instead of DI to preserve the genetic link, and when donor gametes are employed they will probably be used on an anonymous basis. The issues are complex and volatile; the consequences are unknown...

EUGENICS

The final area of concern is the issue of eugenics, the practice of selective breeding intended to 'perfect' the human species. It is generally distinguished by two different methods: positive eugenics and negative eugenics. Positive eugenics is the attempt to increase the number of children born with 'good' characteristics; negative eugenics is the attempt to reduce the number of children born with 'bad' characteristics. An obvious problem arises in deciding what is valued as good or bad, and who is to make these decisions.

At first glance, negative eugenics would seem to be a worthwhile project. Increasingly, genetic screening can detect carriers of diseases such as Huntington's chorea, muscular dystrophy, and cystic fibrosis. Decreasing the incidence of these agonizing diseases would seem social advantageous; however, grey areas abound. Activists in the rights for the disabled movement have pointed out that screening or aborting for 'defects' further devalues individuals considered by society to be 'defective.'[31] One particularly contentious area is the use of prenatal diagnostic techniques such as ultrasound, chronic biopsy, or amniocentesis to identify the sex of a foetus, followed by an abortion if the sex does not accord with parental preference. Viola Roggencamp documents the incidence of this phenomenon in India, where female foetuses are overwhelmingly aborted.[32] Closer to home, a U.S. physician has set up a highly controversial clinic in Vancouver for exactly these purposes.[33]

Although the extent of this practice is unknown in Western industrialized countries, we can speculate that wherever males are valued more highly than females, female foetuses would be aborted more frequently. Research on parental sex preferences overwhelmingly indicates a preference for male over female offspring, a view held more frequently by men than women, and particularly in relation to first-borns.[34] The desire for a child of a particular sex might in itself be sexist and could potentially institutionalize sexism at a new level because, for example, first-borns are known to be high achievers. Other concerns include alterations in the sex ratio, with fewer females born than males. The consequences of this possibility can only be speculated about and include feminist concerns about gynocide.[35]

Preconception sex-selection techniques are an example of 'positive' eugenics. These are less invasive methods than postconception techniques and usually involve theories about the timing of intercourse with ovulation or the separation of X- and Y-bearing spermatozoa.[36] What was once the substance of folklore is increasingly the subject of scientific study. A U.S. company has marketed a package called 'GenderChoice,' available over the counter in drugstores, which the manufacturer claims has a 85 per cent success rate. The product relies on the position of sexual intercourse and the proximity of conception to a woman's ovulation time to predict the sex of a child.

The most extreme example of positive eugenics is the existence in the United States of a Nobel Prize Winner sperm bank from which women or couples of 'superior' intellectual capacities can order sperm. Contractual mothers and gamete donors may be chosen for socially valued traits perceived as genetically inherited. The underlying assumption is that genetics are the key factors in determining personality traits or capacities such as intelligence, athletic abilities, or musical talents. Australian IVF physicians are already claiming that children conceived through IVF are superior to those conceived 'normally.'[37] Statements such as these ignore the obvious influence of environment, including the particular treatment and care these very much wanted children most likely receive from their parents.

The twentieth century has seen the rise of experts advising women how to rear perfect children.[38] Assisted reproduction technologies provide the opportunity for a different level of 'quality control' in the parenting process. Similarly, prenatal diagnostic techniques provide information about a foetus previously unavailable before birth. On the basis of this knowledge a woman in her fifth month of pregnancy may have to choose whether to have an abortion or carry to term and give birth to a child she knows will be disabled—in a society that devalues the 'imperfect.' This instance of choice posed by the new reproductive technologies is a burden carried largely by individual women.

The commercialization of reproductive capacities is inextricably linked to eugenic issues. Through commercialization, the child becomes a commodity, the recipient parents become consumers, and gamete donors and contractual mothers become suppliers. Damaged or defective 'products'— babies who are not 'perfect'—will likely be unacceptable to the consumer. In a preconception contract in 1981, a handicapped child was rejected by both the contracting (presumably) biological father and by the contractual mother. Eventually, a paternity test proved the contractual mother's husband to be the biological father (this destroyed any validity the contract might have had) and the contractual mother and her husband agreed to keep the child. Other problematic instances are bound to arise in the future.

Social policy already lags far behind these rapidly developing medical advances. As the technologies become more sophisticated, the social problems they pose can become more complex—although, in some instances, advances do eliminate earlier difficulties.[39] Medical control over these technologies is already well established and is solidified by recommendations in government reports. Because it is unlikely that a technology will be withdrawn once it has been introduced, all of the technologies are probably here to stay, at least until further technological developments replace them. In cultivating a critical approach to new reproductive technologies, we must consider the point that already scarce health resources are utilized to develop these technologies. As a result it appears that fewer health resources are being channelled into research concerning the causes of infertility.

As with any new social process or technology, we are granted an opportunity, through analysing these technologies, to rethink and reorganize some of our most deeply embedded assumptions. Consequently, the alterations in our traditional assumptions about parenting facilitated by assisted reproduction may have a hidden blessing. They have the potential to make us reflect on, and enhance our understanding of, the meaning and task of parenting. Over the generations parenting has, after all, been one of the principal influences in the reproduction of gender relations.

NOTES

1 *Ultrasound* involves the use of high-frequency sound waves to produce an image of the foetus (or other body parts) on a video screen. Increasingly, particularly in urban areas, it is used routinely in prenatal care and presumed to be safe, although no long-term follow-up studies have been undertaken. *Amniocentesis* is a prenatal diagnostic technique used to detect certain chromosomal abnormalities (such as Down's syndrome). A needle is inserted into the abdomen of a pregnant woman to extract a sample of the amniotic fluid. Amniocentesis, which cannot be used until the second trimester of pregnancy, is becoming a standard practice for women over the age of thirty-five. It can also be used to detect the sex of the foetus. *Chorionic villi sampling* (CVS), or chronic biopsy, is a newer, still experimental method of prenatal diagnosis to detect foetal abnormalities; it can also be used to detect the sex of the foetus. A sample of foetal cells is removed through the pregnant woman's cervix. CVS can be performed in the first trimester of pregnancy and the results are obtainable more quickly than with amniocentesis. *Foetal monitoring* is a method of measuring the foetal heartbeat during pregnancy or labour. *Foetal surgery* is a form of microsurgery to correct foetal defects within the womb.

2 Ruth Hubbard, "The Fetus as Patient," *MS*, October 1982.

3 *See:* Angus McLaren and Arlene Tigar McLaren, *The Bedroom and the State: The Changing Practices and Politics of Contraception and Abortion in Canada, 1880–1980* (Toronto: McClelland and Stewart, 1986) for a historical view of the politics of contraception and abortion in Canada.

4 See, for example, Jan Rehner, *Infertility: Old Myths New Meanings* (Toronto: The Second Story Press, 1989).

5 Barbara Menning, "In Defense of In Vitro Fertilization," in Helen B. Holmes, Betty B. Hoskins, and Michael Gross, eds., *The Custom-Made Child?* (New Jersey: Humana Press, 1981), 263–267.

6   For example, in the "Baby M" trial in 1987 the counsel for a surrogate mother attempted to reassert her custody rights on the basis that the contracting mother was avoiding pregnancy for minor or convenience concerns.

7   Furthermore, the causes of infertility may be socially rooted to some extent in occupational health hazards, environmental pollution, food additives, and the use of specific drugs such as DES and devices such as I.U.D.s.

8   A vasectomy is a simple medical procedure in which the vas deferens is cut so that sperm cannot mix with seminal fluid. It can be done in a doctor's office with a local anesthetic. Tubal ligations are more complex procedures (there are several methods) in which the fallopian tubes are blocked or cut so that the sperm and egg cannot join. Usually a general anaesthetic is employed.

9   For further information on self-insemination *see:* Nancy Adamson, "Self-Insemination," *Healthsharing* 6, no. 4 (1985), 8–9; Francie Hornstein, "Children By Donor Insemination: A New Choice for Lesbians," in Rita Arditti, Renate Duelli Klein, and Shelley Minden, eds., *Test-Tube Women: What Future for Motherhood?* (London: Routledge & Kegan Paul, 1984), 382–390; Gillian E. Hanscombe and Jackie Forster, *Rocking the Cradle* (London: Peter Owen, 1981); Cheri Pies, *Considering Parenthood: A Workbook for Lesbians* (San Francisco: Spinster's Ink, 1985); Susan Robinson and H.F. Pizer, *Having a Baby Without a Man* (New York: Simon & Schuster, 1985); Joy Schulenberg, *Gay Parenting* (Garden City, N.J.: Anchor Press, 1985); Kathleen Lahey, "Alternative Insemination: Facing the Conceivable Options," *Broadside* 8, no. 1 (1986), 8–10.

10   Kathleen Lahey, "Reproduction, Male Technology and 'Lifestyle' Conflicts: The Lesbian Challenge," paper presented at the Sixth National Biennial Conference of the National Association of Women and the Law, February 1985.

11   *See:* Menning, "In Defense of In Vitro Fertilization," for a description of treatments for infertility that are utilized before artificial insemination is attempted.

12   A.T. Gregoire and Robert C. Mayer, "The Impregnators," *Fertility and Sterility* 16, no. I (1965), 130–134.

13   Office of Technology Assessment (OTA), Congress of the United States, *Artificial Insemination: Practice in the United States.* (Washington: U.S. Government, 1988).

14   Elizabeth Noble, *Having Your Baby by Donor Insemination* (Boston: Houghton Miffin, 1987).

15   Rona Achilles, "The Social Meaning of Biological Ties: A Study of Participants in Artificial Insemination by Donor," Ph.D. dissertation, University of Toronto, 1986.

16   George Annas, "Fathers Anonymous: Beyond the Best Interests of the Sperm Donor," *Child Welfare* 60, no. 3 (1981), 161–174.

17   Richard Titmuss, *The Gift Relationship* (London: Allen & Unwin, 1970).

18   OTA, *Artificial Insemination Practice.*

19   Robert Matas, "Court Awards $883,000 to HIV-infected Women," *The Globe and Mail,* November 21, 1991, A.I.

20   Ontario Law Reform Commission, *Report on Human Artificial Reproduction and Related Matters,* (1985), 103. The Commission was requested by Attorney General

Roy McMurtry to "inquire into and consider the legal issues relating to the practice of human artificial insemination, including 'surrogate mothering' and transplantation of fertilized ova to a third party...[and] report on the range of alternatives for resolution of any legal issues that may be identified." The legal issues suggested in the terms of reference for the report included: "(1) The legal status and legal rights of the child and the safeguards for protecting the best interests of the child. (2) The legal rights and legal duties of each biological parent. (3) The legal rights and legal duties of the spouse, if any, of each biological parent. (4) The nature and enforceability of agreements relating to artificial insemination and other related practices. (5) The nature and enforceability of agreements respecting the custody of the child. (6) The legal rights and responsibilities of medical and other personnel involved in performing artificial insemination and other related practices. (7) The legal procedures for establishing and recognizing the biological parentage of the children born as a result of these practices. (8) The applicability of present custody and adoption laws in such cases. (9) The availability of information to identify the child and the parties involved. (10) Such medical and related evidence as may have a bearing on the legal issues raised in these cases."

21 Anecdotal evidence suggests that women bore children for other women long before the practice became organized and a profit-making enterprise for lawyers and physicians.

22 Office of Technology Assessment (OTA), Congress of the United States, *Infertility: Medical and Social Choices* (Washington: Government of the United States, 1988).

23 A. A. Yuzpe, *et al.*, "Rates and Outcome of Pregnancies Achieved in First Four Years of an In Vitro Fertilization Program," *Canadian Medical Association Journal* 140 (1989), 167–172. Cited by H. Bryant, *The Infertility Dilemma* (Ottawa: The Canadian Advisory Council on the Status of Women, 1990), 13.

24 A. Pappert, "Success Rates Quoted by In Vitro Clinics Not What They Seem," *The Globe and Mail*, February 6, 1988, A. 3.

25 Linda S. Williams, "Who Qualifies for In Vitro Fertilization? A Sociological Examination of the Stated Admittance Criteria of Three Ontario IVF Programs," paper presented to the Canadian Sociology and Anthropology Association, 1986.

26 A laparoscopy is a surgical procedure requiring a general anesthetic; eggs are suctioned out through a fiberoptic tube.

27 Anne Mullens, *Missed Conceptions* (Toronto: McGraw-Hill Ryerson, 1990), 273.

28 OTA, *Infertility*.

29 Yet to be clarified are the legal rights and responsibilities of all the participants in artificial reproduction. Traditionally, rights and responsibilities for offspring are assigned to biological parents unless otherwise legislated, as with, for example, adoption. In the practice of DI, the husband of the DI mother is named on the birth certificate as the father of the child, although the sperm donor is the biological father. Further complications arise from the biological and socially defined differences between maternity and paternity. Is an egg donation, for example, the legal equivalent of a sperm donation? What rights do gamete (egg or sperm) donors have over their genetic material? Who 'owns' the extra

embryos that are not implanted? Can physicians, lawyers, or surrogate organizations be liable for inadequate screening procedures or 'damaged goods'? For a discussion of these and other legal issues, *see:* Ontario Law Reform Commission, *Report on Human Artificial Reproduction.*

30 The procedure for an egg donation is much more medically invasive than sperm donation, but it is possible that women simply donate extra eggs removed during the initial phase of IVF. In *The Mother Machine* (New York: Harper & Row, 1985), Gena Corea points out that egg 'donations' might occur unknown to some women during surgery.

31 *See:* Anna Finger, "Claiming Our Bodies: Reproductive Rights and Disabilities," in Arditti, Duelli Klein, and Minden, eds., *Test-Tube Women.*

32 *See:* Jalna Hamner, "Sex Predetermination, Artificial Insemination and the Maintenance of Male-Dominated Culture," in Helen Roberts, ed., *Women, Health and Reproduction* (London: Routledge & Kegan Paul, 1984).

33 Kathleen Kenna, "Couples Wanting Only Boys Flock to MD for Gender Test," *Toronto Star,* December 10, 1990, B.I, B. 3.

34 Nancy Williamson, *Sons or Daughters? A Cross-Cultural Study of Parental Preferences* (Beverly Hills, Cal.: Sage Publications, 1976); Nancy Williamson, "Sex Preferences, Sex Control, and the Status of Women," *Signs: A Journal of Women in Cultural and Society* I, no. 4 (1976), 847–862; Nancy Williamson, "Parental Preference and Sex Control," *Population Bulletin* 33, no. I (1978).

35 *See:* Neil G. Bennett, ed., *Sex Selection of Children* (New York: Academic Press, 1983).

36 *See:* Hammer, "Sex Predetermination," for a more complete discussion of these methods.

37 Fiona Whitlock, "Test-tube Babies are Smarter and Stronger," *The Australian,* May 17, 1984.

38 Barbara Ehrenreich and Deirdre English, *For Her Own Good: 150 Years of the Experts' Advice to Women* (New York: Anchor Books, 1978).

39 As in the example of egg freezing, which will eliminate the more problematic practice of freezing embryos but will create its own problems.

26
Fatherhood and Social Change

Ralph LaRossa

The consensus of opinion in American society is that something has happened to American fathers. Long considered minor players in the affairs of their children, today's fathers often are depicted as major parental figures, people who are expected to—people who presumably want to—*be there* when their kids need them. "Unlike their own fathers or grandfathers," many are prone to say.

But, despite all the attention that the so-called "new fathers" have been receiving lately, only a few scholars have systematically conceptualized the changing father hypothesis, and no one to date has marshalled the historical evidence needed to adequately test the hypothesis (Demos, 1982; Hanson & Bozett, 1985; Hanson & Bozett, 1987; Lamb, 1987; Lewis, 1986; Lewis & O'Brien, 1987; McKee & O'Brien, 1982; Pleck, 1987; Rotundo, 1985)....

THE ASYNCHRONY BETWEEN THE CULTURE AND CONDUCT OF FATHERHOOD

The institution of fatherhood includes two related but still distinct elements. There is the *culture of fatherhood* (specifically the shared norms, values, and beliefs surrounding men's parenting), and there is the *conduct of fatherhood* (what fathers do, their parental behaviors). The distinction between culture and conduct is worth noting because although it is often assumed that the culture and conduct of a society are in sync, the fact is that many times the two are not synchronized at all. Some people make a habit of deliberately operating outside the rules, and others do wrong because they do not know any better (e.g., my 4-year-old son). And in a rapidly changing society like ours, countervailing forces can result in changes in culture but not in conduct, and vice-versa.

The distinction between culture and conduct is especially relevant when trying to assess whether fatherhood has changed because the available evidence on the history of fatherhood suggests that *the culture of fatherhood has changed more rapidly than the conduct.* For example, E. Anthony Rotundo

(1985) argues that since 1970 a new style of American fatherhood has emerged, namely "Androgynous Fatherhood." In the androgynous scheme,

> *A good father is an active participant in the details of day-to-day child care. He involves himself in a more expressive and intimate way with his children, and he plays a larger part in the socialization process that his male forebears had long since abandoned to their wives. [p. 17]*

Rotundo (1985) is describing not what fathers lately have been doing but what some people would *like* fathers to *begin* doing. Later on he says that the new style is primarily a middle-class phenomenon and that "even within the upper-middle class...there are probably far more men who still practice the traditional style of fathering than the new style." He also surmises that "there are more *women* who *advocate* 'Androgynous Fatherhood' than there are *men* who *practice* it" (p. 20). Similarly, Joseph Pleck (1987) writes about the history of fatherhood in the United States and contends that there have been three phases through which modern fatherhood has passed. From the early 19th to mid-20th centuries there was the father as distant breadwinner. Then, from 1940 to 1965 there was the father as sex role model. Finally, since around 1966 there has emerged the father as nurturer. Pleck's "new[est] father," like Rotundo's "androgynous father" is an involved father. He is also, however, more imagined than real. As Pleck acknowledges from the beginning, his analysis is a history of the "dominant *images* of fatherhood." [emphasis added] (p. 84)

Rotundo and Peck are clear about the fact that they are focusing on the culture of fatherhood, and they are careful about drawing inferences about the conduct of fatherhood from their data. Others, however, have not been as careful. John Mogey, for example, back in 1957, appears to have mistaken cultural for behavioral changes when, in talking about the emerging role of men in the family, he asserts that the "newer" father's "behavior is best described as participation, the reintegration of fathers into the conspicuous consumption as well as the child rearing styles of family life" (Mogey, as cited in Lewis, 1986, p. 6). Ten years later, Margaret Mead (1967), too, extolled the arrival of the new father:

> *We are evolving a new style of fatherhood, in which young fathers share very fully with mothers in the care of babies and little children. In this respect American men differ very much from their own grand-fathers and are coming to resemble much more closely men in primitive societies. [p. 36]*

And recently there appeared in my Sunday newspaper the comment that "[Modern men] know more about the importance of parenting. They're aware of the role and how they are doing it. Fifty years ago, fathers didn't think much about what kind of job they were doing' (Harte, 1987, p. 4G).

Neither Mogey nor Mead nor the newspaper presented any evidence to support their views. One can only guess that they were reporting what they assumed—perhaps hoped—was true generally (i.e., true not only for small "pockets" of fathers here and there), for, as was mentioned before, no one to date has carried out the kind of historical study needed to test the changing father hypothesis. If, however, the professional and lay public took seriously the thesis that fathers have changed and if others writing for professional and popular publications have echoed a similar theme, then one can easily understand how the notion that today's fathers are "new" could become implanted in people's minds. Indeed, there is a good chance that this is exactly what has happened. That is to say, Rotundo (1985) and Pleck (1987) probably are correct: there has been a shift in fatherhood—the way fathers and mothers think and feel about men as parents. But what separates a lot of fathers and mothers from Rotundo and Pleck is that, on some level of consciousness, the fathers and mothers also believe (incorrectly) that there has been a proportionate shift in the conduct of fatherhood.

I say on "some" level of consciousness because, on "another" level of consciousness, today's fathers and mothers *do* know that the conduct of fatherhood has not kept pace with the culture. And I include the word "proportionate" because, while some researchers have argued that there have been changes in paternal behavior since the turn of the century, no scholar has argued that these changes have occurred at the same rate as the ideological shifts that apparently have taken place. These two points are crucial to understanding the consequences of the asynchrony between culture and conduct, and they will soon be discussed in more detail. But first another question: If the behavior of fathers did not alter the ideology of fatherhood, then what did?

The answer is that the culture of fatherhood changed primarily in response to the shifts in the conduct of motherhood. In the wake of declines in the birth rates and increases in the percentage of mothers in the labor force, the culture of motherhood changed, such that it is now more socially acceptable for women to combine motherhood with employment outside the home (Margolis, 1984). The more it became apparent that today's mothers were less involved with their children, on a day-to-day basis, than were their own mothers or grandmothers, the more important it became to ask the question: Who's minding the kids? Not appreciating the extent to which substitute parents (day-care centers, etc.) have picked up the slack for mothers, many people (scholars as well as the lay public) assumed that fathers must be doing a lot more than before and changed their beliefs to conform to this assumption. In other words, mother-child interaction was erroneously used as a "template" to measure father-child interaction (Day & Mackey, 1986).

Generally speaking, culture follows conduct rather than vice-versa (Stokes & Hewitt, 1976). Thus, the fact that the culture of fatherhood has changed more rapidly than the conduct of fatherhood would seem to represent an exception to the rule. However, it may not be an exception at all. What may be happening is that culture *is* following conduct, but not in a way we normally think it does. Given the importance that American society places on mothers as parents, it is conceivable that the conduct of fatherhood is accepting the culture of fatherhood, but as a stabilizer rather than a destabilizer. As noted, research suggests that androgynous fatherhood as an ideal has failed to become widespread. One reason for this may be that the conduct of fatherhood is arresting whatever "modernizing" effect the conduct of motherhood is having. Put differently, the conduct of fatherhood and the conduct of motherhood may, on a societal level, be exerting contradictory influences on the culture of fatherhood.

THE CONDUCT OF FATHERHOOD VERSUS THE CONDUCT OF MOTHERHOOD

Contending that the conduct of fatherhood has changed very little over the course of the 20th century flies in the face of what many of us see every day: dads pushing strollers, changing diapers, playing in the park with their kids. Also, what about the men who publicly proclaim that they have made a conscientious effort to be more involved with their children than their own fathers were with them?

What can not be forgotten is that appearances and proclamations (both to others and ourselves) can be deceiving: everything hinges on how we conceptualize and measure parental conduct. Michael Lamb (1987) notes that scholars generally have been ambiguous about what they mean by parental "involvement," with the result that it is difficult to compare one study with the next, and he maintains that if we ever hope to determine whether or not fathers have changed, we must arrive at a definition that is both conceptually clear and comprehensive. The definition which he thinks should be used is one that separates parental involvement into three components: engagement, accessibility, and responsibility. *Engagement* is time spent in one-on-one interaction with a child (whether feeding, helping with homework, or playing catch in the backyard). *Accessibility* is a less intense degree of interaction and is the kind of involvement whereby the parent is doing one thing (cooking, watching television) but is ready or available to do another (respond to the child, if the need arises). *Responsibility* has to do with who is accountable for the child's welfare and care. Responsibility includes things like making sure that the child has clothes to wear and keeping track of when the child has to go to the pediatrician.

Reviewing studies that allow comparisons to be made between contemporary fathers' involvement with children and contemporary mothers' involvement with children, Lamb (1987) estimates that in two-parent families in which mothers are unemployed, fathers spent about one fifth to one quarter as much time as mothers do in an engagement status and about a third as much time as mothers do just being accessible to their children. In two-parent families with employed mothers, fathers spend about 33% as much time as mothers do in an engagement status and 65% as much time becoming accessible. As far as responsibility is concerned, mothers appear to carry over 90% of the load, regardless of whether they are employed or not. Lamb also notes that observational and survey data indicate that the behavioral styles of fathers and mothers differ. Mother-child interaction is dominated by caretaking whereas father-child interaction is dominated by play.

> *Mothers actually play with their children more than fathers do but, as a proportion of the total amount of child-parent interaction, play is a much more prominent component of father-child interaction, whereas caretaking is more salient with mothers. [p. 10]*

In looking for trends, Lamb relies on one of the few studies which allows historical comparisons to be made—a 1975 national survey that was repeated in 1981 (Juster, 1985). No data apparently were collected on parents' accessibility or responsibility levels, but between 1975 and 1981, among men and women aged 18 to 44, there was a 26% increase in fathers' engagement levels and a 7% increase in mothers'. Despite these shifts, paternal engagement was only about one third that of mothers, increasing from 29% in 1975 to 34% in 1981 (Lamb, 1987).

While there is nothing intrinsically wrong with talking about percentage changes, one should be careful about relying on them and them alone. If, for example, one examines the tables from which Lamb drew his conclusions (Juster, 1985), one finds that the number of hours per week that the fathers spent in child care was 2.29 hours in 1975, compared to 2.88 hours in 1981, which is an increase of about 35 minutes per week or 5 minutes per day. The mothers in the sample, on the other hand, spent 7.96 hours per week in child care in 1975, compared to 8.54 hours per week in child care in 1981, which also is an increase of about 35 minutes per week or 5 minutes per day. Thus, in absolute terms, fathers and mothers increased their child care by the same amount.

Bear in mind also that we are still talking about only *one* component of parental involvement, namely engagement. The two national surveys provide little, if any, information about changes in the accessibility and responsibility levels of fathers and mothers. Perhaps I am being overly cautious, but I cannot help but feel that until we gather historical data which would allow us to compare all three components of fatherhood, we should temper our excitement about surveys which suggest changes in the conduct of fatherhood over time. (For a tightly reasoned alternative viewpoint, see Pleck, 1985.)....

What about dads who are seen interacting with their kids in public (see Mackey & Day, 1979)? A thoughtful answer to this question also must address how we conceptualize and measure paternal involvement. Does the paternal engagement level of fathers in public square with the paternal engagement level of fathers in private, or are we getting an inflated view of fatherhood from public displays? If we took the time to scrutinize the behavior of fathers and mothers in public would we find that, upon closer examination, the division of child care is still fairly traditional? When a family with small children goes out to eat, for example, who in the family—mom or dad—is more accessible to the children; that is to say, whose dinner is more likely to be interrupted by the constant demands to "put ketchup on my hamburger, pour my soda, cut my meat"? And how can one look at a family in public and measure who is responsible for the children? How do we know, for instance, who decides whether the kids need clothes; indeed, how do we know who is familiar with the kids' sizes, color preferences, and tolerance levels for trying on clothes? The same applies to studies of parental involvement in laboratory settings (see Parke, 1981). What can a study of father-child interaction in, say, a hospital nursery tell us about father-child interaction in general? The fact that fathers are making their presence known in maternity wards certainly is not sufficient to suggest that the overall conduct of fathers has changed in any significant way. Finally, the fact that fathers can be seen in public with their children may not be as important as the question, How much time do fathers spend *alone* with their children? One recent study found that mothers of young children spent an average of 44.45 hours per week in total child-interaction time (which goes beyond engagement), while fathers spent an average of 29.48 hours per week, a 1.5 to 1 difference. If one looked, however, at time spent alone with children, one discovered that 19.56 hours of mothers' child-interaction time, compared with 5.48 hours of fathers' child-interaction, was solo time, a 3.6 to 1 difference. Moreover, while fathers' total interaction time was positively affected by the number of hours their wives worked, fathers' solo time was not affected at all (Barnett & Baruch, 1987).

As for the public proclamations, almost all the books and articles which tout the arrival of "new" fatherhood are written not by a cross-section of the population but by upper-middle class professionals. Kort and Friedland's (1986) edited book, for instance, has 57 men writing about their pregnancy, birth, and child-rearing experiences. But who are these men? For the most part, they are novelists, educators, sculptors, real estate investors, radio commentators, newspaper editors, publishers, physicians, performers, psychologists, social workers, and attorneys. Not exactly a representative sample. As Rotundo (1985) notes, androgynous fatherhood as an ideal has caught the attention of the upper-middle class more than any other group, but that even in this group, words seem to speak louder than actions.

While the perception of fathers in public and the Kort and Friedland (1986) book may not accurately represent what fathers in general are *doing*, they can most certainly have an effect on what people *think* fathers are doing and should be doing. Which brings us back to the question, What are the consequences that have resulted from the apparent disparity between beliefs and actuality?

THE CONSEQUENCES OF ASYNCHRONOUS SOCIAL CHANGE

....

The Technically Present but Functionally Absent Father

The distinction between engagement and accessibility outlined by Lamb (1987) is similar to the distinction between *primary time* and *secondary time* in our study of the transition to parenthood (LaRossa & LaRossa, 1981). The social organization of a family with children, especially young children, parallels the social organization of a hospital in that both are *continuous coverage social systems* (Zerubavel, 1979). Both are set up to provide direct care to someone (be it children or patients) on a round-the-clock or continuous basis. And both the family and the hospital, in order to give caregivers a break every now and then, will operate according to some formal or informal schedule such that some person or persons will be "primarily" involved with the children or patients (on duty) while others will be "secondarily" involved (on call or accessible).

Like Lamb, we also found that the fathers' levels of engagement, accessibility, and responsibility were only a fraction of the mothers', and that fathers tended to spend a greater part of their care giving time playing with their children. Moreover, we found that the kinds of play that fathers were likely to be involved in were the kinds of activities that could be carried out at a secondary (semi-involved) level of attention, which is to say that it was not unusual for fathers to be primarily involved in watching television or doing household chores while only secondarily playing with their children.

When asked why they wanted to be with their children, the fathers often would answer along the lines that a father has to "put in some time with his kids" (LaRossa, 1983, pp. 585). Like prisoners who "do time" in prison, many fathers see themselves as "doing time" with their children. If, on some level of consciousness, fathers have internalized the idea that they should be more involved with their children, but on another level of consciousness they do not find the idea all that attractive, one would expect the emergence of a hybrid style; the technically present but functionally absent father (cf. Feldman & Feldman, 1975, cited in Pleck, 1983).

The technically present but functionally absent father manifests himself in a variety of ways. One father in our study prided himself on the fact that he and his wife cared for their new baby on an alternating basis, with him "covering" the mornings and his wife "covering" the afternoons. "We could change roles in a night," he said; "it wouldn't affect us." But when this father was asked to describe a typical morning spent alone with his infant son, he gave the distinct impression that he saw fatherhood as a *job* and that while he was "there" in body, he was someplace else in spirit.

I have the baby to be in charge of, [which has] really been no problem for me at all. But that's because we worked out a schedule where he sleeps a pretty good amount of that time…I generally sort of have to be with him in the sense of paying attention to his crying or dirty diapers or something like that for anywhere between 30 to 45 minutes, sometimes an hour, depending. But usually I can have two hours of my own to count on each morning to do my own work, so it's no problem. That's just the breaks that go with it.

Another example: Recently, there appeared an advertisement for one of those mini televisions, the kind you can carry around in your pocket. Besides promoting television as an electronic marvel, the man who was doing the selling also lauded how his mini-TV had changed his life: "Now when I go to my son's track meets, I can keep up with other ball games" (Kaplan, 1987, p. 32a). The question is: Is this father going to the track meets to see his son race, or is he going simply to get "credit" from his son for being in the stands? One more example: A newspaper story about a father jogging around Golden State Park in San Francisco who is so immersed in his running that he fails to notice his 3-year-old daughter—whom he apparently had brought with him—crying "Daddy, Daddy" along the side of the running track. When he finally notices her, he stops only long enough to tell his daughter that it is not his job to watch her, but her job to watch for him (Gustatis, 1982).

What will be the impact of the mixed messages that these children—and perhaps countless others—are getting from their fathers? Research capable of measuring and assessing the complexity of these encounters is needed to adequately answer this question (Pleck, 1983).

Marital Conflict in Childbearing and Child-Rearing Families

Because our study was longitudinal, we were able to trace changes over time; and we found that from the third, to the sixth, to the nine month postpartum, couples became more traditional, with fathers doing proportionately less child care (LaRossa & LaRossa, 1981). It was this *traditionalization process* that provided us with a close-up view of what happens when the bubble bursts; that is, what happens when the romanticized version of dad's involvement starts to break down.

One father, first interviewed around the third month after his daughter's birth, wanted to communicate that he was not going to be an absentee father like some of his friends were:

I've got a good friend of mine, he's the ultimate male chauvinist pig. He will not change a diaper… [But] I share in changing the diapers, and rocking the baby, and in doing those kinds of things…I love babies.

During the sixth month interview, however, it was revealed that he indeed had become very much the absentee father. In fact, almost every evening since the first interview he had left the house after dinner to play basketball, or participate in an amateur theater group, or sing in the local choir.

Since what he was doing contradicted what he said he would do, he was asked by his wife to "account" for his behavior. *Accounts* are demanded of social actors whose behavior is thought to be out of line. By submitting an account, which in common parlance generally takes the form of an excuse or justification, and having it honored or accepted by the offended party, a person who stands accused can manage to create or salvage a favorable impression (Scott & Lyman, 1968). Because the wife did not honor the accounts that her husband offered, the father was put in the position of either admitting he was wrong (i.e., apologizing) or coming up with more accounts. He chose the latter, and in due course offered no fewer than 20 different explanations for his conduct, to include "I help out more than most husbands do" and "I'm not good at taking care of the baby." At one dramatic point during the second interview, the husband and wife got into a verbal argument over how much of the husband's contribution to child care was "fact" and how much was "fancy." (He, with his head: "I *know* I was [around a lot]." She, with her heart: "[To me] it just doesn't *feel* like he was.")

This couple illustrates what may be happening in many homes as a result of the asynchrony between the culture and conduct of fatherhood. In the past, when (as best we can tell) both the culture and conduct of fatherhood were more or less traditional, fathers may not have been asked to account for their low paternal involvement. If the culture said that fathers should not be involved with their children, then fathers were perceived as doing what they should be doing. No need for an explanation. Today, however, the culture and conduct of fatherhood appear to be out of sync. The culture has moved toward (not to) androgyny much more rapidly than the conduct. On some level of consciousness, fathers and mothers believe that the behavior of fathers will measure up to the myth. Usually, this is early in the parental game, before or just after the birth of the first child. In time, however, reality sets in, and on another level of consciousness it becomes apparent that mom is doing more than planned because dad is doing less than planned. The wife challenges the legitimacy of the (more unequal than she had foreseen) division of child care, demanding an explanation from her husband, which may or may not be offered, and if offered may or may not be honored, and so on.

In short, one would expect more conflict in marriage today centered around the legitimacy of the division of child care than, say, 40 years ago because of the shift in the culture of fatherhood that has occurred during this time. Some may say, "Great, with more conflict there will be needed change." And their point is valid. But what must be kept in mind is that conflict also can escalate and destroy. Given that at least one recent study has reported that the most likely conflict to lead a couple to blows is conflict over children (Straus, Gelles, & Steinmetz, 1980), family researchers and practitioners would be well-advised to pay attention to the possibility that violence during the transition to parenthood may be one negative consequence of asynchronous social change.

Fathers and Guilt

[M]any men today experience [feelings of] ambivalence over their performance as fathers.

To feel "ambivalent" about something is to feel alternately good and bad about it. The plethora of autobiographical books and articles written by fathers in the past few years conveys the impression that men do feel and, perhaps more importantly, should feel good about their performance as fathers. A lot of men do seem to be proud of their performance, what with all the references to "new" fatherhood and the like. At the same time, however, men are being almost constantly told—and can see for themselves, if they look close enough—that their behavior does not square with the ideal, which means that they are being reminded on a regular basis that they are *failing* as fathers. Failing not when compared with their own fathers or grandfathers perhaps, but failing when compared with the image of fatherhood which has become part of our culture and which they, on some level of consciousness, believe in.

This is not to suggest that in the past men were totally at ease with their performance as fathers, that they had no doubts about whether they were acting "correctly." For one thing, such an assertion would belie the fact that role playing is, to a large degree, improvisational, that in everyday life (vs. the theater) scripts almost always are ill defined and open to a variety of interpretations (Blumer, 1969). Perhaps more importantly, asserting that men in the past were totally at ease with their performance as fathers would ignore the fact that, contrary to what many think, some of our fathers and grandfathers were ambivalent about the kind of job they were doing. In a study just begun on the history of fatherhood in America, I have come across several cases of men in the early 1900s expressing concern over the quality of their parental involvement. In 1925, for example, one father wrote to a psychologist to ask whether he was *too involved* with his 2-year-old son. Apparently, he had taught the boy both the alphabet and how to count, and he now wondered whether he had forced his son to learn too much too soon (LaRossa, 1988).

So, what *is* the difference between then and now? I would say it is a difference in degree not kind. I would hypothesize that, given the asynchrony between the culture and conduct of fatherhood, the number of fathers who feel ambivalent and, to a certain extent, guilty about their performance as fathers has increased over the past three generations. I would also hypothesize that, given it is the middle class which has been primarily responsible for the changes in the culture of fatherhood, it is the middle-class fathers who are likely to feel the most ambivalent and suffer from the most guilt.

There is a certain amount of irony in the proposition that middle-class men are the ones who are the most likely to experience ambivalence and guilt, in that middle-class men are also the ones who seem to be trying the hardest to act according to the emerging ideal. As noted, the testimonials from the so-called androgynous fathers almost invariably are written by middle-class professionals. But it is precisely because these middle-class professionals are trying to conform to the higher standards that one would expect that they would experience the most ambivalence and guilt. Like athletes training for the Olympics, androgynous-striving fathers often are consumed with how they are doing as fathers and how they can do better. For example:

> *Should I play golf today, or should I spend more time playing with Scott and Julie? Should I stay late in the office to catch up or should I leave early to go home and have dinner with the children? There is an endless supply of these dilemmas each day. (Belsky, 1986, p. 64)*

Some may argue that the parental anxiety that men are beginning to experience is all for the better, that they now may start feeling bad enough about their performance to really change. This argument does have merit. Yes, one positive outcome of asynchronous social change is that ultimately men may become not only more involved with their children but also more sensitive to what it is like to be a mother. After all, for a long time women have worried about *their* performance as parents. It should not be forgotten, however, that the guilt which many women experience as mothers (and which has been the subject of numerous novels, plays, and films) has not always been healthy for mothers—or families. In sum, when it comes to parenthood, today it would appear that both men and women can be victims as well as benefactors of society's ideals.

CONCLUSION

Fatherhood is different today than it was in prior times but, for the most part, the changes that have occurred are centered in the culture rather than in the conduct of fatherhood. Whatever changes have taken place in the behavior of fathers, on the basis of what we know now, seem to be minimal at best. Also, the behavioral changes have largely occurred within a single group—the middle class.

The consequences of the asynchrony between the (comparatively speaking) "modern" culture of fatherhood and the "less modern" or "traditional" conduct of fatherhood are (a) the emergence of the technically present but functionally absent father, (b) an increase in marital conflict in childbearing and child-rearing families and (c) a greater number of fathers, especially in the middle class, who feel ambivalent and guilty about their performance as fathers.

A number of recommendations seem to be in order. First, more people need to be made aware of the fact that the division of child care in America has not significantly changed, that—despite the beliefs that fathers are a lot more involved with their children—mothers remain, far and away, the primary child caregivers. The reason for publicizing this fact is that if our beliefs represent what we want (i.e., more involved fathers) and we mistakenly assume that what we want is what we have, our complacency will only serve to perpetuate the culture-conduct disjunction. Thus, scholars and representatives of the media must commit themselves to presenting a balanced picture of "new fatherhood."

Second, and in line with the above, men must be held responsible for their actions. In our study of the transition to parenthood, we found that the language that couples use to account for men's lack of involvement in infant care does not simply reflect the division of infant care, it constructs that division of infant care. In other words, the account employed by new parents to excuse and justify men's paternal role distance serves as a social lubricant in the traditionalization process (LaRossa & LaRossa, 1981). Thus, when men say things like "I'm not good at taking care of the baby" or "I can't be with Junior now, I have to go to the office, go to the store, go to sleep, mow the lawn, pay the bills, and so forth" the question must be raised, are these reasons genuine (i.e., involving insurmountable role conflicts) or are they nothing more than rationalizations used by men to do one thing (not be with their children) but believe another ("I like to be with my children")? If they are rationalizations, then they should not be honored. Not honoring rationalizations "de-legitimates" actions and, in the process, puts the burden of responsibility for the actions squarely on the person who is carrying out the actions. Only when men are forced to seriously examine their commitment to fatherhood (vs. their commitment to jobs and avocations) can we hope to bring about the kinds of changes that will be required to alter the division of child care in this country (LaRossa, 1983).

What kinds of changes are we talking about? Technically present but functionally absent fathers are products of the society in which we live. So also, the traditionalization process during the transition to parenthood and the conflict and guilt it apparently engenders cannot be divorced from the socio-historical reality surrounding us and of which we are a part. All of which means that if we hope to alter the way men relate to their children, we cannot be satisfied with individualistic solutions which see "the problem" as a private, therapeutic matter best solved through consciousness raising groups and the like. Rather, we must approach it as a public issue and be prepared to alter the institutional fabric of American society (cf. Mills, 1959). For example, the man-as-breadwinner model of fatherhood, a model which emerged in the 19th and early 20th centuries and which portrays fathers primarily as breadwinners whose wages make family consumption and security possible, remains dominant today (Pleck, 1987). This model creates structural barriers to men's involvement with their children, in that it legitimates inflexible and highly demanding job schedules which, in turn, increase the conflict between market work and family work (Pleck, 1985). More flex-time jobs would help to relieve this conflict. So would greater tolerance, on the part of employers, of extended paternity leaves (Levine, 1976). I am not suggesting that the only reason that men are not as involved with their children is that their jobs keep them from getting involved. The fact that many women also contend with inflexible and highly demanding job schedules and still are relatively involved with their children would counter such an assertion. Rather, the point is that the level of achievement in market work expected of men in America generally is higher than the level of achievement in market work expected of women and that this socio-historical reality must be entered into any equation which attempts to explain why fathers are not more involved.

When we will begin to see significant changes in the conduct of fatherhood is hard to say. The past generally provides the data to help predict the future. But, as the historian John Demos (1982) once noted, "Fatherhood has a very long history, but virtually no historians" (p. 425). Hence, our ability to make informed predictions about the future of fatherhood is severely limited. Hopefully, as more empirical research—historical and otherwise—on fatherhood is carried out, we will be in a better position to not only see what is coming but to deal with what is at hand.

REFERENCES

Barnett, R. C., & Baruch, G. K. (1987). Determinants of fathers' participation in family work. *Journal of Marriage and the Family.* 49, 29–40.

Belsky, M. R. (1986). Scott's and Julie's Daddy. In C. Kort & R. Friedland (Eds.), *The father's book: Shared experiences* (pp. 63–5). Boston: G. K. Hall.

Benokraitis, N. (1985). Fathers in the dual-earner family. In S. M. H. Hanson & F. W. Bozett (Eds.), *Dimensions of fatherhood* (pp. 243–268). Beverly Hills, CA: Sage Publications.

Berger, M. (1979). Men's new family roles—Some implications for therapists. *Family Coordinator,* 28, 638–646.

Blumer, H. (1969). *Symbolic interactionism: Perspective and method.* Englewood Cliffs, NJ: Prentice Hall.

Caplow, T. with Bahr, H. M., Chadwick, B. A., Hill, R., & Williamson, M. H. (1982). *Middletown families: Fifty years of change and continuity.* Minneapolis: University of Minnesota Press.

Day, R. D., & Mackey, W. C. (1986). The role image of the American father: An examination of a media myth. *Journal of Comparative Family Studies* 17, 371–388.

Demos, J. (1982). The changing faces of fatherhood: A new exploration in American family history. In S. H. Cath, A. R. Gurwitt, & J. M. Ross (Eds.), *Father and child: Developmental and clinical perspectives* (pp. 425–445). Boston: Little, Brown.

Gustatis, R. (1982, August 15). Children sit idle while parents pursue leisure. *Atlanta Journal and Constitution*, pp. 1D, 4D.

Hanson, S. M. H., & Bozett, F. W. (1985). *Dimensions of fatherhood*. Beverly Hills, CA: Sage Publications.

Hanson, S. M. H., & Bozett, F. W. (1987). Fatherhood: A review and resources. *Family Relations*, 36, 333–340.

Harte, S. (1987, June 21). Fathers and sons. Narrowing the generation gap: Atlanta dads reflect a more personal style of parenting. *Atlanta Journal and Constitution.* pp. 4G, 6G.

Juster, F. T. (1985). A note on recent changes in time use. In F. T. Juster & F. P. Stafford (Eds.), *Time, goods, and well-being* (pp. 313–332). Ann Arbor, MI: Institute for Social Research.

Kaplan, D. (1987, Early Summer). The great $39.00" TV catch. *DAK Industries Inc.* p. 32A.

Kort, C., & Friedland, R. (Eds.). (1986). *The fathers' book: Shared experiences.* Boston: G. K. Hall.

Lamb, M. E. (1987). Introduction: The emergent American father. In M. E. Lamb (Ed.), *The father's role: Cross-cultural perspectives* (pp. 3–25). Hillsdale, NJ: Lawrence Erlbaum.

Lamb, M. E., Pleck, J. H., & Levine, J. A. (1987). Effects of increased paternal involvement on fathers and mothers. In C. Lewis & M. O'Brien (Eds.), *Reassessing fatherhood: New observations on fathers and the modern family* (pp. 109–125). Beverly Hills, CA: Sage Publications.

LaRossa, R. (1983). The transition to parenthood and the social reality of time. *Journal of Marriage and the Family*, 45, 579–589.

LaRossa, R. (1988, November). *Toward a social history of fatherhood in America.* Paper presented at the Theory Construction and Research Methodology Workshop, Annual Meeting of National Council of Family Relations, Philadelphia, PA.

LaRossa, R. & LaRossa, M. M. (1981) *Transition to parenthood: How infants change families.* Beverly Hills, CA: Sage Publications.

LeMasters, E. E. (1957). Parenthood as crisis. *Marriage and Family Living*, 19, 352–355.

LeMasters, E. E. & DeFrain, J. (1983). *Parents in contemporary America: A sympathetic view.* (4th ed.). Homewood, IL: Dorsey.

Levine, J. A. (1976). *Who will raise the children?* New York: Bantam.

Lewis, C. (1986). *Becoming a father.* Milton Keynes, England: Open University Press.

Lewis, C., & O'Brien, M. (1987) *Reassessing fatherhood: New observations on fathers and the modern family.* Beverly Hills, CA: Sage Publications.

Mackey, W. C. & Day, R. O. (1979). Some indicators of fathering behaviors in the United States: A cross-cultural examination of adult male-child interaction. *Journal of Marriage and the Family* 41, 287–297.

Margolis, M. L. (1984). *Mothers and such: Views of American women and why they changed.* Berkeley: University of California Press.

McKee, L., & O'Brien, M. (Eds.). (1982). *The father figure,* London: Tavistock.

Mead, M. (1967). Margaret Mead answers: How do middle-class American men compare with men in other cultures you have studied? *Redbook,* 129, 36.

Mills, C.W. (1959). *The sociological imagination.* London: Oxford University Press.

Parke, R. D. (1981). *Fathers.* Cambridge, MA: Harvard University Press.

Pleck, J. H. (1983). Husbands' paid work and family roles: Current research issues. In H. Z.. Lopata & J. H. Pleck (Eds.), *Research in the interweave of social roles, Vol. 3, Families and jobs.* (pp. 251–333). Greenwich, CT: JAI Press.

Pleck, J. H. (1985). *Working wives/ Working husbands.* Beverly Hills, CA: Sage Publications.

Pleck, J. H. (1987). American fathering in historical perspective. In M. S. Kimmel (Ed.), *Changing men: New directions in research on men and masculinity.* (pp. 83–97). Beverly Hills, CA: Sage Publications.

Rotundo, E. A. (1985). American fatherhood: A historical perspective. *American Behavioral Scientist,* 29, 7–25.

Scott, M. B., & Lyman, S. M. (1968). Accounts. *American Sociological Review,* 33, 46–62.

Stokes, R., & Hewitt, J. P. (1976). Aligning actions. *American Sociological Review,* 41, 838–849.

Straus, M., Gelles, R. J., & Steinmetz, S. K. (1980). *Behind closed doors: Violence in the American family.* New York: Anchor/Doubleday.

Zerubavel, E. (1979). *Patterns of time in hospital life: A sociological perspective.* Chicago: University of Chicago Press.

27

In Whose Best Interest?
The Politics of Joint Custody

Janice Drakich

W hen the nuclear family dissolves through separation or divorce, courts of law reconstitute family relationships by awarding the custody of children to mothers, or fathers, or both parents. Custody embraces the sum of parental rights with respect to the physical, moral, and emotional well-being of the child, including personal care and control (Parry, Broder, Schmitt, and Saunders 1986, 101). The granting of these parental rights to both parents—joint custody—is a new practice in Canada and the subject of this paper.

The underlying guiding principle in the award of custody is "the best interests of the child". Sole custody with preference toward the mother has been the predominant form of child custody since the end of the 1920s (Boyd 1987).This custodial arrangement is increasingly being challenged in Canada with arguments that "joint custody" is a better arrangement than sole custody (see Roman and Haddad 1978 for the typical argument; Henderson 1988). Proponents believe that joint custody is in the best interests of children and parents in almost all cases (Henderson, 1988). Opponents argue that joint custody can only be in the best interests of children and parents in a limited number of cases and under specific conditions.

The debate and politics surrounding joint custody will be examined against the historical background of custody determinations and the contemporary political and social climate. The benefits and risks of joint custody will be assessed from a review of the social science and legal literature. A brief history of the trends in Canadian custody determinations will be presented taking into account impinging social-structural and ideological factors. Following the history discussion, the argument challenging sole custody will provide the backdrop for an explanation of what joint custody means, how it works and the answer to the question—in whose best interests is joint custody?

From Janice Drakich, "In Whose Best Interest? The Politics of Joint Custody," in *Family Bonds and Gender Divisions*, edited by Bonnie Fox, pp. 477–497. Toronto: Canadian Scholar's Press, 1988. Reprinted by permission of the publisher.

HISTORY OF CHILD CUSTODY AWARDS IN CANADA

And when they had brought a sword before the king, he said, "Divide the living child in two, and give half to one and half to the other." But the woman whose child was alive, said to the king, "I beseech thee, my lord, give her the child alive and do not kill it." But the other said, "Let it be neither mine or thine, but divide it." (1 Kings 3)

The parable of King Solomon points to the dilemma facing the courts in awarding custody. In contested custody cases, the competing requests of the parents must be balanced against the interests of the child. The current reality of custody options—sole custody or joint custody—is echoed in the biblical mothers' statements.

Unlike King Solomon, Canadian judges have always been guided by statute or case law in their custody determinations. Canada inherited British Common Law and accepted the reasoning of the English courts in awarding custody in the nineteenth century. Under British Common law, men—husbands and fathers—were the absolute and undisputed heads of the household. Both in law and tradition, men had complete and unquestioned authority over their wives and children. In the event of divorce, "the father was considered the parent naturally endowed to have custody of the children" (MacDonald 1986: 10). According to Backhouse (1981: 216), the judicial approach in the early nineteenth century was to treat the "father's rights to custody as virtually absolute."

One of the best known cases illustrating the indisputable right of the father to his children is the English case of *R v De Manneville* in 1804. In this case, the mother petitioned for custody of her eight-month-old baby after leaving her husband because of his cruelty. The judge refused the mother's petition for custody and denied her access or visitation. The father was awarded custody despite the fact that the child was still breast-fed and that the father's cruelty was proven to have caused the marital breakdown. This case clearly demonstrates that fathers had the indisputable right to the "natural possession" of their children. It further suggests that neither the ability to care for the child nor the degree of attachment felt by the father were relevant to the custody determination. The immutability of the father's custodial right can be seen in a 1824 English case. The mother was denied custody of her child "although the father was in prison and his mistress, who provided child care, brought the child to him for visits" (Polikoff 1983: 186).

Mothers had absolutely no rights to their children. Upon divorce, mothers faced the loss of custody and the real possibility that they would never see their children again. Master Sergeant Talfourd, a British barrister, summarized the powerlessness of women in child custody laws in the nineteenth century:

By the laws of England, the custody of all legitimate children from the hour of their birth belongs to the father. If circumstances however urgent should drive the mother from his roof, not only may she be prevented from tending upon the children in the extremity of sickness, but she may be denied the sight of them; and, if she obtain possession of them by whatever means, she may be compelled by writ of habeas corpus to resign them to her husband or to his agents without condition—without hope. (Chesler 1986: 3)

The changing social landscape in the nineteenth century challenged the common-law right of fathers to their children. The industrial revolution and the entrenchment of the separation of work into two spheres—women's work in the home and men's paid work outside of the home—contributed to changes not only in the role of women but also in their image as mothers. Further, the transformation in family relationships to an emphasis on mutual affection and sentimentality gave the family a psychological and emotional dimension within which parents assumed responsibility for their children's emotional and physical well-being (Anderson, 1987). Perceptions of childhood were also changing. Childhood began to be seen as a distinct stage of development during which time children needed constant care, attention, and love (Ariès, 1962, Anderson, 1987). As men left the home to work for wages, women were left with the responsibility for child care (Cook and Mitchinson 1976). Mothers were increasingly seen as central to their children's development.

The gentle erosion of fathers' automatic right to their children in Canada can be traced to the lawyers' arguments and the judge's decision in the Ontario case of *The Queen* vs. *James Baxter*. In Toronto in 1846, James Baxter, the father of a six-month-old girl and a man alleged to be intemperate and violent, requested that the court order the infant to be taken from the mother and delivered to him. The judge in this case awarded custody to the mother noting that "the child was an infant of very tender age: not more than seven months old, requiring the tender loving care of a mother, and whose health if not its life might be endangered by depriving it of care and of natural food which the mother supplies to it" (Backhouse 1981: 218). This case did not immediately cause a backslide of decisions in favour of mothers. Rather, as Boyd (1987) poignantly reveals, mothers began to receive custody in cases where the father had character or personality flaws and the mothers themselves strictly conformed to the expectations of nineteenth-century womanhood and motherhood. In the Baxter case, for example, the father was alleged to be intemperate and violent. The mother's reputation was not discredited and she had returned to her father's home after the separation. While changes in societal attitudes toward childhood, nurturance and the role of the mother were beginning to influence the judiciary in the mid-nineteenth century, the judiciary was still not convinced that mothers had rights to custody.

In 1855, legislation was passed in Canada that gave the court the discretion to award custody to a mother of infant children up to the age of 12 months in cases where the judges saw fit (Backhouse 1981: 219). This legislation did not deny the father's ownership of the child. It simply recognized the fact that men do not possess the biological equipment necessary to breast-feed. Moreover, it reflected the gender ideology of that time, which held that men did not have the innate psychological disposition to nurture, and the cultural norms that precluded fathers' participation in the care of young children (MacDonald 1986: 10).

The cases that follow this legislation in the ensuing sixteen years reflect the reluctance to award custody to mothers. Backhouse (1981) suggests that visible shifts in judicial perceptions of parenting did not occur until the 1880s. The decisions in Ontario courts in the cases of *Re Ferguson* in 1881, and *Re Murdoch* 1882 illustrate "a departure from the notion of quasi-property paternal rights over children" (Backhouse, 1981: 230) and the emerging concept of "the best interests of the children." By the end of the nineteenth century, the common-law practice of awarding custody to the father was eroding. While mothers were given custody, it is important to recognize that custody was awarded in cases where the fathers were morally delinquent and where maternal custody was viewed to be in the interests of the child's welfare, particularly in the case of very young children.

Systematic research on custody in twentieth-century Canada has yet to be done. However, the major shifts in judicial thinking have been identified in a number of works (Boyd 1987, Mayrand 1985, Abella 1981). Fathers' automatic right to custody was struck down in 1925 by legislation that granted mothers and fathers equal entitlement to custody. In an effort to balance parents' equal entitlement to custody, or from the pressure of pro-children advocates, or simply because of changing attitudes and perceptions, judges increasingly focused on the welfare of the child in custody determinations. One legal translation of the welfare of the child in the twentieth century was the "tender years doctrine." The "tender years doctrine" articulates the belief that children under seven need their mothers more than their fathers to develop emotionally and physically. An Ontario court in 1933 suggested the "tender years doctrine" as a general rule of common sense in awarding custody of children under the age of seven (Abella 1981:14). The "tender years doctrine" was buttressed by the elevation of motherhood to a sacred profession. Judges and lawyers gave some of the finest eulogies to motherhood. MacDonald (1986: 12) provides examples of such statements.

It is not for a Court to rend the most sacred ties of nature which bind a mother to her children, except in extreme cases.

There is but a twilight zone between a mother's love and the atmosphere of heaven.

Mothers were assumed to have greater ability than fathers to parent and nurture. Moreover, the recognition, especially in Freudian psychology, of the mother's role in childhood development influenced the belief that young children were better off with their mothers. From 1933 to the 1970s, the "tender years doctrine" guided judicial decisions and consequently mothers were the preferred custodial parent. The "tender years doctrine" is no longer a legal doctrine, but it still applies as a common-sense rule (Boyd, 1987:9).

In the late 1970s, the "tender years doctrine" was supplanted by "the best interests of the child" doctrine. Justice Mayrand (1981: 160) suggests that the judgments of the Supreme Court of Canada in two custody cases in 1976 established the "paramountcy (*sic*) of the child's welfare in considering to whom custody should be granted." "The best interests of the child" became the single criterion in custody determinations with the passage of the Family Law Reform Act in Ontario 1978 and remains the single standard in both federal and provincial legislation (Abella 1981). The basis of custody determinations in the twentieth century went from common-law paternal rights to the doctrine of "tender years" and finally to the current doctrine of "best interests of the child." Both of the later two doctrines favoured the mother— the primary caregiver of children—as the custodial parent.

Considering contemporary attitudes toward motherhood, it is surprising to learn that mothers enjoyed the preference of the courts in custody cases for fewer than fifty years in Canadian history. Recent challenges in Canada to maternal preference in custody indicate moreover that the situation may change again.

THE CURRENT CHALLENGE TO MATERNAL PREFERENCE

Evidence of women's increased labour force participation and allegations of men's increased participation in the household are used to challenge the maternal preference in custody determinations. It is argued that the maternal preference was formulated at a time when women's primary role was that of homemaker and that changes in women's roles have rendered the maternal preference an anachronism (Miller, 1979). Using the ideology of gender equality, it is argued that fathers as well as mothers are capable, competent parents. Alleging discrimination against men in current custody awards, and borrowing from the experience in the United States, the custodial arrangement of joint custody has been proposed. This section will examine the issue of joint custody in Canada and the supporting argument which is couched in the discourse of equality and the standard of "the best interests of the child."

In 1985, the federal government was considering changes to the *Divorce Act* of 1968. The reforms were intended to ensure that both men and women were given equal rights and obligations, to reduce the hostility between divorcing couples, to consider alternatives to the adversarial system and to consider joint custody of children after divorce. A lobby was mounted by groups—particularly Fathers' Rights Groups—advocating a statutory preference/presumption in favour of joint custody, which amounts to imposing joint custody in situations where one or both parents do not agree to it. In other words, a "presumption" of joint custody is *involuntary* joint custody of children after divorce. Considerable debate ensued over proposals to make joint custody the preferred disposition of child custody disputes (National Association of Women and the Law 1985). In the end the decision was made to retain the principle of the "best interests of the child" and to make joint custody an option rather than a presumption under Section 16(4) of the *Divorce Act* of 1985.

Advocates of joint custody continue to lobby for a presumption of joint custody. In the province of Ontario in 1987 and 1988 there were two initiatives by private members of the provincial parliament, Mr. O'Connor and Dr. Henderson, to introduce a presumption of joint custody as an amendment to the Children's Law Reform Act, 1980. The arguments in favour of a presumption of joint custody at first are appealing and even seductive. The argument favouring joint custody usually begins by claiming that fathers are discriminated against in child custody cases. It claims further that the current adversarial approach to custody makes one parent the winner and the other the loser. Since mothers typically are granted custody, fathers are usually viewed as losers in custody battles and are relegated to the status of visitor in the lives of their children.

After reviewing the problems with the current system, the advocates claim that joint custody will solve the problems experienced by children and mothers as well as fathers, in the divorce/custody process. It is argued that joint custody allows "moms" and "dads" to continue to share the decision-making and responsibilities concerning the children after divorce. In sharing these responsibilities, both parents will continue to have contact with their children after divorce. The proponents of this position, citing the research of Wallerstein and Kelly (1980), maintain the necessity of continued parental contact for children's positive emotional adjustment after divorce. They argue that continued contact is in "the best interests of the child."

The appeal of joint custody and its uncritical acceptance is cause for concern. Joint custody is now a statutory preference or presumption in the majority of states in the United States. The American experience of joint custody and the research on it enjoins us to critically examine the application and the politics of joint custody. The next section presents the arguments and the research used to assess joint custody to be the ideal custodial arrangement and to support the legislation of a presumption of joint custody. These arguments and the research will be critically examined in a later section of the paper that discusses the reality and application of joint custody.

JOINT CUSTODY: THE IDEAL-ARRANGEMENT ARGUMENT

The argument in favour of joint custody is premised on the popular misinterpretation that joint custody means shared physical and legal custody. Joint legal custody refers to the equal rights of both parents to make decisions about the child's education, health care, residence, religious training, and discipline. Joint physical custody refers to parental sharing of the day-to-day responsibilities of childrearing. The application and practice of joint custody do not usually include both aspects. However, the belief that joint custody is both equal sharing of the physical care of the child and joint decision-making—in other words, coparenting—represents an appealing solution to custody disputes. It conforms to our sense of equity by removing the alleged gender discrimination in the courts. It obviates the necessity for judges to possess the wisdom of Solomon, and avoids the unpleasantness of awarding sole custody to only one of the parents. Not surprisingly, joint custody has been promoted as the panacea for the emotional and developmental problems that divorce is assumed to create for children. Its advocates offer six consequences of joint custody that would benefit mothers, fathers and children.

First, it is argued, joint custody promotes continued contact with both parents after divorce. Research on sole-custody arrangements suggests that children desire frequent contact with the noncustodial parent (usually the father) and are disappointed with infrequent contact. And, according to the evidence, the frequency of children's contact with their noncustodial father in sole-custody arrangements decreases over time (Wallerstein and Kelly 1980, Heatherington, Cox and Cox 1978). Proponents conclude that joint custody is a legal prescription for equal contact, which would remedy the problem of decreased visitation in sole custody cases.

The second benefit is assumed to follow from the first benefit. This position maintains that children's emotional adjustment and development will be facilitated through the equal contact resulting from joint custody. And preservation of children's relationships with both parents appears to be central to their post-divorce adjustment. Wallerstein and Kelly's (1980) examination of the effects of divorce on children found that children adjusted positively to divorce when they had frequent interaction with both parents. It has been argued that children in sole-custody arrangements are unable to maintain their attachment to both parents because they are often placed in a position of having to choose, or take sides with one or the other parent. It is believed that the stress of choosing between parents is diminished when children are shared equally with respect to rights and responsibilities. And the children's observations of their parents' joint decision-making will decrease the harmful consequences of divorce.

A third unexpected benefit of joint custody is that shared physical custody will alleviate the burden that mothers, as sole custodial parents, experience. Proponents argue that after divorce mothers with sole custody are overburdened with the day-to-day care of their children. Miller (1979: 364) states that "joint custody allocates to the father a more equitable share of the child rearing burden, and eases the abnormally heavy burden on sole custody mothers." The impression is that shared physical custody gives fathers more responsibilities and mothers more free time.

A fourth presumed benefit is that as a result of shared post-divorce parenting, the relationship between the mother and father will improve. "The need to reach an agreement on all major child rearing decisions, combined with equalized parental power, fosters an atmosphere of detente rather than hostility" (Miller 1979: 364). The belief is that continuing contact for the purpose of decision-making brings harmony to the embittered relationship between divorced parents.

A fifth possible benefit is that the non-custodial parent, again usually the father, will experience less distress and enjoy higher self-esteem under joint custody. It is argued that sole custody has negative effects for the noncustodial parent. Fathers report emotional distress as a result of decreased contact with their children and from their status as marginal parent (Grief, 1979).

Finally, it is assumed that joint custody will lead to greater voluntary compliance with financial support orders. Proponents attribute the high rate of default on child-support orders to the discrimination practiced by the courts and the obstruction of access rights under sole custody.

The early research on sole custody was extremely favourable and fuelled the joint custody argument. Mothers, fathers, and children were thriving, it seemed. Steinman (1981) reported that joint custody allowed mothers to relinquish their full-time mothering roles to pursue their careers and adult social life. For fathers, joint custody was a way to maintain contact with their children, to fulfil their role as fathers, and consequently to feel good about themselves—according to the research. Both mothers and fathers were apparently able to diminish their sense of loss and personal failure, and preserve their self identities as parents and adults within a joint custody arrangement. Grief (1979) found that fathers were less depressed and more satisfied with their post-divorce relationships. Abarbanel (1979) found that parents were satisfied and children were successfully adjusting to the divorce because they had a sense of being loved and wanted by both parents. These findings are impressive and lead one to believe that joint custody is the solution for post-divorce families.

JOINT CUSTODY: A CAVEAT TO THE IDEAL-ARRANGEMENT ARGUMENT

A superficial review of the benefits apparent in the early research on joint custody suggests that a joint custody arrangement is more favourable than marriage itself! Perhaps the appeal of joint custody is that it is better than the marriage that preceded it, or at least that it reproduces marriage and family after divorce. Miller (1979: 365) even cites a case of a joint custody arrangement that was so cooperative and successful that the couple remarried.

Upon closer inspection, however, it is clear that the advantages of joint custody depend on a number of factors. A successful joint custody arrangement requires two important ingredients: parents who have voluntarily entered into the arrangement and parents who are atypical divorcing couples. The subjects in the studies with very positive results were parents who had *voluntarily* chosen joint custody as their way of life after divorce. These parents had a history of cooperation, communication, mutual respect, and commitment to their children. Moreover, they were atypical divorcing couples in that these feelings of mutual respect and communication survived the divorce. They were highly motivated to work together and to sacrifice to make the arrangement successful. This research suggest that joint custody is a viable arrangement when parents voluntarily choose it and make it work.

Proponents of *involuntary* joint custody misuse and misrepresent these research findings by generalizing the benefits of voluntary joint custody to the arrangement itself and by ignoring the qualifiers identified in the research. The joint custody arrangement described by its proponents is the romanticized post-divorce structure of the family. The degree of fit between this romanticized ideal and the reality of joint custody is not examined. Recent evidence suggests that the fit is poor.

THE FIT BETWEEN THE IDEAL AND THE REALITY OF JOINT CUSTODY

The popular notion of joint custody as shared legal and physical custody reflects only the minority of joint custody arrangements. For the most part, a joint custody arrangement involves the sharing of legal custody, but one parent—usually the mother—has physical custody.

This arrangement is virtually indistinguishable from maternal sole custody with liberal access to the father. When physical custody rests with the mother, the mother is still as responsible for the day-to-day care of the children as she was prior to the divorce. Weitzman (1986) studied post-divorce families in California over a ten year period and found that most men did not want custody of their children. One question she was interested in was whether fathers who did not have custody were satisfied with their visitation schedules after divorce. She found that 70 per cent of noncustodial fathers preferred to see their children less often than they actually did, while the remaining 30 per cent liked things the way they were. Not *one* father indicated a desire to see his children more. This should not be surprising if we consider the facts.

Women have traditionally been the primary caregivers of children. Childcare is women's responsibility, not men's. While the media and anecdotal accounts suggest that men are embracing the responsibilities of fatherhood, research does not support this impression. Granted, co-parenting does exist for some men. For the majority of men, however, their role as father in the intact family involves very little caregiving. Men have not assumed an equal share in childcare (Armstrong and Armstrong 1987). In fact, recent research indicates that men continue to do little with respect to childcare or housework (Michelson 1985, Statistics Canada 1985, Connelly and MacDonald 1983, McFarlane 1975, Meissner, Humphreys, Meis and Scheu 1975). There is no reason to believe that men who did not assume childcare responsibilities during marriage will be transformed into "mothers" upon the award of joint custody. Courts can order co-parenting but parents must make it a reality. In those cases where co-parenting did not exist during the marriage, a court order cannot make it happen. The fact that most of the joint custody awards in the United States and Canada are joint *legal* custody and not joint *physical* custody (California State Senate 1987, Richardson 1988) reflects the lack of interest, desire or ability of fathers to share in the day-to-day childcare responsibilities.

Aside from the issue of a father's willingness or ability to co-parent, there are other factors that militate against successful post-divorce co-parenting. The absence of co-parenting prior to divorce clearly predicts problems in co-parenting after divorce. Even if one lives in eternal hope of change, a change to effective co-parenting after divorce is possible only in the absence of inter-parental conflict. Steinman (1981) states that the major undertaking in joint custody is for parents to put aside their marital and divorce-engendered anger. Evidence suggests that benefits from continued contact with both parents occur only when parents are cooperative. Heatherington, Cox and Cox (1978) found that a high level of conflict negates the generally positive effect of frequent visitation by noncustodial fathers. Thus, the argument for joint custody rests on shaky ground when the nature of the relationships of most divorcing parents is taken into account.

For most couples, conflict is inherent in the divorce and the post-divorce process. To expect cooperation between divorcing couples who were unable to maintain their marriage may be unrealistic. In the context of hostile or warring parents, conflict rather than cooperation increases (Steinman, Zimmelman and Knoblauch 1984). Differences of opinion in childrearing, among other joint decisions, have dangerous consequences for children. Heatherington, Cox and Cox (1978) found that children in high-conflict intact and divorced families had more adjustment problems than children in low-conflict families. The researchers conclude that interpersonal conflict may affect the post-divorce adjustment of the children more than the structure of the family. This conclusion is further supported by the number of studies that have shown that children living in conflict-ridden nuclear families are more poorly adjusted than children living in well-functioning, single-parent families (Clingempeel and Reppucci, 1982). Thus, interparental conflict destroys the advantages of continued contact, and makes co-parenting difficult if not impossible. It would seem that the requirement of cooperation in joint custody is inherently contradictory to the reality of the relationships between divorcing couples. A large study of divorce mediation in Colorado found that fully half of joint custody awards had been changed because they were found to be unworkable by the parents (Pearson and Thoennes 1984). Another study showed no differences in a comparison of joint- and sole-custody arrangements with respect to levels of conflict or hostility between couples (Luepnitz 1982).

Another concern about contact in joint custody was voiced by Goldstein, Freud and Solnit (1973). The authors argue that children cannot maintain close emotional ties with both divorced parents, and that visitation rights are artificial and disruptive in a child's life and therefore not in the best interests of the child. Continuity of care with one parent is essential, they argue, and they go so far as to recommend that visitation rights be suspended altogether.

In the majority of post-divorce cases, the standard of living decreases severely for women and increases substantially for men (Weitzman 1985, Richardson 1988). The economic consequences of divorce are detrimental to children and their relationships with their parents. Wallerstein and Kelly (1980) found that the sharp decline in income disrupted children's lives, forced residential moves, and decreased daily contact with the custodial mother. Mothers after divorce are overwhelmed with the responsibility of becoming economically independent, maintaining the children and the home, and facilitating the post-divorce adjustment. In Canada, in 1985, 60.4 per cent of female-headed single-parent families were poor (National Council of Welfare, 1987). Finnbogason and Townson (1985) reviewed existing empirical literature, and found that in Canada default rates on maintenance payments were in excess of 50 per cent. They state the "Law Reform Commission of Canada" estimates true rate to be as high as 75 per cent. The magnitude of default bodes ill for the commitment of fathers to their children after divorce. The premise that "the best interests of children" involves joint custody is suspect in light of the high level of fathers' noncompliance to child-support orders.

Proponents of joint custody argue that fathers default on support payments because of custodial mothers' obstruction of fathers' access rights. The argument contends that with joint custody fathers will willingly make support payments and significantly lower the volume of maintenance order defaults (Lamb, 1987). However, a study of maintenance defaulters conducted by the Alberta Institute of Law Research and Reform in 1981 found no relationship between satisfaction with access and payment status (National Association of Women and the Law 1985). Non-custodial fathers who had no visitation/access problems were as likely to default on support payments as fathers with such problems. Further, Pearson and Thoennes (1984) found in their examination of custody arrangements and support payments in the United States that neither voluntary nor imposed joint custody arrangements resulted in greater compliance with support orders compared to sole-custody arrangements. So, the evidence appears to contradict the assumed benefit of support compliance in joint custody situations. Moreover, it is interesting to note that both in the United States and Canada researchers (Weitzman, 1986, Grief 1985, Richardson 1988) found that the complaints surrounding access/visitation are more commonly voiced by mothers who are disappointed with the infrequency of father visitation than from fathers complaining about inaccessibility to their children.

The potential and real disadvantages of joint custody, as outlined above, demand careful consideration before awarding joint custody and particularly before moving toward a presumption of joint custody (involuntary joint custody) in Canada. The available research on *involuntary* joint custody points to its potential harm. Steinman, Semmelman and Knoblauch (1985) studied voluntary and imposed joint custody families in San Francisco. They found that *none* of the court influenced [mediated] or imposed joint custody arrangements examined were successful. Children in these arrangements were more likely to be stressed or severely at risk of major emotional disturbances. Similarly, parents in imposed joint custody arrangements were unable to set aside their feelings of hostility. The relationship typically involved lack of respect or trust for their ex-spouses as individuals and as parents. The intense conflict between the parents interfered with their acting in accord with the needs of their children. Current research conducted by researchers at the Center for the Family in Transition (1988) in California suggests that *involuntary* joint custody does not promote child adjustment post-divorce. Researchers found that children who had more frequent access to both divorced parents were more emotionally troubled and behaviourally disturbed.

Carefully reviewing the research on joint custody should lead to disenchantment with this arrangement. Such has been the case in the United States. In 1980 California was the first state to enact a joint custody statute. In less than a decade, a California State Senate struck a task force to examine its experience with joint custody. Its report, published in June, 1987, indicated that joint custody is "a complicated arrangement and takes special parents and children to make it work," and that to fail to "appropriately evaluate parents and children results in inappropriate awards or mediated agreements of joint custody that are harmful to children." In response to this re-examination, the Senate Task Force on Family Equity Report (California State Senate, 1987) has recommended amendments to California's joint custody legislation that take into account the parenting skills and co-parenting abilities of the parents.

IN WHOSE BEST INTERESTS?

There is no doubt that the concept of joint custody has an overwhelming appeal. The appeal lies in the rhetoric of gender equality, co-parenting and "best interests of the child." An understanding of joint custody, however,

must be located in the reality of the post-divorce family and not in its fabri-
cation. Research has shown that joint custody can work if parents enter the
arrangement voluntarily with mutual respect, a willingness to cooperate and
communicate, and a commitment to the child and to co-parenting. Joint
custody does not work if these ingredients are absent. And when joint custody does not work it is the children who most suffer the consequences.
Considering the potential harm to children, it is alarming that fathers' rights
groups continue to lobby for a presumption of joint custody. In this final section of the paper, the question that will be addressed is "who is best served by
a presumption of joint custody?"

As we have seen, when the intact family is dissolved, the typical arrangement after divorce is that children live with their mothers and visit with their
fathers. This arrangement is usually made with the mutual consent of both
mothers and fathers. In fact, in 85.6 per cent of cases women receive custody
(McKie, Prentice and Reed, 1983). When custody is contested by the father,
nearly half are awarded sole custody (Richardson, 1988). However, very few
fathers request custody.

The reality of the high percentage of awards to mothers is a result of the
fact that mothers perform the childrearing in our society. This is recognized
by fathers and the courts. An argument could easily be made that the maternal preference evident in the courts in the last half of this century has not
been a preference at all but a reality-based custody decision that conformed
to the "best interests of the child" standard. Men are not and have never
been primary childcare givers. Fathers alleging sex discrimination in custody
awards shift the focus away from parenting to the sex of the parent—in other
words, they turn attention from the "best interests of the child" to the best
interests of the non-custodial parent. Awarding custody to the parent that
has been and will continue to be the primary caregiver would logically
appear to be a custody award that is "in the best interests of the child."

While it is alleged that *involuntary* joint custody will produce two primary
caregivers—fathers and mothers—the experience with voluntary joint custody indicates that this result is unlikely. Morris (1988: 19) studied a sample
of typically middle-class, professional Canadian parents who had legal or *de
facto* joint custody arrangements. She found that mothers continued "to
assume more responsibility for coordinating the routines of their children,
even when in the other home." The co-parenting aspect of joint custody is
left up to the parents to work out, which normally results in an arrangement
identical to sole maternal custody. Even in voluntary joint custody arrangements
continued contact or co-parenting is not guaranteed. It is unrealistic to
believe that it can be imposed by legislation.

Joint custody defined and practised as joint legal custody raises the question of what fathers' rights groups really want in their lobby for a
presumption of joint legal custody. If they want the positive results demonstrated in the research, these can only be realized by actual sharing of day-to-

day responsibilities and decision-making within a cooperative context. Evidence indicates that *most men do not want to have these responsibilities for their children* (NAWL 1985). In this case, it would appear that the application of joint legal custody considers only the best interests of the non-caretaker parent, usually the father. Legal recognition of his authority over his children may serve to raise his self-esteem and control, but what does it do for the children? Moreover, parental rights, without parental responsibilities, calls into question the justice and equity of the control of the absent parent over the primary caregiver's decisions.

Those parents who mutually want a joint custody arrangement can have it. Who, then, are the parents that are lobbying for a presumption of joint custody? Clearly, those parents are the ones who do not have custody and who are unable to reach a mutually agreeable arrangement with their ex-spouse. Embittered by their divorce experience and frustrated by the uncooperative nature of the relationship with their ex-spouse, these parents have sought redress through the courts. Joint custody is seen by them as the solution. Considering the research that has been reviewed in this paper, joint custody holds false promises as the solution. Furthermore, parents engaged in a hostile, warring relationship are, as we have seen, likely to harm the child emotionally and psychologically. That parents are willing to place children in the middle of their battlefields speaks volumes to the question of whose best interests are served by joint custody. Joint custody has been the politicization of the conflict between divorcing mothers and fathers. To debate fathers' rights over the rights of children is to move us back in time to a paternal presumption rather than forward.

Movement toward a presumption of joint custody must be put on hold in Canada until there is empirical support for it. To frame social policy and write legislation on the basis of emotionally appealing rhetoric and selected studies based on unrepresentative samples is to place our children at risk, and in Wallerstein's words, "to experiment with the children of this country" (Polikoff 1985: 4). The social science researchers who study the consequences of divorce (Heatherington, Wallerstein, Weitzman, and Steinman) have all made strong public statements against *involuntary* joint custody. Each one agrees that joint custody is an ideal solution for ideal parents, but that it is not for every divorcing couple. Nor is it in the best interests of the children. To impose joint custody as an arbitrary standard of what constitutes the best interests of the child is to preclude an informed, factual determination of the question in the case of each child.

REFERENCES

Abarbanel, Alice 1979 "Shared Parenting After Separation and Divorce: A Study of Joint Custody." *American Journal of Orthopsychiatry* 49, 2 (1979): 320–9

Abella, Rosalie Silberman 1981 "Family Law in Ontario: Changing Assumptions." *Ottawa Law Review* 13: 1–22

Anderson, Karen 1987 "Historical Perspectives on the Family": 21–39 in K. Anderson *et al.*, eds., *Family Matters*. Toronto: Methuen

Anderson, Karen, H. Armstrong, P. Armstrong, J. Drakich, M. Eichler, C. Guberman, A. Hayford, M. Luxton, J. Peters, E. Porter, C.J. Richardson, G. Tesson 1987 *Family Matters*. Toronto: Methuen

Ariès, Philippe 1962 *Centuries of Childhood: A Social History of Family Life*. New York: Vintage Books

Armstrong, Pat and Hugh Armstrong 1987 "The Conflicting Demands of 'Work' and 'Home'": 133–40 in K. Anderson *et al.*, eds., *Family Matters*. Toronto: Methuen

Backhouse, Constance B. 1981 "Shifting Patterns in Nineteenth-Century Canadian Custody Law": 212–48 in David H. Flaherty, ed. *Essays in the History of Canadian Law*, Vol. 1. Toronto: The Osgoode Society

Boyd, Susan 1987 "Child Custody, Ideologies and Female Employment." Paper presented at the National Association of Women and the Law Biennial Conference. Winnipeg, Manitoba

Center for the Family in Transition 1988 Summary of the Cent[er] for the Family in Transition research presented at the 65th Annual Meeting of the American Orthopsychiatric Association, 30 March 1988

Chesler, Phyllis 1986 *Mothers on Trial: The Battle for Children and Custody*. New York: McGraw-Hill Book Company

Clingempeel, Glenn W. and N. Dickon Reppucci 1982 "Joint Custody After Divorce: Major Issues and Goals for Research." *Psychological Bulletin* 9, 1: 102–27

Connelly, M. Patricia and Martha MacDonald 1983 "Women's Work: Domestic and Wage Labour in a Nova Scotia Community." *Studies in Political Economy* 10 (Winter): 45–72

Cook, Ramsey and Wendy Mitchinson 1976 *The Proper Sphere*. Toronto: Oxford University Press

Finnbogason, Eva and Monica Townson 1985 "The Benefits and Cost Effectiveness of a Central Registry of Maintenance and Custody Orders." Status of Women Canada. Minister of Supply and Services Canada

Goldstein, J., A. Freud, and A. Solnit 1973 *Beyond the Best Interests of the Child*. New York: The Free Press

Grief, Judith Brown 1979. "Fathers, Children and Joint Custody." *American Journal of Orthopsychiatry* 49: 311–19

Heatherington, E., M. Cox, and R. Cox 1978 "The Aftermath of Divorce." In J. H. Stevens Jr. and M. Matthews, eds., *Mother-Child, Father-Child Relationships*. Washington, D.C.: National Association for the Education of the Young

Henderson, J. 1988 "Two Parents are Better than One." *Globe and Mail*, Tuesday, 10 May

Lamb, Louise 1987 "Involuntary Joint Custody: What Mothers will Lose if Fathers' Rights Groups Win". *Herizons* (Jan./Feb.): 20–3, 31

Luepnitz, Deborah Ann 1982 *Child Custody: A Study of Families after Divorce.* Toronto: Lexington Books

MacDonald, James 1986 "Historical Perspective of Custody and Access Disputes": 9–22 in Ruth S. Parry *et al.* eds., *Custody Disputes: Evaluation and Intervention.* Toronto: Lexington Books

Mayrand, Albert 1983 "The Influence of Spousal Conduct on the Custody of Children": 159–73 in Rosalie S. Abella and Claire L'Heureux-Dubé, eds., *Family Law: Dimensions of Justice.* Toronto: Butterworths

McFarlane, Bruce 1975 "Married Life and Adaptations to a Professional Role: Married Women Dentists in Canada:" 359–66 in Pavez S. Wakil, ed., *Marriage, Family and Society.* Toronto: Butterworths

McKie, D. C., B. Prentice, and P. Reed 1983 *Divorce: Law and the Family in Canada.* Ottawa: Statistics Canada, Research and Analysis Division

Meissner, Martin, Elizabeth W. Humphreys, Scott M Meis and William J. Scheu 1975 "No Exit for Wives: Sexual Division of Labour and the Culmination of Household Demands." *The Canadian Review of Sociology and Anthropology* 12: 424–39

Michelson, William 1985 "Divergent Convergent: The Daily Routines of Employed Spouses as a Public Affairs Agenda." *Public Affairs Report* 26, 4: 1–10

Miller, D. 1979 "Joint Custody." *Family Law Quarterly* 13: 345–412

National Association of Women and the Law (NAWL) 1985 A submission to the Senate Standing Committee on Legal and Constitutional Affairs—Bill C–47: Joint Custody, Child Support, Maintenance Enforcement, and Related Issues. Ottawa: National Association of Women and the Law

National Council of Welfare 1987 "Progress Against Poverty." Ottawa: National Council of Welfare

Parry, Ruth S., Elsa Broder, Elizabeth A. G. Schmitt, Elisabeth B. Saunders, and Eric Hood 1986 *Custody Disputes: Evaluation and Intervention.* Toronto: Lexington Books

Pearson, J., and N. [Thoennes] 1984 "Mediating and Litigating Custody Disputes: A Longitudinal Evaluation." *Family Law Quarterly,* 17: 497–524

Polikoff, Nancy 1985 *Brief of Amicus Curiae.* Court of Appeals of Maryland. No. 12, Taylor v. Taylor

1983 "Gender and Child-Custody Determinations: Exploding the Myths": 183–202 in Irene Diamond, ed., *Families, Politics, and Public Policy: A Feminist Dialogue on Women and the State.* New York: Longman, Inc.

Richardson, C. James 1988 *Court-Based Divorce Mediation in Four Canadian Cities: an Overview of Research Results.* Ottawa: Minister of Supply and Services, Canada

Roman, M. and W. Haddad 1978 *The Disposable Parent.* New York: Holt, Rinehart and Winston

Statistics Canada 1985 Women in Canada: A Statistical Report. Ottawa: Supply and Services Canada (Cat. no. 89–503E)

Steinman, Susan 1981 "The experiences of children in a joint custody arrangement: A report of a study." *American Journal of Orthopsychiatry* 51, 3: 403–14

Steinman, Susan B., S. E. Semmelman and T. M. Knoblauch 1985 "A Study of Parents Who Sought Joint Custody Following Divorce: Who Reaches Agreement and Sustains Joint Custody and Who Returns to Court." *Journal of the American Academy of Child Psychiatry* 24, 5: 554–62

Wallerstein, Judith S. and Joan B. Kelly 1980 *Surviving the Breakup: How Children and Parents Cope with Divorce.* New York: Basic Books

Weitzman, Lenore 1986 *The Divorce Revolution: The Unexpected Social and Economic Consequences for Wom[e]n and Children in America.* New York: The Free Press

28

Lone Parenthood: Gender Differences

Jillian Oderkirk and Clarence Lochhead

Most lone-parent families (82%) are headed by a mother. As a result, the characteristics of lone-parent families, in general, tend to reflect those of lone mothers and their children. A small but growing number of lone parents, however, are fathers, whose circumstances differ considerably from those of lone mothers.

Both lone mothers and lone fathers often carry the sole responsibility for the physical and emotional, as well as financial, well-being of their

Lone-parent families as a percentage of all families, 1941–1991

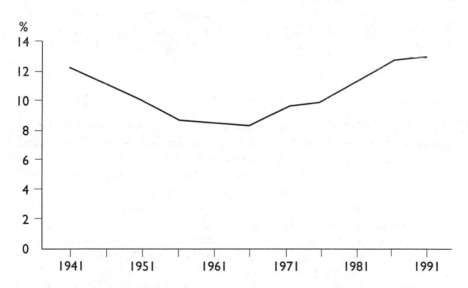

Source: Statistics Canada, Census of Canada.

From Jillian Oderkirk and Clarence Lochhead, "Lone Parenthood: Gender Differences," *Canadian Social Trends,* Cat. No. 11–008E (Spring and Winter 1993): 16–19. Reprinted by permission.

children. Lone mothers tend to be younger, to have less formal education, and to be raising younger children than lone fathers. For them, financial difficulties are often severe. Many young lone parents sacrifice personal educational attainment and career mobility to provide care for children and, as a result, are restricted to earnings from low-wage occupations or income from government transfer payment programs.

NOT A NEW PHENOMENON

According to the 1991 Census, there were almost one million lone-parent families with never-married children of all ages, representing 13% of all families. This proportion has risen since 1966, when 8% of all families were headed by a lone parent. In 1941, however, over 12% of all families had been headed by a lone parent.

Circumstances creating lone-parent families have changed since 1941. During the first half of the 20th century, lower life expectancies, greater risks associated with childbirth, and war contributed to a higher incidence of lone parenthood resulting from the death of a spouse. Today, most episodes of lone parenthood result from marital dissolution (divorce or separation), after which custody of children is generally awarded to mothers, or from never-married women raising children alone. Consequently, a larger proposition of lone parents in 1941 were men (26%) than in 1981 (17%) and 1991 (18%).

GENDER DIFFERENCES

Men are more likely than women to become lone parents through divorce or the death of a spouse. While many lone mothers are also divorced or widowed, a relatively large proportion never have been married.

According to the Survey of Consumer Finances, during the late 1980s, 79% of lone parents were divorced, separated or widowed and 16% never had been married. Few lone parents (5%) were still married or in a common-law relationship but not living with their spouse. Lone fathers (86%) were more likely than lone mothers (78%) to be divorced, separated or widowed. On the other hand, relatively few lone fathers (5%), compared to lone mothers (17%), never had been married.

Divorced lone fathers tend to be older than divorced lone mothers. This may be because husbands, in general, tend to be older than their wives. Also, Canadian courts tend to grant older children a say in their residence following a divorce, increasing the likelihood of custodial retention of older children by fathers, while awarding custody of most young children to mothers.

Measuring gender differences

According to the Survey of Consumer Finances, there were 807,000 lone parents living with never-married children of all ages in 1989. Of these lone-parent families, 16% were living within another relative's household, such as an unmarried mother living with her parents. The remaining 84% were living alone (78%) or with people to whom they were not related (6%).

Because the number of lone fathers is small compared to lone mothers, to focus on differences between male and female lone parents living alone or with non-relatives, data for three survey years (1987, 1988 and 1989) were combined to increase the sample size. The characteristics of lone-parent families were very similar during each of these years, and results from analysis of the combined data (1987, 1988, and 1989) and analysis of each individual year, were not significantly different.

Of all male lone parents, 10% were under age 35, compared with 33% of female lone parents. While there were virtually no male lone parents aged 15–24, there was an average of 38,100 lone mothers that age in each year, representing almost 7% of all lone parents. Male lone parents were also more likely than female lone parents to be aged 55 and over (33% compared with 20%).

MOST LONE MOTHERS HAVE CHILDREN UNDER AGE 18

Of all lone-parent families, almost two-thirds (65%) had at least one child under age 18 living at home. Female lone parents, however, were more likely than male lone parents to have young children. Most lone mothers (68%) had children under age 18, while about one-half of lone fathers had children that young. Furthermore, almost one-third of lone mothers (29%) had children under age 7, compared to very few lone fathers (11%).

Not surprisingly, parents with at least one child under age 18 tend to be relatively young. During the late 1980s, 84% of lone parents with children that age were aged 45 and under. Only 14% of lone mothers with children under age 18 were over age 45, compared with 31% of lone fathers.

LONE FATHERS MORE HIGHLY EDUCATED

Overall, the educational attainment of lone fathers exceeds that of lone mothers. This is likely because the demands of lone parenthood limit or

Lone mothers are younger, have less formal education, and lower incomes than lone fathers

	Lone mothers	Lone fathers
	%	
Age:		
15–24	7	1
25–34	26	9
35–44	29	32
45–54	18	25
55–64	11	18
65 and over	9	15
Education: [1]		
Grade 8 or less	18	20
Grades 9–10	17	15
Grades 11–13	8	3
High-school graduate	21	17
Some postsecondary	10	4
Postsecondary graduate	19	29
University degree	7	12
Income: [2]		
Less than $5,000	3	1
$5,000–$19,999	45	19
$20,000–$29,999	21	16
$30,000 and over	31	64
Total	100	100

1. Data for 1989 only.
2. 1989 dollars.

Source: Statistics Canada, Survey of Consumer Finances Public-Use Microdata, combined income years 1987–1989.

restrict many parents' ability to pursue higher education. As mothers tend to be both younger than fathers, and to have younger children when they become lone parents, they are more likely to interrupt their academic programs or to forego further educational opportunities. This accounts, in part, for the higher proportions of lone mothers who have attended but not graduated from either high school or a postsecondary institution. Lone mothers still in school also contribute to this higher proportion. Considering all types

Major sources of low family income[1]

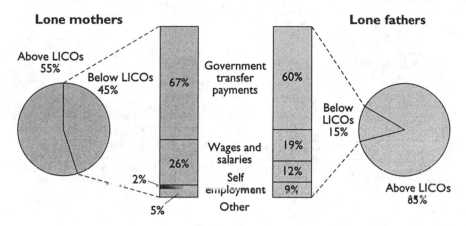

Major income sources

1 Combined years 1987–1989, 1986-based Low Income Cut-offs.

Source: Statistics Canada, Survey of Consumer Finances Public-Use Microdata, unpublished.

of educational institutions, 4% of lone mothers were enrolled full-time and 3% part-time. In contrast, about 1% of male lone parents were enrolled in school either full- or part-time.

MAJOR SOURCES OF INCOME

The major sources of income for most lone-parent families were wages and salaries, followed by income transfers from the government, such as Social Assistance or Unemployment Insurance. More lone fathers (71%), however, than lone mothers (57%) had wages and salaries as their major income source.

Many lone mothers are constrained from employment because of limited work experience and educational attainment, and child-care responsibilities. During the late 1980s, over 41% of lone mothers were not in the labour force, compared with 28% of male lone fathers. Among employed lone parents, mothers (16%) were more likely than fathers (4%) to work part-time.

Women were more than twice as likely as men to have transfer payments as their major income source (35% compared with 16%). Other major sources of income reported by a small minority of lone parents included self-employment earnings (3%), investment income (2%) and pension income (1%).

30% of lone mothers have family incomes $1,000–9,999 below the LICOs[1]

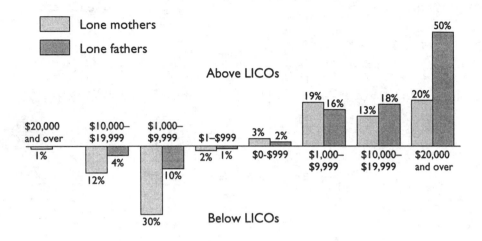

[1] Combined years 1987–1989, 1986-based Low Income Cut-offs.

Source: Statistics Canada, Survey of Consumer Finances Public-Use Microdata, unpublished.

LONE FATHERS HAVE HIGHER EARNINGS

Lone fathers are not only more likely than lone mothers to have wages and salaries as a major income source, their earnings are also higher. This is not surprising considering that lone mothers tend to be younger than lone fathers, and men tend to earn higher salaries, on average, than do women.

During the late 1980s, about one-half (52%) of all male lone parents earned $30,000 [1] or more from wages, salaries and self-employment income, compared with 21% of female lone parents. Female lone parents (33%) were more likely than male lone parents (25%) to earn between $10,000 and $29,000. About 22% of female lone parents and 9% of male lone parents had no income from these sources.

MORE LONE MOTHERS HAVE LOW INCOMES

The incidence of low income is much higher among lone mothers than lone fathers, regardless of the ages of their children. During the late 1980s, 56% of lone mothers with children under age 18, and 20% of lone fathers with children that age, were living with incomes below Statistics Canada's Low Income Cut-Offs (LICOs). Also, among lone parents whose children were

Gap between lone-parent family income and the LICOs,[1] by major source of income and gender of parent

Gap	All income sources		Government transfer payments		Wages and salaries	
	Women	Men	Women	Men	Women	Men
$			%			
Below the LICOs:						
-10,000 and over	12.0	3.9	25.4	11.4	3.4	1.1
-1,000 to -9,999	30.4	10.3	58.3	40.5	14.8	2.7
-1 to -999	2.3	1.0	2.1	5.1	2.2	0.2
Above the LICOs:						
0 to 999	2.6	1.8	2.3	3.9	2.6	1.5
1,000 to 9,999	19.2	15.6	8.8	27.8	25.8	13.7
10,000 to 19,999	13.8	17.8	2.4	9.0	20.7	19.2
20,000 and over	19.7	49.7	0.7	2.3	30.5	61.7
Total	100.0	100.0	100.0	100.0	100.0	100.0

1. Statistics Canada's 1986-based Low Income Cut-offs

Source: Statistics Canada, Survey of Consumer Finances Public-Use Microdata, combined income years 1987–1989.

all aged 18 and over, 20% of mothers and 10% of fathers had family incomes below the LICOs . Most lone mothers (67%) and lone fathers (60%) with low family incomes reported government transfer payments as their major income source.

MANY LONE MOTHERS FAR BELOW THE LICOs

What is even more striking is that a large number of lone-parent families headed by women have total incomes far below the LICOs . More than 11% of all lone mothers (an average of 67,950 families annually during the late 1980s) had incomes $10,000 or more below the LICOs. In contrast, 4% of lone-parent families headed by men had incomes that low. Also, 30% of all lone-parent families headed by women had incomes $1,000–$9,999 below the LICOs, compared with 10% of those headed by men.

Lone-parent families headed by men are not only more likely than those headed by women to have family incomes above the LICOs, but are also much more likely to have incomes exceeding the LICOs by a relatively wide margin. For example, 68% of male-headed lone-parent families had incomes $10,000 or more above the LICOs, compared with 34% of female-headed lone-parent families.

INCOME FROM TRANSFER PAYMENTS VERY LOW

Government transfer payments, such as Social Assistance and Unemployment Insurance, are the second most common major source of income among lone-parent families. Of lone-parent families whose main income source was government transfer payments, those headed by women were more disadvantaged than those headed by men. Of these lone mothers, 84% had family incomes $1,000 or more below the LICOs. In contrast, 52% of lone fathers in similar circumstances had family incomes that low. About one-quarter of these lone mothers, compared with 11% of lone fathers, had family incomes $10,000 or more below the LICOs. An additional 38% of lone mothers and 21% of lone fathers had family incomes between $5,000 and $9,999 below the LICOs.

NOTE

1   All income figures are expressed in 1989 dollars.

29

The Feminization of Poverty: An Old Problem with a New Name

Lesley D. Harman

J ust as things are starting to look better for women, in what many have come to call the "post-feminist" era, the feminization of poverty is being spoken of as a new social problem. In fact, it is an old problem with a new name. Women's poverty, while not new, is taking a new shape. Women have always been poor, but through their dependent roles as wives, mothers, and daughters, their poverty has been concealed as only a potential plight, or as something that only happened to other women, women who did not have a man. But as more and more women live without men, either by choice or by necessity, women's poverty becomes more visible, and their dependency is transferred from the male breadwinner to the state. (Harman)

The apparent gains of the women's movement, including a general shift of women's presence from the domestic ghetto to a growing visibility in the public sphere, have been accompanied by a general complacency, as well as the recently noted backlash against feminism.[1] One often hears that "things have changed"—the battles have been won, equality is here. What implications does this have for the young women about to enter the workforce? Many of these women have been encouraged to be independent and to develop their own careers, a path which they believe will ensure them a good life, in which they will avoid the dependency and potential poverty of their mothers and sisters who had followed the previous generations' role prescriptions. The current mythology is precisely that this life will be possible and attainable. The prospect of being unable to succeed is foreign; the idea that they might be susceptible to poverty, remote. The reality, however, is that in 1987, 59 per cent of poor Canadian adults were women—exactly the same figure as in 1975. (National Council of Welfare, 1) In Canadian society today, 84 per cent of all women will spend part of their adult lives without husbands, supporting themselves as well as their children. (National Council of Welfare, 15) At every stage of their lives, women are more likely to be poor, and are more likely to be trapped in a life of poverty.

From Lesley D. Harman, "The Feminization of Poverty: An Old Problem with a New Name," *Canadian Woman Studies,* vol. 12, no. 4 (1992): 6–9.

What is meant by the feminization of poverty? Simply put, it means that without the support of a man, a woman is likely to be poor. This fact of life is not new. Women's economic dependency on men has been essential to the perpetuation of the system of masculine dominance. Economic dependency produces and is reproduced by women's subordination and powerlessness, which ensures that females conform, silently and passively, to role prescriptions around reproduction (motherhood) and labour (both unpaid domestic labour and work in the paid labour force). As more and more women enter the paid workforce, work and family obligations resulted in conflicts and often economic difficulties for women.

Reproduction factors heavily into women's material existence. As our society is currently organized, women have very little control over their reproductive potential. Women have the children, and childbearing and childrearing are the least valued of all occupations. If we can judge the social value of an occupation by how much those performing it are paid, we will quickly notice that those who get paid for caring for children (domestics, nannies, babysitters, and day care workers) are among the lowest paid of all members of society. Indeed, the pay for most typically 'female' jobs (clerical, service, teaching, nursing and caregiving), reflects the fact that women's work in general is devalued and trivialized in our society. In 1988, 76 per cent of women in the paid labour force worked in these jobs. (National Council of Welfare, 21) Women still earned 65 per cent of what men earned in the paid labour force in Canada. (National Council of Welfare, 27) This work is essential and must be done. However, as long as it is assumed that it will be done, gladly and even gratefully, by women for no money or recognition, then the fundamental structures which reproduce women's dependency will continue to go unchallenged.

In addition to being assumed to be women's 'natural' role and ultimate route to fulfillment (which it may in fact be for many women), reproduction is used to legitimize women's inferior position in the paid labour force. Because it is generally assumed that most women in our society will eventually marry and have children, it is also assumed that their aspirations for career advancement are selfish. It is taken for granted that women will take several years from their careers to spend in full-time mothering. While it is true that over half of all married women in our society are in the paid labour force, and most of them are there because they need the income, it is also true that pregnancy and childbirth guarantee a minimum six-week absence from the workforce. With recent revisions to maternity leave provisions, new mothers can now leave their paid positions for up to six months (or more as unpaid leave). While the new leave provisions are long overdue and should be applauded, we must be careful not to overlook some of the possible implications of women's protracted absence from the paid workforce. It stands to reason that one or more lengthy absences from a career will put a woman "off time" in her own career. (Burman)

The resumption of a career after childbirth usually means employing another person to do the caregiving, although with the current economic recession often hitting male breadwinners, an increasing number of fathers are taking on full-time caregiving roles. Given the gross inequities between salaries in traditional dual-income families, it is usually the woman who receives less money for her work in the paid labour force. Deciding whether or not to go back to work is, therefore, sometimes a difficult decision. It is not unusual to hear a woman say, "I can't afford to work." What does this mean? It means that after taxes, work-related expenses (transportation, wardrobe, and lunches), many women find that having another person to look after their children ends up costing them more than they earn. If they cannot afford to leave their jobs, they may then be heard to say, "I can't afford to have children."

The economic difficulties produced through work and family conflicts have serious implications for women's poverty. On the one hand, this situation can be used to argue that a woman's place is in the home and that we should return to the 'family wage,' an arrangement in which the male bread-winner is seen to be earning enough money through his one paycheque to support the entire family. This idea precludes the necessity of women working for income to share in the support of the family. It also puts the final nail in the coffin of the feminization of poverty, ensuring that women do not have any opportunities for economic independence. Women's poverty thus becomes a self-fulfilling prophecy.

While a return to the family wage would seem to be unlikely in these times of dual-income families, of concern is that paid employment for women has itself become a poverty trap. The prevalent myth that women can compete in the paid labour force, offered equal opportunities to succeed in their careers, and make adequate incomes, is shattered when it is under-stood that for many women it is economically impossible to work in the paid labour force and have children. Economic dependency on either the male breadwinner or the state becomes a necessity, rather than a choice.

The above discussion has assumed a traditional, nuclear familial arrangement in which there are no adult caregivers to stay home during the day with the children, a paid male breadwinner, and a mother who is forced to give up her job in order to look after the children during the day because she cannot afford to work. This is perhaps one of the least visible manifestations of the feminization of poverty because by returning to the private sphere, the women in question are no longer considered to be on the job market and are not categorized as "unemployed." (Burman) Instead, they have resumed their so-called 'natural,' dependent roles in the family. As long as women are economically dependent on men, the opportunities for change are very few.

While female economic dependency is not new, some of the manifestations of what happens when women live in ways other than traditional dependency arrangements, are becoming gradually more visible. Such visibility confirms that the more things change, the more they stay the same. As recent statistics reveal, women's poverty is most striking among those living without men. According to the National Council of Welfare, 75 per cent of never-married female single parents, 52 per cent of previously married female single parents, 44 per cent of unattached women over the age of 65, and 33 per cent of unattached women under 65, are living in poverty in this country. (National Council of Welfare, 9)

Teenage pregnancy is often a direct path to early and long-term poverty for women. For young women who give birth and keep their babies, the label 'single mother' is inevitable. Even when they marry the fathers of their children, the majority of such unions end in early divorce, with the mothers usually taking custody of the children and often ending up as Family Benefits recipients. Family Benefits is another expression of economic dependency on the state. Along with never-married or divorced teenage mothers, all mothers of young children who find themselves 'alone' (read: without a man) may eventually find it necessary to turn to the state for financial support.

Aging and poverty are historically related in our society, particularly for women. Because women tend to outlive men by an average of seven years, it is likely that women will spend at least some portion of their last years alone. Recently, the aged have become more affluent, perhaps due to increases in universal pensions and the tendency for more employed citizens to finance their own retirement through registered retirement plans. However, a woman who has spent her adult life bearing and rearing children and doing unpaid domestic labour in the home may have had little opportunity to save, and is not entitled to the Canada Pension Plan in her old age. While increases in the Guaranteed Income Supplement for low income senior citizens have meant that the poverty rate of elderly women has dropped from 42 percent in 1977, to 22 percent in 1987, we continue to find that many older women who are alone must survive on next to nothing. (National Council of Welfare, 129)

The bleak reality of being old and female is that there is very little hope of ever emerging from a life of poverty. Poverty is more like a life sentence: as long as you are alive, you will be poor. When women are young, the myth of equal opportunity seems more believable. As we have seen, however, myths can be the most insidious traps of all. The myth of equality of opportunity extends to other minority groups as well. If the dominant, privileged, and wealthy group in our society is comprised of white, able-bodied, heterosexual, Anglo-Saxon males somewhere in their middle years with a university education, then we can see that not only is our society sexist and agist, but it is also racist, heterosexist, and ablist.

In our racist society, 'women of colour'[2] are made to feel as if they are 'other' to white women. Immigrant women face difficulties upon arriving in Canada, such as language barriers, lack of education, and racial discrimination in the job market. Domestic workers are one of the most exploited groups of immigrant women. Not only do they perform the most devalued roles in our society, but they are subject to low pay, low status, cruelty, and harassment by their employers. Finally, the double impact of gender and race is nowhere more evident than in the lived experiences of aboriginal women, who belong to the poorest and most discriminated against group in Canadian society.

Discrimination on the basis of sexual preference exists for lesbian women. The Canadian state offers tax advantages to those who marry and have children, resulting in relative economic disadvantage for women who do not. Subtle and not-so-subtle heterosexism may result in lesbian women having to conceal their sexual orientation for fear of losing their jobs or not being hired.

Physical disability is an almost guaranteed route to poverty for women. Disabled women are less likely to be married than are disabled men or able-bodied women; if they are alone, they are less likely to be employed and will therefore have to depend on the state for their material existence. Disabled single mothers often find it difficult to find affordable, accessible housing. (National Council of Welfare, 117)

Perhaps the most visible indication of the breadth and depth of the feminization of poverty is the growing phenomenon of homelessness among women. (Harman) Women who become homeless have basically lost, or never had, the means to support themselves. This is a tragic but inevitable outcome of the feminization of poverty. Homelessness occurs among women from all social classes and a variety of racial and ethnic backgrounds. It is very difficult to gather reliable data on homeless women because they are the group of women in our society which is the most difficult to locate. Their abject poverty, entitling them to membership in the 'underclass,' places them both outside and below the class system, and disenfranchises them from citizenship in this society.

The web of relations that constitutes the rights and duties of citizens (home ownership, taxation, employment, familial relations) also necessitates a series of controls over citizens, in the form of numbers: address, phone, bank account, social insurance, credit card, health insurance, driver's license, passport—the list seems endless. While many such identifiers have taken on the rather perverse connotations of freedom and privilege in our society (the American Express Card), they are really ways of locating and potentially controlling the 'homeful.' When women are 'homeful' they can always be found ("May I speak to the lady of the house, please?"). When women are homeless, what they 'lack,' the source of their 'deficiency,' is precisely a place within these relations of dependency.

The plight of homeless women points to certain contradictions in Canadian society which affect the lives of all women, 'homeful' or not. To be a woman in Canada today is to face a strong likelihood of being poor at some time in one's life. The myth of equality of opportunity conceals the fundamental inequalities which continue to keep women economically dependent on men and the state. While appearing to guarantee women's economic security, the traditional roles of wife and mother in fact only serve to mask how close all women are to a life of poverty. When women attempt to break free of dependency relations, their inferior position in the paid workforce, and the liabilities they will face if they have children, they have a greater likelihood of being economically disadvantaged and of seeking social assistance. Women who are older, non-white, lesbian, or disabled, will find their experiences of poverty compounded.

What is the price of freedom? With all of the courage that it takes to be free of masculine dominance in one's personal life, it is inevitable that it will be replaced by the domination of the state through some form of social assistance. The structural conditions that might guarantee women's financial independence are simply not in place. Does this mean the ultimate freedom is to simply opt out? As Thelma and Louise chose their own death above subjugation to male brutality and the violent state, so it seems that homelessness and abject poverty are the ultimate end for those women who do not have a conventional place within the patriarchy. Is this horrific observation far from the truth? It seems that as long as reproduction and labour power remains in the hands of the patriarchy, so will the material existence of women.

For there to be a glimmer of hope on the horizon, we must look to ways in which women can enrich their own lives. Like all powerless groups, women have found strength in numbers, and empowerment in revaluing what their oppressors devalue. Perhaps the feminization of poverty exists because 'feminine' is defined as impoverishing. Finding our wealth in the very traits which make us poor in this society may be a rewarding path on the road to true equality.

NOTES

1   See Susan Faludi, *Backlash: The Undeclared War Against American Women* (New York: Crown, 1991).

2   I use this term reluctantly because the term itself is implicitly racist. The language lumps all 'women of colour' together as being 'not white,' thus implying that the only normative woman is white.

REFERENCES

Burman, Patrick, *Killing Time: Experiences of Unemployment.* Toronto: Thompson Educational Publishing, 1988.

Harman, Lesley D. *When a Hostel Becomes a Home: Experiences of Women.* Toronto: Garamond, 1989.

National Council of Welfare, *Women and Poverty Revisited.* Ottawa: Ministry of Supply and Services, 1990.

CHAPTER SIX

Private Troubles or Public Issues?

Feminism, like other perspectives, fosters awareness of the linkages between private troubles and public issues. Many private problems are not unique and ultimately cannot be ameliorated through private solutions. Understanding commonalities of experiences develops awareness of underlying social influences producing these private experiences and leads to the realization of a necessity for collective and public solutions. As well, through connecting the private and the public, feminists have begun creating linkages between the experiences of various categories of women and men whose lives were once superficially thought to be separate and distinct.

Sedef Arat-Koc (Article 30) examines problems confronted by immigrant workers who perform child-care duties in the homes of Canadians as a consequence of changing labour force patterns and the demands made on the Canadian household as a result of these changes. Arat-Koc argues that many difficulties experienced by these workers are a consequence of government immigration policies in combination with a lack of policy pertaining to the Canadian domestic situation.

Stuart Hills (Article 31) argues that rather than query what a rape victim wore, or how some aspect of her personality, language, or demeanour supposedly provoked a private act of rape, we should focus on the very nature of the male gender role to understand the social problem of rape. He suggests that certain aspects of the "masculine mystique" provide precipitants for rape such that the act becomes essentially an act of conformity, not deviance. Hills' analysis suggests the necessity of changing male gender expectations in order to reduce the conditions permitting acts of violence against women. Readers are invited to speculate on how much, if at all, male socialization and the larger social environment have changed since this article was first written.

Susan Wendell's presentation (Article 32) forges links between the disadvantages of being a woman and being a person with a disability in our society. Just as women's lives are marginalized by a society that assumes male experience as the norm, so too are people with disabilities relegated to invisibility in a society dominated by assumptions of an able-bodied citizenry. Linda Gerber (Article 33), examines the multiple jeopardies experienced by Canadian women who are also members of Indian, Métis, or Inuit ethnic groups. These women are disadvantaged because they experience the multiplied prejudice and discrimination accorded individuals occupying each stigmatized social category.

Walter DeKeseredy, Hyman Burshtyn, and Charles Gordon (Article 34) respond to a Canadian government initiative that they contend is narrowly framed within a private responsibility perspective that ignores the larger public issues surrounding the abuse of women. These authors contend that such an initiative is myopic and of no real or ultimate value to this pressing issue.

Finally, Peter Marin (Article 35), addressing the issue of "homelessness" among men, turns our attention to the underlying issue of gender expectations held of men in general. He suggests that our negative reaction to the plight of individual homeless men is ultimately founded on our implicit understandings about gender.

30

The Politics of Family and Immigration in the Subordination of Domestic Workers in Canada

Sedef Arat-Koc

Despite marked increases in the participation of women in the labour force, neither the availability and the quality of socialized childcare arrangements nor the division of housework between men and women appear to have changed radically. The structure, demands, and pressures of the labour market in Canada allow for little flexibility in the accommodation of family needs and responsibilities. Under these circumstances, housework and child care remain private problems to be shouldered mainly by women, who must either work double and triple days or find substitutes.

In this context, the employment of live-in domestic workers—a long-abandoned practice in North America—is once again being presented as a solution to the burdens of housework and childcare among high and middle income groups. Yet the way domestic service is organized in capitalist society in general, and the specific conditions of the majority of live-in domestic workers (98 per cent of whom are women), make this type of work particularly oppressive. This "solution" therefore presents a "problem" for "women's liberation" as a collective ideal.

In discussing the implications of the domestic service "solution" to the housework and childcare problem, I will document and analyse the structural and historical conditions of live-in domestic workers in Canada. My primary focus is on foreign domestic workers with temporary work permits. The conditions of this group best demonstrate the complex articulation of gender issues with those of class, race and citizenship.

THE CRISIS OF THE DOMESTIC SPHERE

There has been a very significant increase in women's participation in the labour force in Canada since the 1960s. With around 44.3 per cent of the labour force comprising women (Statistics Canada 1989: B-2), the percent-

From Sedef Arat-Koc, "The Politics of Family and Immigration in the Subordination of Domestic Workers in Canada," in Bonnie J. Fox (ed.), *Family Patterns, Gender Relations*. Toronto: Oxford University Press, 1993, pp. 278–296.

age of couples in the man-the-breadwinner/woman-the-homemaker category has been reduced to less than 16 per cent from around 65 per cent in 1961 (The Task Force on Child Care 1986: 7). What is more dramatic, however, is the change in the participation rates of women with family responsibilities. According to the most recent statistics, 75.7 per cent of married women between the ages of 25 and 44 years are in the labour force (Statistics Canada 1989: B-12). Among women with children of preschool age, 69.6 per cent work outside their homes (Statistics Canada 1989: B–20).

The response of society and the state to these changes in women's employment has been negligible. First, the behaviour of men in the home has changed very little in terms of their contributions to housework and parenting responsibilities. Although attitudes among men have changed positively (Luxton 1986: 20), the actual numbers of men regularly doing some housework have not changed significantly. Moreover, even when men regularly contribute to domestic labour, the sex-typing of duties continues, with men only taking on certain defined tasks and rarely doing any pre-task planning. Overall, the contribution of most men who do some housework does not very often go beyond "helping out" (Luxton 1986, Vanek 1983).

Second, as the Report of the Task Force on Child Care demonstrates, the childcare situation in Canada is in a state of crisis. Over 80 per cent of children receiving non-parental care are in unlicensed arrangements, the quality and dependability of which are unknown. Licensed day-care spaces only serve 9 per cent of children whose parents work or study 20 or more hours each week (The Task Force on Child Care 1986: 45, 277).

Parents also suffer the inflexibility of work arrangements. Canadian employers and the state have provided little accommodation for the family responsibilities of working people. Except for an inadequate parental leave system (which has only recently been extended to fathers, only replaces a relatively small portion of regular income, and covers a relatively short period of time), Canada lacks an official recognition of recent changes in the labour force. In stark contrast to most European countries, there are no systems of extended childcare leave, leave for care of sick children, or other types of family responsibility leave in Canada. Without the rights to refuse shiftwork and overtime and to work reduced hours or flexible work weeks (rights that are almost commonplace for their European counterparts), working parents in Canada find that even privatized solutions fail to meet their needs (The Task Force on Child Care 1986: Chs 11, 12).

As a result of the squeeze on working couples from pressures in the public and private spheres, there are signs that employment of domestic servants, a rare practice since the 1920s, may be becoming widespread again. Several governmental and mass media sources have mentioned the employment of domestic workers as a solution (Hook 1978, Royal Commission on the Status of Women 1970, Vanstone 1986). Indeed, there is evidence to suggest that employers of live-in domestic workers are now overwhelmingly dual-career couples with small children. For 71.4 per cent of the employers the major reason for hiring a domestic has been to "free both spouses for the labour market" (The Task Force on Immigration Practices and Procedures 1981: 35–45). While the majority of employers are in upper-middle to upper income categories, there is a possibility that the demand for live-in domestic servants among middle-income families may rise. An important reason for this is that user fees—as opposed to municipal, provincial or national government financing—constitute a high proportion of childcare costs and middle-class families cannot get subsidies for such services in Canada. Calculations suggest that especially for parents with two or more pre-school children, employment of a live-in nanny would cost significantly less than sending children to a day-care centre or hiring live-out help (Vanstone 1986: 51, Walmsley 1989: 129).

While the demand for domestic workers rises, the conditions of domestic service in general and live-in service in particular are so undesirable that it is very difficult to find Canadians willing to do the job. As a result, the Canadian Department of Immigration has devised mechanisms to bring in domestic workers, usually from the Third World, on temporary status. Since the mid-1970s between 10,000 to 16,000 foreign workers a year have been issued temporary work permits. Almost all (96 per cent) of these workers are in live-in service (The Task Force on Immigration Practices and Procedures 1981: 53).

Although foreign domestic workers have certainly provided some solution to the pressures their employers face in meeting the demands of work and family, this solution is very questionable when one considers the working and living conditions of the workers involved. If these conditions are not changed radically, this solution also has serious implications for the women's movement. With the employment of domestic workers, work in the domestic sphere becomes a source of division, rather than unity and "sisterhood"[1] among women.

This paper starts with a short history of domestic service. The discussion of the conditions of domestic workers is divided into three parts. The first part examines the labour process in domestic service and analyses what the domestic worker shares with the housewife. The second part focuses on the ambiguous status of the domestic as a special type of worker who is neither a member of the family nor an employee in the public sphere enjoying some advantages of socialized work. Finally, the citizenship status of foreign domestic workers in Canada is analysed as a major factor contributing to, as well as perpetuating, the oppressiveness of their conditions.

HISTORY OF DOMESTIC SERVICE

The emergence of domestic service, as service provided by non-family members in the domestic sphere, is relatively recent, corresponding to the public-private split that came about with industrialization. Although servants were very widely employed in feudal Europe, the nature of their work and their status differed significantly from those of later domestic servants.

In feudal Europe, the labour requirements of most households—including those of most peasants and artisans—necessitated, at least during certain phases of their family cycle, the employment of servants. These would be children of poorer families and/or children of other families in different phases of their family life cycle. Social historians like Flandrin (1979) and Mitterauer and Seider (1982) have clearly demonstrated that in an era when "family" was synonymous with household, servants were very much a part of the patriarchal family, owing the same obedience and expecting the same protection and guidance as any family member, especially a child. In households that combined productive and reproductive work, servants performed unspecialized work alongside other family members, little of which had to do with the creation and maintenance of a comfortable domestic environment (Fairchilds 1984: 23–4).

With industrialization, the types of work performed by the family were divided and assigned to separate and gendered spheres. As the middle class home sought to become a "haven" in the competitive and harsh environment of early industrial society, the very purposes and nature of servant-keeping were transformed to serve the new emphasis on domestic comfort. Changes in the structure of society and the family in this period affected domestic service in more ways than one. Parallel to servants' work becoming exclusively "domestic" for the first time, was the "feminization" of the occupation. As the home was defined to be the women's sphere and housework to be women's work, domestic servants as well as their employers became predominantly female.

Another change that characterized this period of transformation was the increased social distance between master and servant. There were two factors. One was the increased privatization of the family that defined it as a nuclear unit of parents and children and excluded servants as "strangers" (Fairchilds 1984: 13–17, Rollins 1985: 33–6). Second, unlike the situation in feudal peasant and artisan households, where masters were direct producers, some of the bourgeois mistresses of the new domestic servants began to separate themselves from manual work. While the majority of middle-class [sic] who could only afford one servant had to work side by side with them to keep up with highly demanding housework, upper-class women, though committed to an ideology of domesticity, began to maintain a clear distinction between their own managerial and supervisory roles in the home and the physical drudgery that servants undertook (Dudden 1983: Ch. 5).

The history of domestic work in both Canada and the United States has been closely connected to histories of racial and ethnic relations and immigration as well as to industrialization and urbanization. During the colonial period in the United States, domestic service was performed mainly by convicts, indentured servants, and black slaves. In this period, the low status and indignities servants suffered were common in both the South and the North (Rollins 1985: 49).

From the American Revolution until about mid-nineteenth century, the exploitative and degrading treatment of black slaves in the U.S. South coincided with relatively egalitarian master/servant relationships in the northern United States and Canada. The term "help" was used for the native-born whites in the North, who partially replaced the foreign or black servants of the colonial period ([Rollins] 1985). Generally employed by farmers and small shopkeepers, the "help" cooperated with the employer in the hard work of the family economy. The relationship of "help" to their employers was quite egalitarian in the sense that they shared the conditions and the tables of the families for whom they worked. Also distinguishing "help" from past and future groups of domestic workers was the fact that theirs was less an occupation and life-long status than an activity that allowed casual temporary and/or part-time employment (Dudden 1983). The conditions contrasted sharply with relations in bourgeois households in the cities where the social distance between employers and employees was growing.[2]

From around the middle of the nineteenth century to the 1920s, the kinds of changes in domestic service that occurred in Europe as a result of the development of industrialization and urbanization also prevailed in North America. As the urban middle-class family became more privatized, its emphasis on domestic comforts and luxury increased and therefore it became more dependent than ever on outsiders to actualize its standard of a private haven. While this substantially increased the demand for domestic workers, changes such as the decline in the general status of the domestic sphere, the "bourgeoisification" of servant employers, and the distinctions drawn between family and non-family members precluded better working and living conditions for domestic workers.

Further contributing to a decline in the status of servants—or, in certain regions, the persistence of their low status—was the availability of groups of vulnerable workers. In the northeastern United States, immigrants like the Irish—many of them single women—were fleeing economic desperation in their own countries, finding almost no alternatives to domestic work, and were thus particularly vulnerable. The term "servant", rarely used in the democratic atmosphere of the post-revolution era in the U.S. North, was reintroduced in this period (Rollins 1985: 51–2, Steinberg 1981: 159). In regions where there were large concentrations of people of colour, it was usually the women of the oppressed racial/ethnic groups who had to take domestic service positions.

Despite differences in the composition of the populations and the mix of industries in the regions, there were important similarities in the situation of Mexicans in the Southwest, African Americans in the South, and Japanese people in northern California and Hawaii.

Each of these groups was placed in a separate legal category from whites, excluded from rights and protections according to full citizens.(Glenn 1992: 8)

Since the turn of the century, changes in the labour market as well as changes in the household have led to a decline in domestic service. First of all, alternative avenues of female employment opened up as industrialization progressed, and some white-collar occupations were feminized. So, women rejected domestic service in favour of better working conditions elsewhere. Even when net wages from clerical, shops, or factory work were lower, women left domestic work to enjoy the relative independence of private life after work (Barber 1985). The demand for domestic workers also began to fall with improvements in household technology, falling birth rates, and market production of goods previously produced in the household (Leslie 1974: 74). Since the beginning of the twentieth century, increased access to electricity, running water, and sewage systems; the mechanization of heating, refrigeration, and laundry; the development of food processing; and the increased use of ready-made clothing meant for middle- and upper-class women that one person alone (in this case, the housewife) could do all the housework (Fox 1980; Luxton 1980). To the extent that domestic service survived, living-out became more wide-spread (Rollins 1985: 54).

In Canada, despite the unwillingness of women to enter domestic service, employers were remarkably successful in maintaining a large supply of servants until World War II. Organized around church groups, YWCA, and other women's clubs and organizations, women seeking domestics were greatly assisted by the Immigration Department (Leslie 1974; Roberts 1979). As domestic service in urban Canada became so undesirable that no native-born whites would do it, and as industrialization diverted women into other occupations, the Immigration Department became increasingly and more directly involved in ensuring a supply of domestics.

Although the demand for domestic workers decreased from the early part of the twentieth century until the late 1960s, it has always exceeded the supply. This has especially been the case for live-in jobs. As a result, the Department of Immigration has had to develop new schemes in the post-war period to bring domestic workers to Canada and to keep them doing domestic work.

THE MATERIAL CONDITIONS OF PRIVATIZED HOUSEHOLD WORK

The geographic, economic, social, and ideological separation of a public work sphere from the home, which developed with socialized commodity production under capitalism, has led to a decline in the status of domestic labour—whether done by housewife or servant. One of the causes of this decline is the physical, economical, and ideological invisibility of domestic labour. Physically, what makes domestic labour "invisible" is the service or maintenance nature of a work whose products are either intangible or consumed very quickly. The domestic labourer is at a disadvantage compared to the factory worker in this regard:

> *The appropriate symbol for housework (and for housework alone) is not the interminable conveyor belt but a compulsive circle like a pet mouse in its cage spinning round on its exercise wheel unable to get off ... (Williams, Twart and Bachelli 1980: 114)*

Also, domestic labour is performed in private, and perhaps is more isolated than ever before in human history. As the production of goods as well as services (such as education and health care) moved out of the home, as the husband and children left, and as the development of household technology made collaboration with other women less necessary, the household worker faced increased isolation, loneliness and invisibility.

Economically, domestic labour is invisible because it is not part of production that utilizes wage labour to produce commodities (for the market) and profit. When performed by the housewife, domestic labour is unpaid; it produces use-value and no profit. In comparison to that of the housewife, the labour of the domestic servant is relatively more visible because it is paid for. As one domestic servant stated, however, it still can remain invisible, even in the eyes of her female employer.

> *You know how housework is; you could tidy up the house and wash the dishes twenty times a day. At the end of each day, especially with three growing boy child, the house look like a hurricane pass through it, so when she is in a bad mood she wants to know what I do all day. (Noreen, in Silvera 1983: 25)*

Domestic labour involves physical and mental work, which goes into the reproduction of labour-power and of the labour force. This is very important and indispensable for the economy. However, intertwined as it is with intimate, personal relations, domestic labour is considered a private matter, a "labour of love". As such, it is ideologically invisible as a form of real and hard work, a status that is hard to change even when it is paid.

Domestic labour generally does not appear on paycheques; or in GNP figures; it is not considered "real work", and is defined as "non-productive". Yet it involves very long working hours.[3] It is work that never ends. Especially for care-givers of young children who must be always on call, there is no clear boundary between work and leisure. For the housewife and the live-in domestic servant, the place of work is also the place of leisure. A domestic does not go to work but wakes up to it. This makes her "leisure" vulnerable to interruptions and her work hours stretchable to 24 hours a day, seven days a week.

Contrary to its image as a place of comfort and safety, the reality of the home for the domestic labourer is one of a hazardous and stressful workplace. Besides working with dangerous chemicals and being involved in several activities that are accident-prone, the domestic worker also experiences stress. Stress is typical for occupations that involve high demand and low control (Rosenberg 1986, 1987). In domestic work, the need to adjust work to the different schedules of family members, and to juggle the conflicting demands of housework and childcare, create stressful conditions. Being her own boss is largely a myth for the housewife. It is probably more so for the domestic worker whose schedule and standards of work are controlled by the employer.

Unlike wage labour which is—at least theoretically—changeable, the labour of the housewife is a life-long or at least marriage-long commitment. Compared to the housewife, the domestic servant should fare better in this respect. This is only the case when we consider the free labourer. Domestic servants in Canada have very often been restricted in their ability to change employers, or even to decide whether or not to sell their labour power.

While domestic labour under capitalism assumes several universal characteristics such as invisibility, isolation and low status, the way these are experienced by individuals performing domestic labour may vary significantly by class, race and citizenship. In the case of foreign domestic workers, the isolation and resulting loneliness imposed by the privatized nature of housework and childcare are perpetuated by racial, cultural and linguistic barriers. Likewise, the invisibility of domestic labour and the low status attached to it are further reinforced by the powerlessness of domestic labourers when they are visible minority women from the Third World on temporary work permits, who lack basic political rights.

NEITHER A WIFE NOR A WORKER

The contradictions of the domestic worker's status

While sharing with the housewife many of the material conditions of privatized housework and child care, the domestic worker also has an ambiguous status: she is neither a wife nor a full-fledged worker with corresponding rights and privileges. Squeezed between the private and public spheres, she belongs to neither one nor the other, and probably experiences the worst aspects of both.

With the privatization of the family, the domestic worker has been excluded from membership in or close bonding with the employing family. Lost are the cooperation and companionship apparently characteristic of relations between "help" and employers in rural North America. The domestic worker today is like a stranger, "being *in* the family, but not *of* it" (Leslie

1974: 87). She is involved in the work of a *house,* but not the pleasures and intimacies of a *home.* Positive traits that are rightly or wrongly attributed to the private sphere—love, intimacy, nurturance, companionship—are not even part of her realistic expectations.

> *I feel as if this is my home. It is my home, this is where I live. It's not like I come to work for them and then eveningtime I leave and go home. When you are living with them, they make you feel as if you really don't belong, and where the devil do you really belong? It's a funny thing to happen to us, because it makes us feel like we don't know if we coming or going. This live-in thing really puts us in a funny situation. (Gail, in Silvera 1983: 113)*

Potentially, lack of intimacy with the employing family is liberating. Since class differences turn close employer-employee relationships into paternalistic ones, many domestic workers actually prefer to maintain a businesslike professionalism. Professionalism in relations, however, is not possible for the domestic worker, since it requires relative power in social, political, and legal terms. Historically, the social construction of domestic work in Canada has deprived domestic workers of these forms of power.

In losing the close relationship to the family and becoming an employee, the domestic worker has not been compensated by the advantages other employees enjoy. The isolation of domestic service makes the organization of workers as well as the standardization and regulation of working conditions very difficult. This difficulty is greater for live-in workers for whom there is no separation between home and work. The result is generally a vulnerable and often exploited worker whose conditions are at the mercy of the employer.

> *Wages are too often regulated by the employer's bank account, hours of service by his personal caprice, and moral questions by his personal convenience. (Salmon, cited in Leslie 1974: 112)*

Labour standards legislation—which is under provincial jurisdiction in Canada and therefore not uniform—either does not apply or only partially applies to domestic workers. Domestic employees in private homes are excluded from labour standards legislation in Alberta, New Brunswick, Nova Scotia, the Northwest Territories, and the Yukon. In other provinces they are only partially covered—in many, only with provisions providing lower than the general minimum wage, longer then the 40-hour-workweek and rarely any overtime pay (Estable 1986: 51–3; The Task Force on Immigration Practices and Procedures 1981: 74–8).

In Ontario, which has about two-thirds of all domestic workers in Canada, the Employment Standards Act finally was extended to domestics in 1984. It set daily and weekly rates of pay based on a standard workweek of 44 hours. This change, however, was almost meaningless for live-in domestic workers because they were not covered by the hours of work and overtime pay provisions of the Act. Since it is not uncommon to see live-in domestic workers working or on call 60 to 80 or more hours per week, the actual hourly wage can in many cases fall substantially below the minimum wage. Working very long hours and having little or no time off are actually some of the most common complaints of live-in domestic workers:

> *I want something where I can go home to my house at night, close my door and pray to my God in peace. I want to know that when I go to bed at night, I don't have to listen out for people shouting at me to come and look after their food or come and change diapers. (Noreen, in Silvera 1983, 26)*

It took the Ontario government two years of negotiations and a Charter of Rights case against itself (filed by the Toronto Organization for Domestic Workers' Rights, INTERCEDE) to produce labour regulation (in October 1987) that gave live-in domestic workers the right to claim overtime pay after a 44-hour workweek.[4] Whether or not the new provision is enforced depends on how much *de facto* bargaining power domestics have in relation to their employers. So far, even when protective legislation exists, governments have generally failed to enforce it. In practice, especially when they are dealing with vulnerable workers who have no choice but to remain in the job, employers are free to set work hours, duties and pay rates.

In Ontario, provincial governments have not only failed to enforce existing legislation, but also prevented domestic workers from defending their rights in an organized, collective way. The Ontario Labour Relations Act denies the domestics employed in private homes the right to unionize.[5] The same act also denies domestics access to an impartial tribunal for unfair practices (Estable 1986: 51).[6]

There are social-psychological dimensions to the subordination of a domestic worker that make it different from the subordination of housewives (who also do domestic work) and workers (who also stand in an unequal class relation to their employers). While a factory worker experiences subordination and control during work, when she leaves her job at the end of the day she is a free person in relation to her employer. The live-in domestic worker, on the other hand, cannot leave her workplace and her employer's supervision. Sharing private space with the employers, and yet not being part of their family, the domestic finds it difficult to create her own private space and private life:

> *Some domestics have to share a room with the children in the household or have their room used as a family room, TV room, sewing room, etc. One woman had to keep her door open at all times in case the chil-*

dren started to cry, others say their employers did not respect their privacy and walk in without knocking. In one case the piano was moved into the domestic's room for the children to practise on! (Epstein 1983: 26)

Living in the employer's home, it is also difficult to invite friends over. Other specific complaints about lack of privacy refer in certain cases to the domestic's mail and phones being watched, personal belongings searched, and inquiries into her activities after days off (Silvera 1981, 1983). With live-in domestic service creating the possibility for total scrutiny over both the work and the lives of domestic workers, it probably is not an exaggeration to call domestic service a "total institution" (Cock 1980, 58–60, Fairchilds 1984: 102–4).

Clearly, during its historical development, domestic service has lost only some of the elements of the childlike status it had in earlier patriarchial households. Gone are the protection, security, and bonding to the family that were typical of service in feudal society. Remaining are the supervision and personal nature of the authority relationship which strip the domestic worker of full adult status. Linguistic practices are often reflective of this. For example, it is very common for both employers and domestics themselves to refer to domestics as "girls", regardless of their age. It is also common for domestic workers to be called by their first names while they are expected to address their employers as Mr or Mrs (Hook 1978: 63, Rollins 1985: 158).

Besides heavy physical work, domestic service involves a personal relationship with the employer. Unlike factory work, which requires completion of clearly defined tasks in clearly defined ways, domestic service is very unstructured. Especially in live-in arrangements, a domestic is not just hired for specific tasks, "but for general availability; above all, a servant ha(s) to take orders as well" (Leslie 1974: 83). Consequently, the deference, obedience, and submissiveness that the domestic is supposed to display can sometimes be as important or a more important part of her job than the actual physical work.[7] The domestic worker, therefore, is hired not for her labour alone but also for her personality traits.

Also unique to the employer-employee relationship in domestic service is that both the domestic and the mistress are designated, on the basis of gender, as responsible for domestic work. In different studies, all the female employers interviewed have indicated that they needed the domestic worker to help them because their husbands would not (Kaplan 1985, Rollins 1985). Employment of a domestic worker has enabled these women to avoid a confrontation with their husbands about sharing domestic work. In this sense, the presence of the domestic worker "emphasizes the fact that women—all women—are responsible for cleaning the house, at the same time that it releases the housewife to become a lady of leisure or a career woman" (Kaplan 1985: 17). Given the gendered division of labour in the household, the labour of the housewife and of the domestic worker is interchangeable: the domestic worker is employed to replace an absent full-time housewife, but when the domestic worker can't work, the housewife must. Given the social degradation of domestic work and the class inequality between the domestic worker and the mistress, however, their shared subordination does not often lead to solidarity.

> *[T]he domestic represents the employer in the most devalued area of the employer's activities. ... Any identification the employer has with the domestic is a negative identification. (Rollins 1985: 185)*

Rather than solidarity, shared subordination can lead to "housewife power strategies" through which "many housewives seek to maintain class and race privileges *vis-à-vis* their domestics" (Kaplan 1985). What characterizes servant-mistress relationships is deference from the worker and maternalism from the employer.

GOOD ENOUGH TO WORK, NOT GOOD ENOUGH TO STAY

Implications of citizenship status for foreign domestic workers

From the nineteenth century on, the Canadian state has been very active in recruiting and controlling a domestic labour force (Barber 1986, Leslie 1974, Lindstrom-Best 1986). The amount of planning and energy that has gone into these activities tells us a great deal about the importance of domestic service for the Canadian economy and society. The low status and unfavourable conditions of the workers involved, however, stand in stark contrast to the attention their recruitment and control have received. In fact, the conditions have been so undesirable that not only has it been difficult to find Canadians interested in the job but the only way of keeping immigrant domestics in domestic work has sometimes been through indenturing them.

Active state involvement in recruitment and control of domestic workers started in the late nineteenth century when industrialization diverted women into other occupations and it became difficult to find enough Canadian-born women interested in domestic service. This involvement ranged from making the immigration of domestics easier by sending immigration employees to England and Scotland to select domestics, to encouraging and even enforcing the so-called "assisted passage" agreements that bonded servants to their employers for a certain period of time (Leslie 1974: 95–105). Bonding became such a necessary part of controlling the domestic labour force that the Department of Immigration sometimes evaded legislation in order to fulfil its policing function. For example, around the turn of the century, most provinces enacted master and servant legislation aimed to protect servants from an exploitative contract that they might have signed in order to immigrate. According to this legislation, contracts signed outside the province were not legally binding. The Immigration Department, however, aiming to enforce bonded status, avoided this legislation by having immigrant domestics re-sign their contracts upon arrival in Canada (Leslie 1974: 122).

Immigration of British and Scottish domestic workers in the late nineteenth and early twentieth century shared with later domestic immigration the practice of bonding. What made immigration practices in this period different from later periods, however, was that recruitment of domestics from abroad was closely linked to Canada's nation-building efforts. Until the 1920s, the middle-class women and social reformers involved in female immigration work voiced racist, nationalist, and moralistic concerns that went beyond a simple interest in meeting demands for the domestic labour force. Through their efforts in selecting, protecting, and supervising domestics, the organizations involved in female immigration wanted to make sure that the recruits would become more than servants: that these women of the "right" national and racial stock and character would, in the long run, constitute the "pure and virtuous mothers of the ideal Canadian home and the foundation of the moral Canadian nation" (Roberts 1979: 188–9). While these expectations were certainly restrictive for domestic workers, they also conveyed the message that these women "belonged" in Canadian society, a message that would be missing in later immigration practices.

The West Indian Domestic Scheme

Although the demand for domestic servants has decreased since the early part of the twentieth century, it has still exceeded the supply. This has especially been the case for live-in jobs. As a result, the Department of Immigration has developed new schemes in the post-war period to bring domestic workers to Canada and to keep them doing domestic work. In 1955, for example, the Domestic Worker Program was started to import domestic workers from the Caribbean region (primarily from Jamaica). Under this scheme single women of good health, between 18 and 40 years of age, with no dependents and of at least grade 8 education, were allowed into Canada as landed immigrants on the condition that they would spend at least one year as domestic servants before being free to choose other types of work (Arnopoulos 1979: 26). Through this program, between 1955 and 1960, an average of 300, and between 1960–1965 around 1,000, domestic workers were admitted per year (Bolaria and Li 1985: 178).

Even though the West Indian Domestic Scheme brought in domestics as landed immigrants, it did involve special "administrative controls" which were missing in previous immigration schemes involving white European domestics. Any domestic who broke her contract or was found "undesirable" (e.g., upon becoming pregnant in her first year) would be deported to her country of origin at the expense of the Caribbean government. Also, unlike preferred domestics from western and northern Europe, West Indian domestics would not be eligible to apply for interest-free travel loans from the Canadian government under the Assisted Passage Loan Scheme (Calliste 1989: 143).

The introduction of temporary status

In the late 1960s, Canadian demand for domestic workers began to increase. This was due to the increasing participation of women in the labour force and insufficient developments in the child care system. In this period, the Department of Immigration started to see the Domestic Worker Program as inadequate in helping to solve the labour shortage in domestic service because most women who came as domestics found their working conditions unacceptable and left service for other work once they fulfilled their one-year obligation. Rather than providing the mechanisms to improve conditions for domestic work and make it attractive for people to stay—through extending and enforcing labour standards and human rights legislation to domestic workers, for example—the Canadian state opted for a solution that would force people to stay in domestic work.

In the 1960s and the early 1970s—in spite of the high and rising demand for domestic workers—immigration authorities arbitrarily lowered the rating for domestic work within the occupational demand category (Bakan and Stasiulis 1992a). In 1973, the government started issuing temporary work permits that would let these workers stay in the country for only a specified period of time (usually a year), doing a specific type of work, for a specific employer. This temporary employment authorization system became a new version of indenture. From 1973 to 1981, foreign domestic workers could only come to Canada as "guest workers"—instead of immigrants. As "guest workers", they had no rights to stay in Canada or claim social security benefits. Although with special permission from immigration authorities foreign domestics could change employers, they could not leave domestic service without also having to leave Canada. Extension of the employment visa beyond the first year was possible and common, but the foreign worker inevitably had to leave Canada. Under this new scheme, increasing numbers of domestic workers were brought into Canada every year. The numbers of employment visas issued to domestics rose consistently from around 1,800 in 1973 to more than 16,000 in 1982 (Bolaria and Li 1985: 178, Silvera 1983: 15).

The official purpose of the employment visa system was to meet the urgent and temporary needs of Canadian employers to fill jobs that cannot be filled domestically without ultimately threatening the employment opportunities of Canadian residents (Wong 1984: 86). When we consider the case of domestic service, however, both the unwillingness of Canadians to take live-in work as well as the century-long efforts of the Canadian state to import domestic workers from abroad, suggest that neither the need nor the solution has been temporary. Despite the persistence of a high demand/low supply situation, domestic workers have, since the 1970s, only been accepted into Canada with temporary status. Except for foreign agricultural workers—who do seasonal work—domestic workers have been the *only* occupational group to whom temporary work permits apply on a permanent basis.

When we look into Canada's immigration practices since the mid-1970s we see an increasing tendency to resort to temporary employment visas as opposed to permanent immigration to meet labour demands not only in domestic service but also in several other job categories. Since 1975 the annual number of people entering Canada on temporary employment visas has consistently exceeded the number of landed immigrants destined for the labour force (Epstein 1983: 237, Wong 1984: 92). Migration to Canada, therefore, has changed in part from a movement of people to a movement of labour power. The benefits of this to Canada as a labour-importing country are enormous. As the literature on migrant workers in Western Europe, South Africa, and California has demonstrated, recipient countries benefit not only by avoiding the costs of developing a young and healthy labour-force, but also by avoiding a commitment to supporting them during old age, sickness and unemployment (Burawoy 1980, Castles and Cosack [sic] 1973, Gorz 1970).

> *Behind the term 'guestworker' [is] a belief that such workers [are] like replaceable parts. Like cogs in a machine, for every part that breaks down, there [is] a seemingly endless supply of replacements. (Rist 1979: 51)*

There are also significant political advantages to employing workers without citizenship rights. Lacking electoral and political rights and freedoms, and dependent on their employers not only for wages but also for their continued stay in the country, workers on employment visas are expected to create a docile and acquiescent labour force. Historically, the presence of migrant workers has also been frequently associated with racist and xenophobic divisions in the working class.

> *Canadians have the feeling that we are coming here to rob them, to take away their jobs, yet we are the ones who clean up their mess, pick up after them. We take the jobs they wouldn't take and yet they hate us so much. (Primrose, in Silvera 1983: 100)*

One significant ideological implication of temporary work permits is that designation of a group of workers as temporary and foreign encourages a desensitized attitude towards their conditions. Hannah Arendt argues that with the development of nation-states and national sovereignty, basic human rights and freedoms were thoroughly implicated with the rights of citizenship (1966: Ch. 9). In liberal democratic society, where emphasis on formal equality has become a part of popular political discourse, separation of people into "citizen" and "non-citizen" categories, into "insiders" (to whom rights apply) and "outsiders", serves to legitimize inferior conditions and lesser rights for the latter group.[8]

The major effect of Canada's employment visa system on domestic workers has been the creation of a captive labour force which has guaranteed that the turnover in domestic service would remain low no matter how bad the working and living conditions. Unable to leave domestic service without losing their rights to stay in Canada, foreign domestics have also found it difficult to change employers. A foreign worker's status in Canada changes to that of visitor if she leaves or loses her job. While in practice workers are generally given a period of two weeks to find a new employer, the decision to issue a new employment visa is at the discretion of the individual immigration officer who judges whether the working conditions with the previous employer have in fact been intolerable (The Task Force on Immigration Practices and Procedures 1981: 26–7).[9] Besides hassles from individual immigration officers, there is a regulation that requires workers on employment visa to have a "release letter" from the former employer before changing employers (Toughill 1986).[10]

Unlike other workers who enjoy the basic freedom to leave a particular job or employer, the only freedom that the foreign worker on an employment visa has is to return to her country of origin. In the case of many Third World women who come to Canada out of conditions of economic desperation, there is no choice but to stay in Canada. As Nancy Hook reported, compared to Canadian workers, foreign domestic workers on employment visa were more likely to live in the homes of their employer, to work more days per week,[11] to work more overtime without pay, and to receive a smaller hourly wage (Hook 1978: 107–8).

Even though their status in Canada is by definition temporary, domestic workers on employment visas have been required to pay Canadian Pension Plan, Unemployment Insurance premiums and income tax (about one month's earnings a year) without being able to claim benefits.[12] The nature of the employment visa has made access to unemployment insurance benefits impossible because the worker losing a job either has to find a new employer or leave the country. Benefits from Canada Pension Plan also have been inaccessible because the "guest worker" is expected to retire in the country of origin (The Task Force on Child Care 1986: 121). For services that they do not expect to receive, foreign domestics have paid a very high price. Revenue Canada has calculated the total of revenues from CPP and UIC premiums collected from foreign domestics between 1973–1979 to be more than 11 million dollars (The Task Force on Immigration Practices and Procedures 1981: 70).[13]

The Foreign Domestic Movement (FDM) Program

In 1981, a federal task force was established to study the conditions of domestic workers on temporary work permits. Its report recommended that the Temporary Employment Authorization system be continued provided that opportunities for landing be broadened (The Task Force on Immigration Policies and Procedures 1981). The Foreign Domestic Movement (FDM) program which came into effect in November 1981 has enabled foreign domestics who have worked in Canada continuously for two years to apply for landed immigrant status without having to leave the country. While this was a progressive step, it failed to solve the problem of foreign domestic workers in Canada. First, the FDM continued to impose a two-year period of bonded service that the domestic had to fulfil before applying. In some ways, the practice of indenturing was strengthened by the entrenchment in the FDM of a mandatory live-in requirement for all participants in the program. Domestic workers who insisted on live-out arrangements would not only lose their rights to apply for landed immigrant status but also would not receive extension on their employment authorization (Employment and Immigration Canada 1988: 17–18).[14]

Another problem with the FDM program has been that it gave no guarantee that landed immigrant status would be granted. Applicants needed to meet Immigration assessment criteria and demonstrate a "potential for self-sufficiency".[15] Reflecting societal notions about domestic labour in general, these women continued to get very low points for both the Specific Vocational Preparation category[16] and, ironically, the Occupational Demand category (The Task Force on Immigration Practices and Procedures 1981: 18–21). As a result, immigration officers required domestic applicants (again without any guarantees to grant them landing) to take upgrading courses (with high foreign-student fees), to demonstrate adaptation and integration into Canadian society (through volunteer work in the community), and to prove financial management skills (through evidence of savings, etc.)—all special requirements applying to domestic workers only. For live-in foreign domestics, it has been difficult to afford both the time and the money to meet these requirements. Another problem has been that domestics with children (in the home country)[17] and older domestics have faced special discrimination during assessment for immigration status.

> *They say Immigration say any woman over 45 soon can't clean house and will be just a burden on the government, and woman with over two children will bring them into the country and take away the opportunities other Canadian children have. (Noreen in Silvera 1983: 29)*

So-called "rationalized" immigration policies, oriented towards the demands of the market, aim to import labour power rather than people. It is not, therefore, surprising to see dependents being treated as "superfluous appendages" (as they are called in South Africa).

The overall effect of the 1981 changes in the Temporary Employment Authorization Program has been to create the possibility for *individual* upward mobility of some domestic workers while providing no *structural* solution to the problems of domestic service or foreign domestic workers in general. Indeed, it is ironic that to accumulate enough points to get landed immigrant status, a domestic has to move out of domestic service altogether. The implicit message that immigration policies and practices give is that domestic workers, as domestic workers, are "good enough to work, but not good enough to stay" in this country. This message surely tells us a great deal about the status of domestic labour in general.

Furthermore, it is interesting to note the parallel between the modern attitude of the Canadian government and the historical treatment of domestic workers. Domestic servants did not receive legal equality and citizenship rights until the late nineteenth or early twentieth century. In France and England, for example, because they were considered to be too dependent on their masters to be recognized as civil persons, domestics (together with women) were the last groups to be enfranchised. Many of the basic workers' rights and freedoms we take for granted and often associate with capitalist society are, in fact, connected to citizenship rights. With the alleged attempt to meet the temporary labour requirements of the Canadian economy without threatening the jobs of Canadians, the Employment Visa system has created a *permanent* temporary work force without citizenship rights.

By treating both the need and the presence of foreign workers as *temporary* the Canadian government has done nothing *permanent* either to improve significantly the conditions of workers or to find other solutions to the problems of housework and child care. As long as it has been able to maintain a captive labour force, without citizenship rights, to do live-in domestic service, the Canadian government has found little incentive for improving the conditions of domestic work. The most recent changes in immigration policy regarding foreign domestic workers further demonstrate this point.

The Live-in Caregiver Program (LCP)

In April 1992, the Ministry of Employment and Immigration introduced several changes to the previous FDM program and renamed it the "Live-in Caregiver Program" LCP. According to the new policy, women intending to do domestic work will be admitted to Canada on the basis of their education and training in the care of children, seniors, and the disabled. Specifically, this involves the successful completion of the equivalent of Canadian Grade 12 education plus proof of six months of full-time formal training in areas such as early childhood education, geriatric care, and pediatric nursing (CEIC 1992, *Domestics' Cross Cultural News* June 1992). The introduction of these new criteria has raised the concerns of domestic workers' advocacy organizations, who fear that many potential applicants from Third World countries will not qualify under the new program. In many countries, basic schooling only goes to Grade 10 or Grade 11 and formal training in the area of child, elderly, and disabled care does not exist (DeMara 1992, *Domestics Cross Cultural News* June 1992).

The new program lifts some of the extra requirements the earlier FDM had placed on foreign domestics for landed immigrant status (i.e. doing skills upgrading, doing volunteer community work, and having to show savings). To become a landed immigrant, a foreign domestic worker now must only demonstrate a minimum of two years employment as a full-time live-in domestic worker. Also, domestic workers no longer need to obtain a "release letter" from their employer in order to change employers. To receive a new employment authorization from immigration officers, domestic workers will now have to get a "record of employment" from their employers showing how long they were employed, and a statement of earnings (CEIC 1992).

Despite limited improvements on freedom of movement and the conditions for landed status, the LCP continues the tradition of immigration policies on domestic workers by imposing the kind of status and conditions on workers that lead to abuse and an unfavourable working environment. Under the LCP, the temporary work permit system and the mandatory live-in requirement still prevail, while women have to prove higher qualifications to work as domestic workers. The new program "enables Canadian employers to obtain higher qualified labour for less pay" (*Domestics' Cross Cultural News* June 1992), while doing little to help domestic workers to improve their conditions.

Conditions of domestic work and the role of the state

In Canada, the state has played a contradictory role in the organization of domestic work. It has under-regulated working conditions while over-regulating the workers. While the provincial labour standards laws, respecting "the sanctity of the home", have either completely ignored or at best unequally treated the home as a workplace, the federal government, with its jurisdiction over immigration, has over-regulated the workers (Luxton, Rosenberg, Arat-Koc 1990: 15). In Canada, therefore, it has not been simply the low status of housework or the nature of the supply of foreign workers that have created the conditions of their vulnerability. As Castells put it:

> *immigrant workers do not exist because there are "arduous and badly paid" jobs to be done, but, rather, arduous and badly paid jobs exist because immigrant workers are present or can be sent to do them. (Castells 1975: 54)*

It is ironic that the consistently high and increasing demand for domestic work has corresponded with a deterioration in workers' conditions. This is due to the active role the state has played in structuring and controlling the volume and also the conditions of these workers. There is a striking contrast between the *laissez-faire* approach the liberal state has taken to problems in the domestic sphere—favouring private solutions—and its rigid intervention in the provision, organization, and control of "help" for that sphere. Given the specific combination of state policies in the areas of childcare provision, labour legislation, and immigration, it is clear that domestic service is a politically constructed solution to the crisis of the domestic sphere.

Recently, the positions put forward by both the federal and provincial governments in policy debates on childcare indicate the persistence of a clear preference for privatized solutions with little concern about the quality and conditions for either children or caregivers. The federal childcare plan, revealed in December 1987, emphasizes a tax-credit approach to childcare with no commitments to providing universal access to dependable and affordable licensed care spaces. The plan proposes to double the number of day-care spaces available in seven years. Even with the number of children remaining constant, this plan would meet less than 20% of the need. While the government claims to have recognized the plurality of parental preferences for childcare arrangements, the lack of socialized childcare spaces means that parents are left with no choice but to make private arrangements.

In Ontario, during the struggle for amendments in the Employment Standards Act to provide set hours and overtime pay for domestic workers, the government fought against the change with "concerns" that the potential increase in costs would "upset the child care arrangements of parents some of whom may already be in financial squeeze" (Fruman 1987). Even the Labour Ministry report, which proposed the amendment, expressed reservations about its extension to all live-out domestic workers, including baby sitters, on the grounds that it would jeopardize the inexpensive informal care arrangements which included 400,000 children in Ontario (Rauhala 1987). While the financial squeeze that many parents face in relation to childcare needs is a real and serious problem, these legislative debates and proposals tacitly assume that domestic workers should subsidize the inadequacy of the social childcare system through their underpaid and overworked conditions.

Current domestic service arrangements bring the interests of employers and employees into conflict. Given the pressures on budget and time that many middle-class working couples face, a domestic service relationship may turn into a zero-sum game in which the improvements in the pay and working conditions of domestic workers mean losses for the employers. As a relationship between female employers and workers, domestic service emphasizes, most clearly, the class, racial/ethnic and citizenship differences among women at the expense of their gender unity.

FEMINISM AND DOMESTIC SERVICE

The domestic service question is a feminist question not just because 98 per cent of domestic workers are women, or because it potentially may create divisions among women that feminism needs to solve to make "sisterhood" a reality. It is also a feminist question because it is so closely implicated in the privatized nature of domestic labour in our society. Domestic service, as it is organized in Canada, is not just a question of human and workers' rights. It is a question of women's oppression and liberation. Women's liberation has been defined by some as the upward *mobility* of individual women *out of* some subordinate positions and occupations. According to this definition, "women's liberation" can be compatible with general devaluation of the subordinate positions and occupations many women hold.[18] If we choose, however, to define women's liberation as a collective and transformative struggle—in addition to being one of individual liberation—that deals with class and racial inequalities and aims to re-structure society to eliminate subordinate positions, live-in domestic service becomes a very conservative solution for the crisis of the domestic sphere.

Domestic service leaves housework and childcare as women's work, still isolating, of low status and low value. Rather than solving the problem of gender inequality, it adds class and racial dimensions to it. Instead of housework and childcare being the responsibility of *all* women, it becomes the responsibility of *some* with subordinate class, racial, and citizenship status, who are employed and supervised by those who they liberate from the direct physical burdens.[19] Reinforcing divisions of mental and manual labour perpetuates low status and pay for domestic service.

The domestic service solution is also conservative because it does not solve the problems posed by the separation of spheres. Given the availability of a cheap source of vulnerable workers, it discourages a struggle for socialized services and more flexible work arrangements.[20] Rather than easing the public/private split in society, therefore, this solution polarizes and deepens it with added class and racial dimensions.

NOTES

This is a revised and updated version of a paper published in *Studies in Political Economy* 28 (Spring 1989) and M. Luxton, H. Rosenberg, S. Arat-Koc, *Through the Kitchen Window* (2nd ed.) Toronto, Garamond, 1990. I am grateful to Pramila Aggarwal, Michal Bodemann, Bonnie Fox, Charlene Gannage, Roberta Hamilton, Mustafa Koc, Meg Luxton, Barb Neis, Lynne Phillips, Ester Reiter, Harriet Rosenberg, Jane Ursel and Fely Villasin for ideas and useful comments on different versions of the paper.

1   Christine Delphy (1984) suggests that the appropriation of women's labour power in housework by men in the "family mode of production" constitutes the major form of women's oppression and the material basis for "sisterhood".

2   *The Canadian Settler's Handbook* advised immigrant domestics that they would enjoy "social amenities" in rural Canada and that "no lady should dream of going

as a home-help in the cities, for there class distinctions (were) as rampant as in England" (cited in Lenskyj 1981: 10).

3   According to one study, in Sweden, 2,340 million hours a year have been spent in housework, as compared to 1,290 million hours in industry (cited in Rowbotham 1973: 68).

4   While these regulations may be a progressive step in recognizing the principle of overtime for domestic workers, they do not necessarily provide standard overtime protection since it is the employers who are given the option to negotiate with their employees to take the overtime in time off rather than in money for actual overtime worked. In this respect, regulations covering domestic workers still deviate from provisions of the provincial Employment Standards Act.

5   Currently, there is a proposal by the new Ontario government to reform the Ontario Labour Relations Act. Among the proposed changes, which are under attack by employers' groups, is the extension of the right to form unions to domestic workers (*Domestics' Cross Cultural News*, December 1991).

6   There is also the "Subversive Activities" provision in the 1977 federal Immigration Act which, through its vague wording, provides an intimidating message to all non-citizen residents in Canada that engaging in union activities may become grounds for deportation. See Arnopoulos 1979: 41–5.

7   It is wrong, however, to confuse this appearance with real thoughts and feelings of the worker. Responding to Lockwood who referred to the domestic worker as the "most socially acquiescent and conservative element" of the working class, Jacklyn Cock emphasizes the need to differentiate between deference and dependence. While the domestic recognizes her dependence on and powerlessness in relation to her employer, her deference is only "a mask which is deliberately cultivated to conform to employer expectations, and shield the workers' real feelings" (Cock 1980: 104–6).

8   Here I have drawn on an argument made by Gerda Lerner in a different context. Commenting on the origins of slavery, Lerner has suggested that the process of marking a group of people as an out-group and "designating th(is) group to be dominated as entirely different from the group exerting dominance", have been essential to the mental constructs involved in institutionalization of slavery. See Gerda Lerner 1986: 76–7.

9   The criteria for tolerability used by immigration officers could sometimes be very flexible. Silvera reports the case of a domestic from the Caribbean who wanted to leave her employer for reasons of sexual assault. Because the assault was less than sexual intercourse, her complaint was not found legitimate and she was deported from Canada. See Silvera 1981:58.

10   Although Employment and Immigration spokespersons have on a number of occasions announced that the practice of requiring release letters would be ended, a survey conducted among foreign domestic workers in Toronto suggests that it is very common (Arat-Koc and Villasin 1990: 12).

11   Recent research also shows that there is a very strong relationship between living-in (a requirement for foreign domestic workers) and working very long hours.

According to a survey among 576 domestic workers in Toronto, only 35% said they worked a standard work week of 44 hours. 40% worked for an average of 45–50 hours a week. 18% worked 50–60 hours and 6% worked more than 60 hours a week. Among the live-in domestics who did overtime work, only 34% received the legal compensation. 22% said they received some, but less than the legal rates of compensation. An overwhelming 44% of those doing overtime work stated that they received no compensation whatsoever! (Arat-Koc and Villasin 1990: 6).

12 In 1987 Canada had international agreements with only six countries (the U.S., Jamaica, Italy, Greece, Portugal and France) whose nationals could combine CPP contributions in Canada with pension contributions in their own countries (INTERCEDE 1987: 12).

13 In January 1986 the immigration department introduced a fee of $50 (later to be raised to $75) for issuing, extension and renewal of employment authorizations. In addition to being underpaid and overtaxed in a society that offers them no privileges and freedoms of citizenship, domestic workers are now being asked to "take the burden off the Canadian taxpayer" and pay the costs of their own processing and policing.

14 The enforcement of the live-in requirement has been so strict that some domestics who lived-out have been threatened by deportation—even if their employer didn't have room and agreed with the arrangement. See: "Patriarch of the Month" 1992.

15 Many workers who have had years of experience supporting themselves (and others) find it very offensive to have to prove such potential: "I supported five children *before* I came here, and I've supported five children *since* I came here, and they want to know if I can manage on my own?" (Mary Dabreo, cited in Ramirez, 1983/84).

16 A point needs to be made about conceptions of the value of different occupations that immigration partly borrows from CCDO. CCDO has a rigid and static conception of skill as a "thing" that is largely determined "objectively" by the time spent in formal education. As Gaskell (1986) has argued, however, "skill", far from being "a fixed attribute of a job or a worker which will explain higher wages or unemployment", is a result of a political process determined by the relative power (through supply/demand advantages, organizational capabilities, etc.) of different groups of workers.

17 The 1978 case of "seven Jamaican women" was fought on the basis that discrimination against women with children was discrimination on the basis of gender. Seven Jamaican women filed a complaint with the Canadian Human Rights Commission after being ordered deported for having failed to list their minor children in their applications to come to Canada. They won their case on the ruling that no married man had ever been deported for having [failed] to list his children (cited in Timoll 1989: 57).

  Although explicit and direct discrimination against women with dependent children has been eliminated, the practice still survives because those women who express their intention to stay in domestic service and also sponsor their dependents to Canada often fail to meet Immigration criteria on the grounds that they would not make enough income to make their families "self-sufficient".

18 This is Betty Friedan's position on housework. She approvingly cites others in *The Feminine Mystique* who think housework can be done by "anyone with a strong enough back (and a small enough brain)" and find it "peculiarly suited to the capacities of feeble-minded girls" (Friedan 1963: 206, 244).

19 With the emergence of surrogate motherhood, the same potential also applies to childbearing. The employment of surrogate mothers of working-class backgrounds may indeed become the solution upper-class and career women opt for to avoid the time and inconvenience a pregnancy would cost.

20 During the 1920s, in southern United States where there were more servants, the growth of commercial bakeries and laundries lagged behind such developments in the North and West. See Katzman 1978: 275.

REFERENCES

Anderson, Doris

1987 "Ontario Should Heed Domestic's Plight", *The Toronto Star,* 24 January 1987

Arat-Koc, Sedef and Fely Villasin

1990 "Report and Recommendations on the Foreign Domestic Movement Program" (Prepared for INTERCEDE, Toronto Organization for Domestic Workers' Rights)

1993 "Immigration policies, Migrant Domestic Workers and the Definition of Citizenship in Canada", forthcoming in Vic Satzewich, ed. *Deconstructing a Nation: Immigration, Multiculturalism and Racism in 1990s Canada.* Toronto: Garamond Press

Arendt, Hannah

1966 *The Origins of Totalitarianism.* New York: Harcourt, Brace and World

Arnopoulos, Sheila McLeod

1979 *Problems of Immigrant Women in the Canadian Labour Force.* Canadian Advisory Council on the Status of Women

Bakan, Abigail and Daiva Stasiulis

1992a "Foreign Domestic Worker Policy in Canada and the Social Boundaries of Citizenship" (Unpublished paper)

1992b "Making the Match: Domestic Placement Agencies and the Racialization of Women's Household Work", paper presented at the 16th Annual CRIAW Conference: "Making the Links: Anti-Racism and Feminism", 13–15 November 1992, Toronto

Barber, Marilyn

1985 "The Women Ontario Welcomed: Immigrant Domestics for Ontario Homes, 1870–1930" in Alison Prentice and Susan Mann Trofimenkoff, eds, *The Neglected Majority. Essays in Canadian Women's History,* Vol. 2. Toronto: McClelland & Stewart

1986 "Sunny Ontario for British Girls, 1900–30" in Jean Burnet, ed., *Looking into My Sister's Eyes: An Exploration in Women's History*. Toronto: The Multicultural History Society of Ontario

Bolaria, B. Singh

1984 "Migrants, Immigrants, and the Canadian Labour Force" in John A. Fry, ed., *Contradictions in Canadian Society*. Toronto: John Wiley and Sons

———— **and Peter S. Li**

1985 *Racial Oppression in Canada*. Toronto: Garamond Press

Branca, Patricia

1974 "Image and Reality: The Myth of the Idle Victorian Woman" in Mary Hartman and Lois Banner, eds, *Clio's Consciousness Raised*. Harper and Row

Burawoy, Michael

1980 "Migrant Labour in South African and the United States" in Theo Nichols, ed., *Capital and Labour*. Glasgow: Fontana

Calliste, Agnes

1989 "Canada's Immigration Policy and Domestics from the Caribbean: The Second Domestic Scheme", *Socialist Studies* 5

Castells, Manuel

1975 "Immigrant Workers and Class Struggles in Advanced Capitalism: The Western European Experience", *Politics and Society* 15, 1: 33–66

Castles, Stephen and Godula Kosack [sic]

1980 "The Function of Labour Immigration in Western European Capitalism" in Theo Nichols, ed. *Capital and Labour*. Glasgow: Fontana

1973 *Immigrant Workers and Class Structure in Western Europe*. London: Oxford University Press

CEIC

1992 *Immigrant Regulations, 1978* as amended by SOR/92–214, P.C. 1992–685 (9 April 1992)

Chodorow, Nancy

1978 *The Reproduction of Mothering: Psychoanalysis and the Sociology of Gender*. Berkeley: University of California Press

Cock, Jacklyn

1980 *Maids and Madams: A Study in the Politics of Exploitation*. [Johannesburg]: Ravan Press

Cohen, Rina

1987 "The Work Conditions of Immigrant Women Live-In Domestics: Racism, Sexual Abuse and Invisibility", *Resources for Feminist Research* 16 (March)

Davis, Angela

1981 *Women, Race and Class*. New York: Random House

Delphy, Christine

1984 "The Main Enemy" in *Close to Home. A Materialist Analysis of Women's Oppression*. Amherst: University of Massachusetts Press

DeMara, Bruce

1992 "New Immigration Rules Racist Domestic Workers Rally Told", *Toronto Star,* 3 February 1992

Diebel, Linda

1973 "Black Women in White Canada: The Lonely Life", *Chatelaine,* March 1973

Dimanno, Rosie

1979 "To Serve and Protest. On Guard Upstairs; Downstairs a Rebellion is Brewing". *The Canadian,* 15–16 September

Domestics' Cross Cultural News

(Monthly newsletter of the Toronto Organization for Domestic Workers' Rights)

Dudden, Faye E.

1983 *Serving Women. Household Service in Nineteenth-Century America.* Middleton: Wesleyan University Press

Employment and Immigration Canada

1986 *Foreign Domestic Workers in Canada. Facts for Domestics and Employers* (Pamphlet). Minister of Supply and Services Canada, Cat. No. MP23–61/1986

Epstein, Rachel

1983 "Domestic Workers: The Experience in B.C." in Linda Briskin and Lynda Yanz, eds., *Union Sisters. Women in the Labour Force.* Toronto: The Women's Press

1980 "I Thought There Was No More Slavery in Canada: West Indian Domestic Workers on Employment Visas", *Canadian Women's Studies* 2, 1: 22–9

Estable, Alma

1986 *Immigrant Women in Canada—Current Issues.* A Background Paper for the Canadian Advisory Council on the Status of Women, March 1986. Ottawa: Minister of Supply and Services Canada

Fairchilds, Cissie

1984 *Domestic Enemies, Servants and Their Masters in Old Regime France.* Baltimore & London: The Johns Hopkins University Press

Flandrin, Jean-Louis

1979 *Families in Former Times.* Cambridge: Cambridge University Press

Fox, Bonnie

1980 "Women's Double Work Day: Twentieth Century Changes in the Reproduction of Daily Life" in Bonnie Fox, ed. *Hidden in the Household: Women's Domestic Labour Under Capitalism.* Toronto: The Women's Press

Friedan, Betty

1963 *The Feminine Mystique.* New York: Dell Publishing

Fruman, Leslie

1987 "Ontario's Domestics: The Fight for Basic Rights", *The Toronto Star,* 30 March, 1987: CI

Gaskell, Jane

1986 "Conceptions of Skill and the Work of Women: Some Historical and Political Issues", in Roberta Hamilton and Michele Barret, eds, *The Politics of Diversity.* Montreal: Book Center

Glenn, Evelyn Nakano

1992 "From Servitude to Service Work: Historical Continuities in the Racial Division of Paid Reproduction Work", *Signs,* 18, 1

Gorz, Andre

1970 "Immigrant Labour", *New Left Review* 61

Hayden, Dolores

1981 *The Grand Domestic Revolution: A History of Feminist Designs for American Homes, Neighbourhoods and Cities.* MIT Press

Henry, Robert

1987 "Domestics to Launch Court Bid on Overtime", *The Globe and Mail.* 8 April 1987

Hook, Nancy C.

1978 *Domestic Service Occupation Study: Final Report.* Submitted to Canada Manpower and Immigration, January, 1978

INTERCEDE

1981 "Domestics Sweep the World", *Wages for Housework Campaign Bulletin* 5, 1 (Spring 1981)

1987 *Know Your Rights (A Guide for Domestic Workers in Ontario).* Toronto: October 1987

Katzman, David M

1978a "Domestic Service: Women's Work" in Ann H. Stromberg and Shirley Harkness, eds, *Women Working. Theories and Facts in Perspective.* Palo Alto, California: Mayfield Pub. Company

1978b *Seven Days a Week. Women and Domestic Service in Industrializing America.* New York: Oxford University Press

Kaplan, Elaine Bell

1985 "I Don't Do No Windows' "*Sojourner* 10, 10 (August)

Knes, Rosemary

1980 "Ontario Government Refuses to Protect Domestic Workers", *Upstream* 4, 2 (January)

[Lenskyj], Helen

1981 "A 'Servant Problem' or a 'Servant-Mistress Problem' ? Domestic Service in Canada, 1890–1930", *Atlantis* 7, 1 (Fall)

Lerner, Gerda

1986 *The Creation of Patriarchy.* Oxford University Press

Leslie, Genevieve

1974 "Domestic Service in Canada, 1880–1920" in *Women at Work, Ontario, 1850–1930.* Toronto: Women's Press

Lindstrom-Best, Varpu

1986 "' I Won't Be a Slave!' —Finnish Domestics in Canada, 1911–30" in Jean Burnet, ed., *Looking into My Sister's Eyes: An Exploration in Women's History*. Toronto: The Multicultural History Society of Ontario

Luxton, Meg

1986 "Two Hands for the Clock: Changing Patterns in the Gendered Division of Labour in the Home" in Meg Luxton and Harriet Rosenbeg, *Through the Kitchen Window. The Politics of Home and Family*. Toronto: Garamond Press

1980 *More Than a Labour of Love*. Toronto: The Women's Press

————, **Harriet Rosenberg, and Sedef Arat-Koc**

1990 *Through the Kitchen Window: The Politics of Home and Family*. Toronto: Garamond Press

Malos, Ellen, ed.

1980 *The Politics of Housework*. London: Allison & Busby

Maychack, Matt

1987 "What Ottawa's New Day-care System Means to Families", *The Toronto Star*. 4 December 1987

McBride, Theresa M.

1976 *The Domestic Revolution. The Modernization of Household Service in England and France 1820–1920*. New York: Holmes and Meier Publishers

McNenly, Pat

"Domestics Seek Provincial Limit on Working Hours", *The Toronto Star*

Mitterauer, Michael and Reinhard Sieder

1982 *The European Family*. Chicago: The University of Chicago Press

"The Nanny Debate",

1987 *The Sunday Star* 15 March 1987: B2

National Conference on Immigrant Women

1981 *The Immigrant Women in Canada: A Right to Recognition*. Part 1, Report of the Proceedings of the Conference. Toronto, 20–2 March

"Patriarch of the Month",

1992 *Herizons*, 6, 3 (Fall)

Ramirez, Judith

1983/1984 "Good Enough to Stay", *Currents* 1, 4

Rauhala, Ann

1987a "House Critics Attack Report on Financing Child-Care Package", *The Globe and Mail* 31 March 1987: A1, 4

1987b "Groups Poised to Fight for Domestics", *The Globe and Mail,* 19 March 1987: A15

1987c "Amended Labor Law Would Give Domestics Overtime, Set Hours", *The Globe and Mail*. 27 January 1987: A1, 12

Rist, Ray C.

1979 "Guestworkers and Post-World War II European Migrations", *Studies in Comparative International Development* 15, 2: 28–53

Roberts, Barbara

1979 "'A Work of Empire': Canadian Reformers and British Female Immigration" in Linda Kealey, ed. *A Not Unreasonable Claim. Women and Reform in Canada, 1880s–1920s.* Toronto: The Women' s Press

Rollins, Judith

1985 *Between Women. Domestics and Their Employers.* Philadelphia: Temple University Press

Romero, Mary

1987 "Domestic Service in the Transition from Rural to Urban Life: the Case of La Chicana", *Women's Studies* 13, 3

Rosenberg, Harriet

1986 "The Home is the Workplace: Hazards, Stress and Pollutants in the Household" in [Meg] Luxton and Harriet Rosenberg, eds, *Through The Kitchen Window.* Toronto: Garamond Press

1987 "Motherwork, Stress, and Depression: The Costs of Privatized Social Reproduction" in Heather J. Maroney and Meg Luxton, eds, *Feminism and Political Economy.* Toronto: Methuen

Rowbotham, Sheila

1973 *Women's Consciousness, Man's World.* Harmondsworth: Penguin

Royal Commission on the Status of Women

1970 *Report of the Royal Commission on the Status of Women.* Ottawa: Minister of Supplies and Services Canada

Scott, Peter

1987 "Minority Women Learn to Lobby", *Share,* 1 April 1987

1986 "Ombudsman Will Fight For Domestics," *Share,* 9 October

Serwonka, Karen

1991 "The Bare Essentials: A Needs Assessment of Foreign Domestic Workers in Ontario" (prepared for INTERCEDE, Toronto Organization for Domestic Workers' Rights)

Sheppard, Robert

1987 "Domestics Guaranteed Overtime Payments", *Globe and Mail,* 10 June 1987: A5

"The Shortage of Domestics",

1976 *U.S. News and World Report* 10 May

Silvera, Makeda

1981 "Immigrant Domestic Workers. Whose Dirty Laundry?" *Fireweed* 9

1983 *Silenced. Talks with Working Class West Indian Women about Their Lives and Struggles as Domestic Workers in Canada.* Toronto: Williams-Wallace Publishers Inc.

Stasiulis, Daiva K.

1987 "Rainbow Feminism: Perspectives on Minority Women in Canada", *Resources for Feminist Research* 16, 1 (March)

Steinberg, Stephen

1981 *The Ethnic Myth: Race Ethnicity and Class in America.* Boston: Beacon Press

Statistics Canada

1989 *The Labour Force, October 1989.* Ottawa: Minister of Supply and Services Canada

Stoffman, Daniel

1992 "'Nanny' Program a Rare Success for Policy Makers", *Toronto Star* 22 September 1992

Sutherland, David E.

1981 *Americans and Their Servants. Domestic Service in the United States from 1800 to 1920.* Louisiana State University Press

The Task Force on Child Care

1986 *Report of the Task Force on Child Care.* Ottawa: Minister of Supply and Services Canada

The Task Force on Immigration Practices and Procedures

1981 *Domestic Workers on Employment Authorizations Report.* April 1981

Timoll, Andrea L.

1989 "Foreign Domestic Servants in Canada" (unpublished research essay, Department of Political Science, Carleton University, Ottawa)

Toughill, Kelly

1986 "Domestic Workers Praise Rule Change", *The Toronto Star.* 22 September 1986: C2

Turittin, Jane Sawyer

1976 "Networks and Mobility: The Case of West Indian Domestics from Montserrat", *Canadian Review of Sociology and Anthropology* 13, 3: 305–20

Vanek, Joann

1983 "Household Work, Wage Work, and Sexual Equality" in A.S. Skolnick and J.H. Skolnick, eds, *Family in Transition,* 4th ed. Little Brown and Company

Vanstone, Ellen

1986 "The Heaven-Sent Nanny", *Toronto Life* (April)

Walmsley, Ann

1989 "Can a Working Mother Afford to Stay Home?" *Chatelaine* (November)

Whisson, Michael G. and William Weil

1971 *Domestic Servants. A Microcosm of "the Race Problem".* Johannesburg: South African Institute of Race Relations

Williams, Jan, Hazel Twart, and Ann Bachelli

1980 "Women and the Family" in Ellen Malos, ed., *The Politics of Housework.* London: Allison and Busby

Wong, Lloyd T.

1984 "Canada's Guestworkers: Some Comparisons of Temporary Workers in Europe and North America", *International Migration Review* 18, 1: 85–97

31
Rape and the Masculine Mystique

Stuart L. Hills

MEDIA IMAGES AND SOCIAL REALITIES

The lower-class sex-crazed *stranger* lurking in the alleys. The crazy, sadistic *psychopath*—the lone mad stalker—masquerading as a delivery man or hiding concealed in the backseat of the parked car. The *freaks* of society. Such is the powerful stereotypical imagery of the typical rapist in the news media. These are the kinds of people we occasionally read about in the big-city newspaper or hear about on the 10 o'clock television news out of New York City. Thus the myth is perpetuated that rape is a rarity—except in certain dangerous urban areas—and is predominantly the result of a small number of psychopaths and weirdos, deviants who are distant strangers to their victims. Rape is not likely to be seen, therefore, as having any further implications for the dominant culture and established social arrangements.

In reality, there are many different kinds of rapists. They vary in their needs, motivations, and approaches to rape. As social scientists devise research methods that go beyond the limited and biased official police statistics, they discover that rape is much more commonplace than most people realize and that it certainly is not the exclusive product of a small number of demented psychopaths or alienated lower-class blacks. In fact, it is quite likely that the majority of rapists are the kinds of men that women from all social classes and communities are likely to *know:* a friend, acquaintance, relative, coworker, employer, date, lover, former-lover, husband—quite *normal* people.

The discussion that follows will particularly explore the "rape date" and some of the cultural patterns that help provoke, justify, and culminate in rape. We shall especially probe some of the idealized attributes of the masculine mystique—the cult of male virility and machismo—the mythical beliefs, values, and expectations that justify treating some women as legitimate targets of violence and contempt.

From Stuart L. Hills, "Rape and the Masculine Mystique," in *Demystifying Social Deviance* (New York: McGraw-Hill Book Company, 1980): 59–77. Reprinted by permission of McGraw-Hill.

SOCIAL STIGMA AND THE REPORTING OF RAPE

Rape typically refers to the oral, anal, or vaginal penetration of a woman by force and without her consent and willingness. It is one of the least studied and most underreported kinds of violent crime in America. For example, a victimization study in the late 1960s by the President's Crime Commission found that women were almost *four times* as likely to report in an interview that they had been raped (in the previous year) than they were to report it to the police.[1] A 1972 study of the five largest American cities, in which respondents were asked if they had ever been victimized by certain crimes, found that of women who were willing to admit that they had been sexually assaulted, only 46 percent (Los Angeles) to 61 percent (NYC) reported it to legal authorities.[2]

Moreover, recent studies reveal that rape is not only more widespread than official records indicate, but also that rapists quite frequently, probably typically, choose women who are *known* to them. ... In a seventeen-city survey done by the National Commission on the Causes of Violence, about one-half of the assailants were strangers.[3] These and other kinds of official and unofficial studies, however, grossly overstate the proportion of rapes involving strangers and vastly understate the actual incidence of rape in America. Certainly stranger-victim rape is much more likely to be reported and admitted—officially or unofficially in interviews—than rape occurring among friends, acquaintances, and relatives. For example, in one study of ninety rape victims, with three exceptions, only women who were raped by strangers reported it to legal authorities.[4] ...

... According to an estimate by the Federal Bureau of Investigation, probably no more than 10 percent of all rape is reported. As the Kinsey Institute for Sex Research points out:

> *These percentages of strangers, acquaintances present ... a false picture of rape. ... It is known that many rape cases go unreported, especially if the two people concerned have been dating. No girl likes to advertise her misfortune through court action, and she is especially loath to do so if the defendant is someone with whom she has been friendly, lest there be some question about the validity of her charge.*[5]

To be raped by a stranger may possibly make one a martyr; to be raped by a friend, business colleague, blind date, or your husband's fishing buddy clearly makes a complaining woman an object of suspicion. The female must convince legal officials that she was coerced, not seduced; that it was a degrading, not a joyful experience. If the woman chooses not to risk serious injury by resisting—or is paralyzed by fear or shock—she becomes even further suspect and often humiliated in a criminal courtroom where the victim's virtue "goes on trial." Even when brutally raped by a stranger, a woman may be compelled to undergo a degradation ceremony and demeaning experience in a male-dominated "criminal-justice" system:

"If I had to do it again, I would never have gone through with the prosecution. I wouldn't even have reported it," said one twenty-seven-year-old woman who suffered through months of legal proceedings and publicity only to see her rapist found innocent because she was unable to prove that she did not consent to the act. Despite extensive body bruises and a wound in her forehead that took six stitches to close, the defense attorney argued that "vigorous love play" did not necessarily indicate nonconsent and, in fact, could even indicate enthusiastic approval and passionate involvement in the act. ...

There are many kinds of motives in the reluctance of women to report that they have been raped: a sense of futility, a fear of reprisal by the rapist, ambivalent feelings of shame, guilt and self-blame, or even a protective, affectionate feeling for the man, not wanting to get him into trouble. The woman may wish to avoid the indignities she may suffer, not only from the police and courts but also from her friends, neighbors, relatives—even her husband. ...

Clearly, there is a strong social *stigma* to being raped. It is one of the few forms of crime in which the victim experiences as much moral devaluation and loss of status as the offender—and sometimes more. The fact that a most intimate but illicit sexual experience becomes a public and open topic for conversation may foster a social identity in the community—and sometimes self-identity—as "the kind of woman who gets raped." Her tainted identity may make her less desirable ("damaged goods") for serious courtship but ripe for further sexual exploitation.[6] ...

THE IMAGE OF MASCULINITY

Feminist sociologist Diana Russell contends that much rape is not so much a *deviant* act as it is an *overconforming* act, an exaggerated form of "normal" relations which often exist between the sexes. Sexual aggression, even violent assault, represents qualities regarded by many men as *super masculine:* strength, power, independence, forcefulness, domination, toughness. To conquer, to be successful, to win, to induce respect through force—all of these attributes are commonly associated with masculinity in our culture (and also in many other societies). Sexual activity particularly is an occasion on which these qualities of masculinity are often most intensely acted out. Especially for men who feel powerless or inadequate in other areas of their lives, the conquest of a woman may become an important instrument for the achievement and maintenance of a man's sense of masculinity, status, and self-esteem.[7]

Growing numbers of feminists and sociologists thus would insist that rape can be adequately understood only by an examination of dominant notions of masculinity and femininity: that in a deeply ingrained sexist culture rape and other forms of aggression are an integral part of a larger sexist ideology that serves to perpetuate the power of men over women.

In the tradition of *machismo,* an extreme version of the masculine image which is widespread, women are to be cynically manipulated and exploited if possible. The opposite sex is viewed as weak, passive, dependent, inferior, and submissive. Such contempt and one-dimensional conceptions of women encourage the use of females as a mere vehicle for a man's pleasure or for an expression of his hostility and feelings of aggression. Although the estimated 200,000 women raped by enemy soldiers in Bangladesh received some publicity, the thousands of Vietnamese women raped by American soldiers have barely received any mention. In Vietnam, one of the few GIs in Charlie Company who was willing to talk candidly about rape said: "That's an everyday affair. You can nail just about everyone on that—at least once. The guys are human, man."[8] For some men who subscribe to the macho perspective, "seduction is for sissies"; as Ogden Nash put it, "a he-man wants his rape." According to Susan Brownmiller, American soldiers who refused to participate in group rapes and subsequent murder of Vietnamese women were regarded as "queers" by their buddies, lacking in sufficient masculinity.[9] For men socialized into the dominant cultural tenets of machismo, "to be dependent on a woman and especially to show her tenderness and consideration because she deserved it as a human being rather than because it is a useful device for overcoming her resistance, is thought to be foolish."[10]

Central to this image of maleness is the belief in a powerful masculine *sexual force* which once unleashed is almost beyond rational control. To be confronted by a "cock teaser" who titillates or suggests but does not deliver is unforgivable. Such perceived female provocation is considered unfair, offensive to male sensibilities, and deserving of retaliation. By *blaming the victim* and by evoking the self-serving belief that the woman's provocation puts the man temporarily "out of control," the rapist shifts the responsibility for the rape to the female. The message communicated is clear: women who walk or talk or dress in a manner that is sexually provocative to men do so at their own risk. Nor do such women have any right to change their mind about sex if they seemingly hint or contemplate such desires. This masculine perspective, of course, puts women in a double bind. Although American society normally *rewards* women for looking sexually attractive—indeed they are *expected* to be enticing and a little "sexy"—if they become a rape victim they are immediately held blameworthy. As one convicted California rapist put it:

> *I believe that women who want to be fashionable in some of the styles that are sexually stimulating to men should try to realize some of the consequences of wearing some of these styles before they wear them. ...*
>
> *Once again, I would say again, by body language—or unconsciously they flirt—sometimes the way they dress—their minds say one thing—*

their bodies say another—or some come on with their seduction-type
overall tone—that says one thing but could possibly mean something
else. Or they put themselves in the position of being alone.[11]

Sexist views which hold the victim responsible are not a monopoly of
rapists but are widely held in American society. Such sentiments are reinforced in the value-laden language of social scientists who emphasize
"victim-precipitated" rape.[12] Or consider the frank remarks of Wisconsin
Judge Archie Simonson. In 1977, he ruled that a boy who raped a schoolgirl
in a stairwell was reacting "normally" to the provocative clothing that women
now wear and sentenced the boy to the protective custody of his parents:

I'm trying to say to women to stop teasing. There should be a restora-
tion of modesty in dress. ... Whether women like it or not they are sex
objects. Are we supposed to take an impressionable person 15 or 16
years of age and punish that person severely because they react to it
(scanty female attire) normally?[13]

The widespread view that girls who exercise their personal freedom by
hitchhiking are really "asking for it" is also the apparent sexist reasoning
applied by a California Court of Appeals recently in reversing the conviction
of an accused rapist. The presiding judge wrote for a unanimous court:

The lone female hitchhiker in the absence of an emergency situation,
as a practical matter, advises all who pass by that she is willing to
enter the vehicle with anyone who stops and in so doing advertises that
she has less concern for the consequences than the average female.
Under such circumstances it would not be unreasonable for a man in
the position of the defendant here to believe that the female would con-
sent to sexual relations.[14]

The force of this sexist mythology in America also contributes to the
common notion that it is mostly "bad girls" that get raped. Yet a District of
Columbia study, for example, reported that 82 percent of the rape victims
had a "good reputation."[15] A common observation accompanying such statistics is for some writers to note that even "nice girls" get raped too. (No
one, of course, ever inquires whether a robbed service station operator
"asked for it" or observes that "nice guys get mugged too.") The chauvinistic
implication is that nice girls follow prescribed and passive sex roles, never
actively seek sexual relationships, and confine their sexual intimacies to only
a husband, a fiancé, or, at best, a single, exclusive, long-term lover. It is precisely such sexist assumptions that the women's movement is attempting to
combat in instigating legal reforms that make prior sexual conduct of the
rape victim inadmissible evidence in court. As Baril and Couchman note,
"Liberation precludes having to convince anyone of one's niceness."[16]

THE DATING GAME AND JUSTIFICATIONS FOR RAPE

Dating is a widespread social practice in American society that sometimes leads to a serious, committed relationship or marriage—and sometimes to rape. The expectations that each partner brings to the encounter may be ambiguous and unfilled. Misunderstandings, confused signals, and misperceptions are a common part of many dating relationships, especially in casual pickups in singles' bars. As Charles McCaghy notes, on many dates,

> *the expectations of the male stem from the attention, time, and money he expends. But it is more than pleasant and witty conversation that is to be his reward. He anticipates a progression of sexual intimacies with each date with the ultimate goal of "going all the way." But somewhere in this progression a point of contention can arise over how much he is "buying" and how much she is "selling." This is particularly likely to occur when there is no emotional commitment to the relationship by either party. For many such couples confrontations over rewards end dramatically, one way or another, with the demand: "Put out or get out!"*[17]

Traditionally, males take the initiative and press for increasing sexual intimacies until stopped by the female. However, in an ambiguously defined social situation where the male may assume that a show of resistance is merely a coquettish ploy or female game of feigning reluctance, many males will pay no heed and continue to persist and cajole. The woman's "no" is not to be taken seriously, especially in a sexually permissive era. Indeed some resistance is *expected* but so is eventual submission. Some men may even assume that the girl may feel less guilty about enjoying sex if she is overwhelmed in caveman style. But regardless, many males are so convinced that women desire sexual intimacies with them that they are unable to hear their protestations to the contrary—even their desperate struggles and cries.

The fact that otherwise respectable and relatively normal males can sexually assault women is facilitated by a vocabulary of socially shared motives or rationalizations that consistently tend to blame the victim. These male justifications for rape typically reflect heavily stereotypical views of women, which enable sexual aggressors to maintain a favorable self-image and to treat some women as *legitimate* targets of violence. McCaghy pinpoints three common kinds of male justifications for forcibly abusing women.[18]

1. "Some Women *Need* to Be Raped."

These accounts given for sexual aggression concern the importance of keeping females in their place—beneath men.

> *These dumb broads don't know what they want. They get you worked up and then they chicken out. You let 'em get away with stuff like that and the next thing you know they'll be walking all over you.*

Women like a strong man who will knock them around once in a while—that way they know the man is in charge.[19]

Or consider the motives offered by this middle-class salesman with two years of college who feels he must prove his superiority and punish an "uppity" woman for being "snobbish and phony:"

> *I met a girl at a party, and I considered her snobbish and phony. She latched onto me at the party, and we laughed and had a good time and went somewhere else. She was an attractive woman in her thirties, but she irritated me. When I took her home to her apartment she was telling me goodnight and I raped her. I didn't really feel the urge. As a matter of fact, I had a hell of a time getting an erection. … I'd had quite a bit of booze. But I forced myself to do it to prove a point to her, to prove that she wasn't as big as she thought she was.*[20]

These sentiments perhaps illustrate what many feminist writers contend: that there is frequently very little sexual desire in such violent assaults. At best, … feminists insist, lustful motives play a minor role in the assault. Rape is more accurately seen as a *power* play, a violent expression of male dominance, a way of subjugating and humiliating women against their will. As Susan Brownmiller succinctly puts it: "Rape is the quintessential act by which a male demonstrates to the female that she is conquered—vanquished—by his superior strength and power."[21]

2. "Some Women *Deserve* to Be **Raped**."

These verbalized motives relate to the social reputation of the victim. A female stigmatized as sexually experienced, as promiscuous or "a slut," may become a legitimate target for all forms of sexual aggression. "Her prior experience qualifies her as public property for all interested males and cancels her prerogative to accept or reject sexual partners."[22] Once the label of "an easy lay" has been affixed, the refusal of a girl to accommodate all comers may threaten fragile male egos and precipitate assault:

> *OK. There was this chick, see. I took her out. It was my first date with her, but I knew from some other dudes that she liked sex, you know what I mean? So I'm driving back to my pad and she says she wants to go home. Well that's a put down. **That's saying to me that I'm not a man.** Well no broad in the world is gonna give me that shit! So I messed her around a little bit.*[23]

When asked to justify his use of force to obtain sex, a college student replied:

> *When a male doesn't respect a girl and knows she is nothing but a whore anyway, I feel he is entitled to use force because he knows it isn't her first time.*[24]

Such tarnished female reputations also may aid males in participating in group rapes—a not uncommon form of sexual assault. The pervasive use of such slang terms as "gang-bangs" or "trains" appears to mitigate the horror of such violence for many young men. Even for assailants who feel some qualms, the fear of losing status in the eyes of their male peers may become a more pressing concern. In one study of group rape, the author describes the dynamics of such peer-group expectations and fears:

> *The leader of the male group ... apparently precipitated and main-tained the activity, despite misgivings, because of a need to fulfill the role that the other two men had assigned to him. "I was scared when it began to happen," he says "I wanted to leave but I didn't want to say it to the other guys—you know—that I was scared."*[25]

3. "Some Women *Want* to Be Raped."

The myth that only willing women get raped, that no female can be actually raped who doesn't wish to be is a fallacious but widely shared chauvinistic contention. This "victim in search of a rapist" perspective is evident in the remarks of this convicted rapist:

> **Interviewer:** *I'd like to know how you can tell if women are suscepti-ble to rape and how they respond.*
>
> **Fred:** *All right, I'd say most of the women that are susceptible to rape are pretty broadminded and pretty sexy. Sometimes a woman who tries to hide sexuality is very susceptible to rape. What she's really saying is, "I'm a woman but I'm not gonna let anybody know about it, but I dare you to find out." So you find that she is a woman and most of the time she's the best lay.*[26]

Some scientific studies may also reinforce the common belief that many women subconsciously desire to be raped. The writer may insist that a woman who claims rape is suffering from self-deceit or selective recall, cam-ouflaging her ambivalent—but real—sexual desires:

> *Even the woman who is quite sane but who is possessed of strong guilt feelings, may convince herself in retrospect that her own conduct was really blameless and she was forced. This conviction is the more easily arrived at because it is quite likely that her conscious response at the time could not accurately be labeled either as consent or non-consent. There may have been an ambivalent and confused mixture of desire and fear, neither of which was clearly dominant. Most women want their lovers to be at least somewhat aggressive and dominating. **Some consciously or unconsciously want to be forced.** Their erotic pleasure is stimulated by preliminary love-play involving physical struggle, slapping, scratching, pinching and biting. The struggle also saves*

face for the girl who fears she would be considered "loose" if she yielded without due maidenly resistance; it also relieves that guilt feeling that might exist if she could not tell herself that "he made me do it." Many of the wrestling matches in parked cars come within this category.[27]

It is perhaps not surprising in a male-dominated society that some women also belittle and scorn raped women by denying the credibility of their claims. Steeped in the notion that only willing women and those who "ask for it" get raped, these women insist that such abused females precipitated their own victimization or that they were not really raped. Indeed, the mystifying power of the male mystique may psychologically so oppress some women that, even when they are assaulted themselves, they may find it difficult to define what occurred as rape. ...

The myth that there is no such thing as rape may also partly explain why some men who rape women maintain a self-concept of lovers rather than rapists. Several days after a young woman had been raped by her friend's husband, the man returned to her home, banged at the door and yelled: "Jane, Jane. You loved it. You know you loved it."[28] ... In one study of rape victims, two women even received marriage proposals from their assailants, who were total strangers. In another instance, after being raped by two men, the victim was asked which of the two rapists she enjoyed the most. Still another victim reported that her rapist was "furious because I wasn't getting turned on."[29]

SEXUAL SOCIALIZATION OF MALES

Many men in American society, perhaps most, have the ability to compartmentalize their purely sexual desires from sentiments of caring, affection, and love. Traditional socialization since preadolescence permits them to separate easily their sexual responsiveness from any feelings of emotional warmth, friendship, commitment, or respect. Men can become "turned on," for example, in the presence of a sexually attractive female. Some males can become sexually aroused to the point of erection from mere pictures of "sexy" scantily clad female bodies (supporting a multimillion-dollar industry of "girlie" magazines such as *Playboy, Hustler, Penthouse,* and *Oui*).[30]

Especially for males who have internalized the importance of appearing virile, and who are unsure of their masculinity, "scoring" with a sexually attractive woman—the more frequently the better—may become a kind of ritualistic test of their manhood. In the lockerroom tradition, the virgin and inexperienced male becomes an object of ridicule, taunted to show that he is a "real man" by "making it" with a woman. ...

In a rather chauvinistic remark, one psychologist was recently quoted as saying: "I don't think there's a man worth his salt who hasn't seen some chick walking by and wanted to screw her."[31] Obviously, not all men forcibly attempt to act out such desires. However, it should not be surprising that

some men socialized into these feelings and attitudes toward women suc-
cumb to the temptation of rape. Such acts of human degradation are to be
expected—regardless of what psychodynamic or situational factors are
involved—as long as our culture continues to equate sexual aggression and
dominance with masculinity, and as long as women are perceived as sex
objects rather than as full human beings.

Yet there *are* cultures in which men are reared to be gentle, tender, nurturing, and sensitive. In these societies, men find rape an incomprehensible
act. Anthropologist Margaret Mead, for example, points out that the
Arapesh, a "primitive" people of New Guinea, "know nothing of rape beyond
the fact that it is the unpleasant custom of the Nugum people to the south-
east of them."[32] As advocates of women's and men's liberation have argued,
radical changes in deeply ingrained values and in the socialization of males
and females must occur if rape is to diminish significantly:

> *If our culture considered it masculine to be gentle and sensitive, to be*
> *responsive to the needs of others, to abhor violence, domination, and*
> *exploitation, to want sex only within a meaningful relationship, to be*
> *attracted by personality and character rather than by physical appear-*
> *ance, to value lasting rather than casual relationships, then rape*
> *would indeed be a deviant act, and ... much less frequent.*[33]

Greater sex-role liberation in America would also reduce the prevalence
of what some feminist writers call "petty rapes" or "the little rapes."[34] This
kind of pervasive female degradation includes sexual exploitation by men
who control promotions and the hiring and firing process in highly desirable jobs. Or the form of sexual blackmail in which men threaten to
discredit a female's reputation by openly talking about her intimate sexual
behavior unless she "comes across." Or the deceit practiced to gain momen-
tary sexual conquest by phony gestures of tenderness and personal interest.
Such petty rapes, as Germaine Greer notes, are a persistent hazard in the
dating game, as are those situations when the man who picks up the tab for
the evening's entertainment and owns the car threatens to throw his date
out on a deserted road if she doesn't respond with the swiftness and degree
of sexual intimacy he desires.

A particularly crass instance of this kind of sexual rip-off is that of a
thirty-six-year-old man who succeeded in "seducing" into bed a twenty-year-
old woman in her own apartment after informing her that he was a psychologist doing research. A New York judge hearing the case stated that a man
may use any nonviolent or nonthreatening means, "even deceit," to gain
female compliance. The judge added, "Bachelors and other men on the
make, fear not. It is still not illegal to feed a girl a line." [35]

Perhaps the most destructive aspect of these insidious "little rapes" is
that they may gradually, almost imperceptibly erode a female's self-esteem
and dignity, and make her more callous and suspect in her dealings with

men. Such self-alienation and "hardening of the heart" may invite still further exploitation in a self-perpetuating manner, deepening her malaise and oppression.[36] ...

NOTES

1   President's Commission on Law Enforcement and Administration of Justice. *The Challenge of Crime in a Free Society* (Washington, D.C.: U.S. Government Printing Office, 1967), 21.

2   U.S. Department of Justice, *Crime in the Nation's Five Largest Cities: National Crime Panel Surveys of Chicago, Detroit, Los Angeles, New York and Philadelphia*, Advance Report (Washington, D.C.: U.S. Department of Justice, April 1974), 28.

3   Donald J. Mulvihill and Melvin M. Tumin, *Crimes of Violence*, Staff Report Submitted to the National Commission on the Causes and Prevention of Violence, Vol. 11 (Washington, D.C.: U.S. Government Printing Office, 1060), 217.

4   Diana E. H. Russell, *The Politics of Rape* (New York: Stein and Day, 1975), 260.

5   Quoted in Erich Goode and Richard R. Troiden, eds., *Sexual Deviance and Sexual Deviants* (New York: William Morrow, 1974), 301.

6   Kurt Weiss and Sandra S. Borges, "Victimology and Rape: The Case of the Legitimate Victim," *Issues in Criminology* 8 (Fall 1973), 103–104.

7   Russell, *The Politics of Rape*, 260. See also Weiss and Borges, "Victimology and Rape," 85–87.

8   Seymour M. Hersh. *My Lai 4: A Report on the Massacre and Its Aftermath* (New York: Vintage Books, 1970), 185.

9   Susan Brownmiller, *Against Our Will* (New York: Simon and Schuster, 1975), Ch. 3.

10   William Goode, "Violence among Intimates," in *Crimes of Violence*, Vol. 13 (Washington, D.C.: U.S. Government Printing Office, 1969), 971.

11   Quoted in Gilbert Geis, "Forcible Rape: An Introduction," in *Forcible Rape*, ed. Duncan Chappel, Robley Geis and Gilbert Geis (New York: Columbia University Press, 1977), 28.

12   See Menachem Amir, *Patterns in Forcible Rape* (Chicago: University of Chicago Press, 1971), Ch. 15.

13   *Time*, Sept. 12, 1977, 41.

14   The *New York Times*, July 24, 1977, 16E.

15   Cited in Susan Griffin, "Rape: The All-American Crime," in *Sexual Deviance and Sexual Deviants*, 315.

16   Cecile Baril and Iain S.B. Couchman, "Legal Rights," *Society* 14 (July/August 1976), 15.

17   Charles McCaghy, *Deviant Behavior* (New York: Macmillan, 1976), 135. See also Weiss and Borges, "Victimology and Rape," 87–89.

18   McCaghy, *Deviant Behavior*, 135–36.

19   Paul II. Gebhard et al., *Sex Offenders: An Analysis of Types* (New York: Harper & Row, 1965), 177–78, 205.

20   Russell, *The Politics of Rape*, 253.

21   Brownmiller, *Against Our Will,* 49.

22   Eugene J. Kanin, "Reference Groups and Sex Conduct Norm Violations," in *Rape Victimology*, ed. L. G. Schultz (Springfield, Ill.: C.C. Thomas, 1975), 502.

23   Quoted in John Perry and Erna Perry, *Face to Face* (Boston: Little, Brown, 1976), 481. Italics added.

24   Kanin, "Selected Dyadic Aspects of Male Sex Aggression," in *Rape Victimology*, 71.

25   Gilbert Geis and Duncan Chappel, "Forcible Rape by Multiple Offenders," *Abstracts on Criminology and Penology* 11 (July/August 1991), 435–36.

26   Robert W. Winslow and Virginia Winslow, *Deviant Reality* (Boston: Allyn and Bacon, 1974), 305.

27   Quoted in Nanette J. Davis, *Sociological Constructions of Deviance* (Dubuque, Iowa: William C. Brown, 1975), 155. Italics added.

28   Griffin, "Rape: The All-American Crime," 308.

29   Russell, *The Politics of Rape*, 258.

30   Russell, *The Politics of Rape*, 263–64.

31   *Newsweek*, Aug. 20, 1973, 67–68.

32   Margaret Mead, *Sex and Temperament in Three Primitive Societies* (New York: Dell, 1935), 110.

33   Russell, *The Politics of Rape*, 264–65.

34   See Germaine Greer, "Seduction Is a Four-Letter Word," in *Sexual Deviance and Sexual Deviants*, 333–42; Andra Medea and Kathleen Thompson, *Against Rape* (New York: Farrar, Straus, & Giroux, 1974), 49–55.

35   *Time*, May 12, 1975, 55.

36   Greer, "Seduction Is a Four-Letter Word," 333.

32
Toward a Feminist Theory of Disability

Susan Wendell

In 1985, I fell ill overnight with what turned out to be a disabling chronic disease. In the long struggle to come to terms with it, I had to learn to live with a body that felt entirely different to me—weak, tired, painful, nauseated, dizzy, unpredictable. I learned at first by listening to other people with chronic illnesses or disabilities; suddenly able-bodied people seemed to be profoundly ignorant of everything I most needed to know. Although doctors told me there was a good chance I would eventually recover completely, I realized after a year that waiting to get well, hoping to recover my healthy body, was a dangerous strategy. I began slowly to identify with my new disabled body and to learn to work with it. As I moved back into the world, I also began to experience the world as structured for people who have no weaknesses.[1] The process of encountering the able-bodied world led me gradually to identify myself as a disabled person, and to reflect on the nature of disability. ...

Disabled women struggle with both the oppressions of being women in male-dominated societies and the oppressions of being disabled in societies dominated by the able-bodied. They are bringing the knowledge and concerns of women with disabilities into feminism and feminist perspectives into the disability rights movement. To build a feminist theory of disability that takes adequate account of our differences, we will need to know how experiences of disability and the social oppression of the disabled interact with sexism, racism, and class oppression. ...

THE SOCIAL CONSTRUCTION OF DISABILITY

If we ask the questions: Why are so many disabled people unemployed or underemployed, impoverished, lonely, isolated; why do so many find it difficult or impossible to get an education (Davis and Marshall 1987; Fine and Asch 1988, 10–11); why are they victims of violence and coercion; why do able-bodied people ridicule, avoid, pity, stereotype and patronize them?, we may be tempted to see the disabled as victims of nature or accident. Feminists should be, and many are, profoundly suspicious of this answer. We are

From Susan Wendell, "Toward a Feminist Theory of Disability," *Hypatia*, vol. 4, no. 2 (Summer 1989): 104–124. Reprinted by permission.

used to countering claims that insofar as women are oppressed they are oppressed by nature, which puts them at a disadvantage in the competition for power and resources. We know that if being biologically female is a disadvantage, it is because a social context makes it a disadvantage. From the standpoint of a disabled person, one can see how society could minimize the disadvantages of most disabilities, and, in some instances, turn them into advantages.

Consider an extreme case: the situation of physicist Stephen Hawking, who has had Amyotrophic Lateral Sclerosis (Lou Gehrig's Disease) for more than 27 years. Professor Hawking can no longer speak and is capable of only the smallest muscle movements. Yet, in his context of social and technological support, he is able to function as a professor of physics at Cambridge University; indeed he says his disability has given him the *advantage* of having more time to think, and he is one of the foremost theoretical physicists of our time. He is a courageous and talented man, but he is able to live the creative life he has only because of the help of his family, three nurses, a graduate student who travels with him to maintain his computer-communications systems, and the fact that his talent had been developed and recognized before he fell seriously ill (*Newsweek* 1988).

Many people consider providing resources for disabled people a form of charity, … in part because the disabled are perceived as unproductive members of society. Yet most disabled people are placed in a double-bind: they have access to inadequate resources because they are unemployed or underemployed, and they are unemployed or underemployed because they lack the resources that would enable them to make their full contribution to society (Matthews 1983; Hannaford 1985). Often governments and charity organizations will spend far more money to keep disabled people in institutions where they have no chance to be productive than they will spend to enable the same people to live independently and productively. In addition, many of the "special" resources the disabled need merely compensate for bad social planning that is based on the illusion that everyone is young, strong, healthy (and, often, male).

Disability is also frequently regarded as a personal or family problem rather than a matter for social responsibility. Disabled people are often expected to overcome obstacles to participation by their own extraordinary efforts, or their families are expected to provide what they need (sometimes at great personal sacrifice). …

In the split between the public and the private worlds, women (and children) have been relegated to the private, and so have the disabled, the sick and the old (and mostly women to take care of them). The public world is the world of strength, the positive (valued) body, performance and production, the able-bodied and youth. Weakness, illness, rest and recovery, pain, death and the negative (de-valued) body are private, generally hidden, and often neglected. Coming into the public world with illness, pain or a de-valued body, we encounter resistance to mixing the two worlds; the split is vividly revealed. Much of our experience goes underground, because there is no socially acceptable way of expressing it and having our physical and psychological experience acknowledged and shared. A few close friends may share it, but there is a strong impulse to protect them from it too, because it seems so private, so unacceptable. I found that, after a couple of years of illness, even answering the question, "How are you?" became a difficult, conflict-ridden business. I don't want to alienate my friends from my experience, but I don't want to risk their discomfort and rejection by telling them what they don't want to know.[2] ...

If the able-bodied saw the disabled as potentially themselves or as their future selves, they would be more inclined to feel that society should be organized to provide the resources that would make disabled people fully integrated and contributing members. They would think that "charity" is as inappropriate a way of thinking about resources for disabled people as it is about emergency medical care or education.

Careful study of the lives of disabled people will reveal how artificial the line is that we draw between the biological and the social. Feminists have already challenged this line in part by showing how processes such as childbirth, menstruation and menopause, which may be represented, treated, and therefore experienced as illnesses or disabilities, are socially constructed from biological reality (Rich 1976; Ehrenreich and English 1979). Disabled people's relations to our bodies involve elements of struggle which perhaps cannot be eliminated, perhaps not even mitigated, by social arrangements. *But,* much of what is *disabling* about our physical conditions is also a consequence of social arrangements (Finger 1983; Browne, Connors and Stern 1985; Fine and Asch 1988) which could, but do not, either compensate for our physical conditions, or accommodate them so that we can participate fully, or support our struggles and integrate us into the community *and our struggles into the cultural concept of life as it is ordinarily lived.* ...

THE OPPRESSION OF DISABLED PEOPLE IS THE OPPRESSION OF EVERYONE'S REAL BODY

Our real human bodies are exceedingly diverse—in size, shape, colour, texture, structure, function, range and habits of movement, and development—and they are constantly changing. Yet we do not absorb or reflect this simple fact in our culture. Instead, we idealize the human body. Our physical ideals change from time to time, but we always have ideals. These ideals are not just about appearance; they are also ideals of strength and energy and proper control of the body. We are perpetually bombarded with images of these ideals, demands for them, and offers of consumer products and services to help us achieve them.[3] Idealizing the body prevents everyone, able-bodied and disabled, from identifying with and loving her/ his real body. Some people can have the illusion of acceptance that comes from believing that their bodies are "close enough" to the ideal, but this illusion only draws them deeper into identifying with the ideal and into the endless task of reconciling the reality with it. Sooner or later they must fail.

Before I became disabled, I was one of those people who felt "close enough" to cultural ideals to be reasonably accepting of my body. Like most feminists I know, I was aware of some alienation from it, and I worked at liking my body better. Nevertheless, I knew in my heart that too much of my liking still depended on being "close enough." When I was disabled by illness, I experienced a much more profound alienation from my body. After a year spent mostly in bed, I could barely identify my body as my own. I felt that "it" was torturing "me," trapping me in exhaustion, pain and inability to do many of the simplest things I did when I was healthy. The shock of this experience and the effort to identify with a new, disabled body, made me realize I had been living a luxury of the able-bodied. The able-bodied can postpone the task of identifying with their *real* bodies. The disabled don't have the luxury of demanding that their bodies fit the physical ideals of their culture. As Barbara Hillyer Davis says: "For all of us the difficult work of finding (one's) self includes the body, but people who live with disability in a society that glorifies fitness and physical conformity are forced to understand more fully what bodily integrity means" (Davis 1984, 3).

In a society which idealizes the body, the physically disabled are marginalized. People learn to identify with their own strengths (by cultural standards) and to hate, fear and neglect their own weaknesses. The disabled are not only de-valued for their de-valued bodies (Hannaford 1985); they are constant reminders to the able-bodied of the negative body—of what the able-bodied are trying to avoid, forget and ignore (Lessing 1981). For example, if someone tells me she is in pain, she reminds me of the existence of pain, the imperfection and fragility of the body, the possibility of my own pain, the *inevitability* of it. The less willing I am to accept all these, the less I want to know about her pain; if I cannot avoid it in her presence, I will avoid her. I may even blame her for it. I may tell myself that she *could have* avoided it, in order to go on believing that I *can* avoid it. I want to believe I am not like her; I cling to the differences. Gradually, I make her "other" because I don't want to confront my real body, which I fear and cannot accept.[4]

Disabled people can participate in marginalizing ourselves. We can wish for bodies we do not have, with frustration, shame, self-hatred. We can feel trapped in the negative body; it is our internalized oppression to feel this. Every (visibly or invisibly) disabled person I have talked to or read has felt this; some never stop feeling it. In addition, disabled women suffer more than disabled men from the demand that people have "ideal" bodies, because in patriarchal culture people judge women more by their bodies than they do men. Disabled women often do not feel seen (because they are often not seen) by others as whole people, especially not as sexual people (Campling 1981; Matthews 1983; Hannaford 1985; Fine and Asch 1988). ...

... In a culture which loves the idea that the body can be controlled, those who cannot control their bodies are seen (and may see themselves) as failures.

When you listen to this culture in a disabled body, you hear how often health and physical vigour are talked about as if they were moral virtues. People constantly praise others for their "energy," their stamina, their ability to work long hours. Of course, acting on behalf of one's health can be a virtue, and undermining one's health can be a vice, but "success" at being healthy, like beauty, is always partly a matter of luck and therefore beyond our control. When health is spoken of as a virtue, people who lack it are made to feel inadequate. I am not suggesting that it is always wrong to praise people's physical strength or accomplishments, any more than it is always wrong to praise their physical beauty. But just as treating cultural standards of beauty as essential virtues for women harms most women, treating health and vigour as moral virtues for everyone harms people with disabilities and illnesses.

The myth that the body can be controlled is not easily dispelled, because it is not very vulnerable to evidence against it. When I became ill, several people wanted to discuss with me what I thought I had done to "make myself" ill or "allow myself" to become sick. At first I fell in with this, generating theories about what I had done wrong; even though I had always taken good care of my health, I was able to find some (rather far-fetched) accounts of my responsibility for my illness. When a few close friends offered hypotheses as to how *they* might be responsible for my being ill, I began to suspect that something was wrong. Gradually, I realized that we were all trying to believe that nothing this important is beyond our control. ...

DISABLED PEOPLE AS "OTHER"

When we make people "other," we group them together as the objects of *our* experience instead of regarding them as fellow *subjects* of experience with whom we might identify. If you are "other" to me, I see you primarily as symbolic of something else—usually, but not always, something I reject and fear and that I project onto you. We can all do this to each other, but very often the process is not symmetrical, because one group of people may have more power to call itself the paradigm of humanity and to make the world suit its own needs and validate its own experiences.[5] Disabled people are "other" to able-bodied people. ...

One recent attempt to reduce the "otherness" of disabled people is the introduction of the term, "differently-abled." I assume the point of using this term is to suggest that there is nothing *wrong* with being the way we are, just different. Yet to call someone "differently-abled" is much like calling her "differently-coloured" or "differently-gendered." It says: "This person is not the norm or paradigm of humanity." If anything, it increases the "otherness" of disabled people, because it reinforces the paradigm of humanity as young, strong and healthy, with all body parts working "perfectly," from which this person is "different." Using the term "differently-abled" also suggests a (polite? patronizing? protective? self-protective?) disregard of the special difficulties struggles and suffering disabled people face. We are *dis-abled*. We live with particular social and physical struggles that are partly consequences of the conditions of our bodies and partly consequences of the structures and expectations of our societies, but they are struggles which only people with bodies like ours experience.

The positive side of the term "differently-abled" is that it might remind the able-bodied that to be disabled in some respects is not to be disabled in all respects. It also suggests that a disabled person may have abilities that the able-bodied lack in virtue of being able-bodied. Nevertheless, on the whole, the term "differently-abled" should be abandoned, because it reinforces the able-bodied paradigm of humanity and fails to acknowledge the struggles disabled people face.

The problems of being "the other" to a dominant group are always politically complex. One solution is to emphasize similarities to the dominant group in the hope that they will identify with the oppressed, recognize their rights, gradually give them equal opportunities, and eventually assimilate them. Many disabled people are tired of being symbols to the able-bodied, visible only or primarily for their disabilities, and they want nothing more than to be seen as individuals rather than as members of the group, "the disabled." Emphasizing similarities to the able-bodied, making their disabilities unnoticeable in comparison to their other human qualities may bring about assimilation one-by-one. It does not directly challenge the able-bodied paradigm of humanity, just as women moving into traditionally male arenas of power does not directly challenge the male paradigm of humanity, although both may produce a gradual change in the paradigms. In addition, assimilation may be very difficult for the disabled to achieve. Although the able-bodied like disabled tokens who do not seem very different from themselves, they may *need* someone to carry the burden of the negative body as long as they continue to idealize and try to control the body. They may therefore resist the assimilation of most disabled people.

The reasons in favour of the alternative solution to "otherness"—*emphasizing difference* from the able-bodied—are also reasons for emphasizing similarities among the disabled, especially social and political similarities. Disabled people share positions of social oppression that separate us from the able-bodied, and we share physical, psychological and social experiences of disability. Emphasizing differences from the able-bodied demands that those differences be acknowledged and respected and fosters solidarity among the disabled. It challenges the able-bodied paradigm of humanity and creates the possibility of a deeper challenge to the idealization of the body and the demand for its control. Invisibly disabled people tend to be drawn to solutions that emphasize difference, because our need to have our struggles acknowledged is great, and we have far less experience than those who are visibly disabled of being symbolic to the able-bodied.

Whether one wants to emphasize sameness or difference in dealing with the problem of being "the other" depends in part on how radically one wants to challenge the value-structure of the dominant group. A very important issue in this category for both women and disabled people is the value of independence from the help of others, so highly esteemed in our patriarchal culture and now being questioned in feminist ethics (see, for example, Sherwin 1984, 1987; Kittay and Meyers 1987) and discussed in the writings of disabled women (see, for example, Fisher and Galler 1981; Davis 1984; Frank 1988). Many disabled people who can see the possibility of living as independently as any able-bodied person, or who have achieved this goal after long struggle, value their independence above everything. Dependence on the help of others is humiliating in a society which prizes independence. In addition, this issue holds special complications for disabled women, reading the stories of women who became disabled as adults, I was struck by their struggle with shame and loss of self-esteem at being transformed from people who took physical care of others (husbands and children) to people who were physically dependent. All this suggests that disabled people need every bit of independence we can get. Yet there are disabled people who will always need a lot of help from other individuals just to survive (those who have very little control of movement, for example), and to the extent that everyone considers independence necessary to respect and self-esteem, those people will be condemned to be de-valued. In addition, some disabled people spend tremendous energy being independent in ways that might be considered trivial in a culture less insistent on self-reliance; if our culture valued *inter-dependence* more highly, they could use that energy for more satisfying activities. ...

When you are very ill, you desperately need medical validation of your experience, not only for economic reasons (insurance claims, pensions, welfare and disability benefits all depend upon official diagnosis), but also for social and psychological reasons. People with unrecognized illnesses are often abandoned by their friends and families.[6] Because almost everyone accepts the cognitive authority of medicine, the person whose bodily experience is radically different from medical descriptions of her/his condition is invalidated as a knower. Either you decide to hide your experience, or you are socially isolated with it by being labelled mentally ill[7] or dishonest. In both cases you are silenced.

Even when your experience is recognized by medicine, it is often re-described in ways that are inaccurate from your standpoint. The objectively observable condition of your body may be used to determine the severity of your pain, for instance, regardless of your own reports of it. For example, until recently, relatively few doctors were willing to acknowledge that severe phantom limb pain can persist for months or even years after an amputation. The accumulated experience of doctors who were themselves amputees has begun to legitimize the other patients' reports (Madruga 1979).

When you are forced to realize that other people have more social authority than you do to describe your experience of your own body, your confidence in yourself and your relationship to reality is radically undermined. What can you know if you cannot know that you are experiencing suffering or joy; what can you communicate to people who don't believe you know even this?[8] Most people will censor what they tell or say nothing rather than expose themselves repeatedly to such deeply felt invalidation. They are silenced by fear and confusion. The process is familiar from our understanding of how women are silenced in and by patriarchal culture.

One final caution: As with women's "special knowledge," there is a danger of sentimentalizing disabled people's knowledge and abilities and keeping us "other" by doing so. We need to bring this knowledge into the culture and to transform the culture and society so that everyone can receive and make use of it, so that it can be fully integrated, along with disabled people, into a shared social life. ...

NOTES

1   Itzhak Perlman, when asked in a recent CBC interview about the problems of the disabled, said disabled people have two problems: the fact that the world is not made for people with weaknesses but for supermen and the attitudes of able-bodied people.

2   Some people save me that trouble by *telling me* I am fine and walking away. Of course, people also encounter difficulties with answering "How are you?" during and after crises, such as separation from a partner, death of a loved one, or a nervous breakdown. There is a temporary alienation from what is considered ordinary shared experience. In disability, the alienation lasts longer, often for a lifetime, and, in my experience, it is more profound.

3   The idealization of the body is clearly related in complex ways to the economic processes of a consumer society. Since it pre-dated capitalism, we know that capitalism did not cause it, but it is undeniable that idealization now generates tremendous profits and that the quest for profit demands the reinforcement of idealization and the constant development of new ideals.

4   Susan Griffin, in a characteristically honest and insightful passage, describes an encounter with the fear that makes it hard to identify with disabled people. See Griffin 1982, 648–649.

5   When Simone de Beauvoir uses this term to elucidate men's view of women (and women's view of ourselves), she emphasizes that Man is considered essential, Woman inessential; Man is the Subject, Woman the Other (de Beauvoir 1952, xvi). Susan Griffin expands upon this idea by showing how we project rejected

aspects of ourselves onto groups of people who are designated the Other (Griffin 1981).

6 Accounts of the experience of relatively unknown, newly-discovered, or hard-to-diagnose diseases and conditions confirm this. See, for example, Jeffreys 1982, for the story of an experience of Chronic Fatigue Syndrome, which is more common in women than in men.

7 Frequently people with undiagnosed illnesses are sent by their doctors to psychiatrists, who cannot help and may send them back to their doctors saying they must be physically ill. This can leave patients in a dangerous medical and social limbo. Sometimes they commit suicide because of it (Ramsay 1986). Psychiatrists who know enough about living with physical illness or disability to help someone cope with it are rare.

8 For more discussion of this subject, see Zaner 1983 and Rawlinson 1983.

REFERENCES

Addelson, Kathryn P. 1983. The man of professional wisdom. In *Discovering reality*. Sandra Harding and Merrill B. Hintikka, eds. Boston: D. Reidel.

Alcoff, Linda. 1988. Cultural feminism versus post-structuralism: The identity crisis in feminist theory. *Signs: Journal of Women in Culture and Society* 13(3): 405–436.

Browne, Susan E., Debra Connors and Nanci Stern, eds. 1985. *With the power of each breath—a disabled women's anthology*. Pittsburgh: Cleis Press.

Bullard, David G. and Susan E. Knight, eds. 1981. *Sexuality and physical disability*. St. Louis: C.V. Mosby.

Bury, M.R. 1979. Disablement in society: Towards an integrated perspective. *International Journal of Rehabilitation Research* 1(1):33–40.

Beauvoir, Simone de. 1952. *The second sex*. New York: Alfred A. Knopf.

Campling, J, ed. 1981. *Images of ourselves—women with disabilities talking*. London: Routledge and Kegan Paul.

Davis, Barbara Hillyer. 1984. Women, disability and feminism: Notes toward a new theory. *Frontiers: A Journal of Women Studies* VIII (1):1–5.

Davis, Melanie and Catherine Marshall. 1987. Female and disabled: Challenged women in education. *National Women's Studies Association Perspectives* 5:39–41.

Deegan, Mary Jo and Nancy A. Brooks, eds. 1985. *Women and disability—the double handicap*. New Brunswick: Transaction Books.

Dinnerstein, Dorothy. 1976. *The mermaid and the minotaur: Sexual arrangements and human malaise*. New York: Harper and Row.

Ehrenreich, Barbara and Dierdre English. 1979. *For her own good: 150 years of the experts' advice to women*. New York: Anchor.

Fine, Michelle and Adrienne Asch, eds. 1988. *Women with disabilities: Essays in psychology, culture and politics*. Philadelphia: Temple University Press.

Finger, Anne. 1983. Disability and reproductive rights. *off our backs* 13(9):18–19.

Fisher, Bernice and Roberta Galler. 1981. Conversation between two friends about feminism and disability. *off our backs* 11(5):14–15.

Frank, Gelya. 1988. On embodiment: A case study of congenital limb deficiency in American culture. In *Women with disabilities.* Michelle Fine and Adrienne Asch, eds. Philadelphia: Temple University Press.

Griffin, Susan. 1981. *Pornography and silence: Culture's revenge against nature.* New York: Harper and Row.

Griffin, Susan. 1982. The way of all ideology. *Signs: Journal of Women in Culture and Society* 8(3):641–660.

Halpern, Sue M. 1988. Portrait of the artist. Review of *Under the eye of the clock* by Christopher Nolan. *The New York Review of Books,* June 30:3–4.

Hannaford, Susan. 1985. *Living outside inside. A disabled woman's experience. Towards a social and political perspective.* Berkeley: Canterbury Press.

Jeffreys, Toni. 1982. *The mile-high staircase.* Sydney: Hodder and Stoughton Ltd.

Kittay, Eva Feder and Diana T. Meyers, eds. 1987. *Women and moral theory.* Totowa, NJ: Rowman and Littlefield.

Kleinman, Arthur. 1988. *The illness narratives: Suffering, healing, and the human condition.* New York: Basic Books.

Lessing, Jill. 1981. Denial and disability. *Off our backs* II(5):21.

Madruga, Lenor. 1979. *One step at a time.* Toronto: McGraw-Hill.

Matthews, Gwyneth Ferguson. 1983. *Voices from the shadows: Women with disabilities speak out.* Toronto: Women's Educational Press.

Moore, Maureen. 1985. Coping with pelvic inflammatory disease. In *Women and Disability.* Frances Rooney and Pat Israel, eds. *Resources for Feminist Research.* 14(1).

Newsweek. 1988. Reading God's mind. June 13:56–59.

Ramsay, A. Melvin. 1986. *Postviral fatigue syndrome, the saga of Royal Free disease.* London: Gower Medical Publishing.

Rawlinson, Mary C. 1983. The facticity of illness and the appropriation of health. In *Phenomenology in a pluralistic context.* William L. McBride and Calvin O. Schrag, eds. Albany: SUNY Press.

Rich, Adrienne, 1976. *Of woman born: Motherhood as experience and institution.* New York: W.W. Norton.

Rooney, Frances and Pat Israel, eds. 1985. *Women and disability. Resources for Feminist Research* 14(1).

Sacks, Oliver. 1988. The revolution of the deaf. *The New York Review of Books,* June 2, 23–28.

Saxton, Marsha and Florence Howe, eds. 1987. *With wings: an anthology of literature by and about women with disabilities.* New York: The Feminist Press.

Shaul, Susan L. and Jane Elder Bogle. 1981. Body image and the woman with a disability. In *Sexuality and physical disability.* David G. Bullard and Susan E. Knight, eds. St. Louis: C.V. Mosby.

Sherwin, Susan. 1984–85. A feminist approach to ethics. *Dalhousie Review* 64(4):704–713.

Sherwin, Susan. 1987. Feminist ethics and in vitro fertilization. In *Science, morality and feminist theory*. Marsha Hanen and Kai Nielsen, eds. Calgary: The University of Calgary Press.

Sontag, Susan. 1977. *Illness as metaphor*. New York: Random House.

U.N. Decade of Disabled Persons 1983–1992. 1983. *World programme of action concerning disabled persons*. New York: United Nations.

Whitbeck, Caroline. 1983. Afterword to the maternal instinct. In *Mothering: Essays in feminist theory*. Joyce Trebilcot, ed. Totowa: Rowman and Allanheld.

Zaner, Richard M. 1983. Flirtations or engagement? Prolegomenon to a philosophy of medicine. In *Phenomenology in a pluralistic context*. William L. McBride and Calvin O. Schrag, eds. Albany: SUNY Press.

33

Indian, Métis, and Inuit Women and Men: Multiple Jeopardy in a Canadian Context

Linda M. Gerber

When the incomes of women and men in Canada are compared, women earn much less than men: those who work full time, all year earn about two-thirds of the income of their male counterparts. While this is true for women in general, one might expect to find that those with combined minority statuses experience multiple jeopardy. On the basis of 1986 census data, this study compares women and men who claim to be Indian, Inuit or Métis (on both paternal and maternal sides). A comparison of the socio-economic characteristics of men and women, across the three Native groups, is undertaken in an attempt to find out if Native women are doubly disadvantaged as women and as members of ethnic (or visible) minorities and if Indian women suffer further disadvantage as a result of the dependent status of Indians and their reserve-based communities.

MULTIPLE JEOPARDY IN EXCHANGE RELATIONSHIPS

In *Exchange and Power in Social Life* (1964: 7), Peter M. Blau limits social exchange to actions that are "contingent on rewarding actions from others and that cease when these expected reactions are not forthcoming" and goes on to point out that:

> *Processes of social attraction, without which associations among men would not occur, give rise to processes of exchange. Unreciprocated exchange leads to the differentiation of power. The exercise of power collectivities, as judged by the social norms of justice, promotes processes of social approval, legitimation, and organization on the one hand, and forces of opposition, conflict, reorganization, and change, on the other.*

Social attraction and the exact nature of exchange relationships among individuals vary with the relative resources of the parties involved in the exchange. Where resources are unequal, the provision of services by the

---

This is an original article written specifically for this volume.

"superior" is met with deference and compliance on the part of the "subordinate" (Blau, 1964: 21). Shared standards of valuation within groups or societies give rise to media of exchange—money being one of them—that facilitate social interaction. Since, in our society, the most widely approved means of acquiring money is through employment, employers find themselves in powerful positions relative to their employees. The employer provides needed jobs and wages to employees who have the appropriate resources (skills, work habits, experience) and they, in turn, perform services and comply with managerial directives (p. 205). Where alternative employment opportunities are lacking, and employees are highly dependent upon existing jobs, assignment to unpleasant duties becomes possible and wages remain low (pp. 119–120).

Among the resources that might shape exchange relationships are socially defined and valued attributes (such as gender, skin colour, or physical attractiveness), education, language facility, skills and contacts. To the extent that resource inequalities give rise to power differentials and power is self-perpetuating, these processes give rise to a class structure (Blau, 1964: 197; Hedican, 1986a).

Those who participate in exchange relations with "inferior" resources (low educational attainment or limited employment experience) or with negatively valued attributes (femaleness or visible minority status) are disadvantaged within the context of those relationships. The multiple jeopardy hypothesis suggests that those disadvantages are additive and that each additional "handicap" further diminishes the individual's position in exchange relationships.

Comparisons of male and female incomes invariably reveal that women trail behind—even when occupation and full- or part-time employment are taken into account (Calzavara, 1985: 521; Ghalam, 1994). Wilson (1986:108) notes that women employed full time have earned approximately 60 percent of men's earnings with an increase from 53 percent in 1911 to 64 percent in 1982. The census of 1986 revealed another slight increase to 66 percent: by 1991 that figure has increased to 70 percent.

The disadvantaged position of women has been explained in terms of the existence of a "double ghetto" or "pink ghetto". Women are segregated, firstly, into the home-making role and, secondly (if they do enter the workforce), into a segregated labour market where "women's work" is paid less (Armstrong and Armstrong, 1984; Fox and Fox, 1989). As late as 1991, despite increased involvement of women in the professions, 71 percent of women continued to be "employed in just five occupational groups—teaching, nursing or related health occupations, clerical, sales and service" (Ghalam, 1994: 143). A dual labour market—relying upon a surplus labour pool[1] of women that enters or retreats from the workforce according to the needs of the economy—ensures that women will continue to be poorly paid (Wilson, 1986: 119). Since discrimination in employment is experienced by women, as well as by various racial and ethnic minorities (Lampkin, 1985; Li,

198; Powless, 1985), one might expect to find that the women of ethnic or racial minorities are doubly disadvantaged. They enter exchange relationships with two devalued attributes—gender and ethnicity.

The concepts of "double whammy" or double jeopardy have been used to deal with the effects of being old and female (Chappell and Havens, 1980; Posner, 1980) or ethnic and female (McMullen, 1981; Elliott and Fleras, 1992:103), while Juteau-Lee and Roberts (1981) call it the "double bind of ethnicity and femininity". Multiple jeopardy has been used to describe the condition of those who are old, ethnic and female (Driedger and Chappell, 1987) or aboriginal, specifically Indian and female (Gerber, 1990). Others have argued that the intersection of race, class and gender exposes immigrant and Native women to multiple disadvantages (Elliott and Fleras, 1992: 109; King, 1988: Wotherspoon and Satzewich, 1993: 62). Whatever the terminology, the basic idea is that some people suffer multiple disadvantages or barriers in their interactions with others—particularly in their economic relations.

Where male-female differences in labour-force participation and income among Natives are discussed (Gerber, 1990; Hedican, 1986b; McDonald, 1994; Wotherspoon and Satzewich, 1993: 60–61), the suggestion is that, like their non-Native counterparts, Native women are less active in the workforce than men and have lower incomes. One would expect Native women, in general, to fare poorly relative to Native men, but there are also reasons to expect that Indians are worse off than Inuit or Métis because of their special status. From a political economy perspective, Frideres (1993: 446–468) argues that the Indian reserve is an exploited internal colony for which external political and economic control creates substantial barriers to development. Thus one can say that Indian women experience triple or multiple jeopardy—as women, as aboriginal people (or as visible minorities), and as members of uniquely dependent communities[2].

On the basis of the multiple jeopardy hypothesis, one would expect to find that all three native groups are disadvantaged compared to Canadians in general, that the women in each category fare poorly relative to the men, and that, on some indicators, Indian women lag behind Inuit and Métis women. These cumulative disadvantages should be apparent in an examination of socio-demographic, educational, occupational and income variables.

THE DATA

A Statistics Canada publication, *Dimensions: Profile of Ethnic Groups* (1989) provides socio-economic profiles—based upon the 1986 census—of roughly 60 ethnic categories. The tables presented below include selected variables (adapted as rates or percentages from *Dimensions*) for single-origin North American Indians, Inuit and Métis[3]. The tables are based upon 286,230 Indians[4], 27,285 Inuit, 56,745 Métis and 25,022,010 Canadians, as enumerated in

1986. The rates and percentages are based upon total populations, populations aged 15 and over, all employed people and so forth, as indicated at the bottom of each table.

OBSERVATIONS

On the basis of selected socio-demographic characteristics (Table 1), Native men and women differ not only from Canadians in general but also among themselves. While all three Native categories are younger than the overall Canadian population, the Inuit are the youngest with more than 14 percent below five years of age and less than 3 percent over 65. The fact that Canadian women have life expectancies about 7 years longer than men is reflected in the higher proportion of females over 65 in the Canadian population: while Métis women are over-represented among the elderly, this is only slightly the case with the Inuit and not at all with Indian women. The relatively high fertility maintained by Native women—under less than ideal conditions—may be responsible in part for their failure to share the longevity of other Canadian women.

The women and men of all three Native groups (Table 1) are less likely to have married than are Canadians overall. Relatively large percentages of Native women 15 years of age and older have never married—about 35 percent compared to 24 percent among Canadian women in general. The combination of low marriage levels and high fertility, suggests the presence of large numbers of single mothers (Siggner, 1980: 40; National Council on Welfare, 1990: 112) who undoubtedly face tremendous barriers to labour-force participation. Within each category, Native men are much more likely to be unmarried than are Native women (or Canadian men in general).

Of the Natives, the Inuit (Table 1) are most likely to speak an aboriginal language at home (about 64 percent) and most likely to be unable to speak either of Canada's official languages (28 percent). Life among the single-origin Inuit is overwhelmingly carried on in Inuktitut. In contrast, less than 25 percent of the Indians speak any of their many languages at home and all but 5 percent can speak one or the other (or both) of our official languages. Linguistic acculturation is most pronounced among the Métis, a mere 1 percent of whom are unable to speak either French or English.

The pattern of residence in Canada's major urban centres (Montreal, Toronto and Vancouver) suggests that the Indian population is most urbanized, the Inuit the least, and that each of the Native categories is much less urbanized than the overall Canadian population (Table 1). Geographic isolation—from centres of population concentration and economic activity—is a reality for the Inuit, less than 3 percent of whom live in the major urban centres: in fact, roughly 85 percent of them live in the Northwest Territories and northern Quebec[5]. One might expect these residence patterns to bring greater educational and employment opportunities to the less isolated

TABLE I

Social and Demographic Characteristics of Native Men and Women, 1986*

	Indian		Métis		Inuit		Canadian	
	Men	Women	Men	Women	Men	Women	Men	Women
Age:								
under 5 years	12.6	11.9	11.4	10.4	14.9	13.8	7.5	7.0
65 yrs. or over	4.0	4.0	3.8	4.3	2.6	2.8	8.7	11.3
Marital status:								
never married**	43.3	34.5	44.8	35.4	46.5	37.5	30.5	23.9
Language:								
mother tongue: not English or French	34.8	33.7	11.9	12.8	74.3	75.4	11.7	11.5
home language: not English or French	25.3	23.0	7.3	7.0	64.3	63.0	5.8	6.0
Able to speak:								
English	84.4	81.4	84.6	84.9	66.7	65.8	67.4	66.2
French	6.2	6.0	6.2	6.2	3.8	3.9	14.8	16.9
both	4.3	4.2	8.5	8.2	1.8	1.6	16.8	16.5
neither	5.1	5.0	0.7	0.8	27.7	28.7	0.9	1.4
Residence:*								
major cities	7.1	7.8	4.8	4.6	2.7	2.6	26.0	26.0

*for single-origin individuals (e.g. Indian on maternal and paternal sides)
** percentages based upon populations 15 years of age and older
*** refers to percentages living in Montreal, Toronto and Vancouver
Note that separate male and female residence figures are not available for Canadians in general.

Source: Statistics Canada: Catalogues 93–154 and 93–155

Indians and severely restrict the opportunities of the Inuit (cf. Gerber, 1984: 152–155).

    Educational attainment figures (Table 2) suggest that, indeed, the Indians and Métis have similar levels of education, whereas the Inuit lag behind. One-third or more of Indian and Métis adults (males and females) have less than grade 9 education—as do about 60 percent of the Inuit—compared to

TABLE 2

Educational Attainment and Occupation of Native Men and Women, 1986

	Indian		Métis		Inuit		Canadian	
	Men	Women	Men	Women	Men	Women	Men	Women
Education:*								
less than grade 9	37.3	35.9	34.9	34.8	57.7	62.2	16.9	7.7
post-secondary certif'n**	14.3	13.4	13.5	11.6	10.7	6.7	34.4	29.5
university degree	1.2	1.4	1.0	1.0	0.2	0.2	11.3	7.9
Occupation:*								
managerial	7.1	5.8	5.3	4.7	7.8	5.8	12.6	7.8
professional	9.0	23.2	6.8	13.6	10.9	24.5	13.1	20.9
clerical	4.3	24.4	4.2	22.0	7.8	26.5	6.8	33.5
sales	2.9	5.7	3.3	5.7	2.9	3.5	8.8	9.4
service	10.0	25.4	10.4	32.1	10.6	28.1	10.2	16.1
primary	17.9	3.0	16.3	2.6	7.6	0.6	7.9	2.5
processing	7.6	3.3	7.5	2.1	3.3	2.5	8.2	2.4
fabricating	5.2	3.4	6.1	2.9	5.7	4.1	9.9	4.2
construction	19.7	1.2	20.4	1.1	18.4	1.1	10.1	0.3
Industry:*								
government service	22.4	21.9	11.4	11.7	27.9	19.7	8.0	5.3

*percentages based upon populations 15 years of age and over
**post-secondary certification refers to all types, including university degrees
*** percentages based upon totals employed in all occupations

Source: Statistics Canada, Catalogues 93–154 and 93–155

---

17 and 8 percent of Canada's men and women respectively. Indians are slightly more likely than the Métis to have less than grade 9 education but, at the other end of the educational scale, they are slightly ahead of the Métis in the attainment of university degrees or post-secondary certification (university and non-university combined). Indian women are alone in being slightly more likely than their male counterparts to have acquired a university degree—though in terms of post-secondary education overall, they are just slightly behind Indian men.[6]

Unlike the measures of educational attainment, the occupational figures in Table 2 are percentages based upon individuals who are employed rather than upon the total populations over 15 years of age. While it is clear that each of the Native categories is less involved in managerial occupations than are Canadian women and men in general, close to 6 percent of the Indian and Inuit women are thus employed. On the other hand, while Native men are less involved in professional occupations than Canadian men in general, working Indian and Inuit women are *more* likely to be classified as professional than is the case with Canadian women overall. Native women are underrepresented in the clerical and sales categories and over-represented in the service category. (Métis women, who are not as well represented in the professional category as are their Indian and Inuit counterparts, are found disproportionately in the service occupations.) Indian and Métis men are more heavily involved in the primary sector (e.g., hunting, fishing, logging or farming) than Inuit or Canadian men but the women are not. And, while Native men (at 20 percent) are twice as likely to be involved in construction as those of Canada, this is true of only 1 percent of Native women. (Note that the latter figure is to be compared with 0.3 percent of Canadian women overall.)

Women and men in each of the aboriginal categories (Table 2) are employed in government service to a greater extent than Canadians in general. For Métis men, the level of overrepresentation is minimal, but Métis women are more than twice as likely as Canadian women to be employed in government service. Government employment is even more important for Indian and Inuit women and men: in each case about 20 percent of the workforce is in government service. These figures reflect the active involvement of government in the political and economic affairs of reserve communities and the north. Public sector employment among status or registered Indians is high. Compared with 25 percent of Canadian workers, more than 50 percent of status Indians, either on or off reserve, are involved in employment that is directly or indirectly funded by government (Wotherspoon and Satzewich, 1993:62).

As indicated in Table 3, labour-force participation rates for Native males and females (15 years of age and older) are about 15 percentage points lower than those for males and females in the general population. In addition, women's participation rates in each Native category are about 20 percentage points lower than those of men. The participation of men is highest among the Métis, while Indian and Inuit rates are identical. This suggests that despite their relative isolation from urban-industrial centres, the Inuit are not the most disadvantaged. Among Native women, Indians have the lowest participation rates of all. In this respect, they are disadvantaged relative to Indian men, Canadians in general and other Native women.

Among young adults (15 to 24 years of age) in the general Canadian population, women are almost as active in the labour force as men (65 and 71 percent respectively) and young women are actually *more* active than older women (Table 3). The fact that, in each of the Native categories,

TABLE 3

Labour-force Participation and Income of Native Men and Women, 1986

	Indian		Métis		Inuit		Canadian	
	Men	Women	Men	Women	Men	Women	Men	Women
Participation rates:*								
15 years and over	59.5	39.0	66.4	44.5	59.5	43.7	77.5	55.9
15–24 years	46.3	34.3	56.2	41.3	45.4	40.2	70.7	64.8
25 years and over	66.3	41.2	71.6	46.0	68.7	45.8	79.4	53.6
Unemployment rates:**								
15 years and over	32.7	28.7	30.3	27.0	28.9	26.0	9.6	11.2
15–24 years	44.5	42.7	39.0	38.8	42.7	34.9	17.3	16.6
25 years and over	28.5	23.1	26.8	21.7	23.0	20.9	7.7	9.6
Employment:***								
full time, all year	17.9	11.6	18.7	12.3	22.0	12.5	37.2	23.3
Income:								
average*****	$23,328	$17,125	$24,701	$17,331	$23,529	$17,842	$30,504	$19,995
above $35,000******	4.6	0.7	6.2	0.9	5.2	1.1	16.1	3.4

*percentage of population in each age category in the labour force (i.e. employed or looking for work)
**percentage of labour force unemployed
*** percentages based upon total population 15 years of age and older
**** average income for those employed full time, all year (1985 income)
*****percentage of population 15 years of age or older with income of $35,000 or more (1985 income)

Source: Statistics Canada: Catalogues 93–154 and 93–155

young adults exhibit *very* low levels of labour-force involvement suggests that, for them, youth is another source of disadvantage or jeopardy. Unless there is a shift in employment patterns, this suggests that the younger generation of Natives—despite gradual increases in educational attainment—may end up being in worse straits than its elders. Note that young Indian women have the lowest participation rates of all and that on this dimension Indian women (older and younger) fare less than their Métis and Inuit counterparts.

Unemployment rates paint an equally dismal picture (Table 3) in that they are up to three times higher for Natives than for adult Canadians in general. Despite the fact that they have the lowest participation rates among Native women (in each age category), Indian women also have the highest unemployment rates (i.e. a large percentage is unemployed out of a relatively small percentage involved in the labour force). It is not surprising then to find that full-time, full-year employment rates are lowest among Indian women—with less than 12 percent of Indian women 15 years of age and older thus employed. The proportions of adult Native men and women employed full time, all year are roughly half those of Canadian men and women. Once again, among the Native categories, Indian women fare worst.

Similar patterns are apparent with respect to income (Table 3). While 16 and 3 percent of Canadian men and women have incomes of $35,000 or more (1985 figures), this is true of about 5 and 1 percent of Native men and women. In other words, Canadian men and women are three times more likely than Native men and women to earn over $35,000 per year. Again, Indian women are less likely than their Métis or Inuit counterparts to earn these high incomes. Average incomes for those employed full-time, all year reveal a similar pattern. The incomes of Native men are substantially lower than those of Canadian men in general, but higher than those of Canadian women overall. Native women have the lowest incomes, with Indian women in particular trailing once again.

SUMMARY AND CONCLUSIONS

On the basis of the above evidence, one may conclude that the three Native groups are disadvantaged relative to the overall Canadian population on many socio-economic and demographic measures. The Native groups have shorter life expectancies, lower marriage rates, higher rates of single parenthood, less education and greater occupational segregation by gender. In addition, for men and women of various ages, the three Native groups have lower rates of labour-force participation coupled with higher unemployment rates. Relatively few Natives are employed full time, all year, and incomes for those who are employed lag far behind those for Canada as a whole.

Comparison of the Inuit, Métis and Indian categories reveals some interesting patterns. Except with respect to educational attainment, the Inuit do not appear to suffer disadvantages resulting from relative isolation or the limited use of English or French. In fact, the Inuit have higher levels of labour-force participation and lower levels of unemployment than the Indians and Métis. The Indians have higher levels of educational attainment in that more of them have post-secondary certification, including university degrees. Despite this level of educational attainment and substantial employment in the government sector, Indian men and women have lower levels of labour-force participation, higher unemployment rates and lower incomes than the Inuit and Métis.

The pattern of differences between women and men support expectations of unequal educational attainment, labour-force participation and income. While Indian women come close to matching their male counterparts with respect to educational attainment, they drop to the lowest levels with respect to labour force involvement and income. Sex segregation in the employment experience of Natives is clearly evident—and even exaggerated relative to that of Canadians in general—especially in service (which employs women) and construction (which employs men). The overall picture suggests that despite relative proximity to employment centres and higher levels of educational attainment than Inuit or Métis women, Indian women in particular are disadvantaged with respect to employment and income.

Within Canada, those who are particularly disadvantaged are: 1) members of visible minorities (in this case Native); 2) Indian rather than Inuit or Métis; and 3) female. Furthermore, where age is taken into account, one finds that *young* Indian women experience by far the lowest labour-force participation and highest unemployment rates. One can argue, then, that Indian women suffer multiple jeopardy with respect to a number of indica tors of social and economic well-being. The fact that Indians, and Indian women in particular, suffer the greatest disadvantages suggests that Indian status, with its historical trappings of colonial dependency, does create additional barriers to economic and social health. The position of Indian women, with respect to labour force involvement and income, suggests that they are the most severely handicapped in their exchange relations with employers.

Our First Nations (or status) Indians, and particularly their women, are clearly among the last when it comes to partaking of what mainstream Canadians might call the "better things of life". While this might be, at least in part, a matter of cultural choice (i.e. a rejection of materialism and its associated ills) or partial reliance upon traditional subsistence economies, the evidence suggests that there are also multiple barriers (including discrimination and a legacy of internal colonialism) that keep Indian men and, to an even greater extent, women from achieving the same standard of living as other Canadians.

NOTES

1 Frideres (1993: 477) and Wotherspoon and Satzewich (1993: 55) argue that Natives as a whole are part of the reserve army of labour or secondary labour pool. As women and as Natives, Native women are twice marginalized with respect to the economy. The political economy argument relating to the intersection of class, race and gender deals, in effect, with triple or multiple jeopardy.

2 Some people who report that they are single-origin Indians may not be registered or status Indians who are entitled to live on reserves. Of those who are, perhaps half currently live off reserve. While this means that not all single-origin Indians lived in dependent communities or internal colonies at the time of the

census, roughly 50 percent did and many of the off-reserve residents grew up on the reserves and/or have maintained close ties with their reserve communities.

3   Single-origin refers to those individuals who report, for example, Indian parentage on both maternal and paternal sides. Data pertaining to those who claim mixed ancestry are provided separately under a multiple origin category.

4   Since a number of Indian communities, especially in Ontario, declined to be included in the 1986 census, the registered Indian population is underrepresented. Nonetheless, the distribution (by province) of single-origin Indians is very similar to that of the registered Indian population (Gerber, 1990).

5   Although the Canadian population is concentrated in Ontario, Quebec and British Columbia, the Indian population is relatively evenly distributed from Quebec to British Columbia. The Métis are to be found mainly in the three prairie provinces.

6   Native women share with other women in Canada a tendency to acquire their post-secondary certification in commerce, education and health. Native men, 60 percent compared to 40 percent of Canadian men, acquire their post-secondary certification in the trades.

REFERENCES

Armstrong, P. and H. Armstrong 1984 *The Double Ghetto,* rev. ed. Toronto: McClelland & Stewart.

Blau, P. M. 1964 *Exchange and Power in Social Life.* New York: Wiley.

Calzavara, L. 1985 "Trends in the Employment Opportunities of Women in Canada, 1930–1980." Pp. 515–36 in R.S. Abella (commissioner) *Research Studies of the Commission on Equality in Employment.* Ottawa: Minister of Supply and Services.

Chappell, N.L. and B. Havens 1980 "Old and Female: Testing the Double Jeopardy Hypothesis." *The Sociological Quarterly* 21(2): 147–71.

Driedger L. and N.L. Chappell 1987 *Aging and Ethnicity; Towards an Interface.* Toronto: Butterworths.

Elliott, J.L. and A. Fleras 1992 *Unequal Relations: An Introduction to Race and Ethnic Dynamics in Canada.* Scarborough, Ontario: Prentice Hall Canada.

Fox, B.J. and J. Fox 1987 "Occupational gender segregation in the Canadian labour force, 1931-1981." *The Canadian Review of Sociology and Anthropology* 24(3): 374–97.

Frideres, J.S. 1993 *Native Peoples in Canada: Contemporary Conflicts.* Scarborough, Ontario: Prentice Hall Canada.

Gerber, L.M. 1984 "Community characteristics and out-migration from Canadian Indian reserves: path analyses." *The Canadian Review of Sociology and Anthropology* 21(2): 145–65.
   1990 "Multiple jeopardy: A socio-economic comparison of men and women among the Indian, Metis and Inuit peoples of Canada." *Canadian Ethnic Studies* XXII (3): 69–84.

Ghalam, N.Z. 1994 "Women in the Workplace." Pp. 141–46 in *Canadian Social Trends: A Canadian Studies Reader* (volume 2). Toronto: Thompson Publishing.

Hedican, E.J.
1986a "Some issues in the anthropology of transaction and exchange." *The Canadian Review of Sociology and Anthropology* 21(2): 97–117.

1986b *The Ogoki River Guides: Emergent Leadership among the Northern Ojibwa.* Waterloo, Ontario: Wilfrid Laurier University Press.

Herberg, E.N. 1990 "The Ethno-Racial Socioeconomic Hierarchy in Canada: Theory and Analysis of the New Vertical Mosaic". *International Journal of Comparative Sociology* 31(3–4): 206–21.

Juteau-Lee, D. and B. Roberts 1981 "Ethnicity and femininity: (d) après nos expériences." *Canadian Ethnic Studies* XIII(1): 1–23.

King, D. 1988 "Multiple Jeopardy, Multiple Consciousness: The Context of Black Feminist Ideology." *Signs* 14(2): 42–49.

Lampkin, L. 1985 "Visible Minorities in Canada." Pp. 651–83 in R.S. Abella (commissioner) *Research Studies of the Commission on Equality in Employment.* Ottawa: Minister of Supply and Services Canada.

Li, P.S. 1988 *Ethnic Inequality in a Class Society.* Toronto: Wall & Thompson.

McDonald, Ryan, J. 1994 "Canada's Off-Reserve Aboriginal Population." Pp. 51–56 in *Canadian Social Trends: A Canadian Studies Reader* (volume 2). Toronto: Thompson Publishing.

McMullen, L. 1981 "Ethnicity and Femininity: Double Jeopardy." *Canadian Ethnic Studies* XIII(1): 52–62.

National Council of Welfare 1990 *Women and Poverty Revisited.* Ottawa: Minister of Supply and Services Canada.

Posner, J. 1980 "Old and Female: the Double Whammy." Pp. 80–87 in V.W. Marshall (ed.) *Aging in Canada: Social Perspectives.* Don Mills: Fitzhenry & Whiteside.

Powless, R.C. 1985 "Native Peoples and Employment: A National Tragedy." Pp. 589–610 in R.S. Abella (commissioner). *Research Studies of the Commission on Equality in Employment.* Ottawa: Minister of Supply and Services Canada.

Siggner, A.J. 1980 "A Socio-Demographic Profile of Indians in Canada." Pp. 31–65 in J.R. Ponting and R. Gibbins. *Out of Irrelevance.* Toronto: Butterworths.

Wilson, S.J. 1986 *Women, the Family and the Economy.* Toronto: McGraw-Hill.

Wotherspoon, T and V. Satzewich 1993 *First Nations: Race, Class and Gender Relations.* Scarborough, Ontario: Nelson Canada.

34

Taking Woman Abuse Seriously: A Critical Response to the Solicitor General of Canada's Crime Prevention Advice

Walter S. DeKeseredy, Hyman Burshtyn, and Charles Gordon

INTRODUCTION

Many Canadian women are psychologically, sexually, and physically victimized by a broad range of male behaviours which occur in a variety of social contexts, such as within intimate, heterosexual relationships, on the streets, and in the workplace (DeKeseredy and Hinch, 1991). Indeed, a review of the growing empirical literature on this problem reveals that there is ample evidence to support Stanko's (1990a; p. 85) contention that 'women's lives rest upon a continuum of unsafety.' While women experience a considerable amount of danger in both public and private settings, the most serious and common threats to their physical and psychological well-being are abusive acts committed by known men. Unfortunately, the federal government's recent crime advice to women fails to take the multifaceted nature of female victimization seriously. A recent example of this 'selective inattention' (Dexter, 1958) is the Solicitor General of Canada's (1990) crime prevention booklet *Woman Alone*, a document which ignores the fact that women are much more likely to be beaten, raped, or killed by their husbands, boyfriends, cohabiting partners, or male friends than by strangers. The safety precautions listed in this document also fail to address many other crimes against women committed by men on the street, in educational contexts, and in the workplace.

The principal objective of this paper is to show how the Solicitor General's advice obscures the reality of women abuse. In the essay which follows, we briefly review survey research on male interpersonal violence against

From Walter S. DeKeseredy, Hyman Burshtyn, and Charles Gordon, "Taking Woman Abuse Seriously: A Critical Response to the Solicitor General of Canada's Crime Prevention Advice," *International Review of Victimology*, vol. 2 (1992): 157–167. Reprinted by permission.

women, summarize and criticise the recommendations presented in *Woman Alone,* and then attempt to explain why the Solicitor General's Office published this pamphlet. We conclude with a call for an alternative crime prevention discourse derived from the First Report of the Standing Committee on Health and Welfare, Social Affairs, Seniors and the Status of Women (1991).

MALE VIOLENCE AGAINST CANADIAN WOMEN

State-sponsored survey research (Solicitor General of Canada, 1985; Sacco and Johnson, 1990) reveals that while Canadian women report high levels of fear of crime, compared to men, their risks of being assaulted are much lower. The main reason for this discrepancy is the fact that Canadian government studies so far have failed to include adequate measures of woman abuse in domestic settings—the most frequent type of violent female victimization (DeKeseredy and Hinch, 1991; DeKeseredy and MacLean, 1991; Smith, 1988). State-sponsored victimization surveys are generally introduced to respondents as 'crime studies.' Unfortunately, many victims do not perceive their partners' violent actions as crimes in the legal sense (Straus, 1989). Thus, the most common acts of violence against women are seriously under-reported and under-recorded (Stanko, 1990b).

Studies specifically designed to examine male assaults on female partners (Brinkerhoff and Lupri, 1988; DeKeseredy, 1988; Kennedy and Dutton, 1989; Lupri, 1990; Smith, 1987) show that women's fear is not subjectively based or irrational because they are at great risk of being harmed by male spouses, dating partners, and friends (Smith, 1988). These surveys, for example, report incidence rates between 11 and 25 percent. Moreover, data like these prompt feminist researchers such as Stanko (1988; p. 86) to ask the following important question: 'Can women feel safe around male strangers when those familiar to them have violated their physical and sexual safety?'

If, as in the U.S. and the U.K., research shows that most interpersonal violent crimes against Canadian women are committed by male intimates,[1] what is the point of devoting most of the state's attention to stranger-to-stranger crimes? Three possible answers to this question warrant attention here. Before we discuss them, however, it is necessary to summarize and evaluate the recommendations outlined in *Woman Alone.*

With *Woman Alone,* the Office of the Solicitor General of Canada attempts to sensitize women to the potential dangers of living and travelling alone. Female readers are advised to take a large number of precautionary measures. Since there are too many of these suggested procedures to describe here, only a few are listed below. The precautions are categorized under eight headings: at home, on the street, in a car, waiting for or travelling on public transit, hitch-hiking, public places, purse snatching, babysitting, and what to do if attacked.

Some of the suggestions listed under these categories are (1990; pp. 2–5):

Never remain alone in an apartment laundry room, mailroom, or parking garage.

Do not put your first name on your mailbox or in the telephone book.

Use two initials and your last name.

Plan your route and avoid short cuts through parks, vacant lots, or unlit areas.

Do not overburden yourself with packages and a bulky purse.

Always lock your car when entering and leaving it.

Do not stop to offer help to a stranded motorist. Stop at the next phone booth and call for assistance.

Try to avoid isolated bus stops.

Sit near other women or near the driver.

Do not hitch-hike.

Use caution in conversations with strangers.

Do not carry large sums of money in your purse.

If you babysit, be escorted home after dark.

If attacked, scream and run to the nearest residence or business.

Of course, precautions such as the above may lessen the risk of being physically and sexually assaulted by the stereotypical, unprovoked stranger. Even so, they do little to deter some of the most 'fear inducing' (Schwartz and DeKeseredy, 1991) male behaviours, such as domestic violence and sexual harassment in both public and private contexts. In fact, the Solicitor General's advice to women has the potential to do more harm than good because it is riddled with limitations.

The limitations of *Woman Alone*

As was stated previously, the most obvious problem with *Woman Alone* is that it ignores the fact that Canadian women are much more likely to be abused by known men rather than strangers. Regardless of the reasons for the Solicitor General's mystification of woman abuse, the outcome is clear. Public attention is diverted away from much of what threatens women's physical and psychological well-being. While there is a growth in public concern about wife abuse and other types of violence against women in intimate relationships, many women will continue to 'suffer in silence' (Pizzey, 1974) because the public will remain more sensitive to public rather than private dangers. The Solicitor General's precautionary strategies also create an exaggerated fear of male strangers and public places which in turn makes women more dependent on their male partners. Ironically, these are the individuals who are most likely to harm them (Hanmer and Saunders, 1984; Smith, 1988).

If physical and sexual violence 'behind closed doors' (Straus *et al.*, 1981) is commonplace, then the same can be said about another frequent 'intimate intrusion' (Stanko, 1985) not addressed in *Woman Alone*—obscene phone calls. The telephone, a necessary instrument of communication for most Canadians,[2] is also a frightening 'tool of sexual intimidation' for many women (Stanko, 1990a). In England and Wales, for example, the British Crime Survey found that approximately 10 percent of females who had access to private phones received obscene phone calls, and some respondents were victimized many times (Pease, 1985). Generally referred to by the police and phone companies as 'nuisance calls' (Stanko, 1990a),[3] these events are not trivial because they induce a fearful state in many victims (DeKeseredy and Schwartz, 1991).

There is a dearth of research on obscene phone calls, and the data which have been captured is 'tantalizingly sketchy' (Pease, 1985). Nevertheless, exploratory British data demonstrate no relationship between receiving offensive phone calls and actually being a victim of physical or sexual assault. This finding may be valid; however, many people do not know how an offensive phone call will end. It is only in retrospect that a caller's intrusion can be designated as insignificant (Kelly and Radford, 1987). At the time of a terrifying call, many women worry that the perpetrator is someone they know and that he will act upon his abusive threats (DeKeseredy and Hinch, 1991; Stanko, 1990a). This is a 'well-founded fear' (Hanmer and Saunders, 1984) because some rapists follow up their attacks with phone calls (Stanko, 1990a).

Also absent from the Solicitor General's advice are methods of dealing with 'non-criminal street violence' (Jones *et al.*, 1986). These are male attacks or acts of sexual harassment in public settings which are not usually defined as violations of the law, such as leers, suggestive comments, being followed for blocks down the street, being yelled at by men in cars, unwanted sexual advances in restaurants and bars, and other types of harassment which cause a large number of women to worry about their safety (DeKeseredy and Hinch, 1991; DeKeseredy and MacLean, 1991; DeKeseredy and Schwartz, 1991; Radford, 1987; Stanko, 1990a) For reasons discussed earlier, concern about these 'little rapes' (Stanko, 1990a) is well-founded. Again, it is only in retrospect that these events are deemed trivial.

Acts of sexual harassment are not only committed by strangers in public settings. *Woman Alone* clearly fails to deal with the painful experiences of women who are sexually harassed by male co-workers, students, peers, and men in powerful positions, such as employers, doctors, lawyers, teachers, psychiatrists, and police officers (DeKeseredy and Hinch, 1991; Gorrie, 1990; Grahame, 1985; Russell, 1984; Stanko, 1990a). Following definitions provided by Fonow (1986) and DeKeseredy and Hinch (1991), sexual harassment by these men is referred to here as unsolicited, unreciprocated behaviour which values a woman's sexuality over her function as a worker, student, client, or platonic friend. Some common examples of this type of victimization are: persistent propositions for dates, employment or promotion contingent upon the provision of sexual favours, unwanted touching, a transfer to a difficult job because sexual favours were not provided, dirty jokes, and repeated references to a woman's sexuality.

Much more attention should be devoted to the victims of sexual harassment because the material, physical and psychological consequences of this key variant of 'everyday violence' (Stanko, 1990a) are staggering. For example, many victims suffer from sleeplessness, nausea, headaches, stomach aches, fatigue, eating disorders, and irritability. Some women quit their jobs, drop courses, and change schools in order to avoid further abuse. Others may blame themselves for their victimization or are so traumatized by their experiences that they attempt suicide (Grahame, 1985; DeKeseredy and Hinch, 1991; Stanko, 1990a). By ignoring these issues, the Solicitor General's office contributes to the maintenance of a '...climate in which women's bodies are routinely objectified and women are continually threatened with sexual assault...' (Houston, 1988).

Woman Alone also implicitly blames women for their victimization by placing on them the burden of trying to prevent various attacks by men. The pamphlet indicates that people facilitate crimes by not using 'target hardening' strategies. No attention is given to the structural, social psychological, and psychological factors that motivate men to abuse women. Consequently, if a person is victimized by a male stranger in a context deemed dangerous by the Solicitor General, she may hold herself responsible for the assault because she did not take what the state regards as appropriate precautions (Walklate, 1989).

An additional negative outcome of victim blaming discourse is that it influences people to curtail their individual freedom. For example, in order to avoid male abuse, people alter their lifestyles and daily routines by staying indoors, change their style of dress, or revise their route to and from work. These strategies, unfortunately, only increase rather than reduce fear of crime (Walklate, 1989).

If people see themselves as mainly responsible for protecting their own well-being, they can be exploited by those seeking to profit from their exaggerated fear of predatory 'street crimes.' In both the U.S. and Canada, there is a growing private security industry which tries to convince people to buy such devices as window locks, infra-red burglar alarms and other products ostensibly designed to make them feel less vulnerable to criminal acts committed by strangers. Commodities such as these are only useful in specific contexts and do not protect women from wife abuse and many other crimes committed by known men (Stanko, 1990a; Walklate, 1989).

In sum, the booklet *Woman Along* is riddled with limitations. It does not contribute to the safety of women in domestic contexts, and it fails to address a wide range of harmful behaviours which occur on the street, in schools, and in the workplace. Indeed, the criticisms presented here suggest that the pamphlet has the potential to do more harm than good. It is to three explanations for its publication that we now turn.

THEORIZING THE SOLICITOR GENERAL'S MYSTIFICATION OF WOMAN ABUSE

The first possible explanation why the Solicitor General's crime prevention advisors avoided the issues of domestic dangers and sexual harassment is that their policy suggestions were mainly informed by their own limited research, such as the Canadian Urban Victimization Survey (CUVS). Since the history of this study and its methodology are well documented elsewhere (DeKeseredy and MacLean, 1991; Solicitor General of Canada, 1983, 1985), only a brief summary of the CUVS research techniques and relevant data will be provided.

With the aid of Statistics Canada, the Ministry of the Solicitor General of Canada administered the CUVS in 1982. A representative sample of approximately 61,000 household residents, 16 years of age or older, were interviewed by telephone in Greater Vancouver, Edmonton, Winnipeg, Toronto, Montreal, Halifax-Dartmouth, and St. John's. The principal objectives of this survey were to gather data on the amount and distribution of reported and unreported crimes which occurred between January 1 and December 31, 1981, the impact of victimization, public perceptions of both crime and the criminal justice system, and public knowledge of, and involvement in crime compensation and crime prevention programs (Solicitor General of Canada, 1983).

The CUVS was not specifically designed to measure the various forms of sexual harassment discussed in the previous section. The operational definition of sexual assault was in fact limited to rape, attempted rape, molesting, and attempted molesting (Solicitor General of Canada, 1985). Capturing comprehensive data on wife abuse was also not a priority. The incidence rate (0.2%),[4] compared to findings reported by Canadian researchers such as Brinkerhoff and Lupri (1988), Kennedy and Dutton (1989), and Smith (1985, 1987), greatly underestimates the amount of husband-to-wife violence.

Because the CUVS data reveal that wife assault and other types of intimate violence are not statistically significant problems, the Solicitor

General's office may have decided to prioritize precautionary measures aimed at curbing only certain attacks by strange men because CUVS findings reveal that many more women experience this problem—35 out of every 1,000. Thus, *Woman Alone* may be purely a product of research rather than a lack of concern for women who endure domestic violence, obscene phone calls, and sexual harassment.

Some radical feminist scholars (e.g. Dobash and Dobash, 1979; MacKinnon, 1982; Stanko, 1985), however, are likely to contend that an alternative explanation best accounts for the Solicitor General's apparent lack of concern about these issues. Radical feminists contend that 'the most important relations in any society are found in patriarchy (masculine control of the labour power and sexuality of women); all other relations (such as class) are secondary and derive from male–female relations' (Beirne and Messerschmidt, 1991; p. 519). While there are a variety of feminist analyses of female victimization and its control (see Daly and Chesney-Lind, 1988), radical feminist research is the most common (Simpson, 1989).

For radical feminists, patriarchal forces rather than empirical factors mainly inform the advice found in *Woman Alone*. Instead of acting as a 'value-free' state institution,[6] the Ministry of the Solicitor General functions on behalf of men to maintain female subordination in intimate heterosexual relationships, the workplace, and in Canadian society as a whole.[7] One way in which it achieves this goal is the publication of ideological messages. By providing crime prevention advice which avoids much of what threatens women's well-being, the pamphlet ideologically supports oppressive gender and class relations: it diverts attention away from the many ways that men abuse women in a wide range of contexts (Edwards, 1989; Messerschmidt, 1986).[8]

Although *Woman Alone* ignores female victimization in intimate relationships and the multifaceted nature of sexual harassment, pamphlets published by other Canadian state agencies, such as the Ministry of Health and Welfare's Family Violence Prevention Division, clearly address these issues. Additionally, this institution and Statistics Canada, with the assistance of several Canadian sociologists, are in the process of conducting a series of representative sample surveys on woman abuse in familial and dating relationships. Perhaps, then, *Woman Alone* is a product of poor communication between government agencies rather than a male conspiracy.

Currie (1985; p. 18) shows that state policy makers tend to 'compartmentalize social problems along bureaucratic lines.' In depth information exchange sessions between state agencies rarely take place. Moreover, as Ellis (1987) points out, some government institutions do not share ideas about the development of strategies aimed at curbing social problems, such as woman abuse, because they are always competing with each other. Consequently, maybe *Woman Alone* is partly a product of intra-state rivalry.

Which one of the above three theories best accounts for the Solicitor General's problematic advice? So far, there is no conclusive evidence to support any of them, and perhaps accurate empirical data on the authors' motivations can never be obtained. Regardless of what influenced state bureaucrats to publish *Woman Alone,* the outcome is clear. Like similar pamphlets produced by Britain's Home Office,[9], the Solicitor General's booklet distorts the reality of male crimes against Canadian women.

SUMMARY AND CONCLUSIONS

This paper articulated the major limitations of the Solicitor General of Canada's recent crime prevention advice to women. While a critical response to this booklet is essential for a better understanding of the 'multidimensional nature of woman abuse in Canada' (DeKeseredy and Hinch, 1991), an alternative crime prevention discourse must be advanced in order effectively to eliminate criminal and non-criminal dangers from both strangers and known men in every social context. Maybe this goal can be achieved if the various branches of both provincial and federal governments work together on media and educational campaigns against various types of woman abuse.

It appears that the federal government is taking some steps to facilitate a coordinated crime prevention strategy. For example, in the summer of 1989, the Standing Committee on Health and Welfare, Social Affairs, Seniors and on the Status of Women created a Sub-Committee on the Status of Women. The Sub-Committee was required to study, over a five-month period, the definitions, incidence, sources, and impact of violence against women. It was also required to examine the ways in which the criminal justice system, community groups, and the government respond to violent female victimization.

The Sub-Committee submitted a report to the Standing Committee which included several important recommendations. Below are three which are relevant to the issues addressed in this paper (1991; p. ii):

1. A national, multi-media education campaign on violence against women which denounces female victimization and emphasizes societal responsibility for its prevention.

2. Discussions between the federal, provincial, and territorial governments to ensure that various communities have adequate resources to meet the demand for services that will result from the multi-media campaign on violence against women.

3. The federal government should work with the provinces, the territories and relevant professions to promote strong and consistent violence-prevention education in schools across the country.

Are these proposals useful? Will they help lower rates of woman abuse? Will they challenge the silence around the abuse of women? These are practical questions which can only be answered practically. The only way of determining the effectiveness of the above recommendations is if they are implemented. As Currie *et al.* (1990; p. 50) point out, 'critical discourse divorced from critical practice degenerates into mere literary criticism, the value of which is a *purely scholastic question.*'

NOTES

1   See Beirne and Messerschmidt (1991), Smith (1987), and Stanko (1990a) for comprehensive reviews of the relevant U.S. and British literature.

2   More than 99 percent of Toronto households, for example, have at least one phone (Smith, 1990; Statistics Canada, 1986).

3   The police do not take victims seriously because the callers' behaviours are considered 'minor' (DeKeseredy and Schwartz, 1991). Furthermore, some criminal justice officials refer to them as the normal actions of virile men (Radford, 1987).

4   For information on other factors which contributed to the low CUVS rate, see DeKeseredy and Hinch (1991), DeKeseredy and MacLean (1991), and Smith (1987).

5   While defining patriarchy is the subject of much debate among feminist scholars, following Eisenstein (1980; p. 16), it is referred to here as '…a sexual system of power in which the male possesses superior power and economic privilege.'

6   For the purpose of this paper, we employ Miliband's (1969; p. 50) definition of the state. The following institutions constitute the state: the government, the bureaucracy, the military, the judiciary, the subcentral government, and parliamentary assemblies.

7. For a comprehensive critique of similar 'functionalist' theories of the state, see Knutilla (1987).

8   For a Marxist analysis of the implicit ideology of criminal justice, see Reiman (1990).

9   See Stanko (1990a, 1990b) for a detailed critique of Home Office's advice to women.

REFERENCES

Beirne, P. and Messerschmidt, J. (1991). *Criminology.* Harcourt Brace Jovanovich; Toronto.

Brinkerhoff, M. and Lupri, E. (1988). Interspousal violence. *The Canadian Journal of Sociology* 13, 407–434.

Currie, D., DeKeseredy, W.S. and MacLean, B.D. (1990). Reconstituting Social Order and Social Control: Police Accountability in Canada. *The Journal of Human Justice* 2, 29–54.

Currie, E. (1985). *Confronting Crime: An American Challenge.* Pantheon; New York.

Daly, K. and Meda Chesney-Lind, M. (1988). Feminism and criminology. *Justice Quarterly* 6, 5–26.

DeKeseredy, W.S. (1988). *Woman Abuse in Dating Relationships: The Role of Male Peer Support.* Canadian Scholars' Press; Toronto.

DeKeseredy, W.S. and Hinch, R. (1991). *Woman Abuse: Sociological Perspectives.* Thompson Educational Publishing; Toronto.

DeKeseredy, W.S. and MacLean, B. (1991). Exploring the gender, race and class dimensions of victimization: A left realist critique of the Canadian Urban Victimization Survey. *International Journal of Offender Therapy and Comparative Criminology* 35, 143–161.

DeKeseredy, W.S. and Schwartz, M.D. (1991). British left realism on the abuse of women: A critical appraisal. In *Criminology as Peacemaking.* (R. Quinney and H. Pepinsky eds.) pp. 154–171. Indiana University Press; Bloomington.

Dexter, L.A. (1958). A note on the selective inattention in social science. *Social Problems* 6, 176–182.

Dobash, R.E. and Dobash, R. (1979). *Violence Against Wives: A Case Against the Patriarchy.* Free Press; N.Y.

Ellis, D. (1987). *The Wrong Stuff: An Introduction to the Sociological Study of Deviance.* Collier Macmillan; Toronto.

Edwards, S (1989). *Policing 'Domestic' Violence: Women, Law and the State.* Sage; London.

Fonow, M.M. (1986). Occupation/steelworker: Sex/female. In *Feminist Frontiers: Rethinking Sex, Gender, and Society.* (L. Richardson and V. Taylor eds.) pp. 209–214. Addison Wesley; Reading, MA.

Gorrie, P. (1990). 'Victim of harassment told she shares blame.' *Toronto Star.* January 23: D1.

Grahame, K.M. (1985). Sexual harassment. In *No Safe Place.* (M. Wolfe and C. Guberman eds.) pp. 109–126. Women's Press; Toronto.

Hanmer, J., Jill Radford and Elizabeth A. Stanko (eds.) (1989). *Women, Policing, and Male Violence: International Perspectives.* Routledge; London.

Hanmer, J. and Saunders, S. (1984). *Well-Founded Fear: A Community Study of Violence to Women.* Hutchinson; London.

Houston, B. (1988). What's wrong with sexual harassment. *Atlantis* 13, 44–7.

Jones, T., MacLean, B.D. and Young, J. (1986). *The Islington Crime Survey.* Gower; Aldershot, England.

Kelly, L. and Radford, J.R. (1987). The problem of men: Feminist perspectives on sexual violence. In *Law, Order and the Authoritarian State: Readings in Critical Criminology.* (P. Scraton ed.) pp. 237–253. Open University Press; Philadelphia.

Kennedy, L. and Dutton, D. (1989). The incidence of wife assault in Alberta. *Canadian Journal of Behavioural Science* 21, 40–54.

Knuttila, M. (1987). *State Theories: From Liberalism to the Challenge of Feminism.* Garamond; Toronto.

Lupri, E. (1990). Male violence in the home. In *Canadian Social Trends* (C. McKie and K. Thompson eds.) pp. 170–172. Thompson Educational Publishing; Toronto.

MacKinnon, C.A. (1982). Feminism, Marxism, method and the State: towards feminist jurisprudence. *Signs: Journal of Women in Culture and Society.* 7, 515–544.

Messerschmidt, J. (1986). *Capitalism, Patriarchy, and Crime: Toward a Socialist Feminist Criminology.* Roman and Littlefield; Totowa, NJ.

Miliband, R. (1969). *The State in Capitalist Society.* Quartet Books; London.

Pease, K. (1985). Obscene telephone calls to women in England and Wales. *The Howard Journal of Criminal Justice.* 24, 275–281.

Pizzey, E. (1974). *Scream Quietly or the Neighbors Will Hear.* Penguin; New York.

Radford, J. (1987). Policing male violence—policing women. In *Women, Violence and Social Control.* (J. Hanmer and M. Maynard eds.) pp. 30–45. Humanities International Press; Atlantic Highlands, NJ.

Reiman, J. (1990). *The Rich Get Richer and the Poor Get Prison.* Macmillan; New York.

Russell, D. (1984). *Sexual Exploitation: Rape, Child Sexual Abuse, and Workplace Harassment.* Sage; Beverly Hills.

Sacco, V.F. and Johnson, H. (1990). *Patterns of Criminal Victimisation in Canada.* Statistics Canada; Ottawa.

Schwartz, M.D. and DeKeseredy, W.S. (1991). Left realist criminology: strengths, weaknesses and the feminist critique. *Crime, Law and Social Change* 15, 51–72.

Simpson, S. (1989). Feminist theory, crime and justice. *Criminology* 27, 605–632.

Smith, M.D. (1985). *Women Abuse: The Case for Surveys by Telephone.* The LaMarsh Research Programme on Violence and Conflict Resolution Report Number 12. York University; North York, Ontario.

Smith, M.D. (1987). The incidence and prevalence of woman abuse in Toronto. *Violence and Victims,* 2, 173–187.

Smith, M.D. (1988). Women's fear of violent crime: An exploratory test of a feminist hypothesis. *Journal of Family Violence,* 31, 29–38.

Smith, M.D. (1990). Sociodemographic risk factors in wife abuse: Results from a survey of Toronto women. *The Canadian Journal of Sociology* 15, 39–58.

Solicitor General of Canada. (1983). *Canadian Urban Victimization Survey: Victims of Crime.* Ministry of the Solicitor General; Ottawa.

Solicitor General of Canada. (1985). *Canadian Urban Victimization Survey: Female Victims of Crime.* Ministry of the Solicitor General; Ottawa.

Solicitor General of Canada. (1990). *Woman Alone.* Ministry of the Solicitor General; Ottawa.

Standing Committee on Health and Welfare, Social Affairs, Seniors and the Status of Women. (1991). *The War Against Women.* House of Commons Canada; Ottawa.

Stanko, E.A. (1985). *Intimate Intrusions: Women's Experience of Male Violence.* Routledge and Kegan Paul; London.

Stanko, E.A. (1988). Fear of crime and the myth of the safe home: A feminist critique of criminology. In *Feminist Perspectives on Wife Abuse.* (K. Yllo and M. Bograd eds.), pp. 75–88. Sage; Beverly Hills.

Stanko, E.A. (1990a). *Everyday Violence: How Women and Men Experience Sexual and Physical Danger.* Pandora; London.

Stanko, E.A. (1990b). The case of fearful women: Gender, personal safety and fear of crime. Paper presented at the annual meeting of the American Society of Criminology, Baltimore; Maryland.

Statistics Canada. (1986). *Household Facilities and Equipment Survey, Household Surveys Division*. Unpublished manuscript. Statistics Canada; Ottawa.

Straus, M.A. (1989). Gender differences in assault in intimate relationships: Implications for the primary prevention of spousal violence. Paper presented at the annual meeting of the American Society of Criminology, Reno; Nevada.

Straus, M.A., Gelles, R. and Steinmetz, S. (1981). *Behind Closed Doors: Violence in the American Family*. Anchor Books; New York.

Walklate, S. (1989). *Victimology: The Victim and the Criminal Justice Process*. Unwin Hyman: London.

35

The Prejudice Against Men

Peter Marin

For the past several years advocates for the homeless have sought public support and sympathy by drawing attention to the large number of homeless families on our streets. That is an understandable tactic. Americans usually respond to social issues on the basis of sympathy for "innocent" victims— those whose blamelessness touches our hearts and whom we deem unable to care for themselves. Families, and especially children, obviously fill the bill.

But the fact remains, despite the claims of advocates, that the problem of chronic homelessness is essentially a problem of *single adult men*. Far more single adults than families, and far more men than women, end up homeless on our streets. Until we understand how and why that happens, nothing we do about homelessness will have much of an impact.

Most figures pertaining to the homeless come from limited studies or educated guesses that tend, when examined, to dissolve in one's hand. The most convincing figures I know can be found in James Wright's book *Address Unknown: The Homeless in America*. According to Wright's data, out of every 1,000 homeless people in America, 120 or so will be adults with children, another hundred will be children and the rest will be single adults. Out of that total, 156 will be single women and 580 will be single men. Now break that down into percentages. Out of all single homeless adults, 78 percent are men; out of all homeless adults, more than 64 percent are single men; and out of all homeless people—adults or children—58 percent are single men.

But even those figures do not give the full story. Our federal welfare system has been designed, primarily, to aid women with children or whole families. That means that most of the families and children on the streets have either fallen through the cracks of the welfare system or have not yet entered it. They will, in the end, have access to enough aid to get them off the streets and into some form of shelter, while most men will be left permanently on their own.

I do not mean to diminish here the suffering of families or children, nor to suggest that welfare provides much more than the meanest alternative to homelessness. It is a form of indentured pauperism so grim it shames the nation. But it does in fact eventually get most families off the streets, and that

From Peter Marin, "The Prejudice Against Men," *The Nation* (8 July 1991). Courtesy of the Alicia Patterson Foundation.

leaves behind, as the chronically homeless, single adults, of whom four-fifths are men. Seen that way, homelessness emerges as a problem involving what happens to men without money, or men in trouble.

Why do so many more men than women end up on the streets? Let me begin with the simplest answers.

First, life on the streets, as dangerous as it is for men, is even more dangerous for women, who are far more vulnerable. While many men in trouble drift almost naturally onto the streets, women do almost anything to avoid it.

Second, there are far better private and public shelters and services available to women.

Third, women are accustomed to asking for help while men are not; women therefore make better use of available resources.

Fourth, poor families *in extremis* seem to practice a form of informal triage. Young men are released into the streets more readily, while young women are kept at home even in the worst circumstances.

Fifth, there are cultural and perhaps even genetic factors at work. There is some evidence that men—especially in adolescence—are more aggressive and openly rebellious than women and therefore harder to socialize. Or it may simply be that men are allowed to live out the impulses women are taught to suppress, and that they therefore end up more often in marginal roles.

More important, still, may be the question of work. Historically, the kinds of work associated with transient or marginal life have been reserved for men. They brought in crops, worked on ships and docks, built roads and railroads, logged and mined. Such labor granted them a place in the economy while allowing them to remain on society's edges—an option rarely available to women save through prostitution.

And society has always seemed, by design, to produce the men who did such work. Obviously, poverty and joblessness forced men into marginality. But there was more to it than that. Schools produced failures, dropouts and rebels; family life and its cruelties produced runaways and throwaways; wars rendered men incapable of settled or domestic life; small-town boredom and provinciality led them to look elsewhere for larger worlds.

Now, of course, the work such men did is gone. But like a mad engine that cannot be shut down, society goes right on producing them. Its institutions function as they always did: The schools hum, the families implode or collapse, the wars churn out their victims. But what is there for them to do? The low-paying service-sector jobs that have replaced manual labor in the economy go mainly to women or high school kids, not the men who once did the nation's roughest work.

Remember, too, in terms of work, that women, especially when young, have one final option denied to men. They can take on the "labor" of being wives and companions to men or of bearing children, and in return they will often be supported or "taken care of" by someone else. Yes, I know: Such roles can often constitute a form of oppression, especially when assumed out of necessity. But nonetheless, the possibility is there. It is permissible (as well as often necessary) for women to become financially, if precariously, dependent on others, while such dependence is more or less forbidden to men.

Finally, there is the federal welfare system. I do not think most Americans understand how the system works, or how for decades it has actually sent men into the streets, creating at least some male homelessness while aiding women and children. Let me explain. There are two main programs that provide care for Americans in trouble. One is Social Security Disability Insurance. It goes to men or women who are unable, because of physical or mental problems, to work or take care of themselves. The other is Aid to Families with Dependent Children (A.F.D.C.). It is what we ordinarily call "welfare." With its roots early in this century, it was established more or less in its present form during the Depression. Refined and expanded again in the 1960s, A.F.D.C. had always been a program meant mainly for women and children and limited to households headed by women. As long as an adult man remained in the household as mate, companion or father, *no aid was forthcoming.* Changes have recently been made in the system, and men may remain in the household if they have a work history satisfying certain federal guidelines. But in poor areas and for certain ethnic groups, where unemployment runs high and few men have a qualifying work history, these changes have not yet had much of an impact and men remain functionally outside the welfare system.

When it comes to single and "able-bodied," or employable, adults, there is no federal aid whatsoever. Individual states and localities sometimes provide their own aid through "general assistance" and "relief." But this is usually granted only on a temporary basis or in emergencies. And in those few places where it is available for longer periods to large numbers of single adults—California, for instance, or New York—it is often so grudging, so ringed round with capricious requirements and red tape, that it is of little use to those in need.

This combination of approaches not only systematically denies men aid as family members or single adults. It means that the aid given to women has sometimes actually deprived men of homes, even as it has provided for women and children. Given the choice between receiving aid for themselves and their children and living with men, what do you think most women do? The regulations as they stand actually force men to compete with the state for women; as a woman in New Orleans once told me: "Welfare changes even love. If a man can't make more at a job than I get from welfare, I ain't even gonna look at him. I can't afford it."

Everywhere in America poor men have been forced to become ghost-lovers and ghost-fathers, one step ahead of welfare workers ready to disqualify families for having a man around. In many ghettos throughout the country you find women and children in their deteriorating welfare apartments, and their male companions and fathers in even worse conditions:

homeless in gutted apartments and abandoned cars, denied even the minimal help granted the opposite sex.

Is it surprising, in this context, that many African-Americans see welfare as an extension of slavery that destroys families, isolates women and humiliates men according to white bureaucratic whim? Or is it accidental that in poor communities family structure has collapsed and more and more children are born outside marriage at precisely the same time that disfranchised men are flooding the streets? Welfare is not the only influence at work in all of this, of course. But before judging men and their failures and difficulties, one must understand that their social roles are in no way supported or made easier by the social policies that in small ways make female roles sustainable.

Is this merely an accidental glitch in the system, something that has happened unnoticed? Or does it merely have something to do with a sort of lifeboat ethic, where our scarce resources for helping people are applied according to the ethics of a sinking ship—women and children first, men into the sea?

I do not think so. Something else is at work: deep-seated prejudices and attitudes toward men that are so pervasive, so pandemic, that we have ceased to notice or examine them.

To put it simply: Men are neither supposed nor allowed to be dependent. They are expected to take care of both others *and* themselves. And when they cannot do it, or "will not" do it, the built-in assumption at the heart of the culture is that they are *less than men* and therefore unworthy of help. An irony asserts itself: Simply by being in need of help, men forfeit the right to it.

Think here of how we say "helpless as a woman." This demeans women. But it also does violence to men. It implies that a man cannot be helpless and still be a man, or that helplessness is not a male attribute, or that a woman can be helpless through no fault of her own, but that if a man is helpless it is or must be his own fault.

Try something here. Imagine walking down a street and passing a group of homeless women. Do we not spontaneously see them as victims and wonder what has befallen them, how destiny has injured them? Do we not see them as unfortunate and deserving of help and *want* to help them?

Now imagine a group of homeless men. Is our reaction the same? Is it as sympathetic? Or is it subtly different? Do we have the very same impulse to help and protect? Or do we not wonder, instead of what befell them, how they have got themselves where they are?

And remember, too, our fear. When most of us see homeless or idle men we sense or imagine danger; they make us afraid, as if, being beyond the pale, they are also beyond all social control—and therefore people to be avoided and suppressed rather than helped.

Here too work plays a crucial role. In his memoirs Hamlin Garland describes the transient farm workers who passed through the countryside each year at harvest time. In good years, when there were crops to bring in, they were tolerated: fed, housed and hired. But when the crops were bad and men weren't needed, then they were forced to stay outside of town or pass on unaided, having become merely threats to peace and order, barbarians at the gates.

The same attitude is with us still. When men work (or when they go to war—work's most brutal form), we grant them a right to exist. But when work is scarce, or when men are of little economic use, then they become in our eyes not only superfluous but a danger. We feel compelled to exile them from our midst, banish them from view, drive them away to shift for themselves in more or less the same way that our Puritan forebears, in their shining city on its hill, treated sinners and rebels.

One wonders just how far back such attitudes go. One thinks of the Bible and the myth of the Garden and the first disobedience, when women were cursed with childbirth and men with the sorrows of labor—destinies still, as if by intention, maintained by our welfare system and private attitudes.

And one thinks too of the Victorian era, when the idealized vision of women and children had its modern beginnings. They were set outside the industrial nexus and freed from heavy labor while being rendered more than ever dependent on and subservient to men. It was a process that obviously diminished women, but it had a parallel effect on men. It defined them as laborers and little else, especially if they came from the lower classes. The yoke of labor lifted from the shoulders of women settled even more heavily on the backs of certain men, confining them in roles as narrow and as oppressive as those to which women were assigned.

We are so used to thinking of ours as a male-dominated society that we tend to lose track of the ways in which some men are as oppressed, or perhaps even more oppressed, than most women. But race and class, as well as gender, play roles in oppression. And while it is true, in general, that men dominate society and women, in practice it is only *certain* men who are dominant; others, usually those from the working class and often darker skinned (at least 50 percent of homeless men are black or Latino), suffer endlessly from forms of isolation and contempt that often exceed what many women experience.

The irony at work in all of this is that what you often find among homeless men, and what seems at the heart of their troubles, is precisely what our cultural myths deny them: a helplessness they cannot overcome on their own. You find vulnerability, a sense of injury and betrayal and, in their isolation, a despair equal to what we accept without question in women.

Often this goes unadmitted. Even when in deep trouble men understand, sometimes unconsciously, that they are not to complain or ask for help. I remember several men I knew in the local hobo jungle. Most of them were vets. They had constructed a tiny village of half-caves and shelters among the trees and brush, and when stove smoke filled the clearing and they stood bare to the waist, knives at their hips, you would swear you were in an army jungle camp. They drank throughout the day, and at dusk there always came a moment when they wandered off individually to sit staring out at the mountains or sea. And you could see on their faces at such moments, if you caught them unawares, a particular and unforgettable look: pensive, troubled, somehow innocent—the look of lost children or abandoned men.

I have seen the same look multiplied hundreds of times on winter nights in huge shelters in great cities, where a thousand men at a time will sometimes gather, each encapsulated in solitude on a bare cot, coughing and turning or sometimes crying all night, lost in nightmares as terrible as a child's or as life on the street. In the mornings they returned to their masked public personas, to the styles of behavior and appearance that often frightened passers-by. But while they slept you could see past all that, and you found yourself thinking: These are still, even grown, *somebody's* children, and many fare no better on their own, as adults, than they would have as children.

I remember, too, a young man in my town who was always in trouble for beating up older drunken men. No one understood his brutality until he explained it one day to a woman he trusted: "When I was a kid my daddy ran off and my mother's drunken brothers disciplined me. Whenever I made a mistake they punished me by slicing my legs with a straight razor." And he pulled up his pant-legs to reveal on each shin a ladder of scars marking each childhood error or flaw.

This can stand for countless stories I've heard. The feeling you get, over and over, is that most men on the street have been "orphaned" in some way, deprived somewhere along the line of the kinds of connection, support and sustenance that enable people to find and keep places in the social order. Of course economics plays a part in this—I do not mean to suggest it does not. But more often than not, something else is also at work, something that cuts close to the bone of social and psychological as well as economic issues: the dissolution of family structures and the vitiation of community; subtle and overt forms of discrimination and racism; and institutions—schools, for instance—that harm or marginalize almost as many people as they help.

For decades now, sociologists have called our attention to rents in our private social fabric as well as our public "safety nets," and to the victims they produce: abused kids, battered women, isolated adults, alcoholics, addicts. Why, I wonder, is it so hard to see homeless men in this context? Why is it so hard to understand that the machinery of our institutions can injure men as permanently as it does women? We know, for instance, that both male and female children are permanently injured by familial abuse and violence and "normal" cruelties of family life. Why, then, do we find it hard to see that grown men, as well as women, can be crippled by childhood, or that they often end up on the edges of society, unable to play expected roles in a world that has betrayed them?

And do not forget here the greatest violence done to men, the tyrannous demand made upon them when young by older and more powerful males: that they kill and die in war. We take that demand for granted in our society and for some reason fail to see it as a form of oppression. But why? Long before the war in Vietnam had crowded our streets with vets—as far back as the Civil War—the male victims of organized state violence wandered across America unable to find or make places in the social world. The fact is that many men never fully recover from the damage done by war, having seen too much of death to ever again do much with life.

Nor is war the only form in which death and disaster have altered the lives of troubled men. They appear repeatedly in the stories men tell. Listening to these tales one thinks of Oedipus and Lear, of tragedy in its classical sense, of the furies and fates that the Greeks believed stalk all human lives and that are still at work among us, no matter how much we deny them.

Gene, a homeless man I know, was conceived when his mother slept with his father's best friend. Neither of his parents wanted him, so he was raised reluctantly by his mother's parents, who saw him only as the living evidence of her disgrace. As an adult he married and divorced twice, had two children he rarely saw later in life, and spent two years in jail for beating nearly to death a friend he found in bed with his second wife. When I first met him he was living in a cave he had dug by hand out of a hillside, and he spent the money he earned on dope or his friends. But then he met a woman on the streets and they moved together to a cheap hotel. He got her pregnant; they planned to marry; but then they argued and she ran off and either had an abortion or spontaneously miscarried—it was never clear which. When Gene heard about it he took to his bed for days and would not sleep, eat or speak. When I later asked him why, he said: "I couldn't stand it. I wanted to die. I was the baby she killed. It was happening to me all over again, that bad stuff back when I was a kid."

Not everything you hear on the street is so dramatic. There are a thousand quiet and gradual ways American lives can fall apart or come to nothing. Often it is simply "normal" life that proves too much for some men. Some have merely failed at or fled their assigned roles: worker, husband, father. Others lacked whatever it takes to please a boss or a woman or else decided it wasn't worth the trouble to learn how to do it. Not all of them are "good" men. Some have brutalized women or left families in the lurch or fled lives in which the responsibility and stress were more than they could handle. "Couldn't hack it," they'll say with a shrug, or "I had to get out." And others have been so cruel to women or proved so unreliable or sometimes so unsuccessful that women fled them, leaving notes on the table or refrigerator such as the one a man in Seattle once repeated to me: "Gone. Took the kids. So long."

Are such men irresponsible? Perhaps. But in working with homeless men over the years, I've seen how many of them are genuinely unable to handle the stress others can tolerate. Many manage, for instance, to steer clear of alcohol or drugs for a certain period of time and then return to them automatically as soon as they are subject again to the kinds of stress they once fled. It is as if their defenses and even their skins are so much thinner than those of the rest of us that they give way as soon as trouble or too much responsibility appears.

The fact is that most such men seem to have tried to make a go of things, and many are willing to try again. But if others have given up and said, inside, *the hell with it* or...*it*, is that really astonishing? The curious world we've compounded in America of equal parts of freedom and isolation and individualism and demands for obedience and submission is a strange and wearing mix, and no one can be startled at the number of victims or recalcitrants it produces or at those who can't succeed at it.

Finally, I must add one more thing. Whatever particular griefs men may have experienced on their way to homelessness, there is one final and crippling sorrow all of them share: a sense of betrayal at society's refusal to recognize their needs. Most of us—men and women—grow up expecting that when things go terribly wrong someone, from somewhere, will step forward to help us. That this does not happen, and that all watch from the shore as each of us, in isolation, struggles to swim and then begins to sink, is perhaps the most terrible discovery that anyone in any society can make. When troubled men make that discovery, as all homeless men do sooner or later, then hope vanishes completely; despair rings them round; they have become what they need not have become: the homeless men we see everywhere around us.

What can be done about this? What will set it right? One can talk, of course, about confronting the root causes of marginalization: the failure of families, schools and communities; the stupidities of war, racism and discrimination; social and economic injustice; the disappearance of generosity and reciprocity among us. But what good will that do? America is what it is; culture has a tenacity of its own; and though it is easy to call for major kinds of renewal, nothing of the sort is likely to occur.

That leaves us with ameliorative and practical measures, and it will do no harm to mention them, though they too are not likely to be tried: a further reformation of the welfare system; the federalization of assistance to single adults; increases in the amount and duration of unemployment insurance; further raises in the minimum wage; expanded benefits for vets; detox centres and vocational education for those who want them; the construction of the kinds of low-cost hotels and boarding houses where men in trouble once stayed.

And remember that back in the Depression when the welfare system was established, it was paralleled by programs providing work for men: the Civilian Conservation Corps and the Works Progress Administration. The idea seems to have been welfare for women, work for men. We still have the welfare for women, but where is the work for those men, or women, who want it? Why no one is currently lobbying for contemporary forms of those old programs remains a mystery. Given the deterioration of the American infrastructure—roads, bridges, public buildings—such programs would make sense from any point of view.

But beyond all this, and behind and beneath it, there remains the problem with which we began: the prejudices at work in society that prevent even the attempt to provide solutions. Suggestions such as those I have made will remain merely utopian notions without an examination and renovation of our attitudes toward men. During the past several decades we have slowly, laboriously, begun to confront our prejudices and oppressive practices in relation to women. Unless we now undertake the same kind of project in relation to men in general and homeless men in particular, nothing whatever is going to change. That's as sure as death and taxes and the endless, hidden sorrows of men.

CHAPTER SEVEN

Where Do We Go From Here?

Attempts to outline a future are obviously fraught with difficulty as projections are frequently confounded with wishes and desires rather than realistic likelihoods. Instead of focusing on specific predictions or arguments, we present a number of articles each of which provides seeds for thought on what might influence future agendas. Joan Acker (Article 36) examines the world of paid work as we move towards the end of the present century. Given the impact of the economy on social life in general, this article deserves its position at the beginning of the chapter. Her suggestions are based on several trends that have developed over the past ten to fifteen years in both Canada and the United States. Acker demonstrates that economic change has different consequences for women and men, a fact that is rarely acknowledged and taken into account by policy makers in both countries.

Various aspects of changing, or unchanging, male gender roles must also be considered when considering our future. We present a classic article by William Goode (Article 37), which seeks to explicate the sources of male resistance to changes wrought by the feminist movement. To the extent to which these conditions still obtain within our society, we can anticipate that future changes will continue to meet resistance. Kenneth Clatterbaugh (Article 38) presents an overview of six strands of the "men's movement," each of which has different implications for the future. Although Clatterbaugh's categorizations have yet to receive unanimous support (the same applies to typologies describing different strands of feminism), we offer them as a heuristic device to promote understanding and discussion. While some of these "submovements" can be seen as regressive in nature, some as reform oriented, and some as radical, each contains a potentially different outcome for the future.

Salome Lucas and her colleagues (Article 39) address the necessity of expanding the focus of the feminist movement so that it will be more inclusive than it has been. Erin Steuter (Article 40) looks at the interaction between feminist and antifeminist social movements over the past hundred years in Canada. With each advance made by the feminist movement, anti-feminists have attempted either to dilute the impact of the change or to nullify the change and return to a prior state. We can anticipate that whatever changes are produced in the future by the feminist movement, antifeminists will attempt to counter them using the beliefs and tactics identified by Steuter.

Much has been made in the mass media of a "backlash" against the feminist movement spawned by countermovements and supported by many segments of mainstream society. Janice Newson (Article 41) contends that constant reference to a backlash creates a mindset that is ultimately counterproductive to the feminist movement. She offers a different perspective for viewing the current and future Canadian situation.

All of these articles, when taken together, point to the obvious: no clear path on which we will walk into the future of gender can be identified. To paraphrase an ancient proverb, it is clear that Canadians will continue to live in interesting times.

36

The Future of Women and Work: Ending the Twentieth Century

Joan Acker

INTRODUCTION

As the 20th century ends, the ongoing global transformation of the division of labor and the organization of production and paid work continues. What does this mean for women and their work? ... What does it mean for gender/race/class relations? Will new opportunities abound in the new participatory workplaces of the future? Will the gender wage gap decline as women and men become more equally distributed in jobs that no longer require physical strength? Or will the supply of "good" jobs continue to disappear, pushing many women and some men into routine work at very low wages and hastening the demise of the family wage for men? What will happen to ... minority women? Although these questions will be answered conclusively only in the future, at the moment, in the early 1990s, we can see how large-scale changes are affecting women's prospects. We can also speculate about what may happen if nothing interrupts the present trajectory, while recognizing that such trajectories are often interrupted. ...

GLOBAL CHANGES

Social and political commentators, generally accepting the notion that a global transformation is in process, analyze its character in a number of ways. They focus on new skills and the reorganization of work (e.g., Wood 1989); the emergence of another critical period of technological innovation comparable to the first industrial revolution (e.g., Marshall 1987); and the exploding acceleration of international competition (e.g., Porter 1990). Most experts see these trends as complexly interconnected. While opinions differ about what is changing and how much (Wood 1989), all contend that new things are happening. Among the claims on which some agreement exists are the following.

From Joan Acker, "The Future of Women and Work: Ending the Twentieth Century," *Sociological Perspectives*, vol. 35, no. 1 (1992): 53–68. Reprinted by permission.

Capital is becoming increasingly internationalized and production is increasingly oriented toward international markets within which competition is intense (Taylor 1991). In the interests of competition and efficiency, both private and public employers pursue lower labor costs and greater "flexibility" (Standing 1989). The search for lower labor costs leads to a shifting global division of labor that is, at the same time, a shifting gender division of labor (Nash 1983; Standing 1989). Technological innovations facilitate these shifts, while they also contribute to creating new products and new markets. Accompanying these changes are the increasing employment of women in the world wage economy, growth of the service sector, and increasing demand for certain kinds of highly skilled labor within a general pattern of deskilling. Political processes facilitate the reorganization of production, including deregulation of business and industry, erosion of labor regulations, decreasing power of organized labor, reductions in welfare state spending, and privatization of social programs and state-owned production. For workers, both women and men, these changes have mixed consequences; some benefit, while others see their present conditions and future prospects undermined.

The Negative View

Looking at these developments, one commentator (Standing 1989) has labelled them the "feminization of labor." Not only is the world's paid labor force increasingly composed of women, but the conditions of work are becoming "feminized" for men as well. Feminization means that a declining proportion of jobs are "good" male jobs that carry the guarantee of lifetime employment with adequate wages and pension guarantees. In highly industrialized countries, technological change results in the deskilling of labor and facilitates the movement of production to areas of cheap labor. Old careers for skilled workers disappear. The family wage sufficient for a single worker to support dependents is fast disappearing; women's paid work is becoming necessary for family survival. Analyzing the United States, Bluestone and Harrison (1988) call this process *"The Great U-Turn."*

Employers achieve the flexibility they need to remain competitive through part-time, contract, and temporary work. On a global level, more people are unemployed, surviving in the informal economy. Unemployment, which creates pools of workers eager for jobs at any wage, also increases the flexibility of employers. Protections against arbitrary dismissal and autocratic control are also disappearing. Organized labor in many countries has decreasing power to protect workers, either because of direct attacks on the right to organize or because changes in production are undermining its bases of power in the old blue-collar, male working class. Finally, the welfare state, the bulwark of protection for workers against the risks of the market (Esping-Andersen 1990), is everywhere under attack on the grounds that too much protection undermines the viability of market capitalism. Already-vulnerable groups, such as women and minorities, suffer the most. All these developments are occurring in the core capitalist countries as well as in the periphery. At the same time, the experience in every country is different, shaped by preexisting political, social, and cultural patterns of power.

The Positive View

Alongside dire predictions about deteriorating conditions for many workers are descriptions of how restructuring has made possible the retention and creation of good jobs for workers as well as for managers and professionals. Restructuring of employment, increased skills and work flexibility, and more worker participation in decision-making are positive consequences of new technology and increased competition. Improved work content and working conditions can result from new technology (Marshal 1987). As old, routine work processes are automated, and as information technology and service industries develop, jobs become more complex and more interesting. New methods of production lead to higher productivity. These changes should lead to higher standards of living, at least for those in the countries that win in global competition.

All of this requires workers with higher-level, more flexible skills. The key to increasing productivity, and to the prosperity that follows, lies in the education of workers and the reorganization of production to allow the most effective use of education (Marshall 1987). Looking to Japan for inspiration, new management thinking emphasizes the importance of teamwork and problem solving. This goes along with reduction of hierarchy and the placement of decision responsibility at lower levels and within work groups. Both Japan and Germany have used these strategies, which have contributed to their success in the process of global transformation.

The positive and negative views of contemporary changes in work and production are not necessarily mutually exclusive. Rising opportunities for professionals, managers, and skilled technicians can emerge side by side with a declining supply of good jobs for the majority of a population. A review of the evidence indicates that this has happened in the United States (Bluestone and Harrison 1988; Appelbaum and Albin 1990) and that these developments have differing impacts along lines of race, class, and gender (Higginbotham 1992).

IDEOLOGICAL UNDERPINNINGS

In Europe, Britain, and the United States, these developments are facilitated by the triumph of neoclassical economics and the blithe belief in "the free market," although it is clear that the most successful economies—Germany and Japan—do not follow many of the precepts of the free-market ideologists. The ideology of emergent capitalism firmly anchored women in the private sphere (Pateman 1988). They were not economic actors or regarded as individuals capable of making rational decisions. However, the concept of the gender-neutral individual, citizen, and worker masked that exclusion, and, later, allowed feminists to claim that women are individuals too, with rights to full participation in society.

Contemporary versions of classical liberal theory tacitly accept women's status as citizens and paid workers, but still retain assumptions that help to perpetuate women's subordinate position in the labor market (Acker 1992). Assuming a gender-neutral worker who has the characteristics of male workers, this ideology cannot incorporate systematic and persistent discrimination against women into its understanding of the economy. Nor can it incorporate the needs of families and the needs of social reproduction more generally into its thinking, except to argue that these should be met through market mechanisms. Thus, deregulation, attacks on labor unions, and other measures to lower wages are justified as beneficial for the market economy.

Opposition to government-supported day care, to mandatory maternity leave, and to other forms of family leave that support women's labor-market participation are consistent with this mode of thinking, as are attacks on existing welfare-state provisions. Similarly, proponents of neoclassical theory oppose comparable-worth arguments and are unwilling to entertain the idea that many women-predominant jobs have been systematically undervalued.

In the United States, the free-market ideology that marginalizes and obscures women's interests has recently been bolstered by the resurgent masculinity of force and violence of the Gulf War. The nineteenth-century entrepreneurial captain of industry resurrected during the Reagan years, shaky because he could not triumph over the Germans and the Japanese, can now join hands with the conquering technological warrior who can defeat everyone. Together they symbolize a twenty-first-century version of a much older hegemonic masculinity (Connell 1988). High-tech military means of domination are welded to a high-tech, aggressive, unregulated, competitive economic manipulation of the world. The other side of this masculinity is woman as the servant-subordinate and protector of caring values, women in the armed forces notwithstanding.

This ideology supports the global developments sketched above, and makes it more difficult to propose and advocate new policies to shape the emerging new world of work. The nineties may bring a weakening of the grip of this ideology as the excesses of the eighties result in economic decline and high unemployment. However, it is still powerful on a global scale and continues to support restructuring policies that undermine equality and encourage attacks on measures that promote gender equality.

CONSEQUENCES FOR WOMEN IN THE UNITED STATES

What does that new world look like for women here in the United States? Most women now have to work to survive, as the alternative of total support from a husband becomes more and more untenable. In 1990, approximately 56 percent of women over the age of 16 were in the paid labor force. Over the preceding 20 years, women's situations at work have improved in minor ways. Sex segregation at the national occupational level has declined somewhat, as has the gender wage gap. Women have broken into many fields formerly monopolized by men and have increased as a proportion of those in most professional and managerial jobs, although they tend to be confined to lower levels and feminine subspecialties. Yet, the majority of women are still in the large, low-wage "women's job" categories where benefits are relatively low and promotion unlikely. The question about the future is whether or not this will change: what kinds of jobs, under what conditions, and at what levels of pay will be available to women? I examine these questions in terms of four characteristics of the present transformations in work: the restructuring of employment, changing skill demands, increasing flexibility, and the reduction of hierarchy along with greater employee participation. ...

Restructuring of Employment

Employment restructuring occurred first in manufacturing production as certain processes in particular industries were moved to areas with cheap labor in the United States as well as in other countries, and as whole industries declined in the United States. The number of blue-collar jobs in female-predominant industries such as garment manufacture and in male-predominant industries such as steel was sharply reduced. This restructuring had a severe impact on women as well as men, and it particularly hit African American men in industrial cities (Wilson 1991), contributing to the emergence of severe ghetto poverty. During the 1980s, however, United States employment increased as service-sector jobs multiplied rapidly. Seventy-nine percent of the 27 million new jobs created between 1973 and 1987 were in services (Appelbaum and Albin 1990). This was the American "miracle": the creation of millions of new jobs even as the old bases of high employment in manufacturing were eroding.

The service sector consists of finance, real estate, insurance, transportation, public utilities, retail and wholesale trade, personal and business services, amusement, health, education, legal and social services, and government. The United States service sector has two tiers (Appelbaum and Albin 1990). According to Appelbaum and Albin, the knowledge-information tier has high technology, high productivity growth, high wages, and is capital-intensive. The other tier has low productivity growth, low technology, and low wages and is labor-intensive. Women are the majority of workers in both sectors and, in both tiers, their wages are lower than the wages of men in comparable jobs. This sector is also structured by race, with minorities disproportionately found in the lower tier. In addition to the service sector, there are service jobs within manufacturing.[1]

During the 1980s, the service sector appeared to be immune to the troubles affecting manufacturing, and, despite heavy investments in computer technology that often reorganized and accelerated work processes, employment did not decline (Roach 1991). Deregulation during the 1980s, leading to hostile competition, takeovers, buyouts, and questionable lending practices, produced crises in this sector. Now, in 1991, service industries, like those in manufacturing, are also restructuring their employment, with the aim of increasing efficiency and reducing their labor costs (Roach 1991). At the same time, reorganization of management in manufacturing is underway. These changes will significantly affect women because they constitute at least 62 percent of service-sector employment (Sweeney and Nussbaum 1989), and because they have made some gains at the entry and middle levels of management.

Restructuring is occurring in communications, banks and other financial services, airlines, entertainment, and retail sales, and in the managerial levels of other kinds of firms. ... Longer trends are evident in employment decline in clerical work between 1988 and 1990, in some instances continuing declines that had begun in the early 1980s. The number of bookkeepers, accounting and auditing clerks, telephone operators, bank tellers, general office clerks, secretaries, and typists all declined over these years.[2] Earlier, declines in these occupations were more than compensated for by increases in other administrative support and clerical areas, but this growth seems to have ended in 1991. ...

Although some of the restructuring of employment in the private service sector is fueled by economic recession, much of it probably represents permanent change in the organization of work and the labor process, made possible by dramatic changes in technology (Baran 1990). ...Volume increased and so did employment. Recently, new systems approaches using computerized master files and on-line data entry eliminated many steps in this process (Baran 1990). The elimination of functions creates the conditions for the reduction of the work force. In another example, a national retail chain reduced its customer service staff by almost two-thirds in the mid-1980s by installing an on-line computer system to access customer accounts. The time for processing a complaint declined from 10 minutes to 2 minutes.

The restructuring process is also underway in the public sector, which has long been the exemplary employer of women and minorities. The federal government undertook employment reductions during the 1980s, as the Reagan regime tried to decrease the size of the welfare state. This is now happening in state and local governments as well, including school districts, as budgetary problems become critical. Budget-slashing in public services may be a temporary phenomenon, but, in the near-term, it further reduces opportunities for women and minorities. Only the health sector seems to be immune: here employment continues to grow. However, the outlook could change rapidly if the demands for reform of the health care system are realized. ...

The consequences for women and minorities are obvious. Women hold the majority of service-sector jobs and most of their job growth has been in this area. Minority women found opportunities in the service sector that enabled some to move away from domestic and factory labor. Women's concentration in these jobs protected them against the consequences of restructuring in manufacturing and pointed to continuing rising employment opportunities. As recently as 1987, Kuhn and Bluestone could write "The greatest cause for optimism lies in the sheer number of jobs being created in occupations and industries that are currently majority female" (1987:21). ... Recent trends make such optimism highly suspect. In addition, as Kuhn and Bluestone (1987) point out, those service-sector jobs are disproportionately at the lower level of work hierarchies, exactly where many of the systems-analysis-generated cuts are coming. Those jobs in the second tier of the service sector that have to do with personal services are more difficult to automate and thus may remain plentiful, but these are the jobs with low pay and few or no benefits. Women of color are disproportionately caught in these dead-end jobs.

Restructuring of manufacturing meant that women's affirmative action path to better jobs through entering male-dominated blue-collar jobs became more and more unrealistic as these jobs disappeared through automation or transfer to other countries. Similarly, movement of women into male-dominated middle-level management and professional jobs may be less and less an option as these jobs also contract. As middle management is cut, there are fewer mobility paths out of the lowest level jobs. Promotion ladders are also truncated as higher-level jobs require more training; employers will look for trained personnel among new graduates rather than promote personnel from the lower levels of their organizations. Reductions in middle-level management will probably also lead to a decrease in entry-level management jobs.

Changes in Skill Demands

New technology is not always used to replace workers' skills and to deskill workers, as critics of Braverman's (1974) deskilling thesis have pointed out (see, for example, Beechey 1987). Often, it requires an upgrading of skills. Some experts believe that not enough skilled workers are being trained in the United States and predict a shortage of such workers in the near future (Marshall and Brock 1990). Forecasts of a shortage of skilled workers are linked to calls to American business to give up its deskilling, low-wage, short-term profit strategy and to embrace instead a longer-term, high-productivity growth strategy. If these prescriptions are followed, an increase in better jobs, at least for some, might be expected. But would these good jobs be available to women as well as to men?

The answer is equivocal. Skill has gendered meanings. As Cockburn (1985) has demonstrated, skill is tied to masculinity in ways that define women as unskilled. In Cockburn's studies, as computerization and other new technologies were introduced into a variety of work processes, men remained in control of the new machines and boundaries between male and female, skilled and unskilled, were redrawn (Cockburn 1985; see also Hacker 1990).

Women's jobs are often perceived by managers, male colleagues, and women workers themselves as requiring less skill than comparable men's jobs when assessed by job evaluation methods (Acker 1989). Thus, new technology may facilitate the upgrading of skill, but this is not necessarily recognized nor rewarded. For example, the development of computerized systems in office work sometimes results in new and more complex jobs that combine components of routine and skilled clerical work along with some previously professional tasks. Baran (1990) documents this for insurance firms in the United States.

I found similar changes in a study of bank jobs in Sweden (Acker and Ask 1989; Acker 1990). In Swedish banks in the late 1980s, old-style tellers were being transformed into multifunctional workers who not only processed deposits and withdrawals, but also took applications for and approved loans, exchanged foreign currency, and provided customers with advice on investments, insurance, and taxes. The variety of tasks, kinds of knowledge required, and levels of responsibility had been substantially increased for these employees, who were almost all women. The process was assisted by on-line, integrated computer systems that provided complete access to client files and other financial information. In effect, formerly professional and managerial functions were being pushed down the organizational hierarchy. At the higher levels of banking, routine functions were reduced as other skill demands increased to meet the increasing challenges of ever more competitive markets. Lower-level employees were more satisfied with their work, but they received no wage increases for their increased skill and added responsibilities. Instead, the wage gap between women and men employees increased during the period of skill increase. These women workers were still at the bottom of the organizational hierarchies and their pay remained there as well.

Of course, computerization has resulted in deskilling as well as in reskilling. In some cases, managers' jobs have been deskilled as lower-level workers take over reorganized managerial tasks and as computer monitoring of errors and numbers of key strokes or transactions replace human supervision. Lower-level jobs have also been deskilled or eliminated. New computer technology can be designed to assist increased autonomy and participation in decision making, or it can be designed to eliminate decision making and to closely control workers (Appelbaum and Albin 1989). ...

The introduction of new technology may also increase skill and income differences among women-predominant jobs. Women's jobs are becoming increasingly polarized into routine, low-wage, highly controlled work and non-routine, relatively autonomous, higher-wage jobs (Kuhn and Bluestone 1987; Sweeney and Nussbaum 1989), reflecting the two tiers in the service sector discussed above. For example, two women-predominant occupations that are predicted to expand most rapidly during the 1990s are nursing and nurses' aides. As Glazer (1991) points out, the skill level of nurses is rising as new technology changes the nature of nursing work and as the profession increasingly requires at least a baccalaureate as certification. At the same time, the work of aides is still defined as unskilled and its pay remains near minimum wage levels (Sweeney and Nussbaum 1989).

Many lower-level women's jobs that cannot be automated still require high skill and responsibility, but are devalued in our society and vastly under-rewarded. The skills that are necessary for caring work and that must be learned through experience rather than through technical, classroom training are those most devalued (see, for example, Acker 1989). An obvious example is child-care work, another occupational area that is expected to expand during the 1990s, in which pay levels are generally not much above minimum wage. Although comparable-worth successes in the public sector have improved wages for many care workers employed there, these efforts have slowed recently and have hardly touched the private sector. Low levels of union organization contribute to low wages, because without union organization, relatively powerless women have no mechanism for pushing for pay levels that reward these skill requirements.

Flexible Work Organization

"Flexibility" is one of private-sector management's answers to the problem of maximizing returns in highly competitive markets. For the public-sector manager, flexibility can mean lower labor costs and budgetary savings. Flexibility has a number of meanings (Standing 1989; Wood 1989), and these meanings have gender implications (Walby 1989; Jenson 1989). Flexibility refers to firms, the organization of work, and to workers' skills. In management theory, the flexible firm should be able to respond rapidly to changes in costs, demand, and technology in a rapidly evolving, competitive world. Workers should have a range of skills and job boundaries should be flexible to make such a response possible. Jenson (1989) points out that the new, flexible workers are apt to be men because patterns of sexual segregation are such that men's jobs have been defined as skilled, while women's have been regarded as unskilled or semi-skilled. Those chosen for new skill training are apt to be those who are already seen as skilled. Cockburn's (1985) studies, discussed above, support this conjecture. There is no reason to think that this will change. The type of flexibility sought through multiple skilling of workers and adaptability to markets is unlikely to benefit women in manufacturing to any great degree, especially women of color and immigrant women. Moreover, as in the banking and insurance examples noted above, although women may develop greater skill and the flexibility to do a variety of tasks, this may not improve their income situation. Gender assumptions allow managers to short-circuit the expected relationship between improved productivity and increased wages.

Another meaning of flexibility is that employers need to be able to increase and decrease the labor force as conditions change. One way to achieve this flexibility is to employ part-time and/or temporary workers who can be easily dismissed and who do not qualify for the same job protections or benefits that labor contracts and legislation grant to regular full-time employees. Women have always comprised the bulk of this "peripheral" or contingent labor force, but the jobs of this type are increasing, particularly with the explosion of the service sector discussed above. ...

Of course, skilled professionals as well as clerical and service workers are part-time and temporary workers. For many women, part-time work is a good solution to problems of combining paid and unpaid responsibilities. For the successful, high-paid professional, independent contracting may have many advantages; on the other hand, it may constitute an undesirable alternative for professionals who cannot find jobs because of organizational downsizing and restructuring. For the low-paid, routine worker, part-time employment has many disadvantages, even though it may make it easier to combine family care and paid work. Flexibility for the employer means frequent job changes, part-time, temporary work, and insecurity for the worker. Lack of benefits in many part-time jobs, inadequate unemployment compensation, absence of other income supports, lack of reasonable child care and parental leave increase the insecurity and stress for women and men, but especially for women. Again, women of color are most vulnerable (Eitzen and Zinn 1992).

Reduction of Hierarchy and Increased Participation

Reduction of hierarchy, as I have argued elsewhere (Acker 1990; also see Kanter 1977), may be a precondition for increased gender equality in the workplace. It is also a precondition for a more contributory and productive organization of work that can achieve flexibility and the effective utilization of new skills. Is it possible that feminist and management goals are converging? To reduce hierarchy, some middle-level management jobs must be eliminated or changed, and jobs that were once closely directed and supervised must be reorganized so that workers may take responsibility for their work, feel empowered to make suggestions that will improve productivity, and feel committed to the workplace and organization. In this scenario, a considerable number of jobs disappear, while the quality of others is enhanced. Since men are likely to have more seniority than women, women are apt to lose their jobs first. Those who are left may be better off because group-organized responsibility and decision-making can empower workers and make work more interesting and satisfying. Experience in Sweden supports this view.

Reduction of hierarchy and increased worker responsibility can also be a new form of increased exploitation and control. Expansion of duties and responsibilities can increase the amount of work that members of a group are expected to do. I take my examples from unpublished accounts from Sweden. In a group of home care workers in Sweden, job redesign resulted in group responsibility for scheduling, ordering supplies, and for contacts with the relatives of patients. These women workers learned the new tasks, including how to use computers to facilitate the work. However, while they shared previous supervisory responsibilities and hierarchy was reduced, no new workers were added to the group. As a consequence, they experienced a self-organized speed-up. There was less time to spend with patients and less time to confer with each other. Control was also transferred from the supervisor to the group. With more work to do, the absence of a group member became more problematic. The workers, now doing their own scheduling, had to find ways of managing such problems. The increased skills and responsibility were gratifying, but worries about the quality of care and sharing of responsibility and control increased tension and dissatisfaction. The public employing organization saved money because supervisory staff were no longer necessary.

In other experiments in group organized work in the care sector, workers were added to groups as tasks increased, allowing the quality of care to be maintained and facilitating ways of sharing the work of absent group members. In these cases, quality of service and worker morale improved, but savings were probably less.

Trends in Wages

Restructuring is having at least two effects on wages that have significance for the future. The wage gap between women and men is declining and jobs with low wages are increasing. While the wage gap between women and men has declined by a few percentage points since 1979, this may not be a cause for great celebration. Three-tenths of the 5-percentage-point decline between 1979 and 1987 was due to the dropping wages of men (National Committee on Pay Equity 1989). Between 1990 and 1991, the wages of white men fell again, even further diminishing the gender and race gap (DeParle 1991). The decline in white men's wages can be attributed to the disappearance of many high-wage production jobs in the course of the global restructuring of manufacturing. A major question is whether the restructuring of management and the service sector will further erode the incomes of white men and undermine women's wage gains as well.

Some of the growth in service-sector jobs was in professional, managerial, and technical fields in which women had relatively good salaries, although lower than those of men. However, 37 percent of job growth between 1979 and 1987 was in service industries with median incomes below $15,000 per year (Appelbaum and Albin 1990). ... In sum, the earnings consequences of economic restructuring are, on the whole, negative for ordinary people, as many others have also observed (Phillips 1990).

CAN WE AVOID A BLEAK FUTURE?

I have drawn a pessimistic picture of the impact of capitalist restructuring on women workers in the United States. As I finish this article in November, 1991, the signs of a severe recession abound, leading me to fear that the trends I have pointed to will only worsen. But, even if the economy has an upturn soon, the underlying processes will continue. Women's recent gains in the service sector and management are apt to stagnate or decline as restructuring continues. At the same time, class and race divisions among women are likely to become greater. The old organization of distribution (Acker 1988) from the male family wage to wives and children is clearly breaking down, as men's incomes decline and two incomes become even more necessary for family survival. No new organization of distribution, such as child allowances, that would provide for more family security in an increasingly low-wage work world has yet been achieved. Nor is there any coherent labor-market policy in the United States to prepare workers for new kinds of work or to create new jobs that are good jobs. With new forms of flexible work that have no long-term employment guarantees and few employee benefits, new forms of redistribution are needed (Standing 1989). Old types of unemployment insurance and retirement benefits linked to continuous and long-term employment do not suffice to guarantee a secure daily life and old age. Workers need protection from the dangers of the free-labor market (Esping-Andersen 1990). These protections are, of course, exactly what has been stripped away with the attack on labor unions and on welfare-state provisions.

The ideology supporting and interpreting these changes, as I argued above, looks more like a nineteenth-century hegemonic masculinity than a twenty-first-century vision of gender equality. This ideology and the organization of power it supports present severe difficulties to those who propose public policies for dealing with these new conditions. Nevertheless, this ideology is being challenged and proposals for reform are now emerging.

Some of these proposals are coming from women workers who have been able to organize in their own interests in the public sector where some protections for organization still exist. They have also been able to form coalitions with women in their communities, as the comparable-worth movement attests. With so many more women in the paid labor market, the structural conditions for more organization exist. In a utopian view of the future, women might be the leaders in a movement for changes that will save the United States from becoming another Third World country that keeps its dominance only because it has a big gun for hire.

In this utopia, the reborn hegemonic masculinity gives way as the recognition of the necessity to do something about our domestic problems returns. Military spending is drastically cut and the savings are allocated to rebuilding our physical infrastructure and our social services. Employment in the public and the private sectors increases, replacing jobs lost to restructuring. Unions are still strong in the public sector, and more women and minorities get good jobs there. New laws protecting the rights of workers are passed and union organization grows in the private sector. Affirmative action efforts are revitalized and comparable-worth reforms of pay structures become commonplace. Rapid change demands flexible workers, and business and public employers collaborate in developing new forms of worker training and education. In many workplaces, the work process is reorganized so that workers have more skill and more responsibility. Controls are reduced or transformed—more people work because it is intrinsically satisfying. New income transfer methods are devised—perhaps a guaranteed annual income is instituted (Standing 1989)—so that people can move from job to job without terror and be assured an income when they stay at home to care for family or when they work part-time. All of this would not necessarily end male domination or achieve equality in the workplace. But it might create a platform of security from which further changes could come.

NOTES

1   The service sector must be distinguished from service occupations. Although the Bureau of Labor Statistics category "Service Occupations" is confined to protective, health, and personal services, if service occupations are more broadly defined to include many of the occupations in the service sector, it is clear that many of these jobs are also found within the manufacturing sector. Manufacturers, for example, hire systems analysts and lawyers.

2   Calculated from *Statistical Abstract of the United States,* 110th edition, 1930; 389–391, and U.S. Department of Labor, *Employment and Earnings* 38: 185–190.

REFERENCES

Acker, Joan. 1988. "Class, Gender, and the Relations of Distribution." *Signs* 13: 473–497.

_____. 1989. *Doing Comparable Worth.* Philadelphia: Temple University Press.

_____. 1990. "Thinking about Wages: The Gendered Wage Gap in Swedish Banks." *Gender and Society* 5: 390–407.

_____. 1992. "Gendering Organizational Theory." In *Gendering Organizational Theory,* edited by Albert Mills and Peta Tancred. Newbury Park: Sage.

Acker, Joan and Ann Marie Ask. 1989. *Wage Differences between Women and Men and the Structure of Work and Wage Setting in Swedish Banks.* Stockholm: Arbetslivscentrum.

Appelbaum, Eileen and Peter Albin. 1990. "Differential Characteristics of Employment Growth in Service Industries." Pp. 36–53 in *Labor Market Adjustments to Structural Change and Technological Progress,* edited by Eileen Appelbaum and Ronald Schettkat. New York: Praeger.

Baran, Barbara. 1990. "The New Economy: Female Labor and the Office of the Future." Pp. 517–534 in *Women, Class, and the Feminist Imagination*, edited by Karen V. Hansen and Ilene J. Philipson. Philadelphia: Temple University Press.

Beechey, Veronica. 1987. *Unequal Work*. London: Verso.

Bluestone, Barry and Bennett Harrison. 1988. *The Great U-Turn: Corporate Restructuring and the Polarizing of America*. New York: Basic Books.

Braverman, Harry. 1974. *Labor and Monopoly Capital*. New York: Monthly Review Press.

Cockburn, Cynthia. 1985. *Machinery of Dominance*. London: Pluto.

Connell, R.W. 1988. *Gender and Power*. Stanford: Stanford University Press.

DeParle, Jason. 1991. "Poverty Rate Rose Sharply Last Year as Incomes Slipped." *New York Times*, 27 September 1991.

Eitzen, D. Stanley and Maxine Baca Zinn. 1992 "Structural Transformation and Systems of Inequality." Pp. 178–182 in *Race, Class, and Gender* edited by Margaret L. Andersen and Patricia Hill Collins. Belmont, CA: Wadsworth.

Esping-Andersen, Gosta. 1990. *Three Worlds of Welfare Capitalism*. Princeton: Princeton University Press.

Glazer, Nona. 1991. "'Between a Rock and a Hard Place': Women's Professional Organizations in Nursing and Class, Racial, and Ethnic Inequalities." *Gender and Society* 5: 351–372.

Hacker, Sally. 1990. *Doing It the Hard Way*. Boston: Unwin Hyman.

Higginbotham, Elizabeth. 1992. "We Were Never on a Pedestal: Women of Color Continue to Struggle with Poverty, Racism and Sexism." Pp. 183–190 in *Race, Class, and Gender*, edited by Margaret L. Andersen and Patricia Hill Collins. Belmont, CA: Wadsworth.

Institute for Women's Policy Studies and National Displaced Homemaker's Network. 1990. *Low Wage Jobs and Workers: Trends and Options for Change*. Washington, DC: National Displaced Homemaker's Network.

Jenson, Jane. 1989. "The Talents of Women, the Skills of Men: Flexible Specialization and Women." Pp. 141–155 in *The Transformation of Work?*, edited by Stephen Wood. London: Unwin Hyman.

Kanter, Rosabeth Moss. 1977. *Men and Women of the Corporation*. New York: Basic Books.

Kuhn, Sarah and Barry Bluestone. 1987. "Economic Restructuring and the Female Labor Market: The Impact of Industrial Change on Women." Pp. 3–32 in *Women, Households, and the Economy*, edited by Lourdes Beneria and Catharine R. Stimpson. New Brunswick: Rutgers University Press.

Marshall, Ray. 1987. *Unheard Voices: Labor and Economic Policy in a Competitive World*. New York: Basic Books.

Marshall, Ray and William E. Brock. 1990. *America's Choice: High Skills or Low Wages*. Rochester, NY: National Center on Education and the Economy's Commission on the Skills of the American Workforce.

Nash, June. 1983. "The Impact of the Changing International Division of Labor on Different Sectors of the Labor Force." Pp. 3–38 in *Women, Men, and the*

International Division of Labor, edited by June Nash and Maria Patricia Fernandez-Kelly. Albany: State University of New York Press.

National Committee on Pay Equity. 1989. *Briefing Paper #1*. Washington, DC: National Committee on Pay Equity.

Norris, Floyd. 1991. "Services: A Boom Area Goes Bust." *The New York Times*, 6 October 1991, 3, 1.

Pateman, Carole. 1988. *The Sexual Contract*. Cambridge: Polity.

Phillips, Kevin. 1990. *The Politics of Rich and Poor*. New York: Random House.

Porter, Michael E. 1990. *The Competitive Advantage of Nations*. New York: The Free Press.

Roach, Steven S. 1991. "Services under Siege: The Restructuring Imperative." *Harvard Business Review* 69: 82–92.

Standing, Guy. 1989. "Global Feminization through Flexible Labor." *World Development* 17: 1077–1095.

Sweeney, John J. and Karen Nussbaum. 1989. *Solutions for the New Work Force*. Cabin John, MD: Seven Locks Press

Taylor, William. 1991. "The Logic of Global Business: An Interview with ABB's Percy Barnevik." *Harvard Business Review* 69: 103–113.

Walby, Sylvia. 1989. "Flexibility and the Changing Sexual Division of Labor." Pp. 127–140 in *The Transformation of Work?*, edited by Stephen Wood. London: Unwin Hyman.

Wilson, William Julius. 1991. "Studying Inner-City Social Dislocations." *American Sociological Review* 56: 1–14.

Wood, Stephen, ed. 1989. *The Transformation of Work?*. London: Unwin Hyman.

Zonana, Victor F. 1991. "Banking Industry Implodes." *Los Angeles Times*. 19 August 1991, Section A:1.

37
Why Men Resist

William J. Goode

Although few if any men in the United States remain entirely untouched by the women's movement, to most men what is happening seems to be "out there" and has little direct effect on their own roles. To them, the movement is a dialogue mainly among women, conferences of women about women, a mixture of just or exaggerated complaints and shrill and foolish demands to which men need not even respond, except now and then. When men see that a woman resents a common male act of condescension, such as making fun of women in sports or management, most males are still as surprised as corporation heads are when told to stop polluting a river.

For the time being, men are correct in this perception if one focuses on the short run only. It is not often than social behavior deeply rooted in tradition alters rapidly. Over the longer run, they are not likely to be correct, and indeed I believe they are vaguely uneasy when they consider their present situation. As against numerous popular commentators, I do not think we are now witnessing a return to the old ways, a politically reactionary trend, and I do not think the contemporary attack on male privilege will ultimately fail. ...

Males will stubbornly resist, but reluctantly adjust, because women will continue to want more equality than they now enjoy and will be unhappy if they do not get it: because men on average will prefer that their women be happy: because a majority of either sex will not find an adequate substitute for the other sex: and because neither will be able to build an alternative social system alone. ...

To many women, the very title of my essay is an exercise in banality, for there is no puzzle. To analyze the peculiar thoughtways of men seems unnecessary, since ultimately their resistance is that of dominant groups throughout history. They enjoy an exploitive position that yields them an unearned profit in money, power, and prestige. Why should they give it up?

The answer contains of course some part of the truth, but we shall move more effectively toward equality only if we grasp much more of the truth that bitter view reveals. If it were completely true, then the greater power of men

---

would have made all societies male-vanity cultures, in which women are kept behind blank walls and forced to work at productive tasks only with their sisters, while men laze away their hours in parasitic pleasure. In fact, one can observe that the position of women varies a good deal by class, by society, and over time, and no one has succeeded in proving that those variations are the simple result of men's exploitation.

Indeed there are inherent socioeconomic contradictions in any attempt by males to create a fully exploitative set of material advantages for all males. Moreover, there are inherent *emotional* contradictions in any effort to achieve full domination in that intimate sphere.

As to the first contradiction, women—and men in the same situation—who are powerless, slavish, and ignorant are most easily exploitable, and thus there are always some male pressures to place them in that position. Unfortunately, such women do not yield much surplus product. In fact, they do not produce much at all. Women who are freer and are more in command of productive skills, as in hunting and gathering societies and increasingly in modern industrial ones, produce far more, but they are also more resistant to exploitation or domination. ...

As to emotional ties, men would like to be lords of their castle and to be loved absolutely—if successful, this is the cheapest exploitative system—but in real life this is less likely to happen unless one loves in return. In that case what happens is what happens in real life: Men care about the joys and sorrows of their women. Mutual caring reduces the degree to which they are willing to exploit their wives, mothers, and sisters. More interesting, their caring also takes the form of wanting to prevent *other* men from exploiting these women when they are in the outside world. That is, men as individuals know that *they* are to be trusted, and so should have great power, but other men cannot be trusted, and so the laws should restrain such fellows. ...

THE RANGE OF SEX ROLES

Let me begin by reminding you of the standard sociological view about the allocation of sex roles. Although it is agreed that we can, with only small error, divide the population into males and females, the biological difference between the two that might affect the distribution of sex roles—which sex is supposed to do which social tasks, which should have which rights—are much too small to determine the large differences in sex-role allocation within any given society or to explain the curious doctrines that serve to uphold it. Second, even if some differences would give an advantage to men (or women) in some tasks or achievements, the overlap in talent is so great that a large minority of men (or women) could do any task as well as could members of the other sex. Third, the biological differences are too fixed in anatomy and physiology to account for the wide diversity of sex-role allocation we observe when we compare different societies over time and cultures.

Consequently, most of sex-role allocation must be explained by how we rear children, by the sexual division of labor, by the cultural definitions of what is appropriate to the sexes, and by the social pressures we put on the two sexes. Since human beings created these role assignments, they can also change them. On the other hand, these roles afford large advantages to men (e.g., opportunity, range of choices, mobility, payoffs for what is accomplished, cultivation of skills, authority, and prestige) in this and every other society we know. Consequently, men are likely to resist large alterations in roles. They will do so even though they understand that in exchange for their privileges, they have to pay high costs in morbidity, mortality, and failure. As a consequence of this fact about men's position, it can be supposed that they will resist unless their ability to rig the system in their favor is somehow reduced. It is my belief that this capacity is in fact being undermined somewhat, though not at a rapid rate.

A first glance at descriptions of the male role, especially as described in the literature about mass media, social stereotypes, family roles, and personality attributes, suggests that the male role is definite, narrow, and agreed upon. Males, we are told, are pressed into a specific mold. ... We are so accustomed to reading such descriptions that we almost believe them, unless we stop to ask, first, how many men do we actually know who carry out these social prescriptions (i.e., how many are emotionally anesthetized, aggressive, physically tough and daring, unwilling or unable to give nurturance to a child)? Second, and this is the test of a social role, do they lose their memberships cards in the male fraternity if they fail in these respects? If socialization and social pressures are so all-powerful, where are all the John Wayne types in our society? Or, to ask a more searching question, how seriously should we take such sex-role descriptions if so few men live up to them?

The key fact is not that many men do not live up to such prescriptions: rather, it is that many other qualities and performances are also viewed as acceptable or admirable, and this is true even among boys, who are often thought to be strong supporters of sex stereotypes. ...

A much more profound observation is that oppressed groups are *typically* given narrow ranges of social roles, while dominant groups afford their members a far wider set of behavior patterns, each qualitatively different but each still accepted or esteemed in varying degrees. One of the privileges granted, or simply assumed, by ruling groups, is that they can indulge in a variety of eccentricities while still demanding and getting a fair measure of authority or prestige. ...

We assert, then, that men manage to be in charge of things in all societies but that their very control permits them to create a wide range of ideal male roles, with the consequence that large numbers of men, not just a few, can locate rewarding positions in the social structure. Thereby, too, they considerably narrow the options left for feminine sex roles. Feminists especially resent the narrowness of the feminine role in informal interaction, where they feel they are dealt with only as women however this may be softened by personal warmth or affection.

We can recognize that general relationship in a widespread male view, echoed over the centuries, that males are people, individuals, while women are lumped together as an aggregate. Or, in more modern language: Women have roles, a delimited number of parts to play, but men cannot be described so simply.

Nor is that particular male view contradicted by the complaint, again found in all major civilizations, that women are mysterious, unpredictable, moved by forces outside men's understanding, and not controllable. Even that master of psychodynamics Sigmund Freud expressed his bewilderment by asking. "What do women want?" Men have found their women difficult to understand for a simple reason: They have continued to try to think of them as a set of roles (above all else, mothers and wives), but in fact women do not fit these roles, not only not now, but not in the past either. Some women were great fighting machines, not compliant; some were competitive and aggressive, not nurturant; many were incompetent or reluctant mothers. They have been queens and astronomers, moralists and nurturers, leaders of religious orders as well as corporations, and so on. At any point, men could observe that women were ignoring or breaking out of their social molds, and men experienced that discrepancy as puzzling. However, it is only recently that many have faced the blunt fact that there is no feminine riddle at all: Women are as complex as men are, and always will escape the confinements of any narrow set of roles.

THE SOCIOLOGY OF SUPERORDINATES

… I believe that there are some general principles or regularities to be found in the view held by superordinates—here, the sex-class called males—about relations with subordinates, in this instance women. These regularities do not justify, but they do explain in some degree, the modern resistance of men to their new social situation. Here are some of them:

1. The observations made by either men or women about members of the other sex are limited and somewhat biased by what they are most interested in and by their lack of opportunity to observe behind the scenes of each others' lives. However, far less of what men do is determined by women; what men do affects women much more. As a consequence, men are often simply less motivated to observe carefully many aspects of women's behavior and activity because women's behavior does not usually affect what men propose to do. By contrast, almost everything men do will affect what women *have* to do, and thus women are motivated to observe men's behavior as keenly as they can.

2. Since any given cohort of men know they did not create the system that gives them their advantages, they reject any charges that they conspired to dominate women.

3. Since men, like other dominants or superordinates, take for granted the system that gives them their status, they are not aware of how much the social structure, from attitude patterns to laws, pervasively yields small, cumulative, and eventually large advantages in most competitions. As a consequence, they assume that their greater accomplishments are actually the result of inborn superiority.

4. As a corollary to this male view, when men weigh their situation, they are more aware of the burdens and responsibilities they bear than of their unearned advantages.

5. Superiors, and thus men, do not easily notice the talents or accomplishments of subordinates, and men have not in the past seen much wisdom in giving women more opportunities for growth, for women are not capable of much anyway, especially in the areas of men's special skills. Thus, in the past, few women have embarrassed men by becoming superior in those areas. When they did, their superiority was seen, and is often still seen, as an odd exception. As a consequence, men see their superior position as a just one.

6. Men view even small losses of deference, advantages, or opportunities as large threats. Their own gains, or their maintenance of old advantages, are not noticed as much.

Although the male view is similar to that of superordinates generally, as the foregoing principles suggest, one cannot simply equate the two. The structural position of males is different from that of superordinate groups, classes, ethnic populations, or castes. Males are, first, not a group, but a social segment or a statistical aggregate within the society. They share much of a common destiny, but they share few if any *group* or *collective* goals (within small groups they may be buddies, but not with all males). Second, males share with certain women whatever gain or loss they experience as members of high or low castes, ethnic groups, or classes. ... They are not fully equal, to be sure, but much more equal than are members of very different castes or social classes.

Moreover, from the male view, women also enjoy certain exemptions: "Freedom from military conscription, whole or partial exemption from certain kinds of heavy work, preferential courtesies of various kinds." Indeed, men believe, on the whole, that their own lot is the more difficult one.

Most important as a structural fact that prevents the male view from being simply that of a superordinate is that these superordinates, like their women, do not live in set-apart communities, neighborhoods, or families. ...

A consequence of this important structural arrangement is that men and women are separated from their own sex by having a stake in the organization that gives each a set of different roles, or a different emphasis to similar roles; women especially come to have a vested interest in the social unit that at the same time imposes inequalities on them. This coalition between the two individuals makes it difficult for members of the same sex to join with large numbers of person of their own sex for purposes of defense or exploitation. This applies equally to men and women. ...

In coalition with their women, they oppose the exploitative efforts of outside men; within the family unit, however, they see little need for such protections against themselves, for they are sure of their own goodheartedness and wisdom.

That men see themselves as bound in a coalition with their families and thus with their daughters and wives is the cause of much common male resistance to the women's movement, while some have instead become angered at the unfair treatment their wives and daughters have experienced. The failure of many women to understand that complex male view has led to much misunderstanding.

RESPONSES OF SUPERORDINATES TO REBELLION

First, men are surprised at the outbreak. They simply had not known the depth of resentment that many women harbored, though of course many women had not known it either. Second, men are also hurt, for they feel betrayed. They discover, or begin to suspect, that the previously contented or pleasant facade their women presented to them was false, that they have been manipulated to believe in that presentation of self. Because males view themselves as giving protection against any one exploiting or hurting their women, they respond with anger to the hostility they encounter, to the discovery that they were deceived, and to the charge that they have selfishly used the dominant position they feel they have rightfully earned.

A deeper, more complex source of male anger requires a few additional comments, for it relates to a central male role, that of jobholder and breadwinner. Most men, but especially most men outside the privileged stratum of professionals and managers, see their job as not yielding much intrinsic satisfaction, not being fun in itself, but they pride themselves on the hard work and personal sacrifice they make as breadwinners. In the male view, men make a gift of all this to their wives and children.

Now they are told that it was not a gift, and they have not earned any special deference for it. In fact, their wives earned what they received, and indeed nothing is owing. If work was a sacrifice, they are told, so were all the services, comforts, and self-deprivations women provided. Whatever the justice of either claim, clearly if you think you are giving or sacrificing much to make gifts to someone over a period of time, and then you learn he or she feels the gifts were completely deserved, for the countergifts are asserted to have been as great and no gratitude or special debt was incurred, you are likely to be hurt or angry.

... Let me go a step further and speculate that the male resentment is the greater because many fathers had already come to suspect that their children, especially in adolescence, were indifferent to those sacrifices, as well as to the values that justified them. Thus, when women too begin to assert that men's gifts are not worth as much as men thought, the worth of the male is further denied.

SOME AREAS OF CHANGE AND NONCHANGE

Although I have not heard specific complaints about it, I believe that the most important change in men's position, as they experience it, is a loss of centrality, a decline in the extent to which they are the center of attention ...

Boys and grown men have always taken for granted that what they were doing was more important than what the other sex was doing, that where they were, was where the action was. Their women accepted that definition. Men occupied the center of the stage, and women's attention was focused on them. Although that position is at times perilous, open to failure, it is also desirable.

Men are still there of course, and will be there throughout our lifetime. Nevertheless, some changes are perceptible. The center of attention shifts to women more now than in the past. I believe that this shift troubles men far more, and creates more of their resistance, than the women's demand for equal opportunity and pay in employment.

The change is especially observable in informal relations, and men who are involved with women in the liberation movement experience it most often. Women find each other more interesting than in the past, and focus more on what each other is doing for they are in fact doing more interesting things. Even when they are not, their work occupies more of their attention, whether they are professionals or factory workers. Being without a man for a while does not seem to be so bereft a state as it once was. I also believe that this change affects men more now than at the time of the suffragist movement half a century ago, not only because more women now participate in it but also because men were then more solidary and could rely on more all-male organizations and clubs: now, they are more dependent on women for solace and intimacy. ...

Although I have noted men's feeling of hurt and anger, I want to emphasize that I believe no backlash of any consequence has been occurring and no trend toward more reactionary male attitudes exists. Briefly, there is a continuing attitude change on the part of both men and women, in favor of more equality. The frequent expressions of male objection, sometimes labeled "backlash" in the popular press, can be attributed to two main sources: (1) The discovery, by some men who formerly did pay lip service to the principle of equality, that they do not approve of its concrete application: and (2) active resistance by men and women who simply never approved of equality anyway and who have now begun to oppose it openly because it can no longer be seen as a trivial threat. Most of this is incorrectly labeled "backlash" which ought instead to refer only to the case in which people begin to feel negative toward a policy they once thought desirable, because now it has led to undesirable results. Those who oppose women's rights like to label any support they get as backlash because thereby they can claim that "women have gone too far." ...

BASES OF PRESENT CHANGES

Most large-scale, objective measures of men's roles show little change over the past decade, but men do feel now and then that their position is in question, their security is somewhat fragile. I believe they are right, for they sense a set of forces that lie deeper and are more powerful than the day-to-day negotiation and renegotiation of advantage among husbands and wives, fathers and children, or bosses and those who work for them. Men are troubled by this new situation.

The conditions we live in are different from those of any prior civilization, and they give less support to men's claims of superiority than perhaps any other historical era. When these conditions weaken that support, men can rely only on previous tradition, or their attempts to socialize their children, to shore up their faltering advantages. Such rhetoric is not likely to be successful against the new objective conditions and the claims of aggrieved women. Thus, men are correct when they feel they are losing some of their privileges. ...

Concretely, because of the increased use of various mechanical gadgets and devices, fewer tasks require much strength. As to those that still require strength, most men cannot do them either. Women can now do more household tasks that men once felt only they could do, and still more tasks are done by repair specialists called in to do them. With the development of modern warfare, there are few if any important combat activities that only men can do. Women are much better educated than before.

With each passing year, psychological and sociological research reduces the areas in which men are reported to excel over women and discloses far more overlap in talents, so that even when males still seem to have an advantage, it is but a slight one. It is also becoming more widely understood that the top posts in government and business are not best filled by the stereotypical aggressive male but by people, male or female, who are sensitive to others' needs, adept at obtaining cooperation, and skilled in social relations. Finally, in one sphere after another, the number of women who try to achieve rises, and so does the number who succeed.

Although the pressure of new laws has its direct effect on these conditions, the laws themselves arise from an awareness of the foregoing forces. Phrased in more theoretical terms, the underlying shift is toward the decreasing marginal utility of males, and this I suspect is the main source of men's resistance to women's liberation. That is, fewer people believe that what the male does is indispensable, nonsubstitutable, or adds such a special value to any endeavor that it justifies his extra "price" or reward. ...

It is not then as individuals, as persons that males will be deemed less worthy in the future or their contributions less needed. Rather, they will be seen as having no claim to *extra* rewards solely because they are members of the male sex-class. This is part of a still broader trend of our generation which will also increasingly deny that being white, or an upper-caste or upper-class person produces a marginally superior result and thus justifies extra privileges. ...

Now, men perceive that they may be losing some of their advantages and that more aspects of their social roles are subject to public challenge and renegotiation than in the past. They resist these changes and we can suppose they will continue to do so. In all such changes, there are gains and losses. Commonly, when people at lower social ranks gain freedom, those at higher ranks lose some power or centrality. When those at the lower ranks also lose some protection, some support, those at the higher ranks lose some of the burden of responsibility. It is also true that the care or help given by any dominant group in the past was never as much as members believed, and their loss in political power or economic rule was never as great as they feared.

On the other hand, I know of no instance when a group or social stratum gained its freedom or moved toward more respect and then had its members decide that they did not want it. Therefore, although men will not joyfully give up their rank, in spite of its burdens, neither will women decide that they would like to get back the older feminine privileges, accompanied with the lack of respect and material rewards that went with those courtesies.

I believe that men perceive their roles as being under threat in a world that is different from any in the past. No society has yet come even close to equality between the sexes, but the modern social forces described here did not exist before either. At the most cautious, we must concede that the conditions favoring a trend toward more equality are more favorable than at any prior time in history. If we have little reason to conclude that equality is at hand, let us at least rejoice that we are marching in the right direction.

38

Contemporary Perspectives on Masculinity

Kenneth Clatterbaugh

THE SIX PERSPECTIVES

It is time now to present a brief sketch of the six major perspectives under study here. Each encompasses a general category within which there are many voices. ... Although some of these perspectives have roots in the social philosophies of the nineteenth century, each has emerged and taken form in response to modern feminist movements. Each has thus developed into a genuinely contemporary perspective on masculinity.

I. The Conservative Perspective

According to conservatives it is perfectly natural for men to be the providers and protectors of women: it is natural for men to be politically and socially dominant. Masculine behaviors and attitudes are manifestations of male nature. According to *moral* conservatives, masculinity is created by society in order to override men's natural antisocial tendencies: it is the civilized role men play when they are fathers, protectors, and providers. According to *biological* conservatives, virtually all social behavior is a manifestation of men's natural tendencies as selected through an evolutionary process.

From the standpoint of moral conservatives, feminist reforms that change the traditional roles of men and women damage society's ability to impose the civilizing masculine role on men. Thus, moral conservatives oppose feminist agendas; they propose their own political and social programs so as to enhance the traditional nuclear family and make the traditional roles for men and women more attractive. Biological conservatives, on the other hand, are less concerned with the impact of feminism or with developing an agenda for social change for the simple reason that they do not believe that biological tendencies are likely to be greatly affected by social movements. Yet biological conservatives do oppose laws and social policies that try to legislate away behaviors that are the result of genetic predispositions.

Excerpted from Kenneth Clatterbaugh, *Contemporary Perspectives on Masculinity: Men, Women, and Politics in Modern Society.* Boulder, Col.: Westview Press, 1990, pp. 9–12, 151–58, 160. Reprinted by permission of Westview Press, Boulder, Colorado.

2. The Profeminist Perspective

Other perspectives are sympathetic to feminism, but adherents of this view are most directly influenced by feminist writing and political organization. Profeminists reject the claim that traditional masculinity is either morally necessary or biologically grounded. For them masculinity is created through male privilege and its corresponding oppression of women, although they allow that traditional masculinity is also harmful to men.

Radical profeminists follow the lead of radical feminism in holding that masculinity is created and maintained by misogyny and violence against women, and that patriarchy is the social and political order in which this masculinity exists. To counter the patriarchal order, radical profeminists believe that it is necessary to repudiate masculinity and to replace it with new behaviors, and attitudes that are informed by feminist values. That is, men may unlearn patriarchal behaviors by working against violence, learning to take on more caretaker roles, and helping to create noncompetitive, nonhierarchical organizations.

Liberal profeminists follow the lead of liberal feminism in maintaining that masculinity is a set of limitations that are imposed on men, much as femininity is a set of limitations that are imposed on women. These limited ways of behaving are encouraged by a system of rewards, punishments, and social stereotypes and ideals. Both men and women are prevented from self-realization by these restrictive roles. The best way for men to combat sexism is to break through their own limitations and to become fully human, just as women have had to struggle to overcome the limitations of femininity. ...

3. The Men's Rights Perspective

This perspective largely concurs with the liberal profeminist account of masculinity, but it defines the principal harm in this role as directed against men rather than women. In fact, its adherents believe that the traditional social role of men has become lethal.

Men's rights advocates also maintain that feminism, instead of helping men or providing a model for male liberation, has actually made things worse. Although it has created new options for women, men have not been given the same range of choices. Thus, a new sexism has come into existence, with men as the victim. In addition, feminism has created guilt in men for their own socialization, which is not their fault. It has not only contributed to false negative images of men but also exacerbated the double binds that afflict them.

The agenda of the men's rights perspective is to bring about an understanding of the new sexism and to create laws that protect men against current injustices, especially in the areas of divorce, child custody, and domestic violence prosecution.

4. The Spiritual Perspective

The spiritual perspective is founded on the conviction that masculinity derives from deep unconscious patterns. These patterns are best revealed through a tradition of stories, myths, and rituals.

The feminist movement has successfully tapped into the unconscious minds of women and found a way to unleash their energy, but men have yet to find a positive and vigorous way of doing the same.

The mythopoetic movement initiated by Robert Bly is the principal spiritual perspective of masculinity today. Bly's view has Freudian underpinnings and is critical of feminine understandings of masculinity. In contrast, there is the smaller Wicca tradition exemplified in the writings of John Rowan. This tradition is more humanistic and openly feminist: it teaches that men have been cut off from a feminine understanding of themselves.

In short, men need to reach down into their psyches and touch an archetypal masculine pattern from which they have been separated. Hence the spiritual perspective is less concerned with developing agendas for social change than with developing an environment in which men can experience growth and self-discovery.

5. The Socialist Perspective

Masculinity is a social reality; as such, it is grounded in economically determined class structures. Today, under patriarchal capitalism, masculinity is determined by who does what work, who controls the labor of others, and who controls the products of that labor. Masculinity is not the same from class to class or from race to race because different classes and races fit into these capitalist structures in different ways. The costs of being masculine, as described by the other perspectives, are nothing but the alienations of men subjected to the relations of production in a capitalist society.

The socialist perspective concurs that the end to the oppression of women can come only when capitalism is replaced by socialism. Classical Marxists tend to think that the change from capitalism to socialism will be sufficient to end the oppression of women. Other socialists, usually identified as "socialist feminists," believe that the structures that oppress women are to some extent independent of capitalism and must therefore be addressed by separate agendas.

The socialists' agenda reflects their commitment to restoring workers' control over their own labor and ending private ownership of the productive force. Those who espouse both the socialist and the feminist perspectives are pursuing strategies for ending men's control over women's labor.

6. The Group-Specific Perspective

Too often the standardized discussions of masculinity presume a universal masculinity that refers to white, heterosexual, and middle-class men. The group-specific perspective began largely as a critique of these standardized discussions. Now it is more than a critique, however, insofar as it points to new explanations of masculinity, to different evaluations of it, and to alternative agendas for change. Thus, the group-specific perspective has been transformed into a sixth contemporary perspective on masculinity.

For black or gay men, for example, the aforementioned framework questions refer to a reality different from their own. Gay profeminists note that as homosexuals do not dominate women sexually, they do not benefit in the same ways as heterosexual men do from their oppression of women. They also point to the important role of homophobia in the formation of heterosexual masculinity. Similarly, black men who explore their own masculinity point to the crushing experience of slavery and to the impact of racism and poverty on the formation of their own masculinity. They are also keenly aware of how dominant white masculinity is shaped and maintained by privilege and antiblack racism. The goal of gay men has been to reduce homophobia in society at large and in organizations of men: the goal of blacks is to reduce antiblack racism.

PREDICTIONS

The Conservative Perspective

The goal of conservatism is the restoration of the traditional nuclear family, with the husband as breadwinner and the wife as homemaker. ... Conservatives...also hope to eliminate the right of women to choose an abortion and to end affirmative-action programs; in short, they oppose *any* policy or legislation that weakens the traditional roles for men and women.

Not the least of recent conservative successes has been control of the White House since 1980. Yet, except for the defeat of the ERA, the major elements of the conservative social agenda have not been achieved. ... Furthermore, the gender roles that characterize the traditional family are continuing to break down. ... Moreover, the conditions needed for a "masculine-affirming" social role, which George Gilder and other conservatives see as important to the restoration of the family, are simply not present. Instead, men are confronting declining wages, more overtime, and work opportunities that do not pay a sufficient family income (Thurow, 1987: 32).

Modern conservatism, which embraces both traditional gender roles and market capitalism, is at odds with itself. On the one hand, it seeks to hold onto the traditional family with its male breadwinner. On the other, it embraces a market capitalism that drives down real wages, makes many workers redundant, and refuses to pay a family wage, thus forcing more and more families to have multiple breadwinners. In other words, capitalism produces the very conditions that prevent the traditional family from surviving. ...

The conservative agenda in the 1980s was nevertheless successful in reducing social programs, limiting women's choices, and undercutting affirmative-action programs. Further successes may yet come, but the conservative goal of restoring the traditional family will likely be frustrated because it fails to meet the needs of corporate society.

The Profeminist Perspective

The goals of the men's movement is to create a substantial social movement that will encourage and support men in their abandonment of a masculinity that is oppressive to women and harmful to themselves. The activists in this movement have worked hard to lessen violence against women and homophobia among men. They have created an impressive number of men's studies course, have conducted national meetings, and have written extensively. But the future of men's studies, as independent programs, is likely to be limited by budgets that are expanding in other directions. And the fear within established women's studies programs that men's studies could become a forum for men's rights groups as some already have, will probably limit the support of women's programs for such courses.

Although the profeminist movement continues to hold national conferences that attract a few hundred men and women…it has failed in its efforts to become a substantial movement. Its membership is largely restricted to "converts" among academics, students, and professional-class psychologists. Some observers believe that the movement exists largely because it meets the personal needs of its members rather than because it features a profeminist agenda (Gross, Smith, and Wallston 1983; Doyle 1989: 306–313). Others argue that formal membership and growth in size should not be a measure of the influence of such a movement (Goldberg 1985: 306; Shiffman 1987: 300). In any case, its influence is much greater than its numbers. The problem with the latter argument is the lack of good evidence to support it. In fact, much of the evidence that American men are changing remains anecdotal.

… Liberal profeminists are inviting men to join a movement that promises to let women participate in society on an equal basis, thus producing more competition for jobs in an economy of lessening opportunities and more power sharing—this in a society where many men already feel relatively alienated and controlled. Radical profeminists, meanwhile, are inviting men to join a movement in which men are distrusted and from which they have been excluded because their masculinity is believed to be premised on violence and woman-hating. It is difficult if not impossible to build a substantial men's movement grounded in these theories. The distance between most men and the women's movement is further exacerbated by the movement's near-exclusive focus on the problems of owning- and professional-class white males.

The Men's Rights Perspective

The goals of the men's rights perspective are to create an awareness of the hazards of being male and to build a substantial movement among men that recognizes the cost and discriminations of being masculine.

... [It] seems to be a movement that meets the needs of its members, who feel victimized in some way. But its growth, its national conferences, and its publications are even more erratic than the comparable structures in the relatively weak profeminist movement. And the split between those interested in fathers' rights and those who prefer to pursue a more general agenda remains unresolved.

The men's rights movement has been successful in keeping its focus on the discriminations against men and the very real costs of being masculine. ... In addition, most states have seen the formation of men's rights lobbies, which are working toward new custody and divorce laws.

The strategic problem confronting this movement is that it is trying to make a case for male oppression in a social reality of male privilege. The lack of oppressive structures aimed at men makes it difficult to politicize men. When the women's movement started, there were many laws, policies, and scientific theories in existence that either assumed the inferiority of women or explicitly advanced it. Indeed, gross inequities still favor men. The fact that the men's rights movement lacks such targets is recognized by some of its advocates (Goldberg 1976: 4). And what efforts have been made to create the impression of male disadvantage, in a society where the reality of male privilege is widely accepted, have not been successful. Indeed, a society that values and depends on wealth is unlikely to equate the poverty of women with the burden for men of being breadwinners. Hence the efforts to create a sense of male "oppression" have given the movement an aura of narcissism and self-pity (Hooks 1984: 79).

The men's rights movement is likely to be short-lived. It not only lacks the dynamism of genuinely oppressed groups but...is also sufficiently at odds with the conservative tradition that it cannot draw on what would be its greatest alliance against the feminist agenda—conservative men. ...

It is entirely conceivable that men from the profeminist movement's liberal wing and the men's rights movement may unite under the cause of ending the burdens of the provider role. This union will become more likely as the provider role loses power and increases in human costs and as the two movements struggle for greater membership. ...

The Spiritual Perspective

Logically speaking, the goal of the mythopoetic perspective must be the restoration of appropriate male initiation rites. Male violence, lack of male vitality, and poor father-son and male-female relations are, from this perspective, caused by the absence of male initiations. Boys need a path into manhood that allows them to come to terms with their wounds and their shadow selves. ...

Men's counseling networks and individual counselors have incorporated these Jungian ideas into their work with some success. But apart from these therapeutic uses, a few rather expensive workshops, and the occasional men's conference, there are few opportunities through which men can receive the appropriate initiations and inspirations. The men attracted to this perspective seem to come mostly from other parts of the men's movement as well as from new-age groups. But its appeal is unlikely to transcend the limited pools represented in these populations.

As a theory of personal development, the Jungian framework is scientifically unacceptable and naive. It provides little insight into how masculinity is formed or how it can be changed, and it seems to lack a willingness to explore historical or cultural differences. As a tool for further exploration of masculinity, it is therefore less attractive than the more social science-oriented liberal movement.

The Socialist Perspective

The short-term goals of socialist feminism are greater worker control in wage labor and a major reduction in men's control over women's labor. The long-term goal of socialism is the end of the class division between workers and owners. ...

Today, socialism faces several problems. First, many people identify socialism with political tyranny (Stalinism). Second, there is a history of sexism within traditional socialist and labor organizations. Third, socialist thought is alien to the dominant liberalism of the major feminist and men's organizations in the United States. And, finally, the job ghettoization of minority women, white women, and minority men has separated them from the situation of white working males. Until these problems are overcome, the working class (which is well over half female, black, Latino, and gay or lesbian) will remain divided.

Certain recent developments may help to alleviate these problems. Repressive Stalinist regimes are currently being dismantled and may be replaced with democratic socialist or mixed structures. Moreover, socialist feminism and civil rights movements have significantly influenced socialist and labor organizations in the United States and Canada, rendering them less sexist and less racist. Finally, the real wages of men are declining while real wages for women are on the rise, thus reducing one major difference between men and women in the area of work. If these trends continue, the possibility of collective action will increase, because men and women within the working class will face more problems in common. And if feminists are correct in their assessment that the economic inequalities between men and women and the differences in the kinds of work they do exacerbate other social and political inequalities, then as men and women are equalized at work, alliances between them on other issues should become easier to create. ...

The Group-Specific Perspective

The group-specific perspective has much to say not only about the conditions of the "outside" groups themselves but also about the creation of society at large. But this perspective must continually struggle to move from a position of invisibility to one of recognition. ...

For profeminist gay men, the struggle against homophobia within particular perspectives has had mixed success. Gay men have won a place in the profeminist men's movement but have been virtually excluded from the men's rights perspective. Socialist groups have been increasingly open to the agenda of gay liberation (Cliff 1984: 221–3). The claim that homophobia is a primary underlying cause of masculinity has become a recognized perspective in its own right.

The success of the gay liberation movement may hinge to some extent on what happens outside of it. For example, if the AIDS panic should deepen institutional and individual homophobia, gay men may find their perspective discounted and their agenda abandoned. ... Yet there remain ominous countervening forces that feed on and encourage homophobia— forces such as conservative legislation that blocks gay men and lesbian women from adopting children, civil rights laws that fail to include gay men and lesbian women, laws that ban gays and lesbians from military service, and insurance companies that attempt to limit and deny payments to AIDS victims. There is also a growing level of street violence against gay man and lesbian women.

For those concerned with exploring black masculinity, the immediate goal is to stop the decimation of black men. The long-term goal is to greatly lessen the antiblack racism that so insidiously afflicts American society. In society at large and within men's organizations, at least some progress has been made. ...

The concern is that society has fundamentally ceased to care about the human consequences of racism and has left a large percentage of black men to struggle against drugs, poverty, and personal and institutionalized violence. Thus, for black men the harsh reality of social oppression may eclipse the successful articulation of their group-specific perspective. ...

At this point, I must reiterate the fact that these perspectives are socio-*political* perspectives. Each perspective is in a political confrontation with the others. Each originated with a need to confront the political realities of feminist theory and practice. Thus, political values and commitments will always enter into the descriptions, explanations, assessment, and agendas of each perspective. There will never be a final perspective on masculinity that is free of political bias and thus completely objective. Such a perspective—or dogma, as the case may be—is not even desirable. But this is not to say that our theories about masculinity cannot be improved. My point is simply that we must be as aware as possible of the values and assumptions underlying our theories. Equally important, we must acknowledge that clearer ideas about masculinity and its causes are potentially achievable through better research.

REFERENCES

Bly, Robert. 1987. *The Pillow and the Key: Commentary on the Fairy Tale of Iron John, Part One*. St. Paul, Minn.: Ally Press.

———. 1988. *When a Hair Turns Gold: Commentary on the Fairy Tale of Iron John, Part Two*. St. Paul, Minn.: Ally Press.

Cliff, Tony. 1984. *Class Struggle and Women's Liberation: 1640 to the Present Day*. London: Bookmarks Publishing Co-operative.

Doyle, James. 1989. *The Male Experience*. 2d ed. Dubuque, Iowa: Wm. C. Brown.

Gilder, George. 1973. *Sexual Suicide*. New York: Bantam.

———. 1986. *Men and Marriage*. London: Pelican.

Goldberg, Herb. 1976. *The Hazards of Being Male: Surviving the Myth of Masculine Privilege*. New York: Signet.

———. 1985. Why the men's movement is not happening. In *Men Freeing Men*, ed. Francis Baumli, p. 306. Jersey City, N.J.: New Atlantis.

Gross, A. E., R. Smith, and B. S. Wallston. 1983. The men's movement: Personal versus political. In *Social Movements of the Sixties and Seventies*, ed. J. Freeman, pp. 71–81. New York: Longman.

Hooks, Bell. 1984. *Feminist Theory from Margin to Center*. Boston: South End.

Rowan, John. 1983. *The Reality Game: A Guide to Humanistic Counseling and Therapy*. London: Routledge & Kegan Paul.

———. 1987. *The Horned God*. New York: Routledge & Kegan Paul.

Shiffman, Michael. 1987. The men's movement: An exploratory empirical investigation. In *Changing Men: New Directions in Research on Men and Masculinity*, ed. Michael S. Kimmel, pp. 285–314. Newbury Park, Calif.: Sage.

Thurow, Lester C. 1987. A surge in inequality. *Scientific American* 256: 5 (May): 30–37.

39

Changing the Politics of the Women's Movement

Salome Lucas, Judy Vashti Persad, Gillian Morton, Sunita Albuquerque, and Nada El Yassir

Within the last few years, the grassroots women's movement has experienced significant changes. These changes are expressed through the issues that are addressed and through the active participation of previously marginalized sectors of the women's movement, such as black women, women of colour, aboriginal women, lesbians and women with disabilities. The issues which affect these sectors have historically been excluded by the narrow vision of the women's movement. For many years, a perspective which reflects these sectors' experiences has been overshadowed by an analysis of feminism which addressed only the lives and experiences of white, middle-class, and able-bodied women.

Feminism, as defined by white middle-class women in North America, is a perspective based on economic and political privilege. White feminists attempted unsuccessfully to impose their definition and analysis on black women, women of colour and aboriginal women. They left unanswered the challenge posed by these groups: what constitutes women's issues and who defines them? To this day, white feminists cling to the false assumption that the women's movement is a homogeneous group experiencing the same forms and degree of oppression. With this assumption, white feminists have not only monopolized the movement with their interests and privileges, but have also carried their equality struggle, in the name of gender, at the expense of aboriginal, black women and women of colour.

Gender comprises only one element of women's identity. We also identify by race, class, sexual orientation and (dis)ability. As women we are not collectively and equally affected by the same issues and therefore we do not benefit equally from the same changes. An example of this is the pay equity issue which is believed to be an issue unique to women. Most aboriginal women, women of colour, black women and women with disabilities how-

The authors of this article are members of the International Women's Day Coalition in Toronto; the article first appeared in the Cross Cultural Communications Centre Newsletter (*Resources for Feminist Research* [RFR/DRF], vol. 20, no. 1/2 [Summer 1991]: 3–4). Reprinted by permission.

ever do not benefit from pay equity programs, since before they receive equal pay they must first be given the opportunity to work!

Black women, women of colour and aboriginal women are oppressed by racism and identify as peoples who have been colonized, historically oppressed and subjected to genocide. In our day-to-day lives, we cannot escape the ugly reality of racism. We recognize it as a product of colonial domination which has been used to justify the raping of the natural and human resources of what became a third world in order to build the economies of the white colonizers. Racism has justified the destruction of the economies and traditions and the genocide of our peoples. Our emancipation therefore must be linked to the equality of our peoples. If we refuse to forget our history or to provide unconditional support to the demands of the privileged white feminists, we do so because neocolonialism is still alive today threatening the future of our peoples and ourselves.

Feminism is an ideology that develops through women's struggles for justice and equality. These struggles cannot be fought apart from the struggles of peoples as a whole and they cannot be separated from the economic and political conditions. It is these conditions and our relations to them that define the "women's issues" and the struggles to be fought. Political developments today have finally forced white feminists to realize their reality, since these developments shake the foundation on which their privileged lives have laid for decades.

There is no longer a debate in the women's movement as to whether issues such as the free trade, the constitution, the cuts of transfer payments to provinces, the UIC benefit cuts, the GST and the country's involvement in the Gulf war are women's issues. These developments cause turmoil in the country's economy and have drastic effects on women's lives. Economic developments have caused the ranks of welfare recipients and the unemployed to soar while transfer payments to provinces have been frozen. Within the context of a bleak economic environment, it is not surprising that we are witnessing a reactionary backlash against anti-racist and feminist politics. Violence against women and children is on the increase, yet federal funding to women's organizations has fallen to the axe. Similarly, many Native programs and organizational funding have been cut. There is also mounting racist violence against peoples who seek justice and equality. This was demonstrated by the attacks against the First Nations peoples near Oka [in 1990], the antagonism shown towards the active opposition of African-Canadians against the Royal Ontario Museum's racist exhibit "Into the Heart of Africa," the harassment of Arab-Canadians during the Gulf crisis and police violence against black, native and other people of colour communities.

The women's movement has also come to realize that in today's world local and international politics can no longer be separated. It is hard to accept the government's argument that the GST and the budget cuts were necessary to reduce the deficit when we paid millions of dollars every day to oppress the Mohawk people [in 1990] and are paying millions more now for our unnecessary involvement in the Gulf war.

As the political and economic dissolution of this country continues the attacks will intensify. To deal with the economic and political changes, it has become necessary not only for the women's movement, but also other social movements, to make the links and to change their form of organization. Instead of building an agenda to respond to priorities set by current governments, the women's movement must set its own agenda. Social and political movements have historically underestimated people's political awareness and have therefore failed to tap into valuable unutilized human resources. As a movement, we also need to be more creative and adopt more participatory forms of action which broaden its accessibility. Certain forms of action such as lobbying, letter writing, consultations, press conferences and rallies have created an elite of activists which works on behalf of people instead of working with people. These forms of organizing are indeed necessary and good but we have to admit that they limit the participation of large numbers of people who have no access to these forms of organization.

The International Women's Day (IWD) coalition in Toronto, of which we are members, strives to make changes in the women's movement. It strives to put forward a politic which reflects the life experience of all women. Its basis of unity ensures that unity and solidarity in the women's movement is not achieved at the expense of First Nations women, black women, women of colour. We want more than lended "support" from white feminists. We want them to take responsibility, and challenge their own racism. Differences do not necessarily divide. They can build unity. They help us to develop actions which deal with all forms of oppression we experience as women.

40

Women Against Feminism: An Examination of Feminist Social Movements and Anti-Feminist Countermovements

Erin Steuter

INTRODUCTION

There is a new interest emerging within feminism in anti-feminist women. It is difficult for feminists to understand how a woman who is intelligent, articulate and strong, as many ardent anti-feminists are, can ignore the vast number of oppressive acts against women and instead fight the very changes which would end that oppression. Women's resistance to a movement which identifies itself as for women is not new. This paper examines the current role played by the pro-family movement in Canada, especially R.E.A.L. Women in opposing contemporary feminist goals and historically situates this contemporary case in the context of previous Canadian and U.S. experiences. By examining the rise of the feminist movement in Canada and the United States and by describing and analysing the anti-feminist counter-movements that have repeatedly arisen in response to it, a pattern emerges that gives insight into the interaction between such groups. These feminist and anti-feminist movements have operated dialectically, shifting and parrying in a continuous effort to achieve dominance. This paper aims to illuminate these processes and suggest some solutions, for feminists must be aware that the process of divide-and-rule benefits patriarchy and contributes to the continuing oppression of women.

Throughout history individuals have banded together to protest against the existing order of society in an attempt to bring about social change. While their aims have been diverse, and their tactics varied, these groups have come to be seen by social scientists as 'social movements'. A social movement is generally understood to be 'a conscious, collective, organized attempt' to bring about large-scale change in the social order (Wilson, 1973:

From Erin Steuter, "Women Against Feminism: An Examination of Feminist Social Movements and Anti-Feminist Countermovements," *Canadian Review of Sociology and Anthropology*, vol. 29, no. 3 (1992): 288–306. Reprinted by permission.

8). While the literature on social movements is extensive and diverse, social movements tend to be generally characterized as having shared values—a goal or objective, sustained by an ideology; a sense of membership or participation; a distinction between those who are for and those who are against the goals of the movement; and an organizational structure of some kind that tends to differentiate between the leaders and followers within the movement (Killian, 1964: 430).

Historically, social movements have been accompanied by 'anti' movements which seek to oppose the changes advocated by the social movement. Tahi Mottl (1980) states that although observers have discussed these movements, few sociologists have analysed them as countermovements, a particular kind of protest movement which is a response to the social change advocated by an initial movement (Mottl, 1980: 620). She argues that reaction is an inevitable part of social conflict and change and that this phenomenon has not received sufficient analytical treatment in the literature of social movements.

Adapting John Wilson's definition of a social movement, Mottl defines a countermovement as 'a conscious, collective, organized attempt to resist or reverse social change' (Mottl, 1980: 620). She sees countermovements as arising out of existing groups whose status is threatened by the gains made specifically by the social movement they organize against, or who are reacting to the more general changes occurring within the society. While countermovements may precede the mobilization of the movement they resist, they neither fully organize as a countermovement nor develop their ideological scope until after the rise and initial success of the movements they attack. Richard Gale, a recent theorist of the phenomenon of countermovements, states that during the growth of the social movement, the ideology of the countermovement crystallizes (Gale, 1986: 209). Both Mottl and Gale see change-oriented social movements as spawning their antitheses: organized efforts to prevent or reverse such change. Thus, change in the existing structure advocated by social movements, followed by counter protests, can be regarded as a dialectical process that needs to be examined in its entirety as part of the continuity of development, conflict and social change. It is with this goal in mind that I will examine the development of the feminist movement[1] in Canada and the United States and the accompanying anti-feminist countermovements that have repeatedly arisen in response to it.

CONCEPTUALIZING THE WOMEN'S MOVEMENT AS A SOCIAL MOVEMENT

While it is clear that the feminist movement corresponds to the definition provided earlier and can thus be considered to be a social movement, nevertheless, treating it as a social movement remains problematic. Recent research into the history of women's struggle for change leaves no doubt that the feminist movement is a conscious, collective, organized attempt to bring about large-scale change in the social order. However, social movements theorists have so long ignored women's struggle for change as an object of research, that it is now questionable whether the traditional models for explaining and interpreting social movements can have any validity for the experience of women. While men's organizations for social change have been characterized as social movements, women's organizations, when studied at all, have generally been characterized as examples of 'collective behaviour' or 'voluntary organizations'. It is important to recognize this differential characterization because it carries with it fundamental ideological implications. Treating women's activities for social change as collective behaviour gives rise to images of a hysterical mass, and to characterize it as a voluntary organization de-politicizes the activity and denotes it as leisure.

Faced with a framework of social movements based largely on male models, feminists have sought to reclaim women's experiences of organizing for social change and characterize them as social movements. These efforts have resulted in an impressive collection of material on women's involvement in social change both historically and cross-culturally. Yet women's anti-feminist countermovements have until recently been ignored as has the inevitable interaction that exists between the two groups. ...

The claim has been made that women are the only group to have actively organized against their own emancipation (Conover and Gray, 1983: 9). While it is not clear that this is in fact true,[2] the fact that some women have organized against the movements of their feminist sisters is of significance and worthy of further investigation. Thus this paper will focus its analysis on the women's anti-feminist countermovements that have arisen in Canada and the United States within the last century in response to gains or perceived gains by the feminist movement. It is my claim that by examining the dialectical relationship that has existed between these movements for the last century, we can further understand the nature and character of the present-day feminist movement and the women who oppose it.

WOMAN SUFFRAGE IN THE U.S. AND CANADA

The American woman suffrage movement, which began in the early part of the 19th century, developed with increasing momentum until it became an active and organized social movement that achieved the enfranchisement of women in 1920. While Ellen DuBois (1979: 139) notes that the movement for women's suffrage began to take on the character of a social movement after the Civil War, it was not until the end of the 19th century and into the early years of the 20th century that it became a mass movement which clearly had the intent and potential to bring about radical social change.

Opposition to the suffrage movement had existed since it began, but the popularity and power of the anti-suffrage movement only developed into a formidable countermovement by 1912. Between 1912 and 1916 the National Association Opposed to Woman Suffrage claimed a membership of 350,000 adult women and counted 25 state organizations working to defeat suffrage. The vast majority of the leaders of this opposition movement were women. It would appear that the momentum toward social change created by the suffrage movement helped to spur on the development of its antithesis—the anti-suffrage countermovement. Anti-suffrage activity developed during the 1890s when several western states (Wyoming, Colorado, Idaho and Utah) adopted woman suffrage amendments, and anti-suffrage organizations were established to halt the migration of suffrage eastward. Once mobilized, the anti-suffrage movement became a powerful force. During the period 1912–1916 21 state-level woman suffrage referenda came to a vote, and only six passed. By 1917, however, this momentum was lost as New York added a woman suffrage amendment to its state constitution, and in the following year the U.S. Congress passed a constitutional amendment which was ratified by the requisite number of states in 1920 (Marshall and Orum, 1986: 14–15).

Women opposed to woman suffrage have been a topic of increasing interest to feminist researchers who are seeking a better understanding of the women opposed to the contemporary women's movement. While these theorists have different priorities in examining this phenomenon, they have identified a number of sources of opposition to woman suffrage that they generally agree upon. The most important of these is the argument that rapid social change was seen by many women as a threat to families and to the traditional function of women. Jeanne Howard (1982: 465) notes that the writings by women engaged in anti-suffrage work reveal that women who resisted the 'burden of the ballot' were involved in a personal battle. They were clinging to traditional roles and patterns of behaviour. They viewed their functions as wives, mothers and keepers of the home as increasingly threatened by the range of progressive movements at the turn of the century.

The fact that an anti-suffragist movement did not ever fully develop in Canada may have been due to the fact that the women who successfully lobbied for suffrage did not attempt to make a concerted attack on these values. Indeed, some historians have argued that the success of the suffrage movement in Canada was in large part due to its highly conservative nature.

Like its American counterpart, the woman suffrage movement in Canada developed early in the 19th century and needed until the latter part of the century to become an active and organized social movement. Drawing much of its support from women active in the Women's Christian Temperance Union (W.C.T.U.) and other temperance organizations across the country, the Canadian suffragists built up strong support and succeeded in winning the federal vote for women in 1918, two years ahead of their American sisters.

Historian Carol Lee Bacchi (1983) makes the claim that the woman suffrage movement in Canada was a protestant, Anglo-Saxon, middle and upper class movement dominated by professionals and the wives of professionals, who endorsed woman suffrage as part of a larger reform program designed to reinstate Puritan morality, Christianity, and the family. In her book *Liberation Deferred*, she describes how this type of moderate movement gained the support of the church and temperance movements which saw votes for women as a means of advancing the cause of social Christianity. Bacchi also makes the claim that many of those supporting woman suffrage in Canada believed that extending the vote to the mainly conservative and Christian women would effectively support the existing status quo against the threat of increased influence of new immigrants with suspect religions and politics.

This interpretation has been criticized by Canadian historians and social scientists who point out that Bacchi underestimates the level of political opposition faced by the Canadian women suffragists and in turn underrepresents the struggle to achieve the vote. Critics also suggest that Bacchi has not taken adequate account of the competing class and gender allegiances that underlay the actions of the women involved in the suffrage movement. Recent feminist scholarship has revealed this issue to be of significance in understanding the complexity of women's social organization. While these criticisms may well be valid and point to a need for further feminist scholarship on the question of the Canadian suffrage movement, Bacchi's hypothesis is worth examining for possible insights into the nature of early social movement/countermovement interaction.

Bacchi states that because the suffrage movement did not fundamentally challenge the existing sexual division of labour in society, it evoked little opposition. She notes (1983: 47) that aside from a few male intellectuals who publicly criticized the suffrage movement, the only organization to oppose it was a group of Toronto women led by Mrs. H.D. Warren. She notes that Mrs. Warren's husband was a prominent businessman who opposed prohibition, and she suggests that the suffragists' predominately pro-temperance position may well have prompted this opposition. Bacchi (1983: 76) argues that while the charge that liquor interests gave support and funding to anti-suffragists has been made in the U.S. and Australia, there is only circumstantial evidence of such a practice in Canada.

It is interesting to note that the Canadian suffragists have been characterized by Bacchi and others as 'maternal feminists'. While other historians provide evidence that more 'radical' feminist suffragists existed in Canada, Bacchi argues that the ones who formed the dominant social movement that ultimately led to women's enfranchisement were maternal feminists. These maternal feminists retained a traditional view of family structure and women's role in it. They strongly believed in the moral integrity of women, and argued that the politics of the nation could only benefit by their sober input and participation. They sought to increase the status of the home and home duties and by extension those responsible for home duties. This type of argument in many ways helps to explain the lack of an anti-suffragist movement in Canada. Bacchi states that,

> *Ideologically, the domination of the movement by men and women who have no intention of upsetting the traditional familial order, and who defended votes for women on the grounds that women's morality, religiosity, and piety were needed in society, took away any sting the issue might once have had (Bacchi, 1983: 133).*

Thus, it is suggested that a women's anti-feminist countermovement will develop only when a feminist social movement threatens or appears to threaten the traditional role and status of women in a given society. Indeed, the powerful and successful opposition to the Equal Rights Amendment (E.R.A.) in the United States provides compelling evidence of this.

THE FIGHT OVER THE EQUAL RIGHTS AMENDMENT

Like their predecessors, contemporary American anti-feminists mobilized in response to the success of the feminist movement in gaining state ratification of the E.R.A. The E.R.A. began its career as a relatively uncontroversial piece of legislation. It was passed overwhelmingly by both houses of Congress in 1972. … Speedy ratification seemed assured, as 22 states passed the E.R.A. in 1972 and another eight followed suit in 1973. The countermovement began to coalesce in late 1972, dedicated to halting ratification in additional states and rescinding the amendment where it had already been ratified. …

While supported by religious and political organizations of the New Right, the rank and file membership as well as the leadership of the contemporary anti-feminist movement in the U.S. remains overwhelmingly female. Numerous ad hoc local and regional anti-feminist groups proliferated throughout the 1970s, but by far the most significant was the Stop-E.R.A. organization headed by Phyllis Schlafly. …

Charging that feminism 'deliberately degrades the homemaker,' Schlafly uplifted the role to one of 'home executive,' and argued that 'marriage and motherhood are the most reliable security the world can offer' (cited in Marshall, 1985: 356). This theme of feminists derogating the housewife and trivializing a women's domestic contributions is found throughout the work of conservative intellectual Midge Decter. It illustrates the important concern of many women who feel their status as homemakers is being threatened by feminist attempts to draw women out of their homes and into the male public sphere.

Jane Mansbridge in her recent and valuable contribution to this issue, *Why We Lost the E.R.A.*, states that in the 20 years leading up to the defeat of the E.R.A., homemakers suffered a tremendous loss of social prestige or 'status deprivation'.

> *Prestige is an important social reward for almost everyone. Since homemakers have never received direct monetary rewards for their work, prestige is especially important to them. During the late 1960s and 1970s they experienced a severe 'pay cut' in prestige. Naturally they were resentful. And consciously or unconsciously they blamed the people who were, at least in part, responsible—their sisters who had deserted the home for paid careers, making the now empty homestead look shabby (Mansbridge, 1986: 108).* ...

Mansbridge states that Schlafly and others capitalized on this view that the E.R.A. was an attack on the home. She argues that this proved to be a promising strategy because in 1977, 42 per cent of American women saw the women's movement as a major cause of family breakdown (Mansbridge, 1986: 104). Thus Schlafly pursued a tactic of 'guilt by association'; linking feminism with the E.R.A., and the E.R.A. with family breakdown. ...

Mansbridge (1986: 13) also notes that although politically distinct, abortion and the E.R.A. were seen to be linked by the Stop-E.R.A. forces. Both were seen to be sponsored by 'women's libbers,' and conservative activists saw abortion and the E.R.A. as two prongs of the libbers' general strategy for undermining traditional American values. This view not only served to mobilize the rank and file anti-E.R.A. women, but it also created a perfect opportunity for the forces of the fundamentalist Christian movement and the New Right conservative movement to join the foray into anti-feminism.

Mansbridge (1986: 5) argues that for many conservative Americans, the personal became the political for the first time when questions of family, children, sexual behaviour, and women's roles became subjects of political debate. Leaders of the 'old' Radical Right, who had traditionally focussed on national defence and the Communist menace, became aware of the organizing potential of these 'women's' issues only slowly. Once assimilated, however, the 'new' issues turned out to have two great organizational virtues. First, they provided a link with fundamentalist churches. Mansbridge (1986: 5) notes that the evangelizing culture and stable geographic base of the fundamentalist churches made them powerful actors in state legislatures once they ventured into the political process. Second, 'women's issues' also gave a focus to the reaction against the changes in child rearing, sexual behaviour, divorce, and the use of drugs that had taken place in the 1960s and 1970s.

The New Right regarded feminists' advocacy of the E.R.A. and of abortion as an attack upon church and family, and ultimately as an attack upon the very basis of an orderly society. Conover and Gray (1983: 73) note that because of the centrality of these issues to core conservatism, the E.R.A. and abortion conflicts provided motivation for an organized and united counter-movement. ...

The powerful mobilization of forces achieved by the New Right was instrumental not only in achieving the defeat of the E.R.A., but also in becoming the central foundation of the pro-family movement that developed in earnest at this time. The pro-family movement is the latest embodiment of anti-feminist countermovements. However, it is distinct from the anti-suffrage and Stop-E.R.A. movements in that it did not develop and exist only to defeat a single feminist issue. The anti-feminist counter-movements discussed so far have tended to develop in response to a specific issue of social change supported by a feminist social movement and in general disbanded when they had either lost their fight as in the case of suffrage, or succeeded in their goal as in the case of the E.R.A. The pro-family movement developed in part out of both of these issues but retained its vitality and organizational structure after the E.R.A. battle in order to act as a constant challenge to all further gains achieved by the feminist movement.

The pro-family movement in the United States has continued the kind of ideology that was instrumental in the other anti-feminist countermovements that preceded it. Members of the pro-family movement dwell upon family breakdown which they blame on the women's movement. They argue that the basis of family life is the exchange of homemaking and mothering by women for financial support by men. Economic independence for women, and its requisite, out-of-the-home child care, both fundamental tenets of contemporary feminism, are defined as threatening to the family because they are threatening to this basic division of labour. In turn, family breakdown is seen as the first step on the road to general societal breakdown. Chafetz and Dworkin (1987: 52–3) identify the development of pro-family movements in other countries and reveal that the ideological focus of the opponents of women's movements there is virtually identical. In contemporary Italy, Eowyn, a group of women split from the neo-fascist party, fights abortion, divorce, and daycare as destructive of the family and argues that women should work outside the home as little as possible. An Australian anti-feminist organization, Women Who Want To Be Women, was formed in 1979 in order to 'enhance the status of uniquely female roles associated with motherhood,' which it seeks to place 'at the center of society'. It is strongly anti-abortion, perceives the roles of the sexes as by 'nature' different and complementary, opposes anti-discrimination legislation, and defines the family as the basic social unit. It justifies its stance with reference to Christian ideals. Feminism is blamed for the low status of women, particularly mothers and housewives.

THE PRO-FAMILY MOVEMENT IN CANADA

While little research has been undertaken to document the nature of the pro-family movement in Canada, it appears to have a similiar ideological disposition.[3] Margrit Eichler (1985: 1) has stated that the pro-family movement in Canada consists of a conglomeration of organizations which are united in their defence of the 'beleaguered' institution of the family.

The largest and best-known of the women's pro-family groups in Canada is R.E.A.L. Women (Realistic, Equal and Active for Life). It was founded in Toronto in 1983 and has affiliates in each province and a self reported membership of 45,000 (Erwin, 1988: 269). While the pro-family movement has male members and includes men's associations it is predominately a movement which is made up of women. R.E.A.L. Women claims to speak for the heretofore silent majority and takes as its motto: 'Women's rights, but not at the expense of human rights'. There are also two pro-family political parties in Canada: the Christian Heritage Party, which operates at the federal level; and, in Ontario, the Family Coalition Party which won 4 per cent of the overall vote in the 1987 Ontario provincial election.

As in the case of the American pro-family movement, religion has played a key role not only in the lives of the constituents of the pro-family movement but also in the mobilization of pro-family forces in Canada. Lorna Erwin's study reveals that the pro-family network is located in the fundamentalist and Catholic churches which provide some important advantages including: a large potential support base of sympathetic, like-minded people, as well as financial support, office space, equipment and free advertising in religious publications.

Not suprisingly, the pro-family movement has its roots in the anti-abortion movement. Erwin (1988: 268) states that her national survey of 1,200 rank and file members of the pro-family movement revealed that 85 per cent of respondents involved in R.E.A.L. Women also belong to 'Right to Life' groups. Eichler (1985) notes that R.E.A.L. Women members are opposed to all forms of birth control other than abstinence and the 'rhythm method' as well as any form of sex education. A R.E.A.L. Women pamphlet states that there is probably a relation between the pill and the suppression of maternal instincts and child battering (cited in Amer, 1987: 8). Eichler (1985: 17) notes that the movement's view of sexuality also explains their abhorrence to homosexuality, which represents 'non-marital, non-procreative sexuality in its purest form'. The movement also rejects explicitly and consistently the notion of sex equality as expressed in the *Charter of Rights and Freedoms*. Even male violence is not seen by some as sufficient grounds for marital breakup. In one of their more horrifying blaming-the-victim statements, one of their leaders has insisted that 'too often a woman is sexually attracted to a man and rushes into marriage within six months. If she had waited a couple of years, she would have realized that he was the type to beat her up' cited in Dubinsky, (1987: 5). The pro-family movement does not support the concept of universally available, government-subsidized day care. Finally, the movement is opposed to the concept of equal pay for work of equal value and rejects the concept of affirmative action. In a speech at the first annual meeting of R.E.A.L. Women Canada, Anne de Vos argued that women are not equal to men, and hiring quotas were therefore unfair (cited in Eichler, 1985: 23).

Thus, it becomes apparent that the pro-family movement in Canada is virulently anti-feminist and in fact explicitly juxtaposes itself against feminism. ...

Eichler (1985: 4) states that according to the spokespeople of the 'so-called pro-family movement,'

> *Feminism and feminists are not only responsible for destroying the family, but also the basic fabric of society, and the well being and health of individual women, men and children. Feminists are, according to this view, responsible for generating those problems feminists have struggled most with, such as abuse, violence, incest, rape and pornography.*

Perhaps more important than these verbal attacks on feminism, is the pro-family movement's increased militancy on the issue of abortion. These groups have embarked on an intensive media campaign, lobbied government officials, and physically blocked the entrance to abortion clinics throughout Canada and the U.S. They have defied court orders banning them from the vicinity of the clinics, continued to harass women entering and exiting the clinics and have even been known to copy down the licence plate numbers of cars in the area of the clinic, acquire (by whatever means) the name and telephone number of the car owner and then make a call to the house informing the person answering the phone that someone of that address has had an abortion today! ....

In addition to the pro-family movement's anti-abortion lobby, groups such as R.E.A.L. Women have also been successfully pressuring the federal government for a share in the scarce resources of the Secretary of State's Women's Program. Traditionally this money has gone to organizations such as the National Action Committee on the Status of Women (N.A.C.), which is an umbrella group representing about 500 feminist-oriented women's organizations throughout the country. Of the approximately $13 million 1987 annual budget of the Women's Program, which was set up in 1973 to implement the recommendations of the Royal Commission on the Status of Women, N.A.C. receives an annual operating grant of between $400,000 and $500,000. While R.E.A.L. Women applied and were turned down three times in their request for funding, in March 1989 they received a federal grant totalling $21,212 to help fund their annual meeting in Ottawa. While their previous applications were denied because their proposals were 'not within the spirit of the objectives of the program' (spokesperson for the Secretary of State cited in *Alberta Report* (A.R.), 1987a; 9), their organization now appears to have the formal recognition of the Secretary of State. According to the mandate of the Women's Program only projects promoting equality as defined under the *Charter of Rights* are to be funded. Yet R.E.A.L. Women have been criticized for failing to demonstrate that their activities will advance the cause of women in Canada. In response to previous funding requests, a spokesperson for the Secretary of State has said:

> *We give funds to organizations whose objective is to promote the advancement of women. Most of their activities are directed against the women's movement (A.R., 1986b: 17).*

The pro-family movement claim to have the support of the majority of the Conservative Party caucus and have sought backing from them in their efforts to acquire Secretary of State funding. A Task Force Report on Government Spending submitted in 1986 by then-Deputy Prime Minister Erik Nielsen seems to lend some truth to this claim. 'We are particularly concerned,' it states, 'that the Women's Program as it has evolved may be addressing the needs of upwardly mobile, middle-class professional women which do not necessarily coincide with the concerns and problems of the majority of the women in Canada' (A.R., 1987a: 12). Gwen Landolt claims that Tory M.P.s tell her that 90 per cent of Conservative M.P.s are behind her. Tory M.P. Sidney Fraleigh said that 'more than 75 per cent of Conservative M.P.s, excluding cabinet ministers,' think the government should fund R.E.A.L. Women. 'There is no group I know,' he says, 'that represents the family better than R.E.A.L. Women' (A.R., 1987b: 12).

Thus, it is now possible to see the positions promoted by the pro-family movement appearing in government policy-making and in the press. Karen Dubinsky (1987b: 5) states that it is common to see R.E.A.L. Women comment[s] included in press reports with a focus on women. She points to the C.B.C.'s 'Morningside' as an example, which began a R.E.A.L. Women panel to 'balance' their regular feminist panel.[4] R.E.A.L. Women have frequently lobbied federal M.P.s and their 1987 'gift' of homemade muffins with pink icing earned national headlines. Dubinsky also points out the way in which the government has used the pro-family opposition as an excuse for inaction. ...

It is very interesting to note that in recent years the pro-family movement has been more careful in its public policy statements than it had been in the past. Past president of R.E.A.L. Women Grace Petrasek's unequivocal statement at their first press conference that a woman's prime responsibility is her family, has been replaced in a recent brief with more flexible and reasonable comments, such as:

> *To support homemaking as an option is not to say that we believe every woman should be in the home. We believe every woman should have the option to remain in the home if she chooses. Neither motherhood or a master's degree is for everyone (cited in Dubinsky, 1987a: 5).*

The social movements literature suggests that this does not represent a major ideological shift in the organization; rather it is characteristic practice of a countermovement at this stage in its relationship with the social movement.

Social movements theorists Ralph Turner and Lewis Killian (1972: 310) state that when the battle between a countermovement and social movement is not quickly won but instead results in an on-going conflict, a pattern of interdependence results. This pattern of interdependence is one in which programs, ideologies, and strategies on each side are continuously adjusted so as to deal with the programs, ideologies, and strategies on the other side and with the changes in ascendance between the two groups. They also note that the effort to defeat or wrest power from the initial movement soon begins to transcend the original program and ideology of the countermovement. The most important determinant of changes in the ideology of a countermovement is the increasing success or failure of the initial social movement. The countermovement begins to adopt popular elements of the initial movement's ideology as its own, attempting thereby to satisfy some of the discontent and also to get the opposed movement identified with only the most extreme portions of its whole program. Where movement and countermovement are of long standing, it is not infrequent for the countermovement eventually to promote everything the early adherents of the initial movement sought. ...

In the case of the pro-family movement in both Canada and the United States, the countermovement has developed into an aggressive and politically astute organization that is successfully parrying the feminist movement. It has become an adept public relations machine that is now striving not to appear too hysterical or overly fervent, and is successfully styling itself as a viable alternative to the feminist movement. As seen in the turnabout of R.E.A.L. Women's language concerning women's place in the home, the pro-family movement have co-opted feminism's use of the term 'choice' and used it for their own ideological agenda. Feminist Susan Cole, who debated Gwen Landolt in a university lecture series notes that it became very difficult to pin a political label on Landolt.

> *Never once did she say women were naturally suited to the role of housewife and men born to run the world. She never sided with God. Her vision, at least the one she revealed on the podium, did not have any of the fundamentalist fervour we tend to associate with the right wing (Cole, 1987: 35).*

Not surprisingly, feminists have reacted with a great deal of concern over the attacks by the pro-family movement and against the growing publicity that surrounds them. Norma Scarborough, former President of the Canadian Abortion Rights Action League (C.A.R.A.L.), spoke for many feminists when she said that R.E.A.L. Women represent 'a real threat to the gains we have made and to our future progress.' Ottawa lawyer and past N.A.C. President Louise Dulude stated that 'there will always be some females who will join groups like R.E.A.L. Women, which espouses traditional, conservative views. What worries us,' she says, 'is their influence with members of Parliament. They are not trying to advance the status of women,' says Dulude, 'it is just one of their fronts when they say they are promoting the rights of homemakers' (cited in A.R., 1986: 11). In 1986 the annual N.A.C. convention at Carleton University in Ottawa held a workshop on the 'New Right' which observers say turned into a 90-minute debate on how to cope with the problem of R.E.A.L. Women. The workshop was the first in the history of the N.A.C. to be devoted to 'the other side,' and demonstrates the rising credibility and influence of the pro-family movement.

CONCLUSION

In light of these concerns, what can feminists learn about the nature of anti-feminist countermovements and their relationship to feminist social movements? The historical record shows that the two groups have remained firm in their commitment to their policies and strategies over time, yet in recent years, the countermovements have shown increased political and strategic acumen in their relationship with the feminist social movement, and this may in fact account for some of their recent successes.

The suffrage debate showed that the countermovement could launch a daunting challenge to the momentum of a feminist social movement by focussing public attention on perceived threats to the traditional role and status of women that feminism represented. While the American anti-suffrage movement did not succeed in their goal to prevent the vote for women, popular support for the maintenance of women's traditional roles was popular enough that Canadian maternal feminists incorporated these claims into their own policies and thus successfully avoided serious opposition to their cause. The lessons of the E.R.A. also showed that when countermovement advocates linked feminism to the disruption and decline of the family, opposition to feminism increased. Feminists have expressed concern that the countermovement forces are winning the public relations battle because of this kind of pro-family rhetoric. This has caused some feminists to consider reinforcing support for the family in their program. Others point out that this would only alienate the single, divorced and lesbian supporters of the movement. But perhaps, the most persuasive argument is made by feminists who respond that it is important not to fall into an 'us-versus-them' trap, in which the countermovement defines itself in opposition to the feminist social movement and thereby defines the image of the feminist movement. Feminists argue that there is an urgent need to clarify who and what they are and not become or accept the caricature that the other side paints. Dubinsky (1987a: 5) states that the image of feminism that these groups are trying to exploit must be challenged.

This us-versus-them trap becomes dangerous when it puts feminists in the position of being seen as being against homemakers. Feminists have noted that this is exactly the kind of affirmation that the countermovement forces need in order to claim a legitimate representation of women's interests. Eichler (1985: 5) points out that while feminists' critique of the patriarchal family may lead some to conclude that feminists are against the family, it is important to make clear that it is feminist organizations and individuals who have drawn attention to such things as unpaid work performed by women in the home. Feminists are the ones who have identified this work as socially necessary and important work that should be recognized as such. Indeed, upgrading the status of housewives, wives, and mothers have been feminist concerns from the very beginning of the movement.

Eichler states that it is important for feminists to make clear that they are critical of the patriarchal family and not all kinds of families. She states that it is time for the feminist movement to come to terms with its own ambiguity towards families by making clear distinctions between what types of families are seen as unacceptable (where there is exploitation, violence, abuse, incest, stifling of growth) and which ones are not only acceptable but indeed deserving of social support (where there is mutual caring, support, respect, commitment and growth)—irrespective of their structure and composition (Eichler, 1985: 29).

A final challenge raised by the countermovement is the strategy of modification of political rhetoric. As has been clearly illustrated by the case of R.E.A.L. Women, the countermovement has tried to occupy the 'middle ground' of the debate between themselves and feminists, thus forcing the feminist social movement into occupying the politically more marginal space. ...

Social movements theorists have pointed out that sustained contention between a social movement and a countermovement often transforms the initial movement in the direction of moderation (Turner and Killian, 1972: 312). Feminists must be aware of this and make a conscious decision if they will in any way lessen their demands and apologize for or temper their desire for radical social change. ...

NOTES

1   In this paper, I refer to women's organization for progressive social change as the 'feminist movement' in order to distinguish it from the women's anti-feminist countermovements to which it will be compared. Referring to women's activities in the 19th century as 'feminist' has become problematic, for while these women may well have earned that label at the time, theorists assessing their activities by today's standard of feminism have often accused them of

conservativism and lack of real commitment to feminism. Feminist historian Ellen DuBois (1979) points out that it is important to situate women's organization for progressive social change in its own historical context so that its radicalism can be appreciated and its failures understood. Thus while the 'radicalism' and 'feminism' of the various women's organizations to be discussed will be assessed individually, the totality of the organizations for progressive change for women will be referred to as the feminist movement.

2   Some minority groups as well as workers opposed to the labour movement have also been divided and have acted in a similiar manner. Industrial labour history and recent shifts in the attitudes of African-Americans reveal examples of members of oppressed groups who have opposed the attempts of their leaders for progressive social change.

3   The valuable contributions that do exist are so far limited to English Canada. They include Margrit Eichler's (1985) debate over whether the 'pro-family' movement is really pro-family, and Lorna Erwin's (1988) recently published national survey of 1,200 rank and file members of the pro-family movement in Canada.

4   On this point it has been argued that it is especially disturbing when the media, politicians and even social scientists treat groups such as R.E.A.L. Women, whose self-reported and unconfirmed membership is 40,000, as an equal counterpart to feminist organizations such as N.A.C. which represent hundreds of groups translating into approximately three million women. While this is an important point and must be taken into consideration when giving coverage to the two groups, it is still valuable to recognize that the numbers themselves may be deceptive. Both N.A.C. and R.E.A.L. Women represent polarized bodies of opinion with substantial support in Canadian society. Clearly N.A.C. is much better organized than R.E.A.L. Women by virtue of its status as an umbrella organization but this fact alone does not make R.E.A.L. Women as irrelevant as the numbers alone suggest. The strength of support for R.E.A.L. Women's ideology can be seen by the fact that in a 1982 special anti-abortion supplement to New Brunswick newspapers, over 30,000 or 5 per cent of New Brunswickers paid $2 and up to have their names published as publicly opposing abortion. These numbers may not be equal to feminist support in Canada but they are nevertheless considerable.

REFERENCES

Alberta Report 1986a 'Feminists aim at R.E.A.L. foes,' 13(7): 11–12
   1986b 'Not REAL enough,' 13(12): 17
   1987a 'REALists versus feminists,' 14(13): 8–13
   1987b 'A Tory slap to R.E.A.L. Women,' 14(7): 12–13

Amer, Elizabeth 1987 'Muffin Lobby Goes Home Empty-Handed.' *This Magazine* 21(1): 7–8

Bacchi, Carol Lee 1983 *Liberation Deferred: The Ideas of the English-Canadian Suffragists 1877–1918*, Toronto: University of Toronto Press

Chafetz, Janet Saltzman and Anthony Gary Dworkin 1986 *Female Revolt.* Totowa, NJ: Rowman and Allenheld
1987 'In the Face of Threat: Organized Antifeminism in Comparative Perspective.' *Gender and Society* 1: 33–60

Cole, Susan G. 1987 'On Muffins and Misogyny: R.E.A.L. Women get Real.' *This Magazine* 21(4): 33–36

Conover, Pamela J., and Virginia Gray 1983 *Feminism and the New Right Conflict Over the American Family.* New York: Praeger

Dubinsky, Karen 1987a 'Really Dangerous: The Challenge of R.E.A.L. Women.' *Canadian Dimension* 21(6): 4–7

1987b 'Forces of Opposition.' *Broadside* 8(6): 5–6

DuBois, Ellen 1979 'The Nineteenth-Century Woman Suffrage Movement and the Analysis of Women's Oppression,' Pp. 137–50 in Zillah Eisenstein (ed.), *Capitalist Patriarchy and the case for Socialist Feminism.* New York: Monthly Review Press

Eichler, Margrit 1985 'The Pro-Family Movement: Are they For or Against Families?' C.R.I.A.W. working paper, pp. 1–37

Erwin, Lorna K. 1988 'What Feminists Should Know About the "Pro-Family" Movement in Canada: A Report On a Recent Survey of Rank and File Members.' Pp. 266–78 in Peta Tancred-Sheriff (ed.), *Feminist Research: Prospect and Retrospect,* Montreal: McGill-Queens University Press

Gale, Richard 1986 'Social Movements and the State: The Environmental Movement, Countermovements, and Government Agencies.' *Sociological Perspectives* 29: 202–40

Howard, Jeanne 1982 'Our Own Worst Enemies: Women Opposed to Woman Suffrage.' *Journal of Sociology and Social Welfare* 9: 463–74

Killian, Lewis M. 1964 'Social Movements.' In Robert E.L. Faris (ed.), *Handbook of Modern Sociology,* Chicago: Rand McNally and Co.

Mansbridge, Jane 1986 *Why We Lost the E.R.A.* Chicago: University of Chicago Press

Marshall, Susan 1985 'Ladies Against Women: Mobilization Dilemmas of Anti-feminist Movements.' *Social Problems* 32: 348–62

Marshall, Susan, and Anthony Orum 1986 'Opposition Then and Now: Countering Feminism in the Twentieth Century.' In G. Moore and G. Spitze (eds.), *Research in Politics and Society* Vol. 2, Greenwich, CT: JAI Press

Mottl, Tahi L. 1980 'The Analysis of Countermovements.' *Social Problems* 27:620–35

Petchesky, Rosalind 1981 'Antiabortion, Antifeminism and the Rise of the New Right.' *Feminist Studies* 7: 206–46

Turner, Ralph, and Lewis Killian 1972 *Collective Behaviour.* Englewood Cliffs, NJ: Prentice-Hall

Wilson, John 1973 *Introduction to Social Movements.* New York: Basic Books

41

"Backlash" Against Feminism: A Disempowering Metaphor

Janice Newson

> *As I look at the human story, I see two stories. They run parallel and never meet. One is of people who live, as they can or must, the events that arrive; the other is of people who live, as they intend, the events they create.*
> —Margaret Anderson, *The Fiery Fountains*

The purpose of this paper is simple. I want to eliminate the use of the word "backlash" as a metaphorical account of resistance and opposition to women's efforts to advance in society. I offer it as a small contribution to developing a language of social transformation which moves away from viewing women as victims of forces beyond control and moves toward affirming the position of women as being actively engaged in shaping and transforming social relations.

Before beginning, two things must be clearly said about the project itself. First, I am not denying the existence of powerful social forces which are major obstacles to our efforts to create a better place for ourselves in the world. On the contrary, my intention is to make visible the nature of our struggle with these very forces and to validate the power that we exercise as social agents in challenging and undermining them. Second, I don't believe that the kind of social transformation that we are engaged in will be achieved by simply changing our language. However, our language has a great deal to do with how we perceive, and therefore how we position ourselves in relation to, these powerful, contending forces. It often constructs the terrain of the struggle and it is one of the few things over which we can exercise relatively unobstructed choice. Therefore, by choosing language which locates us at the centre rather than at the margins of social transformation, we are claiming the space to create a world that more closely approximates our language.

My argument for eliminating the use of "backlash" is also quite simple: it centres our energy in the motion of those who oppose and resist our efforts, rather than in our own forward motion, and it tends to reinforce the idea

From Janice Newson, "'Backlash'" Against Feminism: A Disempowering Metaphor," *Resources for Feminist Research (RFR/DRF)*, vol. 29, no. 3/4 (1991): 93–97. Reprinted by permission.

that we are victims of forces disconnected from our own agency. In order to better elaborate on these general points, I first need to tell the story about how I came to think in this way about the "backlash" metaphor.

Three proximate events form the plot of this story. The first (not in time, but in its place in the story) was the viewing of a videotape in a session of the 1990 Learned Societies Meetings. The second was a lecture by Dorothy Smith at the Canadian Sociology and Anthropology Meetings, entitled "Whistling Women: Reflections on Objectivity, Science and the Exclusion of Women," given the day before I viewed the videotape. The third was the appearance of an article a few weeks earlier in the Op. Ed. section of *The Globe and Mail*, written by well known Canadian historian Ramsay Cook, entitled, "A Peace Proposal for the War of the Sexes." While viewing the videotape, a line of thinking began which tied together these three events.

The videotape was of a late January 1990 campus forum at Bishop's University in Lennoxville, Québec, which focused on the killing of 14 female engineering students at L'École Polytechnique at the Université de Montréal on December 6, 1989. Three faculty members—a woman sociologist, a male psychologist, and a male Dean of Students—provided their versions of the meaning of these killings. As I listened to their presentations, I was at once struck by a strange and uncomfortable sense that everything that was being said and the manner in which it was being said, and the rapt attention of the largely student audience, was dated. I tried at first to shake the feeling. After all, this was no history lesson, recounting events that had taken place a decade or a century age. They had happened less than six months earlier. Nevertheless, the relentless, overflowing-with-words, spellbinding talk about violence against women, about media representations of women that invite violence, about the statistics on rape and battered wives, about the cultural supports for male aggression—this kind of talk, reproduced through a video-tape in early June—seemed painfully remote, amazing, almost inconceivable, yet oddly familiar. It was talk which had engaged our whole society for a brief moment of time in a single conversation. But six months later, I felt that the flow of this conversation had been broken or interrupted.

To understand why I felt this way, I carried myself back to the events of six months before, when the forum I was viewing would have been experienced as an episode of that conversation. I quickly surveyed my memory of how I had come to first hear about the 14 women shot dead early on the evening of December 6, through a CBC news bulletin while driving off my campus. I remembered the rest of that evening too: with a friend, plugged into CBC Newsworld, phoning other friends to tell them to turn on their TVs or radios, leaving messages on answering machines, checking on a dear friend in Montréal who told us that another of our friends had been at L'École Polytechnique earlier that evening but had not been involved in the shootings, feeling glad for her safety but not relieved, being moved by Denis Trudeau's refusal (or inability) to maintain the professional cool of the news reporter on national television, and finally going to bed when Newsworld signed off.

I remembered tuning in to CBC "Commentary" the next morning and hearing the strong, breaking voice of Francine Pelletier, a Québécoise journalist, unrelentingly placing the events of the previous evening in the context of women's ongoing struggle to find a place of equality and respect in our society. That's when, for me at least, the conversation began. In the days and weeks that followed, it carried on in an endless stream of news reports, media interviews with panels and experts, all trying to place these killings in perspective. I recalled the mix of anguished and arrogant and angry voices on phone-in shows, answering back to each other, or to the previous day's editorial, or to the latest "facts" about the biography of the killer, Marc Lépine. My memory of these events appeared to hang together by a single thread. But from the vantage point of "now," watching back on "then" through a videotape, I felt the sense of an abrupt discontinuity.

In order to account for this sense of discontinuity, I tried to recall what I had heard in the conversation which followed the Montréal killings. In the earliest stages, the talk reflected intense shock, anguish, and a sense of incredulity. But as time evolved, the conversation became more predictable, consolidating the various reactions that had been voiced from the beginning. I especially recalled two recurring themes which emerged in this consolidation.[1] The first was that Lépine's action on December 6 was an excessive example of the "backlash" against feminism. The second was a related recurring theme, that it was the action of an irrational, rampaging psychopath. Both of these themes entered very early in the conversation and re-appeared through the weeks that followed as person after person, commentator after commentator, tried to interpret what had taken place. Not surprisingly, these themes were present in the commentary on the videotape. But some things did not fit these themes. In fact, some things seemed to be excluded—things that provide the basis of a different interpretation altogether.

For example, in spite of comments which attempted to locate his actions in the context of patriarchal, male privileged social relationships, much of the public talk returned to the issue of Lépine's mental state. In fact, I recalled how frequently newspaper headlines and other media summations characterized the killings in terms of the mad rampage of an *irrational* psychotic—with emphasis on "irrational"—regardless of the content of the talk which preceded or followed. Sharply reminded of this, I recalled Dorothy Smith's lecture of the day before.

Smith's talk was about a male-centred, male-empowering, male-privileging "regime of rationality" that, over the last two to three centuries, had become entrenched at the centre of knowledge construction. Her argument was not against rationality *per se*, but against a particular social organization of rationality that has been constructed in the interest of male power and male authority. This "regime of rationality" until recently has successfully accomplished the exclusion of women in modern centres of authorized knowledge production, like universities. In fact, she argued, women in universities appear as "whistling women"[2] whose presence inflames a sense of danger and threat to the appropriate "order" of things—an order which is defined, maintained and reproduced by "the regime of rationality." This sense of danger and threat incited Lépine's actions.

It then occurred to me that representing Lépine as irrational effectively camouflages the relationship between his actions and the "rational" practices that maintain male privilege and male power in the everyday, routine aspects of our lives. In other words, rather than being understood as an irrational psychopathic outburst—which could have taken place anywhere, not only on a university campus—Lépine's killing of the 14 women at L'École Polytechnique might be better understood as an action in the interest of Smith's "regime of rationality": Lépine, the loyal foot soldier to the ideology of women-in-universities as infidels, as invaders of the authorized and exclusive space of men, as depriving men of their entitlement. If this is a possible construction of the meaning of [Lépine's] action, then what is accomplished by adopting a representation of him as an irrational, deranged, damaged by bad-parentage, psychotic killer?

One thing it accomplishes is to drive us into fear. During the weeks that followed December 6, someone insightfully pointed out that women's fear had shifted from a fear of dark, secret spaces to a fear of open, public spaces. Anyone out there could be the next assassin. Being in well lighted places, joining together with allies, and thus, taking some personal responsibility for our own safety, not only does not guarantee "safety" (if it ever did) but in fact, may be the very trigger that incites the "rampage." Not even the power of *reasonable men* can control this sudden explosion of misogyny!

A second accomplishment is to disconnect Lépine's action from any "intention" other than his personal motive of irrational hatred and thus to suggest that no one and nothing could have been (or could be) done to prevent it. It invites no useful response or intervention except perhaps to ensure that its perpetrator never again has the opportunity to vent his rage—and Lépine took care of that himself. None of our strategies aimed at changing the pattern of social relationships, and little of our previous experience of collective struggle, appear relevant or suitable to this circumstance. It leaves us only with an intense desire for protection and ensuring our physical safety.

Thirdly, it leads us away from exploring the connection which was embedded in Dorothy Smith's talk. That is, that Lépine's apparent outburst of rage and revenge could (and should) be linked not to an irrational, uncontrollable impulse[3] but to a rational, logically implemented set of practices that sustain women's exclusion from the authorized domain of male privilege.

Is there any evidence for making this kind of link? At this point, the article that had appeared in *The Globe and Mail* just three weeks earlier came into focus for me. With the reasoned, careful logic of a skilled academic, Ramsay Cook had taken up a question Marc Lépine left behind: that is, if women are now to be given "special" access to the university because of the historic pattern of their exclusion, how will justice be meted out for the young men who may now be deprived of access by programs like affirmative action and employment equity?

I am not suggesting that Cook was endorsing Lépine's apparent hatred of women and feminists, nor his method for solving this problem. In fact, like many other reasonable, civilized, "decent" men, I am sure that he was repelled, alarmed, and outraged by this violence. Nevertheless, whatever the arguments that are mounted to represent his action as being motivated by irrational psychotic rage, we are stuck with the fact that Lépine *defined himself* as "a rational erudite (person)" [*sic*] who has been "forced to take extreme acts." However much men of reason may disassociate themselves from Lépine by trying to assign to him a flawed nature unlike their own, Lépine certainly associated his actions with them! In fact, it is even arguable that he saw himself as their emissary, acting on behalf of men everywhere whose lives have been unjustly ruined by opportunistic feminists.

In this sense, it is important to consider the link between what Cook offered as "A Peace Proposal for the War of the Sexes" and the sense of injustice to which Lépine saw himself responding. Perhaps Cook felt compelled to write this piece precisely because of the extremity and gravity of Lépine's actions and the many other serious attacks on women students and faculty members that were reported on campuses in the weeks following the Montreal killings. That is, perhaps he saw himself as trying to head off the intense competition for access between men and women that is "doubly dangerous because it threatens to become a battle of the sexes." Whatever his motivations, his concern is very clearly a concern for aspiring young male academics.

> *The young men are in a difficult position. Most admit there are serious imbalances between men and women in the universities. Yet they, too, have invested heavily in preparing for academic work. Must they pay the price of past injustice? (Cook, 1990, p. A7)*

The "dangerous" situation to which Cook refers is not the historic imbalance which reflects women's exclusion from the academy, but rather the approach taken by many universities in trying to "even up the balance sheet in a hurry." Employment equity and affirmative action programs, although "laudable," are part of the danger, according to Cook, because they seem to have only the goal of appointing more women: "No men need apply."

Cook's solution to this problem—presumably one that will defuse the danger—appears on the surface to be eminently reasonable: to remove the job security acquired through tenure from the mainly male, mainly middle-aged professoriat in order to open up space for the more vital and productive energy of younger women *and* men. In its place, a system of periodic reviews should be installed to test the ongoing contribution of academics and provide a strong incentive for improved performance. Such a solution would not only ensure that "more posts would become available *than could be easily filled by young women*, thus making discriminatory employment practices unnecessary" (italics mine). It would also provide a more just solution, since it would place the cost of greater sex balance on "the old men who presumably did the discriminating" rather than on the young men who are now precluded from obtaining the few posts that are available.

Much could be said (and has been[4]) in response to this "peace proposal." Rather than being treated as one of many opinion pieces on matters of public concern, Cook's article provides us with a "reading" on the response of the "regime of rationality" to women's recent success in gaining access to the academy. It is probably not coincidental that Cook speaks from his experience in university—the same one I work in —at which an affirmative action program for the appointment of women has been in place since 1987. During this time, the percentage of women in the fulltime tenure stream increased from approximately 21 percent to a little over 26 percent in less than three years.[5] Academic units have been required to account for their hiring decisions and to offer appointments to women candidates who are "substantially equal" to the best male candidates. Perhaps most important, the monitoring provisions of the program have begun to expose the hiring practices of academic units and to make it less possible for them to practice exclusion without being detected and subjected to intervening vetoes. Clearly, this program has produced some positive results in the struggle of women[6] to gain access to the academy, although undeniably at the cost of departmental "peace."

The question which Cook's article plainly begs is whether "peace" is desirable at this particular moment, a moment when, finally, women's struggle for access is becoming effective. Understood in this way, Cook is trying on a counter-strategy for dealing with the "problem" of women's success at entering what he describes as "traditionally, a male domain" and in the process, of creating unfair, unjust consequences for men. Was this not the same problem that Marc Lépine also addressed, although admittedly through means that would be utterly rejected by "reasonable," "ethical," "civilized" men? Lépine's own words answers this question best:

> *Please note that if I am committing suicide today … it is … for political reasons. For I have decided to send Ad Patres (to the fathers, or death) the feminists who have always ruined my life …*
>
> *[T]he feminists always have a talent to enrage me. They want to keep the advantages of women (e.g., cheaper insurance, extended maternity leave preceded by a preventative retreat) **while trying to grab those of men.***
>
> *Thus it is an obvious truth that if the Olympic Games removed the MenWomen distinction, there would be Women only in the graceful event. **So the feminists are not fighting to remove that barrier. They***

are so opportunistic they neglect to profit from the knowledge accumu-
lated by men through the ages. ...

   Thus the other day, I heard they were honoring the Canadian
men and women who fought at the frontline during the world wars.
How can you explain then that women were not authorized to go to the
frontline??? Will we hear of Caesar's female legions and female galley
slaves who of course took up 50 percent of the ranks of history, though
they never existed. ...

   —Marc Lépine, *as reprinted in* The Globe and Mail, *Novem-*
   ber 27, 1990, p. A21 [emphasis mine].

How does what I have been describing relate to the second recurring theme of the conversation which followed the Montréal killings, that Lépine's action is an extreme illustration of a "backlash" against women? I have been drawing a connecting line through Cook's "peace proposal," Lépine's own sense of injustice in response to women's entry into male domains, and the recent progress toward gaining access for women into the academy. In the same way that the recurring discussion of Lépine's mental state camouflages a relationship between his actions and the "regime of rationality," I want to show how the "backlash" metaphor not only fails to comprehend the significance of this line but, to our disadvantage, may render it invisible and lead us to engage in strategies that have been constructed by those who oppose, or who wish to undermine, our efforts.

   In my view, this connecting line signifies forward rather than backward movement. Cook's article betrays this point clearly. He calls for "peace" precisely at the time that advances have been made for women entering the academy. Even though the terms of his proposal are designed to undermine, contain, and limit these advances, the article clearly confirms that women's struggle to gain access to a masculine domain is having some effect. The term "backlash," however, draws our attention away from this reality of advancement and focuses it instead on the resistance to it. In the process, it has emotionally and politically disempowering effects.

   For one thing, it heightens our awareness of the opposition and focuses our energy on dealing with that, rather than on pressing ahead. The conversation carried on by commentators and journalists following the Montréal killings frequently employed the term "backlash" as an account of what had taken place. Since other similar, though less extreme, actions involving male aggression toward women on university campuses occurred both before and after the killings, they added up to a convincing picture of a "backlash" against feminism, or feminists, or women's presence in a traditionally male domain, the university. Much of the conversation focused on these acts of aggression.

   I will not deny that, in the context of that conversation, the idea of a "backlash" had some attractive features. It not only underlined the violent, jarring and extreme nature of these acts of aggression, but it also allowed that they are a response to something. They are not, as some tried to argue, isolated, random acts of violence focused on women for no particular reason. By the same token, however, the idea of "backlash" also made space for a debate about whether the "something" these actions are responding to might not also have been "extreme," having "gone too far," or "too quickly."[7] In the process of debating this point, "feminism," "feminists," and any women (or men, for that matter) who support women's struggle for equality, whether in the domain of the university or elsewhere, were placed in the position of defending their claims to *ground already gained,* not to ground yet to be taken. Energy was diverted from arguing, not for where we have yet to go, but for where we have already gone!

Secondly, in focusing attention on the opposition and defending ground already gained, it becomes a relatively small step to perceiving women in the position of "victims," being driven "backwards" by the aggression of our opposition, rather than being carried forward by our own agency. Ironically, one way this small step is taken is through debating who or what is "responsible" for the backlash. On the one hand, in the case of the Montréal killings, many agreed that Lépine's action, and other similar, less extreme, acts of male aggression on university campuses, was against these women, against feminists and feminism, and against their struggle to gain access to a male domain. On the other hand, by pushing too hard, too fast, it was also argued that these very women and this very struggle have brought the reprisal upon themselves. Do they also, therefore, share "responsibility" for "the backlash"?

The reply to this question is critical. More often than not, those who support women's struggle respond by representing women as the victims of male aggression and reprisal and adamantly insist that any effort to implicate them in causing the "backlash" is "blaming the victim." But surely something is distorted here. The women who entered joyfully into their studies at L'École Polytechnique by no means carry the mark of being "victims" in any general sense: they were boldly striding forward into a future that once excluded members of their sex. Nor do those many women who have struggled over decades to gain an equal place for women convey the impression of being "victims."

I am by no means suggesting that women *are* responsible for the resistance and opposition in which others *choose* to engage. The problem emerges when the denial of responsibility reifies the resistance and opposition as something to which we have no connection. Resistance and opposition appear to come "out of the air" suddenly and without the possibility of anticipation—springing if anything from the out-of-control irrational rage of a misogynist.

I want to locate this problem in the lines of argument which are drawn by the "backlash" metaphor itself. The etymology of "backlash" locates the term in the realm of mechanics. It was originally used to describe a violent, jarring motion in a mechanical device, usually a wheel, which results from loose or worn parts. In this original sense, both the backlash and the cause of the backlash are aspects of the same motion. The jarring, violent reaction is "of" the loose and worn parts that create the condition for the backlash. In other words, the condition is a direct "cause" of the reaction. This mechanistic cause and effect sequence is distorting when imported as a metaphor into a description or account of a social process such as the one being discussed here. It suggests that the jarring reaction—the backlash—and what that is a reaction to, are all part of the same, unified motion and therefore, can be seen in a cause-effect way.

Instead of this representation of women's struggle and the resistance and opposition to it, I am proposing a representation that sees two lines of motion, not one. The first is a line of motion that incorporates the many struggles[8] to advance women's claims to equality and respect. The second is rooted in the many forms of male privilege and power which resist and oppose women's advancement. These two lines of motion are entwined in a struggle in which the action carried forward by one line is responded to by the other. But the relationship between them is not a simple cause and effect relationship since they represent lines of motion that are independently propelled, being rooted in different, often contradictory and opposing, social processes.

From this understanding of the social (as opposed to mechanical) dynamics of the struggle, we women can (and should) fully claim our responsibility for the advances and successes to which male resistance and opposition respond, while at the same time holding men responsible for their opposition and resistance. Moreover, being centred in our own forward motion makes it less likely that we will be drawn into the motion of our opposition and thereby pushed "backwards," defending the ground which we have already won. In fact, precisely at the moment that we encounter resistance and opposition, we will understand that, through our own agency, we have been effective. We will not be caught by surprise when opposed, but rather will anticipate it and even be able to predict where and when it might take place. Most importantly, centred in our own motion and sense of agency, we will not be as easily overwhelmed by those forces that are beyond our control because we will be able to use our own momentum to respond.[9]

It is with this kind of awareness of our own power and agency that we should understand the link between Ramsay Cook's "peace proposal" and the acts of aggression against women in universities which have almost become commonplace. In the guise of cleverly constructed logic, Cook presents himself as someone who is putting forward a "reasonable" proposition. But he fearmongers. He warns of the dangers of a war that is on the verge of breaking out and urges us to pull back from unjustly dislodging deserving young men from their (entitled) place in the academy. It's a view from the other side: a view located in a different line of motion than that in which we, as women, are located. We know (and, by the way, so does he!) that the "war" broke out some time ago and that acts of aggression which we have already experienced signal resistance and opposition. We also know that we are gaining ground and that we will not stop now! Affirmative action and employment equity are among the means that have helped us come this far. They need to be strengthened and improved, not abandoned.[10]

Cook wants us to believe that, if we set aside these tools, and turn our efforts to displacing the old men from their privileged positions, thereby providing access to deserving young men as well as young women, then the struggle will be no longer necessary. Does he really intend us to believe that these young men will be magically free from practices that exclude women? Does he really expect that we will give up a strategy that is gaining us ground, in exchange for an alliance that we have too much reason to doubt—one that gives us no guarantee that the same priority will be given to correcting the imbalance between men and women in the academy as it will to ensuring that men retain their place? And who or what are we being asked to ally ourselves with? Since he appears to be neither among the young men who are being denied access, nor the old men who deserve to be expunged, who or what is he representing?

I believe that Cook's offer is on behalf of the "regime of rationality"—the very regime that has been able, through rational and routine practices, to exclude women from the academy for centuries. What would it mean to accept his "reasonable" strategy for avoiding the "war"? It would ensure that the "old men" who discriminated will only be replaced by "young men" who will soon learn to discriminate (it they don't know how already), since they will be inserted into the "regime of rationality" in the same ways as were their predecessors. It would ensure the continuation of the regime, something that has currently been placed under threat by, among other things, the success of women in gaining greater control over the hiring process. It would even enhance the power of the regime in that the same "rational" practices that have excluded women will now be used to "turf out" members of the middle-aged, tenured professoriat! Those who wish to preserve this regime consider our success to be too much. But for those of us who have been excluded by it and seek to dismantle it, it is nowhere near enough.

The actions of Marc Lépine and others who have tried to preserve men's space in the academy through violence and aggression no doubt alert us to the need to secure ourselves from physical harm. However, it is perhaps most important for us to be wary of the rapprochement that is offered by the kind of peace proposal that Cook puts forward. It builds on the fears that Lépine and others engender and it creates a false sense of our location in a unitary movement in which we must contain our own motion in order to avoid the dangers of a jarring response. The fact is, we are *not* centred in the preservation of the "regime of rationality." What threatens it does not threaten us. On the contrary, we are centred in a struggle to dismantle the regime and its power to reproduce itself, not only in the academy but in society as a whole.

NOTES

Originally presented at a joint session of the Canadian Association of Sociology and Anthropology, and the Socialist Studies Society, June 1991.

1 It is very instructive to compare the substance of the talk contained in Francine Pelletier's CBC "Commentary" on the morning after the killings, and subsequent interactions between her and other public interpreters of Lépine's actions on two separate editions of CBC's "Morningside." The second of these episodes took place in early February 1990, around the time that the public conversation began to subside. I cannot explore this matter here, but the shift is striking between the position that Francine Pelletier was able to articulate clearly on December 7, and the position she was able to articulate in subsequent episodes of the public conversation.

2 This phrase is taken from an old rhyme: "A whistling woman and a crowing hen lets the devil out of the pen."

3 It should be clear that I am not concerned with Lépine's own psychology, which, for my purpose here, is irrelevant. I am attempting to consider the question of how his action was taken up and accounted for by talk in the public domain which tried to interpret his actions and to draw conclusions about what kind of response it calls for. This issue was at the heart of the "conversation" to which I have referred. Could a link be drawn between the Montréal killings and the more general character of male privilege and female exclusion in our society?

4 Some letters to the editor were published in *The Globe and Mail* in response to Cook's article. As well, the Canadian History Association devoted a large portion of its September/October 1990 newsletter to responses to Professor Cook's proposal.

5 This increase is especially dramatic when we consider that the first Status of Women report was published in 1975, which clearly pointed to the serious sex imbalance in academic appointments and which urged that some means be adopted for improving it. From that time on, it was often claimed that a kind of "voluntary" approach was being followed, based on academic units being "sensitive" and "aware" of the possibility of discrimination and exclusion. In 1987, the contractually binding affirmative action program was adopted. The voluntary approach had resulted in little meaningful change in the statistics in the previous 12 years. Although it is true that few hirings had taken place in those years on the average, by the early 1980s more hirings had been taking place, and still the statistics had not been meaningfully affected.

6 I am not suggesting, however, that *all* women have benefited from this program. For example, race and class backgrounds still exist as barriers.

7 A woman colleague informed me of a conversation with a male colleague who said about Lépine's actions, "I don't of course condone what he did but he had reason. Women have been going too far. They are taking over." This kind of comment was not uncommon and is precisely the kind of comment that the "backlash" metaphor makes room for.

8 I am acknowledging that the women's "movement" is not monolithic.

9   I am not arguing that we should ignore the opposing responses to our advances. In fact, we can learn a great deal from them. For example, these responses can help us decide which move to make next and they may even lead us to conclude that a particular tactic or approach is not effective. However, we must make this kind of strategic assessment from the perspective of being centred in the motion of our advancement rather than in the motion of our opposition. Another paper would be required to further elaborate what this means in practice.

10   See note 6.

REFERENCES

Cook, Ramsay. "A Peace Proposal for the War of the Sexes," *The Globe and Mail*, May 10, 1990, p. A7.

Lépine, Marc. "Last Words from a Woman Hater," *The Globe and Mail*, November 27, 1990, p. A21.

Smith, Dorothy. "Whistling Women: Reflections on Objectivity, Science and the Exclusion of Women." Paper presented at the Canadian Sociology and Anthropology Association annual meeting, University of Victoria, Victoria, BC, June 1990.